The Broadview Reader

Third Edition

The
Broadview Reader

Third Edition

edited by

Herbert Rosengarten and Jane Flick

broadview press

Canadian Cataloguing in Publication Data

Main entry under title:

The Broadview reader
3rd ed.

Includes bibliographical references and index.

ISBN 1-55111-114-4

1. English essays. 2. College readers. 3. English
language - Rhetoric. I. Rosengarten, Herbert. II. Flick, Jane, 1944-
PE1417.B76 1997   814.008   C97-930471-7

broadview press
P.O. Box 1243
Peterborough, Ontario
K9J 7H5   Canada

broadview press
3576 California Road
Orchard Park, NY
14127   USA

B.R.A.D. Book Representation
& Distribution Ltd.
244a, London Road
Hadleigh, Essex
SS7 2DE United Kingdom

Bruce Watson,
St. Clair Press
P.O. Box 287
Rozelle, NSW
2039 Australia

Table of Contents

Preface   ix
Guide to Rhetorical Patterns and Devices   xiii
Chronological Table of Contents   xviii
Acknowledgements   xxi

Language and Communication
Woody Allen   Slang Origins   3
Russell Baker   Little Red Riding Hood Revisited   7
Richard Hoggart   The Case Against Advertising   11
Samuel Johnson   The Abuses of Advertising   17
George Orwell   Politics and the English Language   21

Literature and Audience
Sir Francis Bacon   Of Studies   37
Thomas De Quincey   The Literature of Knowledge and
                         the Literature of Power   40
Northrop Frye   The Motive for Metaphor   47
Margaret Laurence   Where the World Began   58
Mordecai Richler   An Unquiet Awakening   65
Barbara Tuchman   The Historian's Opportunity   72
Guy Vanderhaeghe   Influences   87
Virginia Woolf   How Should One Read a Book?   95

Film and the Media
Martin Amis   Blown Away   109
Kurt Andersen   The Origin of Alien Species   117
Bruno Bettelheim   The Art of Moving Pictures   123
Edward D. Castillo   *Dances With Wolves:* Review   131
Gertrude Himmelfarb   A Neo-Luddite Reflects on the Internet   147
Pauline Kael   New Age Daydreams [*Dances With Wolves*]   153
X.J. Kennedy   Who Killed King Kong?   156
Joseph Natoli   *The Unforgiven:* Histories and "Indians"   162
Rick Salutin   Loose Canons   179

Nature and Humankind

Rachel Carson	The Obligation to Endure	191
Loren Eiseley	The Bird and the Machine	199
Stephen Leacock	Roughing it in the Bush (My Plans for Moose-Hunting in the Canadian Wilderness)	209
Farley Mowat	The Nature of the North	215
Mark Twain	A River Pilot Looks at the Mississippi	224
E.B. White	Death of a Pig	228
Edward O. Wilson	Storm Over the Amazon	238

Patterns of Social Behaviour

Gail Anderson-Dargatz	Errington, B.C.	245
Sir Francis Bacon	Of Marriage and Single Life	250
Hugh Brody	A Hearing	253
Daniel Francis	Re-hanging the National Wallpaper: The Group of Seven and the Public Mind	266
J.H. Plumb	De Mortuis	280
Witold Rybczynski	Nostalgia	286
Garry Trudeau	To Our Valued Customers	297
George Woodcock	The Tyranny of the Clock	301

Politics and Morality

Joseph Addison	On Party-lying	309
Margaret Atwood	The Writer's Responsibility	314
George Orwell	Shooting an Elephant	319
Mike Royko	Another Accolade for Charter Arms Corp.	328
Alan Sillitoe	Sport and Nationalism	332
Jonathan Swift	A Modest Proposal	338
Henry David Thoreau	Civil Disobedience	348

Society and the Individual

Ken Dryden	The Game	371
E.M. Forster	My Wood	379
Patricia Highsmith	Child's Play 4?	384
Russell Hoban	Thoughts on a Shirtless Cyclist, Robin Hood and One or Two Other Things	392
Edith Iglauer	Bella Coola	401
Hugh MacLennan	The Shadow of Captain Bligh	411
Jan Morris	St John's	418
Wallace Stegner	Specifications for a Hero	430

Women in Society

Regina Barreca	How Many Feminists Does It Take to Change a Light Bulb?	445
Moira Farr	Dangerous Determination	464
Janet Flanner	Murder Among the Lovebirds	474
Alison Lurie	Women's Clothes — Towards Emancipation	482
Noretta Koertge	Are Feminists Alienating Women from the Sciences?	492
Gloria Steinem	Marilyn Monroe: The Woman Who Died Too Soon	498
Helen Taylor	Women and Criticism	505
Margaret Visser	Feeding, Feasts and Females	515

Ethnicity and Culture

Neil Bissoondath	I Am Canadian	529
Susan Crean	Taking the Missionary Position	543
Kildare Dobbs	Matata	554
Fil Fraser	Black Like Me	559
Carole Giangrande	Allowing the Mind to Wander	568
Basil H. Johnston	Is That All There Is? Tribal Literature	572
Lenore Keeshig-Tobias	Stop Stealing Native Stories	583
Amy Tan	In the Canon, For All the Wrong Reasons	587
Martin Walker	Westward Oh!	593
Christine Welsh	Women in the Shadows: Reclaiming a Métis Heritage	603

The World of Science

Geoffrey Bibby	The Body in the Bog	619
Jacob Bronowski	The Real Responsibilities of the Scientist	631
David H. Freedman	The Aggressive Egg	641
Stephen Jay Gould	Posture Maketh the Man	650
J.B.S. Haldane	Some Enemies of Science	657
Jay Ingram	The Cathedral Square	666
Richard Selzer	The Discus Thrower	675
David Suzuki	The Pain of Animals	680
Lewis Thomas	Humanities and Science	686
James Trefil	Unexpected Vistas	696

Notes on the Authors	701
Glossary	710
Index of Authors and Titles	718

Preface to the Third Edition

Despite the proliferation of electronic communications in recent years, most readers still rely heavily on printed materials. The Internet has infinite and unimagined resources, and surely anyone involved in the study of language and communications must become adept in negotiating this new universe of ideas. However, the rapid emergence of web-pages and interactive writing programs, of hot links and on-line chat rooms, has not yet displaced the printed word in all its hard-copy embodiments, and it is to our traditional sources — to books, newspapers, magazines — that we have turned to find new materials for the third edition of *The Broadview Reader*.

We have been guided as before by the tastes and preferences of our readers, and by our wish not to create too much upheaval in the process of revision. We have therefore retained the structure of earlier editions, with essays gathered loosely in topic groups. Some pieces formerly in different sections are now brought together, with several new essays, in a section on "Women in Society." We have also changed the emphasis in the group of essays dealing with film, in an effort to give a broader sense of the movies' handling of social issues.

Friendly nudges from several quarters have helped to remind us that "modern" issues often have a long and honourable history, and so we have included a number of nineteenth-century essays that articulate concerns of continuing relevance as we approach the twenty-first century: the struggle between the private citizen and the state (Thoreau), the opportunities for women to realize their potential (Taylor), the power of great literature to move and inspire (De Quincey). We hope that readers find in these and other selections the inspiration to map out and develop their own ideas in writing, whether on paper or on-line.

HJR
JMF

Preface to the Second Edition

For this new edition we are pleased to have been able to preserve much of the first. We have kept representative pieces by such writers as George Orwell, Virginia Woolf, E.B. White and E.M. Forster, not only because they are recognized as "classics" that are touchstones of style and substance, but also because they can be relied on to offer something fresh and exciting to each new set of readers. As teachers, we turn to such pieces as to old friends. Many of the other essays included in the first edition have also become old friends; consequently, fewer than a dozen items from that edition have been cut.

At the same time, we have sought to include a selection of new essays from the recent past. In particular, we wanted to reflect in the book some of the stimulating and often controversial changes that have spread through society — and enlivened the study of English — over the past five years. A new section, "Ethnicity and Culture," signals the inclusion of a variety of essays on such topics as appropriation of voice, the conflict of cultures, and the representation of First Nations' peoples in art, history, and the cinema. Elsewhere, the reader will find a range of materials on other issues of current concern, including animal rights, "political correctness," and questions of race and gender.

We have retained the format of the first edition, including a thematic table of contents, a set of questions following each selection, and a glossary of terms used in the analysis of prose discourse.

HJR
JMF

Preface to the First Edition

Like many anthologies, *The Broadview Reader* was born out of a conviction that most other collections of this kind failed in one way or another to meet students' needs, and that it would not be difficult to improve on the efforts of our predecessors. In the event, the experience proved to be a humbling one. What began as an almost casual enterprise, to be completed in a short time, turned into a year-long search through books, magazines, newspapers, indexes, and catalogues. The process of selection became more and more complicated as we proceeded; many of the essays we had first chosen were edged out by later discoveries; categories formed and reformed with bewildering frequency; firm favorites suddenly lost their appeal and found their way into an ever-growing discard file. But for the exigencies of publishers' deadlines, *The Broadview Reader* might still be gestating in a hundred dog-eared yellow folders.

In making our final choices, we were guided by three considerations: would the essay be interesting to a variety of readers? would it lend itself to discussion and analysis? would it demonstrate some of the techniques and strategies of effective writing? We have not sought to present a history of the prose essay; though a few of our examples have been drawn from earlier periods, the emphasis is very much on twentieth-century writing. Nor have we attempted to assemble a "manual of styles" of the kind sometimes offered to students as models for their own writing. Our hope is rather that student writers will be stimulated by the ideas and issues presented in the essays, and be encouraged to search for ways of articulating their own ideas effectively.

The essays are grouped by subject to facilitate a thematic focus and a comparison of writers, attitudes, and approaches. Each essay is followed by a list of questions intended to help the reader identify the main lines of thought, and recognize some of the writer's strategies of language and organization. The questions are not comprehensive, or chosen with some particular rhetorical prescription in mind; rather, their function is to prepare the reader for more detailed discussion and analysis in the classroom, and to suggest writing exercises that might form a natural culmination of the critical process.

To help the reader focus on salient aspects of technique, we have also provided a "Guide to Rhetorical Patterns and Devices," and a glossary of terms commonly used in the critical analysis of prose discourse.

HJR
JMF

Guide to Rhetorical Patterns and Devices

Essays which employ analogy

Frye	The Motive for Metaphor
Crean	Taking the Missionary Position
Hoban	Thoughts on a Shirtless Cyclist, Robin Hood and One or Two Other Things
Swift	A Modest Proposal
Taylor	Women and Criticism
Trefil	Unexpected Vistas
Freedman	The Aggressive Egg
Woolf	How Should One Read a Book?

Essays which employ analysis

Bettelheim	The Art of Moving Pictures
Castillo	*Dances With Wolves:* Review
Dryden	The Game
Ingram	The Cathedral Square
Lurie	Women's Clothes — Towards Emancipation
Orwell	Politics and the English Language
Richler	An Unquiet Awakening
Rybczynski	Nostalgia
Salutin	Loose Canons
Steinem	Marilyn Monroe: The Woman Who Died Too Soon
Walker	Westward Oh!

Essays which employ argumentation and persuasion

Amis	Blown Away
Atwood	The Writer's Responsibility
Barreca	How Many Feminists Does It Take to Change a Light Bulb?
Bissoondath	I Am Canadian
Bronowski	The Real Responsibilities of the Scientist
Carson	The Obligation to Endure
De Quincey	The Literature of Knowledge and the Literature of Power
Dryden	The Game
Farr	Dangerous Determination
Giangrande	Allowing the Mind to Wander
Haldane	Some Enemies of Mankind
Hoggart	The Case Against Advertising

Keeshig-Tobias	Stop Stealing Native Stories
Kennedy	Who Killed King Kong?
Koertge	Are Feminists Alienating Women from the Sciences?
Natoli	*The Unforgiven:* Histories and "Indians"
Sillitoe	Sport and Nationalism
Suzuki	The Pain of Animals
Swift	A Modest Proposal
Taylor	Women and Criticism
Thomas	Humanities and Science
Thoreau	Civil Disobedience
Woodcock	The Tyranny of the Clock

Essays which employ cause and effect

Addison	On Party-lying
Bronowski	The Real Responsibilities of the Scientist
Carson	The Obligation to Endure
Crean	Taking the Missionary Position
Forster	My Wood
Gould	Posture Maketh the Man
Himmelfarb	A Neo-Luddite Reflects on the Internet
Ingram	The Cathedral Square
Kennedy	Who Killed King Kong?
Koertge	Are Feminists Alienating Women from the Sciences?
MacLennan	The Shadow of Captain Bligh
Orwell	Politics and the English Language
Richler	An Unquiet Awakening
Rybczynski	Nostalgia
Sillitoe	Sport and Nationalism
Suzuki	The Pain of Animals
Tan	In the Canon, For All the Wrong Reasons
Taylor	Women and Criticism
Thoreau	Civil Disobedience
Vanderhaeghe	Influences
Walker	Westward Oh!
Woodcock	The Tyranny of the Clock

Essays which employ classification

Addison	On Party-lying
Andersen	The Origin of Alien Species
De Quincey	The Literature of Knowledge and the Literature of Power
Bacon	Of Studies
Lurie	Women's Clothes — Towards Emancipation
Orwell	Politics and the English Language
Woolf	How Should One Read a Book?

Essays which employ comparison and contrast

Anderson- Dargatz	Errington, B.C.
Bacon	Of Marriage and Single Life
Barreca	How Many Feminists Does It Take to Change a Light Bulb?
Brody	A Hearing
De Quincey	The Literature of Knowledge and the Literature of Power
Eiseley	The Bird and the Machine
Flanner	Murder Among the Lovebirds
Freedman	The Aggressive Egg
Frye	The Motive for Metaphor
MacLennan	The Shadow of Captain Bligh
Plumb	De Mortuis
Twain	A River Pilot Looks at the Mississippi
Vanderhaeghe	Influences

Essays which employ definition

Allen	Slang Origins
De Quincey	The Literature of Knowledge and the Literature of Power
Forster	My Wood
Leacock	Roughing It in the Bush (My Plans for Moose-Hunting in the Canadian Wilderness)
Salutin	Loose Canons
Stegner	Specifications for a Hero
Tuchman	The Historian's Opportunity

Essays which employ description

Anderson- Dargatz	Errington, B.C.
Brody	A Hearing
Dobbs	Matata
Iglauer	Bella Coola
Laurence	Where the World Began
Lurie	Women's Clothes — Towards Emancipation
Morris	St John's
Mowat	The Nature of the North
Trudeau	To Our Valued Customers
Twain	A River Pilot Looks at the Mississippi
Welsh	Women in the Shadows: Reclaiming a Métis Heritage
Wilson	Storm Over the Amazon

Essays which employ example and illustration

Allen	Slang Origins
Barreca	How Many Feminists Does It Take to Change a Light Bulb?

Bettelheim   The Art of Moving Pictures
Bissoondath   I Am Canadian
Francis   Re-hanging the National Wallpaper: The Group of Seven and
                   the Public Mind
Giangrande   Allowing the Mind to Wander
Hoban   Thoughts on a Shirtless Cyclist, Robin Hood and One or Two
                   Other Things
Johnson   The Abuses of Advertising
Johnston   Is That All There Is? Tribal Literature
Lurie   Women's Clothes — Towards Emancipation
Natoli   *The Unforgiven:* Histories and "Indians"
Orwell   Politics and the English Language
Salutin   Loose Canons
Suzuki   The Pain of Animals
Thomas   Humanities and Science
Tuchman   The Historian's Opportunity
Visser   Feeding, Feasts and Females
Walker   Westward Oh!

Essays which employ induction and deduction

Bibby   The Body in the Bog
Dryden   The Game
Kennedy   Who Killed King Kong?
Orwell   Politics and the English Language
Rybczynski   Nostalgia
Sillitoe   Sport and Nationalism
Trefil   Unexpected Vistas
Woodcock   The Tyranny of the Clock

Essays which employ narration

Barreca   How Many Feminists Does It Take to Change a Light Bulb?
Bibby   The Body in the Bog
Brody   A Hearing
Dobbs   Matata
Eiseley   The Bird and the Machine
Francis   Re-hanging the National Wallpaper: The Group of Seven and
                   the Public Mind
Freedman   The Aggressive Egg
Flanner   Murder Among the Lovebirds
Highsmith   Child's Play 4?
Iglauer   Bella Coola
Orwell   Shooting an Elephant
Selzer   The Discus Thrower
Stegner   Specifications for a Hero

Tan	In the Canon, For All the Wrong Reasons
Thoreau	Civil Disobedience
Welsh	Women in the Shadows: Reclaiming a Métis Heritage
White	Death of a Pig

Essays which employ humour and satire

Allen	Slang Origins
Andersen	The Origin of Alien Species
Baker	Little Red Riding Hood Revisited
Barreca	How Many Feminists Does It Take to Change a Light Bulb?
Forster	My Wood
Kael	New Age Daydreams [*Dances With Wolves*]
Leacock	Roughing it in the Bush (My Plans for Moose-Hunting in the Canadian Wilderness)
Royko	Another Accolade for Charter Arms Corp.
Salutin	Loose Canons
Swift	A Modest Proposal
Trudeau	To Our Valued Customers

Chronological Table of Contents

1613	BACON, Sir Francis	Of Marriage and Single Life
1613	BACON, Sir Francis	Of Studies
1712	ADDISON, Joseph	On Party-lying
1729	SWIFT, Jonathan	A Modest Proposal
1759	JOHNSON, Samuel	The Abuses of Advertising
1848	DE QUINCEY, Thomas	The Literature of Knowledge and the Literature of Power
1849	THOREAU, Henry David	Civil Disobedience
1866	TAYLOR, Helen	Women and Criticism
1875	TWAIN, Mark	A River Pilot Looks at the Mississippi
1923	LEACOCK, Stephen	Roughing it in the Bush (My Plans for Moose-Hunting in the Canadian Wilderness)
1926	FORSTER, E.M.	My Wood
1928	HALDANE, J.B.S.	Some Enemies of Science
1932	WOOLF, Virginia	How Should One Read a Book?
1936	FLANNER, Janet	Murder Among the Lovebirds
1936	ORWELL, George	Shooting an Elephant
1944	WOODCOCK, George	The Tyranny of the Clock
1946	ORWELL, George	Politics and the English Language
1947	WHITE, E.B.	Death of a Pig
1953	MacLENNAN, Hugh	The Shadow of Captain Bligh
1955	EISELEY, Loren	The Bird and the Machine
1955	STEGNER, Wallace	Specifications for a Hero
1956	BRONOWSKI, Jacob	The Real Responsibilities of the Scientist
1960	KENNEDY, X.J.	Who Killed King Kong?
1962	CARSON, Rachel	The Obligation to Endure
1962	DOBBS, Kildare	Matata
1963	FRYE, Northrop	The Motive for Metaphor
1967	MOWAT, Farley	The Nature of the North
1967	PLUMB, J.H.	De Mortuis
1967	TUCHMAN, Barbara	The Historian's Opportunity
1968	BIBBY, Geoffrey	The Body in the Bog
1970	HOGGART, Richard	The Case Against Advertising
1971	HOBAN, Russell	Thoughts on a Shirtless Cyclist, Robin Hood and One or Two Other Things

1971	LAURENCE, Margaret	Where the World Began
1972	SILLITOE, Alan	Sport and Nationalism
1972	STEINEM, Gloria	Marilyn Monroe: The Woman Who Died Too Soon
1973	GOULD, Stephen Jay	Posture Maketh the Man
1975	ALLEN, Woody	Slang Origins
1977	SELZER, Richard	The Discus Thrower
1979	BAKER, Russell	Little Red Riding Hood Revisited
1980	ROYKO, Mike	Another Accolade for Charter Arms Corp.
1981	ATWOOD, Margaret	The Writer's Responsibility
1981	BETTELHEIM, Bruno	The Art of Moving Pictures
1981	BRODY, Hugh	A Hearing
1981	LURIE, Alison	Women's Clothes — Towards Emancipation
1983	DRYDEN, Ken	The Game
1983	THOMAS, Lewis	Humanities and Science
1983	TREFIL, James	Unexpected Vistas
1984	VANDERHAEGHE, Guy	Influences
1986	RICHLER, Mordecai	An Unquiet Awakening
1986	RYBCZYNSKI, Witold	Nostalgia
1986	WILSON, Edward O.	Storm Over the Amazon
1987	FRASER, Fil	Black Like Me
1988	IGLAUER, Edith	Bella Coola
1989	MORRIS, Jan	St John's
1989	SUZUKI, David	The Pain of Animals
1990	GIANGRANDE, Carole	Allowing the Mind to Wander
1990	KAEL, Pauline	New Age Daydreams
1990	KEESHIG-TOBIAS, Lenore	Stop Stealing Native Stories
1991	BARRECA, Regina	How Many Feminists Does It Take to Change a Light Bulb?
1991	CASTILLO, Edward D.	*Dances With Wolves:* Review
1991	CREAN, Susan	Taking the Missionary Position
1991	FARR, Moira	Dangerous Determination
1991	JOHNSTON, Basil H.	Is That All There Is? Tribal Literature
1991	SALUTIN, Rick	Loose Canons
1991	VISSER, Margaret	Feeding, Feasts and Females
1991	WALKER, Martin	Westward Oh!
1992	FREEDMAN, David H.	The Aggressive Egg
1994	AMIS, Martin	Blown Away
1994	BISSOONDATH, Neil	I Am Canadian
1994	HIGHSMITH, Patricia	Child's Play 4?
1994	INGRAM, Jay	The Cathedral Square

1994	KOERTGE, Noretta	Are Feminists Alienating Women from the Sciences?
1994	NATOLI, Joseph	*The Unforgiven:* Histories and "Indians"
1995	WELSH, Christine	Women in the Shadows: Reclaiming a Métis Heritage
1996	ANDERSON-DARGATZ, Gail	Errington, B.C.
1996	FRANCIS, Daniel	Re-hanging the National Wallpaper
1996	HIMMELFARB, Gertrude	A Neo-Luddite Reflects on the Internet
1996	TAN, Amy	In the Canon, For All the Wrong Reasons
1996	TRUDEAU, Garry	To Our Valued Customers
1997	ANDERSEN, Kurt	The Origin of Alien Species

Acknowledgements

Woody Allen, "Slang Origins," from *Without Feathers* © 1975 by Woody Allen. Reprinted by permission of Random House Inc.

Martin Amis, "Blown Away," from *The New Yorker*, May 30, 1994. Reprinted with permission.

Kurt Andersen, "The Origin of Alien Species," from *The New Yorker*, July 14, 1997. Reprinted with permission.

Gail Anderson-Dargatz, "Errington, B.C.," from *Western Living*, December 1996; copyright © 1996 by Gail Anderson-Dargatz.

Margaret Atwood, "The Writer's Responsibility," published as "Amnesty International: An Address" in *Second Words: Selected Critical Prose* (Toronto: House of Anansi Press, 1982).

Russell Baker, "Little Red Riding Hood Revisited," Copyright © 1980 by The New York Times Company. Reprinted by permission.

Regina Barreca, "How Many Feminists Does It Take to Change a Light Bulb?" from *They Used to Call Me Snow White ... But I Drifted: Women's Strategic Use of Humor.* Copyright © 1991 by Regina Barreca. Used by permission of Viking Penguin, a division of Penguin Books USA Inc.

Bruno Bettelheim, "The Art of Moving Pictures," reprinted by permission of the author and his agents. This article originally appeared in *Harper's Magazine.* Copyright © 1981 by Bruno Bettelheim.

Geoffrey Bibby, "The Body in the Bog," from the Winter 1968 issue of *Horizon.* Reprinted with permission from *Horizon*, Volume X, Number 1. Copyright 1968 by American Heritage, a division of Forbes Inc.

Neil Bissoondath, "I Am Canadian," from *Saturday Night*, October 1994. Copyright © 1994 by Neil Bissoondath. Reprinted by permission of the author.

Hugh Brody, "A Hearing," from *Maps and Dreams* by Hugh Brody. Copyright © 1981 Douglas & McIntyre Ltd. Reprinted by permission.

Jacob Bronowski, "The Real Responsibilities of the Scientist," reprinted by permission of the *Bulletin of Atomic Scientists*, a magazine of science and world affairs. Copyright © 1956 by the Educational Foundation for Nuclear Sciences, 6042 South Kimbark, Chicago, IL 60637.

Rachel Carson, "The Obligation to Endure," from *Silent Spring* by Rachel Carson. Copyright © 1962 by Rachel L. Carson. Copyright © renewed 1990 by Roger Christie. Reprinted by permission of Houghton Mifflin Company. All rights reserved.

Edward D. Castillo, "*Dances With Wolves:* Review." *Film Quarterly* 44.4 (Summer 1991): 14–23. Reprinted by permission.

Susan Crean, "Taking the Missionary Position," *This Magazine* 24.6 (February 1991): 23–28. Reprinted by permission.

Kildare Dobbs, "Matata," from *Running to Paradise* by Kildare Dobbs. Copyright © Oxford University Press 1962. Reproduced by permission of the publisher.

Ken Dryden, "The Game," from *The Game*, © 1983 Ken Dryden. Reprinted by permission of Macmillan of Canada, a division of Canada Publishing Corporation.

Loren Eiseley, "The Bird and the Machine," from *The Immense Journey* by Loren Eiseley, Copyright © 1955 by Loren Eiseley. Reprinted by permission of Random House Inc.

Moira Farr, "Dangerous Determination." *This Magazine* 24.7 (March/April 1991): 10–15. Reprinted by permission.

Janet Flanner, "Murder Among the Lovebirds," from *Paris Was Yesterday* by Janet Flanner, Copyright © 1940 by Janet Flanner, renewed 1968 by Janet Flanner. Reprinted by permission of Viking Penguin Inc.

E.M. Forster, "My Wood," from *Abinger Harvest* by E.M. Forster; reprinted by permission of Edward Arnold (Publishers) Ltd.

Daniel Francis, "Re-hanging the National Wallpaper: The Group of Seven and the Public Mind," from *Geist* 21, Spring 1996. Copyright © 1996.

Fil Fraser, "Black Like Me." *Saturday Magazine*, January 1987. *Between Worlds*, ed. Maggie Groh and Craig Stephenson. Oakville, Ont.: Rubicon, 1989, 101–111. Reprinted by permission.

David H. Freedman, "The Aggressive Egg," from *Discover Magazine*, June 1992. Reprinted by permission.

Northrop Frye, "The Motive for Metaphor," excerpted from *The Educated Imagination* by Northrop Frye (C.B.C., 1963). Reprinted with permission.

Carole Giangrande, "Allowing the Mind to Wander." *The Globe and Mail*, 19 September 1990. Reprinted by permission.

Language and Communication

Slang Origins

by Woody Allen

How many of you have ever wondered where certain slang expressions 1
come from? Like "She's the cat's pajamas," or to "take it on the lam."
Neither have I. And yet for those who are interested in this sort of thing
I have provided a brief guide to a few of the more interesting origins.

Unfortunately, time did not permit consulting any of the established 2
works on the subject, and I was forced to either obtain the information
from friends or fill in certain gaps by using my own common sense.

Take, for instance, the expression "to eat humble pie." During the 3
reign of Louis the Fat, the culinary arts flourished in France to a degree
unequaled anywhere. So obese was the French monarch that he had to
be lowered onto the throne with a winch and packed into the seat itself
with a large spatula. A typical dinner (according to DeRochet) consisted
of a thin crêpe appetizer, some parsley, an ox, and custard. Food became the court obsession, and no other subject could be discussed under penalty of death. Members of a decadent aristocracy consumed
incredible meals and even dressed as foods. DeRochet tells us that M.
Monsant showed up at the coronation as a weiner, and Étienne Tisserant
received papal dispensation to wed his favorite codfish. Desserts grew
more and more elaborate and pies grew larger and larger until the minister of justice suffocated trying to eat a seven-foot "Jumbo pie." *Jumbo*
pie soon became *jumble* pie and "to eat a jumble pie" referred to any
kind of humiliating act. When the Spanish seamen heard the word
jumble, they pronounced it "humble," although many preferred to say
nothing and simply grin.

Now, while "humble pie" goes back to the French, "take it on the 4 lam" is English in origin. Years ago, in England, "lamming" was a game played with dice and a large tube of ointment. Each player in turn threw dice and then skipped around the room until he hemorrhaged. If a person threw seven or under he would say the word "quintz" and proceed to twirl in a frenzy. If he threw over seven, he was forced to give every player a portion of his feathers and was given a good "lamming." Three "lammings" and a player was "kwirled" or declared a moral bankrupt. Gradually any game with feathers was called "lamming" and feathers became "lams." To "take it on the lam" meant to put on feathers and later, to escape, although the transition is unclear.

5   Incidentally, if two of the players disagreed on the rules, we might say they "got into a beef." This term goes back to the Renaissance when a man would court a woman by stroking the side of her head with a slab of meat. If she pulled away, it meant she was spoken for. If, however, she assisted by clamping the meat to her face and pushing it all over her head, it meant she would marry him. The meat was kept by the bride's parents and worn as a hat on special occasions. If, however, the husband took another lover, the wife could dissolve the marriage by running with the meat to the town square and yelling, "With thine own beef, I do reject thee. Aroo! Aroo!" If a couple "took to the beef" or "had a beef" it meant they were quarreling.

6   Another marital custom gives us that eloquent and colorful expression of disdain, "to look down one's nose." In Persia it was considered a mark of great beauty for a woman to have a long nose. In fact, the longer the nose, the more desirable the female, up to a certain point. Then it became funny. When a man proposed to a beautiful woman he awaited her decision on bended knee as she "looked down her nose at him." If her nostrils twitched, he was accepted, but if she sharpened her nose with pumice and began pecking him on the neck and shoulders, it meant she loved another.

7   Now, we all know when someone is very dressed up, we say he looks "spiffy." The term owes its origin to Sir Oswald Spiffy, perhaps the most renowned fop of Victorian England. Heir to treacle millions, Spiffy squandered his money on clothes. It was said that at one time he owned enough handkerchiefs for all the men, women and children in Asia to blow their noses for seven years without stopping. Spiffy's sartorial innovations were legend, and he was the first man ever to wear gloves on his head. Because of extra-sensitive skin, Spiffy's underwear had to be made of the finest Nova Scotia salmon, carefully sliced by one particular tailor. His libertine attitudes involved him in several notorious scan-

dals, and he eventually sued the government over the right to wear ear-muffs while fondling a dwarf. In the end, Spiffy died a broken man in Chichester, his total wardrobe reduced to kneepads and a sombrero.

Looking "spiffy," then, is quite a compliment, and one who does is 8 liable to be dressed "to beat the band," a turn-of-the-century expression that originated from the custom of attacking with clubs any symphony orchestra whose conductor smiled during Berlioz. "Beating the band" soon became a popular evening out, and people dressed up in their fin-est clothes, carrying with them sticks and rocks. The practice was fi-nally abandoned during a performance of the *Symphonie Fantastique* in New York when the entire string section suddenly stopped playing and exchanged gun-fire with the first ten rows. Police ended the melee but not before a relative of J.P. Morgan's was wounded in the soft pal-ate. After that, for a while at least, nobody dressed "to beat the band."

If you think some of the above derivations questionable, you might 9 throw up your hands and say, "Fiddlesticks." This marvelous expres-sion originated in Austria many years ago. Whenever a man in the bank-ing profession announced his marriage to a circus pinhead, it was the custom for friends to present him with a bellows and a three-year sup-ply of wax fruit. Legend has it that when Leo Rothschild made known his betrothal, a box of cello bows was delivered to him by mistake. When it was opened and found not to contain the traditional gift, he exclaimed, "What are these? Where are my bellows and fruit? Eh? All I rate is fid-dlesticks!" The term "fiddlesticks" became a joke overnight in the tav-erns amongst the lower classes, who hated Leo Rothschild for never removing the comb from his hair after combing it. Eventually "fiddle-sticks" meant any foolishness.

Well, I hope you've enjoyed some of these slang origins and that they 10 stimulate you to investigate some on your own. And in case you were wondering about the term used to open this study, "the cat's pajamas," it goes back to an old burlesque routine of Chase and Rowe's, the two nutsy German professors. Dressed in oversized tails, Bill Rowe stole some poor victim's pajamas. Dave Chase, who got great mileage out of his "hard of hearing" specialty, would ask him:

Chase: Ach, Herr Professor. Vot is dot bulge under your pocket?
Rowe: Dot? Dot's de chap's pajamas.
Chase: The cat's pajamas? Ut mein Gott?

Audiences were convulsed by this sort of repartee and only a prema- 11 ture death of the team by strangulation kept them from stardom.

(1975)

The Writer's Subject

1. Allen's essay is an example of literary burlesque. What form of writing is Allen burlesquing in this essay?

2. The essay depends for its effect upon inventing incredible etymologies for well-known phrases such as "to eat humble pie" or "to look down one's nose." With the help of a dictionary of etymology, choose any of the words or phrases that Allen pretends to explain, and trace its real origin.

The Writer's Style and Strategy

1. What assumptions does Allen make about his audience in paragraph 1?

2. What methods associated with sociology does Allen pretend to employ in his study of word origins?

3. Allen uses a variety of techniques to achieve his humorous effects, such as inflating the trivial, reversing the reader's expectations, juxtaposing sense and nonsense, mixing real names (Morgan, Rothschild) with invented ones (Sir Oswald Spiffy), or combining objects or ideas in unexpected ways. Take one of Allen's explanations (e.g., "to eat humble pie" in para. 3), and try to pinpoint the means by which he creates humour.

4. Allen imposes an apparent order on his material by means of transitions. Examine some of these transitions and comment on their logic.

Suggested Topics for Writing and Discussion

1. Allen pokes fun at odd customs, as well as at essays on the curiosities of language. For example, the "custom" he describes in paragraph 5 concerning the use of a slab of meat in courtship and marriage during the Renaissance is not significantly more ridiculous than such real customs as a girl's putting a slice of wedding cake under her pillow, or having baby shoes coated in bronze. Discuss one or two odd or peculiar customs you are familiar with, and trace their origins as far as you can.

2. Choose one of the following slang expressions, and make up your own derivation in the style of Allen's essay: off his rocker; round the bend; dressed fit to kill.

3. Give a description of a group of slang terms which you or your friends currently use. Write explanations of these terms for a member of the older generation.

Little Red Riding Hood
Revisited

by Russell Baker

In an effort to make the classics accessible to contemporary readers, I am translating them into the modern American language. Here is the translation of *Little Red Riding Hood:* 1

Once upon a point in time, a small person named Little Red Riding 2 Hood initiated plans for the preparation, delivery and transportation of foodstuffs to her grandmother, a senior citizen residing at a place of residence in a wooded area of indeterminate dimension.

In the process of implementing this program, her incursion into the 3 area was in mid-transportation process when it attained interface with an alleged perpetrator. This individual, a wolf, made inquiry as to the whereabouts of Little Red Riding Hood's goal, as well as inferring that he was desirous of ascertaining the contents of Little Red Riding Hood's foodstuffs basket, and all that.

"It would be inappropriate to lie to me," the wolf said, displaying his 4 huge jaw capability. Sensing that he was a mass of repressed hostility intertwined with acute alienation, she indicated.

"I see you indicating," the wolf said, "but what I don't see is what- 5 ever it is you're indicating at, you dig?"

Little Red Riding Hood indicated more fully, making one thing per- 6 fectly clear — to wit, that it was to her grandmother's residence and with a consignment of foodstuffs that her mission consisted of taking her to and with.

At this point in time the wolf moderated his rhetoric and proceeded 7 to grandmother's residence. The elderly person was then subjected to the disadvantages of total consumption and transferred to residence in the perpetrator's stomach.

8   "That will raise the old woman's consciousness," the wolf said to himself. He was not a bad wolf, but only a victim of an oppressive society, a society that not only denied wolves' rights, but actually boasted of its capacity for keeping the wolf from the door. An interior malaise made itself manifest inside the wolf.

9   "Is that the national malaise I sense within my digestive tract?" wondered the wolf. "Or is it the old person seeking to retaliate for her consumption by telling wolf jokes to my duodenum?" It was time to make a judgment. The time was now, the hour had struck, the body lupine cried out for decision. The wolf was up to the challenge. He took two stomach powders right away and got into bed.

10   The wolf had adopted the abdominal distress recovery posture when Little Red Riding Hood achieved his presence.

11   "Grandmother," she said, "your ocular implements are of an extraordinary order of magnitude."

12   "The purpose of this enlarged viewing capability," said the wolf, "is to enable your image to register a more precise impression upon my sight systems."

13   "In reference to your ears," said Little Red Riding Hood, "it is noted with the deepest respect that far from being underprivileged, their elongation and enlargement appear to qualify you for unparalleled distinction."

14   "I hear you loud and clear, kid," said the wolf, "but what about these new choppers?"

15   "If it is not inappropriate," said Little Red Riding Hood, "it might be observed that with your new miracle masticating products you may even be able to chew taffy again."

16   This observation was followed by the adoption of an aggressive posture on the part of the wolf and the assertion that it was also possible for him, due to the high efficiency ratio of his jaw, to consume little persons, plus, as he stated, his firm determination to do so at once without delay and with all due process and propriety, notwithstanding the fact that the ingestion of one entire grandmother had already provided twice his daily recommended cholesterol intake.

17   There ensued flight by Little Red Riding Hood accompanied by pursuit in respect to the wolf and a subsequent intervention on the part of a third party, heretofore unnoted in the record.

Due to the firmness of the intervention, the wolf's stomach under- 18
went ax-assisted aperture with the result that Little Red Riding Hood's
grandmother was enabled to be removed with only minor discomfort.

The wolf's indigestion was immediately alleviated with such effec- 19
tiveness that he signed a contract with the intervening third party to perform with grandmother in a television commercial demonstrating the
swiftness of this dramatic relief for stomach discontent.

"I'm going to be on television," cried grandmother. 20

And they all joined her happily in crying, "What a phenomena!" 21

(1979)

The Writer's Subject

1. Baker takes the traditional folktale of "Little Red Riding Hood" and
   "translates" it into an inflated jargon-ridden English. What is his purpose
   in doing this?

2. What are the objects of Baker's satire in his opening sentence?

3. In the original story, the wolf was clearly the villain, but in Baker's version he is described as "a victim of an oppressive society" (para. 8). What
   is Baker making fun of through this change?

4. The traditional story ends with the death of the wolf at the hands of a
   woodsman. What is the point Baker makes through the changed ending?

5. What comment on modern American values is Baker making in this essay?

The Writer's Style and Strategy

1. Why does Russell Baker use the phrase "the modern American language"
   in paragraph 1?

2. The inflated language of this essay draws attention to the abuse of English
   by writers who use jargon, euphemism, and needlessly elaborate diction.
   Pick out examples of each of these abuses as they are mimicked by Baker,
   and suggest what areas they might be drawn from (e.g., politics, law, psychology, advertising).

3. At what kind of audience is Baker aiming his essay?

4. What effect is created by the sudden injection of slang in paragraphs 5
   and 14?

5. Comment on Baker's use of clichés in this essay.

6. "Translate" one of the paragraphs of the essay (e.g., paras. 2, 3, 7, 16) into

plain English, and compare the number of words you require with the number in the original.

7. Baker uses many passive constructions (e.g., "it is noted that ..."; "it might be observed that ..."; "this observation was followed by ..."). What is Baker's purpose?

8. Comment on the closing sentence of the essay.

Suggested Topics for Writing and Discussion

1. Choose a well known folktale or fairy tale, and "translate it for a modern reader" in the way that Baker has done with "Little Red Riding Hood."

2. Discuss the ways in which Baker's essay is similar to Orwell's "Politics and the English Language" in its attitude to the uses and abuses of language.

3. Choose a well known folktale or fairy tale and write a satirical modern ending of the kind which Baker has provided in "Little Red Riding Hood Revisited." Explain why you have changed the ending.

4. Baker's treatment of "Little Red Riding Hood" suggests that he does not think such classics need "updating." One area in which "updating" is taking place is in literature for children. What is your view of the current trend to update classic children's stories, notably to remove elements now thought to be sexist or violent? Consult your local library for information on this movement.

The Case Against Advertising

by Richard Hoggart

By turns hurt, defiant, apologetic and self-justifying, advertising men   1
seem particularly sensitive to criticism just now. Criticism has certainly
been heavy in the last few years, perhaps because the number of reasonably well-informed people is somewhat greater than it used to be.
You need a fairly widespread critical public opinion to get the Consumers' Association, the Advertising Inquiry Council and similar organizations started. Yet few people in advertising have taken the measure of
this development. Some have seen its superficial aspects and made their
advertising more self-conscious and sophisticated; but the moderate
widening of critical opinion has so far escaped almost all of them.

I will try to sum up as directly as I can the case against advertising.   2
Even so, I do not expect to have much, if any, effect. None of us likes
our profession to be attacked, and we fight back when it is. But usually
someone somewhere in a profession steps out of line and says that he
does see some justice in the criticisms, that some things in his particular house do need to be put in order. This can be seen in the quite fierce
arguments about the function and financing of universities today. But I
have not heard any spokesman of the advertising (or public relations)
industry admit to other than minor faults (that claims are sometimes a
bit exaggerated, say, or not strictly truthful); I have not heard any spokesman of the industry take the full measure of the case against advertising, let alone answer it.

Why is this? Is it because a profession which lives by manipulating   3
reality, by weaving attractive but deceptive verbal links between products and potential consumers, gets taken in by its own sleight-of-hand?

And that, by-and-large, such a trade gets the servants it needs, who fit its demands and are suited by them? For such men, when they find themselves criticized, the temptation to sell themselves a rationalization, like an outfitter clothing himself from stock, must be strong. Still, if the case against advertising is going to be seen (not necessarily accepted, but at least seen), then people in advertising have to make a harder effort than they have made so far. The time for easy rides, especially for the big public spokesman of advertising, is past.

4   To get a few red herrings out of the way first. There can be some unexceptionable advertising (and it need not be dull). It has not been proved that advertising in its present form (the kind of advertising that is being criticized) is essential to the economy, or reduces costs. It is true that the industry has done some self-policing; but only at an innocuous, true-or-false level. Last, no one in his senses is proposing censorship; anyway, the important problems could not be touched by censorship.

5   The really serious questions raised by advertising are much wider than advertising itself. If critics spend a lot of time attacking advertising this is not because advertising is a peculiar kind of vice, but because it is a symptom, because it exhibits more plainly and persistently than anything else the issues raised by mass persuasion. At bottom the case against advertising is the same as that against political propaganda, much religious proselytizing and any other form of emotional blackmail.

6   The case is this: that advertising tries to achieve its ends by emotionally abusing its audiences. Recognizing that we all have fears, hopes, anxieties, aspirations, insecurities, advertisers seek not to increase our understanding of these feelings and so perhaps our command of them, but to use their existence to increase the sales of whatever product they happen to have been paid to sell at any particular time. They exploit human inadequacy, and we have the right to say to them what Hamlet said to Guildenstern: "Why look you now, how unworthy a thing you make of me; you would play upon me; you would seem to know my stops; you would pluck out the heart of my mystery; you would sound me from my lowest note, to the top of my compass.... Why do you think that I am easier to be played on, than a pipe?"

7   There is no point in illustrating, since illustrations are all around, nor in elaborating on the occasional exceptions. The basic charge is indisputable, unless you adopt a purely predatory — every man for himself — attitude; in which case there is no basis for argument. But if you accept some responsibility in your conduct towards others then

you have problems, in advertising, which verbal manoeuvres can only evade, not solve.

Some apologists seek to rebut all this by taking up the Stance of the 8
Licensed Pantaloon. You are too solemn, they argue. No one really believes what we say. The ordinary chap is much more subtle than you give him credit for. He recognizes that we add to the amusement and colour of his life — and that's all there is to it.

Coming from anyone who has read the research literature this is dis- 9
ingenuous. The evidence shows, and a reasonably close acquaintance with 'ordinary people' will tell you anyway, that a lot of people do literally believe what they read in the ads. A surprising number, when you think of the effort which goes into training in literacy. Still, that effort has been long delayed and is still small in proportion to the need. Most men in advertising are, of course, more effectively trained, more articulate and mentally quicker than their audiences — which doesn't make the business any pleasanter. What usually passes for sophisticated advertising (e.g. in the Sunday glossies) is at bottom as simple in its appeals as the stuff in the mass circulation papers; its stage-properties and snobberies are different, that's all. Outside that range there is, I suppose, a small core of self-aware intellectuals who do enjoy, or claim to enjoy, advertisements as aesthetic objects, as sources of verbal, sociological or psychological fun. Most talk of this kind strikes me as disingenuous; but men in advertising are grateful for it. It confirms their status as harmless amusers and pays tribute to their verbal inventiveness. Since there is a poet or novelist manqué inside many a copywriter, this is a benison. And an outsider may feel that, though it is a sad little claim they are making, at least it isn't portentous.

It is easy to appreciate the excitement, even the glamour, which ad- 10
vertising can have. Playing with words, making them do tricks for you within narrowly prescribed rules (this product, this target audience, this number of words), is obviously fascinating and in some ways similar to working within the rules of a simple literary form. I once passed hours, on a sticky hot journey by troop-train from Italy, inventing copy (with a man who is now a very popular columnist) for 'Critch,' a mythical powder which would eliminate the awful persistent itch in our crutches. Still, how long can that sort of fun satisfy a man? A long time, I suppose, if the rewards are good, and if you find something cathartic for your spare time. But it's a shabby business.

Which is why the least attractive people in the whole advertising busi- 11
ness are the front men with the public relations voices — the men who

cheer up conferences with fighting keynote speeches about the public-service element in advertising and make prepared palliative statements on all other suitable occasions. Their routine is usually predictable. They assert that advertising is the linch-pin or lubricant of a modern progressive economy. They use words like 'creative', 'dedicated' and 'sincere', so much that you remember Hemingway's *A Farewell to Arms:* "I was always embarrassed by the words. There were many words that you could not stand to hear and finally only the names of places had dignity. Abstract words were obscene...." They take a few cheering-up-the-troops swipes at critics (this is a fairly recent development), and offer the services of advertising to promote any good cause the community can name — citizenship, education, religion.

12   With people like that you are really up against it. They seem to have no sense of the difficulty of truth and of the need to respect other people's effort after it: "There's no limit to the wonderful things advertising can be made to sell ... religion, social conscience, racial tolerance, education...." How do you explain that if religion is to mean anything it must be founded on personal commitment, arrived at with any help others can disinterestedly give, but in the end arrived at personally and in the fullest possible emotional clarity? Or how do you explain that illicit manoeuvres (associating religion with togetherness or smartness) cannot really convert anyone and only prepare the ground for equally illicit manoeuvres with more questionable ends. As 'professionals', Goebbels' ad men were very efficient indeed.

13   There is, of course, good persuasion as well as bad persuasion; and advertisers keep the debate murkier than it should be by sliding between the two types. In one sense, any good book is an act of persuasion. But the gap between that and the persuasion of advertisers is so large as to make virtually a difference of kind. Good persuasion, whether in dispassionate argument or in a powerfully moving novel, has two root qualities: respect for the reality of the subject, and respect for the listener's right to judge for himself his attitude to the subject. This definition does not rule out emotional engagement; any important commitment is a mixture of emotion and intellect. But it insists on emotional relevance — that the emotion, in both its nature and its intensity, fit the theme.

14   Naturally, the line between this and illicit emotional persuasion is a continuous one, and it is difficult to decide just where the watershed comes. But look at each end of the line and you see the distinction at once, and see its importance; and this makes it all the more important not to blur distinctions in the large middle area (which is where most of

the battles about persuasion are fought), but to try to make them clearer.

It is important for outside critics not to use advertisers as scapegoats 15
for bigger social problems; they reflect more than they affect in society.
There are a lot of reasons why a society such as this throws up so much
persuasion, and so to many people in advertising theirs seems as respectable a trade as many others.

That much can be granted. But it is just as important not to make 16
easy accommodations. The overriding fact is that much of the work of
this profession, as it is at present practised, consists of exploiting weakness, through language. Anyone who thinks it is better to try to understand one's weaknesses than to indulge them, anyone who thinks that
language (the articulation of our thoughts and feelings in communica-
ble form) can help in that better grasp, anyone with these two premises
must regard most modern advertising as, at the best, a waste of good
human resources and, at the worst, a misuse of other people.

(1970)

The Writer's Subject

1. Why, in Hoggart's view, have advertisers failed to criticize themselves?
   (paras. 2–3)

2. How, according to Hoggart, do advertisers emotionally abuse their audiences? (para. 6)

3. What kind of apology for advertising does Hoggart discuss in paragraph
   8? How does he regard such an apology?

4. What is Hoggart's view of "sophisticated advertising"? (para. 9)

5. Why, in speaking of the apparently limitless possibilities of advertising,
   does Hoggart end his paragraph with a reference to Goebbels? (para. 12)

6. How does Hoggart distinguish between good persuasion and bad persuasion in paragraphs 12–14?

The Writer's Style and Strategy

1. What kind of audience is implied in this essay? (See, for example, paragraphs 7 and 16.)

2. A way of dealing with opponents to an argument is to denigrate their views
   by making them seem trivial, irrelevant, or absurd. Find instances in this
   essay of Hoggart's use of this strategy.

3. Do you think Hoggart presents his "case" fairly and objectively?

4. Comment on Hoggart's use of the two literary references to works by Shakespeare and Hemingway. (paras. 6, 11)

5. What use does Hoggart make of personal anecdote to support his case against advertising?

Suggested Topics for Writing and Discussion

1. Write an argument in defense of advertising.

2. Hoggart sees advertising as merely one example of the workings of mass persuasion in our society. (para. 5) Discuss another example of mass persuasion (e.g., election campaigns, religious broadcasting), showing how it makes use of the techniques commonly used to sell products.

3. Hoggart says a few individuals "claim to enjoy advertisements as aesthetic objects." Can a serious claim be made for advertising as an art form? Give examples to support your view.

4. Describe an advertisement which has wide currency (i.e., on television, in national magazines) as "a source of verbal, sociological or psychological fun" and discuss the nature of its appeal.

The Abuses of Advertising

by Samuel Johnson

The Idler No. 40 - Saturday, 20 January 1759

The practice of appending to the narratives of public transactions, more 1
minute and domestic intelligence, and filling the news-papers with advertisements, has grown up by slow degrees to its present state.

Genius is shewn only by invention. The man who first took advan- 2
tage of the general curiosity that was excited by a siege or battle, to
betray the readers of news into the knowledge of the shop where the
best puffs and powder were to be sold, was undoubtedly a man of great
sagacity, and profound skill in the nature of man. But when he had once
shewn the way, it was easy to follow him; and every man now knows a
ready method of informing the publick of all that he desires to buy or
sell, whether his wares be material or intellectual; whether he makes
cloaths, or teaches the mathematics; whether he be a tutor that wants a
pupil, or a pupil that wants a tutor.

Whatever is common is despised. Advertisements are now so numer- 3
ous that they are very negligently perused, and it is therefore become
necessary to gain attention by magnificence of promises, and by eloquence sometimes sublime and sometimes pathetic.

Promise, large promise, is the soul of an advertisement. I remember 4
a "wash-ball" that had a quality truly wonderful, it gave "an exquisite
edge to the razor." And there are now to be sold "for ready money only,"
some "duvets for bed-coverings, of down, beyond comparison superior
to what is called otter down," and indeed such, that its "many excellen-
cies cannot be here set forth." With one excellence we are made ac-

quainted, "it is warmer than four or five blankets, and lighter than one."

5   There are some, however, that know the prejudice of mankind in favour of modest sincerity. The vendor of the "Beautifying Fluid" sells a
lotion that repels pimples, washes away freckles, smooths the skin, and
plumps the flesh; and yet, with a generous abhorrence of ostentation,
confesses, that it will not "restore the bloom of fifteen to a lady of fifty."

6   The true pathos of advertisements must have sunk deep into the heart
of every man that remembers the zeal shewn by the seller of the ano-
dyne necklace, for the ease and safety "of poor toothing infants," and
the affection with which he warned every mother, that "she would never
forgive herself" if her infant should perish without a necklace.

7   I cannot but remark to the celebrated author who gave, in his noti-
fications of the camel and dromedary, so many specimens of the genuine sublime, that there is now arrived another subject yet more worthy
of his pen. "A famous Mohawk Indian warrior, who took Dieskaw the
French general prisoner, dressed in the same manner with the native
Indians when they go to war, with his face and body painted, with his
scalping knife, tom-ax, and all other implements of war: a sight worthy the curiosity of every true Briton!" This is a very powerful description; but a critic of great refinement would say that it conveys rather
"horror" than "terror." An Indian, dressed as he goes to war, may bring
company together; but if he carries the scalping knife and tom-ax, there
are many true Britons that will never be persuaded to see him but
through a grate.

8   It has been remarked by the severer judges, that the salutary sorrow
of tragick scenes is too soon effaced by the merriment of the epilogue;
the same inconvenience arises from the improper disposition of advertisements. The noblest objects may be so associated as to be made ridiculous. The camel and dromedary themselves might have lost much
of their dignity between "The True Flower of Mustard" and "The Original Daffy's Elixir"; and I could not but feel some indignation when I
found this illustrious Indian warrior immediately succeeded by "A Fresh
Parcel of Dublin Butter."

9   The trade of advertising is now so near to perfection, that it is not
easy to propose any improvement. But as every art ought to be exercised in due subordination to the publick good, I cannot but propose it
as a moral question to these masters of the publick ear, whether they do
not sometimes play too wantonly with our passions, as when the register of lottery tickets invites us to his shop by an account of the prize
which he sold last year; and whether the advertising controvertists do

not indulge asperity of language without any adequate provocation; as in the dispute about "straps for razors," now happily subsided, and in the altercation which at present subsists concerning *Eau de Luce.*

In an advertisement it is allowed to every man to speak well of him- 10 self, but I know not why he should assume the privilege of censuring his neighbour. He may proclaim his own virtue or skill, but ought not to exclude others from the same pretensions.

Every man that advertises his own excellence, should write with some 11 consciousness of a character which dares to call the attention of the publick. He should remember that his name is to stand in the same paper with those of the King of Prussia, and the Emperor of Germany, and endeavour to make himself worthy of such association.

Some regard is likewise to be paid to posterity. There are men of dili- 12 gence and curiosity who treasure up the papers of the day merely because others neglect them, and in time they will be scarce. When these collections shall be read in another century, how will numberless contradictions be reconciled, and how shall fame be possibly distributed among the tailors and boddice-makers of the present age.

Surely these things deserve consideration. It is enough for me to have 13 hinted my desire that these abuses may be rectified; but such is the state of nature, that what all have the right of doing, many will attempt without sufficient care or due qualifications.

(1759)

The Writer's Subject

1. What are Johnson's speculations on how advertising began?

2. Explain what Johnson means by "Genius is shewn only by invention." (para. 2)

3. According to Johnson, what means do advertisers employ to attract attention to their products? (paras. 3–7)

4. In paragraphs 5 and 6, what styles or techniques of advertising does Johnson illustrate?

5. In paragraphs 7 and 8 Johnson describes an advertisement for the public exhibition of a Mohawk Indian Warrior. What aspects of advertising does he comment on through reference to this example?

6. In paragraphs 9 and 10, what faults of advertisers does Johnson point to?

7. Why, according to Johnson, should advertisers be concerned about "posterity"? (para. 12)

The Writer's Style and Strategy

1. Find an example of parallel structure in paragraph 2.

2. Johnson, it is often said, is excessively fond of lengthy, complex structures, yet in this essay he makes pointed use of the short simple sentence. Find several short sentences and comment upon their effectiveness.

3. What is the tone of the first sentence of paragraph 9?

4. How does Johnson structure the long sentence that makes up most of paragraph 9?

5. How does Johnson use sentence structure to present opposing views in paragraph 10?

6. What clues in paragraph 12 suggest that Johnson's concerns about posterity may not be entirely serious?

Suggested Topics for Writing and Discussion

1. Johnson complains of the state of advertising in his day — the mid-eighteenth century. In what ways are advertisements of today similar to those which Johnson discusses? Provide specific examples to support your view.

2. Johnson states that "Promise, large promise, is the soul of an advertisement." Choose one or two advertisements in which you feel the "promise" of the advertisement is a false one. Discuss the way in which language either exaggerates, distorts, or misrepresents the product being sold.

3. Johnson talks about the advertisers' unfair appeals to emotion in selling their products. Discuss one or two advertisements that seem to you to indulge in this same reprehensible practice. Identify the nature of these appeals to emotion.

Politics and the English Language
by George Orwell

Most people who bother with the matter at all would admit that the English language is in a bad way, but it is generally assumed that we cannot by conscious action do anything about it. Our civilization is decadent and our language — so the argument runs — must inevitably share in the general collapse. It follows that any struggle against the abuse of language is a sentimental archaism, like preferring candles to electric light or hansom cabs to aeroplanes. Underneath this lies the half-conscious belief that language is a natural growth and not an instrument which we shape for our own purposes.   1

Now, it is clear that the decline of a language must ultimately have political and economic causes: it is not due simply to the bad influence of this or that individual writer. But an effect can become a cause, reinforcing the original cause and producing the same effect in an intensified form, and so on indefinitely. A man may take to drink because he feels himself to be a failure, and then fail all the more completely because he drinks. It is rather the same thing that is happening to the English language. It becomes ugly and inaccurate because our thoughts are foolish, but the slovenliness of our language makes it easier for us to have foolish thoughts. The point is that the process is reversible. Modern English, especially written English, is full of bad habits which spread by imitation and which can be avoided if one is willing to take the necessary trouble. If one gets rid of these habits one can think more clearly, and to think clearly is a necessary first step towards political regeneration: so that the fight against bad English is not frivolous and is not the exclusive concern of professional writers. I will come back to this pres-   2 ently, and I hope that by that time the meaning of what I have said here will have become clearer. Meanwhile, here are five specimens of the English language as it is now habitually written.

3   These five passages have not been picked out because they are especially bad — I could have quoted far worse if I had chosen — but because they illustrate various of the mental vices from which we now suffer. They are a little below the average, but are fairly representative samples. I number them so that I can refer back to them when necessary:

"(1) I am not, indeed, sure whether it is not true to say that the Milton who once seemed not unlike a seventeenth-century Shelley had not become, out of an experience ever more bitter in each year, more alien *[sic]* to the founder of that Jesuit sect which nothing could induce him to tolerate."

Professor Harold Laski (Essay in *Freedom of Expression*).

"(2) Above all, we cannot play ducks and drakes with a native battery of idioms which prescribes such egregious collocations of vocables as the Basic *put up with* for *tolerate* or *put at a loss* for *bewilder*."

Professor Lancelot Hogben *(Interglossa)*.

"(3) On the one side we have the free personality: by definition it is not neurotic, for it has neither conflict nor dream. Its desires, such as they are, are transparent, for they are just what institutional approval keeps in the forefront of consciousness; another institutional pattern would alter their number and intensity; there is little in them that is natural, irreducible, or culturally dangerous. But *on the other side,* the social bond itself is nothing but the mutual reflection of these self-secure integrities. Recall the definition of love. Is not this the very picture of a small academic? Where is there a place in this hall of mirrors for either personality or fraternity?"

Essay on psychology in *Politics* (New York).

"(4) All the 'best people' from the gentlemen's clubs, and all the frantic fascist captains, united in common hatred of Socialism and bestial horror of the rising tide of the mass revolutionary movement, have turned to acts of provocation, to foul incendiarism, to medieval legends of poisoned wells, to legalize their own destruction of proletarian organizations, and rouse the agitated petty-bourgeoisie to chauvinistic fervour on behalf of the fight against the revolutionary way out of the crisis."

Communist pamphlet.

"(5) If a new spirit *is* to be infused into this old country, there is one thorny and contentious reform which must be tackled, and that is the humanization and galvanization of the B.B.C. Timidity here will bespeak canker and atrophy of the soul. The heart of Britain may be sound and of strong beat, for instance, but the British lion's roar at present is like that of Bottom in Shakespeare's *Midsummer Night's Dream* — as gentle as any sucking dove. A virile new Britain cannot continue indefinitely to be traduced in the eyes or rather ears, of the world by the effete languors of Langham Place, brazenly masquerading as 'standard English'. When the Voice of Britain is heard at nine o'clock, better far and infinitely less ludicrous to hear aitches honestly dropped than the present priggish, inflated, inhibited, school-ma'amish arch braying of blameless bashful mewing maidens!"

Letter in Tribune.

Each of these passages has faults of its own, but, quite apart from avoidable ugliness, two qualities are common to all of them. The first is staleness of imagery: the other is lack of precision. The writer either has a meaning and cannot express it, or he inadvertently says something else, or he is almost indifferent as to whether his words mean anything or not. This mixture of vagueness and sheer incompetence is the most marked characteristic of modern English prose, and especially of any kind of political writing. As soon as certain topics are raised, the concrete melts into the abstract and no one seems able to think of turns of speech that are not hackneyed: prose consists less and less of *words* chosen for the sake of their meaning, and more and more of *phrases* tacked together like the sections of a prefabricated hen-house. I list below, with notes and examples, various of the tricks by means of which the work of prose-construction is habitually dodged:

Dying Metaphors. A newly invented metaphor assists thought by evoking a visual image, while on the other hand a metaphor which is technically "dead" (e.g. *iron resolution*) has in effect reverted to being an ordinary word and can generally be used without loss of vividness. But in between these two classes there is a huge dump of worn-out metaphors which have lost all evocative power and are merely used because they save people the trouble of inventing phrases for themselves. Examples are: *Ring the changes on, take up the cudgels for, toe the line, ride roughshod over, stand shoulder to shoulder with, play into the hands of, no axe to grind, grist to the mill, fishing in troubled waters, on the order of the day, Achilles' heel, swan song, hotbed.* Many of these are used without knowledge of their meaning (what is a "rift", for instance?), and incompatible metaphors are frequently mixed, a sure sign that the writer is not interested in what he is saying. Some metaphors now current have been twisted out of their original meaning without those who use them even being aware of the fact. For example, *toe the line* is sometimes written *tow the line*. Another example is *the hammer and the anvil*, now always used with the implication that the anvil gets the worst of it. In real life it is always the anvil that breaks the hammer, never the other way about: a writer who stopped to think what he was saying would be aware of this, and would avoid perverting the original phrase.

6   *Operators* or *verbal false limbs*. These save the trouble of picking out appropriate verbs and nouns, and at the same time pad each sentence with extra syllables which give it an appearance of symmetry. Characteristic phrases are: *render inoperative, militate against, make contact with, be subjected to, give rise to, give grounds for, have the effect of, play a leading part (role) in, make itself felt, take effect, exhibit a tendency to, serve the purpose of, etc., etc.* The keynote is the elimination of simple verbs. Instead of being a single word, such as *break, stop, spoil, mend, kill*, a verb becomes a *phrase*, made up of a noun or adjective tacked on to some general-purposes verb such as *prove, serve, form, play, render.* In addition, the passive voice is wherever possible used in preference to the active, and noun constructions are used instead of gerunds *(by examination of* instead of *by examining).* The range of verbs is further cut down by means of the *-ize* and *de-* formations, and the banal statements are given an appearance of profundity by means of the *not un-* formation. Simple conjunctions and prepositions are replaced by such phrases as *with respect to, having regard to, the fact that, by dint of, in view of, in the interests of, on the hypothesis that;* and the ends of sentences are saved from anti-climax by such resounding commonplaces as *greatly to be desired, cannot be left out of account, a development to be expected in the near future, deserving of serious consideration, brought to a satisfactory conclusion,* and so on and so forth.

7   *Pretentious diction.* Words like *phenomenon, element, individual* (as noun), *objective, categorical, effective, virtual, basic, primary, promote, constitute, exhibit, exploit, utilize, eliminate, liquidate,* are used to dress up simple statements and give an air of scientific impartiality to biased judgments. Adjectives like *epoch-making, epic, historic, unforgettable, triumphant, age-old, inevitable, inexorable, veritable,* are used to dignify the sordid processes of international politics, while writing that aims

at glorifying war usually takes on an archaic colour, its characteristic words being: *realm, throne, chariot, mailed fist, trident, sword, shield, buckler, banner, jackboot, clarion.* Foreign words and expressions such as *cul de sac, ancien régime, deus ex machina, mutatis mutandis, status quo, gleichschaltung, weltanschauung,* are used to give an air of culture and elegance. Except for the useful abbreviations *i.e., e.g.,* and *etc.,* there is no real need for any of the hundreds of foreign phrases now current in English. Bad writers, and especially scientific, political and sociological writers, are nearly always haunted by the notion that Latin or Greek words are grander than Saxon ones, and unnecessary words like *expedite, ameliorate, predict, extraneous, deracinated, clandestine, subaqueous* and hundreds of others constantly gain ground from their Anglo-Saxon opposite numbers.[1] The jargon peculiar to Marxist writing *(hyena, hangman, cannibal, petty bourgeois, these gentry, lacquey, flunkey, mad dog, White Guard,* etc.) consists largely of words and phrases translated from Russian, German or French; but the normal way of coining a new word is to use a Latin or Greek root with the appropriate affix and, where necessary, the -ize formation. It is often easier to make up words of this kind *(deregionalize, impermissible, extramarital, non-fragmentatory* and so forth) than to think up the English words that will cover one's meaning. The result, in general, is an increase in slovenliness and vagueness.

Meaningless words. In certain kinds of writing, particularly in art criticism and literary criticism, it is normal to come across long passages which are almost completely lacking in meaning.[2] Words like *romantic, plastic, values, human, dead, sentimental, natural, vitality,* as used in art criticism, are strictly meaningless, in the sense that they not only do not point to any discoverable object, but are hardly ever expected to do so by the reader. When one critic writes, "The outstanding feature of Mr. X's work is its living quality", while another writes, "The immediately striking thing about Mr. X's work is its peculiar deadness", the reader accepts this as a simple difference of opinion. If words like *black* and *white* were involved, instead of the jargon words *dead* and *living,* he would see at once that language was being used in an improper way. Many political words are similarly abused. The word *Fascism* has now no meaning except in so far as it signifies "something not desirable". The words *democracy, socialism, freedom, patriotic, realistic, justice,* have each of them several different meanings which cannot be reconciled with one another. In the case of a word like *democracy,* not only is there no agreed definition, but the attempt to make one is resisted from all sides. It is almost universally felt that when we call a country democratic we are praising it: consequently the defenders of every kind of régime claim that it is a democracy, and fear that they might have to stop using the word if it were tied down to any one meaning. Words of this kind are often used in a consciously dishonest way. That is, the person who uses them has his own private definition, but allows his hearer to think he means something quite different. Statements like *Marshal Pétain was a true patriot, The Soviet Press is the freest in the world, The Catholic Church is opposed to persecution,* are almost always made with intent to deceive. Other words used in variable meanings, in most cases more or less dishonestly, are: *class, totalitarian, science, progressive, reactionary, bourgeois, equality.*

9   Now that I have made this catalogue of swindles and perversions, let me give another example of the kind of writing that they lead to. This time it must of its nature be an imaginary one. I am going to translate a passage of good English into modern English of the worst sort. Here is a well-known verse from *Ecclesiastes:*

"I returned and saw under the sun, that the race is not to the swift, nor the battle to the strong, neither yet bread to the wise, nor yet riches to men of understanding, nor yet favour to men of skill; but time and chance happeneth to them all."

10   Here it is in modern English:

"Objective consideration of contemporary phenomena compels the conclusion that success or failure in competitive activities exhibits no tendency to be commensurate with innate capacity, but that a considerable element of the unpredictable must invariably be taken into account."

11   This is a parody, but not a very gross one. Exhibit (3), above, for instance, contains several patches of the same kind of English. It will be seen that I have not made a full translation. The beginning and ending of the sentence follow the original meaning fairly closely, but in the middle the concrete illustrations — race, battle, bread — dissolve into the vague phrase "success or failure in competitive activities". This had to be so, because no modern writer of the kind I am discussing — no one capable of using phrases like "objective consideration of contemporary phenomena" — would ever tabulate his thoughts in that precise and detailed way. The whole tendency of modern prose is away from concreteness. Now analyse these two sentences a little more closely. The first contains forty-nine words but only sixty syllables, and all its words are those of everyday life. The second contains thirty-eight words of ninety syllables: eighteen of its words are from Latin roots, and one

from Greek. The first sentence contains six vivid images, and only one phrase ("time and chance") that could be called vague. The second contains not a single fresh, arresting phrase, and in spite of its ninety syllables it gives only a shortened version of the meaning contained in the first. Yet without a doubt it is the second kind of sentence that is gaining ground in modern English. I do not want to exaggerate. This kind of writing is not yet universal, and outcrops of simplicity will occur here and there in the worst-written page. Still, if you or I were told to write a few lines on the uncertainty of human fortunes, we should probably come much nearer to my imaginary sentence than to the one from *Ecclesiastes.*

As I have tried to show, modern writing at its worst does not consist 12 in picking out words for the sake of their meaning and inventing images in order to make the meaning clearer. It consists in gumming together long strips of words which have already been set in order by someone else, and making the results presentable by sheer humbug. The attraction of this way of writing is that it is easy. It is easier — even quicker, once you have the habit — to say *In my opinion it is a not unjustifiable assumption that* than to say *I think.* If you use ready-made phrases, you not only don't have to hunt about for words, you also don't have to bother with the rhythms of your sentences, since these phrases are generally so arranged as to be more or less euphonious. When you are composing in a hurry — when you are dictating to a stenographer, for instance, or making a public speech — it is natural to fall into a pretentious, Latinized style. Tags like *a consideration which we should do well to bear in mind* or *a conclusion to which all of us would readily assent* will save many a sentence from coming down with a bump. By using stale metaphors, similes and idioms, you save much mental effort, at the cost of leaving your meaning vague, not only for your reader but for yourself. This is the significance of mixed metaphors. The sole aim of a metaphor is to call up a visual image. When these images clash — as in *The Fascist octopus has sung its swan song, the jackboot is thrown into the melting pot* — it can be taken as certain that the writer is not seeing a mental image of the objects he is naming; in other words he is not really thinking. Look again at the examples I gave at the beginning of this essay. Professor Laski (1) uses five negatives in fifty-three words. One of these is superfluous, making nonsense of the whole passage, and in addition there is the slip *alien* for akin, making further nonsense, and several avoidable pieces of clumsiness which increase the general vagueness. Professor Hogben (2) plays ducks and drakes with a battery which is able to write prescriptions, and, while disapproving of the everyday phrase *put up with,* is unwilling to look *egregious* up in the dictionary and see what it means. (3), if one takes an uncharitable attitude towards it, is simply meaningless: probably one could work out its intended meaning by reading the whole of the article in which it occurs. In (4), the writer knows more or less what he wants to say, but an accumulation of stale phrases chokes him like tea leaves blocking a sink. In (5), words and meaning have almost parted company. People who write in this manner usually have a general emotional meaning — they dislike one thing and want to express solidarity with another — but they are not interested in the detail of what they are saying. A scrupulous writer, in every sentence that he writes, will ask himself at least four questions, thus: What am I trying to say? What words will express it? What image or idiom will make it clearer? Is this image fresh enough to have an effect? And he will probably ask himself two more: Could I put it more shortly? Have I said anything that is avoidably ugly? But you are not obliged to go to all this trouble. You can shirk it by simply throwing your mind open and letting the ready-made phrases come crowding in. They will construct your sentences for you — even think your thoughts for you, to a certain extent — and at need they will perform the important service of partially concealing your meaning even from yourself. It is at this point that the special connection between politics and the debasement of language becomes clear.

13   In our time it is broadly true that political writing is bad writing. Where it is not true, it will generally be found that the writer is some kind of rebel, expressing his private opinions and not a "party line". Orthodoxy, of whatever colour, seems to demand a lifeless, imitative style. The political dialects to be found in pamphlets, leading articles, manifestos, White Papers and the speeches of under-secretaries do, of course, vary from party to party, but they are all alike in that one almost never finds in them a fresh, vivid, home-made turn of speech. When one watches some tired hack on the platform mechanically repeating the familiar phrases — *bestial atrocities, iron heel, bloodstained tyranny, free peoples of the world, stand shoulder to shoulder* — one often has a curious feeling that one is not watching a live human being but some kind of dummy: a feeling which suddenly becomes ·stronger at moments when the light catches the speaker's spectacles and turns them into blank discs which seem to have no eyes behind them. And this is not altogether fanciful. A speaker who uses that kind of phraseology has gone some distance towards turning himself into a machine.

The appropriate noises are coming out of his larynx, but his brain is not involved as it would be if he were choosing his words for himself. If the speech he is making is one that he is accustomed to make over and over again, he may be almost unconscious of what he is saying, as one is when one utters the responses in church. And this reduced state of consciousness, if not indispensable, is at any rate favourable to political conformity.

In our time, political speech and writing are largely the defence of **14** the indefensible. Things like the continuance of British rule in India, the Russian purges and deportations, the dropping of the atom bombs on Japan, can indeed be defended, but only by arguments which are too brutal for most people to face, and which do not square with the professed aims of political parties. Thus political language has to consist largely of euphemism, question-begging and sheer cloudy vagueness. Defenceless villages are bombarded from the air, the inhabitants driven out into the countryside, the cattle machine-gunned, the huts set on fire with incendiary bullets: this is called *pacification.* Millions of peasants are robbed of their farms and sent trudging along the roads with no more than they can carry: this is called *transfer of population* or *rectification of frontiers.* People are imprisoned for years without trial, or shot in the back of the neck or sent to die of scurvy in Arctic lumber camps: this is called *elimination of unreliable elements.* Such phraseology is needed if one wants to name things without calling up mental pictures of them. Consider for instance some comfortable English professor defending Russian totalitarianism. He cannot say outright, "I believe in killing off your opponents when you can get good results by doing so". Probably, therefore, he will say something like this:

"While freely conceding that the Soviet regime exhibits certain features which the humanitarian may be inclined to deplore, we must, I think, agree that a certain curtailment of the right to political opposition is an unavoidable concomitant of transitional periods, and that the rigours which the Russian people have been called upon to undergo have been amply justified in the sphere of concrete achievement."

The inflated style is itself a kind of euphemism. A mass of Latin words **15** falls upon the facts like soft snow, blurring the outlines and covering up all the details. The great enemy of clear language is insincerity. When there is a gap between one's real and one's declared aims, one turns as it were instinctively to long words and exhausted idioms, like a cuttlefish squirting out ink. In our age there is no such thing as "keeping out of politics". All issues are political issues, and politics itself is a mass

of lies, evasions, folly, hatred and schizophrenia. When the general atmosphere is bad, language must suffer. I should expect to find — this is
a guess which I have not sufficient knowledge to verify — that the German, Russian and Italian languages have all deteriorated in the last ten
or fifteen years, as a result of dictatorship.

16   But if thought corrupts language, language can also corrupt thought.
A bad usage can spread by tradition and imitation, even among people
who should and do know better. The debased language that I have been
discussing is in some ways very convenient. Phrases like *a not unjustifiable assumption, leave much to be desired, would serve no good purpose, a consideration which we should do well to bear in mind,* are a
continuous temptation, a packet of aspirins always at one's elbow. Look
back through this essay, and for certain you will find that I have again
and again committed the very faults I am protesting against. By this
morning's post I have received a pamphlet dealing with conditions in
Germany. The author tells me that he "felt impelled" to write it. I open
it at random, and here is almost the first sentence that I see: "(The Allies) have an opportunity not only of achieving a radical transformation
of Germany's social and political structure in such a way as to avoid a
nationalistic reaction in Germany itself, but at the same time of laying
the foundations of a co-operative and unified Europe." You see, he "feels
impelled" to write — feels, presumably, that he has something new to
say — and yet his words, like cavalry horses answering the bugle, group
themselves automatically into the familiar dreary pattern. This invasion
of one's mind by ready-made phrases (*lay the foundations, achieve a
radical transformation*) can only be prevented if one is constantly on
guard against them, and every such phrase anaesthetizes a portion of
one's brain.

17   I said earlier that the decadence of our language is probably curable.
Those who deny this would argue, if they produced an argument at all,
that language merely reflects existing social conditions, and that we cannot influence its development by any direct tinkering with words and
constructions. So far as the general tone or spirit of a language goes, this
may be true, but it is not true in detail. Silly words and expressions have
often disappeared, not through any evolutionary process but owing to the
conscious action of a minority. Two recent examples were *explore every
avenue* and *leave no stone unturned,* which were killed by the jeers of a
few journalists. There is a long list of flyblown metaphors which could
similarly be got rid of if enough people would interest themselves in the
job; and it should also be possible to laugh the *not un-* formation out of

existence,[3] to reduce the amount of Latin and Greek in the average sentence, to drive out foreign phrases and strayed scientific words, and, in general, to make pretentiousness unfashionable. But all these are minor points. The defence of the English language implies more than this, and perhaps it is best to start by saying what it does *not* imply.

To begin with it has nothing to do with archaism, with the salvaging **18** of obsolete words and turns of speech, or with the setting up of a "standard English" which must never be departed from. On the contrary, it is especially concerned with the scrapping of every word or idiom which has outworn its usefulness. It has nothing to do with correct grammar and syntax, which are of no importance so long as one makes one's meaning clear, or with the avoidance of Americanisms, or with having what is called a "good prose style". On the other hand it is not concerned with fake simplicity and the attempt to make written English colloquial. Nor does it even imply in every case preferring the Saxon word to the Latin one, though it does imply using the fewest and shortest words that will cover one's meaning. What is above all needed is to let the meaning choose the word, and not the other way about. In prose, the worst thing one can do with words is to surrender to them. When you think of a concrete object, you think wordlessly, and then, if you want to describe the thing you have been visualizing you probably hunt about till you find the exact words that seem to fit it. When you think of something abstract you are more inclined to use words from the start, and unless you make a conscious effort to prevent it, the existing dialect will come rushing in and do the job for you, at the expense of blurring or even changing your meaning. Probably it is better to put off using words as long as possible and get one's meaning as clear as one can through pictures or sensations. Afterwards one can choose — not simply *accept* — the phrases that will best cover the meaning, and then switch round and decide what impression one's words are likely to make on another person. This last effort of the mind cuts out all stale or mixed images, all prefabricated phrases, needless repetitions, and humbug and vagueness generally. But one can often be in doubt about the effect of a word or a phrase, and one needs rules that one can rely on when instinct fails. I think the following rules will cover most cases:

   (i)   Never use a metaphor, simile or other figure of speech which you are used to seeing in print.

  (ii)   Never use a long word where a short one will do.

 (iii)   If it is possible to cut a word out, always cut it out.

   (iv) Never use the passive where you can use the active.

   (v) Never use a foreign phrase, a scientific word or a jargon word if you can think of an everyday English equivalent.

   (vi) Break any of these rules sooner than say anything outright barbarous.

These rules sound elementary, and so they are, but they demand a deep change of attitude in anyone who has grown used to writing in the style now fashionable. One could keep all of them and still write bad English, but one could not write the kind of stuff that I quoted in those five specimens at the beginning of this article.

19   I have not here been considering the literary use of language, but merely language as an instrument for expressing and not for concealing or preventing thought. Stuart Chase and others have come near to claiming that all abstract words are meaningless, and have used this as a pretext for advocating a kind of political quietism. Since you don't know what Fascism is, how can you struggle against Fascism? One need not swallow such absurdities as this, but one ought to recognize that the present political chaos is connected with the decay of language, and that one can probably bring about some improvement by starting at the verbal end. If you simplify your English, you are freed from the worst follies of orthodoxy. You cannot speak any of the necessary dialects, and when you make a stupid remark its stupidity will be obvious, even to yourself. Political language — and with variations this is true of all political parties, from Conservatives to Anarchists — is designed to make lies sound truthful and murder respectable, and to give an appearance of solidity to pure wind. One cannot change this all in a moment, but one can at least change one's own habits, and from time to time one can even, if one jeers loudly enough, send some worn-out and useless phrase — some *jackboot, Achilles' heel, hotbed, melting pot, acid test, veritable inferno* or other lump of verbal refuse — into the dustbin where it belongs.

                                                 (1946)

Notes

1. An interesting illustration of this is the way in which the English flower names which were in use till very recently are being ousted by Greek ones, *snapdragon* becoming *antirrhinum*, *forget-me-not* becoming *myosotis*, etc. It is hard to see any practical reason for this change of fashion; it is probably due to an instinctive turning-away from the more homely word and a vague feeling that the Greek word is scientific.

2. Example: "Comfort's catholicity of perception and image, strangely Whitmanesque in range,

almost the exact opposite in aesthetic compulsion, continues to evoke that trembling atmospheric accumulative hinting at a cruel, an inexorably serene timelessness ... Wrey Gardiner scores by aiming at simple bull's-eyes with precision. Only they are not so simple, and through this contented sadness runs more than the surface bitter-sweet of resignation. (*Poetry Quarterly*)

3. One can cure oneself of the *not un-* formation by memorizing this sentence: *A not unblack dog was chasing a not unsmall rabbit across a not ungreen field.*

The Writer's Subject

1. What cause and effect relationship does Orwell perceive between language and thought? (paras. 2, 16)

2. What vices of bad writing does Orwell illustrate in citing the five passages given in paragraph 3? (See paras. 4, 12)

3. Why is Orwell so critical of "dying metaphors"? (para. 5)

4. What is Orwell's objection to the use in English writing of foreign words and phrases? (para. 7)

5. Why, according to Orwell, are words like "democracy," "freedom," and "patriotic" used dishonestly? (para. 8)

6. What is Orwell's point in comparing a political speaker with a dummy or a machine? (para. 13)

7. Why, according to Orwell, is it necessary for modern political language to consist largely of "euphemism, question-begging, and sheer cloudy vagueness"? (para. 14)

8. What connection does Orwell see between the decline of language and the rise of modern dictatorships? (para. 15)

9. Why, in Orwell's view, must one be on guard against the ready-made phrases found in political writing? (para. 16)

The Writer's Style and Strategy

1. What purposes are served by the first two paragraphs of the essay?

2. In paragraph 16, Orwell invites the reader to "look back through this essay, and for certain you will find that I have again and again committed the very faults I am protesting against." Why does Orwell make this statement?

3. Orwell constantly emphasizes the need for concrete images in place of vague abstractions or ready-made phrases. Does his own writing exemplify this principle? Find examples of Orwell's attempt to give concrete

expression to his ideas.

4. In paragraph 9 and again in paragraph 22 Orwell demonstrates the misuse of language by modern writers. How does he do this?

5. What is the tone of Orwell's essay? Does it change in any way as he moves from a consideration of language to a discussion of politics?

6. How effectively does the final paragraph sum up the main points of Orwell's argument? Why, in the last sentence, does Orwell use the words "verbal refuse" and "dustbin"?

Suggested Topics for Writing and Discussion

1. Find a printed version of a political speech, and analyze it along the lines of Orwell's comments about political writing. Is it guilty of any of the sins he attributes to political speakers or writers, such as stale images, imprecision, ready-made phrases, meaningless words, or euphemisms?

2. Choose an issue that has aroused controversy, such as abortion, capital punishment, or sex education, and write a speech that might be delivered on the subject by a politician hoping to win votes. Then offer an analysis of the speech, showing where you have used the kind of language attacked by Orwell.

3. Read Russell Baker's "Little Red Riding Hood Revisited" in this reader. Write an essay in which you demonstrate how much Baker's "translation" of the traditional tale owes to the bad habits discussed by Orwell.

Literature and Audience

Of Studies
by Francis Bacon

Studies serve for delight, for ornament, and for ability. Their chief use 1
for delight is in privateness and retiring; for ornament, is in discourse;
and for ability, is in the judgement and disposition of business. For expert men can execute and perhaps judge of particulars, one by one; but
the general counsels and the plots and marshalling of affairs come best
from those that are learned. To spend too much time in studies is sloth;
to use them too much for ornament is affectation; to make judgement
wholly by their rules is the humour of a scholar. They perfect Nature
and are perfected by experience. For natural abilities are like natural
plants, that need pruning by study; and studies themselves do give forth
directions too much at large, except they be bounded in by experience.
Crafty men condemn studies; simple men admire them; and wise men
use them; for they teach not their own use, but that is a wisdom without
them and above them, won by observation. Read not to contradict and
confute, nor to believe and take for granted, nor to find talk and discourse, but to weigh and consider. Some books are to be tasted, others
to be swallowed, and some few to be chewed and digested: that is, some
books are to be read only in parts; others to be read but not curiously;
and some few to be read wholly and with diligence and attention. Some
books also may be read by deputy, and extracts made of them by others, but that would be only in the less important arguments and the
meaner sort of books; else distilled books are like common distilled
waters, flashy things. Reading maketh a full man; conference a ready
man, and writing an exact man. And therefore if a man write little, he
had need have a great memory; if he confer little, he had need have a

present wit; and if he read little, he had need have much cunning to seem to know that he doth not. Histories make men wise; poets, witty; the mathematics, subtle; natural philosophy, deep; moral, grave; logic and rhetoric, able to contend. *Abuent studia in mores.*[1] Nay there is no stond or impediment in the wit but may be wrought out by fit studies, like as diseases of the body may have appropriate exercises. Bowling is good for the stone and reins; shooting for the lungs and breast; gentle walking for the stomach; riding for the head; and the like. So if a man's wit be wandering, let him study the mathematics, for in demonstrations, if his wit be called away never so little, he must begin again. If his wit be not apt to distinguish or find differences, let him study the schoolmen, for they are *Cymini sectores.*[2] If he be not apt to beat over matters and to call up one thing to prove and illustrate another, let him study the lawyers' cases. So every defect of the mind may have a special receipt.

(1613)

Notes

1. Studies are transformed into behaviour.

2. Hair-splitters. "Schoolmen" in this context refers to medieval scholars such as Thomas Aquinas and John Duns Scotus, who spent much time arguing very subtle theological distinctions.

The Writer's Subject

1. What is the difference between a learned man and an expert, according to Bacon?

2. In Bacon's view, what are the possible evils of study?

3. Why do "Crafty men condemn studies, simple men admire them, and wise men use them"?

4. What uses of reading does Bacon warn against?

5. What does Bacon mean when he says "some books may be read by deputy"?

6. What particular virtues does Bacon see in specific types of reading?

7. What "prescriptions" for reading does Bacon provide?

The Writer's Style and Strategy

1. How does Bacon develop his opening assertion?

2. What figure of speech does Bacon employ when he writes, "for natural abilities are like natural plants, that need pruning by study"? How is this figure of speech "explained" by Bacon?

3. How does Bacon develop the analogy between "diseases" of the wit and those of the body?

4. Consider Bacon's sentence style. Find instances of parallel structures and balanced structures. What rhetorical effects are gained by using these sentence strategies?

Suggested Topics for Writing and Discussion

1. In "Of Studies" Bacon says, "Reading maketh a full man." What do you understand by this statement? Use specific details to explain your view.

2. Bacon says, "Some books are to be tasted, others to be swallowed, and some few to be chewed and digested." Write an essay in which you develop Bacon's classification by means of reference to and discussion of particular books.

The Literature of Knowledge and the Literature of Power

by Thomas De Quincey

1   What is it that we mean by *literature?* Popularly, and amongst the thoughtless, it is held to include everything that is printed in a book. Little logic is require to disturb *that* definition; the most thoughtless person is easily made aware that in the idea of *literature* one essential element is — some relation to a general and common interest of man, so that what applies only to a local — or professional — or merely personal interest, even though presenting itself in the shape of a book, will not belong to literature. So far the definition is easily narrowed; and it is as easily expanded. For not only is much that takes a station in books not literature; but inversely, much that really *is* literature never reaches a station in books. The weekly sermons of Christendom, that vast pulpit literature which acts so extensively upon the popular mind — to warn, to uphold, to renew, to comfort, to alarm, does not attain the sanctuary of libraries in the ten thousandth part of its extent. The drama again, as, for instance, the finest of Shakspere's plays in England, and all leading Athenian plays in the noontide of the Attic stage, operated as a literature on the public mind, and were (according to the strictest letter of that term) *published* through the audiences that witnessed[1] their representation some time before they were published as things to be read; and they were published in this scenical mode of publication with much more effect than they could have had as books, during ages of costly copying or of costly printing.

2   Books, therefore, do not suggest an idea co-extensive and interchange-

able with the idea of literature; since much literature, scenic, forensic, or didactic, (as from lecturers and public orators,) may never come into books; and much that *does* come into books, may connect itself with no literary interest. But a far more important correction, applicable to the common vague idea of literature, is to be sought — not so much in a better definition of literature, as in a sharper distinction of the two functions which it fulfils. In that great social organ, which collectively we call literature, there may be distinguished two separate offices that may blend and often *do* so, but capable severally of severe insulation, and naturally fitted for reciprocal repulsion. There is first the literature of *knowledge*, and secondly, the literature of *power*. The function of the first is — to *teach*; the function of the second is — to *move*: the first is a rudder, the second an oar or a sail. The first speaks to the *mere* discursive understanding; the second speaks ultimately it may happen to the higher understanding or reason, but always *through* affections of pleasure and sympathy. Remotely, it may travel towards an object seated in what Lord Bacon calls *dry* light; but proximately it does and must operate, else it ceases to be a literature of *power*, on and through that *humid* light which clothes itself in the mists and glittering *iris* of human passions, desires, and genial emotions. Men have so little reflected on the higher functions of literature, as to find it a paradox if one should describe it as a mean or subordinate purpose of books to give information. But this is a paradox only in the sense which makes it honourable to be paradoxical. Whenever we talk in ordinary language of seeking information or gaining knowledge, we understand the words as connected with something of absolute novelty. But it is the grandeur of all truth which *can* occupy a very high place in human interests, that it is never absolutely novel to the meanest of minds: it exists eternally by way of germ or latent principle in the lowest as in the highest, needing to be developed but never to be planted. To be capable of transplantation is the immediate criterion of a truth that ranges on a lower scale. Besides which, there is a rarer thing than truth, namely, *power* or deep sympathy with truth. What is the effect, for instance, upon society — of children? By the pity, by the tenderness, and by the peculiar modes of admiration, which connect themselves with the helplessness, with the innocence, and with the simplicity of children, not only are the primal affections strengthened and continually renewed, but the qualities which are dearest in the sight of heaven — the frailty for instance, which appeals to forbearance, the innocence which symbolizes the heavenly, and the simplicity which is most alien from the worldly, are kept up in per-

petual remembrance, and their ideals are continually refreshed. A purpose of the same nature is answered by the higher literature, viz. the literature of power. What do you learn from Paradise Lost? Nothing at all.
What do you learn from a cookery-book? Something new, something that
you did not know before, in every paragraph. But would you therefore
put the wretched cookery-book on a higher level of estimation than the
divine poem? What you owe to Milton is not any knowledge, of which
a million separate items are still but a million of advancing steps on the
same earthly level; what you owe — is *power*, that is exercise and expansion to your own latent capacity of sympathy with the infinite, where
every pulse and each separate influx is a step upwards — a step ascending as upon a Jacob's ladder from earth to mysterious altitudes above
the earth. *All* the steps of knowledge, from first to last, carry you farther on the same plane, but could never raise you one foot above your
ancient level of earth: whereas, the very *first* step in power is a flight —
is an ascending into another element where earth is forgotten.

3   Were it not that human sensibilities are ventilated and continually
called out into exercise by the great phenomena of infancy, or of real
life as it moves through chance and change, or of literature as it recom-
bines these elements in the mimicries of poetry, romance, &c., it is certain that, like any animal power or muscular energy falling into disuse,
all such sensibilities would gradually droop and dwindle. It is in relation to these great *moral* capacities of man that the literature of power,
as contradistinguished from that of knowledge, lives and has its field of
action. It is concerned with what is highest in man: for the Scriptures
themselves never condescend to deal by suggestion or co-operation, with
the mere discursive understanding: when speaking of man in his intellectual capacity, the Scriptures speak not of the understanding, but of
"the understanding heart," — making the heart, *i.e.* the great *intuitive*
(or non-discursive) organ, to be the interchangeable formula for man in
his highest state of capacity for the infinite. Tragedy, romance, fairy-
tale, or epopee, all alike restore to man's mind the ideals of justice, of
home, of truth, of mercy, of retribution, which else, (left to the support
of daily life in its realities,) would languish for want of sufficient illustration. What is meant for instance by *poetic justice*? — It does not mean
a justice that differs by its object from the ordinary justice of human
jurisprudence; for then it must be confessedly a very bad kind of justice; but it means a justice that differs from common forensic justice by
the degree in which it *attains* its object, a justice that is more omnipo-
tent over its own ends, as dealing — not with the refractory elements of

earthly life — but with elements of its own creation, and with materials flexible to its own purest preconceptions. It is certain that, were it not for the literature of power, these ideals would often remain amongst us as mere arid notional forms; whereas, by the creative forces of man put forth in literature, they gain a vernal life of restoration, and germinate into vital activities. The commonest novel, by moving in alliance with human fears and hopes, with human instincts of wrong and right, sustains and quickens those affections. Calling them into action, it rescues them from torpor. And hence the pre-eminency over all authors that merely *teach*, of the meanest that *moves*; or that teaches, if at all, indirectly *by* moving. The very highest work that has ever existed in the literature of knowledge, is but a *provisional* work: a book upon trial and sufferance, and *quamdiu bene se gesserit*. Let its teaching be even partially revised, let it be but expanded, nay, even let its teaching be but placed in a better order, and instantly it is superseded. Whereas the feeblest works in the literature of power, surviving at all, survive as finished and unalterable amongst men. For instance, the *Principia* of Sir Isaac Newton was a book *militant* on earth from the first. In all stages of its progress it would have to fight for its existence: 1*st*, as regards absolute truth; 2*ndly*, when that combat is over, as regards its form or mode of presenting the truth. And as soon as a La Place, or anybody else, builds higher upon the foundations laid by this book, effectually he throws it out of the sunshine into decay and darkness; by weapons won from this book he superannuates and destroys this book, so that soon the name of Newton remains, as a mere *nominis umbra*, but his book, as a living power, has transmigrated into other forms. Now, on the contrary, the Iliad, the Prometheus of Æschylus, — the Othello or King Lear, — the Hamlet or Macbeth, — and the Paradise Lost, are not militant but triumphant for ever as long as the languages exist in which they speak or can be taught to speak. They never *can* transmigrate into new incarnations. To reproduce *these* in new forms, or variations, even if in some things they should be improved, would be to plagiarize. A good steam-engine is properly superseded by a better. But one lovely pastoral valley is not superseded by another, nor a statue of Praxiteles by a statue of Michael Angelo. These things are not separated by imparity, but by disparity. They are not thought of as unequal under the same standard, but as differing in *kind*, and as equal under a different standard. Human works of immortal beauty and works of nature in one respect stand on the same footing: they never absolutely repeat each other: never approach so near as not to differ; and they differ not as better and worse, or simply by more and less: they differ by undecipherable and incommunicable differences, that cannot be caught by mimicries, nor be reflected in the mirror of copies, nor become ponderable in the scales of vulgar comparison.

4   Applying these principles to Pope, as a representative of fine literature in general, we would wish to remark the claim which he has, or which any equal writer has, to the attention and jealous winnowing of those critics in particular who watch over public morals. Clergymen, and all the organs of public criticism put in motion by clergymen, are more especially concerned in the just appreciation of such writers, if the two canons are remembered, which we have endeavoured to illustrate, viz., that all works in this class, as opposed to those in the literature of knowledge, 1*st*, work by far deeper agencies; and, 2*ndly*, are more permanent; in the strictest sense they are κτηματα εζ αει [possessions forever]: and what evil they do, or what good they do, is commensurate with the national language, sometimes long after the nation has departed. At this hour, 500 years since their creation, the tales of Chaucer,[2] never equalled on this earth for tenderness, and for life of picturesqueness, are read familiarly by many in the charming language of their natal day, and by others in the modernizations of Dryden, of Pope, and Wordsworth. At this hour, 1800 years since their creation, the Pagan tales of Ovid, never equalled on this earth for the gaiety of their movement and the capricious graces of their narrative, are read by all Christendom. This man's people and their monuments are dust: but *he* is alive: he has survived them, as he told us that he had it in his commission to do, by a thousand years; "and *shall* a thousand more."

5   All the literature of knowledge builds only ground-nests, that are swept away by floods, or confounded by the plough; but the literature of power builds nests in aerial altitudes of temples sacred from violation, or of forests inaccessible to fraud. *This* is a great prerogative of the *power* literature: and it is a greater which lies in the mode of its influence. The *knowledge* literature, like the fashion of this world, passeth away. An Encyclopædia is its abstract; and, in this respect, it may be taken for its speaking symbol — that, before one generation has passed, an Encyclopædia is superannuated; for it speaks through the dead memory and unimpassioned understanding, which have not the *rest* of higher faculties, but are continually enlarging and varying their phylacteries. But all literature, properly so called — literature κατ εξοχηυ [i.e., great literature], for the very same reason that it is so much more durable than the literature of knowledge, is (and by the very same

proportion it is) more intense and electrically searching in its impressions. The directions in which the tragedy of this planet has trained our human feelings to play, and the combinations into which the poetry of this planet has thrown our human passions of love and hatred, of admiration and contempt, exercises a power bad or good over human life, that cannot be contemplated when seen stretching through many generations, without a sentiment allied to awe.[3] And of this let every one be assured — that he owes to the impassioned books which he has read, many a thousand more of emotions than he can consciously trace back to them. Dim by their origination, these emotions yet arise in him, and mould him through life like the forgotten incidents of childhood.

Notes

1. Charles I, for example, when Prince of Wales, and many others in his father's court, gained their known familiarity with Shakspere — not through the original quartos, so slenderly diffused, nor through the first folio of 1623, but through the court representations of his chief dramas at Whitehall.

2. The Canterbury Tales were not made public until 1380 or thereabouts: but the composition must have cost 30 or more years; not to mention that the work had probably been finished for some years before it was divulged.

3. The reason why the broad distinctions between the two literatures of power and knowledge so little fix the attention, lies in the fact, that a vast proportion of books — history, biography, travels, miscellaneous essays, &c., lying in a middle zone, confound these distinctions by interblending them. All that we call "amusement" or "entertainment," is a diluted form of the power belonging to passion, and also a mixed form; and where threads of direct *instruction* intermingle in the texture with these threads of *power*, this absorption of the duality into one representative *nuance* neutralises the separate perception of either. Fused into a *tertium quid*, or neutral state, they disappear to the popular eye as the repelling forces, which in fact they are.

(Note: This was originally part of a review of the works of Alexander Pope, and appeared in *The North Briton Review*, August 1848.)

The Writer's Subject

1. How does De Quincey define literature? (para. 1)

2. What are the chief differences between the "literature of knowledge" and the "literature of power," as De Quincey describes them? Why are these categories "naturally fitted for reciprocal repulsion"? (para. 2)

3. How does the "literature of power" operate on our "great *moral* capacities," according to De Quincey? (para. 3)

4. Why does De Quincey regard "tragedy, romance, fairy-tale, or epopee" as "literature of power"? (para. 3)

5. Why, according to the author, is any work in the literature of knowledge to be regarded as "provisional"? (para. 3) What examples does De Quincey provide to illustrate this idea?

6. Explain the point De Quincey wishes to make in comparing Newton's *Principia* to works by Homer, AEschylus, Shakespeare, and Milton. (para. 3)

7. "A good steam-engine is properly superseded by a better. But one lovely pastoral valley is not superseded by another, nor a statue of Praxiteles by a statue of Michael Angelo." (para. 3) Explain De Quincey's meaning here.

8. What, according to De Quincey, are the two "canons" (i.e., decrees or laws) that characterize works of fine literature? How does he support his point? (para. 5)

9. Why does De Quincey call the encyclopaedia a "speaking symbol" of the literature of knowledge? (para. 5)

The Writer's Style and Strategy

1. Discuss De Quincey's use of figurative language in this essay. How does he make use of metaphor to enliven his discussion?

2. Explain the metaphor of the rudder and the sail in para. 2; also the metaphor of nests in para. 5.

3. How does De Quincey define the terms "knowledge" and "power" in this essay? How does he illustrate his definitions? How does he relate them to the idea of "truth"?

4. Discuss De Quincey's use of comparison and contrast. Where do you find these devices to be most effective in the essay?

Suggested Topics for Writing and Discussion

1. De Quincey argues that literature gives life and force to human ideals, so that they "germinate into vital activities" (para. 3). Do you think that the study of literature helps to develop our ideals and shape our conduct? Or do you think that its importance has been exaggerated?

2. Choose a work of literature from either of De Quincey's categories that you feel has had a positive impact on your life, and explain in some detail what you have gained from studying that work.

3. De Quincey observes that "an Encyclopaedia is superannuated" before one generation has passed (para. 5). Choose a major encyclopaedia (e.g., the *Encyclopaedia Britannica*) you have used for reference purposes; focus on one article and note any features that already seem outdated.

The Motive for Metaphor

by Northrop Frye

For the past twenty-five years I have been teaching and studying Eng-   1
lish literature in a university. As in any other job, certain questions stick
in one's mind, not because people keep asking them, but because they're
the questions inspired by the very fact of being in such a place. What
good is the study of literature? Does it help us to think more clearly, or
feel more sensitively, or live a better life than we could without it? What
is the function of the teacher and scholar, or of the person who calls
himself, as I do, a literary critic? What difference does the study of literature make in our social or political or religious attitude? In my early
days I thought very little about such questions, not because I had any of
the answers, but because I assumed that anybody who asked them was
naïve. I think now that the simplest questions are not only the hardest
to answer, but the most important to ask, so I'm going to raise them and
try to suggest what my present answers are. I say try to suggest, because there are only more or less inadequate answers to such questions
— there aren't any right answers. The kind of problem that literature
raises is not the kind that you ever 'solve'. Whether my answers are
any good or not, they represent a fair amount of thinking about the questions. As I can't see my audience, I have to choose my rhetorical style
in the dark, and I'm taking the classroom style, because an audience of
students is the one I feel easiest with.

There are two things in particular that I want to discuss with you. In   2
school, and in university, there's a subject called 'English' in English-
speaking countries. English means, in the first place, the mother tongue.
As that, it's the most practical subject in the world: you can't under-

stand anything or take any part in your society without it. Wherever
illiteracy is a problem, it's as fundamental a problem as getting enough
to eat or a place to sleep. The native language takes precedence over
every other subject of study: nothing else can compare with it in usefulness. But then you find that every mother tongue, in any developed
or civilized society, turns into something called literature. If you keep
on studying 'English', you find yourself trying to read Shakespeare and
Milton. Literature, we're told, is one of the arts, along with painting
and music, and, after you've looked up all the hard words and the Classical allusions and learned what words like imagery and diction are supposed to mean, what you use in understanding it, or so you're told, is
your imagination. Here you don't seem to be in quite the same practical and useful area: Shakespeare and Milton, whatever their merits, are
not the kind of thing you must know to hold any place in society at all.
A person who knows nothing about literature may be an ignoramus,
but many people don't mind being that. Every child realizes that literature is taking him in a different direction from the immediately useful,
and a good many children complain loudly about this. Two questions I
want to deal with, then, are, first: what is the relation of English as the
mother tongue to English as a literature? Second: what is the social value
of the study of literature, and what is the place of the imagination that
literature addresses itself to, in the learning process?

3   Let's start with the different ways there are of dealing with the world
we're living in. Suppose you're shipwrecked on an uninhabited island
in the South Seas. The first thing you do is to take a long look at the
world around you, a world of sky and sea and earth and stars and trees
and hills. You see this world as objective, as something set over against
you and not yourself or related to you in any way. And you notice two
things about this objective world. In the first place, it doesn't have any
conversation. It's full of animals and plants and insects going on with
their own business, but there's nothing that responds to you: it has no
morals and no intelligence, or at least none that you can grasp. It may
have a shape and a meaning, but it doesn't seem to be a human shape or
a human meaning. Even if there's enough to eat and no dangerous animals, you feel lonely and frightened and unwanted in such a world.

4   In the second place, you find that looking at the world, as something
set over against you, splits your mind in two. You have an intellect that
feels curious about it and wants to study it, and you have feelings or
emotions that see it as beautiful or austere or terrible. You know that
both these attitudes have some reality, at least for you. If the ship you

were wrecked in was a Western ship, you'd probably feel that your intellect tells you more about what's really there in the outer world, and that your emotions tell you more about what's going on inside you. If your background were Oriental, you'd be more likely to reverse this and say that the beauty or terror was what was really there, and that your instinct to count and classify and measure and pull to pieces was what was inside your mind. But whether your point of view is Western or Eastern, intellect and emotion never get together in your mind as long as you're simply looking at the world. They alternate, and keep you divided between them.

The language you use on this level of the mind is the language of consciousness or awareness. It's largely a language of nouns and adjectives. You have to have names for things, and you need qualities like 'wet' or 'green' or 'beautiful' to describe how things seem to you. This is the speculative or contemplative position of the mind, the position in which the arts and sciences begin, although they don't stay there very long. The sciences begin by accepting the facts and the evidence about an outside world without trying to alter them. Science proceeds by accurate measurement and description, and follows the demands of the reason rather than the emotions. What it deals with is there, whether we like it or not. The emotions are unreasonable: for them it's what they like and don't like that comes first. We'd be naturally inclined to think that the arts follow the path of emotion, in contrast to the sciences. Up to a point they do, but there's a complicating factor. 5

That complicating factor is the contrast between 'I like this' and 'I don't like this'. In this Robinson Crusoe life I've assigned you, you may have moods of complete peacefulness and joy, moods when you accept your island and everything around you. You wouldn't have such moods very often, and when you had them, they'd be moods of identification, when you felt that the island was a part of you and you a part of it. That is not the feeling of consciousness or awareness, where you feel split off from everything that's not your perceiving self. Your habitual state of mind is the feeling of separation which goes with being conscious, and the feeling 'this is not a part of me' soon becomes 'this is not what I want'. Notice the word 'want': we'll be coming back to it. 6

So you soon realize that there's a difference between the world you're living in and the world you want to live in. The world you want to live in is a human world, not an objective one: it's not an environment but a home; it's not the world you see but the world you build out of what you see. You go to work to build a shelter or plant a garden, and as soon as 7 you start to work you've moved into a different level of human life. You're not separating only yourself from nature now, but constructing a human world and separating it from the rest of the world. Your intellect and emotions are now both engaged in the same activity, so there's no longer any real distinction between them. As soon as you plant a garden or a crop, you develop the conception of a 'weed', the plant you don't want in there. But you can't say that 'weed' is either an intellectual or an emotional conception, because it's both at once. Further, you go to work because you feel you have to, and because you want something at the end of the work. That means that the important categories of your life are no longer the subject and the object, the watcher and the things being watched: the important categories are what you have to do and what you want to do — in other words, necessity and freedom.

8   One person by himself is not a complete human being, so I'll provide you with another shipwrecked refugee of the opposite sex and an eventual family. Now you're a member of a human society. This human society after a while will transform the island into something with a human shape. What that human shape is, is revealed in the shape of the work you do: the buildings, such as they are, the paths through the woods, the planted crops fenced off against whatever animals want to eat them. These things, these rudiments of city, highway, garden and farm, are the human form of nature, or the form of human nature, whichever you like. This is the area of the applied arts and sciences, and it appears in our society as engineering and agriculture and medicine and architecture. In this area we can never say clearly where the art stops and the science begins, or vice versa.

9   The language you use on this level is the language of practical sense, a language of verbs or words of action and movement. The practical world, however, is a world where actions speak louder than words. In some ways it's a higher level of existence than the speculative level, because it's doing something about the world instead of just looking at it, but in itself it's a much more primitive level. It's the process of adapting to the environment, or rather of transforming the environment in the interests of one species, that goes on among animals and plants as well as human beings. The animals have a good many of our practical skills: some insects make pretty fair architects, and beavers know quite a lot about engineering. In this island, probably, and certainly if you were alone, you'd have about the ranking of a second-rate animal. What makes our practical life really human is a third level of the mind, a level where consciousness and practical skill come together.

This third level is a vision or model in your mind of what you want 10 to construct. There's that word 'want' again. The actions of man are prompted by desire, and some of these desires are needs, like food and warmth and shelter. One of these needs is sexual, the desire to reproduce and bring more human beings into existence. But there's also a desire to bring a social human form into existence: the form of cities and gardens and farms that we call civilization. Many animals and insects have this social form too, but man knows that he has it: he can compare what he does with what he can imagine being done. So we begin to see where the imagination belongs in the scheme of human affairs. It's the power of constructing possible models of human experience. In the world of the imagination, anything goes that's imaginatively possible, but nothing really happens. If it did happen, it would move out of the world of imagination into the world of action.

We have three levels of the mind now, and a language for each of 11 them, which in English-speaking societies means an English for each of them. There's the level of consciousness and awareness, where the most important thing is the difference between me and everything else. The English of this level is the English of ordinary conversation, which is mostly monologue, as you'll soon realize if you do a bit of eavesdropping, or listening to yourself. We can call it the language of self-expression. Then there's the level of social participation, the working or technological language of teachers and preachers and politicians and advertisers and lawyers and journalists and scientists. We've already called this the language of practical sense. Then there's the level of imagination, which produces the literary language of poems and plays and novels. They're not really different languages, of course, but three different reasons for using words.

On this basis, perhaps, we can distinguish the arts from the sciences. 12 Science begins with the world we have to live in, accepting its data and trying to explain its laws. From there, it moves towards the imagination: it becomes a mental construct, a model of a possible way of interpreting experience. The further it goes in this direction, the more it tends to speak the language of mathematics, which is really one of the languages of the imagination, along with literature and music. Art, on the other hand, begins with the world we construct, not with the world we see. It starts with the imagination, and then works towards ordinary experience: that is, it tries to make itself as convincing and recognizable as it can. You can see why we tend to think of the sciences as intellectual and the arts as emotional: one starts with the world as it is, the other with the world we want to have. Up to a point it is true that science gives an intellectual view of reality, and that the arts try to make the emotions as precise and disciplined as sciences do the intellect. But of course it's nonsense to think of the scientist as a cold unemotional reasoner and the artist as somebody who's in a perpetual emotional tizzy. You can't distinguish the arts from the sciences by the mental processes the people in them use: they both operate on a mixture of hunch and common sense. A highly developed science and a highly developed art are very close together, psychologically and otherwise.

13   Still, the fact that they start from opposite ends, even if they do meet in the middle, makes for one important difference between them. Science learns more and more about the world as it goes on: it evolves and improves. A physicist today knows more physics than Newton did, even if he's not as great a scientist. But literature begins with the possible model of experience, and what it produces is the literary model we call the classic. Literature doesn't evolve or improve or progress. We may have dramatists in the future who will write plays as good as *King Lear*, though they'll be very different ones, but drama as a whole will never get better than *King Lear*. *King Lear* is it, as far as drama is concerned; so is *Oedipus Rex*, written two thousand years earlier than that, and both will be models of dramatic writing as long as the human race endures. Social conditions may improve: most of us would rather live in nineteenth-century United States than in thirteenth-century Italy, and for most of us Whitman's celebration of democracy makes a lot more sense than Dante's *Inferno*. But it doesn't follow that Whitman is a better poet than Dante: literature won't line up with that kind of improvement.

14   So we find that everything that does improve, including science, leaves the literary artist out in the cold. Writers don't seem to benefit much by the advance of science, although they thrive on superstitions of all kinds. And you certainly wouldn't turn to contemporary poets for guidance or leadership in the twentieth-century world. You'd hardly go to Ezra Pound, with his fascism and social credit and Confucianism and anti-semitism. Or to Yeats, with his spiritualism and fairies and astrology. Or to D. H. Lawrence, who'll tell you that it's a good thing for servants to be flogged because that restores the precious current of blood-reciprocity between servant and master. Or to T.S. Eliot, who'll tell you that to have a flourishing culture we should educate an elite, keep most people living in the same spot, and never disestablish the Church of England. The novelists seem to be a little closer to the world they're living in, but not much. When Communists talk about the decadence of bourgeois cul-

ture, this is the kind of thing they always bring up. Their own writers don't seem to be any better, though; just duller. So the real question is a bigger one. Is it possible that literature, especially poetry, is something that a scientific civilization like ours will eventually outgrow? Man has always wanted to fly, and thousands of years ago he was making sculptures of winged bulls and telling stories about people who flew so high on artificial wings that the sun melted them off. In an Indian play fifteen hundred years ago, *Sakuntala*, there's a god who flies around in a chariot that to a modern reader sounds very much like a private aeroplane. Interesting that the writer had so much imagination, but do we need such stories now that we have private aeroplanes?

This is not a new question: it was raised a hundred and fifty years 15 ago by Thomas Love Peacock, who was a poet and novelist himself, and a very brilliant one. He wrote an essay called *Four Ages of Poetry*, with his tongue of course in his cheek, in which he said that poetry was the mental rattle that awakened the imagination of mankind in its infancy, but that now, in an age of science and technology, the poet has outlived his social function. 'A poet in our times,' said Peacock, 'is a semi-barbarian in a civilized community. He lives in the days that are past. His ideas, thoughts, feelings, associations, are all with barbarous manners, obsolete customs, and exploded superstitions. The march of his intellect is like that of a crab, backwards.' Peacock's essay annoyed his friend Shelley, who wrote another essay called *A Defence of Poetry* to refute it. Shelley's essay is a wonderful piece of writing, but it's not likely to convince anyone who needs convincing. I shall be spending a good deal of my time on this question of the relevance of literature in the world of today, and I can only indicate the general lines my answer will take. There are two points I can make now, one simple, the other more difficult.

The simple point is that literature belongs to the world man constructs, 16 not to the world he sees; to his home, not his environment. Literature's world is a concrete human world of immediate experience. The poet uses images and objects and sensations much more than he uses abstract ideas; the novelist is concerned with telling stories, not with working out arguments. The world of literature is human in shape, a world where the sun rises in the east and sets in the west over the edge of a flat earth in three dimensions, where the primary realities are not atoms or electrons but bodies, and the primary forces not energy or gravitation but love and death and passion and joy. It's not surprising if writers are often rather simple people, not always what we think of as intellectuals, and certainly not always any freer of silliness or perversity than anyone else. What concerns us is what they produce, not what they are, and poetry, according to Milton, who ought to have known, is 'more simple, sensuous and passionate' than philosophy or science.

17   The more difficult point takes us back to what we said when we were on that South Sea island. Our emotional reaction to the world varies from 'I like this' to 'I don't like this'. The first, we said, was a state of identity, a feeling that everything around us was part of us, and the second is the ordinary state of consciousness, or separation, where art and science begin. Art begins as soon as 'I don't like this' turns into 'this is not the way I could imagine it'. We notice in passing that the creative and the neurotic minds have a lot in common. They're both dissatisfied with what they see; they both believe that something else ought to be there, and they try to pretend it is there or to make it be there. The differences are more important, but we're not ready for them yet.

18   At the level of ordinary consciousness the individual man is the centre of everything, surrounded on all sides by what he isn't. At the level of practical sense, or civilization, there's a human circumference, a little cultivated world with a human shape, fenced off from the jungle and inside the sea and the sky. But in the imagination anything goes that can be imagined, and the limit of the imagination is a totally human world. Here we recapture, in full consciousness, that original lost sense of identity with our surroundings, where there is nothing outside the mind of man, or something identical with the mind of man. Religions present us with visions of eternal and infinite heavens or paradises which have the form of the cities and gardens of human civilization, like the Jerusalem and Eden of the Bible, completely separated from the state of frustration and misery that bulks so large in ordinary life. We're not concerned with these visions as religion, but they indicate what the limits of the imagination are. They indicate too that in the human world the imagination has no limits, if you follow me. We said that the desire to fly produced the aeroplane. But people don't get into planes because they want to fly; they get into planes because they want to get somewhere else faster. What's produced the aeroplane is not so much a desire to fly as a rebellion against the tyranny of time and space. And that's a process that can never stop, no matter how high our Titovs and Glenns may go.

19   For each of these six talks I've taken a title from some work of literature, and my title for this one is 'The Motive for Metaphor', from a poem of Wallace Stevens. Here's the poem:

> You like it under the trees in autumn,
> Because everything is half dead.
> The wind moves like a cripple among the leaves
> And repeats words without meaning.
>
> In the same way, you were happy in spring,
> With the half colors of quarter-things,
> The slightly brighter sky, the melting clouds,
> The single bird, the obscure moon —
>
> The obscure moon lighting an obscure world
> Of things that would never be quite expressed,
> Where you yourself were never quite yourself
> And did not want nor have to be,
>
> Desiring the exhilarations of changes:
> The motive for metaphor, shrinking from
> The weight of primary noon,
> The A B C of being,
>
> The ruddy temper, the hammer
> Of red and blue, the hard sound —
> Steel against intimation — the sharp flash,
> The vital, arrogant, fatal, dominant X.

What Stevens calls the weight of primary noon, the A B C of being, and the dominant X is the objective world, the world set over against us. Outside literature, the main motive for writing is to describe this world. But literature itself uses language in a way which associates our minds with it. As soon as you use associative language, you begin using figures of speech. If you say this talk is dry and dull, you're using figures associating it with bread and breadknives. There are two main kinds of association, analogy and identity, two things that are like each other and two things that are each other. You can say with Burns, 'My love's like a red, red rose', or you can say with Shakespeare:

> Thou that art now the world's fresh ornament
> And only herald to the gaudy spring.

One produces the figure of speech called the simile; the other produces the figure called metaphor.

In descriptive writing you have to be careful of associative language. You'll find that analogy, or likeness to something else, is very tricky to handle in description, because the differences are as important as the resemblances. As for metaphor, where you're really saying 'this *is* that', you're turning your back on logic and reason completely, because logically two things can never be the same thing and still remain two things. The poet, however, uses these two crude, primitive archaic forms of thought in the most uninhibited way, because his job is not to describe nature, but to show you a world completely absorbed and possessed by the human mind. So he produces what Baudelaire called a "suggestive magic including at the same time object and subject, the world outside the artist and the artist himself". The motive for metaphor, according to Wallace Stevens, is a desire to associate, and finally to identify, the human mind with what goes on outside it, because the only genuine joy you can have is in those rare moments when you feel that although we may know in part, as Paul says, we are also a part of what we know.

The Writer's Subject

1. What does the title of this essay mean?

2. In paragraph 2, Frye distinguishes between English as "the mother tongue, the most practical subject in the world," and "English as a literature." How does he illustrate this distinction in the paragraphs that follow?

3. What is the distinction Frye draws between the intellectual response and the emotional response to the world? (para. 4) How does he think these responses might be shaped by a Western or an Eastern view?

4. Frye uses an extended analogy of life on a desert island as a model to discuss levels of thought and language. What are the stages of human development that Frye identifies through use of this analogy? (paras. 3–11)

5. Frye identifies three levels of the mind and, correspondingly, three levels of language. What are these? (paras. 4–11)

6. According to Frye, how do the sciences deal with the external world differently than do the arts? (para. 5)

7. What turns the external objective world into a human world? What gives the human world its "human shape"? (paras. 7–8)

8. What processes of thought distinguish the artist's approach from the scientist's? (para. 12)

9. In paragraph 14 Frye asks the question, "Is it possible that literature, especially poetry, is something that a scientific civilization like ours will eventually outgrow?" How does he answer this question in paragraphs 16–18?

10. Why, according to Frye, does the poet make use of metaphor and simile? (paras. 19–20)

The Writer's Style and Strategy

1. This essay is the first of six published lectures. How does Frye establish the context for his discussion? Where, in the essay, are you aware that this essay is an introduction to the series?

2. Frye says, "I'm taking the classroom style." How is the classroom style demonstrated in the tone, structure, and diction of the essay?

3. Analyze the structure of Frye's essay as a whole. Indicate the major stages of the essay. How does Frye effect the transitions from one part to another?

4. What is the function of paragraph 11?

5. What means does Frye use to demonstrate his point that literary artists don't serve as useful social guides? (para. 14)

6. How does the lengthy reference to Thomas Love Peacock in paragraph 15 contribute to Frye's arguments at this point?

7. What is Frye's purpose in including the poem by Wallace Stevens?

Suggested Topics for Writing and Discussion

1. In an age of science and technology, does the poet have a role to play?

2. Frye talks about the imaginative processes involved in scientific thinking. Do you think that scientific advances depend upon the imagination as much as upon the analytical process of thought? Provide an example to support your point of view.

3. Many students going on to college feel they already "know" enough English to get on in the world without studying more — especially literature. What are your views on the place of literature courses in colleges and universities?

4. Choose an article from a popular magazine (e.g., *Time, Maclean's, Saturday Night, Science Digest*) and analyze the article to determine the extent to which the writer uses metaphorical language.

Where the World Began

by Margaret Laurence

1   A strange place it was, that place where the world began. A place of incredible happenings, splendours and revelations, despairs like multitudinous pits of isolated hells. A place of shadow-spookiness, inhabited by the unknowable dead. A place of jubilation and of mourning, horrible and beautiful.

2   It was, in fact, a small prairie town.

3   Because that settlement and that land were my first and for many years only real knowledge of this planet, in some profound way they remain my world, my way of viewing. My eyes were formed there. Towns like ours, set in a sea of land, have been described thousands of times as dull, bleak, flat, uninteresting. I have had it said to me that the railway trip across Canada is spectacular, except for the prairies, when it would be desirable to go to sleep for several days, until the ordeal is over. I am always unable to argue this point effectively. All I can say is — well, you really have to live there to know that country. The town of my childhood could be called bizarre, agonizingly repressive or cruel at times, and the land in which it grew could be called harsh in the violence of its seasonal changes. But never merely flat or uninteresting. Never dull.

4   In winter, we used to hitch rides on the back of the milk sleigh, our moccasins squeaking and slithering on the hard rutted snow of the roads, our hands in ice-bubbled mitts hanging onto the box edge of the sleigh for dear life, while Bert grinned at us through his great frosted moustache and shouted the horses into speed, daring us to stay put. Those mornings, rising, there would be the perpetual fascination of the frost feathers on windows, the ferns and flowers and eerie faces traced there

during the night by unseen artists of the wind. Evenings, coming back
from skating, the sky would be black but not dark, for you could see a
cold glitter of stars from one side of the earth's rim to the other. And
then the sometime astonishment when you saw the Northern Lights flaring across the sky, like the scrawled signature of God. After a blizzard,
when the snowploughs hadn't yet got through, school would be closed
for the day, the assumption being that the town's young could not possibly flounder through five feet of snow in the pursuit of education. We
would then gaily don snowshoes and flounder for miles out into the white
dazzling deserts, in pursuit of a different kind of knowing. If you came
back too close to night, through the woods at the foot of the town hill,
the thin black branches of poplar and chokecherry now meringued with
frost, sometimes you heard coyotes. Or maybe the banshee wolf-voices
were really only inside your head.

Summers were scorching, and when no rain came and the wheat be-   5
came bleached and dried before it headed, the faces of farmers and
townsfolk would not smile much, and you took for granted, because it
never seemed to have been any different, the frequent knocking at the
back door and the young men standing there, mumbling or thrusting
defiantly their request for a drink of water and a sandwich if you could
spare it. They were riding the freights, and you never knew where they
had come from, or where they might end up, if anywhere. The Drought
and Depression were like evil deities which had been there always. You
understood and did not understand.

Yet the outside world had its continuing marvels. The poplar bluffs   6
and the small river were filled and surrounded with a zillion different
grasses, stones, and weed flowers. The meadowlarks sang undaunted
from the twanging telephone wires along the gravel highway. Once we
found an old flat-bottomed scow, and launched her, poling along the
shallow brown waters, mending her with wodges of hastily chewed
Spearmint, grounding her among the tangles of soft yellow marsh mari-
golds that grew succulently along the banks of the shrunken river, while
the sun made our skins smell dusty-warm.

My best friend lived in an apartment above some stores on Main Street   7
(its real name was Mountain Avenue, goodness knows why), an elegant
apartment with royal-blue velvet curtains. The back roof, scarcely sloping at all, was corrugated tin, of a furnace-like warmth on a July afternoon, and we would sit there drinking lemonade and looking across the
back lane at the Fire Hall. Sometimes our vigil would be rewarded. Oh
joy! Somebody's house burning down! We had an almost-perfect cal-

lousness in some ways. Then the wooden tower's bronze bell would clonk and toll like a thousand speeded funerals in a time of plague, and in a few minutes the team of giant black horses would cannon forth, pulling the fire wagon like some scarlet chariot of the Goths, while the firemen clung with one hand, adjusting their helmets as they went.

8   The oddities of the place were endless. An elderly lady used to serve, as her afternoon tea offering to other ladies, soda biscuits spread with peanut butter and topped with a whole marshmallow. Some considered this slightly eccentric, when compared with chopped egg sandwiches, and admittedly talked about her behind her back, but no one ever refused these delicacies or indicated to her that they thought she had slipped a cog. Another lady dyed her hair a bright and cheery orange, by strangers often mistaken at twenty paces for a feather hat. My own beloved stepmother wore a silver fox neckpiece, a whole pelt, *with the embalmed (?) head still on.* My Ontario Irish grandfather said, "sparrow grass," a more interesting term than asparagus. The town dump was known as "the nuisance grounds," a phrase fraught with weird connotations, as though the effluvia of our lives was beneath contempt but at the same time was subtly threatening to the determined and sometimes hysterical propriety of our ways.

9   Some oddities were, as idiom had it, "funny ha ha"; others were "funny peculiar." Some were not so very funny at all. An old man lived, deranged, in a shack in the valley. Perhaps he wasn't even all that old, but to us he seemed a wild Methuselah figure, shambling among the underbrush and the tall couchgrass, muttering indecipherable curses or blessings, a prophet who had forgotten his prophesies. Everyone in town knew him, but no one knew him. He lived among us as though only occasionally and momentarily visible. The kids called him Andy Gump, and feared him. Some sought to prove their bravery by tormenting him. They were the medieval bear baiters, and he the lumbering bewildered bear, half blind, only rarely turning to snarl. Everything is to be found in a town like mine. Belsen, writ small but with the same ink.

10   All of us cast stones in one shape or another. In grade school, among the vulnerable and violet girls we were, the feared and despised were those few older girls from what was charmingly termed "the wrong side of the tracks." Tough in talk and tougher in muscle, they were said to be whores already. And may have been, that being about the only profession readily available to them.

11   The dead lived in that place, too. Not only the grandparents who had, in local parlance, "passed on" and who gloomed, bearded or bonneted,

from the sepia photographs in old albums, but also the uncles, forever eighteen or nineteen, whose names were carved on the granite family stones in the cemetery, but whose bones lay in France. My own young mother lay in that graveyard, beside other dead of our kin, and when I was ten, my father, too, only forty, left the living town for the dead dwelling on the hill.

When I was eighteen, I couldn't wait to get out of that town, away from 12 the prairies. I did not know then that I would carry the land and town all my life within my skull, that they would form the mainspring and source of the writing I was to do, wherever and however far away I might live.

This was my territory in the time of my youth, and in a sense my life 13 since then has been an attempt to look at it, to come to terms with it. Stultifying to the mind it certainly could be, and sometimes was, but not to the imagination. It was many things, but it was never dull.

The same, I now see, could be said for Canada in general. Why on 14 earth did generations of Canadians pretend to believe this country dull? We knew perfectly well it wasn't. Yet for so long we did not proclaim what we knew. If our upsurge of so-called nationalism seems odd or irrelevant to outsiders, and even to some of our own people (what's all the fuss about?), they might try to understand that for many years we valued ourselves insufficiently, living as we did under the huge shadows of those two dominating figures, Uncle Sam and Britannia. We have only just begun to value ourselves, our land, our abilities. We have only just begun to recognize our legends and to give shape to our myths.

There are, God knows, enough aspects to deplore about this country. 15 When I see the killing of our lakes and rivers with industrial wastes, I feel rage and despair. When I see our industries and natural resources increasingly taken over by America, I feel an overwhelming discouragement, especially as I cannot simply say "damn Yankees." It should never be forgotten that it is we ourselves who have sold such a large amount of our birthright for a mess of plastic Progress. When I saw the War Measures Act being invoked in 1970, I lost forever the vestigial remains of the naive wish-belief that repression could not happen here, or would not. And yet, of course, I had known all along in the deepest and often hidden caves of the heart that anything can happen anywhere, for the seed of both man's freedom and his captivity are found everywhere, even in the microcosm of a prairie town. But in raging against our injustices, our stupidities, I do so as family, as I did, and still do in writing, about those aspects of my town which I hated and which are always in some ways aspects of myself.

16   The land still draws me more than other lands. I have lived in Africa
and in England, but splendid as both can be, they do not have the power
to move me in the same way as, for example, that part of southern Ontario where I spent four months last summer in a cedar cabin beside a
river. "Scratch a Canadian, and you find a phony pioneer," I used to say
to myself in warning. But all the same it is true, I think, that we are not
yet totally alienated from physical earth, and let us only pray we do not
become so. I once thought that my lifelong fear and mistrust of cities
made me a kind of old-fashioned freak; now I see it differently.

17   The cabin has a long window across its front western wall, and sitting at the oak table there in the mornings, I used to look out at the river
and at the tall trees beyond, green-gold in the early light. The river was
bronze; the sun caught it strangely, reflecting upon its surface the near-
shore sand ripples underneath. Suddenly, the crescenting of a fish, gone
before the eye could clearly give image to it. The old man next door
said these leaping fish were carp. Himself, he preferred muskie, for he
was a real fisherman and the muskie gave him a fight. The wind most
often blew from the south, and the river flowed toward the south, so
when the water was wind-riffled, and the current was strong, the river
seemed to be flowing both ways. I liked this, and interpreted it as an
omen, a natural symbol.

18   A few years ago, when I was back in Winnipeg, I gave a talk at my
old college. It was open to the public, and afterward a very old man
came up to me and asked me if my maiden name had been Wemyss. I
said yes, thinking he might have known my father or my grandfather.
But no. "When I was a young lad," he said, "I once worked for your
great-grandfather, Robert Wemyss, when he had the sheep ranch at
Raeburn." I think that was a moment when I realized all over again something of great importance to me. My long-ago families came from Scotland and Ireland, but in a sense that no longer mattered so much. My
true roots were here.

19   I am not very patriotic, in the usual meaning of that word. I cannot
say "My country right or wrong" in any political, social or literary context. But one thing is inalterable, for better or worse, for life.

20   This is where my world began. A world which includes the ancestors — both my own and other people's ancestors who became mine. A
world which formed me, and continues to do so, even while I fought it
in some of its aspects, and continue to do so. A world which gave me
my own lifework to do, because it was here that I learned the sight of
my own particular eyes.   (1971)

The Writer's Subject

1. On what grounds does Laurence reject the stereotypical description of the prairie as "dull, bleak, flat, uninteresting"?

2. In referring to the child's response to the Depression, Laurence says, "You understood and did not understand" (para. 5). Explain what she means by this statement.

3. What is revealed about small-town attitudes in Laurence's description of the town dump? (para. 8)

4. Why does Laurence say that she would carry the land and town within her all her life? (paras. 12–13)

5. What connections does Laurence perceive between small town prairie life and Canadian life on the national scale? (paras. 14–15)

6. Why is Laurence drawn so strongly to "the land"?

7. Suggest possible interpretations of what Laurence calls "a natural symbol," the river's flowing both ways. (para. 17)

8. What does Laurence mean by "patriotic, in the usual meaning of that word"? (para. 19)

9. Why is the essay entitled "Where the World Began" (and not "Where My World Began," for example)?

The Writer's Style and Strategy

1. Why does Laurence begin her description of a small prairie town with a series of fragments?

2. The second paragraph consists of only one sentence. Why?

3. How does Laurence make the reader see the prairie winter through a child's eyes? (para. 4)

4. How does Laurence recreate the romantic excitement the child felt at the prospect of a fire? Where is the consciousness of the writer as adult apparent? (para. 7)

5. Discuss the shift in tone at the end of paragraph 9. How is this shift achieved? What is its purpose?

6. How does Laurence achieve the transition from a discussion of mistaken perceptions of the prairie town and the land to a discussion of perceptions of Canada?

7. Why does Laurence describe the small prairie town as a microcosm? (para. 15)

8. There are obvious similarities between the opening and concluding paragraphs. What are these similarities? What are the differences?

Suggestions for Writing and Discussion

1. Where did your world begin? Write an essay introducing and explaining what you believe to be the beginnings of your particular world.

2. Margaret Laurence writes about a very personal place that carries special significance for her. Describe a place that has particular significance for you and explain its importance.

3. Laurence suggests that Canada is commonly viewed as dull. Defend Canada — or your region — against this common view.

4. Laurence writes with obvious pleasure of the adventures of childhood in winter and in summer. If you could return to childhood, what season would you choose, and why? ·

An Unquiet Awakening

by Mordecai Richler

Reading was not one of my boyhood passions. Girls, or rather the ab- 1
sence of girls, drove me to it. When I was 13 years old, short for my
age, more than somewhat pimply, I was terrified of girls. They made
me feel sadly inadequate.

Retreating into high seriousness, I acquired a pipe, which I chewed 2
on ostentatiously, and made it my business to be seen everywhere, even
at school basketball games, absorbed by books of daunting significance.
The two women who ran the lending library, possibly amused by my
pretensions, tried to interest me in fiction.

"I want fact. I can't be bothered with stories," I protested, waving 3
my pipe at them affronted, "I just haven't got the time for such nonsense."

Novels, I knew, were mere romantic make-believe, not as bad as po- 4
etry, to be fair, but bad enough.

I fell ill with a childhood disease, I no longer remember which, but 5
obviously I meant it as a rebuke to those girls in tight sweaters who
continued to ignore me. Never mind, they would mourn at my funeral,
burying me with my pipe. Too late, they would say, "Boy, was he ever
an intellectual."

The women from the lending library, concerned, dropped off books 6
for me at our house. The real stuff. Fact-filled. Providing me with the
inside dope on Theodore Herzl's childhood and *Brazil Yesterday, Today, and Tomorrow*.

One day they brought me a novel: *All Quiet on the Western Front* by 7
Erich Maria Remarque. The painting on the jacket that was taped to the

book showed a soldier wearing what was unmistakably a German Army helmet. What was this, I wondered, some sort of bad joke?

8   Nineteen forty-four that was, and I devoutly wished every German left on the face of the earth an excruciating death. The Allied invasion of France had not yet begun, but I cheered every Russian counterattack, each German city bombed, and — with the help of a map tacked to my bedroom wall — followed the progress of the Canadian troops fighting their way up the Italian boot. Boys from our street had already been among the fallen. Izzy Draper's uncle. Harvey Kegelmass' older brother. The boy who was supposed to marry Gita Holtzman.

9   *All Quiet on the Western Front* lay unopened on my bed for two days. Finally, I was driven to picking it up out of boredom. I never expected that a mere novel, a stranger's tale, could actually be dangerous, creating such turbulence in my life, obliging me to question so many received ideas. About Germans. About my own monumental ignorance of the world. About what novels were.

10   At the age of 13 in 1944, happily as yet untainted by English 104, I couldn't tell you whether Remarque's novel was
   a. a slice of life
   b. symbolic
   c. psychological
   d. seminal.
I couldn't even say if it was well or badly written. In fact, as I recall, it didn't seem to be "written" at all. Instead, it just flowed. Now, of course, I understand that writing that doesn't advertise itself is art of a very high order. It doesn't come easily. But at the time I wasn't capable of making such distinctions. I also had no notion of how *All Quiet on the Western Front* rated critically as a war novel. I hadn't read Stendhal or Tolstoy or Crane or Hemingway. I hadn't even heard of them. I didn't know that Thomas Mann, whoever he was, had praised the novel highly. Neither did I know that in 1929 the judges at some outfit called the Book-of-the-Month Club had made it their May selection.

11   But what I did know is that, hating Germans with a passion, I had read only 20, maybe 30, pages before the author had seduced me into identifying with my enemy, 19-year-old Paul Baumer, thrust into the bloody trenches of the First World War with his schoolmates: Muller, Kemmerich and the reluctant Joseph Behm, one of the first to fall. As if that weren't sufficiently unsettling in itself, the author, having won my love for Paul, my enormous concern for his survival, then betrayed me in the last dreadful paragraphs of his book:

"He fell in October 1918, on a day that was so quiet and still on the   12
whole front, that the army report confined itself to the single sentence:
All Quiet on the Western Front.

"He had fallen forward and lay on the earth as though sleeping. Turn-   13
ing him over one saw that he could not have suffered long; his face had
an expression of calm, as though almost glad the end had come."

The movies, I knew from experience, never risked letting you down   14
like that. No matter how bloody the battle, how long the odds, Errol
Flynn, Robert Taylor, even Humphrey Bogart could be counted on to
survive and come home to Ann Sheridan, Lana Turner or — if they were
sensitive types — Loretta Young. Only character actors, usually Brooklyn
Dodger fans, say George Tobias or William Bendix, were expendable.

Obviously, having waded into the pool of serious fiction by accident,   15
I was not sure I liked or trusted the water. It was too deep. Anything
could happen.

There was something else, a minor incident in All Quiet on the West-   16
ern Front that would not have troubled an adult reader but, I'm embarrassed to say, certainly distressed that 13-year-old boy colliding with
his first serious novel:

Sent out to guard a village that has been abandoned because it is be-   17
ing shelled too heavily, Katczinsky, the incomparable scrounger, sur-
faces with suckling pigs and potatoes and carrots for his comrades, a
group of eight altogether:

"The suckling pigs are slaughtered, Kat sees to them. We want to   18
make potato cakes to go with the roast. But we cannot find a grater for
the potatoes. However, that difficulty is soon over. With a nail we punch
a lot of holes in a pot lid and there we have a grater. Three fellows put
on thick gloves to protect their fingers against the grater, two others
peel the potatoes, and business gets going."

The business, I realized, alarmed — not affronted — was the mak-   19
ing of potato latkes, a favorite of mine as well as Paul Baumer's, a dish
I had always taken to be Jewish, certainly not a German concoction.

What did I know? Nothing. Or, looked at another way, my real edu-   20
cation, my life-long addiction to fiction, began with the trifling discovery that the potato latke was not of Jewish origin, but something
borrowed from the German and now a taste that Jew and German shared
in spite of everything.

I felt easier about my affection for the German soldier Paul Baumer   21
once I was told by the women from the lending library that when Hitler
came to power in 1933 he had burned all of Erich Maria Remarque's

books and in 1938 he took away his German citizenship. Obviously Hitler had grasped that novels could be dangerous, something I learned when I was only 13 years old. He burned them; I began to devour them. I started to read at the breakfast table and on streetcars, often missing my stop, and in bed with benefit of a flashlight. It got me into trouble.

22   I grasped, for the first time, that I didn't live in the centre of the world but had been born into a working-class family in an unimportant country far from the cities of light: London, Paris, New York. Of course this wasn't my fault, it was my inconsiderate parents who were to blame. But there was, I now realized, a larger world out there beyond St. Urbain Street in Montreal.

23   Preparing myself for the Rive Gauche, I bought a blue beret, but I didn't wear it outside, or even in the house if anybody else was at home. I looked at but lacked the courage to buy a cigarette holder.

24   As my parents bickered at the supper table, trapped in concerns now far too mundane for the likes of me — what to do if Dworkin raised the rent again, how to manage my brother's college fees — I sat with but actually apart from them in the kitchen, enthralled, reading for the first time, "All happy families are alike but an unhappy family is unhappy after its own fashion."[1]

25   Erich Maria Remarque, born in Westphalia in 1897, went off to war, directly from school, at the age of 18. He was wounded five times. He lost all his friends. After the war he worked briefly as a schoolteacher, a stonecutter, a test driver for a tire company and an editor of *Sportbild* magazine. His first novel, *Im Westen Nichts Neues*, was turned down by several publishers before it was brought out by the Ullstein Press in Berlin in 1928. *All Quiet on the Western Front* sold 1.2 million copies in Germany and was translated in 29 languages, selling some four million copies throughout the world. The novel has been filmed three times; the first time, memorably by Lewis Milestone in 1930. The Milestone version, with Lew Ayres playing Paul Baumer, won Academy Awards for best picture and best direction.

26   Since *All Quiet on the Western Front* once meant so much to me, I picked it up again with a certain anxiety. After all this time, I find it difficult to be objective about the novel. Its pages still evoke for me a back bedroom with a cracked ceiling and a sizzling radiator on St. Urbain Street: mice scrabbling in the walls, and a window looking out on the sheets frozen stiff on the laundry line.

27   Over the years the novel has lost something in shock value. The original jacket copy of the 1929 Little, Brown & Company edition of *All*

Quiet on the Western Front warns the reader that it is "at times crude" and "will shock the supersensitive by its outspokenness." Contemporary readers, far from being shocked, will be amused by the novel's discretion, the absence of explicit sex scenes, the unbelievably polite dialogue of the men in the trenches.

The novel also has its poignant moments, both in the trenches and 28 when Paul Baumer goes home on leave, an old man of 19, only to find insufferably pompous schoolmasters still recruiting the young with mindless prattle about the fatherland and the glory of battle. Strong characters are deftly sketched. Himmelstoss, the postman who becomes a crazed drillmaster. Tjaden, the peasant soldier. Kantorek, the schoolmaster.

On the front line the enemy is never the Frogs or the Limeys, but the 29 insanity of the war itself. It is the war, in fact, and not even Paul Baumer, that is the novel's true protagonist. In a brief introduction to the novel Remarque wrote: "This book is to be neither an accusation nor a confession, and least of all an adventure, for death is not an adventure to those who stand face to face with it. It will try simply to tell of a generation of men who, even though they may have escaped its shells, were destroyed by the war."

Since the First World War we have become altogether too familiar 30 with larger horrors. The Holocaust, Hiroshima, the threat of a nuclear winter. Death by numbers, cities obliterated by decree. At peace, as it were, we live the daily dread of the missiles in their silos, ours pointed at them, theirs pointed at us. None of this, however, diminishes the power of *All Quiet on the Western Front*, a novel that will endure because of its humanity, its honor and its refusal to lapse into sentimentality or strike a false note.

(1986)

Note

1. The opening sentence of *Anna Karenina* by Leo Tolstoy.

The Writer's Subject

1. What was Richler's attitude to novels before he had read *All Quiet on the Western Front?* What *did* he read, and why? (paras. 1–6)

2. Why did the young Richler react with anger when Remarque's novel was first lent to him? (paras. 7–8)

3. Why did Richler feel betrayed by "the last dreadful paragraphs" of the novel? Why had he expected a different ending? (paras. 11–15)

4. Why was Richler so distressed by the episode describing the making of potato cakes? (paras. 18–21)

5. Why does Richler twice use the word "dangerous" in connection with the reading of novels? (paras. 9, 21)

6. How did his reading of *All Quiet on the Western Front* change Richler's view of his own life? Why did he prepare himself for the "Rive Gauche" (the Left Bank, an area in Paris associated with the bohemian life)? (paras. 22–24)

7. Why, in Richler's view, has the novel lost something of its original "shock value"? What makes it, nevertheless, a work that will endure? (paras. 27–30)

The Writer's Style and Strategy

1. Discuss the appropriateness of the essay's title.

2. The essay was adapted from an introduction to a new edition of *All Quiet on the Western Front*. What elements of the essay reflect that function? What might the reader expect to find in the introduction to a reprinted novel?

3. Spending the first six paragraphs on his own conduct, Richler does not mention Remarque's novel until the seventh paragraph. What is Richler's purpose in adopting this strategy?

4. What is Richler burlesqueing in paragraph 10? What is the function of the paragraph in its context?

5. Discuss Richler's use of direct quotation from the novel and from its author's introduction. Why did he choose the passages he quotes?

6. What differences in tone are evident between the essay's opening section and its conclusion? Relate the shift in tone to the shape of Richler's essay.

Suggested Topics for Writing and Discussion

1. *All Quiet on the Western Front*, both as a novel and as a film, presents a powerful indictment of the waste and insanity of war. Choose another novel or film that seems to you to have a similar intention, and assess its treatment of the subject.

2. Richler feels that Remarque's novel may have lost some of its "shock value" for modern readers. Do you agree with his view that events in modern history may have hardened us to horror? Have film, literature, and the media made us more aware of the horrors of war and violence, or have they somehow dulled our moral and emotional responses?

3. Richler claims that Remarque's novel began the process of his "real education." From your own reading experience, select a work of literature that you found memorable, and attempt to account for its impact on you.

4. Richler was deeply affected by the ending of Remarque's novel, noting that it had shown him a picture of reality very different from what he had previously encountered in war movies. How faithfully, in your view, does the modern war movie reflect the reality of war?

The Historian's Opportunity
by Barbara Tuchman

1   Given the current decline of the novel and the parallel decline of poetry
and the drama, public interest has turned toward the literature of actuality. It may be that in a time of widening uncertainty and chronic stress
the historian's voice is the most needed, the more so as others seem
inadequate, often absurd. While the reasons may be argued, the opportunity, I think, is plain for the historian to become the major interpreter
in literary experience of man's role in society. The task is his to provide
both the matter to satisfy the public interest and those insights into the
human condition without which any reading matter is vapid.

2   Historians have performed this role before. Although we have no figures on readership in classical Greece and Rome, it is evident from their
continuers and imitators and from later references that Herodotus,
Thucydides and Xenophon, Tacitus, Polybius, Josephus, Plutarch, Livy,
and the others were significant voices to their contemporaries. Since
the outbreak of World War II the statistics of the book trade reflect the
growing appetite of the public for biography, autobiography, science,
sociology, and history — especially contemporary history.

3   The last category, as we have lately been made rather tiresomely
aware, has its special problems, although in the long tradition of authorized biography a subject's family has usually found quieter means
than legal recourse for retaining control over personal matters. The simple way to keep private affairs private is not to talk about them — to the
authorized, or even the "hired," writer.

4   I do not cite as evidence of the public interest in the literature of actuality the fact that since 1964 nonfiction, so called, has outsold fiction

by two to one, because that merely reflects the mass buying of cook-books and peace-of-mind books (the two front runners), plus voyeur books — that is, the sex life of everybody else — cartoon books, and how-to books on baby care, home decorating, curing arthritis, counting calories, golf, etiquette, and that recent sleeper, avoiding probate. Non-books aside, by whatever criterion you use — number of titles published and book-club choices, hardcovers and paperbacks, new titles and re-prints — the categories concerned with reality all show greater increases than fiction.

People are turning to the books of reality for a truer image of man 5 and society than is offered by contemporary novels. To look for the rea-son why fictional truth has gone askew is part of the historian's task. The novelists' failure is a consequence, I believe, of the historical expe-rience of the twentieth century, which since the First World War has been one of man's cumulative disillusionment in himself. The idea of progress was the greatest casualty of that war, and its aftermath was cynicism, confirmed by a second round of world conflict and by the implications of the Nazis' gas chambers. Then the advent into man's hands of unlimited lethal power has been topped by the frightening pres-sure of overpopulation, so that now we live under the weight of a weird paradox which threatens us simultaneously with too many people in the world and too much power to destroy them. Finally, we are faced with mounting evidence — in pollution of air and water, in destruction of the balance of nature, in the coming ear-shattering boom of supersonic flight — that we cannot refrain from despoiling our environment.

The experience has been enough to destroy in many of our genera- 6 tion their inherited belief in human goodness. Gilbert Murray found the same despair of the world overtaking the Greeks after their own period of prolonged internecine warfare and ascribed it to a sense of "the pres-sure of forces that man could not control or understand."

Man in the twentieth century is not a creature to be envied. Formerly 7 he believed himself created by the divine spark. Now, bereft of that proud confidence, and contemplating his recent record and present problems, he can no longer, like the Psalmist, respect himself as "a little lower than the angels." He cannot picture himself today, as Michelangelo did on the Sistine ceiling, in the calm and noble image of Adam receiving the spark from the finger of God. Overtaken by doubt of human pur-pose and divine purpose, he doubts his capacity to be good or even to survive. He has lost certainty, including moral and ethical certainty, and is left with a sense of footloose purposelessness and self-disgust which literature naturally reflects. The result is what the *Times Literary Supplement* has named the "Ugh" school of fiction.

8   Writers who dislike their fellow men have taken over the literary world. The mainstream of their work is epitomized by the recent novel advertised as an "engrossing" treatment of "more or less random adventures touching on thievery, homosexuality, pimping, sadism, voyeurism, a gang bang." Unaccountably, drug addiction was missing. As we all know, this is not exceptional, but run-of-the-mill, and the drama, in the dreary examples that reach the stage today, does its best to keep pace. The preferred characters of current fiction are the drifters and derelicts of life in whose affairs or ultimate fate it is impossible to sustain interest. They do not excite the question that is the heart of narrative — "What happens next?" — because one cannot care what happens to them.

9   Perhaps the fault is not in the novelists but in the times that their characters are underlings; anti-heroes who reflect a general sense of man as victim. Perhaps the novelist today cannot honestly create a protagonist who is master of his fate and captain of his soul because man in the image of Henley seems obsolete. That man belonged to the self-confident nineteenth century, whereas the twentieth finds its exponent in losers, "beautiful losers" according to the title of a recent novel, although few seem to deserve the adjective. Oedipus was a loser and so was King Lear, but their losing was universal and profound, not pointless.

10   Since fiction and drama no longer present a true balance of human activity and motive, it is not to be wondered that they are losing their audience. According to a recent report from the capital, "Official Washington does not read contemporary novels" for the reason given by a sub-Cabinet officer in these words: "I try to read them and give up. Why should I spend my time on [books] ... where the central character spends 350 pages quivering about whether to cross the street or go to the toilet?"

11   He has a point. Reading, which is to say writing, is the greatest gift with which man has endowed himself, by whose means we may soar on unlimited voyages. Are we to spend it picking through the garbage of humanity? Certainly the squalid and worthless, the mean and depraved are part of the human story just as dregs are part of wine, but the wine is what counts. Sexual perversion and hallucinatory drugs, as Eliot Fremont-Smith said of a recent novel, "are not what drives us, not what human history is about."

12   The task then devolves upon historians to tell what human history *is* about and what are the forces that *do* drive us. That is not to say that history excludes the squalid and depraved, but, being concerned as it is

with reality and subject as it is to certain disciplines, it deals with these in proportion to the whole.

Historians start with a great advantage over fiction in that our characters, being public, are invested with power to affect destiny. They are the captains and kings, saints and fanatics, traitors, rogues and villains, pathfinders and explorers, thinkers and creators, even, occasionally, heroes. They are significant — if not necessarily admirable. They may be evil or corrupt or mad or stupid or even stuffed shirts, but at least, by virtue of circumstance or chance or office or character, they *matter*. They are the actors, not the acted upon, and are consequently that much more interesting. 13

Readers want to see man shaping his destiny or, at least, struggling with it, and this is the stuff of history. They want to know how things happened, why they happened, and particularly what they themselves have lived through, just as after a record heat or heavy snow the first thing one turns to in the morning paper is the account of yesterday's weather. And now more than ever, when man's place in the world has never been so subject to question, when "alienation" is the prevailing word, the public also hopes to find some guidelines to destiny, some pattern or meaning to our presence on this whirling globe. Whether or not, as individuals, historians believe in one pattern or another, or some of us in none, the evidence we have to present provides reassurance in showing that man has gone through his dark ages before. 14

When I was a young parent a series of books appeared on child behavior by Dr. Arnold Gesell and his associates of the Yale Clinic in which one discovered that the most aberrant, disturbing, or apparently psychotic behavior of one's own child turned out to be the common age pattern of the group innocently disporting itself behind Dr. Gesell's one-way observation screen. Nothing was ever so comforting. Historians provide a one-way screen on the past through which one can see man, at one time or another, committing every horror, indecency, or idiocy that he is capable of today. It is all already on his record, in kind if not in degree. I do not suggest that history can be as comforting as Gesell because the difference in degree that we face today is so great — in the speed and impact of the mechanisms we have created — that problems and dangers multiply faster than we can devise solutions. Henry Adams' law of acceleration is proving perilously true. Nevertheless, Adams' law is one of those guidelines historians have to offer. The story and study of the past, both recent and distant, will not reveal the future, but it flashes beacon lights along the way and it is a useful nostrum against despair. 15

16   Historians cannot expect to take over the leading role in literature without competition. Last summer Albert Rosenfeld, science editor of *Life*, wrote in an editorial that creative writers must turn to science to revive literature because "That is where the action is." There is a relevant and challenging truth in his statement. Science is formidably relevant and dynamic. "Great writing in any age," Rosenfeld continued, "casts some illumination on the major contemporary dilemmas." That is equally cogent. If science can evoke great creative writers who will do for space aeronautics or genetics or nuclear energy what Rachel Carson, for example, did for the sea around us, they will certainly win a large share of the public interest. The chief obstacle is language. Great writing in science must come from inside the discipline, and everything will depend on the rare talent which can break through the meshes of a technical vocabulary and express itself in words of common usage.

17   Here, too, we have a head start. Historians can — though not all do — make themselves understood in everyday English, the language in use from Chaucer to Churchill. Let us beware of the plight of our colleagues, the behavioral scientists, who by use of a proliferating jargon have painted themselves into a corner — or isolation ward — of unintelligibility. *They* know what they mean, but no one else does. Psychologists and sociologists are the farthest gone in the disease and probably incurable. Their condition might be pitied if one did not suspect it was deliberate. Their retreat into the arcane is meant to set them apart from the great unlearned, to mark their possession of some unshared, unsharable expertise. No matter how illuminating their discoveries, if the behavioral scientists write only to be understood by one another, they must come to the end of the Mandarins.

18   Communication, after all, is what language was invented for. If history is to share its insights with a public in need of them, it must practice communication as an art, as Gibbon did, or Parkman. History has, of course, other parts; like that other famous property, it is divisible into three: the investigative or research, the didactic or theory, and the narrated or communication. The elements that enter into communication are what I want to discuss, because history, it seems to me, is nothing if not communicated. Research provides the material, and theory a pattern of thought, but it is through communication that history is heard and understood

19   At the risk of stating the obvious, it is worth remarking that success of communication depends upon the charm (I use the word in its most serious sense) of the narrative. "Writings are useless," declared Theodore

Roosevelt, speaking as president of the American Historical Association in 1912, "unless they are read, and they cannot be read unless they
are readable."

The history most successfully communicated, as far as the public is   20
concerned, can in one sense be determined by the annual lists of the top
best-sellers. Up to 1960 the all-time best-seller in history was H. G.
Wells's *Outline of History*, first published in 1921, which stayed among
the top ten for three years in a row and reappeared on the list in a cheaper
edition in 1930. It is the only book of history up to 1960 to have sold
more than two million copies — more, oddly enough, than *The Kinsey
Report*. Since then the leading work in history has been William L.
Shirer's *Rise and Fall of the Third Reich*, which has sold, at last report,
close to three million copies in the United States alone.

These names suggest what the evidence confirms: During the 1920s   21
and 1930s, when serious books had a better chance of reaching the top
ten, the best-sellers in historical biography and straight history (as distinct from personal history and current events) included four academics, James Harvey Robinson, Charles Beard, Carl Van Doren, and James
Truslow Adams three times over; and twelve non-academics, Emil
Ludwig with four books, Hendrik van Loon with three, Lytton Strachey,
Claude Bowers, Van Wyck Brooks, Andre Maurois, Francis Hackett,
Stefan Zweig with two each, Will Durant, Frederick Lewis Allen,
Margaret Leech, and Douglas Southall Freeman with one each. During
the 1940s, when the war books took over, one academic, Arnold Toynbee
(with his one-volume condensation) and one non-academic, Catherine
Drinker Bowen, made the top ten. After that, except for Shirer and
Frederic Morton's *The Rothschilds*, the swamping effect of the non-books
begins and one has to look just beneath the top ten to the books which
have been best-sellers during the course of the year without making the
final list. Taking only the 1960s, these included three academics, Garrett
Mattingly, Samuel Eliot Morison, Arthur Schlesinger, Jr., and nine independent writers, Winston Churchill, Bruce Catton, Alan Moorehead,
Thomas Costain, Walter Lord, Cecil Woodham-Smith, and myself with
two or more books each, Stewart Holbrook and George Kennan each
with one.

To be a best-seller is not necessarily a measure of quality, but it *is* a   22
measure of communication. That the independent writers have done
better is hardly surprising, since communicating is their business; they
know how. To capture and hold the interest of an audience is their object, as it has been that of every storyteller since Homer. Perhaps the

academic historian suffers from having a captive audience, first in the
supervisor of his dissertation, then in the lecture hall. Keeping the reader
turning the page has not been his primary concern.

23   My intention is not to exacerbate the distinction between the professional historian and the so-called amateur but to clarify its terms. "Professional" — meaning someone who has had graduate training leading
to a professional degree and who practices within a university — is a
valid term, but "amateur" — used to mean someone outside the university without a graduate degree — is a misnomer. Graduate training certainly establishes a difference of which I, who did not have it, am deeply
aware, sometimes regretfully, sometimes thankfully. But I would prefer
to recognize the difference by distinguishing between academics and
independents, or between scholars and writers, rather than between professionals and amateurs, because the question is not one of degree of
professionalism but which profession. The faculty people are professional historians, we outside are professional writers. Insofar as they
borrow our function and we borrow their subject, each of us has a great
deal to learn from the other.

24   An objection often made to the independents is that they are insufficiently acquainted or careless with the facts. An extreme case is the
Cortez of Keats, staring at the Pacific with a wild surmise, silent upon a
peak in Darien. Keats, of course, got the name wrong but the idea right.
Through the power of marvelous phrasing and the exercise of a poet's
imagination he immortalized a historic moment. It is possible that his
vision of the man on the peak is more important, for conveying history,
than the name of the man. Poets aside, historians of course should offer
both. There is no need to choose between accuracy and beauty; one
should be clothed in the other.

25   In pockets of survival there may be some historians who still retain
the old notion imposed by scientific history that, as another president
of the American Historical Association, Walter Prescott Webb, put it,
"There is something historically naughty about good writing," that "a
great gulf exists between truth and beauty and the scholar who attempts
to bridge it deserves to fall in and drown," and that "the real scholar
must choose truth and somehow it is better if it is made so ugly that
nobody could doubt its virginity." If some still believe this, communication is not for them.

26   For the first element in communication, Webb gave the perfect triple
criterion: a writer's belief that he has something to say, that it is worth
saying, and that he can say it better than anyone else — and, he added,

"not for the few but for the many." For coupled with compulsion to write must go desire to be read. No writing comes alive unless the writer sees across his desk a reader, and searches constantly for the word or phrase which will carry the image he wants the reader to see and arouse the emotion he wants him to feel. Without consciousness of a live reader, what a man writes will die on his page. Macaulay was a master of this contact with the reader. His sister Hannah cried when he read the *History of England* aloud to her. What writer could ask for more?

When it comes to content, inspiration, what Webb calls the moment 27 of synthesis — the revealing flash of a synthesizing idea — is obviously a help. Webb describes his own moment of insight when the idea came to him that the emergence of Americans from the life of the forests to the life of the plains was of dramatic significance. Admiral Mahan had his moment when, from the study of Hannibal's failure to control sea communication with Carthage, the idea flashed on him of the influence of sea power on history. The moment is exciting but not, I think, essential. A theme may do as well to begin with as a thesis and does not involve, like the overriding theory, a creeping temptation to adjust the facts. The integrating idea or insight then evolves from the internal logic of the material, in the course of putting it together. From the gathering of the particulars one arrives at the general, at that shining grail we are all in search of, the historical generalization. To state it in advance does not seem necessary to me. The process is more persuasive and the integrating idea more convincing if the reader discovers it for himself out of the evidence laid before him.

All theses run the risk of obsolescence. The pathways of history, said 28 the great historian of the frontier, Frederick Jackson Turner, are "strewn with the wrecks" of once known and acknowledged truths, discarded by a later generation. Revision and counter-revision roll against the shores of history as rhythmically as waves. Even so, a true inspiration or integrating idea such as Mahan's or Turner's will be valid and enlightening for its time, regardless of subsequent fortune.

Though some will debate it, intuition, too, is an aid. The intuitive 29 historian can reach an understanding of long-past circumstance in much the same way as Democritus, the predecessor of Aristotle, arrived at the idea of the atom. His mind, mulling over observed phenomena, worked out a theory of matter as composed of an infinite number of mobile particles. The process may have been cerebral, but its impetus was intuitive. Strict disciples of history as a science may scorn the intuitive process, but that attitude comes from being more Catholic than the Pope.

True scientists know its value. It is an arrow shot into the air, which will often pierce the same target that the scientific historian with his nose on the ground will take months to reach on foot.

30   Of all the historian's instruments, belief in the grandeur of his theme is the most compelling. Parkman, in his preface to *Montcalm and Wolfe*, describes his subject, the Seven Years' War in the American theater, as "the most momentous and far-reaching question ever brought to issue on this continent." Its outcome determined that there would be an American Revolution. "With it began a new chapter in the annals of the world." That is the way an author should feel about his subject. It ensures that no reader can put the book down.

31   Enthusiasm, which is not quite the same thing, has a no less leavening effect. It was recognized by Admiral Mahan, who, in the course of studying Britain's contest with Napoleon, developed a particular admiration for Pitt. "His steadfast nature," Mahan wrote, "aroused in me an enthusiasm which I did not seek to check; for I believe enthusiasm no bad spirit in which to realize history to yourself and to others."

32   Mahan's prescription disposes of the myth of "pure objectivity" when used to mean "without bias." As John Gunther once said of journalism, "A reporter with no bias at all would be a vegetable." If such a thing as a "purely objective" historian could exist, his work would be unreadable — like eating sawdust. Bias is only misleading when it is concealed. After reading *The Proud Tower*, a onetime member of the Asquith government scolded me in a letter for misrepresenting as he thought, his party. "Your bias against the Liberals sticks out," he wrote. I replied that it was better to have it stick out than be hidden. It can then be taken into account. I cannot deny that I acquired a distaste for Mr. Asquith as, for other reasons, I did for Henry Adams. There are some people in history one simply dislikes, and as long as they are not around to have their feelings hurt, I see no reason to conceal it. To take no sides in history would be as false as to take no sides in life.

33   A historian tries to be objective in the sense of learning as much as possible, and presenting as sympathetically as possible the motives and conditions of both sides, because to do so makes the drama more intense — and more believable. But let us not pretend that this is being without bias — as if historians were mere recorders who have given up the exercise of judgment. Bias means a *leaning* which *is* the exercise of judgment as well as a source of insight. Admittedly, it is usually helped by emotional conditioning, but that is what makes for commitment. The great historians more often than not have been passionately committed

to a cause or a protagonist, as Mommsen was to Julius Caesar or Michelet to the glorious power of the people.

How commitment can generate insight and heighten communication 34 is nowhere better shown than in G. M. Trevelyan's *Garibaldi and the Thousand*, one of the finest works of history, I think, both for investigation and narrative, produced in this century. Trevelyan's commitment to his hero is explicit. Describing the foot track from the Villa Spinola down to the embarkation point in Genoa, he writes in a footnote, "I had the honor of going down it" with a veteran of the Thousand. There is no doubt where he stands. His feeling of personal involvement led Trevelyan to visit every place connected with the Garibaldini, to walk in their footsteps, to interview those still living, until he knew the persons, terrain, view, sounds, smells, sights, distances, weather — in short, the feel — of every scene of action he was to write about.

As the Thousand marched to the Battle of Calatafimi, Trevelyan 35 writes, "Their hearts were light with the sense that they were enviable above all Italians, that their unique campaign was poetry made real." The quality of emotion here is not, as so often, created out of the historian's feelings and foisted onto his characters, but drawn from the evidence. A footnote gives the original from a letter of one of the Garibaldini to his mother telling her, "*Questa spedizione è così poetica.*" ("This expedition is a poetical thing") Approaching the battle, they pass through a green valley at early morning. "In the bloom of the early Sicilian summer," Trevelyan writes, "the vale fresh from last night's rain, and sung over by the nightingale at dawn, lay ready to exhale its odors to the rising sun. Nature seemed in tune with the hearts of Garibaldi and his men." Here, too he worked from evidence in diaries and letters that it had rained the night before and that the nightingale had sung. In these two passages he has conveyed the sense of miraculous freshness and noble enterprise which the Garibaldi expedition signalized for the liberal spirit of the nineteenth century. He could accomplish this, first, because of his quick sensitivity to source material, and second, because he himself was in tune with the hearts of Garibaldi and his men.

Again, when Garibaldi's bugler blew reveille, "the unexpected mu- 36 sic rang through the noonday stillness like a summons to the soul of Italy." In the verb of sound, "rang," the reader hears the bugle and in the phrase "like a summons to the soul of Italy" feels the emotion of the listener. Without knowing that he is being told, he has learned the meaning to history of the expedition.

To visit the scene before writing, even the scene of long-dead adven- 37 tures, is, as it were, to start business with money in the bank. It was said of Arthur Waley, the great Orientalist who died a few months ago, that he had never visited Asia, explaining that he was content with the ideal image of the East in his imagination. For a historian that would be a risky position. On the terrain motives become clear, reasons and explanations and origins of things emerge that might otherwise have remained obscure. As a source of understanding, not to mention as a corrective for fixed ideas and mistaken notions, nothing is more valuable than knowing the scene in person, and, even more so, living the life that belongs to it. Without that intimacy Francis Parkman would not have been the master he was.

38   Parkman's hero was really the forest. Through experience he learned passion for it, and fear, and understood both its savagery and beauty. In those long days of intermittent blindness when he was not allowed to write, his mind must have worked over remembered visions of the forest so that they come through on the page with extra clarity. As a scout paddles across the lake in autumn, "the mossed rocks double in the watery mirror" and sumachs on the shore glow like rubies against the dark green spruce. Or the frontier settler, returning at evening, sees a "column of blue smoke rising quietly in the still evening air" and runs to find the smoldering logs of his cabin and the scalped bodies of his murdered wife and children.

39   Vision, knowledge, experience will not make a great writer without that extra command of language which becomes their voice. This, too, was Parkman's. When the English are about to descend the rapids of the upper St. Lawrence, they look on the river whose "reckless surges dashed and bounded in the sun, beautiful and terrible as young tigers at play." In choice of verbs and nouns and images that is a masterpiece. It is only physical description, to be sure, not a great thought, but it takes perfect command of words to express great thoughts in the event one has them.

40   Steeped in the documents he spent his life collecting, as he was steeped in the forest, Parkman understood the hardship and endurance, grim energy, and implacable combat that underlay the founding of the American nation. He knew the different groups of combatants as if he had lived with each, and could write with equal sympathy of French or Indians, English or colonials. Consider his seventeenth-century French courtiers, "the butterflies of Versailles ... facing death with careless gallantry, in their small three-cornered hats, powdered perukes, embroidered coats, and lace ruffles. Their valets served them with ices in the

trenches, under the cannon of besieged towns." In this case the ices in the trenches is a specimen of the historian's selective insight at work. He has chosen a vivid item to represent a larger whole. It distills an era and a culture in a detail.

Distillation is selection, and selection, as I am hardly the first to af- 41
firm, is the essence of writing history. It is the cardinal process of composition, the most difficult, the most delicate, the most fraught with error as well as art. Ability to distinguish what is significant from what is insignificant is *sine qua non*.[1] Failure to do so means that the point of the story, not to mention the reader's interest, becomes lost in a morass of undifferentiated matter. What it requires is simply the courage and self confidence to make choices and, above all, to leave things out.

In history as in painting, wrote the great stylist Macaulay, to put in 42
everything achieves a less, rather than a more, truthful result. The best picture and best history, he said, are those "which exhibit such parts of the truth as most nearly produce the effect of the whole." This is such an obvious rule that it is puzzling why so many historians today seem to practice a reverse trend toward total inclusion. Perhaps the reason is timidity: fear of being criticized for having left something out, or, by injudicious selection, of not conforming to the dominant thesis of the moment. Here the independent writer has an advantage over the professional historian: He need not be afraid of the outstuck neck.

Finally, the historian cannot do without imagination. Parkman, in- 43
tense as always in his effort to make the reader "feel the situation," chose to picture the land between the Hudson and Montreal as it would look to a wild goose flying northward in spring. He sees the blue line of the river, the dark mass of forests and shimmer of lakes, the geometric lines and mounds of man-made forts, "with the flag of the Bourbons like a flickering white speck" marking Ticonderoga, and the "mountain wilderness of the Adirondacks like a stormy sea congealed." On reading that passage I feel the excitement of the Count of Monte Cristo when he opened the treasure chest. It would not be remarkable for one of us who has traveled in airplanes to think of the device of the bird's-eye view, but Parkman had never been off the ground. It was a pure effort of imagination to put himself behind the eye of the goose, to see the flag as a flickering white speck and the mountains, in that perfect phrase, as "a stormy sea congealed."

Great as this is, the more necessary use of imagination is in applica- 44
tion to human behavior and to the action of circumstance on motive. It becomes a deliberate effort at empathy, essential if one is to understand

and interpret the actions of historical figures. With antipathetic characters it is all the more necessary. The historian must put himself inside
them, as Parkman put himself inside the wild goose, or as I tried to do
inside Sir John French in an effort to understand the draining away of
his will to fight. As soon as the effort was made, the explanation offered itself. I could feel the oppression, the weight of responsibility, the
consciousness of the absence of any trained reserves to take the place
of the BEF if it were lost.[2] The effort to get inside is, obviously enough,
a path to insight. It is the *Einfühlung* that Herder demanded of historians: the effort to "feel oneself into everything." The interpreter of the
Hebrew scriptures, as he put it, must be "a shepherd with shepherds, a
peasant in the midst of an agricultural people, an oriental with the primitive dwellers of the East."

45   To describe the historian's task today in terms of narrative history
and two romantic practitioners, Parkman and Trevelyan, will seem old-
fashioned at a time when interdisciplinary techniques, and horizontal
subjects such as demography, and the computerized mechanics of quantification are the areas of fresh endeavor. These are methods of research,
not of communication, for one reason because the people who use them
tend to lose contact with ordinary language; they have caught the jargon disease. Their efforts are directed, I take it, toward uncovering underlying patterns in history and human behavior which presumably might
help in understanding the past and managing the future, or even the
present. Whether quantification will reveal anything which could not
have been discerned by deduction is not yet clear. What seems to be
missing in the studies that I have seen is a certain element of common
sense.

46   The new techniques will, I am sure, turn up suggestive material and
open avenues of thought, but they will not, I think, transform history
into a science, and they can never make it literature. Events happen: but
to become history they must be communicated and understood. For that,
history needs writers — preferably great writers — a Trevelyan who
can find and understand the *cosi poetica* in a soldier's letter and make
the right use of it, a Parkman who can see and feel, and report with
Shakespeare's gift of words; both, I need not add, assemblers of their
own primary material. To be a really great historian, Macaulay said, "is
the rarest of intellectual distinctions." For all who try, the opportunity
is now and the audience awaits.

(1967)

Notes

1. sine qua non: "without which, nothing"

2. BEF — British Expeditionary Force of World War I, headed in 1914 by Sir John French. Tuchman is referring in this paragraph to her Pulitzer prize winning book, *The Guns of August.*

The Writer's Subject

1. What does Tuchman mean by "the literature of actuality"? (paras. 1–4)

2. What cause and effect relation does Tuchman draw between "man's cumulative disillusionment in himself" (para. 5) and the state of contemporary fiction and drama? Why, in her view, are fiction and drama losing their audience? (paras. 5–11)

3. How, according to Tuchman, does the historian take account of "the squalid and worthless" differently from the contemporary novelist? (paras. 11–12)

4. How may the historian, in Tuchman's view, offer reassurance to the modern reader disturbed by the problems of contemporary life? (paras. 14–15)

5. What contrast does Tuchman draw between the writing of historians and that of behavioural scientists? (para. 17)

6. Why, in Tuchman's view, have the independent, non-academic historical writers been more successful with the reading public than the professional, academic historians? (paras. 20–24)

7. What are the most important attributes for a good historian, according to Tuchman? (paras. 26–44)

8. What is Tuchman's response to the idea that a historian should be completely objective and without bias? (paras. 32–33)

9. What qualities does Tuchman admire in the historians G. M. Trevelyan and Francis Parkman? (paras. 34–40)

10. What does Tuchman mean in asserting that "selection ... is the essence of writing history"? (paras. 41–42)

11. What importance does Tuchman ascribe to the historian's ability to empathize with historical figures? (para. 44)

12. Of what value are computers and statistical approaches to the study of history, in Tuchman's view? (para. 45)

The Writer's Style and Strategy

1. How does Tuchman's title reflect her purposes in this essay?

2. What is Tuchman's thesis, and where is it most clearly stated?

3. What evidence does the essay provide of its origin as an address to the American Historical Association? What assumptions does Tuchman make about her audience?

4. Tuchman observes that the study of the past can throw light upon the present. Where does she exemplify this principle in the course of her discussion?

5. Show how Tuchman uses the works of other historians to illustrate the principles of good historical writing.

6. Tuchman alludes to W. E. Henley's poem "Invictus" (para. 9) and Keats's poem "On First Looking into Chapman's Homer" (para. 24). Look up the poems, and discuss the appropriateness of Tuchman's references to them for her argumentative purposes.

7. Tuchman believes that historians should "make themselves understood in everyday English" (para. 17). What qualities of "everyday English" does Tuchman's own writing display? Choose one or two paragraphs for the purpose of your analysis.

Suggested Topics for Writing and Discussion

1. Find a work of history by a noted historian of the nineteenth or twentieth century. Choose two or three pages for analysis and indicate whether the writer, in your opinion, exhibits the qualities that Tuchman maintains are needed for good historical writing.

2. Tuchman, writing this essay in 1967, says that most works of literature of the time were characterized by "the squalid and the worthless, the mean and depraved." Choose any well-known work of imaginative literature written in the last twenty years and indicate whether the work fits the generalized pattern described by Tuchman.

3. Tuchman says: "To be a best-seller is not necessarily a measure of quality, but it *is* a measure of communication." Consult a bestseller list in a national magazine or newspaper to locate a work of non-fiction which has been on the list for several months. Find two or three reviews of the book and report on its capacity to "communicate" its subject.

Influences
by Guy Vanderhaeghe

It was only after I published a book that I was forced to consider the   1
question of influence on my writing. Until that point I had merely written. But reviewers made me aware of the problem of influence, drawing as they did convincing parallels between my short stories and the
work of writers I had never read. Interviewers, too, were keen to un-
earth literary debts. Which writers and books, they asked, had most influenced me?

It was a question I wanted to answer honestly. But I was not sure I   2
could. For one thing I had the impression I was really being asked which
books and writers I admired most, asked that in the certainty that the
answer to both questions was the same. That might be so, but isn't necessarily. *Ulysses*, for instance, is one of those universally admired works
which has influenced writers less than one would think. *Remembrance
of Things Past* is another.

What I was coming to suspect was that literary influences are more   3
various and varied than I had imagined. In my case, the threads of these
influences resolved themselves into a Gordian knot which stubbornly
resisted all my efforts to untangle it. For instance, when asked to produce
a list of those authors whom I particularly admired I was inevitably struck
by the heterogeneity of the list I compiled. I could not but help imagine
these authors incongruously yoked in conversation at literary cocktail
parties. Flannery O'Connor and Anthony Powell? Christopher Isherwood
and Rudy Wiebe? Alice Munro and Evelyn Waugh?

I could not see how these converging vectors of probable influence   4
had shaped my writing. Worse, I felt I was suppressing another, per-

haps equally important list of names. Names such as Zane Grey, Walter Scott, John Buchan, and Robert Louis Stevenson came immediately to mind. Yet I was afraid of being thought facetious if I gave these writers the nod of acknowledgement.

5   It was only when I read Vladimir Nabokov's autobiography *Speak, Memory* that I seriously began to define and elaborate a dim suspicion I had been harbouring: that "bad" writing is as influential in the development of a writer as "good" writing. A brief reference of Nabokov's to an article he had read as a child in the *Boy's Own Paper* strengthened that suspicion because it helped carry me back, back beyond my first acquaintance with Zane Grey, Stevenson, Buchan, and Scott, back to my earliest reading, to my introduction to the *Boy's Own Annual*.

6   During Nabokov's Edwardian childhood the *Boy's Own Paper* was one of those bellicose boys' magazines which tub-thumped for the British Empire and the "right little, tight little Island!" It may seem strange that such a paper found its way into the Nabokov home, but Vladimir Nabokov's father was a wealthy anglophile who insisted on English governesses, governesses who, in turn, insisted that their little Russian charges read and write English before they read and write Russian. Thus the *Boy's Own Paper*.

7   All this smacks a bit of Alice in Wonderland. There is surely something absurd in the notion of a young Russian aristocrat, citizen of a xenophobe empire, reading, in English, the rival claims to glory of a competing xenophobe empire. The only thing possibly more absurd is that almost exactly fifty years later, in 1957 or thereabouts, I was poring over a like-minded publication, the *Boy's Own Annual*. My volume too was Edwardian, an issue that Nabokov might conceivably have read on dark St. Petersburg winter evenings, a book that had lost its covers and was coming apart in my hands and which I, at the age of six, took to be a reasonably accurate account of the world outside my bailiwick. No one told me that the fabulous world described in its pages had expired in the mud of Flanders more than forty years before.

8   Or perhaps it was just that I refused not to believe in what I was reading. In any case, I held on to the illusion for something like three years before it evaporated. During that time I confined my reading basically to two books (aside from the insipid things assigned in school) and those books were an old school text of my mother's, *A History of the World*, and the previously mentioned volume of the *Boy's Own Annual*. In the beginning I found *A History of the World* the more intriguing because of its illustrations: photographs of antiquities such as Mycenaean dag-

gers and Etruscan coins, and reproductions of "historical" paintings which showed Egyptian charioteers dramatically dying, transfixed by Hittite arrows. The *Boy's Own Annual* supplanted the *History* in my affections only as my ability to read improved. Only then did it become the staple nourishment of my imagination. I never read, or had read to me, for instance, any of the children's classics such as *Winnie the Pooh*, *The Jungle Book*, or *The Wind in the Willows*. In retrospect I can say it would have been a good thing if I had read other books, but at the time I certainly didn't suffer from these omissions. My pre-World War I issue of the *Boy's Own Annual* kept me entranced. I needed no other books. I was like a fundamentalist with his Bible.

The *Boy's Own Annual* fell into my hands by way of an elderly English lady who was cleaning out her attic. This lady was typically English — or at least what North American readers of Agatha Christie mysteries might imagine as typically English. A widow, she lived for her huge garden, her budgerigars, and a cocker spaniel named Rusty. She presented me the tattered copy with the assurance that it was "just the thing for a lively young fellow." Against all odds it was.

The contents of the *Boy's Own*, as I remember it, divided fairly evenly into three broad categories. Practical knowledge; historical yarns which even I recognized as historical; and "contemporary" tales which were, at the time I read them, already more than forty years old. The latter I insisted on thinking of as accurate reflections of life in the British Isles and Empire. With hindsight I conclude that this misconception of mine probably continued to flourish primarily because my parents didn't own a television. A TV set would have rubbed my nose in the grit of reality. But I also must have practised self-delusion on a grand scale, some part of my mind censoring all evidence that contradicted the *Boy's Own* picture of the world. Still, in my defence I can say that this was the age of Tarzan movies.

Anyway, who wouldn't wish to keep alive such magnificent delusions? How well I recall the *Boy's Own* article on self-defence. Here was practical knowledge indeed, a step by step, blow by blow account of the proper use of one's walking stick in repulsing assailants. The reader was enjoined to strike *glancing* blows off threatening blackguards because glancing blows foil any attempts at seizing one's walking stick, wresting it from one's grasp, and turning it against one. (It being understood that blackguards were clearly not the kind of fellows to carry walking sticks of their own.) Recommended targets for such glancing blows were elbows, shins, and, of course, the crown of the head. As a bonus several policeman's grips were described and illustrated. When applied these grips promised to bring about the instant submission of felons. Young readers were reminded to use minimum force when practising such grips on their chums.

12   The article incited in me a powerful longing. I knew that there were no interesting blackguards stalking the streets of Esterhazy, Saskatchewan, of the type depicted in *Boy's Own*. Nor did I own an ashplant. However, that didn't mean I oughtn't to study the article very closely. Particularly since I had, on the spot, determined to go to England where there apparently was an abundance of blackguards, villains, and ruffians. All suitable for thrashing.

13   The rest of *Boy's Own* was, if possible, even better, stuffed plum-full to bursting with plucky youths. There were the plucky youths of the past: a ferreter-out of the Gunpowder Plot, an alarm-raiser at the Great Fire of London, an aider and abettor of the escape of Bonny Prince Charlie to France. Then there were the plucky youths I mistook for my contemporaries. My favourite among these was a lad who had stained his skin with berry juice, wrapped his head in a turban, and embarked on a steamer ferrying pilgrims to Mecca. His mission? To uncover a ring of Arab slavers dealing in British subjects. After making fog-bound London streets safe for respectable strollers I thought I might lend this chap a hand tidying up the Red Sea. My future bloomed.

14   If it was Nabokov's perfunctory comment about the *Boy's Own Paper* that resurrected memories which had lain mute under the dead weight of all the books that followed this one volume, books deposited year by year, strata upon strata, it was something else in *Speak, Memory* that made me consider whether my writing hadn't been flavoured by this early infatuation of mine with the *Boy's Own Annual*.

15   Reading Nabokov's autobiography I was struck by a curious thing. I noted that although Nabokov makes frequent reference to the authors of the great European and Russian masterpieces, he devotes more space to a man called Captain Mayne Reid than he does to either Blok, Pushkin, Tolstoy, Gogol, Kafka, Flaubert, Dostoevsky, or for that matter, any other writer.

16   Who was Captain Mayne Reid? Captain Mayne Reid (1818–83), Nabokov informs us, was a writer of Wild West romances. At the turn of the century translations of his work were enormously popular with Russian schoolchildren. Young Vladimir Nabokov was, however, because of the diligence of his governesses, fluent enough in English to have the privilege of reading them in the original language. His favourite, he tells his readers, was *Headless Horseman*.

From what Nabokov has to say in *Speak, Memory* it is possible to 17
deduce that Mayne Reid completely captivated his young reader.
Nabokov even admits to re-reading *Headless Horseman* as an adult, and
he maintains that the book has its points. It is instructive to note what
these points are.

First of all Nabokov takes delight in the artificiality and intricacy of 18
Captain Mayne Reid's plots. Second, several passages of prose are
quoted with approval. There is the Whiskey decanter behind a Texan
barman which looks like "an iris sparkling behind his shoulder," and
the barman himself is improbably graced with "an aureole surrounding
his perfumed head." Now it is true that in all this Nabokovian applause
there is more than a trace of the familiar Nabokovian mockery. But two
things came to my mind also: Nabokov's own prose, touched as it is
with the fantastic and a tincture of the archaic, and his own taste for
studied melodrama and gloriously coincidental plots. One has, after all,
only to think of how improbably the nymphet's mother was despatched
in *Lolita* to leave the field free for Humbert Humbert.

On such slender, even feeble evidence it would be foolhardy to ar- 19
gue a connection between Reid and Nabokov, to see the romancer's taste,
filtered and purified by Nabokov's genius, later making a bow in the
shadows of Nabokov's novels. But I sensed that, if clearly unprovable,
it was still possible. Nabokov himself is frank in admitting that many
of the books he later read resonated with Reidian echoes. Dwelling on
Louise Pointdexter, a young lady equipped with lorgnette that he discovered in *Headless Horseman*, Nabokov writes,

> That lorgnette I found afterward in the hands of Madame Bovary,
> and later Anna Karenin had it, and then it passed into the posses-
> sion of Chekhov's Lady with the Lapdog and was lost by her on
> the pier at Yalta. When Louise held it, it was directed toward the
> speckled shadows under the mesquites, where the horseman of her
> choice was having an innocent conversation with the daughter of
> a wealthy haciendado, Doña Isidora Covarubio de los Llanos
> (whose 'head of hair in luxuriance rivalled the tail of a wild steed').

In just this manner the turbaned heads of Moslem pilgrims that I had
met in the *Boy's Own Annual* sprang into view when I read *Lord Jim*,
and walking sticks in the hands of Henry James' characters were suddenly transformed from the innocent appurtenances of dandies into
menacing clubs.

There was something else, too. I had come to wonder if I had not 20 begun the process of learning to write long ago with the *Boy's Own*. The one problem with the magazine was that it was a serial, and I possessed only a single volume. Some of the stories had no beginning. Worse, some had no end. Several of the more harrowing tales had appended to their last page a cruel joke: To be continued. My favourite character, the berry-stained boy, I had to leave manacled in the bottom of an Arab dhow on the point of being pitched overboard to sharks. What, I asked myself in torments of anxiety, had happened to him?

21   I like to think now that he would have remained forever frozen in that queer limbo of near death if I hadn't assumed the responsibility of rescuing him. Because at some point in my childhood I came to realize that what I was reading was fiction, a structure created by the imagination. If I were daring enough I might collaborate in the making of it. Or as I saw it then: the boy can be saved. So at about the age of seven or eight I set about saving him, manufacturing ploys and desperate acts of desperate courage that would deliver him from implacable fate. In other words, I began an apprenticeship. I was learning to write.

22   Perhaps all my subsequent fiction has been marked by this experience, this revelation. Certain reviewers have remarked on my "traditionalism." Others have gently chided me for my interest in plot and "story." Is the *Boy's Own Annual* the obscure root of these tendencies? Have the stratagems concocted to elude the wicked slavers become, in some sense, second nature?

23   I don't know. The only testimony I can offer is the confession that when I sit down to write it is only with the greatest effort of will I manage to force the turbaned heads down, out of sight below the bulwarks of the dhows, or manage to master the violent and intoxicating urge to conclude every chapter with a clear suggestion of imminent peril.

24   It is, I suppose, only a matter of time before the will weakens and the long serialization begun twenty-five years ago resumes under a slightly different guise. I find that once acquired the taste is hard to lose.

(1984)

The Writer's Subject

1. What difficulties did Vanderhaeghe encounter when he first considered the question of influences on his writing? (paras. 1–4)

2. Explain the meaning and relevance of Vanderhaeghe's allusion to a "Gordian knot." (para. 3)

3. In paragraphs 3 and 4 Vanderhaeghe describes two lists he made up, of writers he admired. Why was he "afraid of being thought facetious" if he acknowledged the writers on the second list?

4. What parallels does Vanderhaeghe draw between Nabokov's childhood reading and his own? Why does he find something absurd about their respective experiences? (paras. 5–7)

5. How does Vanderhaeghe's reference to "the mud of Flanders" reinforce his point about the vision of the world conveyed in the *Boy's Own Annual*? (para. 7)

6. Why, in speaking of his "self-delusion," does Vanderhaeghe say that "in my defence I can say that this was the age of Tarzan movies"? (para. 10)

7. Vanderhaeghe draws attention to the frequent references in Nabokov's autobiography to Captain Mayne Reid, a minor English writer of Wild West romances. What influence did Mayne Reid's work have on Nabokov? What parallel does Vanderhaeghe draw between Nabokov's reading experience and his own? (paras. 14–19)

8. How does Vanderhaeghe conclude that his own writing may have been shaped to some extent by his childhood reading of the single volume of the *Boy's Own Annual* in his possession? (paras. 20–24)

The Writer's Style and Strategy

1. What is Vanderhaeghe's thesis? How does he introduce it, and at what point does he make his thesis explicit? (paras. 1–5)

2. How does Vanderhaeghe convey the chauvinistic nature of the *Boy's Own Paper*? (paras. 6 and 7) What does the repeated phrase "xenophobe empire" tell you about the values of the *Boy's Own Paper*?

3. Why does Vanderhaeghe use the word "fabulous" to describe the world in the pages of the *Boy's Own Annual*? (para. 7)

4. How does Vanderhaeghe convey the flavour of the articles in the *Boy's Own Annual*? (para. 11) How does he create a sense of the romantic excitement he felt as a youthful reader of such articles? (paras. 12 and 13)

5. Vanderhaeghe begins his essay by saying that he wants to answer honestly the questions of interviewers concerning which writers and books most influenced him. What is the connection between Vanderhaeghe's statement of purpose and the essay's conclusion?

Suggested Topics for Writing and Discussion

1. Vanderhaeghe observes that "bad" writing may be as influential in the development of a writer as "good" writing. Drawing from your own reading experience, offer your views of what constitutes "bad" literature. Does "bad" literature have any redeeming qualities?

2. In discussing his misconceptions about reality derived from the *Boy's Own Annual*, Vanderhaeghe observes that these flourished in part because his parents did not own a TV set: "A TV set would have rubbed my nose in the grit of reality." To what extent, in your view, does television present us with a true picture of the real world?

3. Vanderhaeghe notes that as a child he did not read such children's classics as *Winnie the Pooh*, *The Jungle Book*, or *Wind in the Willows*. Choose one of these works, or another acknowledged children's classic, and offer your views about its possible appeal for young readers today.

4. Choose a contemporary magazine intended for children or teenagers, and analyze its contents. What assumptions does it make about its audience? What "picture of the world" does it create? How accurately does it reflect the values or circumstances of our society? In your assessment, you might consider whether the contents are likely to excite a young reader's curiosity and imagination.

How Should One Read a Book?
by Virginia Woolf

In the first place, I want to emphasize the note of interrogation at the   1
end of my title. Even if I could answer the question for myself, the answer would apply only to me and not to you. The only advice, indeed,
that one person can give another about reading is to take no advice, to
follow your own instincts, to use your own reason, to come to your own
conclusions. If this is agreed between us, then I feel at liberty to put
forward a few ideas and suggestions because you will not allow them
to fetter that independence which is the most important quality that a
reader can possess. After all, what laws can be laid down about books?
The battle of Waterloo was certainly fought on a certain day; but is *Hamlet* a better play than *Lear*? Nobody can say. Each must decide that question for himself. To admit authorities, however heavily furred and
gowned, into our libraries and let them tell us how to read, what to read,
what value to place upon what we read, is to destroy the spirit of freedom which is the breath of those sanctuaries. Everywhere else we may
be bound by laws and conventions — there we have none.

But to enjoy freedom, if the platitude is pardonable, we have of course   2
to control ourselves. We must not squander our powers, helplessly and
ignorantly, squirting half the house in order to water a single rose-bush;
we must train them, exactly and powerfully, here on the very spot. This,
it may be, is one of the first difficulties that faces us in a library. What
is "the very spot"? There may well seem to be nothing but a conglom-
eration and huddle of confusion. Poems and novels, histories and memoirs, dictionaries and blue-books; books written in all languages by men
and women of all tempers, races, and ages jostle each other on the shelf.

And outside the donkey brays, the women gossip at the pump, the colts gallop across the fields. Where are we to begin? How are we to bring order into this multitudinous chaos and so get the deepest and widest pleasure from what we read?

3   It is simple enough to say that since books have classes — fiction, biography, poetry — we should separate them and take from each what it is right that each should give us. Yet few people ask from books what books can give us. Most commonly we come to books with blurred and divided minds, asking of fiction that it shall be true, of poetry that it shall be false, of biography that it shall be flattering, of history that it shall enforce our own prejudices. If we could banish all such preconceptions when we read, that would be an admirable beginning. Do not dictate to your author; try to become him. Be his fellow-worker and accomplice. If you hang back, and reserve and criticise at first, you are preventing yourself from getting the fullest possible value from what you read. But if you open your mind as widely as possible, then signs and hints of almost imperceptible fineness, from the twist and turn of the first sentences, will bring you into the presence of a human being unlike any other. Steep yourself in this, acquaint yourself with this, and soon you will find that your author is giving you, or attempting to give you, something far more definite. The thirty-two chapters of a novel — if we consider how to read a novel first — are an attempt to make something as formed and controlled as a building: but words are more impalpable than bricks; reading is a longer and more complicated process than seeing. Perhaps the quickest way to understand the elements of what a novelist is doing is not to read, but to write; to make your own experiment with the dangers and difficulties of words. Recall, then, some event that has left a distinct impression on you — how at the corner of the street, perhaps, you passed two people talking. A tree shook; an electric light danced; the tone of the talk was comic, but also tragic; a whole vision, an entire conception, seemed contained in that moment.

4   But when you attempt to reconstruct it in words, you will find that it breaks into a thousand conflicting impressions. Some must be subdued; others emphasized; in the process you will lose, probably, all grasp upon the emotion itself. Then turn from your blurred and littered pages to the opening pages of some great novelist — Defoe, Jane Austen, Hardy. Now you will be better able to appreciate their mastery. It is not merely that we are in the presence of a different person — Defoe, Jane Austen, or Thomas Hardy — but that we are living in a different world. Here, in *Robinson Crusoe*, we are trudging a plain high road; one thing happens

after another; the fact and the order of the fact is enough. But if the open air and adventure mean everything to Defoe they mean nothing to Jane Austen. Hers is the drawing-room, and people talking, and by the many mirrors of their talk revealing their characters. And if, when we have accustomed ourselves to the drawing-room and its reflections, we turn to Hardy, we are once more spun round. The moors are round us and the stars are above our heads. The other side of the mind is now exposed — the dark side that comes uppermost in solitude, not the light side that shows in company. Our relations are not towards people, but towards Nature and destiny. Yet different as these worlds are, each is consistent with itself. The maker of each is careful to observe the laws of his own perspective, and however great a strain they may put upon us they will never confuse us, as lesser writers so frequently do, by introducing two different kinds of reality into the same book. Thus to go from one great novelist to another — from Jane Austen to Hardy, from Peacock to Trollope, from Scott to Meredith — is to be wrenched and uprooted; to be thrown this way and then that. To read a novel is a difficult and complex art. You must be capable not only of great fineness of perception, but of great boldness of imagination if you are going to make use of all that the novelist — the great artist — gives you.

But a glance at the heterogeneous company on the shelf will show   5
you that writers are very seldom "great artists"; far more often a book makes no claim to be a work of art at all. These biographies and autobiographies, for example, lives of great men, of men long dead and forgotten, that stand cheek by jowl with the novels and poems, are we to refuse to read them because they are not "art"? Or shall we read them, but read them in a different way, with a different aim? Shall we read them in the first place to satisfy that curiosity which possesses us sometimes when in the evening we linger in front of a house where the lights are lit and the blinds not yet drawn, and each floor of the house shows us a different section of human life in being? Then we are consumed with curiosity about the lives of these people — the servants gossiping, the gentlemen dining, the girl dressing for a party, the old woman at the window with her knitting. Who are they, what are they, what are their names, their occupations, their thoughts, and adventures?

Biographies and memoirs answer such questions, light up innumerable   6
such houses; they show us people going about their daily affairs, toiling, failing, succeeding, eating, hating, loving, until they die. And sometimes as we watch, the house fades and the iron railings vanish and we are out at sea; we are hunting, sailing, fighting; we are among savages and sol-

diers; we are taking part in great campaigns. Or if we like to stay here in
England, in London, still the scene changes; the street narrows; the house
becomes small, cramped, diamond-paned, and malodorous. We see a
poet, Donne, driven from such a house because the walls were so thin that
when the children cried their voices cut through them. We can follow him,
through the paths that lie in the pages of books, to Twickenham; to Lady
Bedford's Park, a famous meeting-ground for nobles and poets; and then
turn our steps to Wilton, the great house under the downs, and hear Sidney
read the *Arcadia* to his sister; and ramble among the very marshes and
see the very herons that figure in that famous romance; and then again
travel north with that other Lady Pembroke, Anne Clifford, to her wild
moors, or plunge into the city and control our merriment at the sight of
Gabriel Harvey in his black velvet suit arguing about poetry with Spenser.
Nothing is more fascinating than to grope and stumble in the alternate
darkness and splendour of Elizabethan London. But there is no staying
there. The Temples and the Swifts, the Harleys and the St. Johns beckon
us on; hour upon hour can be spent disentangling their quarrels and de-
ciphering their characters; and when we tire of them we can stroll on, past
a lady in black wearing diamonds, to Samuel Johnson and Goldsmith and
Garrick; or cross the channel, if we like, and meet Voltaire and Diderot,
Madame du Deffand; and so back to England and Twickenham — how
certain places repeat themselves and certain names! — where Lady Bedford had her Park once and Pope lived later, to Walpole's home at Strawberry Hill. But Walpole introduces us to such a swarm of new
acquaintances, there are so many houses to visit and bells to ring that we
may well hesitate for a moment, on the Miss Berrys' doorstep, for example, when behold, up comes Thackeray; he is the friend of the woman
whom Walpole loved; so that merely by going from friend to friend, from
garden to garden, from house to house, we have passed from one end of
English literature to another and wake to find ourselves here again in the
present, if we can so differentiate this moment from all that have gone
before. This, then, is one of the ways in which we can read these lives
and letters; we can make them light up the many windows of the past;
we can watch the famous dead in their familiar habits and fancy sometimes that we are very close and can surprise their secrets, and sometimes
we may pull out a play or a poem that they have written and see whether
it reads differently in the presence of the author. But this again rouses
other questions. How far, we must ask ourselves, is a book influenced by
its writer's life — how far is it safe to let the man interpret the writer?
How far shall we resist or give way to the sympathies and antipathies that

the man himself rouses in us — so sensitive are words, so receptive of the character of the author? These are questions that press upon us when we read lives and letters, and we must answer them for ourselves, for nothing can be more fatal than to be guided by the preferences of others in a matter so personal.

But also we can read such books with another aim, not to throw light 7 on literature, not to become familiar with famous people, but to refresh and exercise our own creative powers. Is there not an open window on the right hand of the bookcase? How delightful to stop reading and look out! How stimulating the scene is, in its unconsciousness, its irrelevance, its perpetual movement — the colts galloping round the field, the woman filling her pail at the well, the donkey throwing back his head and emitting his long, acrid moan. The greater part of any library is nothing but the record of such fleeting moments in the lives of men, women, and donkeys. Every literature, as it grows old, has its rubbish-heap, its record of vanished moments and forgotten lives told in filtering and feeble accents that have perished. But if you give yourself up to the delight of rubbish-reading you will be surprised, indeed you will be overcome, by the relics of human life that have been cast out to moulder. It may be one letter — but what a vision it gives! It may be a few sentences — but what vistas they suggest! Sometimes a whole story will come together with such beautiful humour and pathos and completeness that it seems as if a great novelist had been at work, yet it is only an old actor, Tate Wilkinson, remembering the strange story of Captain Jones; it is only a young subaltern serving under Arthur Wellesley and falling in love with a pretty girl at Lisbon; it is only Maria Allen letting fall her sewing in the empty drawing-room and sighing how she wishes she had taken Dr. Burney's good advice and had never eloped with her Rishy. None of this has any value; it is negligible in the extreme; yet how absorbing it is now and again to go through the rubbish-heaps and find rings and scissors and broken noses buried in the huge past and try to piece them together while the colt gallops round the field, the woman fills her pail at the well, and the donkey brays.

But we tire of rubbish-reading in the long run. We tire of searching 8 for what is needed to complete the half-truth which is all that the Wilkinsons, the Bunburys, and the Maria Allens are able to offer us. They had not the artist's power of mastering and eliminating; they could not tell the whole truth even about their own lives; they have disfigured the story that might have been so shapely. Facts are all that they can offer us, and facts are a very inferior form of fiction. Thus the desire grows upon us to have done with half-statements and approximations;

to cease from searching out the minute shades of human character, to
enjoy the greater abstractness, the purer truth of fiction. Thus we create
the mood, intense and generalised, unaware of detail, but stressed by
some regular, recurrent beat, whose natural expression is poetry; and
that is the time to read poetry — when we are almost able to write it.

> Western wind, when wilt thou blow?
> The small rain down can rain.
> Christ, if my love were in my arms,
> And I in my bed again!

9   The impact of poetry is so hard and direct that for the moment there is
no other sensation except that of the poem itself. What profound depths
we visit then — how sudden and complete is our immersion! There is
nothing here to catch hold of; nothing to stay us in our flight. The illusion of fiction is gradual; its effects are prepared; but who when they read
these four lines stops to ask who wrote them, or conjures up the thought
of Donne's house or Sidney's secretary; or enmeshes them in the intricacy of the past and the succession of generations? The poet is always
our contemporary. Our being for the moment is centred and constricted,
as in any violent shock of personal emotion. Afterwards, it is true, the sensation begins to spread in wider rings through our minds; remoter senses
are reached; these begin to sound and to comment and we are aware of
echoes and reflections. The intensity of poetry covers an immense range
of emotion. We have only to compare the force and directness of

> I shall fall like a tree, and find my grave,
>   Only remembering that I grieve,

with the wavering modulation of

> Minutes are numbered by the fall of sands,
> As by an hour glass; the span of time
> Doth waste us to our graves, and we look on it;
> An age of pleasure, revelled out, comes home
> At last, and ends in sorrow; but the life,
> Weary of riot, numbers every sand,
> Wailing in sighs, until the last drop down,
> So to conclude calamity in rest,

or place the meditative calm of

> whether we be young or old,
> Our destiny, our being's heart and home,
> Is with infinitude, and only there;

With hope it is, hope that can never die,
Effort, and expectation, and desire,
And something evermore about to be,

beside the complete and inexhaustible loveliness of

The moving Moon went up the sky,
And no where did abide:
Softly she was going up,
And a star or two beside —

or the splendid fantasy of

And the woodland haunter
Shall not cease to saunter
     When, far down some glade,
Of the great world's burning,
One soft flame upturning
Seems, to his discerning,
     Crocus in the shade.

to bethink us of the varied art of the poet; his power to make us at once actors and spectators; his power to run his hand into character as if it were a glove, and be Falstaff or Lear; his power to condense, to widen, to state, once and for ever.

"We have only to compare" — with those words the cat is out of the bag, and the true complexity of reading is admitted. The first process, to receive impressions with the utmost understanding, is only half the process of reading; it must be completed, if we are to get the whole pleasure from a book, by another. We must pass judgment upon these multitudinous impressions; we must make of these fleeting shapes one that is hard and lasting. But not directly. Wait for the dust of reading to settle; for the conflict and the questioning to die down; walk, talk, pull the dead petals from a rose, or fall asleep. Then suddenly without our willing it, for it is thus that Nature undertakes these transitions, the book will return, but differently. It will float to the top of the mind as a whole. And the book as a whole is different from the book received currently in separate phrases. Details now fit themselves into their places. We see the shape from start to finish; it is a barn, a pigsty, or a cathedral. Now then we can compare book with book as we compare building with building. But this act of comparison means that our attitude has changed; we are no longer the friends of the writer, but his judges; and just as we cannot be too sympathetic as friends, so as judges we cannot be too severe. Are they not criminals, books that have wasted our time and sympathy; are they not the most insidious enemies of society, corrupters, defilers, the writers of false books, faked books, books that fill the air with decay and disease? Let us then be severe in our judgments; let us compare each book with the greatest of its kind. There they hang in the mind, the shapes of the books we have read solidified by the judgments we have passed on them — *Robinson Crusoe*, *Emma*, *The Return of the Native*. Compare the novels with these — even the latest and least of novels has a right to be judged with the best. And so with poetry — when the intoxication of rhythm has died down and the splendour of words has faded, a visionary shape will return to us and this must be compared with *Lear*, with *Phèdre*, with *The Prelude*; or if not with these, with whatever is the best or seems to us to be the best in its own kind. And we may be sure that the newness of new poetry and fiction is its most superficial quality and that we have only to alter slightly, not to recast, the standards by which we have judged the old.

11   It would be foolish, then, to pretend that the second part of reading, to judge, to compare, is as simple as the first — to open the mind wide to the fast flocking of innumerable impressions. To continue reading without the book before you, to hold one shadow-shape against another, to have read widely enough and with enough understanding to make such comparisons alive and illuminating — that is difficult; it is still more difficult to press further and to say, "Not only is the book of this sort, but it is of this value; here it fails; here it succeeds; this is bad; that is good." To carry out this part of a reader's duty needs such imagination, insight, and learning that it is hard to conceive any one mind sufficiently endowed; impossible for the most self-confident to find more than the seeds of such powers in himself. Would it not be wiser, then, to remit this part of reading and to allow the critics, the gowned and furred authorities of the library, to decide the question of the book's absolute value for us? Yet how impossible! We may stress the value of sympathy; we may try to sink our own identity as we read. But we know that we cannot sympathise wholly or immerse ourselves wholly; there is always a demon in us who whispers, "I hate, I love," and we cannot silence him. Indeed, it is precisely because we hate and we love that our relation with the poets and novelists is so intimate that we find the presence of another person intolerable. And even if the results are abhorrent and our judgments are wrong, still our taste, the nerve of sensation that sends shocks through us, is our chief illuminant; we learn through feeling; we cannot suppress our own idiosyncrasy without impoverishing it. But as time goes on perhaps we can train our taste; perhaps we can make it submit to some con-

trol. When it has fed greedily and lavishly upon books of all sorts — poetry, fiction, history, biography — and has stopped reading and looked for long spaces upon the variety, the incongruity of the living world, we shall find that it is changing a little; it is not so greedy, it is more reflective. It will begin to bring us not merely judgments on particular books, but it will tell us that there is a quality common to certain books. Listen, it will say, what shall we call *this*? And it will read us perhaps *Lear* and then perhaps the *Agamemnon* in order to bring out that common quality. Thus, with our taste to guide us, we shall venture beyond the particular book in search of qualities that group books together; we shall give them names and thus frame a rule that brings order into our perceptions. We shall gain a further and a rarer pleasure from that discrimination. But as a rule only lives when it is perpetually broken by contact with the books themselves — nothing is easier and more stultifying than to make rules which exist out of touch with facts, in a vacuum — now at last, in order to steady ourselves in this difficult attempt, it may be well to turn to the very rare writers who are able to enlighten us upon literature as an art. Coleridge and Dryden and Johnson, in their considered criticism, the poets and novelists themselves in their unconsidered sayings, are often surprisingly relevant; they light up and solidify the vague ideas that have been tumbling in the misty depths of our minds. But they are only able to help us if we come to them laden with questions and suggestions won honestly in the course of our own reading. They can do nothing for us if we herd ourselves under their authority and lie down like sheep in the shade of a hedge. We can only understand their ruling when it comes in conflict with our own and vanquishes it.

If this is so, if to read a book as it should be read calls for the rarest 12 qualities of imagination, insight, and judgment, you may perhaps conclude that literature is a very complex art and that it is unlikely that we shall be able, even after a lifetime of reading, to make any valuable contribution to its criticism. We must remain readers; we shall not put on the further glory that belongs to those rare beings who are also critics. But still we have our responsibilities as readers and even our importance. The standards we raise and the judgments we pass steal into the air and become part of the atmosphere which writers breathe as they work. An influence is created which tells upon them even if it never finds its way into print. And that influence, if it were well instructed, vigorous and individual and sincere, might be of great value now when criticism is necessarily in abeyance; when books pass in review like the procession of animals in a shooting gallery, and the critic has only one second in which to load and aim and shoot and may well be pardoned if he mistakes rabbits for tigers, eagles for barndoor fowls, or misses altogether and wastes his shot upon some peaceful cow grazing in a further field. If behind the erratic gunfire of the press the author felt that there was another kind of criticism, the opinion of people reading for the love of reading, slowly and unprofessionally, and judging with great sympathy and yet with great severity, might this not improve the quality of his work? And if by our means books were to become stronger, richer, and more varied, that would be an end worth reaching.

13   Yet who reads to bring about an end, however desirable? Are there not some pursuits that we practise because they are good in themselves, and some pleasures that are final? And is not this among them? I have sometimes dreamt, at least, that when the Day of Judgment dawns and the great conquerors and lawyers and statesmen come to receive their rewards — their crowns, their laurels, their names carved indelibly upon imperishable marble — the Almighty will turn to Peter and will say, not without a certain envy when He sees us coming with our books under our arms, "Look, these need no reward. We have nothing to give them here. They have loved reading."

                                                                                                    (1932)

The Writer's Subject

1. Why does Woolf put her title in the form of a question?

2. What is the difficulty facing a reader in a library? (para. 2)

3. What, according to Woolf, should be the reader's attitude to the author whose work one is reading? (para. 3)

4. What, according to Woolf, is "the quickest way to begin to understand the elements of what a novelist is doing"? (paras. 3–4)

5. What accounts for the interest most readers have in works of biography and autobiography? (paras. 5–6)

6. What does Woolf mean by "the delight of rubbish-reading"? What is missing from such reading? (paras. 7–8)

7. What does Woolf mean by the statement, "The poet is always our contemporary"? (para. 9)

8. What are the two halves of the process of reading, as Woolf sees it? (para. 10) How does the second half of the process alter the reader's relationship with the writer which she describes in paragraph 3?

9. What importance does Woolf attach to individual taste? How is this taste

formed? (para. 11)

10. At what stage in reading may the reader wish "to turn to the very rare writers who are able to enlighten us upon literature as an art"? (para. 11)

11. In what way may readers have an effect upon writers? (para. 12)

12. What, finally, is the reward of reading? (para. 13)

The Writer's Style and Strategy

1. How does Woolf organize her ideas in this essay? How does she divide and sub-divide her materials? What are the stages by which Woolf moves from her opening rejection of critical advice and judgment to her eventual assertion of their importance?

2. In paragraph 2, Woolf introduces the donkey, the women, and the colts outside the library window. What is her purpose, and what use does she make of them elsewhere in her essay?

3. What is Woolf's purpose in beginning over a third of her paragraphs with the word "But"?

4. What extended analogies does Woolf use to clarify her ideas about the appeal of biography? (paras. 5–6)

5. Discuss the ways in which Woolf makes use of example. What purposes do the examples serve in paragraph 4? in paragraph 6? in paragraph 7?

6. Discuss the effectiveness of Woolf's use of poetic quotation in paragraph 9.

7. Comment on Woolf's use of metaphorical language in paragraph 10. How does the writer's use of images here enhance her ideas?

8. Although Woolf's paragraphs are unusually long, they are all highly unified. Choose one paragraph and show how Woolf achieves this unity.

Suggested Topics for Writing and Discussion

1. Woolf speaks of the delight of "rubbish-reading." Choose two or three books that you think might be placed in such a category, and explain what pleasure a reader might derive from them.

2. Woolf says, "The poet is always our contemporary." Using the work of one poet not alive today, write an essay supporting this view.

3. Woolf says that books "return" to us at unexpected moments. Is there a book which has returned to you in this way? Try to account for its power over you.

4. Woolf ends her essay by saying that reading is its own reward. Do you agree?

Film and the Media

Blown Away

by Martin Amis

In the cinema, if not elsewhere, violence started getting violent in 1966. **1**
The films that marked the escalation, in my memory, were Arthur Penn's
"Bonnie and Clyde" (1967) and Sam Peckinpah's "The Wild Bunch"
(1969). And I was delighted to see it, all this violence. I found it volup-
tuous, intense, and (even then) disquietingly humorous; it felt subversive and counter-cultural. Violence had arrived. There was also, I noticed, a sudden flowering of sex and swearing. The future looked bright.

Before then, violence wasn't violent. People often talk, usually dis- **2**
approvingly, about the way violence has become "stylized" on film. But
the old violence was stylized, too: it simply wore the soft gloves of much
gentler conventions. Writing in the fifties, Nabokov noted the ineffec-
tuality of the "ox-stunning fisticuffs" of an average cinematic rumble,
and remarked on the speed with which the hero invariably recovered
from "a plethora of pain that would have hospitalized a Hercules." Few
of us are in a position to say which style is the more lifelike: the
cartoonish invulnerability of the old violence or the cartoonish
besplatterings of the new. We imagine that reality lies somewhere in
between—that it is less dramatic, less balletic, and, above all, quicker.
In life, the average fistfight, for instance, lasts about a second and consists of one blow. The loser gets a broken nose, the winner gets a broken hand, and they both trudge off to the outpatient clinic. Thus the
great Stallone joins the queue at the trauma unit, while Chuck Norris
fumbles with his first-aid kit. It just wouldn't play.

What happens, how, if you drag out the old movies and look again at **3**
even their most violent violence? I gained my first solid apprehension

of earthly mortality not from the death of a relative or a pet but from the death of Jim Bowie in "The Alamo" (1960). Richard Widmark's skirling death cry haunts me still. I also remember my audible "Jesus," when I saw Paul Newman smash his rifle butt into the raised glass of the saloon Okie, in "Hombre" (1967). And who can forget the various torments meted out to Marlon Brando in "On the Waterfront" (1954), "One Eyed Jacks" (1961), and "The Chase" (1966)? (Brando, always well known for having his artistic "say," definitely has a thing about getting beaten up.) Look again at such scenes and you marvel at your earlier susceptibility. They seem tame partly because they *are* tame (not dramatically but technically tame), and also because, in the interim, you have yawned and blinked your way through a thirty-year Passchendaele of slaughter. You have become, in other words, irreversibly desensitized. Macbeth—and let's make that Polanski's Macbeth—speaks for you when he says:

> I am in blood
> Stepp'ed in so far, that, should I wade no more,
> Returning were as tedious as go o'er.

4   In real life, interestingly, desensitization is precisely the quality that empowers the violent: empowers them to bear it away. In the moments leading up to violence, the nonviolent enter a world drenched with unfamiliar revulsions. The violent know this. Essentially, they are taking you to where they feel at home. You are leaving your place and going over to their place.

5   Screen violence, we might notice, has close affinities with the weapons business, and, to borrow an aging phrase from the nuclear-arms community, is often technology-led. "Bullitt" (1968) is justly remembered for its car chase, which, astonishingly, remains unsurpassed, despite bigger budgets, bigger engines, and the existence of furiously literal-minded actors willing to spend years of their lives bonding with racing drivers and crash dummies. But there was another standard-setting scene in "Bullitt": the shotgun slaying of the underground witness, which entrains the incomprehensible plot. Suddenly, the door of the murky hotel room is kicked open; the police guard is shot in the thigh; the camera glances at this wound and then turns on the swarthy stoolie, who retreats with his hands raised, clambering up onto the foot of the low bed. As the gun is fired he is lifted off his feet and jerked through the air, smashing back-first into the wall in a nebula of blood. Soon after the film appeared, I happened to meet its director, Peter Yates, and when I

asked him about this scene he took me through the mechanics of it—
the blood pouch, the steel wires: in the old days, an actor who stopped
a bullet would merely crush a ketchup sachet to the supposed entry
wound and look indignant. If he was a bad guy, he would roll to the
floor and decorously close his eyes. If he was a good guy, he would get
really mad, then later assure the gasping blonde at his side that the bullet hole was just a "scratch" or, better, a "flesh wound." Well, after 1968
there were no more scratches, no more flesh wounds. With the elec-
tronically ignited plasma-brimmed sandwich Baggie, the lurch cables
and jolt harnesses, and so on, death by shotgun ceased to look like something you could quickly recover from.

In this context, the recent "Schindler's List" marks a progression, or 6
maybe a retrogression. Here the point-blank pistol shot to the head results in a tubular spout of blood followed by a tragic curtsy to the ground
almost as girlish and theatrical as Uma Thurman's swoon in "Dangerous Liaisons." One feels sure that this rendition was the result of close
research, part of the carapace of verisimilitude that Spielberg needed to
allow him artistic passage to the Holocaust. (Nearing the Holocaust, a
trespasser finds that his imagination is decently absenting itself, and
reaches for documentation and technique. The last thing he wants to
do, once there, is make anything up.) In general, the escalation of violence in war films is not much questioned. Even the squeamish accept
that a mechanized heartlessness forms the natural background—a civilian obedience, perhaps, to the hawkish axiom "What did you expect?
This is *war*." We know more and more about the horror and pity of war,
but we still seem to need persuading about the horror and pity of, for
example, bank robbing, drug trafficking, serial murders, and chainsaw
massacres.

To the extent that screen violence is technology-led, a specialized 7
value system will tend to assert itself. As in the weapons industry, you
will get no moral guidance from the specialist, the salaried expert. What
you will get is the explanation "Everyone *else* does it," because, when
up against can-do, don't-do will always finish second. Still, the prop-
shop eggheads at places like Praxis and Visual Concept Engineering,
the morphers and animators at Industrial Light & Magic or Dream Quest
Images are mere hirelings: somebody has to *want* that particular splat
or spatter, that cute decapitation, that ginchy evisceration. There is this
half-formed view of Hollywood as an acropolis of conglomerates, of
marketers and targeters, unsmilingly supplying the public with what it
has come to want and need: more violence. But it doesn't work like

that. "Projects" swim around the movie community until someone with power gets connected to them. Then they get "developed" by writers, producers, and directors, and then get sent upstairs to the "suits"—these supposedly pitiless bottom-liners. But what happens up there remains a mystery to everyone, the suits included. Some projects go ahead, and some don't. "The only films they make," a director once told me, "are the films they can't get out of making." The final decision, then, is the result of fatalism, embarrassment, or inertia—office politics, maybe, but not policy. So violence is director-led, or auteur-led. Films are violent because the talent wants it that way.

8   Who else does, apart from me? One of the few points that survives the battering of Michael Medved's beleaguered monograph "Hollywood vs. America" is that the moviegoing public *doesn't* like violence. In his introduction to the paperback edition Medved writes in heroic cadences about "the passionate intensity of the public response to my work"; yes, he has taken his share of "intemperate anger" and "personal abuse," but on the whole, says Medved, "I am grateful for whatever contribution my arguments have made to facilitating this discussion." Certainly, "Hollywood vs. America" got Hollywood thinking, at least for a weekend or two (late nights in the dens of the Moorish mansions). And it got America thinking, too, and the controversy that gathered around it managed to trickle up as high as Janet Reno and Bill Clinton. It was a book, and a mood, whose time had come: the feeling that Hollywood had gone too far in its divergence from the American mainstream; the feeling that Hollywood—that faceless monolith—loved everything that America hated (violence, sex, swearing, drugging, drinking, and smoking), and hated everything that Americans loved (religion, parents, marriage, and monogamy, plus the military, policemen, businessmen, and America). Now, I'm sure that Mr. Medved seldom, if ever, gets into fights, which is just as well. After three hundred pages of his pedantry and sarcasm, I imagine him tooled up like the loathed Schwarzenegger, and spray-firing from either hip. His argumentative style is so strident that even his own intelligence, you suspect, is cowed and deafened by it. Why, oh, why, he typically asks, is Hollywood so obsessed by Vietnam and so unmoved by the struggle in Kuwait, which, "amazingly enough," has yet to be celebrated on film? If Dan Quayle were a lot brighter, this is what he would sound like.

9   Despite its contemporary attire, Medved's theme, or plaint, is as old as time. It is *Ubi sunt?* all over again. Where are they now, the great simplicities of yesterday?

In years past, in the heyday of Gary Cooper and Greta Garbo, Jimmy Stewart and Katharine Hepburn, the movie business drew considerable criticism for manufacturing personalities who were larger than life, impossibly noble and appealing individuals who could never exist in the real world. Today, the industry consistently comes up with characters who are *smaller* than life—less decent, less intelligent, and less likeable than our own friends and neighbors.

Medved's "beat is the entertainment industry." He knows about the entertainment industry, but does he know about art—about literature, for example, which has been following exactly the same graph line for two thousand years? If art has an arrow, then that is the way it points: straight downward, from demigod to demirep.   10

Cinema is a young form, and has been obliged to make this same journey in less than a century. I said earlier that violence got violent in 1966, because that was the year the Hays Production Code was revised, and film edged closer to being a director's medium, freer to go where the talent pushed it. As we now know, the talent pushed it away from the mainstream of America and toward the mainstream of contemporary art, while playing to its own strengths—action, immediacy, affect. So the great current debate is caught in a confusion of categories. If cinema is just mass entertainment, then Medved is an eloquent awakener. If cinema is art, then Medved is just a noisy philistine.   11

We now enter a world of closed circles. By 1966, movie audiences halved, and they have stayed that way. Proportionately, auteurism did more damage to the industry than the arrival of television. Medved, with his polls and his content analysis, gathers plenty of evidence to confirm what he wants to believe: that Americans don't like violence—and violent themes and violent language—and won't pay money to see it. (A final analogy with weaponry: Americans have always been avowedly pro–gun-control but somehow never pro enough to make any difference.) Americans don't want violence. They probably don't want art, either. What Americans want is escape—especially from American violence. American violence "travels," it's said, and enthralls audiences all over the planet, but Americans have to live in America, where all the violence is. Does screen violence provide a window or a mirror? Is it an effect or is it a cause, an encouragement, a facilitation? Fairly representatively, I think, I happen to like screen violence while steadily deploring its real-life counterpart. Moreover, I can tell the difference between the two. One is happening, one is not. One is earnest, one is   12 play. But we inhabit the postmodern age, an age of mass suggestibility, in which image and reality strangely interact. This is now perhaps the most vulnerable area in the common mind. There is a hole in the credulity layer, and it is getting wider.

13   In Britain, in recent months, two of the most sensational murder trials of the century have involved discussion of the same rental video; namely, "Child's Play 3." The first case was that of James Bulger, a toddler who was beaten to death by two ten-year-olds; the second case was that of Suzanne Capper, a teen-ager who was kidnapped, strenuously tortured, and finally set alight by a clique of young acquaintances. "Child's Play 3" has therefore been much in the news, and therefore much in demand. It, too, has been set alight, semi-ritualistically, by public-spirited managers of video-rental stores. When my two children (aged seven and nine) noticed "Child's Play 3" in its package, up on a high shelf, they regarded it with reverent dread. In their schoolyard voodoo, "Child's Play 3" was considered potent, venomous, toxic. It was like angel dust—a ticket to frenzy.

14   So one afternoon I duly settled down to watch a routine little horror film about a children's doll called Chucky that comes to life and starts killing people. The modicum of horror it inspires can be traced back to Freud's definition of the uncanny: ambiguity about the extent to which something is, or is not, alive. Equally conventionally, such frights and shrieks as the film elicits have to do not with very scary things happening but with mildly scary things happening very suddenly. As the credits rolled in "Child's Play 3," I felt no urge or prompting to go out and kill somebody. And I knew why, too. It's nothing to boast about, but there is too much going on in my head for Chucky to gain sway in there. Probably the worst that Chucky could do to me is to create an appetite to see more Chucky, or more things like Chucky.

15   What we have to imagine is a mind that, on exposure to Chucky, is already brimful of Chucky and things like Chucky. Then, even if you mix in psychopathology, stupidity, moral deformation, dreams of omnipotence and sadism, and whatever else, Chucky is unlikely to affect anything but the *style* of your subsequent atrocities. Murderers have to have something to haunt them: they need their internal pandemonium. A century ago, it might have been the Devil. Now it's Chucky. When the killers tortured Suzanne Capper, they chanted the catchphrase "I'm Chucky. Wanna play?" When the ten-year-old boy began to throw bricks, James Bulger fell down and stood up again. "Just stand there," said the killer, "and we'll get you a plaster." And then he threw another brick.

This is Chucky's way: the worthless joke, the worthless swagger. Here was a mind that had seen a lot of things like Chucky, and had nothing much in prospect but more things like Chucky. Perhaps, also, the child didn't understand the meaning of earnest. As a result, he was all too ready to play.

(1994)

The Writer's Subject

1. What marked the change in modern cinematic representations of violence, according to Amis?

2. How does Amis describe cinematic violence before the movies of the mid-sixties and later? (paras. 2–3)

3. What is Amis's point in noting that in life, the average fistfight "lasts about a second and consists of one blow"? (para. 2)

4. Why do the "old movies" listed in para. 3 now seem so tame to Amis?

5. Explain the phrase "a thirty-year Passchendaele of slaughter" in para. 3.

6. What does Amis mean by his point that screen violence "is often technology-led"? (para. 5) How does he support this assertion? (para. 5)

7. Explain the phrase "carapace of verisimilitude" in para. 6. Why, according to Amis, was verisimilitude so important to *Schindler's List*?

8. What connection does Amis draw between the video *Child's Play 3* and the work of Sigmund Freud, the founder of modern psychoanalysis? (para. 14)

9. How does Amis respond to the argument that movies like *Child's Play* may encourage or facilitate violent acts in real life? (paras. 12–15) Compare his view to that expressed in Highsmith's essay "Child's Play 4?"

The Writer's Style and Strategy

1. What is the predominant tone of Amis's essay? Discuss its suitability for the kind of audience he has in mind, and for the argument he wishes to make.

2. What is Amis's point in quoting *Macbeth* at the end of para. 3? Why does he refer specifically to "Polanski's Macbeth"?

3. Explain Amis's use of the term "auteur." (para. 7)

4. How does Amis back up his assertion that today "image and reality strangely interact" in terms of the impact of cinema on people's minds? (para. 12)

5. Discuss Amis's use of metaphor (e.g., "There is a hole in the credulity layer, and it is getting wider," para. 12, or "It was like angel dust — a ticket to frenzy," para. 13).

6. Why does the essay end with a reference to the distinction between "earnest" and "play"? (para. 15)

Suggested Topics for Writing and Discussion

1. Try to find a few Westerns, war movies, or adventure movies made in the period 1940–1965. Would you agree with Amis's point at the beginning of para. 2 that "Before then [the mid-sixties], violence wasn't violent"?

2. Amis sets cinematic violence in the context of the debate concerning whether cinema is art or entertainment (paras. 10-11). Choose one or two movies that include violent scenes, and offer your own view: does the violence have aesthetic justification, or is it merely "entertainment"?

3. Amis cites Michael Medved's view that "Americans don't want violence … What Americans want is escape — escape from American violence" (para. 12). How far does this accord with your own sense of what Americans want, based on American movies currently showing?

4. Amis asks, "Does screen violence provide a window or a mirror?" (para. 12) Explain the meaning of the metaphors in this statement. What is your own view concerning this matter?

5. Amis cites the book *Hollywood vs. America* (1992) by Michael Medved. What is the book's main point, as summarized by Amis? What is Amis's attitude towards Medved's book, and how is his attitude conveyed? (para. 8)

The Origin of Alien Species
by Kurt Andersen

During the past several years, evolutionary biologists have proved that the disparate creatures of our planet are, at a fundamental genetic level, very similar to one another. The genes that differentiate the top and the bottom of a bug, for instance, are the same ones that differentiate our fronts from our backs. According to the paleontologist Stephen Jay Gould, this new understanding is among "the most stunning evolutionary discoveries of the decade," and is clearly "a dominant theme in evolution." **1**

The same law applies, it appears, to the extraterrestrial creatures that come out of Hollywood. As is true of biological evolution, the evolution of movie aliens is constrained by a limited range of modes and materials: skeletons are aluminum, steel, or fibreglass; skins are foam rubber, polyurethane, silicone, or gels. In the evolutionary pseudobiology of the cinema, memes, rather than genes, circumscribe the forms that a new alien creature can take. "The process of designing aliens always takes you back to variations on a theme," Laurie MacDonald, the coproducer of the new film "Men in Black," told me. "They all look similar." There may be more than one way to skin an extraterrestrial, in other words, but not a lot more. **2**

Is the current alien mania in films ("Men in Black," "The Fifth Element," "Contact"), on television ("The X-Files," "3rd Rock from the Sun"), and in the news (Heaven's Gate, Roswell reminiscences) some kooky by-product of the end of the Cold War? Or can it be an epiphenomenon of the turn of the millennium? That's what commentators have been asking lately. Perhaps the more interesting question is: Why are **3** so many of the new movie aliens so ... gooey? A preliminary taxonomy indicates that Hollywood aliens may be classified into six distinct phyla.

4   Type One, *more or less normal-looking people,* includes most aliens in episodic network television, from the original "Star Trek" to "3rd Rock from the Sun." A subcategory is the alien lollapalooza, usually a blonde: Zsa Zsa Gabor in "The Queen of Outer Space" (1958), say, or Natasha Henstridge, the star of "Species" (1995). In many instances, of course, aliens assume human form only in order to charm Earthlings (as in the forthcoming Jodie Foster movie, "Contact") or to keep below-the-line production costs under control.

5   Type Two consists of *hulking humanoids with enormous bald heads,* which are (a) anatomically expressionist, (b) faux leprous, or (c) shaped like a chef's toque. Originally a product of suspicious nineteen-fifties anti-intellectualism — giant skull equals genius equals Communist — Type Twos include the (balding) Klingons and Ferengi from "Star Trek," the diva in "The Fifth Element," and, in overtly parodic mode, the Coneheads and the exposed-brain aliens in "Mars Attacks" (1996).

6   Type Three, which has emerged only during the past few decades, is the modern classic: *the small, gray, hairless, chinless, big-eyed waif,* resembling the woman from Munch's "The Scream" on antidepressants or a member of a children's mime group. These wan, innocent, naked creatures appeared during the Woodstock era and after — and, tellingly, supplanted the scheming, sinister, aggressively superhuman aliens typical of the anti-Communist fifties. The definitive portrayal appeared in Steven Spielberg's "Close Encounters of the Third Kind" (1977), but those aliens surely bear some cinemagenetic relation to the space fetus at the end of "2001" (1967) and to the aliens in "The X-Files," even down to the portentous backlighting.

7   As it happens, the great majority of "real" aliens today are also Type Threes, including the ones who abducted Whitley Streiber in his book "Communion: A True Story," and the ones who performed experiments on the abductees treated by the Harvard Medical School professor John Mack during the past decade. Is it unfair to assume that suggestible people began seeing Spielbergian aliens in real life during the eighties as a result of having seen the aliens in "Close Encounters" during the late seventies? No more unfair than to assume that it was only after McCaulay Culkin pumped his arm triumphantly and said "Yesss!" in "Home Alone" (1990) that millions of American eleven-year-olds acquired the habit of pumping an arm triumphantly and saying "Yesss!"

8   Hollywood Extraterrestrial Type Four is *the comic-relief plush toy.*

The tiny, furry tribbles in the original "Star Trek" series may have been the first appearance of this type. Other instances include the title character in "Alf" and most of the memorable secondary characters in "Star Wars," such as Chewbacca and the Ewoks. A prominent Type Four subgroup is the evil, rotund comic-relief plush toy, such as the creatures in "Gremlins" (1984) and the churlish bovine/porcine warriors in both "Return of the Jedi" and "The Fifth Element." It seems no accident that Type Four aliens, clownish but winning, achieved their peak of popularity at the very moment we were giving a landslide reëlection to Ronald Reagan, our clownish but winning plush-toy President.

Type Five is *the swamp creature* — reptiles and amphibians who walk   9 upright. This was a standard form of the fifties, and reëmerged with a vengeance, like just about every other fifties cultural artifact, during the eighties. The nicer aliens of this type are apt to be more amphibian than reptilian. The major examples — E.T. (1982) and Yoda (1983) — both arguably have strains of Type Three (big eyes) and Type Four (tactile, seriocomic cuteness) as well. The evolutionary semiotics seem straightforward: frogs and turtles are homely but cute and unthreatening. Conversely, snakes and lizards are scary, so reptilian extraterrestrials are bad, notable recent examples being the reptilian queen alien in "Aliens" (1986) and the man-killing lizard girl Sil in "Species." Sil and the creatures in the original, 1979 "Alien" were designed by the Swiss artist H.R. Giger, but the director and creature designer of its sequel "Aliens" were James Cameron and Stan Winston, respectively. "Jim Cameron had the concept that there would be a queen," Winston told me. "He'd done a painting of her. The big change from that first concept was an added joint to the leg that gave her feet the look of high-heeled shoes. This was a queen. This was a bitch." Antifeminist backlash as a Hollywood-alien design parameter seems not to have caught on, but the lizardy, slightly bug-like "Aliens" queen undoubtedly led to the lizardy, slightly buglike "Independence Day" (1996) extraterrestrials and to the lizardy aliens in Robin Cook's novel and TV miniseries "Invasion." (Some ostensible real-life abductees, according to C.D.B. Bryan's 1995 book "Close Encounters of the Fourth Kind," have reported experiences with menacing, six-to-eight-foot-tall reptilian aliens.)

Hollywood Extraterrestrial Type Six consists of hypertrophied arthro-   10 pods, or, in lay terms, *really, really big shellfish and insects.* Again, as with the reptilian aliens they sometimes resemble, the genesis seems clear: bugs are gross. The title character in "Predator" (1987) was a hybrid that Stan Winston, its creator, describes as a "Rastafarian insectoidhumanoid alien." The movie's producer, Joel Silver, suggested the Rasta notion, and James Cameron, who wasn't even working on the picture, inspired the rest. "Jim and I were on a flight to Japan to speak at a symposium on creatures in movies," Winston told me. "I remember drawing my first sketches on the plane, and he looked over my shoulder and said, 'I'd like to see a creature with mandibles'." Today, a decade later, giant alien insects are everywhere, threatening to destroy mankind not only in "Men in Black" (a twelve-foot-tall neo-cockroach) but in next fall's "Starship Troopers" (hordes of ten-foot-tall grasshoppers). An emerging alien metatype that blurs the categories is the morphing extraterrestrial, the creature who visibly changes on-screen from human being to bug or bug to lizard. The morphing extraterrestrial is almost wholly a function of technology — in this case, computer-generated imagery. The other unmistakable trend in aliens is of a piece with gross-out explicitness in pop culture generally. Extraterrestrials today tend to be *wet,* the glycerine sheen variously suggesting evisceration, birth, mucus, dangerous bodily fluids, otherworldly goo. "Slime?" Stan Winston said when I asked if he thought he had helped usher in the current Wet Era with his work on "Aliens." "I would say yes, there is something visceral that comes from seeing drool — maybe you relate it to a rabid animal."

11   "Men in Black," which posits Earth as an intergalactic Switzerland (and Earthlings like Elvis Presley as incognito extraterrestrials in exile), represents an alien-morphology apotheosis. For the first time in the history of film, every one of the six alien types is represented. And the movie is full of alien goo. Indeed, "Men in Black" doesn't seem to *want* its extraterrestrials to look too original: it intends to be familiar in a hep "Nick at Night" fashion, and assembles a pastiche of extraterrestrial archetypes to do its postmodern business.

12   Laurie MacDonald coproduced the film with her husband, Walter Parkes. "We always knew Edgar was going to be a bug," Parkes told me, speaking about their main alien villain.

13   "The first design looked too much like our house cat," MacDonald recalled.

14   "We moved it scarier," Parkes said. They also moved it away from the design of the "Independence Day" aliens. "When we heard that their main alien was going to be a lot like ours, there was some substantial redesigning of Edgar," he explained. "If you look at Edgar now, he has that protruding jaw and those enormous teeth. But we didn't want to go too far into the territory of 'Alien'."

15   Stan Winston's aliens have been more imitated than imitative, but

even he admitted, "It's impossible not to be influenced by things you have experienced in the past." His other major conclusion about creating movie aliens is that the creatures have to be able to express feelings. "You must relate to it with something you can relate emotion to."

"Human form is an interesting issue in this," Walter Parkes said about **16** the challenge of designing aliens for "Men in Black." "On the one hand, you want to be able to relate to these creatures, so you want some semblance of human form. But you don't want the audience to say, 'It's just a man in a suit'." Steven Spielberg, as the film's executive producer, also helped decide how the aliens in "Men in Black" would look. "Steven's main note," Parkes told me, "tended to be that the alien faces should somewhere and somehow reflect human structure." He paused. "And that's because, of course, he's an alien himself."

The Writer's Subject

1. What evolutionary law does the writer apply to the extraterrestrial creatures developed by Hollywood? (paras. 1–2)

2. "... memes, rather than genes, circumscribe the forms that a new alien creature can take" (para. 2). Explain the writer's meaning here.

3. What explanations have been offered for "the current alien mania in films"? (para. 3)

4. What are the general categories into which Andersen fits the space creatures he finds in American movies?

5. Explain the analogy that Andersen develops in discussing the origin of the aliens many people claimed to have seen in real life in the nineteen-eighties. (para. 7)

6. What distinction does the writer draw between amphibian aliens and reptilian extraterrestrials? (para. 9) On what does he suggest this distinction is based?

7. What is a "morphing extraterrestrial"? (para. 10)

8. Andersen asserts that the movie *Men in Black* "represents an alien-morphology apotheosis" (para. 11). Explain his meaning.

9. Why do film-makers seek to endow their monsters with human qualities? (paras. 15–16)

The Writer's Style and Strategy

1. Discuss the writer's choice of title.

2. Andersen states that "Hollywood aliens may be classified into six distinct phyla" (3). Why does he use the word "phyla" instead of "classes" or "categories"?

3. Andersen structures his discussion of movie monsters as if it were a scientific description and analysis. What effect do you think the writer is aiming at in his use of this strategy? Is he successful?

4. What is the writer's attitude to the "Type Three" aliens he describes at the beginning of para. 6? How is that attitude conveyed?

5. What is the dominant tone of Andersen's essay? How is it achieved?

6. Discuss Andersen's use of words and phrases such as "gooey" (para. 3), "bugs are gross" (para. 10), "gross-out explicitness" (para. 10), "otherworldly goo" (para. 10), "alien goo" (para. 11). How do such words operate in their respective contexts? How do they affect tone?

Suggested Topics for Writing and Discussion

1. Andersen notes trends in alien design that suggest the influence of social or political movements in society: the anti-Communism of the 1950s, the Woodstock era, the presidencies of Ronald Reagan. Choose any of the alien creatures mentioned in the article, and examine its characteristics in terms of the time in which it first appeared.

2. After viewing any movie that includes a creature of the kind described in this article, summarise your own responses to the alien creature, and try to account for the feelings you experienced.

3. Choose a major film about or including aliens of the type mentioned in this article, and look for two or three reviews published in magazines or newspapers at the time of the film's first showings. Compare the treatment by different critics of the monster or alien theme.

4. Devise your own set of sub-categories for movie characters in any of the following groups: gangsters; teachers; children; animals; scientists.

5. This article was originally printed in *The New Yorker*. Examine any issue of the magazine, and say what kind of audience the magazine is trying to appeal to. Does the implied audience for Andersen's article match the profile you have drawn for readers of *The New Yorker*?

The Art of Moving Pictures
by Bruno Bettelheim

Whether we like it or not — and many may disagree with my thesis   1
because painting, or music, or some other art is more important to them
— the art of the moving image is the only art truly of our time, whether
it is in the form of the film or television. The moving picture is our
universal art, which comprises all others, literature and acting, stage
design and music, dance and the beauty of nature, and, most of all, the
use of light and of color.

It is always about us, because the medium is truly part of the mes-   2
sage and the medium of the moving image is uniquely modern. Everybody can understand it, as everyone once understood religious art in
church. And as people used to go to church on Sundays (and still do),
so the majority today go to the movies on weekends. But while in the
past most went to church only on some days, now everybody watches
moving images every day.

All age groups watch moving pictures, and they watch them for many   3
more hours than people have ever spent in churches. Children and adults
watch them separately or together; in many ways and for many people,
it is the only experience common to parents and children. It is the only
art today that appeals to all social and economic classes, in short, that
appeals to everybody, as did religious art in times past. The moving picture is thus by far the most popular art of our time, and it is also the
most authentically American of arts.

When I speak here of the moving picture as the authentic American   4
art of our time, I do not think of art with a capital A, nor of "high" art.
Putting art on a pedestal robs it of its vitality. When the great medieval

and Renaissance cathedrals were erected, and decorated outside and in with art, these were popular works, that meant something to everybody.

5   Some were great works of art, others not, but every piece was significant and all took pride in each of them. Some gain their spiritual experience from the masterpiece, but many more gain it from the mediocre works that express the same vision as the masterpiece but in a more accessible form. This is as true for church music or the church itself as for paintings and sculptures. This diversity of art objects achieves a unity, and differences in quality are important, provided they all represent, each in its own way, the overarching vision and experience of a larger, important cosmos. Such a vision confers meaning and dignity on our existence, and is what forms the essence of art.

6   So among the worst detriments to the healthy development of the art of the moving image are efforts by aesthetes and critics to isolate the art of film from popular movies and television. Nothing could be more contrary to the true spirit of art. Whenever art was vital, it was always equally popular with the ordinary man and the most refined person. Had Greek drama and comedy meant nothing to most citizens, the majority of the population would not have sat all day long entranced on hard stone slabs, watching the events on the stage; nor would the entire population have conferred prizes on the winning dramatist. The medieval pageants and mystery plays out of which modern drama grew were popular entertainments, as were the plays of Shakespeare. Michelangelo's David stood at the most public place in Florence, embodying the people's vision that tyranny must be overthrown, while it also related to their religious vision, as it represented the myth of David and Goliath. Everybody admired the statue; it was simultaneously popular and great art but one did not think of it in such disparate terms. Neither should we. To live well we need both: visions that lift us up, and entertainment that is down to earth, provided both art and entertainment, each in its different form and way, are embodiments of the same visions of man. If art does not speak to all of us, common men and elites alike, it fails to address itself to that true humanity that is common to all of us. A different art for the elites and another one for average man tears society apart, it offends what we most need: visions that bind us together in common experiences that make life worth living.

7   When I speak of an affirmation of man, I do not mean the presentation of fake images of life as wonderfully pleasant. Life is best celebrated in the form of battle against its inequities, of struggles, of dignity in defeat, of the greatness of discovering oneself and the other.

Quite a few moving pictures have conveyed such visions. In 8
Kagemusha, the great beauty of the historical costumes, the cloak-and-
dagger story with its beguiling Oriental settings, the stately proceedings, the pageantry of marching and fighting armies, the magnificent
rendering of nature, the consummate acting — all these entrance us and
convince us of the correctness of the vision here: the greatness of the
most ordinary of men. The hero, a petty thief who turns impostor, grows
before our eyes into greatness, although it costs him his life. The story
takes place in sixteenth-century Japan, but the hero is of all times and
places: he accepts a destiny into which he is projected by chance and
turns a false existence into a real one. At the end, only because he wants
to be true to his new self, he sacrifices his life and thus achieves the
acme of suffering and human greatness. Nobody wants him to do so.
Nobody but he will ever know that he did it. Nobody but the audience
observes it. He does it only for himself; it has no consequences whatsoever for anybody or anything else. He does it out of conviction; this is
his greatness. Life that permits the lowest of men to achieve such dignity is life worth living, even if in the end it defeats him, as it will defeat all who are mortal.

Two other films, very different, render parallel visions that celebrate 9
life, a celebration in which we, as viewers, vicariously participate although we are saddened by the hero's defeat. The first was known in
the United States by its English name, *The Last Laugh*, although its original title, *The Last Man*, was more appropriate. It is the story of the door-
man of a hotel who is demoted to cleaning washrooms. The other movie
is *Patton*. In one of these films the hero stands on the lowest rung of
society and existence; in the other, he is on society's highest level. In
both pictures we are led to admire a man's struggle to discover who he
really is, for, in doing so, he achieves tragic greatness. These three films,
as do many others, affirm man and life, and so inspire in us visions that
can sustain us.

My choice of these three films out of many is arbitrary. What I want 10
to illustrate is their celebration of life in forms appropriate to an age in
which self-discovery may exact the highest possible price. Only through
incorporating such visions can we achieve satisfaction with our own life,
and defeat and transcend existential despair.

What our society suffers from most today is the absence of consen- 11
sus about what it and life in it ought to be. Such consensus cannot be
gained from society's present stage, or from fantasies about what it ought
to be. For that the present is too close and too diversified, and the future

too uncertain, to make believable claims about it. A consensus in the present hence can be achieved only through a shared understanding of the past, as Homer's epics informed those who lived centuries later what it meant to be Greek, and by what images and ideals they were to live their lives and organize their societies.

12   Most societies derive consensus from a long history, a language all their own, a common religion, common ancestry. The myths by which they live are based on all of these. But the United States is a country of immigrants, coming from a great variety of nations. Lately, it has been emphasized that an asocial, narcissistic personality has become characteristic of Americans, and that it is this type of personality that makes for the malaise, because it prevents us from achieving a consensus that would counteract a tendency to withdraw into private worlds. In his study of narcissism, Christopher Lasch says that modern man, "tortured by self-consciousness, turns to new cults and therapies not to free himself of his personal obsessions but to find meaning and purpose in life, to find something to live for." There is wide-spread distress because national morale has declined, and we have lost an earlier sense of national vision and purpose.

13   Contrary to rigid religions or political beliefs, as are found in totalitarian societies, our culture is one of great individual differences, at least in principle and in theory. But this leads to disunity, even chaos. Americans believe in the value of diversity, but just because ours is a society based on individual diversity, it needs consensus about some overarching ideas more than societies based on the uniform origin of their citizens. Hence, if we are to have consensus, it must be based on a myth — a vision — about a common experience, a conquest that made us Americans, as the myth about the conquest of Troy formed the Greeks. Only a common myth can offer relief from the fear that life is without meaning or purpose. Myths permit us to examine our place in the world by comparing it to a shared idea. Myths are shared fantasies that form the tie that binds the individual to other members of his group. Such myths help to ward off feelings of isolation, guilt, anxiety, and purposelessness — in short, they combat isolation and anomie.

14   We used to have a myth that bound us together; in *The American Adam*, R.W.B. Lewis summarizes the myth by which Americans used to live:

> God decided to give man another chance by opening up a new world
> across the sea. Practically vacant, this glorious land had almost inex-
> haustible natural resources. Many people came to this new world. They

were people of special energy, self-reliance, intuitive intelligence, and
purity of heart... This nation's special mission in the world would be to
serve as the moral guide for all other nations.

The movies used to transmit this myth, particularly the westerns, 15
which presented the challenge of bringing civilization to places where
before there was none. The same movies also suggested the danger of
that chaos; the wagon train symbolized the community men must form
on such a perilous journey into the untamed wilderness, which in turn
became a symbol for all that is untamed within ourselves. Thus the western gave us a vision of the need for cooperation and civilization, because without it man would perish. Another symbol often used in these
westerns was the railroad, which formed the link between wilderness
and civilization. The railroad was the symbol of man's role as civilizer.

Robert Warshow delineates in *The Immediate Experience* how the 16
hero of the western — the gunfighter — symbolizes man's potential: to
become either an outlaw or a sheriff. In the latter role, the gunfighter
was the hero of the past, and his opening of the West was our mythos,
our equivalent of the Trojan War. Like all such heroes, the sheriff experienced victories and defeats, but, through these experiences, he grew
wiser and learned to accept the limitations that civilization imposes.

This was a wonderful vision of man — or the United States — in 17
the New World; it was a myth by which one could live and grow, and it
served as a consensus about what it meant to be an American. But although most of us continue to enjoy this myth, by now it has lost most
of its vitality. We have become too aware of the destruction of nature
and of the American Indian — part of the reality of opening the West
— to be able to savor this myth fully; and, just as important, it is based
on an open frontier that no longer exists. But the nostalgic infatuation
with the western suggests how much we are in need of a myth about
the past that cannot be invalidated by the realities of today. We want to
share a vision, one that would enlighten us about what it means to be
an American today, so that we can be proud not only of our heritage but
also of the world we are building together.

Unfortunately, we have no such myth, nor, by extension, any that re- 18
flects what is involved in growing up. The child, like the society, needs
such myths to provide him with ideas of what difficulties are involved
in maturation. Fairy tales used to fill this need, and they would still do
so, if we would take them seriously. But sugar-sweet movies of the Disney variety fail to take seriously the world of the child — the immense
problems with which the child has to struggle as he grows up, to make

himself free from the bonds that tie him to his parents, and to test his own strength. Instead of helping the child, who wants to understand the difficulties ahead, these shows talk down to him, insult his intelligence, and lower his aspirations.

19   While most of the popular shows for children fall short of what the child needs most, others at least provide him with some of the fantasies that relieve pressing anxieties, and this is the reason for their popularity. Superman, Wonder Woman, and the Bionic Woman stimulate the child's fantasies about being strong and invulnerable, and this offers some relief from being overwhelmed by the powerful adults who control his existence. The Incredible Hulk affords a confrontation with destructive anger. Watching the Hulk on one of his rampages permits a vicarious experience of anger without having to feel guilty about it or anxious about the consequences, because the Hulk attacks only bad people. As food for fantasies that offer temporary relief, such shows have a certain value, but they do not provide material leading to higher integration, as myths do.

20   Science-fiction movies can serve as myths about the future and thus give us some assurance about it. Whether the film is *2001* or *Star Wars*, such movies tell about progress that will expand man's powers and his experiences beyond anything now believed possible, while they assure us that all these advances will not obliterate man or life as we now know it. Thus one great anxiety about the future — that it will have no place for us as we now are — is allayed by such myths. They also promise that even in the most distant future, and despite the progress that will have occurred in the material world, man's basic concerns will be the same, and the struggle of good against evil — the central moral problem of our time — will not have lost its importance.

21   Past and future are the lasting dimensions of our lives; the present is but a fleeting moment. So these visions about the future also contain our past; in *Star Wars*, battles are fought around issues that also motivated man in the past. There is good reason that Yoda appears in George Lucas's film: he is but a reincarnation of the teddy bear of infancy, to which we turn for solace; and the Jedi Knight is the wise old man, or the helpful animal, of the fairy tale, the promise from our distant past that we shall be able to rise to meet the most difficult tasks life can present us with. Thus any vision about the future is really based on visions of the past, because that is all we can know for certain.

22   As our religious myths about the future never went beyond Judgment Day, so our modern myths about the future cannot go beyond the search

for life's deeper meaning. The reason is that only as long as the choice between good and evil remains man's paramount moral problem does life retain that special dignity that derives from our ability to choose between the two. A world in which this conflict has been permanently resolved eliminates man as we know him. It might be a universe peopled by angels, but it has no place for man.

What Americans need most is a consensus that includes the idea of 23 individual freedom, as well as acceptance of the plurality of ethnic backgrounds and religious beliefs inherent in the population. Such consensus must rest on convictions about moral values and the validity of overarching ideas. Art can do this because a basic ingredient of the aesthetic experience is that it binds together diverse elements. But only the ruling art of a period is apt to provide such unity: for the Greeks, it was classical art; for the British, Elizabethan art; for the many petty German states, it was their classical art. Today, for the United States, it has to be the moving picture, the central art of our time, because no other art experience is so open and accessible to everyone.

The moving picture is a visual art, based on sight. Speaking to our 24 vision, it ought to provide us with the visions enabling us to live the good life; it ought to give us insight into ourselves. About a hundred years ago, Tolstoy wrote, "Art is a human activity having for its purpose the transmission to others of the highest and best feelings to which men have risen." Later, Robert Frost defined poetry as "beginning in delight and ending in wisdom." Thus it might be said that the state of the art of the moving image can be assessed by the degree to which it meets the mythopoetic task of giving us myths suitable to live by in our time — visions that transmit to us the highest and best feelings to which men have risen — and by how well the moving images give us that delight which leads to wisdom. Let us hope that the art of the moving image, this most authentic American art, will soon meet the challenge of becoming truly the great art of our age.

(1981)

The Writer's Subject

1. Why does Bettelheim regard the moving picture as the "only art truly of our time"? (paras. 1–4)

2. What is the point of the analogy between going to the movies and going to church? (para. 2)

3. Why does Bettelheim insist that mediocre works of art are as important as masterpieces in conferring "meaning and dignity on our existence"? (para. 5) Why does Bettelheim argue against an art for the elite?

4. What common qualities of heroes does Bettelheim identify in the movies *Kagemusha*, *The Last Laugh*, and *Patton*? Why does he attach such importance to movies of this kind? (paras. 8 and 9)

5. Why, according to Bettelheim, does a society need common myths? (paras. 10–14)

6. Bettelheim says that Americans used to be bound together by a myth. What was this myth? In what ways was this myth expressed in the Western movie? Why has the Western lost its vitality as myth? (paras. 15–17)

7. What mythic qualities are embodied in science fiction movies, according to Bettelheim? (paras. 20–21)

8. Why does Bettelheim compare the art of the moving picture in the United States to classical art in Greece and Elizabethan art in Britain? (para. 23)

The Writer's Style and Strategy

1. Bettelheim asserts that the efforts of aesthetes and critics to distinguish the art of film from popular movies and television are "contrary to the true spirit of art." (para. 6) What method does he use to support his argument?

2. "Vision" is a key word in this essay. Examine Bettelheim's use of this word, and show its importance to his central argument.

3. What use does Bettelheim make of examples to demonstrate his point that, for modern audiences, science fiction films have taken over the role of myth?

4. Show the relationship between the opening and closing sentences of the essay, and comment on their different emphases.

Suggested Topics for Writing and Discussion

1. Choose a science fiction film with which you are familiar and argue for it as myth.

2. According to Bettelheim, the American myth focused on a new world, a myth often embodied in Westerns. What myth do you think characterizes the Canadian experience? In what form has this myth found expression?

3. Do you agree with Bettelheim's assertion that movies of the Disney variety "talk down to [the child], insult his intelligence, and lower his aspirations"? Use specific examples to explain your view.

4. The heroes of television programs, films and books can tell us a great deal about the values and attitudes of our society. Choose one hero from a contemporary television program, film or book and explain what that hero tells us about our values and attitudes. Be specific and detailed in your response.

Dances With Wolves: Review
by Edward D. Castillo

Dances With Wolves is not only a well-crafted film by a first-time di-   1
rector, but it also touches on a number of important spiritual, social,
and environmental issues vital to all Americans at the end of this century. American Indian historians have long been well aware of many
important stories that resulted from the encounters between native peoples and Euro-Americans in the last century. Hope, fear, hatred, dread,
humor, guilt, and loathing can be found in nearly every such encounter.
From a native point of view, we have long been mystified as to why
this rich mine of human experience has been studiously avoided by
Hollywood film-makers. Within the Indian world, Costner's powerful
directing debut is for certain the most talked about mainstream Hollywood Indian film in two decades. Despite some negative reviews by
jaded Eurocentric urbanites, Costner's vision of an alternate Lakota encounter with Americans has captured the imagination of Americans from
a variety of social, economic, and racial backgrounds.

From a native viewpoint, the film's primary virtue is its sensitive ex-   2
ploration of a native culture. The screenplay, without preaching, engen-
ders understanding, acceptance, and sympathy for Lakota culture. I am
thinking especially here of small scenes, as when Kicking Bird and his
wife get into bed and we sense concern and confusion in his face; then
he pulls out one of his children's dolls that he has lain upon. This vignette
tells us in purely cinematic terms of the humanity of this family, and rings
warmly familiar to all parents in the audience. With such small touches
the director achieved his goal of demonstrating the most important aspect
of the picture was "... the sentiment, the humanity, not the politics."[1]

3   As non-Indian archaeologists, ethnographers, and historians have been painfully reminded over the last 20 years, all contemporary endeavors to interpret Indian history and culture have the dual potential of possibly hurting or helping contemporary Indians. In this respect most native peoples seem pleased with Costner in this most recent portrayal of our people in the last century. However, those expecting immediate reform in the social, economic, and political fortunes of the Sioux or any other tribe are sure to be disappointed. This film may help bring about much-needed reform in our nation and our tribes, but true reform will always require more than Hollywood can offer. Nevertheless, to minimize the power of the mass media to generate sympathy, concerns, and demands for reform is to ignore reality. For that reason alone it seems worthwhile to devote some thoughtful reflection to the shadows of the Indians whom Costner and screenwriter Michael Blake have lyrically dance upon the screen, thrusting us backward in time for a fleeting moment.

4   The characters portrayed are both engaging and varied. Kicking Bird is of course the most sympathetic of the Lakotas, the father figure who rescues and raises the small white girl (Christine/Stands With Fists) who had escaped a Pawnee raiding party, and eventually opens communication between Dunbar and the Lakota. He is a shaman/warrior whose poised and convincing portrayal by Canadian-born Oneida Indian Graham Greene rivals Costner's, and gained him an Academy Award nomination. The archetype Lakota warrior in the story is Wind In His Hair, played by Omaha Indian Rodney Grant. His commanding presence is sexually charged, with an aura of danger just beneath his angry bluster. Early on in the film his character is dramatically revealed in a confrontation with Dunbar: he charges on horseback directly toward Dunbar, stopping only feet from the soldier, shouts his defiance and lack of fear of this strange white man, and disdainfully turns his back on a cocked pistol to demonstrate his contempt for Dunbar — who promptly faints.

5   The most familiar Native American actor is folk singer/activist Floyd Red Crow Westerman, a Lakota Indian. He plays Ten Bears, chief of the film's Lakota band. His understated performance is in sharp contrast to his real character: for those who know him, he is nearly always smiling and a performer with an easygoing demeanor. Perhaps reflecting the growing dominance of warriors in Lakota society as the crisis of the frontier enveloped the plains Indian societies, the film offers few prominent parts for Indian women. The most important Indian female part is Canadian Cree/Chippewa Tantoo Cardinal as Black Shawl, wife of Kicking Bird. It is a small part which she performs skillfully. She

delivers one of the best one-liners in the film: when Kicking Bird declares that his crying stepdaughter, Stands With Fists, is being difficult, Black Shawl observes sardonically that it is perhaps Kicking Bird who is being difficult, since Stands With Fists is the one who is crying. While women in the audience will find this an appropriate rejoinder, it offers little comfort for the curious lack of strong females or for that matter, any young Indian women/children roles in the remainder of the screenplay. On the other hand, young viewers will be especially pleased with the trio of pre-pubescent Lakota boys led by Lakota Indian Nathan Lee Chasing His Horse (Smiles A Lot), who appropriately displays the independence, foolishness, and self-sacrificing courage typical of Indian youth both then and today. The other Lakota characters inhabiting Ten Bears' village, while undeniably likeable, are rather conventional and lack the delightfully quirky characters found in *Little Big Man*'s Cheyenne camp — a saucy berdache (homosexual) and the frustrated contrary warrior.

The "enemy" Pawnee portrayal has generated a good deal of discussion among Indians. Some viewers have decried the one-dimensional and negative portrait of Pawnee so badly maligned earlier in *Little Big Man* (1970). Despite a largely negative image, careful viewers will note the Pawnee war party that attacks the mule skinner Timmons is led by the unidentified actor and character I call "Violent Leader" who seeks both to humiliate and drive his hesitant followers into attacking the yet unseen whites. Later we see the Pawnee scouts helping the soldiers track down Ten Bears' people. One recalls Jack Crabbe's acerbic declaration, "Pawnees always were sucking up to whites," from *Little Big Man*. In reality much of Indian frontier history is characterized by a native survival response that varied between fight, flight, and accommodation. Earlier, the Pawnee offered considerable armed resistance to white encroachment upon their territory while later they assisted the US government in pursuing their traditional enemies, the Sioux. These unfortunate people were subjected to the purposeful introduction of smallpox by traders along the Santa Fe trail in 1831.[2] The film makes it too easy to dismiss these much maligned Indians as stereotypical "bad Indians." Their kind of imprudent judgment is today often chided by those living comfortably with full bellies and not faced with the horrible leadership decisions that could spell violent death or starvation for their men, women, and children. In the last quarter of the nineteenth century various bands of Sioux faced these terrible choices too and ultimately cooperated with federal authorities, riding with the blue coats

as scouts, auxiliaries, and even as U.S. soldiers.[3] Thoughtful viewers
wishing to know more about the tortuous history of the Pawnee can find
the works of Pawnee authors James Murie and Gene Weltfish in a recently published Pawnee bibliography.[4]

7   The non-Indian characters present some striking contrasts as well.
I've discussed this film with some colleagues who claim the whites in
it were negatively portrayed throughout its three-hour running time. That
type of generalization does not do justice to Michael Blake's subtly tex-
tured screenplay. In fact, the film is really about the transformation of
the white soldier Lt. John Dunbar into the Lakota warrior Dances With
Wolves. Kevin Costner's sensitive and convincing character transformation earned him an Oscar. What Blake has done with Dunbar's character is to assume that, as in the race- and class-conscious
nineteenth-century James Fenimore Cooper leatherstocking tales, largely
white American audiences will not endure a story centered around Indians only. Therefore a white central character is mandatory to capture
audience sympathy. However, unlike Cooper's protagonist Natty
Bumppo, a white frontiersman of common social origin, Blake at first
sight provides us with another type of frontier hero, the "military aristocrat" — a hero who combines high status and potential leadership in
Eastern society with the ability to both survive and triumph in the wilderness. This traditional type of frontier hero has a future in a post-fron-
tier America beginning to evolve into a rather rigid system divided by
class and race, based on land ownership and wealth. He has the resourcefulness and skills to fight and conquer Indians as well as the wilderness. He is supposed to be able to do this without developing savage
traits nor forgetting that he is the agent of progress and order in the
wild. But that is precisely what Costner's character ultimately rejects.
Dunbar does the unthinkable: he breaks out of the rigid confines of the
Frontier Aristocrat prototype. The widespread abhorrence of Indians and
their wilderness empire shared by all classes of frontier whites is slyly
demonstrated by Blake's screenplay that has the illiterate and sadistic
Private Spivey (Tony Pierce) stealing Dances With Wolves/Dunbar's
journal of his gradual evolution into a Lakota Warrior and using it for
toilet paper![5]

8   Stands With Fists is of course the other major non-Indian character
in the story. However, it could be argued that she is in fact "Lakota,"
her family having been killed by marauding Pawnee (again!) and rather
completely assimilated into Ten Bears' band as a mourning widow of a
recently killed Lakota warrior. It is to the film-maker's credit that such

a skilled and mature actress as Mary McDonnell was cast in this pivotal role. Costner recently revealed his reasoning in selecting McDonnell: "The key word in characterizing Stands With Fists was woman not girl. I wanted someone with lines on her face. That's not an easy thing to explain to a studio."[6] While the character is inherently likeable, McDonnell's skillful performance adds immeasurably to her appeal; strong yet vulnerable, possessing beauty without vanity. Especially noteworthy is the actress's authentic Lakota cadence and accent throughout the film. Her scenes where she relearns English are skillfully executed with pathos and conviction. For all of the above reasons she has gained the respect and acknowledgement of her peers who nominated her for the Academy's Best Supporting Actress category.

Other white characters in the film also show a great deal of variety. 9 The flatulent mule skinner Timmons (Robert Pastorelli), despite limited screen time, manages to steal scenes from Costner. His role evokes humor, disgust, and ultimately pathos. One can only suppose it was someone of Timmons's character that prompted Thomas Jefferson to observe that when the Indians encountered the typical frontiersman in the wilderness it was hardly an elevating experience for the Indians. Screenwriter Blake juxtaposes Timmons's painfully detailed violent death with his unexpected plea that his killers not hurt his mules. Just when the audience is ready to see the dirty, disgusting, crude, and racist Timmons killed, Blake introduces us to an unexpectedly compassionate side of the character and leaves the audience the disquieting reflection on our eagerness to see this low-lifer killed. That scene also clearly shows us that in the Pawnee "Violent Leader" scalping of Timmons, there is no honor.

Even among the soldiers we find all types — good, bad, insane, and 10 brutal. The enlisted men at the beginning of the film are shown to be tired, disgusted, and demoralized by the indecisiveness of their leaders. While we are witness to General Tide's personal pledge to save the "hero" of St. David's Field, the majority of the military leaders are shown to be cruel, brutal, or alcoholic. The suicidal Major Fambrough is quickly shown to be an isolated and insane alcoholic; he perhaps serves as a warning to Dunbar that the same fate awaits him at Fort Sedgewick. Blake perhaps went over the top with having his pathetic individual announce he had wet his pants! However, we can be reasonably sure that the audience clearly recognizes Fambrough's alcoholic insanity. Unquestionably the most brutal soldiers were to be found near the end of the film at the regarrisoned Fort Sedgewick. The film-makers leave no question in our minds that this is a particularly unsavory and dangerous bunch. This group kills Dances With Wolves' magnificent buckskin Cisco. They repeatedly brutalize Dances With Wolves, and threaten to hang him if he does not lead them to the "hostiles." Finally, they kill the partly domesticated wolf Two Sox. The film-makers show us by this senseless act the all too familiar fear and hatred in the American psyche of the natural world. Yet even among this motley crew, careful observers will find Lt. Elgin (Charles Rocket). Perhaps out of military respect for a fellow officer of equal rank, or sense of common decency, he repeatedly acts to curb the excesses of enlisted men as well as the indifferent Major in command.

11   While the characters in Blake's screenplay are satisfactorily varied, some violence has been done to the historical realities in which this story is set. Blake's original novel centered on the Comanche of the Southern Plains, not the Lakota. According to producer Jim Wilson, the change of tribes occurred because the production company gained access to a 3,500-strong herd of buffalo available on the private ranch of former Lieutenant Governor Roy Houck of South Dakota. Yet we are still presented with a Lakota chief called Ten Bears. In fact the real Ten Bears (Par-Roowah Sermehno) was a Southern Plains Yapparika Comanche chief and signer of the Medicine Lodge Treaty of 1867.[7] One rather obvious overlooked transitional casualty of the relocation of the story to the Northern Plains is revealed when Ten Bears shows Dances With Wolves and Kicking Bird an aged Spanish morion and explains, "The men who wore this came in the time of my grandfather's grandfather. Eventually we drove them out. Then came the Mexicans. They do not come here anymore. In my own time, the Texans...." The Lakota could never have encountered this assemblage of Southern colonists on the Northern Plains. The real Kicking Bird was a principal chief (not shaman) of the Kiowas, yet another Southern Plains tribe. Blake is said to have fashioned the film's Kicking Bird after the Kiowa chief because he favored peace with whites. Ironically the real Kicking Bird was believed to have been poisoned by a rival Kiowa shaman/warrior called Ma Man-ti (Skywalker) for his role in imprisoning resisting tribesmen in 1875.[8] Perhaps the film's most glaring factual inaccuracy is the depiction of a winter military campaign by soldiers hunting for Dances With Wolves and Ten Bears' band in the winter of 1864. In fact no U.S. Army winter campaign was undertaken on the Plains until November of 1868. Interestingly enough, this was Lieutenant Colonel George A. Custer's 7th Cavalry massacre of Cheyenne at Washita Creek on Thanks-

giving Day. That massacre, which killed 38 warriors and 67 women and children of the luckless Chief Black Kettle's people (earlier subjected to yet another massacre at Sand Creek, 1864) was portrayed with chilling authenticity in *Little Big Man*.[9]

In addition to factual errors, the film contains a number of unlikely 12 absurdities. Audiences are asked to believe that the Confederate infantry at the St. David's battlefield in 1863 could not hit a lone Union officer at a slow gallop within 50 feet of its picket lines. Viewers literate in Civil War battlefield history will have difficulty reconciling the known Confederate accuracy in small arms fire with the film's myopic troopers. We are also asked to believe that an Eastern neophyte would need to inform a highly skilled, hungry, and presumably alert band of Indians that a thunderously noisy herd of buffalo was in their neighbourhood.

The costumes have received wide praise and were beautifully executed 13 by Kathy Smith and Larry Belitz. Costume designer Elso Zamparelli has received a much deserved Academy Award nomination as well. Indeed they appear to have sprung to life from the works of nineteenth-century painters Karl Bodmer and George Catlin. And that may be precisely the problem: all of the Indian characters appear to be wearing their finest ceremonial regalia all the time, everyday! While it makes for colorful and picturesque village life, it certainly would have been impractical. In a similar vein we witness the marriage of Stands With Fists to Dances With Wolves taking place in the middle of the day, and in a white buckskin dress. The latter is certainly outside of acknowledged Lakota culture norms. Finally we are asked to believe that Army rifles buried in the ground for weeks and soaked from a fierce storm could be used functionally by Lakota who within hours of an impending attack had only used war clubs, bows and arrows, and lances. It makes for great drama but presses the limits of our willing suspension of disbelief.

A little acknowledged aspect of the appeal this film has for both In- 14 dian and non-Indian audiences is its sly sense of humor. A good part of that humor is at the expense of non-Indians. Nervous chuckles are heard among audiences as the mad Major Fambrough scavenges through his bottle-laden "files" and disjointedly converses with a bewildered and shocked Lt. Dunbar. We are disgustingly amused by the ill-mannered ignorance of the mule skinner Timmons and his bizarre behaviour. Costner himself provides a good many laughs. Audiences are delighted with Dunbar's buffalo pantomime and coffee-grinding antics as he desperately attempts to communicate with an incredulous Lakota visiting party. Indians in the audience are especially amused by Dunbar's perplexed reaction to the Lakota ritual of eating the raw buffalo liver following Dunbar's kill.

15   Perhaps director Costner's best remembered amusing visuals are a series of delightful sight jokes centered around the many Lakota attempts to steal Dunbar's magnificent buckskin mare Cisco. Much of the humor here is in fact at the expense of the Indians. A naked Lt. Dunbar confronts a startled Kicking Bird and causes him to flee. A trio of Lakota youth led by Smiles A Lot gallops away leading Cisco and boasting of their soon-to-be-acknowledged warrior status when abruptly their dreams of glory are literally yanked out of their hands and instead of acclaim, they consequently face a whipping. Even Wind In His Hair has Cisco's persistent loyalty to Lt. Dunbar thwart his best efforts to capture the prized mount. Yet the best belly laugh of this running gag is the delayed realization that during one of the attempts to steal Cisco, Dunbar has knocked himself unconscious on the low door jamb of his Fort Sedgewick sod house.

16   Perhaps in the same vein, although in this instance made ironically poignant, is Wind In His Hair's boastful soliloquy, "When I heard that more whites are coming, more than can be counted, I wanted to laugh. We took 100 horses from those people, there was no honor in it. They don't ride well, they don't shoot well, they're dirty. They have no women, no children. They could not even make it through one winter in our country. And these people are said to flourish? I think they will be dead in ten years." These moments of humor relieve the tension of early contact and eventual hunted lives that the Indians, we all know, were inevitably subjected to.

17   The film's phenomenal popularity can be attributed to a number of factors. Thoughtful viewers are conscious of the film's powerfully evocative images of our country in the mid-nineteenth century, including the struggle with the persistent issue of slavery and the ubiquitous "Indian Problem." Those problems have unrelentingly dogged the American psyche for over 100 years and remain largely unresolved to this day. But perhaps more to the point, the character of Lt. Dunbar is very appealing to today's audience precisely because he is a 1990s man, not an 1860s white man. Dunbar is for the Baby Boomer generation the disillusioned soldier seeking personal redemption in a wilderness experience. In the process he is literally transformed before our eyes from an Army officer to a Lakota warrior. He tells the quietly deranged Major Fambrough

that he wants to be stationed in the west to "see the frontier … before it's gone." That simple childlike desire touches an unspoken yearning in many Americans, young and old. Who can blame Dunbar for wanting to escape the mass killing of the Civil War battlefields?

Confronting the solitude of Fort Sedgewick we are only provided with **18** a presumption that the military post had been abandoned, not plundered by Indians. Actually the film-makers reportedly filmed a segment showing the nearly starving and desertion-ridden garrison abandoning the fort. Nevertheless, as Dunbar surveys his post we are treated to an elevated back panning shot revealing a disturbing foreground scene of the former soldiers' hovels burrowed in the hill, a fouled water source littered with trash and partially devoured animal carcasses. It is clear the white men from the East have been reduced to a condition that is truly barbaric by their attempt to attempt to conquer the Indians and their natural world. We witness Lt. Dunbar cleaning up the animal carcasses and the trash and filling in the burrow holes, just as sensible Americans everywhere work to heal the ecological mess the first wave of Euro-Americans have left in their frenzy to possess the American landscape. Still, Lt. Dunbar's growth in ecological consciousness and personal transformation into a "native" is gradual and incremental. First his beard, then his jacket, his hat, and then his moustache is exchanged for Lakota breastplate armor, knife, and long hair with feathers. His journal entries speak of his awe and love of this new territory, though he habitually longs for company. Done entirely on location, Dean Semler's stunning cinematography effectively captures the unspoiled plains biosphere. It becomes apparent to Dunbar and the audience that he can find an unexpected satisfaction in relationships with animals (Two Sox and Cisco) as well as the natural world around him. His first instinct upon seeing the wolf later called "Two Sox" is to raise his rifle and kill it. Only as he pauses do we begin to realize he is truly changing, perhaps driven by loneliness to allow the magnificent predator to live.

The pivotal event in Dunbar's transformation is just prior to the mag- **19** nificently photographed buffalo hunt. As Ten Bears' band approaches the herd they come upon two dozen buffalo carcasses, shot for their hides with the bodies left to rot upon the plains. Although the mass slaughter of buffalo became rampant a few years later, the scene evokes strong emotions — we know this is only the beginning. Dunbar notes in his journal, "Who would do such a thing? The field was proof enough that it was a people without value and without soul, with no regard for Sioux rights. The wagon tracks leading away left little doubt, and my heart sank as I knew it could only be white hunters." Not seen in the theatrical release is a scene of Dunbar coming upon Ten Bears' hunting camp as a scalp dance is in progress. Fresh white scalps are seen and the suggestion is that the white buffalo hunters have been discovered and killed.

20   In the buffalo hunt audiences are treated to a sight not witnessed for over 120 years. To be sure it was for Native Americans the high point of the movie. Bareback Lakota hunters are shown charging among a thunderous avalanche of large and dangerous bison. Non-Indians are shown that this too is a part of the natural order, a world of predator and game animals. In the feasting and celebrations that follow, we see Dunbar begin to exchange his uniform for native attire. When Dunbar returns to Fort Sedgewick he builds a fire and dances around it alone. Powerful drumbeats rhythmically signal a deeper transformation of Dunbar as he joins in the rhythm of the earth and perhaps harks back to a race memory of his own neolithic ancestors.

21   It is the next day that Kicking Bird gives Dunbar his Indian name, Dances With Wolves, after the Indians witness his extraordinary relationship with the wolf Two Sox. Interestingly enough, it is the white captive Stands With Fists who mentors and entices Dances With Wolves deeper into Lakota culture, teaching him the language and thus opening up communication between the Indians and this newcomer to their land. The significance of this should not be underestimated. Those who wish to physically and spiritually embrace the land must first learn how from its native people. When Dances With Wolves and Stands With Fists first embrace near a stream we cannot ignore the cattail pollen that fills the air around them — symbolizing germination of their new love for one another and also a new ecological consciousness among the Euro-Americans who have embraced the Indians. Their marriage follows and represents not only the union of the white woman who had preceded Dunbar in her own transformation into an "Indian woman," but also a final rite of passage of Dances With Wolves into a tribal citizen.

22   Yet another scene missing from the theatrical release occurred after the marriage. In this instance, Kicking Bird and Dances With Wolves encounter a sacred forested area that whites had recently despoiled. The bloated bodies of dozens of small animals killed for target practice swarming with flies, half-consumed deer, and empty whisky bottles littered the landscape. It was this senseless carnage that ultimately prompts Dances With Wolves to tell Kicking Bird that whites will be coming, "more than can be counted, ... like the stars." When this frightening specter is revealed to Ten Bears he seems unable to grasp the terrible

physical and ecological carnage that we know will eventually envelop the Lakota and all other Indians.

Perhaps because that scene was excised from the print of the film the 23 public saw, the shock value of the capture of Dances With Wolves by the regarrisoned Fort soldiers is more powerful. As if to underscore the ominous hints of the impending campaigns to ruthlessly exploit or destroy the winged creatures, those that crawled, the two-legged, and the four-legged, we witness the recently metamorphized Dances With Wolves/Dunbar captured after the soldiers heartlessly kill his beloved buckskin Cisco. In the brutal interrogation that follows, despite kicks, punches, and clubbing with a rifle Dances With Wolves refuses to cooperate in "hunting hostiles and returning white captives." We know Dances With Wolves has completely assumed his Lakota persona when he refuses to speak English to his captors. As he is being transported back to Fort Hays his brutal escorts stop long enough to kill his companion Two Sox. In a shot that cinematically tells us all we need to know, as this scene progresses the camera reveals that just behind the ridge on which Two Sox is killed a Lakota rescue party is tracking the soldiers. Naturally the brutal despoilers of Lakota territory are summarily dispatched in stylish Hollywood fashion. This is a very satisfying scene for 1990s audiences. The Indians on an ecologically moral high ground become a kind of environmental SWAT team for the future Americans.

If there is any lingering question about the meaning of all this personal 24 transformation and evolution of ecological ethos among this new white man and woman who have internalized Lakota culture, it is confirmed in the film's final scene. Deciding his presence will only further endanger his Lakota brothers, Dances With Wolves and Stands With Fists sadly leave their mentors to their inevitable fate and strike off on their own, perhaps to search for an America where they can live in peace and flourish with a new ecological ethos. While exchanging parting gifts, Dances With Wolves tells Kicking Bird, "You were the first man I ever wanted to be like. I will not forget you." Indians know that no white man or woman can become Indian, but many of us hope those who have learned of our cultures and appreciate their unique humanity will be our friends and allies in protecting the earth and all of her children. An interesting postscript to this tale of personal transformation and rebirth of an ecologically sound ethos for the Plains has a parallel in real life. Currently efforts are underway to create a "buffalo commons" amid the failed federal-subsidized farming that replaced the great Plains buffalo range. Imagine, a huge area where buffalo could again roam free! Perhaps the

Ghost Dance prophets were right: the buffalo may be returning after all.

25   While Hollywood has a dismal record of employing Indian actors and technical staff, *Dances With Wolves* has clearly demonstrated that an American Indian presence in a film can make it work. The Native American actors naturally lent an air of authenticity to the work. This viewer, like thousands of other Native Americans, remains mystified as to why Hollywood still continues to employ non-Indian actors in redface to play major speaking parts (e.g. Trevor Howard in *Windwalker*). Many of us had hoped that Dan George's endearing performance of "Old Lodgeskins" in Arthur Penn's *Little Big Man* would throw open the doors of opportunity for Indian actors. It didn't happen then, but happily today we again have a major film with a number of important and significant roles for Native Americans. Certainly Tantoo Cardinal, Nathan Lee Chasing His Horse, Graham Greene, Rodney Grant, and Floyd Red Crow Westerman created memorable performances and demonstrated there is a significant pool of talented Native American actors out there. Responsible for a good deal of the authenticity of the Indian roles was South Dakota's Sinte Gleska Indian College Linguist, Doris Leader Charge. She is the Lakota linguist who translated Michael Blake's screenplay into Lakota, coached the actors in the language, and played a small role in the film. This was no small feat, since none of the actors spoke Lakota fluently. However, the Indian grapevine reports that among the Plains Indians it was the 24 Native American bareback stunt riders who charged in among a 3500-strong herd of buffalo (a feat that had not been accomplished in more than a century) who were the true heroes of the film. My Cheyenne and Comanche friends tell me the buffalo hunt alone was worth the price of admission. No doubt about it, Costner counted coup (gained honor by taking risks) on all Hollywood Indian movies and touched something deeply significant in the Plains Indian cultures with that magnificent buffalo hunt.

26   Some audiences and critics have commented on the violence in the film and called it excessive. Especially disturbing and painful to watch is the Pawnee killing of the mule skinner Timmons. In Stands With Fists's childhood flashback, we witness a hatchet murder of a white farmer. When Pretty Shield (Doris Leader Charge) crushes a Pawnee skull with a burning log and Stands With Fists shoots another Pawnee during an attack, we clearly see these women are not to be messed with. The soldiers at the end of the film are particularly sadistic and themselves meet a brutal end. Even youth get in the act; after being pistol-whipped Smiles A Lot kills the sadistic Sgt. Bauer by burying a hatchet

into his chest to the hilt. As awful as these and other violent acts are, they hardly compare to the violence of the real American frontier. Despite a highly romantic and mythologized popular view of the American past, the American Indian frontier was an incredibly heartless, sordid, violent, and chaotic scramble by Euro-Americans to get something (Indian land and resources) for nothing. For viewers upset over this cinematic tip of an iceberg of violence that Costner reveals for the popcorn-eating masses, I suggest they stick to Roy Rogers westerns or similar pablum. Costner has reminded all popular culture consumers of the violent underpinnings of the American Indian policy.

I suppose it is inevitable and perhaps *de rigueur* that comparisons 27 will be made between Costner's epic and other recent films that prominently feature Indian culture and actors or themes. Thematically perhaps *Windwalker* (1973) makes the best comparison. That film also featured a mythological death and rebirth. Furthermore it also took pains to show Indian society in a positive light, where grandparents, children, and families dominate the portrait of Cheyenne society just prior to sustained colonial contact. While *Windwalker* does feature a touching love story, it is somewhat troublesome to Indians that its most important leads are played by non-Indians. Many writers have commented on the extensive use of the Lakota language in Costner's film, but it was not the first such use in Indian films; in fact *Windwalker* holds that distinction. (*Little Big Man* began using Cheyenne but soon switched over to English.) However, it is probably the brooding and melancholy American Playhouse epic *Roanoak* (1986) that best utilized an Indian language effectively to demonstrate communication problems between whites and America's native people.

A film that may not be considered by critics as an Indian film but 28 nevertheless shows some important links to mainstream Indian films is Clint Eastwood's *The Outlaw Josey Wales* (1975). This last great American Western was adapted from Cherokee writer Forrest Carter's novel *Gone to Texas*. On the surface it is about an embittered and extremely violent Civil War guerilla's attempt to escape the madness of the Reconstruction South. It could be interpreted as another attempt to retell the familiar story of a lone white man on the Indian frontier who ultimately attracts an ethnically diverse following, ultimately makes peace with local Indians, and finds physical and spiritual refuge in that diverse milieu. Especially memorable in the Phillip Kaufman–Sonia Chernuss adaptation of Carter's story is the charming performance of Dan George as Confederate Cherokee Lone Watie and Will Sampsom in a powerful and menacing role as the Comanche chief Ten Bears.

29   One can almost feel sorry for the "creative talents" that recently completed the four-hour miniseries adaptation of Evan S. Connell's *Son of Morning Star* (1991). This utterly boring, dramaless, flat, one-dimensional, and totally humorless attempt to tell the story of Lt. Col. George Armstrong Custer's career and his fateful encounter at Little Big Horn is a lesson for film-makers everywhere. While it was laudable for its conscientious attempt to give an even-handed account of the clash of Americans and Plains Indians, its Indians were not allowed to speak. All native reactions and motivations are relegated to a voice-over narration (Buffy St. Marie) that instead of providing insights further isolates the Indians by denying them a voice in history. It is perhaps symptomatic of the contempt network moguls hold for their audiences. In contrast, PBS programmers offered the haunting *Roanoak* where more than two-thirds of the film is in the Chippewa dialect.

30   Unquestionably the film that invites most comparison is Arthur Penn's 1970 classic *Little Big Man*. Again we find the theme of a white man encountering the Indians and discovering their humanity. Yet that bawdy parody of the American frontier only focused on Indians for less than one-third of its screen time. The real similarities of the two films lie in their unusual juxtaposition of humor and drama. Jack Crabbe's humorous sexual encounter with his wife's three sisters is immediately followed by Custer's murderous attack upon the Cheyenne camp at Washita River where his wife and newborn child are massacred along with many others. In a similar vein, *Dances With Wolves* invites us to laugh both with and at the ignorant mule skinner Timmons only to shortly witness his frightening murder by Pawnee. Both films featured an elaborate and memorable set piece; for Costner it was the buffalo hunt, in Arthur Penn's film it was the reenactment of the Battle of Greasy Grass (Custer's Last Stand). However, significant differences exist. Penn's film was made at the height of the Vietnam War and emphasized the military assault on America's native peoples. Costner's film on the other hand is concerned with the re-establishment of a spiritual and ecologically sound American ethic with which Euro-Americans can enter the twenty-first century. Costner has been widely quoted as calling his film his personal love letter to the past. It also seems to offer one artist's optimistic blueprint for a new America, where a spiritually based and ecologically sound future awaits those willing to learn from this land's first children.

(1991)

Notes

1. Costner, Kevin et al., *Dances With Wolves, The Illustrated Story of the Epic Film*. New York: New Market Press, 1990.

2. Miles, William. "Enamored with Civilization: Isaac McCoy's Plan for Indian Reform."*Kansas Historian* Vol. 38, 1972: 268–286.

3. Dunlay, Thomas W. *Wolves for the Blue Soldiers: Indian Scouts and Auxiliaries with the United States Army, 1860–90*. Lincoln: University of Nebraska Press, 1987.

4. Blaine, Martha Royce. *The Pawnees: A Critical Bibliography*. Bloomington: Indiana University Press, 1979.

5. Drinnon, Richard. *Facing West: The Metaphysics of Indian Hating and Empire Building*. New York: New Americans Library, 1980.

6. Costner, ibid., 44.

7. Utley, Robert M. *Frontier Regulars, The United States Army and the Indian, 1866–1891*. New York: Macmillan, 1973.

8. Nye, Wilber S. *Bad Medicine and Good, Tales of the Kiowas*. Norman: University of Oklahoma Press, 1962.

9. Utley, ibid., 150–156.

The Writer's Subject

1. *Dances With Wolves* is set in the 1860s. Why then does Castillo see the film as important to Americans at the end of the 20th century?

2. How does Castillo deal with the film's depiction of the Pawnee Indians who attack the Lakotas? Does he offer any defence of their conduct?

3. Explain what Castillo means by the "military aristocrat" type of frontier hero. (para. 7)

4. How does Castillo deal with the charge that all the white characters in the film are negatively portrayed throughout? (para. 7)

5. What are some of the film's factual inaccuracies and "unlikely absurdities"?

6. In what ways, according to Castillo, does the principal white character, Lieutenant Dunbar, represent Americans of the 1990s?

7. What significance does the reviewer attach to the film's depiction of the buffalo hunt? (paras. 19–20, 24)

8. How, according to Castillo, does the film convey a sense of a "new ecological ethos"? (para. 24)

9. In what respects, in Castillo's opinion, does the film offer an "optimistic blueprint for a new America"? (para. 30)

The Writer's Style and Subject

1. In what ways, if any, is the review affected by the fact that the writer is himself a native North American?

2. What is meant by the phrase "jaded Eurocentric urbanites" (para. 1), and what does it convey about the writer's attitude?

3. What use does Castillo make of other films about North American Indians?

4. Castillo's review of *Dances With Wolves* first appeared in *Film Quarterly*. In what respects does it go beyond the usual bounds of a movie review?

Suggested Topics for Writing and Discussion

1. Compare Castillo's review of *Dances With Wolves* with the comments by Pauline Kael elsewhere in this anthology.

2. Castillo notes that in *Dances With Wolves* the main white character breaks out of the rigid confines of the "Frontier Aristocrat" type of hero. Compare this or other recent films about native North American life to earlier films in this genre, and indicate what differences you see in the portrayal of white characters.

3. Castillo believes that *Dances With Wolves* reflects the emergence of a "new ecological order" in our time. What evidence is there of such an order in other recent films?

4. What in your view is gained by having native North American characters in films speak in their own languages?

A Neo-Luddite Reflects on the Internet
by Gertrude Himmelfarb

On the subject of our latest technological revolution, cyberspace, I am 1
a neo-Luddite. Not a true Luddite; my Luddism is qualified, compromised. I revel in the word processor; I am grateful for computerized
library catalogues; I appreciate the convenience of CD-ROMs; and I
concede the usefulness of the Internet for retrieving information and
conducting research. But I am disturbed by some aspects of the new
technology — not merely by the moral problems raised by cybersex,
which have occupied so much attention recently, but also by the new
technology's impact on learning and scholarship.

Revolutions come fast and furious these days. No sooner do we adapt 2
to one than we are confronted with another. For almost half a millennium, we lived with the product of the print revolution — the culture of
the book. Then, a mere century ago, we were introduced to the motion
picture; a couple of decades later, to radio and then to television. To a
true Luddite, those inventions were the beginning of the rot, the decline
of Western civilization as we have known it. To a true revolutionary,
such as Marshall McLuhan, they were giant steps toward a brave new
world liberated from the stultifying rigidities of an obsolete literacy. To
the rest of us, they were frivolities, diversions, often meretricious (as
some popular culture has always been), but not threatening to the life
of the mind, the culture associated with books.

Not that the book culture has been immune from corruption. When the 3
printing press democratized literature, liberating it from the control of
clerics and scribes, the effects were ambiguous. As the historian Elizabeth Eisenstein pointed out in her seminal 1979 work *The Printing Press*

as an Agent of Change, the advent of printing facilitated not only the production of scientific works, but also of occult and devotional tracts. It
helped create a cosmopolitan secular culture and, at the same time, distinctive national and sectarian cultures. It stimulated scholarship and high
culture, as well as ephemera and popular culture. It subverted one intellectual elite, the clergy, only to elevate another, the "enlightened" class.

4   Yet for all of its ambiguities, printing celebrated the culture of the
book — of bad books, to be sure, but also of good books and great books.
Movies, radio, and television made the first inroads on the book, not
only because they distracted us from reading, but also because they began to train our minds to respond to oral and visual sensations of brief
duration rather than to the cadences, nuances, and lingering echoes of
the written word. The movie critic Michael Medved has said that even
more detrimental than the content of television is the way that it habitu-
ates children to an attention span measured in seconds rather than minutes. The combination of sound bites and striking visual effects shapes
the young mind, incapacitating it for the longer, slower, less febrile tempo
of the book.

5   And now we have the Internet to stimulate and quicken our senses
still more. We channel-surf on television, but that is as naught compared
with cyber-surfing. The obvious advantage of the new medium is that it
provides access to an infinite quantity of information on an untold
number and variety of subjects. How does one quarrel with such a pleni-
tude of goods?

6   As an information-retrieval device, the Internet is unquestionably an
asset, assuming that those using it understand that the information retrieved is only as sound as the original sources — an assumption that
applies to all retrieval methods, but especially to one whose sources are
so profuse and indiscriminate. Yet children and even older students, encouraged to rely upon the Internet for information and research, may
not be sophisticated enough to question the validity of the information
or the reliability of the source. A child whom I saw interviewed on television said that it was wonderful to be able to ask a question on one's
home page and have "lots of people answer it for you." Before the age
of the Internet, the child would have had to look up the question in a
textbook or encyclopedia, a source that he would have recognized as
more authoritative than, say, his older brother or sister (or even his mother
or father).

7   As a learning device, the new electronic technology is even more
dubious — indeed, it may be more bad than good. And it is dubious at

all levels of learning. Children who are told that they need not learn how to multiply and divide, spell, and write grammatical prose, because the computer can do that for them, are being grossly miseducated. More important, young people constantly exposed to "multimedia" and "hypermedia" replete with sound and images often become unable to concentrate on mere "texts" (known as books), which have only words and ideas to commend them. Worse yet, the constant exposure to a myriad of texts, sounds, and images that often are only tangentially related to each other is hardly conducive to the cultivation of logical, rational, systematic habits of thought.

At the more advanced level of learning and scholarship, the situation is equally ambiguous. Let me illustrate this from my own experience. I used to give (in the pre-electronic age) two sequences of courses: one on social history, the other on intellectual history. In a course on social history, a student might find electronic technology useful, for example, in inquiring about the standard of living of the working classes in the early period of industrialization, assuming that the relevant sources — statistical surveys, diaries, archival collections, newspapers, tracts, journals, books, and other relevant materials — were on line (or at least that information about their location and content was available). **8**

This kind of social history, which is built by marshaling social and economic data, is not only facilitated, but actually is stimulated, by the new technology. One might find oneself making connections among sources of information that would have had no apparent link had they not been so readily called up on the computer screen (on the other hand, now one might not make the effort to discover other kinds of sources that do not appear). **9**

But what about intellectual history? It may be that the whole of Rousseau's *Social Contract* and Hegel's *Philosophy of History* are now on line. Can one read such books on the screen as they should be read — slowly, carefully, patiently, dwelling upon a difficult passage, resisting the temptation to scroll down, thwarting the natural speed of the computer? What is important in the history of ideas is not retrieving and recombining material, but understanding it. And that requires a different relation to the text, a different tempo of reading and study. **10**

One can still buy the book (or perhaps print out a "hard copy" from the computer), read it, mark it up, and take notes the old-fashioned way. The difficulty is that students habituated to surfing on the Internet, to getting their information in quick easy doses, to satisfying their curiosity with a minimum of effort (and with a maximum of sensory stimula- **11** tion) often do not have the patience to think and study this old-fashioned way. They may even come to belittle the intellectual enterprise itself, the study of the kinds of books — "great books," as some say derisively — that require careful thought and study.

12   Perhaps I am exaggerating the effect of the electronic revolution, just as critics have said that Elizabeth Eisenstein has exaggerated the effect of the print one. She sometimes seems to suggest that printing was not only *an* agent of change, but *the* primary agent. Without the printing press, she has implied, the Renaissance might have petered out or the Reformation been suppressed as yet another medieval heresy. "The advent of printing," she notes, preceded "the Protestant revolt."

13   The electronic media cannot make that claim to priority. The intellectual revolution of our time, postmodernism, long antedated the Internet. Nonetheless, the Internet powerfully reinforces postmodernism: It is the postmodernist technology *par excellence*. It is as subversive of "linear," "logocentric," "essentialist" thinking, as committed to the "aporia," "indeterminacy," "fluidity," "intertextuality," and "contextuality" of discourse, as deconstruction itself. Like postmodernism, the Internet does not distinguish between the true and the false, the important and the trivial, the enduring and the ephemeral. The search for a name or phrase or subject will produce a comic strip or advertising slogan as readily as a quotation from the Bible or Shakespeare. Every source appearing on the screen has the same weight and credibility as every other; no authority is "privileged" over any other.

14   The Internet gives new meaning to the British expression describing intellectuals, "chattering classes." On their own home pages, subscribers can communicate to the world every passing reflection, impression, sensation, obsession, or perversion.

15   Michael Kinsley, editor of the new cyberspace journal *Slate*, defensively insists that his magazine will retain the "linear, rational thinking" of print journalism. To have to make that claim is itself testimony to the non-linear, non-rational tendency of the new medium. Each article in *Slate* gives the date when it was "posted" and "composted" (archived). Composted! One recalls the computer-programming acronym a few years ago — "GIGO," for "garbage in, garbage out." (As it happens, the articles in *Slate* are not garbage, but much on the Internet is.)

16   One need not be a Luddite, or even a neo-Luddite, to be alarmed by this most useful, most potent, most seductive, and most equivocal invention.

                                                                        (1996)

The Writer's Subject

1. What does Himmelfarb mean by saying that she is "not a true Luddite"? (paras. 1–2)

2. What does Himmelfarb mean by stating that the printing press "democratized literature"? (para. 3) Why were the effects of that democratization "ambiguous"?

3. What, according to the writer, has been the impact of movies, television and radio on the culture of the book? (para. 4)

4. What limitation does Himmelfarb attach to the use of the Internet as a source of information? (para. 6)

5. What are the drawbacks of the new electronic technology, as perceived by Himmelfarb? (para. 7)

The Writer's Style and Strategy

1. Why does Himmelfarb juxtapose "the moral problems raised by cybersex" and "the new technology's impact on learning and scholarship" in the opening paragraph of the essay?

2. Himmelfarb writes, "Perhaps I am exaggerating the effect of the electronic revolution" (para. 12). What preceding details might support this comment?

3. What is Himmelfarb's strategy in saying that "the search for a name or phrase or subject will produce a comic strip or advertising slogan as readily as a quotation from the Bible or Shakespeare"? (para. 13)

4. How would you sum up Himmelfarb's attitude to computer technology and the Internet? How is that attitude conveyed?

5. What is the implied audience for this essay?

6. Discuss the appropriateness of Himmelfarb's title.

Suggested Topics for Writing and Discussion

1. Find out what you can about Marshall McLuhan, to whom Himmelfarb refers in para. 2. In what respects was McLuhan a "true revolutionary"?

2. Do you agree with Himmelfarb that exposure to multimedia and hypermedia work against the development of "logical, rational, systematic habits of thought"? (para. 7)

3. Drawing on her own experience as a teacher, Himmelfarb describes the effects of computer technology on courses in social history and intellectual history. What differences does she perceive? (paras. 8–10) From your

own experience, do you find that the distinction she draws applies to courses you are taking?

4. Do you agree with Himmelfarb that students accustomed to surfing on the Internet may lack the patience necessary to study a text in depth and detail? (para. 11)

5. Himmelfarb believes that postmodernism, rather than electronic technology, is "the intellectual revolution of our time" (para. 13). What exactly is postmodernism? What is its relation to deconstruction, as described here? In what ways does the Internet reinforce postmodernism, in Himmelfarb's view?

6. In criticizing computer technology, Himmelfarb is speaking from the perspective of a scholar in the humanities. How might scholars in other fields — the sciences, for example, or commerce, or law — respond to her charge that the computer has a bad impact on study habits and the capacity for rational thinking?

7. On 11 February 1969, two hundred students occupied a building of Sir George Williams University in Montreal and destroyed the University's computer. Find out what you can about this incident as an example of "neo-Luddism."

New Age Daydreams [*Dances With Wolves*]
by Pauline Kael

A friend of mine broke up with his woman friend after they went to see   1
Field of Dreams: she liked it. As soon as I got home from *Dances With Wolves*, I ran to the phone and warned him not to go to it with his new woman friend. Set during the Civil War, this new big Indians-versus-Cavalry epic is about how the white men drove the Native Americans from their land. But Kevin Costner, who directed *Dances With Wolves* and stars in it, is not a man who lets himself be ripped apart by the violent cruelty of what happened. He's no extremist: it's a middle-of-the-road epic. Lieutenant Dunbar (Costner), a Union officer, sees that the Sioux have a superior culture — they're held up as models for the rest of us — and he changes sides. Costner must have heard Joseph Campbell on PBS advising people to "follow your bliss." This is a nature-boy movie, a kid's daydream of being an Indian. When Dunbar has become a Sioux named Dances With Wolves, he writes in his journal that he knows for the first time who he really is. Costner has feathers in his hair and feathers in his head.

Once our hero has become an Indian, we don't have to feel torn or   2
divided. We can see that the white men are foulmouthed, dirty louts. The movie — Costner's début as a director — is childishly naïve. When Lieutenant Dunbar is alone with his pet wolf, he's like Robinson Crusoe on Mars. When he tries to get to know the Sioux, and he and they are feeling each other out, it's like a sci-fi film that has the hero trying to communicate with an alien race. But in this movie it's the white men who are the aliens: the smelly brutes are even killing each other, in the war between the North and the South. Luckily, we Indians are part of a

harmonious community. Dances With Wolves has never seen people "so dedicated to their families." And he loves their humor.

3   At the beginning, there's a bizarre Civil War battle sequence with the wounded Lieutenant Dunbar riding on horseback between rows of Union and Confederate soldiers, his arms outstretched, welcoming bullets in a Christlike embrace, and throughout the movie he is brutalized, seems dead, but rises again. (Does getting beaten give Costner a self-righteous feeling? Even when it's as unconvincingly staged as it is here?) There's nothing really campy or shamelessly flamboyant after the opening. There isn't even anything with narrative power or bite to it. This Western is like a New Age social-studies lesson. It isn't really revisionist; it's the old stuff toned down and sensitized.

4   Costner and his friend Michael Blake, who worked up the material with him in mind and then wrote the novel and the screenplay, are full of good will. They're trying to show the last years of the Sioux as an independent nation from the Sioux point of view. And it's that sympathy for the Indians that (I think) the audience is responding to. But Costner and Blake are moviemaking novices. Instead of helping us understand the Sioux, they simply make the Sioux like genial versions of us. The film provides the groovy wisdom of the Sioux on the subjects of peace and togetherness: you never fight among yourselves — you negotiate. Each of the Indian characters is given a trait or two; they all come across as simple-minded, but so does the hero. Even the villains are endearingly dumb, the way they are in stories children write.

5   There's nothing affected about Costner's acting or directing. You hear his laid-back, surfer accent; you see his deliberate goofy faints and falls, and all the close-ups of his handsomeness. This epic was made by a bland megalomaniac. (The Indians should have named him Plays with Camera.) You look at that untroubled face and know he can make everything lightweight. How is he as a director? Well, he has moments of competence. And the movie has an authentic vastness. The wide-screen cinematography, by Dean Semler, features the ridges, horizons, and golden sunsets of South Dakota; it is pictorial rather than emotionally expressive, but it is spacious and open at times, and there are fine images of buffalo pounding by.

6   Mostly, the action is sluggish and the scenes are poorly shaped. Crowds of moviegoers love the movie, though — maybe partly because the issues have been made so simple. As soon as you see the Indians, amused, watch the hero frolicking with his wolf, you know that the white men will kill it. Maybe, also, crowds love this epic because it is so in-

nocent: Costner shows us his bare ass like a kid at camp feeling one with the great outdoors. He is the boyish man of the hour: the Sioux onscreen revere him, because he is heroic and modest, too. TV interviewers acclaim him for the same qualities. He is the Orson Welles that everybody wants — Orson Welles with no belly.

(1990)

The Writer's Subject

1. What does Kael mean by calling *Dances With Wolves* a "middle-of-the-road epic"? (para. 1)

2. Why is the movie, in Kael's opinion, "childishly naïve"? (para. 2)

3. What is the writer's principal criticism of the movie's depiction of the Sioux?

4. Given that she herself is so critical in her estimate, why does Kael think that the movie is so popular?

The Writer's Style and Strategy

1. Why does Kael begin her review of *Dances With Wolves* with an anecdote about a friend?

2. Clearly, the reviewer did not like *Dances With Wolves*. How does she seek to persuade the reader to share her point of view?

3. What is the predominant tone of the review? How is it established?

4. Discuss the intended effect of the following phrases: "like Robinson Crusoe on Mars" (para. 2); "a New Age social-studies lesson" (para. 3); "the groovy wisdom of the Sioux" (para. 4).

5. A favourite device of critics is to "damn with faint praise." Where does Kael make use of this technique?

Suggested Topics for Writing and Discussion

1. Compare Kael's views about *Dances With Wolves* with those of Castillo. Are there any points of agreement?

2. Find other examples of hostile or critical film reviews, and discuss the methods by which the writers convey their unfavourable response.

3. Write your own review of a film you have seen recently.

4. Choose a film that has been widely reviewed, and compare the styles of the reviewers in a number of different magazines or newspapers.

Who Killed King Kong?
by X.J. Kennedy

1   The ordeal and spectacular death of *King Kong*, the giant ape, undoubtedly has been witnessed by more Americans than have ever seen a performance of *Hamlet*, *Iphigenia at Aulis*, or even *Tobacco Road*. Since
RKO-Radio Pictures first released *King Kong*, a quarter-century has gone
by; yet year after year, from prints that grow more rain-beaten, from
sound tracks that grow more tinny, ticket-buyers by thousands still pursue Kong's luckless fight against the forces of technology, tabloid journalism and the DAR. They see him chloroformed to sleep, see him
whisked from his jungle isle to New York and placed on show, see him
burst his chains to roam the city (lugging a frightened blonde), at last to
plunge from the spire of the Empire State Building, machine gunned
by model airplanes.

2   Though Kong may die, one begins to think his legend unkillable. No
clearer proof of his hold upon the popular imagination may be seen than
what emerged one catastrophic week in March 1955, when New York
WOR-TV programmed Kong for seven evenings in a row (a total of
sixteen showings). Many a rival network vice-president must have
scowled when surveys showed that Kong — the 1933 B-picture — had
lured away fat segments of the viewing populace from such powerful
competitors as Ed Sullivan, Groucho Marx and Bishop Sheen.

3   But even television has failed to run *King Kong* into oblivion. Cof-
fee-in-the-lobby cinemas still show the old hunk of hokum, with the
apology that in its use of composite shots and animated models the film
remains technically interesting. And no other monster in movie history
has won so devoted a popular audience. None of the plodding mum-

mies, the stultified draculas, the whitecoated Lugosis with their shiny
pinball-machine laboratories, none of the invisible stranglers, berserk
robots, or menaces from Mars has ever enjoyed so many resurrections.

Why does the American public refuse to let *King Kong* rest in peace? 4
It is true, I'll admit, that Kong outdid every monster movie before or
since in sheer carnage. Producers Cooper and Schoedsack crammed into
it dinosaurs, headhunters, riots, aerial battles, bullets, bombs,
bloodletting. Heroine Fay Wray, whose function is mainly to scream,
shuts her mouth for hardly one uninterrupted minute from first reel to
last. It is also true that Kong is larded with good healthy sadism, for
those whose joy it is to see the frantic girl dangled from cliffs and har-
ried by pterodactyls. But it seems to me that the abiding appeal of the
giant ape rests on other foundations.

Kong has, first of all, the attraction of being manlike. His simian na- 5
ture gives him one huge advantage over giant ants and walking vegeta-
bles in that an audience may conceivably identify with him. Kong's
appeal has the quality that established the Tarzan series as American
myth — for what man doesn't secretly imagine himself a huge hairy
howler against whom no other monster has a chance? If Tarzan recalls
the ape in us, then Kong may well appeal to that great-granddaddy pri-
mordial brute from whose tribe we have all deteriorated.

Intentionally or not, the producers of *King Kong* encourage this iden- 6
tification by etching the character of Kong with keen sympathy. For the
ape is a figure in a tradition familiar to moviegoers: the tradition of the
pitiable monster. We think of Ion Chaney in the role of Quasimodo, of
Karloff in the original *Frankenstein*. As we watch the Frankenstein monster's fumbling and disastrous attempts to befriend a flower-picking
child, our sympathies are enlisted with the monster in his impenetrable
loneliness. And so with Kong. As he roars in his chains, while barkers
sell tickets to boobs who gape at him, we perhaps feel something more
deep than pathos. We begin to sense something of the problem that engaged Eugene O'Neill in *The Hairy Ape*: the dilemma of a displaced
animal spirit forced to live in a jungle built by machines.

King Kong, it is true, had special relevance in 1933. Landscapes of 7
the depression are glimpsed early in the film when an impresario, seeking some desperate pretty girl to play the lead in a jungle movie, visits
souplines and a Woman's Home Mission. In Fay Wray — who's been
caught snitching an apple from a fruitstand — his search is ended. When
he gives her a big feed and a movie contract, the girl is magic-carpeted
out of the world of the National Recovery Act. And when, in the film's

climax, Kong smashes that very Third Avenue landscape in which Fay had wandered hungry, audiences of 1933 may well have felt a personal satisfaction.

8   What is curious is that audiences of 1960 remain hooked. For in the heart of urban man, one suspects, lurks the impulse to fling a bomb. Though machines speed him to the scene of his daily grind, though IBM comptometers ("freeing the human mind from drudgery") enable him to drudge more efficiently once he arrives, there comes a moment when he wishes to turn upon his machines and kick hell out of them. He wants to hurl his combination radioalarmclock out the bedroom window and listen to its smash. What subway commuter wouldn't love — just for once — to see the downtown express smack head-on into the uptown local? Such a wish is gratified in that memorable scene in Kong that opens with a wide-angle shot: interior of a railway car on the Third Avenue El. Straphangers are nodding, the literate refold their newspapers. Unknown to them, Kong has torn away a section of trestle toward which the train now speeds. The motorman spies Kong up ahead, jams on the brakes. Passengers hurtle together like so many peas in a pail. In a window of the car appear Kong's bloodshot eyes. Women shriek. Kong picks up the railway car as if it were a rat, flips it to the street and ties knots in it, or something. To any commuter the scene must appear one of the most satisfactory pieces of celluloid ever exposed.

9   Yet however violent his acts, Kong remains a gentleman. Remarkable is his sense of chivalry. Whenever a fresh boa constrictor threatens Fay, Kong first sees that the lady is safely parked, then manfully thrashes her attacker. (And she, the ingrate, runs away every time his back is turned.) Atop the Empire State Building, ignoring his pursuers, Kong places Fay on a ledge as tenderly as if she were a dozen eggs. He fondles her, then turns to face the Army Air Force. And Kong is perhaps the most disinterested lover since Cyrano: his attentions to the lady are utterly without hope of reward. After all, between a five-foot blonde and a fifty-foot ape, love can hardly be more than an intellectual flirtation. In his simian way King Kong is the hopelessly yearning lover of Petrarchan convention. His forced exit from his jungle, in chains, results directly from his single-minded pursuit of Fay. He smashes a Broadway theater when the notion enters his dull brain that the flashbulbs of photographers somehow endanger the lady. His perilous shinnying up a skyscraper to pluck Fay from her boudoir is an act of the kindliest of hearts. He's impossible to discourage even though the love of his life can't lay eyes on him without shrieking murder.

The tragedy of King Kong then, is to be the beast who at the end of   10
the fable fails to turn into the handsome prince. This is the conviction
that the scriptwriters would leave with us in the film's closing line. As
Kong's corpse lies blocking traffic in the street, the entrepreneur who
brought Kong to New York turns to the assembled reporters and pro-
claims: "That's your story, boys — it was Beauty killed the Beast!" But
greater forces than those of the screaming Lady have combined to lay
Kong low, if you ask me. Kong lives for a time as one of those persecuted near-animal souls bewildered in the middle of an industrial order,
whose simple desires are thwarted at every turn. He climbs the Empire
State Building because in all New York it's the closest thing he can find
to the clifftop of his jungle isle. He dies, a pitiful dolt, and the army
brass and publicity men cackle over him. His death is the only possible
outcome to as neat a tragic dilemma as you can ask for. The machine
guns do him in, while the manicured human hero (a nice clean Dartmouth
boy) carries away Kong's sweetheart to the altar. O, the misery of it all.
There's far more truth about upper-middle-class American life in *King
Kong* than in the last seven dozen novels of John P. Marquand.

A Negro friend from Atlanta tells me that in movie houses in colored   11
neighborhoods throughout the South, Kong does a constant business.
They show the thing in Atlanta at least every year, presumably to the
same audiences. Perhaps this popularity may simply be due to the fact
that Kong is one of the most watchable movies ever constructed, but I
wonder whether Negro audiences may not find some archetypical appeal in this serio-comic tale of a huge black powerful free spirit whom
all the hardworking white policemen are out to kill.

Every day in the week on a screen somewhere in the world, King   12
Kong relives his agony. Again and again he expires on the Empire State
Building, as audiences of the devout assist his sacrifice. We watch him
die, and by extension kill the ape within our bones, but these little deaths
of ours occur in prosaic surroundings. We do not die on a tower, New
York before our feet, nor do we give our lives to smash a few flying
machines. It is not for us to bring to a momentary standstill the civilization in which we move. King Kong does this for us. And so we kill him
again and again, in much-spliced celluloid, while the ape in us expires
from day to day, obscure, in desperation.

                                                                    (1960)

The Writer's Subject

1. What evidence does Kennedy bring in support of his contention that "no other monster in movie history has won so devoted a popular audience" as Kong? (paras. 1–3)

2. Summarize what Kennedy believes to be the reasons for "the abiding appeal of the giant ape."

3. Why does Kennedy refer to the Tarzan series as an American myth? What connection does this myth have with *King Kong*? (para. 5)

4. What does Kennedy mean by "the tradition of the pitiable monster"? (para. 6)

5. Why, in Kennedy's view, did the film have particular appeal to audiences during the Depression? (para. 7)

6. Why does Kennedy believe that the violent episode he describes in paragraph 8 would be satisfying to audiences in modern cities?

7. What use does Kennedy make of the well known fairytale, "Beauty and the Beast"? (para. 10)

8. What larger social significance does Kennedy perceive in the ordeal and the inevitable death of Kong? (para. 10)

9. To what does Kennedy attribute the popularity of King Kong with black audiences? (para. 11)

10. What does Kennedy mean when he says, in paragraph 12, that Kong's celluloid death is a "sacrifice"? Relate his comment to his choice of title.

The Writer's Style and Strategy

1. What details of phrasing and diction in the first four paragraphs reveal Kennedy's attitude to *King Kong* as film?

2. In paragraph 3 Kennedy compares Kong to other movie monsters. How does his description of Kong's rivals convey his sense of their inferiority?

3. What use does Kennedy make of analogy in paragraph 6 to convey Kong's "pitiable" qualities?

4. Discuss the organization of paragraph 8. How does Kennedy relate his assertion about modern urban man to the scene he describes from *King Kong*?

5. What is the tone of paragraph 9, and how is it established? Why does Kennedy describe Kong as "a gentleman" with a "sense of chivalry," and as "the hopelessly yearning lover of Petrarchan convention"?

6. The tone and language of this essay are informal, even colloquial, for the most part, but they change dramatically in the closing paragraphs (compare, for example, paragraphs 4 and 12). Why does Kennedy adopt this strategy?

7. Identify the major stages of Kennedy's discussion. At what point does he move from his introduction to his principal arguments? How is the reader prepared for the conclusion?

Suggested Topics for Writing and Discussion

1. Kennedy points to a number of reasons for the success of *King Kong*, including psychological, political and social. Choose a popular movie and discuss those elements which might claim for the film a deeper significance.

2. Choose a genre other than monster movies (e.g., Westerns, science fiction movies, spy thrillers, ninja and kung-fu movies) and account for the genre's popularity.

3. Many of the modern equivalents of *King Kong* are notable for their realistic violence and brutality, aided by the use of special effects. Do you think there is a case for the censoring of such films?

4. Locate reviews of the "remake" of *King Kong* which appeared in 1980 and the "sequel," *King Kong Lives!* which appeared in 1986. What do these reviews suggest about the continuing popularity of *King Kong*?

The Unforgiven: Histories and "Indians"
by Joseph Natoli

How to tell and show the story is more than ever contested.

— Dell Hymes

If we have survived the 'death of God' and the 'death of man,' we will surely survive the 'death of history' — and of truth, reason, morality, society, reality, and all the other verities we used to take for granted and that have now been 'problematized' and 'deconstructed.' We will even survive the death of postmodernism.

— Gertrude Himmelfarb

[T]he open discussion of scholarly research has made it rather difficult to conceal or to manufacture facts without arousing the skepticism or the scorn of colleagues. There are, after all, canons of evidence and standards of argument.

— Mary Lefkowitz

Logic is the attempt to comprehend the actual world by means of a scheme of being posited by ourselves; more correctly, to make it formulatable and calculable for us.

— Friedrich Nietzsche

1   I expected to see a remake of the 1960 John Huston Western classic *The Unforgiven*, but Clint Eastwood's 1992 *The Unforgiven* was an entirely different movie. Audrey Hepburn is unforgiven in the Huston film because she's an Indian living among whites and endangering those whites because her people want her back. Two cowpokes are unforgiven in Eastwood's film because one of them cut up a whore's face and the

madam, Strawberry Alice, isn't satisfied with the punishment the sheriff, Little Bill, has meted out. Two entirely different movies.

Why did Eastwood help himself to the Huston title and distance his   2
own movie so completely from it? I think it has to do with the nature of
unforgiving, what and why. Audrey Hepburn can't be forgiven for being an Indian and that failure haunts the film. In 1960 we're at the beginning of representing to ourselves that in regard to Native Americans
we're the ones who can't possibly be forgiven. We're at the beginning
of actually shaping a discourse, a saying that says we cannot be acquitted here for our actions nor can we efface from our memories our state
of being unforgiven.

Ten years later Arthur Penn's *Little Big Man* will straddle — in the   3
person of Jack Crabb, white pioneer and adopted Indian — the worlds
of those who are unforgiven and those who cannot forgive. In Kevin
Costner's 1990 *Dances with Wolves* the issue is no longer straddled. The
only release from the unbearable weight of being unforgiven is to give
up one's whiteness and become an Indian. In 1991 — coming fast and
furious now — *Black Robe* gives us an Indian view of white men: stupid, weak, unable to survive. While the Jesuit lives in the dream of a
Christian paradise, he cannot live in it as something connected to the here
and now. The Indians, on the other hand, link their dreams and the waking world. The Black Robe has never seen the paradise he speaks of but
he knows its laws: no women, no tobacco, a welcoming of death, and
nothing afterward but sitting on a cloud contemplating the face of God.
This dream that fails to enrich the white man's life but rather diminishes
it, is totally unacceptable to the Indians who recognize the hardships of
life but also its gifts; who leave this world reluctantly but do so with a
more vivid understanding of the spirit world they go to than the white
man. It is vivid because dream and imagination, the world as ceaseless
symbol of what lies unseen, of the working connection between visible
and invisible, has permeated their lives. Not the laws of the Church or
the inculcated dictates of conscience shape reality for them but the
crisscrossings of world and dream. "Nothing is more real than a dream."
The white man's reality is too thin, too lifeless a world for the Indian.

In 1992 a remake of *The Last of the Mohicans* blights the bright be-   4
ginning of a white New World with the darkness of the last days of the
Indians. In our beginning is already a disruption from the ecological
order of things, an impossible stepping away from the flux of order and
disorder that we, as well as all nature, are already and always within —
a place the Indian did not spend energy in moving out of or against, but

rather lived in concert with and within. Things were better before we even began to become Americans in our brave new world — a very unforgiving politics indeed.

5   A grand, lavish, heavily publicized 1992 version of *The Last of the Mohicans* does not come to the screen innocently, apolitically. Our culture's trek to the stars from *2001: A Space Odyssey* to the *Star Wars* trilogy and *The Right Stuff* had us looking toward the technological future, not our rapidly unraveling past. But a series of sci-fi films — *Blade Runner,* the *Alien* trilogy, and the *Terminator* films — dramatically displays the darkness of our cyberspace future, a darkness permeating William Gibson's "book of the year! winner of the Hugo, Nebula, and Philip K. Dick Awards," *Neuromancer.* A Baby Boom generation now in its Jean Brody prime was reared on Saturday afternoon Westerns at the local cinema. The Thoreauvian natural simplicity of life there at the frontier beginnings of our country, out west, living in concert with and within nature, and so on — all Saturday afternoon simulacra — becomes a place to run to as one runs from this: "Cyberspace. A consensual hallucination experienced daily by billions of legitimate operators, in every nation, by children being taught mathematical concepts.... A graphic representation of data abstracted from the banks of every computer in the human system. Unthinkable complexity. Lines of light ranged in the nonspace of the mind, clusters and constellations of data. Like city lights, receding."

6   In the lush greenery and agile heroism of Michael Mann's *Last of the Mohicans* we are treated to subliminal desires of the Baby Boom generation and, at the same time, the clear imagery of what they know never was but could have been. So doubly haunted by past and future, it is nevertheless those beginnings in nature, in multiple frontiers extending ever westward, which leave us unforgiving of ourselves. While there is something fated and inexorable regarding our cyberspace future, the past remains a ghostly garden of forking paths, all turns taken, wrong turns. We yearn to begin again, to rewrite our history. Yet again.

7   The West is being revisited in these films at the very beginning of the final decade of the century, as it is in Eastwood's film *The Unforgiven.* But there is a startling difference: Eastwood is not rewriting the historical account, scrutinizing more closely the nature of our guilt, our Western conscience, confounding our origins and our manifest destinies. He is, instead, marking the evanescence of our historical consciousness, the half-baked and half-blurred and half-heard accounts that form our present

perceptions of the past, including the West. The flow of past events, words, and contingencies can never forgive us our representation of them. Western films, from *High Noon* to *True Grit,* remain unforgiven. History is unforgivable because it cannot rid itself of the burden of its own deceits, its own lies, its own misrepresentations.

If I were to link both *Unforgivens* it would be thusly: we cannot in   8
the present attain a proper state of guilt, a true sense of being unforgiven in regard to what we have done to Native Americans because our representations are inevitably a barricade standing between what we are now and what we have been. History only enables us to live with ourselves.

Eastwood therefore doesn't offer another rewriting but rather gives   9
us a look at the way we form our lies, the way we write ourselves and envision ourselves within a state of either extending forgiveness or able to be forgiven. But the whole terrible muddle of telling and showing the American West — from heroes like William Munny and English Bob to heroic acts they performed to whores with hearts of gold — is invariably ensconced in the conscience, or lack thereof, of the teller and picked at by the conscience of the listener/reader/viewer.

Mr. W.W. Beauchamp, dime novel chronicler of the West, follows   10
English Bob the way Boswell followed Johnson. And W.W. recounts Bob's life with a smidgen of poetic license, all of which is contested by Little Bill who reads the account of McCorkle's death, laughs, and gives W.W. the "true story." Because he was there at the time. English Bob, who did the deed, doesn't contest Little Bill's account because he's been too badly beaten by Little Bill to speak. He's been unarmed by Little Bill and several of his deputies and then kicked viciously up and down Main Street until he's a bloody mess. We watch and wonder what account W.W. will give of this beating or what Little Bill will say about it later. Because he was there.

Perhaps we can draw back from the center of town and get a more   11
objective chronicle of the West from Eastwood the director, from the film as a whole, from Eastwood's own telling. Does that telling lead us down the road of truth to the truth? Is there a metanarrative positioning that points us not only to what the West was really like but how we can indisputably narrate what it was really like? Is there a way of showing or telling the past that after many detours we've finally discovered? After all, Eastwood debunks everything he can focus a lens on. What remains after this debunking — isn't that the truth, an accurate, reliable, historical retrieval? What's unforgivable, then, are the inaccurate, unreliable accounts, all those past stories we've heard about the West that

we swallowed. Why didn't we cut through the bunk and see the Truth? Like Clint Eastwood has done in *The Unforgiven?*

12   Or has he? I mean, how could he? Has he in this film appealed to the real historical facts or has he simply replaced an older ideological lens with a newer one? Has he cut through the stereotypes and found the real West? Has he exposed a prior frame of reference by standing on a solidly grounded, stable one? I think he has done a little of this, namely, the debunking, but rather than settle into a stable frame of sorting through the facts he has left us with a sense that there is no such inherently stable frame, that we narrate facts and in that narration fail to tell what that narrative frame doesn't see, can't conceive of, as part of the story. The transparency of historical events and texts gives way to mere reflections of the cultural frames we are in. The transparency of the Rodney King tape turns out to be nothing more than a reflection of the jury's cultural frame.

13   In this matter both the stereotypical real West, marvelously 'typed' in Huston's *The Unforgiven*, as well as the contesting of such stereotypes, notable for example in the 1991 National Museum of American Art "The West as America" exhibit, ground themselves in the notion that they can distinguish reality from illusion. In Huston's film, there is no marked space between the film's representation and the real West. The story may be artfully presented — this is what makes a great director like Huston great — but the essence of life as it was lived is not belied. In the case of the exhibit, there is an acknowledged recognition that while ideology is determining, we can still from a present nonideological perspective look back and see that imposition of ideology upon the real. In other words, we can see how an illusionary real West was assumed in the past to be the real West.

14   But unlike Eastwood's film, that exhibit of paintings of the West, mostly American Indians, winds up talking about each painting as if *now* the real story can be told, as if we had now jumped out of our cultural frames and taken up headquarters in that much talked of Archimedean point, that ideology-free perspective upon which we can look back and see the real West. So the commentary about the paintings seems like it comes from where Kevin Costner is at in *Dances with Wolves:* it wants to tell the story the Indians would tell, not the relatively few Indians alive today who have already been culturally severed, but the Indians back then. Back then when they were real Indians and the West, of course, was equally real.

Before saying something more about the real American West I want to   15
stray wider along the history path and discuss two 1992 Columbus films:
Christopher Columbus: The Discovery and *1492*. Point of immediate
connection: here we have a telling of the first encounter of Indian and
white man. But the whole matter of the present's positioning in 1992
and our revisiting of 1492 creates other interesting intersections. How
much of the 1992 cultural agenda can be read in these tales of
Columbus's voyage? Here we have a deeply embedded cultural narrative: the discovery of our own country. The most important date one
learns in elementary school. "In fourteen hundred and ninety-two,
Columbus sailed the ocean blue." How, we now say, could he discover
a land and people that had already been there for eons. From a Western
point of view, he discovered. From the point of view of the Indians who
were already there, he invaded. Columbus invaded and claimed a land
and people for Spain that was already inhabited. Since we are in 1992
quite sensitive to our history as the imposition of Western cultural values upon the Third World, we cannot unabashedly celebrate the folklore origin of our country. You might say that here our need to be politically correct shapes our historical correctness. We deem it necessary to
give the people who were already there their due and thus refrain from
seeing them as savage heathens needing to be Christianized, or as soul-
less and therefore subject to enslavement.

Decentering Columbus and centering the Native Americans he dis-   16
covered is a ticklish matter, especially since we as Americans would be
revisiting the discovery of America five hundred years after not to
deconstruct it as a point of origin but to celebrate it. How to celebrate a
beginning that can only be represented as sordid if we decenter the Europeans and center the Indians? How to celebrate a beginning that is
not a beginning, or only a beginning of the end for the people who were
already there? It is not surprising then that for the most part during 1992
we have been undecided about celebration. Already under economic attack by the Pacific Rim, the West does not particularly welcome this
occasion to rewrite-in-small its Great Age of Exploration and Discovery, a prominent section in every elementary school history book.

Mario Puzo, who wrote the screenplay for *Christopher Columbus:*   17
The Discovery, does not take on Columbus the way Oliver Stone took
on JFK or Costner took on the American West. While they progress along
a vertical path with a definite end in sight and a clear map to follow,
Christopher Columbus depicts this origin of the New World as broadly
layered, as a path intersecting numerous other paths, as much a middle

of many things, and a natural culmination of others, as a beginning. There would be no voyage to the New World if Isabella had not succeeded in destroying the Moorish hegemony in Spain and looting the Moorish coffers. In the name of Christianity. And in that name and with the profits of war she supports Cristobal Colon's voyage. Not before both Isabella and Ferdinand have agreed to the immodest demands of Colon, including a tenth of all the wealth of the Indies and the title of Admiral of the Ocean Sea.

18   The Church does not see Colon as its apostle but rather as a possible heretic, a free-thinker who challenges the teachings of the Church Fathers. Colon stands before the Inquisitorial bulk of no less than Marlon Brando as Torquemada wrapped in forty yards of black cloth, a seminal presence in the Court of Ferdinand and Isabella. St. Augustine had written there were no human souls a certain distance from Spain; Colon disagreed with this, pointing out the discovery of humans in Africa. Colon's beginning is thus already muddied. It already lies in an act of domination — the victory of Christianity over Islam. His course is also a deviation from established truths of the Church. But those truths have Spain in thrall. At the moment Colon's ships finally depart from port, there is a shipload of Jews who have refused to accept the Church's offer to become Christians or to give up their possessions (to Church and Crown) and leave Spain. Brando blesses them both, regretting the fact that the Jews have missed the opportunity to become Christians, and hoping that Colon gets lost at sea.

19   Europe, thusly, is the birthplace of discovery, the origin of exploration but it is itself fractious, caught between dominating and liberating impulses, between the order of absolute narratives and the interrogation of those narratives.

20   Colon is also entangled in this garden of forking paths and he never emerges, as does Jim Garrison and Lt. Dunbar, as a hero, romanticized, stereotyped, idealized, Hollywoodized. No mean feat considering he is our eponymous character, the agent of discovery. The decentering here is achieved not by villainizing him as Costner villainizes white men, but rather by depicting him as an ambitious man who has convinced himself that he has a correct map of the world, a man also with a secret, a very practical secret that indeed makes his voyage a success where others had failed. He has knowledge of what he calls "rivers of wind" that will drive him westward and then enable him to return. In short, he wants wealth and power and has the perseverance and know-how to succeed. If given the chance. While this is enough to get him across the

waters, it is not enough to see him through when he reaches land and encounters his Indians.

There our historical narrative gives up its multifocused lens and zooms 21 in on "the truth." Whereas the Europe and Columbus that shaped the voyage seem each to fork off in many directions and thus deny us both a definite point of origin — a sequence of events and/or a propelling, hidden force — or a well-documented historical understanding, the Indians and white men who first confront each other in the New World are dominated by a strong metanarrative. The Indians are marvelous, joyful, loving, trusting people and the white men are rapacious and violent. These Indians are the forebears of Kevin Costner's Indians. The daughter of the chief, sent as an envoy of peace to Columbus, is almond-eyed and bare breasted, large well-shaped breasts, and wonderful, innocent clear eyes, a lovely face full of natural innocence. Eve before the fiasco. She is met by a rapist and patricide, a tortured, divided soul — a harbinger of what angst awaits *Homo sapiens* in America's technological future, in its reign of *Machina sapiens*. He needs a shrink or Prozac but neither is as yet available on the shores of what will become Club Med.

  1492 is an exception in its refusal to undemonize the Indian while 22 demonizing the invader. Ridley Scott's *1492* is less troubled a film than *Christopher Columbus,* although Gerard Depardieu's Columbus is certainly troubled within a great romantic tradition of troubled heroes, of tortured souls, of rare individuals who have dreams that enable them to see further and deeper than the rest of us, who cannot give up their dreams regardless of the forces set against them. A very classic realist rendering this attempt to assert Columbus as a controlling presence. Someone is hoping that *1492* will be seen as it would have been when we went to the movies in the '50s, as if Depardieu's energy — and he is almost a force of nature — would seduce us away from our present uneasiness with not only this discovery but with a great romantic tradition of troubled heroes.

  Strangely, in spite of Depardieu's overbearing presence, his wresting 23 our attention from the dark corners of the event being narrated, the narrative is lackluster, dead-in-the-water. There is no fire here, no clash of what we in the audience are already troubled by. There is no playing into the dark corners of our culture's need to be unforgiving to itself. The angst of Depardieu's Columbus intersects deadened Hollywoodized angst. The voyage has been made too many times, always in less self-reflective times.

24   A hackneyed conflict of hero and villain conceals the real conflicts
with this voyage and this voyager. Armand Assante conspires against
Columbus but this villain in the end admits that his name will only be
recorded in history because it was linked to Columbus's. Villainy, too,
must bow to the presence of canonized history. Because this moral ri-
valry is foregrounded we do not in *1492* get a playing out of the tur-
moil of the European stage as we do in *Christopher Columbus*. But
inertia is disrupted at one point in the film: the representation of Indians whom Columbus meets.

25   In contrast to the Indians of *Christopher Columbus,* who are edenic,
these *1492* Indians are described by one Spanish nobleman as "monkeys." They are scrawny, dark, with twisted features and look very much
like World War II racist caricatures of the Japanese. Every time
Depardieu/Columbus speaks with the Indians, he is told that they are
lying. Ridley Scott's camera plays on their scowling features, as if we,
too, should believe they are liars, that this Other-ness is to be feared.

26   The most electrically charged scene is when Depardieu wanders as
if in a dream through a fight between the Europeans and the Indians.
Like frightening monsters from the Id, the Indians appear and then disappear before Depardieu's eyes. It is as if not only he but the viewer
were engaged in an unrepresentational confrontation with the people
we conquered, demonized, and then destroyed. It is as if we were still
trying to grapple — but in an unspecified, unrealized way — with the
people we dominated. At the same time there is visual buzz that links
that originary New World Western domination of nonwhites, that first
move on the Manifest Destiny chessboard, with a present '90s economic
domination of the West by the East. Destiny has transferred itself to the
Pacific Rim, back to Asia, the conjectured home of our Native Americans. If there is no easy way to continue in 1991 to demonize the Indian, then the appropriate Hollywood move to make is to translate old
demons into new ones. This is a brief scene, a brief departure from a
romanticized narrative that tries to package itself the way heroes and
commemorative, cultural-legacy narratives have always been packaged.

27 Judging by the "West as America" exhibit, Costner's acclaimed *Dances
with Wolves,* and the New World narrative of *Christopher Columbus:
The Discovery* we are now ready to revise the history of our relations
with Native Americans. We're finally telling the truth. We're finally separating stereotypes from hard realities, fictions from facts, and so on.
Before I go along that road I want to take up Arthur Scheslinger Jr.'s

notion that we can take sides on historical matters — and therefore sort
through the good and bad of the past, guilt and innocence — by applying certain humanitarian, democratic guidelines that foster "liberal democratic political regimes" that we believe are "expressions of the natural
order of things." What we want to sort through in the past is the workings of a progressive emancipatory spirit, a growing acknowledgment
of individual worth and freedom, a movement away from oppression,
chauvinism, superstition. Can we, in other words, agree to a fixed humane narrative of historical review, a perceptual lens that looks for the
fulfillment of these certain ideals? Our historical accounts would then
be relative to this communicative rationality — the past would be filtered to us through it — but that would be okay because it would be
encouraging us or chastising us in a way that does us the most good.
History becomes our culture's report card and the criteria of evaluation
are at the highest, most estimable level.

In his *Atlantic* article, "Was America a Mistake. Reflections on the 28
Long History of Efforts to Debunk Columbus and His Discovery," Arthur
Schlesinger Jr. defines the criteria by which we can judge the past and
according to which we can know what perspective on the past to take.
The issue of whether we have any reliable way to retrieve the past becomes irrelevant; the important thing is that we have the means to sort
through conflicting representations of the past and to attach ourselves
to the one that moves us further along this inscribed path of what we
should be, or what any culture should be moving toward. We move along
by distinguishing what impedes and what hinders a culture from achieving "the great liberating ideas."

What are they in Schlesinger's view? "Individual dignity, political 29
democracy, equality before the law, religious tolerance, cultural pluralism, artistic freedom ... ideas to which most of the world today aspires."
Before we begin to inscribe matters in a pro-Aztecs manner, Schlesinger
argues, we should realize that both Europe and Mexico in 1492 suppressed individual freedom and human rights and that Latin America's
failure "to achieve humane, stable, and progressive democracies" cannot be blamed on Columbus. But while we cannot know whether the
Aztecs would have "learned to read and write and would have abandoned their commitment to torture, obsidian knives, and blood-stained
pyramids," Europe did evolve "great liberating ideas" out of anguish,
self-criticism, and bad conscience.

The issue here, as Schlesinger presents it, is not whether European 30
culture ever did wean itself away from mass extermination ("ethnic

cleansing"), high-tech weaponry, and blood-stained jungles and deserts. The issue rather is whether we can settle on these "great liberating ideas" as a means of sifting through history and establishing historical accounts that clearly show the ebb and flow of these. We encase the past within the metanarrative of these ideals and recount it within the implicit universal rule of judgment such a framing affords. The actual grasp of the past in itself is too clearly a visionary enterprise. But the capacity to grasp it within a certain order of things, within a universal thrust of all cultures, gives us a rod by which we bend history. We bend it but only for the purpose of placing it within the compass of "a new and generous vision of our common life on this interdependent planet." This is not a little and local bending of history that perhaps is not so generous to those in other locales. No, it is presented to us as natural and universal.

31   What is presently in 1992 going on in a balkanized Yugoslavia between Serbs and Croats, Muslim and Christian, clearly indicates that Europe's ethnic rivalries produce Aztec-size bloodbaths. Democracy is foundering in a contemporary America of rich and poor while the Soviet attempt to ground *its* "great liberating ideas" in economic equality has collapsed. The play of the market is indifferent to any liberation except its own liberation from "great liberating ideals" that intrude the common life of humankind into market play. Western cultural hegemony has achieved no determinate, fixed, absolute hold on individual freedom and dignity, human rights, political democracy, equality before the law, religious tolerance, cultural pluralism, and artistic freedom.

32   We are propelled, however, by our own cultural linkages of these, linking them with vague but grand chunks of reality whenever we narrate what we're all about. That we are now sensitive to the local positioning of our own cultural linkages is, of course, demonstrative of our present self-reflexiveness — our urge to jump back from the results of our own real-izing. But this acknowledgment of cultural relativity is a new shifting and while it is carried through in Eastwood's film it is not present in Schlesinger's ostensibly more astute meditations in *The Atlantic,* which claim to have a firm hold on the natural order of things.

33   The point is that we don't get to the other side of our culture's local biases by, for instance, going at history under the guidance of a series of inflated and floating, puffy, and abused signifiers like "individual freedom" and "equality before the law." We can't do so because at the present moment the power of the free market reconnects grandiose notions of individual freedom to matters of product choice. We become free of any

regulations that will hamper needs creation and the ethos of "I shop, therefore I am." That ethos makes all past demands for individual freedom forgettable, unrecognizable, of little interest. We fail, for instance, to recognize the lack of freedom of the underclass nonconsumer. That feeling is repressed by the play of the market.

History becomes a long fight to get us to this point — market seduction and repression. And because we have a fallen sense of individual freedom, there is no way that we can preserve that equality which makes individual freedom possible and also tempers it with a recognition of the existence of others no less important than ourselves. Instead of supporting cultural pluralism, this economic privileging reduces it to a new moral hierarchy: consumption matters most, those who can consume the most matter the most, those who cannot consume have no existence, although they remain tantalized by the whole culture's urgings to fulfill themselves through consumption. 34

Enough. Sufficient to undermine our confidence in "great liberating ideas" as the way to deal with the past. The day of blithely imposing a grand narrative scrutiny of the past, of weighing and discarding, is now itself past. To do history now is to observe how one cultural inscription is exposed by another, how a questioning of stereotypes exposes its own shaky premises, and how our narratives of the past must foreground the narrative protocols we have assumed. 35

Let's head west once again. 36

Huston's *The Unforgiven* and Costner's *Dances with Wolves* are two contesting Western narratives while Eastwood's *The Unforgiven* is about how history itself is narrated. How does Huston's film abide by the stereotypes that Costner exposes? Doesn't in fact Huston show us that how we see and respond to things emerges from where and how we're brought up? No one can assume an objective position from which to observe and recount the truth. Ben, the older brother, can't hate his sister Rachel when she's revealed to be an Indian because the way he sees and responds to her is already shaped by his love for her. Cash, another brother, rejects Rachel when he finds out about her because his real-izing is already contorted by his hatred for all Indians. Rachel herself cannot jump out of her upbringing within the white narrative and suddenly see the world as an Indian. She can neither see herself nor her own brother, a Kiowa chief who comes to claim her, as they are, as real Indians. The mother, the only one who has always known Rachel to be an Indian, cannot see Rachel as anything other than as that sweet baby girl who, 37 in reality, died at birth. The truth emerges in every case from a frame of representation, different frames producing different truths. Indeed, the film has begun with the Voice of One Crying in the Wilderness, a fiery prophet who announces himself to be the God of Vengeance so that "Truth Be Told and Wrong Righted." It is this promise to reveal the truth, to fix guilt and establish the right, to lay bare what must not be forgiven but damned, that Huston's film does not fulfill. All that is laid bare as the film ends as it begins — with the flight of geese overhead observed by the players below — is the multiplicity of narrative worlds both individuals and cultures are already in and the drama of their collisions, as many histories as there are collisions.

38 Costner, on the other hand, clings to many classic realist formula elements: immediate and steadfast identification with Costner, clear-cut opposition of good and evil, presence of a historical record (Dunbar's journal) that says this is not illusion but reality, and a determinate moral closure. In his zeal to set the record straight and to allow the Indians a chance to tell their side of things, to relate a countermemory, Costner falls prey to some prevalent Western stereotyping he wishes to debunk. Indians become noble; nature naturally fills them with good humor. They have a deep, abiding sense of brotherhood and equality, a grounding tradition of ancient wisdom, a harmonious relationship with nature, and so on. White men are guilt-ridden, sadistic, debauched, and just plain unnatural.

39   While Huston is aware of the difficulties in the telling, in showing the past, Costner just wants to tell his side of things and tell it so that it doesn't seem like a positioned telling but the real truth at last. It is not the tentativeness of making such pronouncements regarding the truth here in the '90s that Costner reflects but an absolutely unfissured certitude, an infectious bravado that doesn't take a moment out to doubt itself. In this he intersects that same desire for a determinate past and present, a return to firm categories of right and wrong, truth and falsehood, which propelled Ronald Reagan into office. And just as Reagan turned out to be launching balloons full of hot air, Costner's dance with the real West is danced to a tune of his own.

40 But views of the past must always be forgiven because we cannot hope to assert that unpositioned truth of the past, that stable record of historical reference, which would have no need of forgiveness because it is the truth. By means of this truth it would be possible to point out which

stories of the past, which histories, are so pernicious, so destructive of our humanity, so deceitful and beguiling, that they must remain unforgiven. Blessed are we when the truth of the past is revealed, when no conflicting narratives emerge.

When has that been? Skinheads today venerate Hitler while others 41 assert Hitler was not a fascist but a liberal. Others assert that the Jewish holocaust did not happen and challenge anyone to prove it did. Truman has been evoked by both Clinton and Bush as a historical mentor — clashing evocations, same historical entity. The very foundations of Western culture are being rocked by histories of Asian and African origins. Serbs recount a different history than Croats, Croats than Bosnians. The American South still has a different history of the War between the States (Civil War?) than the North. And the assassination of JFK has led to a state of parallel historicizing that continues into the present. Everything from Vietnam to the Reagan-Bush era is recounted in multiple ways from these universes of parallel history. These conflicts are orchestrated — sounded or silenced — by the present, another disturbing feature of a postmodern history.

The past draws us to it not because of its variable vividness but be- 42 cause we wish to bring something in the present to life and often find it easiest to do so in terms of a record of life we have already lived. In making the present vivid, often for political and/or economic reasons, we use the past like a palette of colors. We take what we need, win the day, or sell the product despite the fact that someone will always be protesting our exploitation of the past, challenging its historical accuracy from the presumed pedestal of totalizing truth telling and determinate retrieval of the past.

We are always in the process of transgressing someone else's con- 43 struction of what really happened. Accounts other than our own are always unforgiven. Their history is always unforgiven. It is to Clint Eastwood's credit that he shows us that all stories about the past are equally unreliable and therefore equally unforgiven. It is the universality of this plight that must render all our histories forgivable. Even those of the real American West.

(1992)

The Writer's Subject

1. Who is "unforgiven" in John Huston's movie of 1960, and who in Clint Eastwood's movie of 1992? What significance does the writer attach to this difference? (paras. 1–2)

2. In what way is the Indian view of life different from that of the white man, as depicted in *The Black Robe*? (para. 3)

3. In what way is Eastwood's *The Unforgiven* different from other movie Westerns in its handling of the subject of the American West? (paras. 7–9)

4. Does Eastwood's film, in Natoli's opinion, provide us with a picture of "what the West was really like"? If not, what *has* Eastwood shown us? (paras. 10–12)

5. What do the 1962 film *The Unforgiven* and the 1991 exhibit "The West as America" have in common despite their differing versions of the old West? (paras. 13–14)

6. What, according to the writer, was the problem facing Americans in 1992 who wished to celebrate Columbus's voyage of 1492? (paras. 15–16)

8. What are the chief differences between the two Columbus movies, as described by Natoli? (paras. 17–26)

9. What point is Natoli making by describing the daughter of the Indian chief in *Christopher Columbus: The Discovery* as "Eve before the fiasco"? (para. 21)

10. In what ways does the movie *1492* present American Indians differently from their representation in *Christopher Columbus: The Discovery*? (paras. 21–26)

11. Natoli summarizes the "great liberating ideas," the criteria or guidelines by which, according to the historian Arthur Schlesinger, we can judge "the good and bad of the past." (para. 27) What are these liberating ideas, as Natoli presents them? Does he agree that such ideas do offer a means of judging history? (paras. 31–35)

12. What, according to the writer, has "the play of the market" done to notions of individual freedom and cultural pluralism? (paras. 33–34)

13. According to Natoli, Costner's *Dances With Wolves* "falls prey to some prevalent Western stereotyping he wishes to debunk." In what ways? (para. 38)

14. What parallel does Natoli draw between Ronald Reagan and Kevin Costner? (para. 39)

15. Why must views of the past "always be forgiven"? (paras. 40–43)

The Writer's Style and Strategy

1. What is the thesis of Natoli's essay? Show where it is given explicit expression, and trace the main points of its development.

2. Discuss the use Natoli makes of the passage from *Neuromancer* at the end of para. 5.

3. Discuss the contrast Natoli describes in para. 5, between "the darkness of our cyberspace future" and "the Thoreauvian natural simplicity of life" in the early settlement of the U.S. by European immigrants.

4. Why does Natoli move from a discussion of movie representations of the old West to an analysis of two 1992 films about Christopher Columbus? (para. 15)

5. Natoli contrasts the figure of Christopher Columbus as drawn by Mario Puzo to Jim Garrison (from the movie *JFK*) and Lieutenant Dunbar (the hero of *Dances With Wolves*). What is the point of this contrast? (para. 20)

6. Natoli often uses the first-person pronouns "I" and "we." What effects is he perhaps striving for by employing this strategy?

7. How does Natoli relate the issues he has raised about representations of the old West to broader questions of contemporary politics and social change? See particularly the concluding section of the essay, paras. 40–43.

Suggested Topics for Writing and Discussion

1. The author discusses the difficulties experienced by Americans attempting to celebrate the "discovery" of America in 1492. Compare his account with others in magazines or newspapers published in 1992. How did Americans reconcile their wish to commemorate Columbus's voyage with a need to acknowledge the subsequent fate of the native peoples after first contact?

2. Natoli lists some notable "conflicting narratives" of events in our own century, evidence of the difficulty of ever arriving at an objective and "true" account of the past. (para. 41) Choose a major event in recent history and examine three or four different accounts of it. Indicate where significant differences occur in the narratives, and say why you think those differences are present.

3. What makes Clint Eastwood's movie *The Unforgiven* so significant in Natoli's eyes? Has he, in your opinion, exaggerated the film's importance?

4. Natoli notes how today Americans are sensitive to their history "as the imposition of Western cultural values upon the Third World" (para. 15), and have revised some of the older notions about the origin of their country in accordance with the current "cultural agenda." Do you see any parallel here with the history of the relations between French and English in Canada, and changing views of those relations?

5. Choose another movie about the old West, and offer your own views about its portrayal of the society there portrayed. Ask yourself whether the filmmaker has been able to rise above clichés and stereotypes to an objective view of the past.

6. Examine Natoli's statement that "To do history now is to observe how one cultural inscription is exposed by another" (para. 35) Take another historical period or event dramatized on film (e.g., World War II, or the Vietnam War), and compare two screen versions made at different times. Is the later version any "truer" than the earlier version?

Loose Canons

by Rick Salutin

The first time I heard the phrase was in a Chinese restaurant during the 1
*late 1960s, after a political meeting or protest march. Those things built
an appetite. Someone always has to take charge when you're ordering
Chinese food, and someone did. She listed a number of dishes and asked
if it sounded okay. "I don't know," somebody else said, "whether that's
a politically correct order." It got a little laugh, as a touch of slightly
self-conscious left-wing humour. But it worked because the cuisine was
Chinese, and Maoism was then the most popular fare on the left's ideological menu.*

Around the same time, a comic strip called Korrect Line Komix ap- 2
*peared in the alternative press along with the Fabulous Furry Freak
Brothers. A chubby little Mao face in the corner of each panel said things
like, "Where do correct ideas come from?" Next panel he'd ask, "Do
they fall from the sky?" Then some guy would get bonked on the head
by a falling idea and Mao would chirp, "Nope!" A nice send-up. It's a
shame really: people on the left concoct a phrase that pokes fun at themselves — a healthy instinct — and more than twenty years later every
mass medium in the triumphant capitalist West is using it to pummel
whatever spirit of opposition remains in the post-Cold War world.*

The media frenzy over political correctness, or PC, has consumed 3
most of 1991. It started before the Gulf War and outlasted it. It must be
trying to tell us something. To me the best way to treat the subject is to
start with that media reaction before going back to have a look at the
thing itself. I'm not saying the object of all the attention doesn't exist;

it does, and I'll get to it. But the reality of political correctness is minuscule compared to the orgy of media attention — the overkill — launched in its name. I mean, how big should a story be to rate cover or feature treatment in *Newsweek*, *New York*, *Time*, *The Atlantic*, *The New Republic*, and (wait for it, because you had to) *Maclean's*? We're talking about World War III or the fall of the Berlin Wall. At least you'd think so.

4   The first cover story showed up like a grim Christmas present in the December 24, 1990, issue of *Newsweek*, wrapped in the words, "Watch What You Say: THOUGHT POLICE." The story centred on universities, where, as *Time* later put it, "a troubling number of teachers, at all levels, regard the bulk of American history and heritage as racist, sexist, and classist and believe their purpose is to bring about social change." The evidence was mainly anecdotal. Check that: entirely anecdotal. In fact, *all* the coverage has revealed nothing more than a batch of scary tales: some students or professors being criticized or harassed for using certain language; some changes in curriculum to de-emphasize certain authors and stress others. No statistics to show how widespread the phenomenon is, no studies or surveys, no coherent theory to explain the thing and put it in perspective. (One of the few stats I did find said 100 to 200 U.S. colleges and universities — out of 3,600 — had tried to restrict speech on PC grounds, and a number of those restrictions had now been withdrawn.) Even the anecdotes were often feeble. "If I was at lunch [in the dorm]," a Stanford student told *Newsweek*, "and we started talking about something like civil rights, I'd get up and leave.... I knew they didn't want to hear what I had to say." Now, into each life a little rain must fall, but for these stories, newsmagazine correspondents all over America are asked to submit reports, which are exhaustively culled by editors at head office — and *this* tale made the cut?

5   There was also some light analysis in *Newsweek*. Like: "PC is, strictly speaking, a totalitarian philosophy." Huh? Where is it taught? Name a single thinker or book that expounds this philosophy. Elsewhere, PC was called a "movement." So what are its organizational structures or publications or membership? For Pete's sake, "Star Trek" is more of a movement than PC. It makes better sense to call racism a movement or philosophy; you could name spokesmen, institutions, guiding thoughts, and thinkers. *Newsweek* also struggled to uncloak the obscure literary technique called deconstruction, seen as a deadly weapon in the PC armament, and expose its threat to, gasp, The Canon. Some of this gets pretty unreal. The foes of PC are furious over challenges to the list of

literary and philosophical classics taught as the Western "canon" and
the attempts to add on, say, "testimonials written by oppressed Guate-
malan women" — as Ray Conlogue of *The Globe and Mail* put it in a
fine show of Western open-mindedness. They're terrified that Shakespeare and, of all things, Rabelais will be tossed out with the morning
garbage. Yet even the notion of canonization in its original sense — establishing the text of the Bible — is controversial: the Catholic canon
differs from the Protestant, which differs from the Jewish. The revered
canon of Western literature wasn't even set until the 1930s, in the case
of its British component; and until the 1950s, for the American. I don't
mean there's not a lot of good stuff in there — I'm partial to Shakespeare myself, though I doubt he'd be peeing his pants over whether he
made the canon — but there's mediocrity, too: did you ever try reading
The Pilgrim's Progress?

The whole investigation by *Newsweek* had a thumb-sucking quality,   6
a sulky sense of grievance that anyone would dare challenge the prevailing value system in the West, and especially "the single most compelling idea in human history, individual liberty, which as it happens is
just now sweeping the entire world." *Hey, we're number one, our product is wiping the competition, how come they're raining on our parade?*
Still, *Newsweek* wasn't entirely one-sided. It ran an interview with a
prof who supported curriculum change, and an account from someone
who'd worked on a campus program to combat traditional prejudices.
In retrospect, *Newsweek* starts to look good.

New York magazine's January 21, 1991, cover showed a bespecta-   7
cled white fellow tortured by the question "Are you Politically Correct?"
There were photographs of Hitler Youths burning books in the 1930s,
along with student guidelines handed out by Smith University, and wash-
room graffiti at Brown. Imagine how swamped you'd be if you decided
to go after racism or sexism on the basis of such "evidence?" *Time*'s
long essay on April 1 agreed that universities should be "centers for the
critical examination of Western beliefs," but said this had now taken a
"strident turn" — as if upping the volume were cause for declaring a
national emergency. It singled out an assistant professor who teaches a
course on white male writers; she argues that since there are courses on
women writers and black writers, why not one on white men? Personally, I don't see the fallacy. In *The New Republic*, historian Eugene
Genovese called the PC people "storm troopers" and demanded
counterterror in response. Others referred to PC as "fascism of the left"
and "the new McCarthyism." A little overstated, perhaps, since, unlike

German, Italian, or Japanese fascism, or the original McCarthyism, the PC movement has no government representing it, no money behind it, no mass media or propaganda presence, no paramilitary forces. What would fascism have amounted to with so little support? Something like the PC "movement" — maybe. The *Atlantic*'s March cover story, by a former Reagan staffer, Dinesh D'Souza, quoted a teacher at Duke University who hopes "to create a Marxist culture in this country, to make Marxism an unavoidable presence in American social, cultural and intellectual life." A man and his dream, to be sure, but enough to make an entire society tremble? At a time when even the Soviet Communist Party had ditched Uncle Karl? The worst, though, was yet to come.

8   In late May, "Canada's Weekly Newsmagazine" became the last on its block to get a PC cover. It showed a young white couple in graduation garb with gags over their mouths and hurt expressions. The title was "The Silencers." In his note to readers, *Maclean's* editor, Kevin Doyle, condemned the "vociferous intolerance" of what he called "the Nons." Though he found many practices they were protesting (racism, sexism, fascism) "distasteful" — "in the extreme," actually — he said their own actions represented "a far more insidious evil." Doyle relied for backup, as did the cover story, on what he called "a recent, little noticed speech" by George Bush. The speech was about as little noticed as the heart scare Bush had later the same day he gave it. It was valuable in one way though: it summed up the shallowness and hypocrisy of much of the assault against PC.

9   Bush criticized political correctness for declaring off limits certain topics, expressions, "and even certain gestures." Yet he himself had run against Michael Dukakis on the issue of the pledge of allegiance, and had tried to introduce a constitutional amendment forbidding gestures demeaning the U.S. flag. Bush attacked those who'd set "citizens against one another on the basis of their class or race" — after using mug shots of the convicted black killer Willie Horton to create white anxiety about Dukakis. He denounced "the temptation to assign bad motives to people who disagree with us," yet had called Saddam Hussein *worse* than Hitler and the war against him a simple case of good versus evil. Bush warned of "the growing tendency to use intimidation rather than reason in settling disputes," but rejected sanctions against Iraq despite evidence that they were working. And he praised the freedom to speak one's mind as "the most fundamental and deeply revered of all liberties," after attacking Dukakis as a "card-carrying member" of the American Civil Liberties Union. Bush, just like Kevin Doyle, found the desire to com-

bat racism and sexism "laudable," apparently forgetting that after his 1988 television debate with Geraldine Ferraro he had told the world that he'd "kicked some feminist ass." Bush's speech was normal political pap. What's remarkable is the deference with which Doyle and *Maclean's* — alone in all of journalism — treated it. Two weeks later, even *Maclean's* own American columnist, Fred Bruning, ridiculed the speech.

The text of the *Maclean's* cover story was mostly a rehash, larded **10** with weasel words ("many academics," "some feminists," "some social commentators," "critics say," "lots of people") to hide the absence of specifics. A psychology prof at the University of Western Ontario grumbled "I have to measure my words carefully" — which doesn't sound like such a horrid burden for a teacher and scholar. Besides Bush, the piece peddled one other U.S. authority, an employee of the National Association of Scholars, which is an anti-PC organization funded by several seriously right-wing American foundations. *Maclean's* quoted him seven times in two pages, and included his photo. Speaking of pictures, one could do a little deconstruction of the juxtaposition of George and Barbara Bush at a graduation, waving and smiling with open hands, set across the page from a sea of mostly black graduates raising clenched fists. Then, there was one of those joyous generalizations only *Maclean's* has the staff to research: "From Vancouver to Miami, people say that they are constantly being harangued or induced to change." I'd love to see the transcripts. Historian Michael Bliss lamented that, these days, "You're not allowed to sin against gender equality." Pity. But as the mag assured us, in another breathtaking *aperçu,* "off-color and ethnic jokes are now as rare in mixed company as the three-martini lunch." If you think you've heard the odd such joke lately, well, you probably just drank too much at lunch.

What's a touch hard to take is how distressed Doyle and his employ- **11** ees get about "The Silencers" when they've been known to practise some, let's say, restraint themselves. Merely on the level of editing, *Maclean's,* as Robert Fulford has said, "is the most rigidly edited magazine in Canadian history." Or have you never wondered why all those reporters write in *exactly* the same style? One former correspondent says any time he proudly reported anything that hadn't appeared elsewhere, the editors would say, "Good. We'll cut that." Or there was the time *Maclean's* airbrushed the genitals out of a painting by Attila Richard Lukacs, after Doyle had warned the art department to stay alert for "objectionable details." In fact, *Maclean's* own employees have formed an "Editorial Integrity Committee" evincing a certain lack of confidence in their leader.

A survey taken in-house by that committee showed widespread alarm over "lack of balance" in the political-correctness cover story itself. For another case of "Stifling," as the subhead on the cover put it, consider Kevin Doyle's own, ah, alteration to an exclusive interview with President Bush himself in the summer of 1990. Bush referred to a dinner he'd had with Brian Mulroney, "and a couple of drinks, I might add" — an interesting reference since there'd been much speculation at that time about whether Mulroney had returned to his old drinking habits because of Meech and Oka. Then Bush added, "Oh, I hope I'm not getting the prime minister into trouble," or words to that effect. It showed an impressive awareness of Mulroney's medical and political problems, but Doyle cut the line from the story.

12   And for a sample of political correctness of a different sort, just glance at *Maclean's* cover two weeks later. "The Private Prime Minister" featured seven pages of exclusive photos of a day in the life of Brian. It came in the wake of this year's spate of rumours and reports about the PM, which centred on marital breakdown. Strangely enough, nine of the twenty-eight pictures included Mila or the kids — with lots of kissyface and popping in unexpectedly on hubby at the office. The shots were taken by a *Maclean's* photo editor who happened to have been Mulroney's official photographer during his first year in office.

13   There's been some other Canadian comment on PC. "How long might it take to repair the damage wrought by the PC movement?" fretted Conlogue in *The Globe and Mail*, neatly assuming a devastation of the campuses that had nowhere been established. On CTV's "W5," the regular political panel also grumped about the subject. The New Democrats' Gerry Caplan was sure they all regretted that everybody on their panel was a white man in a suit, but no one volunteered to step down and improve the balance. In an impassioned column, Dalton Camp said he could remember "when it was considered politically correct for anyone to say anything that came to mind and when outrageous opinion was not only indulged, but encouraged." Funny, I don't. He never said when that happened, but you got the impression he was thinking of the *fifties*.

14   All those poor fellows in suits with columns and tenure are twitching frantically about a lost golden age that never was, except maybe for them; and about a new McCarthyism, or worse, for which there's only meagre evidence. Sure there are some students and profs making demands. Ranged against them are the entire mass media, most of the academic establishment, and politicians starting at the level of the president of the U.S. You get the idea the anti-PCs might manage to hold their

own. Could that really be what it's all about: a bunch of guys sitting there in their bastions of privilege, at the *Globe* or the university, with tenure or a by-line they've worked and schemed to acquire, and feeling so incredibly insecure they go wild to protect that privilege against — not even a threat but a mild and fairly marginal challenge?

You don't hear much from these same people about a different threat 15 to university independence: the invasion of business influence, for which there's lots of evidence — joint academic-corporate councils and forums, grants to encourage research that will increase profits, "joint-venture discovery parks" on campus just like the industrial parks cities build to compete for business, deals profs negotiate with companies on patents and discoveries, university-business liaison, and real-estate officers alongside the deans and registrars. You could say there are signs of a threat to academic independence there — but no magazine covers.

And finally, there's the mainstream media's own version of PC, though 16 they never call it that. As Thomas Walkom of the *Toronto Star* wrote, "This year's most telling examples of political correctness come not from the dispossessed but from the powerful: the media jingos who treated any criticism of the Gulf War as treasonous; and the business lobbies that — regardless of the circumstances — rail against government deficits."

So, having established that the entire media offensive against the so- 17 called PC movement is overblown, dishonest, and hypocritical, I'd like to turn to the phenomenon itself. Personally and politically, I find it a pain in the ass.

It can be irksome and picky, for starters, especially concerning lan- 18 guage: doing search-and-destroy missions on phrases like "a nip in the air," or "a chink in the armour," or words like "blackmail." And I can't get comfortable with the phrase "people of colour." It sounds prissy and self-congratulatory to me. I feel like the San Francisco writer who was upbraided for dumping on the term, and said he didn't want to discuss it until he'd had his coffee of morning.

It gets more serious though. People or groups with rigid, "politically 19 correct" attitudes and demands on matters like racism and sexism really can be a threat — but *not* to pillars of the establishment like *Newsweek*, *Maclean's*, and George Bush, who've been responding to them with the equivalent of the war against Iraq. The politically correct people are generally pretty marginal and powerless, striving for a toe-hold in the curriculum or hiring policy, or just to be noticed. They pose no serious danger to the right, or the establishment; but they can be a real problem for the left, and for efforts actually to combat forces like racism and sexism. They muddy the water, set people of goodwill against each other, create disunity, and present a version of their causes that alienates potential allies and provides a big fat target for their enemies.

20   This is an old story. It happened even to Maoism, to go back to where we started. Just twenty years ago, it didn't look all that implausible, in China or elsewhere. But the mindless and parodic versions of it mouthed by students and others during the Cultural Revolution made it impossible to ever take seriously again. Mao himself, who had a sense of humour — just read some of his unofficial speeches — wondered if there wasn't a plot to make his ideas look ridiculous.

21   The PC mind-set is just a phoney nuisance for the establishment, but it can make real trouble for serious movements of social change. Consider, for instance, the battle of the Women's Press, a small feminist publisher painstakingly created over a period of sixteen years. A few years ago it nearly died in a virtual blood bath of political correctness about who was racist. There were demands for public confessions, stacked meetings, and the lock on the door got changed. In the end eight women who'd put their life's effort into building a useful feminist institution were driven out, and the bitterness and infighting are still going on. Not exactly the way you build an alternative movement to challenge the status quo.

22   Then there's the case of June Callwood, who until the end of 1989 was a rare voice of social conscience at the new, Darwinian *Globe and Mail*. Publisher Roy Megarry had been trying to ditch her for years, unsuccessfully. Then, outside a writers' convention, the black author Marlene Nourbese Philip harangued Callwood for racism — a ludicrous charge. In frustration, Callwood told Philip to "fuck off," which was duly reported, re-reported, and editorialized about in our newspaper of record. The upshot was that Callwood left the paper, not really a great victory for the cause of reform — though Marlene Philip was the subject of a flattering profile in the paper a few days after Callwood departed.

23   Or take even the case of the playwright Joanna Glass, a person of talent and goodwill, but little experience of political action, who attended a Women Playwrights Conference in Toronto recently. She was so alienated by the posturing and bullying that went on concerning colour, and men, and the "correct" views on women in the arts that she "came away from it deploring (for a change) not man's inhumanity to man, but women's inhumanity to women." My own feeling is that so much needs changing in this society — and the larger world society too — and the forces in power are so cocky and entrenched that it's sheer idi-

ocy to drive away potential supporters like Joanna Glass, while creating deep divisions among those already committed.

The scariest part of all is who you find yourself agreeing or disa- 24
greeing with — for instance, when the well-meaning advisers to York University on the status of women, and race and ethnic relations, write, in the style of an encyclical, "White males cannot be victims of racism or sexism. Discrimination results from systemic oppression." Sorry, but racism and sexism are more flexible than that, which is what makes them hard to eradicate. Oppression can be practised by victims; in fact, victims are powerfully motivated to victimize others in turn — if they can get away with it. On the other hand, I reluctantly nod my head to Lorrie Goldstein, in the odious (and often racist and sexist) *Toronto Sun*, when he says, "Political correctness isn't just good liberal intentions run amok.... It is racism and, for that matter, sexism.... Accept that only blacks can teach African history or that only men can be sexist and you are not very far from accepting that blacks have rhythm, that women make lousy drivers, and that Jews are good with money." Ouch. The *Toronto Sun* gets it right?

So a pox on both their houses, both the media hysterics of the main- 25
stream and the self-righteous crusaders of PC. It will, however, require a considerably larger pox to deal with the former than with the latter.

(1991)

The Writer's Subject

1. What is the nature of "political correctness," as it is described in Salutin's article?

2. What deficiencies does Salutin point to in the coverage of "political correctness" by such magazines as *Newsweek*, *Time*, *The New Republic*, and *The Atlantic*?

3. What fears are expressed by the foes of political correctness concerning the possible fate of the classics of Western literature? (para. 5) Does Salutin think this fear is justified?

4. On what grounds does Salutin attack *Maclean's* handling of the political correctness issue?

5. What does Salutin mean by his reference to "political correctness of a different sort" in the pages of *Maclean's*? (para. 12)

6. What in Salutin's view is a greater threat than "political correctness" to the independence of thought at universities?

7. What dangers do "the politically correct people" pose to our society, in Salutin's view?

The Writer's Style and Strategy

1. Discuss the play on words in Salutin's title.

2. "Loose Canons" first appeared in the weekly magazine *Saturday Night*. What aspects of its style indicate its journalistic origins?

3. How does Salutin's vocabulary in paragraph 3 reflect his attitude towards the handling of political correctness by the press?

4. Why does Salutin give such prominence to a speech by George Bush, reported in detail by *Maclean's*? (paras. 8–9)

5. Why does Salutin spend so long criticizing the various media assaults on political correctness before he turns to examine the phenomenon itself?

6. Discuss the way in which Salutin mocks the excessive concerns about "politically correct" language in paragraph 18.

Suggested Topics for Writing and Discussion

1. Examine some of the magazine articles cited by Salutin, and say whether his summary of them is a fair representation of their content.

2. Has any aspect of "political correctness," as described in Salutin's article, had an effect on you, your circle of acquaintance, or your community?

3. Examine the essays in this book by Susan Crean, Moira Farr, or Lenore Keeshig-Tobias. Do you see in their arguments anything of what might be called "political correctness"?

4. Salutin speaks of "frenzy" and "hysterics" in media treatments of the issue of political correctness. Discuss another example of frenzied or hysterical reporting of an issue of public interest (e.g., the private life of political candidates; drug abuse in professional sport; royal marriages or divorces). Point to instances of distortion, exaggeration, or sensationalism.

Nature and Humankind

The Obligation to Endure
by Rachel Carson

The history of life on earth has been a history of interaction between   1
living things and their surroundings. To a large extent, the physical form
and the habits of the earth's vegetation and its animal life have been
moulded by the environment. Considering the whole span of earthly
time, the opposite effect, in which life actually modifies its surroundings, has been relatively slight. Only within the moment of time represented by the present century has one species — man — acquired
significant power to alter the nature of his world.

During the past quarter century this power has not only increased to   2
one of disturbing magnitude but it has changed in character. The most
alarming of all man's assaults upon the environment is the contamination of air, earth, rivers, and sea with dangerous and even lethal materials. This pollution is for the most part irrecoverable; the chain of evil it
initiates not only in the world that must support life but in living tissues
is for the most part irreversible. In this now universal contamination of
the environment, chemicals are the sinister and little recognized partners of radiation in changing the very nature of the world — the very
nature of its life. Strontium 90, released through nuclear explosions into
the air, comes to earth in rain or drifts down as fallout, lodges in soil,
enters into the grass or corn or wheat grown there, and in time takes up
its abode in the bones of a human being, there to remain until his death.
Similarly, chemicals sprayed on croplands or forests or gardens lie long
in soil, entering into living organisms, passing from one to another in a
chain of poisoning and death. Or they pass mysteriously by underground
streams until they emerge and, through the alchemy of air and sunlight,

combine into new forms that kill vegetation, sicken cattle, and work unknown harm on those who drink from once pure wells. As Albert Schweitzer has said, "Man can hardly even recognize the devils of his own creation."

3   It took hundreds of millions of years to produce the life that now inhabits the earth — eons of time in which that developing and evolving and diversifying life reached a state of adjustment and balance with its surroundings. The environment, rigorously shaping and directing the life it supported, contained elements that were hostile as well as supporting. Certain rocks gave out dangerous radiation; even within the light of the sun, from which all life draws its energy, there were shortwave radiations with power to injure. Given time — time not in years but in millennia — life adjusts, and a balance has been reached. For time is the essential ingredient; but in the modern world there is no time.

4   The rapidity of change and the speed with which new situations are created follow the impetuous and heedless pace of man rather than the deliberate pace of nature. Radiation is no longer merely the background radiation of rocks, the bombardment of cosmic rays, the ultraviolet of the sun that have existed before there was any life on earth; radiation is now the unnatural creation of man's tampering with the atom. The chemicals to which life is asked to make its adjustment are no longer merely the calcium and silica and copper and all the rest of the minerals washed out of the rocks and carried in rivers to the sea; they are the synthetic creations of man's inventive mind, brewed in his laboratories, and having no counterparts in nature.

5   To adjust to these chemicals would require time on the scale that is nature's; it would require not merely the years of a man's life but the life of generations. And even this, were it by some miracle possible, would be futile, for the new chemicals come from our laboratories in an endless stream; almost five hundred annually find their way into actual use in the United States alone. The figure is staggering and its implications are not easily grasped — 500 new chemicals to which the bodies of men and animals are required somehow to adapt each year, chemicals totally outside the limits of biologic experience.

6   Among them are many that are used in man's war against nature. Since the mid-1940's over 200 basic chemicals have been created for use in killing insects, weeds, rodents, and other organisms described in the modern vernacular as "pests": and they are sold under several thousand different brand names.

7   These sprays, dusts, and aerosols are now applied almost universally

to farms, gardens, forests, and homes — nonselective chemicals that have the power to kill every insect, the "good" and the "bad," to still the song of birds and the leaping of fish in the streams, to coat the leaves with a deadly film, and to linger on in soil — all this though the intended target may be only a few weeds or insects. Can anyone believe it is possible to lay down such a barrage of poisons on the surface of earth without making it unfit for all life? They should not be called "insecticides," but "biocides."

The whole process of spraying seems caught up in an endless spiral. 8 Since DDT was released for civilian use, a process of escalation has been going on in which ever more toxic materials must be found. This has happened because insects, in a triumphant vindication of Darwin's principle of the survival of the fittest, have evolved super races immune to the particular insecticide used. Hence a deadlier one has always to be developed — and then a deadlier one than that. It has happened also because, for reasons to be described later, destructive insects often undergo a "flareback," or resurgence, after spraying, in numbers greater than before. Thus the chemical war is never won, and all life is caught in its violent crossfire.

Along with the possibility of the extinction of mankind by nuclear 9 war, the central problem of our age has therefore become the contamination of man's total environment with such substances of incredible potential for harm — substances that accumulate in the tissues of plants and animals and even penetrate the germ cells to shatter or alter the very material of heredity upon which the shape of the future depends.

Some would-be architects of our future look toward a time when it 10 will be possible to alter the human germ plasm by design. But we may easily be doing so now by inadvertence, for many chemicals, like radiation, bring about gene mutations. It is ironic to think that man might determine his own future by something so seemingly trivial as the choice of an insect spray.

All this has been risked — for what? Future historians may well be 11 amazed by our distorted sense of proportion. How could intelligent beings seek to control a few unwanted species by a method that contaminated the entire environment and brought the threat of disease and death even to their own kind? Yet this is precisely what we have done. We have done it, moreover, for reasons that collapse the moment we examine them. We are told that the enormous and expanding use of pesticides is necessary to maintain farm production. Yet is our real problem not one of *overproduction*? Our farms, despite measures to remove acreages from production and to pay farmers not to produce, have yielded such a staggering excess of crops that the American taxpayer in 1962 is paying out more than one billion dollars a year as the total carrying cost of the surplus-food storage program. And is the situation helped when one branch of the Agriculture Department tries to reduce production while another states, as it did in 1958, "It is believed generally that reduction of crop acreages under provisions of the Soil Bank will stimulate interest in use of chemicals to obtain maximum production on the land retained in crops"?

12   All this is not to say there is no insect problem and no need of control. I am saying, rather, that control must be geared to realities, not to mythical situations, and that the methods employed must be such that they do not destroy us along with the insects.

13   The problem whose attempted solution has brought such a train of disaster in its wake is an accompaniment of our modern way of life. Long before the age of man, insects inhabited the earth — a group of extraordinarily varied and adaptable beings. Over the course of time since man's advent, a small percentage of the more than half a million species of insects have come into conflict with human welfare in two principal ways: as competitors for the food supply and as carriers of human disease.

14   Disease-carrying insects become important where human beings are crowded together, especially under conditions where sanitation is poor, as in time of natural disaster or war or in situations of extreme poverty and deprivation. Then control of some sort becomes necessary. It is a sobering fact, however, as we shall presently see, that the method of massive chemical control has had only limited success, and also threatens to worsen the very conditions it is intended to curb.

15   Under primitive agricultural conditions the farmer had few insect problems. These arose with the intensification of agriculture — the devotion of immense acreages to a single crop. Such a system set the stage for explosive increases in specific insect populations. Single-crop farming does not take advantage of the principles by which nature works; it is agriculture as an engineer might conceive it to be. Nature has introduced great variety into the landscape, but man has displayed a passion for simplifying it. Thus he undoes the built-in checks and balances by which nature holds the species within bounds. One important natural check is a limit on the amount of suitable habitat for each species. Obviously then, an insect that lives on wheat can build up its population to

much higher levels on a farm devoted to wheat than on one in which wheat is intermingled with other crops to which the insect is not adapted.

The same thing happens in other situations. A generation or more 16 ago, the towns of large areas of the United States lined their streets with the noble elm tree. Now the beauty they hopefully created is threatened with complete destruction as disease sweeps through the elms, carried by a beetle that would have only limited chance to build up large populations and to spread from tree to tree if the elms were only occasional trees in a richly diversified planting.

Another factor in the modern insect problem is one that must be 17 viewed against a background of geologic and human history: the spreading of thousands of different kinds of organisms from their native homes to invade new territories. This worldwide migration has been studied and graphically described by the British ecologist Charles Elton in his recent book *The Ecology of Invasions*. During the Cretaceous Period, some hundred million years ago, flooding seas cut many land bridges between continents and living things found themselves confined in what Elton calls "colossal separate nature reserves." There, isolated from others of their kind, they developed many new species. When some of the land masses were joined again, about 15 million years ago, these species began to move out into new territories — a movement that is not only still in progress but is now receiving considerable assistance from man.

The importation of plants is the primary agent in the modern spread 18 of species, for animals have almost invariably gone along with the plants, quarantine being a comparatively recent and not completely effective innovation. The United States Office of Plant Introduction alone has introduced almost 200,000 species and varieties of plants from all over the world. Nearly half of the 180 or so major insect enemies of plants in the United States are accidental imports from abroad, and most of them have come as hitchhikers on plants.

In new territory, out of reach of the restraining hand of the natural 19 enemies that kept down its numbers in its native land, an invading plant or animal is able to become enormously abundant. Thus it is no accident that our most troublesome insects are introduced species.

These invasions, both the naturally occurring and those dependent 20 on human assistance, are likely to continue indefinitely. Quarantine and massive chemical campaigns are only extremely expensive ways of buying time. We are faced, according to Dr. Elton, "with a life-and-death need not just to find new technological means of suppressing this plant or that animal"; instead we need the basic knowledge of animal populations and their relations to their surroundings that will "promote an even balance and damp down the explosive power of outbreaks and new invasions."

21   Much of the necessary knowledge is now available but we do not use it. We train ecologists in our universities and even employ them in our governmental agencies but we seldom take their advice. We allow the chemical death rain to fall as though there were no alternative, whereas in fact there are many, and our ingenuity could soon discover many more if given opportunity.

22   Have we fallen into a mesmerized state that makes us accept as inevitable that which is inferior or detrimental, as though having lost the will or the vision to demand that which is good? Such thinking, in the words of the ecologist Paul Shepard, "idealizes life with only its head out of water, inches above the limits of toleration of the corruption of its own environment ... Why should we tolerate a diet of weak poisons, a home in insipid surroundings, a circle of acquaintances who are not quite our enemies, the noise of motors with just enough relief to prevent insanity? Who would want to live in a world which is just not quite fatal?"

23   Yet such a world is pressed upon us. The crusade to create a chemically sterile, insect-free world seems to have engendered a fanatic zeal on the part of many specialists and most of the so-called control agencies. On every hand there is evidence that those engaged in spraying operations exercise a ruthless power. "The regulatory entomologists ... function as prosecutor, judge and jury, tax assessor and collector and sheriff to enforce their own orders," said Connecticut entomologist Neely Turner. The most flagrant abuses go unchecked in both state and federal agencies.

24   It is not my contention that chemical insecticides must never be used. I do contend that we have put poisonous and biologically potent chemicals indiscriminately into the hands of persons largely or wholly ignorant of their potentials for harm. We have subjected enormous numbers of people to contact with these poisons, without their consent and often without their knowledge. If the Bill of Rights contains no guarantee that a citizen shall be secure against lethal poisons distributed either by private individuals or public officials, it is surely only because our forefathers, despite their considerable wisdom and foresight, could conceive of no such problem.

25   I contend, furthermore, that we have allowed these chemicals to be used with little or no advance investigation of their effect on soil, water,

wildlife, and man himself. Future generations are unlikely to condone our lack of prudent concern for the integrity of the natural world that supports all life.

There is still very limited awareness of the nature of the threat. This is an era of specialists, each of whom sees his own problem and is unaware of or intolerant of the larger frame into which it fits. It is also an era dominated by industry, in which the right to make a dollar at whatever cost is seldom challenged. When the public protests, confronted with some obvious evidence of damaging results of pesticide applications, it is fed little tranquilizing pills of half truth. We urgently need an end to these false assurances, to the sugar coating of unpalatable facts. It is the public that is being asked to assume the risks that the insect controllers calculate. The public must decide whether it wishes to continue on the present road, and it can do so only when in full possession of the facts. In the words of Jean Rostand, "The obligation to endure gives us the right to know." 26

(1962)

The Writer's Subject

1. What does Carson mean by "the chain of evil" initiated by chemical pollution? (para. 2) How does she illustrate her point?

2. Why does Carson believe that we cannot adjust to the various chemicals we have introduced into the environment? (paras. 3–5)

3. Why does Carson say that insecticides should be called "biocides"? (para. 7)

4. Why does Carson believe that the chemical war against insects may never be won? (para. 8)

5. What does Carson mean by saying that "control must be geared to realities, not to mythical situations" (para. 12)?

6. How do modern agricultural practices help to increase specific insect populations rather than curb them? (para. 15)

7. Carson says that we have the knowledge necessary to control troublesome insects without polluting the environment. Why, in her view, have we not used this knowledge?

8. What changes in attitudes and government policies does Carson imply must take place if the dangers of chemical pollution are to be checked?

The Writer's Style and Strategy

1. What is the tone of this essay? How is it established?

2. The essay is both an exposition of the effects of chemicals and an argument against their uncontrolled use. Identify those elements which are primarily expository and those which are particularly calculated to appeal to the reader's emotions.

3. Carson makes use of a number of devices to lend weight and add emphasis to her argument: rhetorical questions, the citing of authorities, references to statistical information. Find an example of each of these and comment on its effectiveness.

Suggested Topics for Writing and Discussion

1. This essay is taken from Rachel Carson's book *Silent Spring*, published in 1962. In what respects are we still threatened by the dangers which Carson pointed out 35 years ago?

2. We are a society accustomed to the free use of chemicals in the home as well as in industry and agriculture. Drawing on your own experience, show how chemical products play a part in our daily lives. To what extent do any of these products constitute a threat to human life or the natural environment?

3. Compare the concerns of Carson in "The Obligation to Endure" with those of Bronowski in "The Real Responsibilities of the Scientist." Both are concerned with the need to keep the public well informed about scientific research. How might this be accomplished?

4. Carson says that ours is "an era dominated by industry, in which the right to make a dollar at whatever cost is seldom challenged." Do you agree with Carson's assessment?

The Bird and the Machine

by Loren Eiseley

I suppose their little bones have years ago been lost among the stones   1
and wind of those high glacial pastures. I suppose their feathers blew
eventually into the piles of tumbleweed beneath the straggling cattle
fences and rotted there in the mountain snows, along with dead steers
and all the other things that drift to an end in the corners of the wire. I
do not quite know why I should be thinking of birds over the *New York
Times* at breakfast, particularly the birds of my youth half a continent
away. It is a funny thing what the brain will do with memories and how
it will treasure them and finally bring them into odd juxtapositions with
other things, as though it wanted to make a design, or get some meaning out of them, whether you want it or not, or even see it.

It used to seem marvelous to me, but I read now that there are ma-   2
chines that can do these things in a small way, machines that can crawl
about like animals, and that it may not be long now until they do more
things — maybe even make themselves — I saw that piece in the *Times*
just now. And then they will, maybe — well, who knows — but you
read about it more and more with no one making any protest, and already they can add better than we and reach up and hear things through
the dark and finger the guns over the night sky.

This is the new world that I read about at breakfast. This is the world   3
that confronts me in my biological books and journals, until there are
times when I sit quietly in my chair and try to hear the little purr of the
cogs in my head and the tubes flaring and dying as the messages go
through them and the circuits snap shut or open. This is the great age,
make no mistake about it; the robot has been born somewhat appropri-

ately along with the atom bomb, and the brain they say now is just another type of more complicated feedback system. The engineers have its basic principles worked out; it's mechanical, you know; nothing to get superstitious about; and man can always improve on nature once he gets the idea. Well, he's got it all right and that's why, I guess, I sit here in my chair, with the article crunched in my hand, remembering those two birds and that blue mountain sunlight. There is another magazine article on my desk that reads "Machines Are Getting Smarter Every Day." I don't deny it, but I'll stick with the birds. It's life I believe in, not machines.

4   Maybe you don't believe there is any difference. A skeleton is all joints and pulleys, I'll admit. And when man was in his simpler stages of machine building in the eighteenth century, he quickly saw the resemblances. "What," wrote Hobbes, "is the heart but a spring, and the nerves but so many strings, and the joints but so many wheels, giving motion to the whole body?" Tinkering about in their shops it was inevitable in the end that men would see the world as a huge machine "subdivided into an infinite number of lesser machines."

5   The idea took on with a vengeance. Little automatons toured the country — dolls controlled by clockwork. Clocks described as little worlds were taken on tours by their designers. They were made up of moving figures, shifting scenes, and other remarkable devices. The life of the cell was unknown. Man, whether he was conceived as possessing a soul or not, moved and jerked about like these tiny puppets. A human being thought of himself in terms of his own tools and implements. He had been fashioned like the puppets he produced and was only a more clever model made by a greater designer.

6   Then in the nineteenth century, the cell was discovered, and the single machine in its turn was found to be the product of millions of infinitesimal machines — the cells. Now, finally, the cell itself dissolves away into an abstract chemical machine, and that into some intangible, inexpressible flow of energy. The secret seems to lurk all about, the wheels get smaller and smaller, and they turn more rapidly, but when you try to seize it the life is gone — and so, by popular definition, some would say that life was never there in the first place. The wheels and the cogs are the secret and we can make them better in time — machines that will run faster and more accurately than real mice to real cheese.

7   I have no doubt it can be done, though a mouse harvesting seeds on an autumn thistle is to me a fine sight and more complicated, I think, in his multiform activity than a machine "mouse" running a maze. Also, I

like to think of the possible shape of the future brooding in mice, just
as it brooded once in a rather ordinary mousy insectivore who became
man. It leaves a nice fine indeterminate sense of wonder that even an
electronic brain hasn't got, because you know perfectly well that if the
electronic brain changes, it will be because of something man has done
to it. But what man will do to himself he doesn't really know. A certain
scale of time and a ghostly intangible thing called change are ticking in
him. Powers and potentialities like the oak in the seed, or a red and
awful ruin. Either way, it's impressive; and the mouse has it, too. Or
those birds, I'll never forget those birds — yet before I measured their
significance, I learned the lesson of time first of all. I was young then
and left alone in a great desert — part of an expedition that had scattered its men over several hundred miles in order to carry on research
more effectively. I learned there that time is a series of planes existing
superficially in the same universe. The tempo is a human illusion, a subjective clock ticking in our own kind of protoplasm.

As the long months passed, I began to live on the slower planes and to   8
observe more readily what passed for life there. I sauntered, I passed
more and more slowly up and down the canyons in the dry baking heat
of midsummer. I slumbered for long hours in the shade of huge brown
boulders that had gathered in tilted companies out on flats. I had forgotten the world of men and the world had forgotten me. Now and then
I found a skull in the canyons, and these justified my remaining there. I
took a serene cold interest in these discoveries. I had come, like many
naturalists before me, to view life with a wary and subdued attention. I
had grown to take pleasure in the divested bone.

I sat once on a high ridge that fell away before me into a waste of   9
sand dunes. I sat through hours of a long afternoon. Finally, as I glanced
beside my boot an indistinct configuration caught my eye. It was a coiled
rattlesnake, a big one. How long he had sat with me I do not know. I
had not frightened him. We were both locked in the sleep-walking tempo
of the earlier world, baking in the same high air and sunshine. Perhaps
he had been there when I came. He slept on as I left, his coils, so ill-
discerned by me, dissolving once more among the stones and gravel
from which I had barely made him out.

Another time I got on a higher ridge, among some tough little wind-   10
warped pines half covered over with sand in a basinlike depression that
caught everything carried by the air up to those heights. There were a
few thin bones of birds, some cracked shells of indeterminable age, and

the knotty fingers of pine roots bulged out of shape from their long and agonizing grasp upon the crevices of the rock. I lay under the pines in the sparse shade and went to sleep once more.

11   It grew cold finally, for autumn was in the air by then, and the few things that lived thereabouts were sinking down into an even chillier scale of time. In the moments between sleeping and waking I saw the roots about me and slowly, slowly, a foot in what seemed many centuries, I moved my sleep-stiffened hands over the scaling bark and lifted my numbed face after the vanishing sun. I was a great awkward thing of knots and aching limbs, trapped up there in some long, patient endurance that involved the necessity of putting living fingers into rock and by slow, aching expansion bursting those rocks asunder. I suppose, so thin and slow was the time of my pulse by then, that I might have stayed on to drift still deeper into the lower cadences of the frost, or the crystalline life that glistens pebbles, or shines in a snowflake, or dreams in the meteoric iron between the worlds.

12   It was a dim descent, but time was present in it. Somewhere far down in that scale the notion struck me that one might come the other way. Not many months thereafter I joined some colleagues heading higher into a remoter windy tableland where huge bones were reputed to protrude like boulders from the turf. I had drowsed with reptiles and moved with the century-long pulse of trees; now, lethargically, I was climbing up some invisible ladder of quickening hours. There had been talk of birds in connection with my duties. Birds are intense, fast-living creatures — reptiles, I suppose one might say, that have escaped out of the heavy sleep of time, transformed fairy creatures dancing over sunlit meadows. It is a youthful fancy, no doubt, but because of something that happened up there among the escarpments of that range, it remains with me a lifelong impression. I can never bear to see a bird imprisoned.

13   We came into that valley through the trailing mists of a spring night. It was a place that looked as though it might never have known the foot of man, but our scouts had been ahead of us and we knew all about the abandoned cabin of stone that lay far up on one hillside. It had been built in the land rush of the last century and then lost to the cattlemen again as the marginal soils failed to take to the plow.

14   There were spots like this all over that country. Lost graves marked by unlettered stones and old corroding rim-fire cartridge cases lying where somebody had made a stand among the boulders that rimmed the valley. They are all that remain of the range wars; the men are under the stones now. I could see our cavalcade winding in and out through

the mist below us: torches, the reflection of the truck lights on our collecting tins, and the far-off bumping of a loose dinosaur thigh bone in
the bottom of a trailer. I stood on a rock a moment looking down and
thinking what it cost in money and equipment to capture the past.

We had, in addition, instructions to lay hands on the present. The 15
word had come through to get them alive — birds, reptiles, anything. A
zoo somewhere abroad needed restocking. It was one of those reciprocal matters in which science involves itself. Maybe our museum needed
a stray ostrich egg and this was the payoff. Anyhow, my job was to help
capture some birds and that was why I was there before the trucks.

The cabin had not been occupied for years. We intended to clean it 16
out and live in it, but there were holes in the roof and the birds had
come in and were roosting in the rafters. You could depend on it in a
place like this where everything blew away, and even a bird needed some
place out of the weather and away from coyotes. A cabin going back to
nature in a wild place draws them till they come in, listening at the eaves,
I imagine, pecking softly among the shingles till they find a hole, and
then suddenly the place is theirs and man is forgotten.

Sometimes of late years I find myself thinking the most beautiful 17
sight in the world might be the birds taking over New York after the last
man has run away to the hills. I will never live to see it, of course, but I
know just how it will sound because I've lived up high and I know the
sort of watch birds keep on us. I've listened to sparrows tapping tenta-
tively on the outside of air conditioners when they thought no one was
listening, and I know how other birds test the vibrations that come up
to them through the television aerials.

"Is he gone?" they ask, and the vibrations come up from below, "Not 18
yet, not yet."

Well, to come back, I got the door open softly and I had the spotlight 19
all ready to turn on and blind whatever birds there were so they couldn't
see to get out through the roof. I had a short piece of ladder to put against
the far wall where there was a shelf on which I expected to make the
biggest haul. I had all the information I needed, just like any skilled
assassin. I pushed the door open, the hinges squeaking only a little. A
bird or two stirred — I could hear them — but nothing flew and there
was a faint starlight through the holes in the roof.

I padded across the floor, got the ladder up and the light ready, and 20
slithered up the ladder till my head and arms were over the shelf. Everything was dark as pitch except for the starlight at the little place back of
the shelf near the eaves. With the light to blind them, they'd never make

it. I had them, I reached my arm carefully over in order to be ready to seize whatever was there and I put the flash on the edge of the shelf where it would stand by itself when I turned it on. That way I'd be able to use both hands.

21   Everything worked perfectly except for one detail — I didn't know what kind of birds were there. I never thought about it at all, and it wouldn't have mattered if I had. My orders were to get something interesting. I snapped on the flash and sure enough there was a great beating and feathers flying, but instead of my having them, they, or rather he, had me. He had my hand, that is, and for a small hawk not much bigger than my fist he was doing all right. I heard him give one short metallic cry when the light went on and my hand descended on the bird beside him; after that he was busy with his claws and his beak was sunk in my thumb. In the struggle I knocked the lamp over on the shelf, and his mate got her sight back and whisked neatly through the hole in the roof and off among the stars outside. It all happened in fifteen seconds and you might think I would have fallen down the ladder, but no, I had a professional assassin's reputation to keep up, and the bird, of course, made the mistake of thinking the hand was the enemy and not the eyes behind it. He chewed my thumb up pretty effectively and lacerated my hand with his claws, but in the end I got him, having two hands to work with.

22   He was a sparrow hawk and a fine young male in the prime of life. I was sorry not to catch the pair of them, but as I dripped blood and folded his wings carefully, holding him by the back so that he couldn't strike again, I had to admit the two of them might have been more than I could have handled under the circumstances. The little fellow had saved his mate by diverting me, and that was that. He was born to it and made no outcry now, resting in my hand hopelessly but peering toward me in the shadows behind the lamp with a fierce, almost indifferent glance. He neither gave nor expected mercy and something out of the high air passed from him to me, stirring a faint embarrassment.

23   I quit looking into that eye and managed to get my huge carcass with its fist full of prey back down the ladder. I put the bird in a box too small to allow him to injure himself by struggle and walked out to welcome the arriving trucks. It had been a long day, and camp still to make in the darkness. In the morning that bird would be just another episode. He would go back with the bones in the truck to a small cage in a city where he would spend the rest of his life. And a good thing, too. I sucked my aching thumb and spat out some blood. An assassin has to get used to these things. I had a professional reputation to keep up.

In the morning, with the change that comes on suddenly in that high 24
country, the mist that had hovered below us in the valley was gone. The
sky was a deep blue, and one could see for miles over the high
outcroppings of stone. I was up early and brought the box in which the
little hawk was imprisoned out on to the grass where I was building a
cage. A wind as cool as a mountain spring ran over the grass and stirred
my hair. It was a fine day to be alive. I looked up and all around and at
the hole in the cabin roof out of which the other little hawk had fled.
There was no sign of her anywhere that I could see.

"Probably in the next county by now," I thought cynically, but before 25
beginning work I decided I'd have a look at my last night's capture.

Secretively, I looked again all around the camp and up and down and 26
opened the box. I got him right out in my hand with his wings folded
properly and I was careful not to startle him. He lay limp in my grasp
and I could feel his heart pound under the feathers but he only looked
beyond me and up.

I saw him look that last look away beyond me into a sky so full of light 27
that I could not follow his gaze. The little breeze flowed over me again,
and nearby a mountain aspen shook all its tiny leaves. I suppose I must
have had an idea then of what I was going to do, but I never let it come
up into consciousness. I just reached over and laid the hawk on the grass.

He lay there a long minute without hope, unmoving, his eyes still 28
fixed on that blue vault above him. It must have been that he was already so far away in heart that he never felt the release from my hand.
He never even stood. He just lay with his breast against the grass.

In the next second after that long minute he was gone. Like a flicker 29
of light, he had vanished with my eyes full on him but without actually
seeing a premonitory wing beat. He was gone straight into that tower-
ing emptiness of light and crystal that my eyes could scarcely bear to
penetrate. For another long moment there was silence. I could not see
him. The light was too intense. Then from far up somewhere a cry came
ringing down.

I was young then and had seen little of the world, but when I heard 30
that cry my heart turned over. It was not the cry of the hawk I had captured; for, by shifting my position against the sun I was now seeing farther up. Straight out of the sun's eye, where she must have been soaring
restlessly above us for untold hours, hurtled his mate. And from far up,
ringing from peak to peak of the summits over us, came a cry of such
unutterable and ecstatic joy that it sounds down across the years and
tingles among the cups on my quiet breakfast table.

31   I saw them both now. He was rising fast to meet her. They met in a
great soaring gyre that turned to a whirling circle and a dance of wings.
Once more, just once, their two voices, joined in a harsh wild medley
of question and response, struck and echoed against the pinnacles of
the valley. Then they were gone forever somewhere into those upper
regions beyond the eyes of men.

32   I am older now, and sleep less, and have seen most of what there is to
see and am not very much impressed any more, I suppose, by anything.
"What Next in the Attributes of Machines?" my morning headline runs.
"It Might Be the Power to Reproduce Themselves."

33   I lay the paper down and across my a mind a phrase floats insinuat-
ingly: "It does not seem that there is anything in the construction, constituents, or behavior of the human being which it is essentially
impossible for science to duplicate and synthesize. On the other hand...."

34   All over the city the cogs in the hard, bright mechanisms have begun
to turn. Figures move through computers, names are spelled out, a
thoughtful machine selects the fingerprints of a wanted criminal from
an array of thousands. In the laboratory an electronic mouse runs swiftly
through a maze toward the cheese it can neither taste nor enjoy. On the
second run it does better than a living mouse.

35   "On the other hand...." Ah, my mind takes up, on the other hand the
machine does not bleed, ache, hang for hours in the empty sky in a tor-
ment of hope to learn the fate of another machine, nor does it cry out
with joy nor dance in the air with the fierce passion of a bird. Far off,
over a distance greater than space, that remote cry from the heart of
heaven makes a faint buzzing among my breakfast dishes and passes
on and away.

                                                                    (1955)

The Writer's Subject

1. What fears about the "new world" does Eiseley express in the first three
    paragraphs?

2. Eiseley says that man has come to see himself as a mechanism. What, in
    Eiseley's opinion, are the limitations of this view? (paras. 4–7)

3. Eiseley describes time as "a series of planes existing superficially in the
    same universe" and speaks of his own experience in the desert where he
    "began to live on the slower planes." How did Eiseley become aware of
    these "slower planes" of time? (para. 7–11)

4. In speaking of time at the beginning of paragraph 12, what does Eiseley mean by "one might come the other way"?

5. What feelings are stirred in Eiseley by the resistance of the male sparrow hawk? (paras. 22–23)

6. Why did Eiseley let the bird go?

7. In his description of the release of the sparrow hawk, Eiseley gives special prominence to the sky. Why? (paras. 24–31)

8. Why does Eiseley place his reflections in the mundane setting of his breakfast table?

The Writer's Style and Strategy

1. Eiseley treats the machine age in ironic terms. How is this irony conveyed? (paras. 2–3)

2. How does Eiseley move from general observations about men and machines to the more personal element of his narrative?

3. How does Eiseley's use of co-ordinated clauses in paragraph 11 help to convey his experience of the slowing down of time?

4. What is Eiseley's attitude to the expedition's secondary task, that the researchers "lay hands on the present"? (para. 15) How is this attitude conveyed?

5. Why does Eiseley refer to himself at several points as a skilled assassin with a professional reputation to keep up? (paras. 19, 21, and 23) What is the significance of his description of himself as a "huge carcass with a fistful of prey"? (para. 23)

6. Discuss the tone and language of the final paragraph. What makes the paragraph a fitting conclusion to Eiseley's reflections?

7. Comment on Eiseley's title. What emphasis does he gain by using the definite article?

Suggested Topics for Writing and Discussion

1. Eiseley seems disturbed at the notion that he must send the sparrow hawk to the city, to spend the rest of its life in a zoo. What is your own attitude to zoos? Do you think they serve a useful function?

2. Eiseley expresses concern at scientists' attempts to duplicate life forms. Do you believe that scientists should he given unrestricted freedom to pursue their experiments in genetic engineering and artificial intelligence?

3. Relate an incident which led to a change in your perspective. Use specific details of the experience to develop your narrative.

4. Eiseley is not enamoured of humanity's achievements in the modern age. Do you share his view? Choose one achievement of modern technology and show whether its benefits outweigh its drawbacks.

Roughing It in the Bush

My Plans for Moose Hunting in the Canadian Wilderness

by Stephen Leacock

The season is now opening when all those who have a manly streak in   1
them like to get out into the bush and "rough it" for a week or two of
hunting and fishing. For myself, I never feel that the autumn has been
well spent unless I can get out after the moose. And when I go I like to
go right into the bush and "rough it" — get clear away from civilization, out in the open, and take fatigue or hardship just as it comes.

So this year I am making all my plans to get away for a couple of   2
weeks of moose hunting along with my brother George and my friend
Tom Gass. We generally go together because we are all of us men who
like the rough stuff and are tough enough to stand the hardship of living
in the open. The place we go to is right in the heart of the primitive
Canadian forest, among big timber, broken with lakes as still as glass,
just the very ground for moose.

We have a kind of lodge up there. It's just a rough place that we put   3
up, the three of us, the year before last, built out of tamarack logs faced
with a broad axe. The flies, while we were building it, were something
awful. Two of the men that we sent in there to build it were so badly
bitten that we had to bring them out a hundred miles to a hospital. None
of us saw the place while we were building it, — we were all busy at
the time, — but the teamsters who took in our stuff said it was the worst
season for the black flies that they ever remembered.

Still we hung to it, in spite of the flies, and stuck at it till we got it   4
built. It is, as I say, only a plain place but good enough to rough it in.

We have one big room with a stone fireplace, and bedrooms round the sides, with a wide verandah, properly screened, all along the front. The verandah has a row of upright tamaracks for its posts and doesn't look altogether bad. In the back part we have quarters where our man sleeps. We had an ice-house knocked up while they were building and water laid on in pipes from a stream. So that on the whole the place has a kind of rough comfort about it, — good enough anyway for fellows hunting moose all day.

5   The place, nowadays, is not hard to get at. The government has just built a colonization highway, quite all right for motors, that happens to go within a hundred yards of our lodge.

6   We can get the railway for a hundred miles, and then the highway for forty, and the last hundred yards we can walk. But this season we are going to cut out the railway and go the whole way from the city in George's car with our kit with us.

7   George has one of those great big cars with a roof and thick glass sides. Personally none of the three of us would have preferred to ride in a luxurious darned thing like that. Tom says that as far as he is concerned he'd much sooner go into the bush over a rough trail in a buckboard, and for my own part a team of oxen would be more the kind of thing that I'd wish.

8   However the car is there, so we might as well use the thing especially as the provincial government has built the fool highway right into the wilderness. By taking the big car also we can not only carry all the hunting outfit that we need but we can also, if we like, shove in a couple of small trunks with a few clothes. This may be necessary as it seems that somebody has gone and slapped a great big frame hotel right there in the wilderness, not half a mile from the place we go to. The hotel we find a regular nuisance. It gave us the advantage of electric light for our lodge (a thing none of us care about), but it means more fuss about clothes. Clothes, of course, don't really matter when a fellow is roughing it in the bush, but Tom says that we might find it necessary to go over to the hotel in the evenings to borrow coal oil or a side of bacon or any rough stuff that we need; and they do such a lot of dressing up at these fool hotels now that if we do go over for bacon or anything in the evening we might just as well slip on our evening clothes, as we could chuck them off the minute we get back. George thinks it might not be a bad idea, — just as a way of saving all our energy for getting after the moose, — to dine each evening at the hotel itself. He knew some men who did that last year and they told him that the time saved for moose hunting in that way is extraor-

dinary. George's idea is that we could come in each night with our moose, — such and such a number as the case might be — either bringing them with us or burying them where they die, — change our things, slide over to the hotel and get dinner and then beat it back into the bush by moonlight and fetch in the moose. It seems they have a regular two dollar table d'hôte dinner at the hotel, — just rough stuff of course but after all, as we all admit, we don't propose to go out into the wilds to pamper ourselves with high feeding: a plain hotel meal in a home-like style at two dollars a plate is better than cooking up a lot of rich stuff over a camp fire.

If we *do* dine at the hotel we could take our choice each evening 9 between going back into the bush by moonlight to fetch in the dead moose from the different caches where we had hidden them, or sticking round the hotel itself for a while. It seems that there is dancing there. Nowadays such a lot of women and girls get the open air craze for the life in the bush that these big wilderness hotels are crowded with them. There is something about living in the open that attracts modern women and they like to get right away from everybody and everything; and of course hotels of this type in the open are nowadays always well closed in with screens so that there are no flies or anything of that sort.

So it seems that there is dancing at the hotel every evening, — nothing 10 on a large scale or pretentious, — just an ordinary hardwood floor, — they may wax it a little for all I know — and some sort of plain, rough Italian orchestra that they fetch up from the city. Not that any of us care for dancing. It's a thing that personally we wouldn't bother with. But it happens that there are a couple of young girls that Tom knows that are going to be staying at the hotel and of course naturally he wants to give them a good time. They are only eighteen and twenty (sisters) and that's really younger than we care for, but with young girls like that, — practically kids, — any man wants to give them a good time. So Tom says, and I think quite rightly, that as the kids are going to be there we may as well put in an appearance at the hotel and see that they are having a good time. Their mother is going to be with them too, and of course we want to give her a good time as well; in fact I think I will lend her my moose rifle and let her go out and shoot a moose. One thing we are all agreed upon in the arrangement of our hunting trip, is in not taking along anything to drink. Drinking spoils a trip of that sort. We all remember how in the old days we'd go out into a camp in the bush (I mean before there used to be any highway or any hotel) and carry in rye whiskey in demijohns (two dollars a gallon it was) and sit around the camp fire drinking it in the evenings.

11   But there's nothing in it. We all agree that the law being what it is, it is better to stick to it. It makes a fellow feel better. So we shall carry nothing in. I don't say that one might not have a flask or something in one's pocket in the car; but only as a precaution against accident or cold. And when we get to our lodge we all feel that we are a darned sight better without it. If we *should* need anything, — though it isn't likely, — there are still three cases of old Scotch whiskey, kicking around the lodge somewhere; I think they are kicking round in a little cement cellar with a locked door that we had made so as to use it for butter or anything of that sort. Anyway there are three, possibly four, or maybe, five, cases of Scotch there and if we should for any reason want it, there it is. But we are hardly likely to touch it, — unless we hit a cold snap, or a wet spell; — then we might; or if we strike hot dry weather. Tom says he thinks there are a couple of cases of champagne still in the cellar; some stuff that one of us must have shot in there just before prohibition came in. But we'll hardly use it. When a man is out moose hunting from dawn to dusk he hasn't much use for champagne, not till he gets home anyway. The only thing that Tom says the champagne might come in useful for would be if we cared to ask the two kids over to some sort of dinner; it would be just a rough kind of camp dinner (we could hardly ask their mother to it) but we think we could manage it. The man we keep there used to be a butler in England, or something of the sort, and he could manage some kind of rough meal where the champagne might fit in.

12   There's only one trouble about our plans for our fall camp that bothers us just a little. The moose are getting damn scarce about that place. There used, so they say, to be any quantity of them. There's an old settler up there that our man buys all our cream from who says that he remembers when the moose were so thick that they would come up and drink whiskey out of his dipper. But somehow they seem to have quit the place. Last year we sent our man out again and again looking for them and he never saw any. Three years ago a boy that works at the hotel said he saw a moose in the cow pasture back of the hotel and there were the tracks of a moose seen last year at the place not ten miles from the hotel where it had come to drink. But apart from these two exceptions the moose hunting has been poor.

13   Still, what does it matter? What we want is the *life*, the rough life just as I have described it. If any moose comes to our lodge we'll shoot him, or tell the butler to. But if not, — well, we've got along without for ten years, I don't suppose we shall worry.

                                                                                                                (1923)

The Writer's Subject

1. What image of himself does the narrator create in the first two paragraphs?

2. At what point in the essay does the reader see that the narrator is not all that he professes to be?

3. What are the "rough comforts" that the narrator reluctantly feels that he and his companions must take advantage of?

4. Under what conditions does the narrator indicate that he and his companions might partake of a little alcohol? (paras. 10–11)

5. How important to the narrator and his friends is the prospect of shooting a moose?

The Writer's Style and Strategy

1. This is clearly a humorous essay. What seems to you to be its chief humorous effect? How is this effect achieved?

2. What expectations are set up by the title of the essay? Comment on the subtitle.

3. In paragraphs 3 and 4, the narrator uses such phrases as "a kind of lodge," "just a rough place," "only a plain place," and "a kind of rough comfort." Why does the narrator use such vague phrases? Find other examples.

4. What effect does the narrator wish to create by his references to "the fool highway" and "these fool hotels"? (para. 8)

5. How does the narrator suggest again and again that the unfortunate luxuries of life in the bush are not of his choosing? How does Leacock's use of expletive constructions (i.e., "it is," "there are," "it seems that") convey the narrator's apparent reluctance?

6. Discuss the appropriateness to the essay as a whole of the concluding paragraph.

Suggested Topics for Writing and Discussion

1. Though Leacock's essay is humorous, it touches on the serious subject of our encroachment on the wilderness. Discuss one form of such encroachment (e.g., tourism, hunting, logging) and show how it threatens a particular wilderness area.

2. The myth of "the great outdoors" as an important part of North American life is still kept alive in films and on television. Discuss one TV programme or movie and show how it perpetuates this myth.

3. Camping has come a long way from the original idea of "getting away from it all" with a tent and a campfire. Write an essay showing the extent to which modern camping equipment and supplies have taken the "roughing it" element out of camping.

4. Write a humorous account of a camping or holiday experience.

The Nature of the North
by Farley Mowat

Somewhere far to the north of Newfoundland, the St. Lawrence Sea- 1
way, Place Ville Marie, the Macdonald-Cartier Freeway, the bald-headed
prairie and Stanley Park lies an unreal world conceived in the mind's
eye, born out of fantasy and cauled in myth. It is a weird and terrible
land where nothing is as it may seem. Home of the ice worm and the
igloo, of mad trappers and mushing Mounties, of pingos and polar bears,
of the legions of the damned that were conjured into being by Robert
Service, its voice is the baleful whisper of the aurora borealis, the eerie
howl of Jack London's malemutes and the whining dirge of C.B.C. wind
machines. It is a "white hell", "the ultimate desolation", a "howling
wasteland", "the Land that God Forgot" and "the Land God Gave to
Cain." It is a region almost wholly of our contriving, and we have made
of it so inimical a world that the truly alien moon, even as seen on television screens and in picture magazines, seems to have more reality.

This North, this Arctic of the mind, this frigid concept of a flat and 2
formless void of ice and snow congealed beneath the impenetrable black-
ness of the polar night, is pure illusion. Behind it lies a lost world obscured in drifts of literary drivel, obliterated by blizzards of bravado
and buried under an icy weight of obsessive misconceptions. The magnificent reality behind the myth has been consistently rejected by Canadians since the day of our national birth and is rejected still. Through
almost a century the Far North has meant to Canadians either a night-
marish limbo or an oppressive polar presence looming darkly over southern Canada and breathing icily down our necks. During most of that
century the handful of people who called themselves Canadians were

engrossed in the occupation of the apparently limitless spaces on the southern fringes of the country. When that space was finally circumscribed and its limits reached, Canadians did not look northward to the challenge of the unknown half of their share of the continent. The northern myth seemed more than they could face, even as it had in the past. They shunned it then — they shun it still. With the exception of a very few outstanding individuals, most of them employed by the Geological Survey of Canada, the exploration of the High North was accomplished, not by Canadians, but by British, French, Scandinavian, German, American and even Portuguese adventurers — men who mastered the myth, faced the reality, and took their knowledge home with them to their native lands. Those who followed in the paths of the explorers and made use of their discoveries, the traders and merchant exploiters, were English, Scotch, French and American, and the companies that employed them (such as the Hudson's Bay Company, Revillon Frères, Canalaska Trading Company) operated out of London, Paris, New York and Seattle. Even the missionaries, coming in time-honoured manner in the wake of trade, were aliens. Moravians from Germany, and Grenfell from England, worked the Labrador coast; throughout the rest of the North, Oblate priests from Belgium and France competed for souls with Anglican priests straight out from England. Meanwhile the seas of the Canadian North were being exploited by Scotch and American whalers. In the Yukon the placer gold fields were overrun by men of half a hundred lands — and there were precious few Canadians among them. White trappers, moving in on the Eskimos and Indians, were almost exclusively northern Europeans. Even Canada's standard-bearers of a token sovereignty in the Arctic, the North West (later the Royal Canadian) Mounted Police, got most of their first recruits from England, Scotland, Newfoundland and even farther afield.

3   The pattern is old and well established. A century after the nation's birth, about three-quarters of the exploration and exploitation of the Canadian North is being carried out by consortiums controlled by American, European and Japanese companies. Military occupation of the North, while nominally a joint undertaking, remains effectively American. Until the middle of the twentieth century almost the only Canadians in the Arctic were Indians and Eskimos; but they were people born to the reality and in any case were, and are, "Canadians" only by courtesy.

4   Only since the early 1950's have southern Canadians begun to glance over their shoulders northward. As yet only a handful have made the

effort to penetrate to the reality behind the myth and to actually go north, not to make a quick buck and then flee south as if the very hounds of hell were on their heels, but to attempt to make themselves integral parts of a gigantic and exciting world spurned by the nation that pretends to own it.

They are very few indeed. Apart from government employees and 5
similar transients employed by mines and military installations, there are not more than a few thousand Canadians of other than Eskimo or Indian ancestry living in a land that is larger than the ten provinces. And most of these few are concentrated in southern Yukon Territory and around Great Slave lake. In the central and eastern reaches, themselves ten times as vast as Texas, only a few hundred southern Canadians make the North their abiding home.

These are the true pioneers in a nation that is fond of boasting about 6
her pioneering spirits. Men like Bob Williamson at Rankin Inlet, Terry Ryan at Cape Dorset, Ross Peyton at Pangnirtung, Ernie Lyall at Spence Bay, Fred Ross at Cambridge Bay, Tom Butters at Inuvik, Allan Innis-Taylor at Dawson, Bob Engles at Yellowknife, Don Stuart at Hay River — these are of the few, the dedicated ones, who have committed their lives to a land the rest of us reject. They are trying desperately to neutralize the apathy and ignorance of southern Canada, to destroy the suffocating myth so that we others may come to know the North for what it really is. So that we may come to recognize it as a part of our nation.

Men like these believe that la dolce vita is the way of death for any 7
country. They would have us face resolutely north to a world that offers us — if we are men and women enough to recognize and grasp the opportunity — not only the material wealth we crave, but a fighting chance of finding the greatness of spirit that Canada so signally lacks.

* * *

The first difficulty that must be mastered in coming to grips with the 8
Far North is to decide just where "north" begins and to ascertain its boundaries. Modern man has tried to evade the issue by separating the northern regions into sections, like a layer cake, so that he can deal with each part as a separate entity. Ask a scientist for a definition of "north" and you are instantly ears deep in boreal, subarctic and arctic zones, in isotherms, degree-days and permafrost limits. The truth is that the region has no arbitrary southern boundary except insofar as one exists in us as a state of mind. The situation is akin to that of an astronaut shot up in a rocket. At what point does he enter space? At no point, but only when he has become aware that he has entered an alien environment.

9   Since Canadians generally regard the Far North as an alien environment, they enter it when they leave their familiar world of the South behind them. The entry takes place in the upper reaches of the broad band of sombre coniferous forest that stretches across the entire breadth of Canada. Beginning near the Yukon–British Columbia border, this transition region slopes southeastward to Hudson Bay near Churchill where it swings sharply south, paralleling the coast around James Bay. It then angles northeastward across Ungava to reach the Atlantic in the general vicinity of Nain on the Labrador coast. At its southernmost point (the top of James Bay) there are polar bears, seals, tundra, and caribou. The North embraces the arctic zone but it is not limited to that region, nor to the Yukon and the Northwest Territories. It includes a sliver of northern Alberta, rather more of northern Saskatchewan, a goodly bite of northern Manitoba, a nibble of Ontario, a large part of Quebec, and the upper portion of Labrador.

10   It comprises a huge section of the earth's surface. Measuring from the north tip of Ellesmere Island (less than five hundred miles from the North Pole), the northern land mass strikes southward nearly two thousand miles to Cape Henrietta Maria on Hudson Bay — roughly the distance between Montreal and Calgary! And from the Alaska-Yukon border to Cape Dyer on the coast of Baffin Bay it stretches about the same distance east and west. It encompasses about one million, seven hundred thousand square miles — nearly half the total area of Canada.

11   The Canadian North reaches from Atlantic to Pacific but, more important, it extends almost to the heart of the Arctic Ocean. Canada fronts on this third ocean, which is a true mediterranean sea, in exactly the same way that North Africa fronts on the European Mediterranean. This is a startling idea but one we would be well advised to get used to since Asia, Europe and North America all face each other across the almost land-locked polar sea and it is here that the three continents lie closest together. The orientation we get from looking at standard maps that show the North Pole at the top of beyond is arbitrary and wrong. This is not the way the world really is. The polar region is actually the centre of the northern hemisphere, and the geographic centre of Canada is in the Keewatin tundra 250 miles north-northwest of Churchill. Consequently when we turn our back on the North in the belief that there isn't much of interest in that direction, we are turning our backs on Europe and Asia, as well as on a great part of our own country. So far only the military men, preoccupied with death and destruction, have grasped this vital fact. When and if Canadians have the sense to appreciate its peaceful

significance we may become a nation at the centre, instead of remaining a sycophantic satellite at the back door of the United States.

One of the particularly cockeyed misconceptions we have about our **12** North is that it is all of a piece — or, at the most, of two pieces: a bleak expanse of frozen sea and a dreary wilderness of frozen plain. The truth is that the Arctic displays as much variety as any other great natural realm on earth. Stretching from central Labrador to Baffin Island, the up-tilted eastern edge of the Canadian Shield forms a shaggy range of glacier-encrusted mountains that are as formidable, as massively overwhelming in appearance, as anything in the Rockies. There is nothing to match them in eastern North America; yet they are almost unknown to us. They form the eastern wall of the North. Far to the westward, beyond the Mackenzie River, rise range after range of mountains that culminate in the St. Elias Range whose glacier-shrouded peaks soar to nearly twenty thousand feet in Canada and twenty-four thousand in Alaska. This is the western wall. Between these walls sprawls the worn and pitted face of the Canadian Shield composed of some of the oldest rocks on earth and so eroded by the work of the eons that only the time-smoothed stubs of its once-mighty mountains remain as undulating hills, giving relief to the naked, ancient rock. Here, in the shield country, lies the greatest assemblage of lakes upon our planet. Between the western edge of the Shield and the risers of the Yukon Cordillera lies a broad tongue of lowlands that extends north from the Great Central Plains of North America, and down it one of the world's greatest rivers, the Mackenzie, carries the waters of the Peace, the Liard, and many lesser rivers to the Arctic Ocean.

North of the mainland lies the Arctic Archipelago, some nine hun- **13** dred thousand square miles of lands constituting the largest island group in the world. These islands, too, have their variety. Some are mountainous, others are low and grassy plains, still others are bald stone and gravel deserts. Surrounding them lies a complex of sounds and channels as intricate as the most sophisticated maze.

Contained within the arctic lands of Canada is the vast inland sea of **14** Hudson Bay, in which the British Isles could be sunk without a trace. East of the main northern land mass a tremendous river carried on the Labrador Current flows down through Baffin Bay and Davis Strait, stretching an arctic tentacle as far south as Nova Scotia. The polar ocean is itself a species of "land", for it is perpetually ice covered and, though the ice moves, men can and do travel over it, and four-engine aircraft can land upon it.

15   Although the bone structure of most of the North, the Canadian Shield, is perhaps five million years old, much of the land looks raw and new. This is because a mere ten thousand years ago the entire region, except for the northwestern corner, lay buried beneath a gigantic ice sheet. The dome of the Keewatin District ice sheet was two miles thick. Its own titanic weight made the ice sheet plastic and it flowed implacably in all directions outwards from several high-domed centers. It scoured and gouged the ancient rocks, shearing off the surface soil layers and leaving behind an incredibly intricate pattern of water-filled valleys, basins, and deep coastal fiords. When the ice eventually melted it left the land littered with debris that ranged from barn-sized boulders to vast fields of shattered rock, and it embossed the naked bones of the country with a complex design of morainic ridges, drumlins, and long sinuous eskers of sand and gravel.

16   The ice had another, unseen effect. It deep-froze the rock beneath it, producing what we call permafrost. In the extreme northern islands permafrost penetrates fifteen hundred feet into the primeval rock. Even as far south as northern Manitoba the ancient frost remains, unyielding, only a few feet below the shallow surface layers that thaw in summer.

17   Remnants of the ice sheet itself also survive. In the wall of the eastern mountains some sixty thousand square miles of ice crown the heights and fill great valleys. Other remnants of ice persist in the mountains of the west.

18   Another generally held misconception about the North is that its climate is so hostile that only polar bears and Eskimos can endure it. Yet winter blizzards on the western prairies can match, in ferocity if not in intensity, the worst weather the North produces. Northern residents who have subsequently endured a winter at Saskatoon or Winnipeg have been heard to refer with nostalgia to the North as "the banana belt". Surprisingly, it is a dry world with very little rain or snowfall. Winter snows often lie deeper in Toronto or Montreal than in most parts of the North. Although not even the Yellowknife Chamber of Commerce would call northern winters balmy, summers can be lovely. There are only two true seasons: winter and summer, the transitions between them being so brief as to be negligible. Near and north of the Arctic Circle the midsummer sun never sets and temperatures sometimes persist in the comfortable sixties and higher for days on end. In winter above the Arctic Circle the sun vanishes for weeks or months, but this "long night" is seldom really dark. The Northern Lights often give a pervading luminosity and the glitter of the stars in a lucid atmosphere combined with bright moonlight provides

enough light for almost normal activity, including hunting.

The concept of the Far North as a lifeless land is another of our more 19
grotesque illusions. Its southern fringes include the upper reaches of
the taiga forests — mainly black and white spruce, larch, birch and poplar. The northward-marching trees of the taiga grow sparser and more
stunted until they fade out in the vast open plains called tundra. There
is no absolute line of demarcation between taiga and tundra — no real
"timberline". The two regions interpenetrate like the clasped fingers of
gigantic hands. There are pockets of tundra deep inside the forest, and
oases of trees far out on the sweep of the tundra. Nor is the tundra all of
a kind. There is alpine tundra high on mountain slopes, shrub tundra
close to the taiga region, sedge tundra to the north, moss-and-lichen tundra still farther north and, on the extreme northern islands, fell-field tundra where vegetation finally gives up its stubborn attempt to occupy the
remote lands that lie surrounded by unyielding polar ice. But in sum-
mertime most tundra regions boast an array of flowering plants of infinite number and delight. Although they are small, they mass in such
profusion that they suffuse hundreds of square miles with shifting colour. They form a Lilliputian jungle where hunting spiders, bumblebees,
small and delicate moths and butterflies abound. Black flies and mosquitoes abound too, alas, and there is no evading the fact that they are
the bane of summer in the North.

Birds breed almost everywhere. Mammals of many species, ranging 20
from squat, rotund lemmings to massive muskox occupy the lands. The
seas are home to whales, seals, obese walrus and sinuous white bears.
The seas are also rich in fishes as are the numberless inland lakes. For
those with eyes to see, the North is vitally and vividly alive. Long, long
ago, men of other races out of another time recognized this truth and
learned to call the northern regions "home".

(1967)

The Writer's Subject

1. What does Mowat mean by his assertion that the North is "a region almost wholly of our contriving"? (para. 1)

2. Why, in Mowat's view, have Canadians consistently rejected "the magnificent reality behind the myth" of the North? (para. 2)

3. Mowat outlines the pattern of early exploration and development of the
   Canadian North, pointing out how little was the contribution made by Canadians themselves. What, in his view, is the current situation?

4. What contrast does Mowat draw in paragraphs 4–7 between southern Canadians and those who live and work in the North? Why does he believe that southern Canadians must "face resolutely north"?

5. What analogy does Mowat use in paragraph 8 to show the difficulty of establishing where the North begins?

6. What is the "vital fact" about the Canadian North that is so far understood only by the military?

7. What are the principal misconceptions about the North that Mowat addresses from paragraph 12 onwards? What evidence does he produce to dispose of these misconceptions?

The Writer's Style and Strategy

1. Why does Mowat begin the essay with a list of the various images associated with the North?

2. What effect is he seeking by using such phrases as "mad trappers and mushing Mounties" or "the whining dirge of C.B.C. wind machines"? What is the point Mowat is making with the five phrases in quotation marks? (para. 1)

3. What is the tone of the first two sentences of paragraph 2? What figure of speech does Mowat use in the second sentence of paragraph 2? What response does Mowat hope to arouse in the reader by this strategy?

4. What words or phrases convey most clearly Mowat's critical attitudes to southern Canadians?

5. What audience has Mowat in mind for this essay? Provide specific evidence for your point of view.

6. Much of this essay is devoted to a description of the North. How does the descriptive element of this essay serve Mowat's argumentative purpose?

7. Discuss the means by which Mowat establishes the size and magnificence of the Arctic landscape in paragraphs 12–15. Comment on his use of adjectives, particularly superlatives.

8. How does Mowat convey the rich variety of plant life on the tundra in paragraph 19? Identify instances of personification, simile, and metaphor in this paragraph, and comment on the description of the flowering plants as "a Lilliputian jungle."

Suggested Topics for Writing and Discussion

1. Find a recent newspaper or magazine article about Canada's North and discuss how it confirms or contradicts Mowat's thesis that Southern Canadians have constructed a false myth about the North.

2. Mowat says somewhat bitterly that Canada lacks greatness of spirit. Do you agree?

3. Choose a nation, national group or geographic region (e.g., China, the Russians, the Sahara) and discuss the stereotypical images and myths associated with it. Can you, as Mowat has done, account for the formation of such myths and offer an opposing view?

4. In paragraph 4, Mowat says that it is only since the 1950s that southern Canadians have "begun to glance over their shoulders northward"; he implies that Canadians habitually face south. Indeed, he goes on to condemn Canada as a "sycophantic satellite" of the United States. Has the situation changed since Mowat wrote this essay in 1967? Does the North figure more prominently in our national consciousness, or is our orientation still primarily to the south?

A River Pilot Looks at the Mississippi

by Mark Twain

1   The face of the water, in time, became a wonderful book — a book that was a dead language to the uneducated passenger, but which told its mind to me without reserve, delivering its most cherished secrets as clearly as if it uttered them with a voice. And it was not a book to be read once and thrown aside, for it had a new story to tell every day. Throughout the long twelve hundred miles there was never a page that was void of interest, never one that you could leave unread without loss, never one that you would want to skip, thinking you could find higher enjoyment in some other thing. There never was so wonderful a book written by man; never one whose interest was so absorbing, so unflagging, so sparklingly renewed with every re-perusal. The passenger who could not read it was charmed with a peculiar sort of faint dimple on its surface (on the rare occasions when he did not overlook it altogether); but to the pilot that was an *italicized* passage; indeed, it was more than that, it was a legend of the largest capitals, with a string of shouting exclamation-points at the end of it, for it meant that a wreck or a rock was buried there that could tear the life out of the strongest vessel that ever floated. It is the faintest and simplest expression the water ever makes, and the most hideous to a pilot's eye. In truth, the passenger who could not read this book saw nothing but all manner of pretty pictures in it, painted by the sun and shaded by the clouds, whereas to the trained eye these were not pictures at all, but the grimmest and most dead-earnest of reading-matter.

2   Now when I had mastered the language of this water, and had come to know every trifling feature that bordered the great river as familiarly

as I knew the letters of the alphabet, I had made a valuable acquisition. But I had lost something, too. I had lost something which could never be restored to me while I lived. All the grace, the beauty, the poetry, had gone out of the majestic river! I still keep in mind a certain wonderful sunset which I witnessed when steamboating was new to me. A broad expanse of the river was turned to blood; in the middle distance the red hue brightened into gold, through which a solitary log came floating, black and conspicuous; in one place a long, slanting mark lay sparkling upon the water; in another the surface was broken by boiling, tumbling rings, that were as many-tinted as an opal; where the ruddy flush was faintest, was a smooth spot that was covered with graceful circles and radiating lines, ever so delicately traced; the shore on our left was densely wooded, and the somber shadow that fell from this forest was broken in one place by a long, ruffled trail that shone like silver; and high above the forest wall a clean-stemmed dead tree waved a single leafy bough that glowed like a flame in the unobstructed splendor that was flowing from the sun. There were graceful curves, reflected images, woody heights, soft distances; and over the whole scene, far and near, the dissolving lights drifted steadily, enriching it every passing moment with new marvels of coloring.

I stood like one bewitched. I drank it in, in a speechless rapture. The 3 world was new to me, and I had never seen anything like this at home. But as I have said, a day came when I began to cease from noting the glories and the charms which the moon and the sun and the twilight wrought upon the river's face; another day came when I ceased altogether to note them. Then, if that sunset scene had been repeated, I should have looked upon it without rapture, and should have commented upon it, inwardly, after this fashion: "This sun means that we are going to have wind tomorrow; that floating log means that the river is rising, small thanks to it; that slanting mark on the water refers to a bluff reef which is going to kill somebody's steamboat one of these nights, if it keeps on stretching out like that; those tumbling 'boils' show a dissolving bar and a changing channel there; the lines and circles in the slick water over yonder are a warning that that troublesome place is shoaling up dangerously; that silver streak in the shadow of the forest is the 'break' from a new snag, and he has located himself in the very best place he could have found to fish for steamboats; that tall dead tree, with a single living branch, is not going to last long, and then how is a body ever going to get through this blind place at night without the friendly old landmark?"

4   No, the romance and beauty were all gone from the river. All the value any feature of it had for me now was the amount of usefulness it could furnish toward compassing the safe piloting of a steamboat. Since those days, I have pitied doctors from my heart. What does the lovely flush in a beauty's cheek mean to a doctor but a "break" that ripples above some deadly disease? Are not all her visible charms sown thick with what are to him the signs and symbols of hidden decay? Does he ever see her beauty at all, or doesn't he simply view her professionally, and comment upon her unwholesome condition all to himself? And doesn't he sometimes wonder whether he has gained most or lost most by learning his trade?

                                                                    (1875)

The Writer's Subject

1. Why did Twain find the river so absorbing and interesting? (para. 1)

2. What contrast does Twain draw between the perceptions of a passenger and those of a river pilot? (para. 1)

3. What does Twain feel he lost when he had "mastered the language of this water"? (para. 2)

4. How did Twain respond to a beautiful sunset on the river when steamboating was still a new experience? How did his response change with experience? (paras. 3–4)

5. Why does Twain say that he pities doctors? (para. 4) What is the relation between this observation and his account of his river-boat experiences?

The Writer's Style and Strategy

1. How does Twain use an extended metaphor in paragraph 1 to describe the features of the river?

2. How does Twain effect a transition from paragraph 1 to paragraph 2?

3. Paragraphs 2 and 3 present two different views of the river. How does Twain organize the details of the contrast?

4. How does the language of paragraph 2 convey the sense of "rapture" that Twain first felt about the river at sunset? What details in paragraph 3 convey a change of tone?

5. Discuss the function of the concluding paragraph. By what means does Twain reinforce the connection between this paragraph and what has preceded it?

Suggested Topics for Writing and Discussion

1. Twain shows how a writer may convey his feelings about a landscape by a careful selection of detail and descriptive words. Describe a place or landscape in such a way as to help the reader share your feelings about the scene (e.g., a city seen from an airplane; a mountain range; a building).

2. Twain's closing comment suggests that professional training and education involve losses as well as gains. Choose a career or profession that interests you, and speculate what gains and losses it may entail.

3. Choose a place or a person that impressed you in childhood, and write an essay contrasting your early impressions with those you hold now.

Death of a Pig

by E.B. White

1   I spent several days and nights in mid-September with an ailing pig and
I feel driven to account for this stretch of time, more particularly since
the pig died at last, and I lived, and things might easily have gone the
other way round and none left to do the accounting. Even now, so close
to the event, I cannot recall the hours sharply and am not ready to say
whether death came on the third night or the fourth night. This uncertainty afflicts me with a sense of personal deterioration; if I were in
decent health I would know how many nights I had sat up with a pig.

2   The scheme of buying a spring pig in blossomtime, feeding it through
summer and fall, and butchering it when the solid cold weather arrives,
is a familiar scheme to me and follows an antique pattern. It is a tragedy enacted on most farms with perfect fidelity to the original script.
The murder, being premeditated, is in the first degree but is quick and
skillful, and the smoked bacon and ham provide a ceremonial ending
whose fitness is seldom questioned.

3   Once in a while something slips — one of the actors goes up in his
lines and the whole performance stumbles and halts. My pig simply
failed to show up for a meal. The alarm spread rapidly. The classic outline of the tragedy was lost. I found myself cast suddenly in the role of
pig's friend and physician — a farcical character with an enema bag for
a prop. I had a presentiment, the very first afternoon, that the play would
never regain its balance and that my sympathies were now wholly with
the pig. This was slapstick — the sort of dramatic treatment that instantly appealed to my old dachshund, Fred, who joined the vigil, held
the bag, and, when all was over, presided at the interment. When we

slid the body into the grave, we both were shaken to the core. The loss we felt was not the loss of ham but the loss of pig. He had evidently become precious to me, not that he represented a distant nourishment in a hungry time, but that he had suffered in a suffering world. But I'm running ahead of my story and shall have to go back.

My pigpen is at the bottom of an old orchard below the house. The   4
pigs I have raised have lived in a faded building that once was an icehouse. There is a pleasant yard to move about in, shaded by an apple tree that overhangs the low rail fence. A pig couldn't ask for anything better — or none has, at any rate. The sawdust in the icehouse makes a comfortable bottom in which to root, and a warm bed. This sawdust, however, came under suspicion when the pig took sick. One of my neighbors said he thought the pig would have done better on new ground — the same principle that applies in planting potatoes. He said there might be something unhealthy about that sawdust, that he never thought well of sawdust.

It was about four o'clock in the afternoon when I first noticed that   5
there was something wrong with the pig. He failed to appear at the trough for his supper, and when a pig (or a child) refuses supper a chill wave of fear runs through any household, or ice-household. After examining my pig, who was stretched out in the sawdust inside the building, I went to the phone and cranked it four times. Mr. Dameron answered. "What's good for a sick pig?" I asked (There is never any identification needed on a country phone; the person on the other end knows who is talking by the sound of the voice and by the character of the question.)

"I don't know, I never had a sick pig," said Mr. Dameron, "but I can   6
find out quick enough. You hang up and I'll call Henry."

Mr. Dameron was back on the line again in five minutes. "Henry says   7
roll him over on his back and give him two ounces of castor oil or sweet oil, and if that doesn't do the trick give him an injection of soapy water. He says he's almost sure the pig's plugged up, and even if he's wrong, it can't do any harm."

I thanked Mr. Dameron. I didn't go right to the pig, though. I sank   8
into a chair and sat still for a few minutes to think about my troubles, and then I got up and went to the barn, catching up on some odds and ends that needed tending to. Unconsciously I held off, for an hour, the deed by which I would officially recognize the collapse of the perform-ance of raising a pig; I wanted no interruption in the regularity of feed-ing, the steadiness of growth, the even succession of days. I wanted no interruption, wanted no oil, no deviation. I just wanted to keep on rais-

ing a pig, full meal after full meal, spring into summer into fall. I didn't even know whether there were two ounces of castor oil in the place.

9   Shortly after five o'clock I remembered that we had been invited out to dinner that night and realized that if I were to dose a pig there was no time to lose. The dinner date seemed a familiar conflict: I move in a desultory society and often a week or two will roll by without my going to anybody's house to dinner or anyone's coming to mine, but when an occasion does arise, and I am summoned, something usually turns up (an hour or two in advance) to make all human intercourse seem vastly inappropriate. I have come to believe that there is in hostesses a special power of divination, and that they deliberately arrange dinners to coincide with pig failure or some other sort of failure. At any rate, it was after five o'clock and I knew I could put off no longer the evil hour.

10   When my son and I arrived at the pigyard, armed with a small bottle of castor oil and a length of clothesline, the pig had emerged from his house and was standing in the middle of his yard, listlessly. He gave us slim greeting. I could see that he felt uncomfortable and uncertain. I had brought the clothesline thinking I'd have to tie him (the pig weighed more than a hundred pounds) but we never used it. My son reached down, grabbed both front legs, upset him quickly, and when he opened his mouth to scream I turned the oil into his throat — a pink, corrugated area I had never seen before. I had just time to read the label while the neck of the bottle was in his mouth. It said Puretest. The screams, slightly muffled by oil, were pitched in the hysterically high range of pig-sound, as though torture were being carried out, but they didn't last long: it was all over rather suddenly, and, his legs released, the pig righted himself.

11   In the upset position the corners of his mouth had been turned down, giving him a frowning expression. Back on his feet again, he regained the set smile that a pig wears even in sickness. He stood his ground, sucking slightly at the residue of oil; a few drops leaked out of his lips while his wicked eyes, shaded by their coy little lashes, turned on me in disgust and hatred. I scratched him gently with oily fingers and he remained quiet, as though trying to recall the satisfaction of being scratched when in health, and seeming to rehearse in his mind the indignity to which he had just been subjected. I noticed, as I stood there, four or five small dark spots on his back near the tail end, reddish brown in color, each about the size of a housefly. I could not make out what they were. They did not look troublesome but at the same time they did not look like mere surface bruises or chafe marks. Rather they seemed blemishes of internal origin. His stiff white bristles almost completely hid

them and I had to part the bristles with my fingers to get a good look.

Several hours later, a few minutes before midnight, having dined well 12
and at someone else's expense, I returned to the pighouse with a flashlight. The patient was asleep. Kneeling, I felt his ears (as you might put
your hand on the forehead of a child) and they seemed cool, and then
with the light made a careful examination of the yard and the house for
signs that the oil had worked. I found none and went to bed.

We had been having an unseasonable spell of weather — hot, close 13
days, with the fog shutting in every night, scaling for a few hours in
midday, then creeping back again at dark, drifting in first over the trees
on the point, then suddenly blowing across the fields, blotting out the
world and taking possession of houses, men, and animals. Everyone kept
hoping for a break, but the break failed to come. Next day was another
hot one. I visited the pig before breakfast and tried to tempt him with a
little milk in his trough. He just stared at it, while I made a sucking sound
through my teeth to remind him of past pleasures of the feast. With very
small, timid pigs, weanlings, this ruse is often quite successful and will
encourage them to eat; but with a large, sick pig the ruse is senseless
and the sound I made must have made him feel, if anything, more miserable. He not only did not crave food, he felt a positive revulsion to it.
I found a place under the apple tree where he had vomited in the night.

At this point, although a depression had settled over me, I didn't sup- 14
pose that I was going to lose my pig. From the lustiness of a healthy pig
a man derives a feeling of personal lustiness; the stuff that goes into the
trough and is received with such enthusiasm is an earnest of some later
feast of his own, and when this suddenly comes to an end and the food
lies stale and untouched, souring in the sun, the pig's imbalance becomes
the man's, vicariously, and life seems insecure, displaced, transitory.

As my own spirits declined, along with the pig's, the spirits of my 15
vile old dachshund rose. The frequency of our trips down the footpath
through the orchard to the pigyard delighted him, although he suffers
greatly from arthritis, moves with difficulty, and would be bedridden if
he could find anyone willing to serve him meals on a tray.

He never missed a chance to visit the pig with me, and he made many 16
professional calls on his own. You could see him down there at all hours,
his white face parting the grass along the fence as he wobbled and stum-
bled about, his stethoscope dangling — a happy quack, writing his vil-
lainous prescriptions and grinning his corrosive grin. When the enema
bag appeared, and the bucket of warm suds, his happiness was complete, and he managed to squeeze his enormous body between the two

lowest rails of the yard and then assumed full charge of the irrigation. Once, when I lowered the bag to check the flow, he reached in and hurriedly drank a few mouthfuls of the suds to test their potency. I have noticed that Fred will feverishly consume any substance that is associated with trouble — bitter flavor is to his liking. When the bag was above reach, he concentrated on the pig and was everywhere at once, a tower of strength and inconvenience. The pig, curiously enough, stood rather quietly through this colonic carnival, and the enema, though ineffective, was not as difficult as I had anticipated.

17   I discovered, though, that once having given a pig an enema there is no turning back, no chance of resuming one of life's more stereotyped roles. The pig's lot and mine were inextricably bound now, as though the rubber tube were the silver cord. From then until the time of his death I held the pig steadily in the bowl of my mind; the task of trying to deliver him from his misery became a strong obsession. His suffering soon became the embodiment of all earthly wretchedness. Along toward the end of the afternoon, defeated in physicking, I phoned the veterinary twenty miles away and placed the case formally in his hands. He was full of questions, and when I casually mentioned the dark spots on the pig's back, his voice changed its tone.

18   "I don't want to scare you," he said, "but when there are spots, erysipelas has to be considered."

19   Together we considered erysipelas, with frequent interruptions from the telephone operator, who wasn't sure the connection had been established.

20   "If a pig has erysipelas can he give it to a person?" I asked.

21   "Yes, he can," replied the vet.

22   "Have they answered?" asked the operator.

23   "Yes, they have," I said. Then I addressed the vet again. "You better come over here and examine the pig right away."

24   "I can't come myself," said the vet, "but McFarland can come this evening if that's all right. Mac knows more about pigs than I do anyway. You needn't worry too much about the spots. To indicate erysipelas they would have to be deep hemorrhagic infarcts."

25   "Deep hemorrhagic what?" I asked.

26   "Infarcts," said the vet.

27   "Have they answered?" asked the operator.

28   "Well," I said, "I don't know what you'd call these spots, except they're about the size of a housefly. If the pig has erysipelas I guess I have it, too, by this time, because we've been very close lately."

"McFarland will be over," said the vet.   29

I hung up. My throat felt dry and I went to the cupboard and got a   30
bottle of whiskey. Deep hemorrhagic infarcts — the phrase began fastening its hooks in my head. I had assumed that there could be nothing
much wrong with a pig during the months it was being groomed for
murder; my confidence in the essential health and endurance of pigs
had been strong and deep, particularly in the health of pigs that belonged
to me and that were part of my proud scheme. The awakening had been
violent and I minded it all the more because I knew that what could be
true of my pig could be true also of the rest of my tidy world. I tried to
put this distasteful idea from me, but it kept recurring. I took a short
drink of the whiskey and then, although I wanted to go down to the
yard and look for fresh signs, I was scared to. I was certain I had erysipelas.

It was long after dark and the supper dishes had been put away when   31
a car drove in and McFarland got out. He had a girl with him. I could
just make her out in the darkness — she seemed young and pretty. "This
is Miss Owen," he said. "We've been having a picnic supper on the shore,
that's why I'm late."

McFarland stood in the driveway and stripped off his jacket, then his   32
shirt. His stocky arms and capable hands showed up in my flashlight's
gleam as I helped him find his coverall and get zipped up. The rear seat
of his car contained an astonishing amount of paraphernalia, which he
soon overhauled, selecting a chain, a syringe, a bottle of oil, a rubber
tube, and some other things I couldn't identify. Miss Owen said she'd
go along with us and see the pig. I led the way down the warm slope of
the orchard, my light picking out the path for them, and we all three
climbed the fence, entered the pighouse, and squatted by the pig while
McFarland took a rectal reading. My flashlight picked up the glitter of
an engagement ring on the girl's hand.

"No elevation," said McFarland, twisting the thermometer in the light.   33
"You needn't worry about erysipelas." He ran his hand slowly over the
pig's stomach and at one point the pig cried out in pain.

"Poor piggledy-wiggledy!" said Miss Owen.   34

The treatment I had been giving the pig for two days was then re-   35
peated, somewhat more expertly, by the doctor, Miss Owen and I hand-
ing him things as he needed them — holding the chain that he had looped
around the pig's upper jaw, holding the syringe, holding the bottle stop-
per, the end of the tube, all of us working in darkness and in comfort,
working with the instinctive teamwork induced by emergency condi-

tions, the pig unprotesting, the house shadowy, protecting, intimate. I went to bed tired but with a feeling of relief that I had turned over part of the responsibility of the case to a licensed doctor. I was beginning to think, though, that the pig was not going to live.

36 He died twenty-four hours later, or it might have been forty-eight — there is a blur in time here, and I may have lost or picked up a day in the telling and the pig one in the dying. At intervals during the last day I took cool fresh water down to him and at such times as he found the strength to get to his feet he would stand with head in the pail and snuffle his snout around. He drank a few sips but no more; yet it seemed to comfort him to dip his nose in water and bobble it about, sucking in and blowing out through his teeth. Much of the time, now, he lay indoors half buried in sawdust. Once, near the last, while I was attending him I saw him try to make a bed for himself but he lacked the strength, and when he set his snout into the dust he was unable to plow even the little furrow he needed to lie down in.

37 He came out of the house to die. When I went down, before going to bed, he lay stretched in the yard a few feet from the door. I knelt, saw that he was dead, and left him there: his face had a mild look, expressive neither of deep peace nor of deep suffering, although I think he had suffered a good deal. I went back up to the house and to bed, and cried internally — deep hemorrhagic intears. I didn't wake till nearly eight the next morning, and when I looked out the open window the grave was already being dug, down beyond the dump under a wild apple. I could hear the spade strike against the small rocks that blocked the way. Never send to know for whom the grave is dug, I said to myself, it's dug for thee. Fred, I well knew, was supervising the work of digging, so I ate breakfast slowly.

38 It was Saturday morning. The thicket in which I found the gravediggers at work was dark and warm, the sky overcast. Here, among alders and young hackmatacks, at the foot of the apple tree, Lennie had dug a beautiful hole, five feet long, three feet wide, three feet deep. He was standing in it, removing the last spadeful of earth while Fred patrolled the brink in simple but impressive circles, disturbing the loose earth of the mound so that it trickled back in. There had been no rain in weeks and the soil, even three feet down, was dry and powdery. As I stood and stared, an enormous earthworm which had been partially exposed by the spade at the bottom dug itself deeper and made a slow withdrawal, seeking even remoter moistures at even lonelier depths. And

just as Lennie stepped out and rested his spade against the tree and lit a cigarette, a small green apple separated itself from a branch overhead and fell into the hole. Everything about this last scene seemed overwritten — the dismal sky, the shabby woods, the imminence of rain, the worm (legendary bedfellow of the dead), the apple (conventional garnish of a pig).

But even so, there was a directness and dispatch about animal burial, **39** I thought, that made it a more decent affair than human burial: there was no stopover in the undertaker's foul parlor, no wreath nor spray; and when we hitched a line to the pig's hind legs and dragged him swiftly from his yard, throwing our weight into the harness and leaving a wake of crushed grass and smoothed rubble over the dump, ours was a business-like procession, with Fred, the dishonorable pallbearer, staggering along in the rear, his perverse bereavement showing in every seam in his face; and the post-mortem performed handily and swiftly right at the edge of the grave, so that the inwards that had caused the pig's death preceded him into the ground and he lay at last resting squarely on the cause of his own undoing.

I threw in the first shovelful, and then we worked rapidly and with- **40** out talk, until the job was complete. I picked up the rope, made it fast to Fred's collar (he is a notorious ghoul), and we all three fled back up the path to the house, Fred bringing up the rear and holding back every inch of the way, feigning unusual stiffness. I noticed that although he weighed far less than the pig, he was harder to drag, being possessed of the vital spark.

The news of the death of my pig traveled fast and far, and I received **41** expressions of sympathy from friends and neighbors, for no one took the event lightly and the premature expiration of a pig is, I soon discovered, a departure which the community marks solemnly on its calendar, a sorrow in which it feels fully involved. I have written this account in penitence and in grief, as a man who failed to raise his pig, and to explain my deviation from the classic course of so many raised pigs. The grave in the woods is unmarked, but Fred can direct the mourner to it unerringly and with immense good will, and I know he and I shall often revisit it, singly and together, in seasons of reflection and despair, on flagless memorial days of our own choosing.

(1947)

The Writer's Subject

1. From White's reference to "the pigs I have raised" (para. 4), it is clear that he was no novice in the business of fattening up and slaughtering pigs. Why, then, is he so affected by the illness and death of the pig described in this essay?

2. Why did the pig's illness mean that "the classic outline of the tragedy was lost"? (para. 3) What "tragedy" is White referring to here?

3. Explain the importance of White's statement that "the loss we felt was not the loss of ham but the loss of pig." (para. 3)

4. What is revealed by White's reluctance to administer the castor oil? (para. 8)

5. Discuss the role of Fred the dachshund. Why did he seem to enjoy the pig's illness and death? Why does White call him "a happy quack"? (para. 16)

6. Why did White become obsessed with the task of saving the pig from its misery? (para. 17)

7. Why was White so disturbed by the preliminary diagnosis of erysipelas? In what way did this news affect his attitude to life? (paras. 18–30)

8. Why did everything about the pig's burial seem "overwritten" in White's eyes? (para. 38)

9. White states that he is writing his account of the pig's death "in penitence and in grief." (para. 41) Why should he feel penitent? Do you think he means this statement to be taken seriously?

The Writer's Style and Strategy

1. White's essay is a subtle blend of humour, irony, and pathos. Find examples of these differing tones in the essay, and explain their appropriateness.

2. Why does White "run ahead of his story" in the first three paragraphs? What function is performed by these paragraphs?

3. Discuss White's use of analogy in paragraphs 2 and 3. How does the analogy contribute to our understanding of White's feelings about the death of his pig?

4. Discuss the terms in which White describes the pig. What is conveyed by the use of the pronoun "he" rather than "it" in White's references to the animal? Why does he twice draw analogies between the pig and a child? (paras. 5, 12)

5. Examine the effect of each of the following statements in their respective contexts:

   (a) "I found myself cast suddenly in the role of pig's friend and physician — a farcical character with an enema bag for a prop." (para. 3)

   (b) "A pig couldn't ask for anything better — or none has, at any rate." (para. 4)

   (c) "I went back up to the house and to bed, and cried internally — deep hemorrhagic intears." (para. 37)

   (d) "'Poor piggledly-wiggledy!' said Miss Owen." (para. 34)

   (e) "Never send to know for whom the grave is dug, I said to myself, it's dug for thee." (para. 37)

6. In the concluding paragraph, White states that the whole community feels sorrow at "the premature expiration of a pig." How does he create a sense of that community in the course of his essay?

7. Discuss the essay's final paragraph. What makes it a fitting conclusion to the account that has preceded it?

Suggested Topics for Writing and Discussion

1. Most people have at one time or another suffered the loss of a pet. Working from a real or an imaginary experience, describe your own response to such an event.

2. As White explains in his essay, the breeding and butchering of animals for food is a commonplace feature of life on a farm. In recent years, however, animal activists have questioned our right to exploit animals, even in this way. Do you believe that we have the right to use animals as we see fit?

3. As White presents him, Fred the dachshund is more than a dog; he is a character in the drama of the pig's death. Describe an animal you have known that might be regarded as "a character."

Storm Over the Amazon
by Edward O. Wilson

1   The Amazonian forest of Brazil whipsaws the imagination. After two or three days there I grow familiar with the earthy smell and vegetation as though in a Massachusetts woodlot, so that what was recently new and wonderful starts to fade from my senses. Then some small event occurs to shift my conceptual framework, and the mystery comes back in its original force. One night I walked into the forest north of Manaus with a headlamp to study the ground surface and everywhere I saw — diamonds! At regular intervals of several yards, intense pinpoints of white light flashed on and off with each turning of the lamp. They were reflections from the eyes of wolf spiders on the prowl. When the spiders were spotlighted they froze into stillness, allowing me to peer at them from inches away. I could distinguish a wide variety of species by size, color, and hairiness. Where did they all come from? What was their prey, and how could so many kinds exist there in these numbers? By morning they would retreat into the leaf litter and soil, yielding the microterrain to a new set of predators. Because I had come for other purposes, I abandoned their study to the arachnologists who would surely follow.

2   Each evening after dinner I carried a folding chair to a clearing to escape the noise and stink of the camp I shared with Brazilian field hands. The forest around us was in the process of being clearcut northward along an east-west line, mostly to create short-lived pastures. Even so, what remained was and is one of the few great wildernesses of the world, stretching almost unbroken from where I sat across five hundred miles to the Venezuelan savannas.

Just knowing I was on the edge of that immensity deepened the sense   3
of my own purpose. I stared straight into the dark for hours at a time,
thinking in spurts about the ecological research that had attracted me
there, dreaming pleasantly about the forest as a reservoir of the unknown,
so complicated that its measure will not be taken in my lifetime. I was
a would-be conquistador of sorts, searching not for Amazonian gold but
for great discoveries to be made in the interior. I fantasized about new
phenomena and unborn insights. I confess this without embarrassment,
because science is built on fantasies that can be proved true. For me the
rainforest is the greatest of fantasy lands, a place of hope still unchained
by exact knowledge.

And I strained to catch any trace of sound or light. The rainforest at   4
night is an experience in sensory deprivation, black and silent as a tomb.
Life is moving out there all right, but the organisms communicate chiefly
by faint chemical trails laid over the surface, puffs of odor released into
the air, and body scents detected downwind. Most animals are geniuses
in this chemical channel where we are idiots. On the other hand, we are
masters of the audiovisual channel, matched in that category only by a
few odd groups like birds and lizards. At the risk of oversimplification,
I can say that this is why we wait for the dawn while they wait for the
fall of darkness.

So I welcomed every meteorite's streak and distant mating flash from   5
luminescent beetles. Even the passage of a jetliner five miles up was
exciting, having been transformed from the familiar urban irritant to a
rare sign of the continuance of my own species.

Then one August night in the dry season, with the moon down and   6
starlight etching the tops of the trees, everything changed with wrench-
ing suddenness. A great storm came up from the west and moved quickly
toward where I sat. It began as a flickering of light on the horizon and a
faint roll of thunder. In the course of an hour the lightning grew like a
menacing organism into flashes that spread across the sky and illumi-
nated the thunderhead section by section. The sound expanded into focused claps to my left, front, and right. Now the rain came walking
through the forest with a hiss made oddly soothing by its evenness of
pitch. At this moment the clouds rose straight up and even seemed to
tilt a little toward me, like a gigantic cliff about to topple over. The bril-
liance of the flashes was intimidating. Here, I knew, was the greatest
havoc that inanimate nature can inflict in a short span of time: 10,000
volts dropping down an ionizing path at 500 miles an hour and a
countersurge in excess of 30,000 amperes backup the path at ten times

that speed, then additional back-and-forth surges faster than the eye can follow, all perceived as a single flash and crack of sound.

7   In the midst of the clamour something distracted my attention off to the side. The lightning bolts were acting like photoflashes to illuminate the wall of the rainforest. In glimpses I studied its superb triple-tiered structure: top canopy a hundred feet off the ground, middle tree layer below that, and a scattering of lowest trees and shrubs. At least 800 kinds of trees had been found along a short transect eastward from the camp, more than occur natively in all of North America. A hundred thousand or more species of insects and other small animals were thought to live in the same area, many of which lack scientific names and are otherwise wholly unstudied. The symmetry was complete: the Amazonian rainforest is the most that life has been able to accomplish within the constraints of this stormy planet.

8   Large splashing drops turned into sheets of water driven by gusts of wind. I retreated into the camp and waited with my *mateiros* friends under the dripping canvas roof. In a short time leptodactylid frogs began to honk their territorial calls in the forest nearby. To me they seemed to be saying rejoice! rejoice! The powers of nature are within our compass.

9   For that is the way it is in the nonhuman world. The greatest powers of the physical environment slam into the resilient forces of life and nothing much happens. The next morning the forest is still there, and although a few old trees have fallen to create clearings and the way to new plant growth, the profile stays the same. For a very long time, approximately 150 million years, the species of the rainforest evolved to absorb precisely this form and magnitude of violence. They even coded its frequent occurrence into their genes. Organisms use heavy rain and floods to time their mating and other episodes of the life cycle.

10   Awe is what I am talking about here. It is the most peculiar human response, an overwhelming feeling of reverence or fear produced by that which is sublime or extremely powerful, sometimes changing perception in a basic way. I had experienced it by seeing a living system in a dramatic and newly symbolic fashion. Far larger storms occur on Venus and Jupiter, but they disclose no life underneath. Nothing like the forest wall exists anywhere else we will ever visit. To drop onto another planet would be a journey into death.

11   A few days later the grinding of gears announced the approach of the truck sent to return me and two workers to Manaus. We watched it coming across the pastureland, a terrain strewn with fire-blackened stumps and logs, the battlefield the rainforest finally lost. On the ride

back I tried not to look at it. No awe there, only defeat and decay. I think that the ultimate irony of organic evolution is that in the instant of achieving self-understanding through the mind of man, it doomed its most beautiful creations.

(1986)

The Writer's Subject

1. Why is the Brazilian rain forest of such importance to the writer?

2. In what respect are animals "geniuses" and humans "idiots"? (para. 4)

3. What aroused the writer's awe during his experience of the storm? (para. 10)

4. What is "the ultimate irony of organic evolution" to which Wilson refers to in the last paragraph of the essay?

The Writer's Style and Strategy

1. Explain the meaning of the opening sentence of Wilson's essay. In what sense does he use "whipsaw" here?

2. Why does Wilson call himself "a would-be conquistador of sorts"? (para. 3) Who were the conquistadors?

3. What details in Wilson's account give readers a sense of the power of the storm? Why does he place such emphasis on that power?

4. Why does Wilson describe the frogs' honking in the forest during the storm?

5. What words or phrases in the essay best convey the writer's feelings about the Amazonian forest?

6. What is the tone of the concluding paragraph? How is it created?

Suggested Topics for Writing and Discussion

1. Find out what you can about the ecological importance of the Amazonian forest, and show what is being lost through the process of its destruction.

2. The destruction of the Amazonian forest is an issue that has raised worldwide concern. However, similar concerns about the need to protect and enhance our natural environment are evident on a more local scale. Examine a conservation issue that has aroused debate in your community (e.g., the preservation of a park or marshland, the felling of old trees, the use of aerial sprays), and outline the principal arguments presented by both sides.

3. At some time in their lives, most people have been moved, frightened, or excited by an experience in nature. Describe one such experience in your life.

Patterns of Social Behaviour

Errington, B.C.

by Gail Anderson-Dargatz

To tell you about my home is to tell you about my self. I live in a house   1
trailer surrounded by corn fields, dairy cows and forest that I did not
choose to live in but now call home. No one is allowed in my writing
room, not even my beloved Floyd, and we wrangle over this bit of territory: he slips in for a book, I flick my hand and tell him to scram. Yet
in the kitchen I welcome all of visiting society and here we take meals,
drink tea and listen to CBC radio. There's a window in this kitchen
looking over the cats in the window box, the front deck on which we
grow sad apple trees, and beyond the deck our flower garden and the
corn field that hides us from our landlord and employer (who is one
and the same).

The kitchen is dominated by a floor-to-ceiling pine shelf, that Floyd   2
built, crowded with all manner of things: my maternal grandmother's
wooden cutting board and green weight scales; vats of dried flowers
from which I will make paper; jars and jars of foodstuffs that keep us
fed even in lean times; cards from friends; squash and gourds; ripening
pears; binoculars my lover uses to spy on cows in heat; and a brass
candlestick one of my British ancestors stole from a church.

To tell you about my garden is to tell you about my soul: it is a tum-   3
ble of green mint, planted two years ago as a handful of ragged yellow
roots and now woolly in flower, that is maneuvering a takeover, an up-
rising, a coup of my gentle, planned flower bed. It is crowded with flowering chives and wild in marjoram and left to its own devices, though
once a year, in spring, I plunge in to taming it with a vengeance that is
truly Herculean. It is bothered by grasshoppers and busy in bees and

full of strawberries that grew weedy and sour this spring, lacking the sweetness a bit of lazy sun might have provided.

4   To tell you about my neighbourhood is to tell you about my world: It is the road leading up to the post office and convenience store all housed in one large and rustic log building. It is the café where, once a day, we sit next to burly, black-faced grease monkeys and take bitter coffee in an effort to purge the literary pretence from our bowels. It is the three-store mall named, in rude salute to the Edmonton monster, West Errington Mall. It is Errington Farmer's Market to which we parade each Saturday in our ugly green truck (named Fugly) and where I drink too much coffee and mingle with irritating tourists (strangers) who know me for my writing, and locals (friends and farmers) who know only that I do write and could care less (and are therefore equally as irritating).

5   My husband's home, *his* soul — though we live in the same house, amble through the same garden and roam the same neighbourhood — is very different. Floyd is the automotive shop, the tractor next door, the cows whose lives he saves, replicates and milks. But he is also the African print he bought in Nairobi and the sunflowers he planted whose stalks, severe as temple columns, are made friendly by sunny yellow heads. He is nestled comfortably in cabbage, leaping up in stalks of corn and hidden in potato plants. He is as haughty as the bird-of-paradise, but can be as frivolous and fruitful as the pompom dahlias. He is all this and still the shy, contemplative solace of our hidden forest pond.

6   Some time ago Floyd became very ill and could not work and we became homeless. Not the homeless of the street, thank god, for we still had friends and family who would offer us sanctuary. But we came very close to that sort of homelessness. There were many moves, many uprootings. Our things were kept in storage. Without a home I became aware, perhaps for the first time, of the nature of home. With each move I didn't only lose a few precious possessions, I lost bits of myself. I became unsure. Who was I, without my surroundings, the knick-knacks and memories all packed away? I wasn't the Gail of my grandmother's cutting board, nor was I Gail of the brass candlestick. I was homeless Gail. This is when I came to see home and soul as one and the same. I realized home is not only a place in which we live; home is what defines us. It is, in a sense, who we are. How much less of myself, I wondered, would I feel if I were truly homeless, on the street, or in an ugly tenement house. How much less of myself am I now when I stumble across other souls in my neighbourhood who are shackled in homelessness?

7   In the 1950s my grandfather moved my grandmother from the farm

life she knew into the city of Vancouver, into a small house. Imagine this move: from a spread of fertile land down to an acre of struggling couch grass and concrete. All that she knew as home was gone: her friends, her community, her garden. I would have raged against the isolation of the city. I would have gathered myself into a corner and sulked. My soul would have shrunk to fit that acre. She, however, went around to her neighbours and asked them to collect fat: the tailings of bacon, the milky lard at the bottom of roasters, the white layer skimmed from chilled stock. What did her city neighbours think of her, I wonder? Did they see her as a backward farm woman, or down on her luck? Did they think she might make lard sandwiches for herself and her immigrant husband? Whatever they thought of her, they gave her the collected fat, and when she had enough she mixed the fat with water, coal oil, powdered ammonia, borax, sugar and lye to make soap. She then went around to the neighbours who had taken pity on her and at the moment she gave them the lovely gift of homemade soap she took back the dignity she had lent when she asked for the fat. She had an instinctive understanding of the dance that conjures community: the waltzing exchange of indebtedness and favour, and with this knowledge she not only made friends, she extended the realm of what was familiar, she extended what was home.

How is your home? Is it small and tidy, neatly confined? Or does 8 your clutter of possessions spew willy-nilly to intermingle artfully, or lustfully, with the possessions of your mate? Are your neighbours familiar? Are they friends? Do you borrow from them and give them small gifts? Are there homeless souls in the neighbourhood in which you live? Do you walk by them as you shop? What story does the city in which you live tell on you?

When my life is careening out of my control I am driven to clean 9 house. I organize drawers, sweep floors, ship half-finished craft projects to the thrift shop. At the time, and to my family, it can seem a needless diversion. But I must do it and when I am done it is not only my house that is organized. I can now handle problems I could not otherwise. If my home is in order, so too, it seems am I. If there are great changes in my life, things to which I must adjust, I dream of a house, old and feeble, rickety, creaking and lilting to the side. The house may collapse at any moment and yet I must do something in this house, find someone, or gain some object, and so I search the many rooms. Always there is a secret room that I stumble across, a part of the house I didn't know was there, a section of myself I'd never imagined I possessed.

10   I submit we all have rooms in our souls we don't recognize, and that
many of those rooms are out there, in the world of our senses: in our
homes, our gardens, even on the street. We may walk past cafés and
tube steak vendors, buskers and bums — and not recognize them as bits
of ourselves. We may refuse to volunteer to clean up our neighbourhood and not realize the harm we are inflicting on ourselves. Or, conversely, we may pluck flowers from our gardens, root out weeds, plant
a chrysanthemum, and never fully realize the good we are doing. For
our selfhood does not end at our skin, or at our clothes. It extends outward to the walls in which we live and we call this home, and home
extends still further to all that is familiar: to our place of work, to the
streets on which we walk, to the restaurants and theatres and bookstores
we chose to haunt, to the people we meet or pass by, to the gardens that
we tend. Our environment is not only a reflection of us, nor does it simply shape us. Our environment *is* us, the very soul of us, and we would
do well to care for it, tend it, show it affection as we would a beloved.
To show our surroundings — ourselves — such care is at the heart of
living graciously, to living with grace.

                                                                    (1996)

The Writer's Subject

1. What is the difference between the writer's "self" and her "soul" as she
   images these in the first three paragraphs of the essay?

2. Describe the character of the writer's husband, as conveyed through the
   details in para. 4.

3. What is it about the nature of "home" that the writer discovers when she
   and her husband must move? (para. 6)

4. How did the writer's grandmother cope with the move from a spacious
   farm to a small house in the city? What is the relevance of this reminiscence to the main point of the essay? (para. 7)

5. What connection does the writer draw between cleaning house and dealing with her problems? (para. 9)

6. What is the importance of the "secret room" that the writer sees in her
   dreams?

7. "For our selfhood does not end at our skin, or at our clothes" (para. 10).
   Explain what the writer means by this statement.

The Writer's Style and Strategy

1. How does the writer order her ideas in this essay?

2. Discuss the writer's use of descriptive detail in the first four paragraphs of the essay.

3. Does "the brass candlestick one of [her] British ancestors stole from a church" tell us anything about the writer's self? (para. 2)

4. What details does the writer choose to show us the kind of community she lives in? What is her attitude towards that community, and how is it conveyed? (para. 4)

5. What is the writer's purpose in asking the reader a series of questions in para. 8?

6. Discuss the writer's use of metaphor in para. 9.

Suggested Topics for Writing and Discussion

1. Describe your home environment as it reflects aspects of your "self" and "soul." If you share your home with others, describe one of them in the same way that the writer portrays her husband, through the details of his everyday environment.

2. Choose one room in your house and describe it through a selection of descriptive details. Try to make the description coherent by tying the details to your sense of the room's overall character.

3. The writer emphasizes the importance of community as an extension of self and home. Do you have a sense of your community as in some way a part of yourself?

4. Discuss a significant move you have made, and say how you adjusted to your "new home" — whether it be a rented room, a dorm, a new house, a new neighbourhood, a new city or country.

5. Anderson-Dargatz says that "We may refuse to volunteer to clean up our neighbourhood and not realize the harm we are inflicting on ourselves" (para. 10). Describe a neighbourhood with which you are familiar, and say what the impact might be of "cleaning it up."

Of Marriage and Single Life
by Francis Bacon

He that hath wife and children hath given hostages to Fortune, for they are impediments to great enterprises either of virtue or mischief. Certainly the best works and of greatest merit for the public have proceeded from the unmarried or childless men, which both in affection and means have married and endowed the public. Yet it were great reason that those that have children should have greatest care of future times, unto which they know they must transmit their dearest pledges. Some there are who though they lead a single life, yet their thoughts do end with themselves and account future times impertinences. Nay, there are some other that account wife and children but as bills of charges. Nay more, there are some foolish rich covetous men that take a pride in having no children, because they may be thought so much the richer. For perhaps they have heard some talk, "Such an one is a great rich man," and another except to it, "Yea, but he hath a great charge of children," as if it were an abatement to his riches. But the most ordinary cause of a single life is liberty, especially in certain self-pleasing and humorous minds which are so sensible of every restraint as they will go near to think their girdles and garters to be bonds and shackles. Unmarried men are best friends, best masters, best servants, but not always best subjects, for they are light to run away, and almost all fugitives are of that condition. A single life doth well with Church men, for charity will hardly water the ground where it must first fill a pool. It is indifferent for judges and magistrates, for if they be facile and corrupt, you shall have a servant five times worse than a wife. For soldiers I find the generals, commonly in their hortatives, put men in mind of their wives and children. And I think the despising of marriage amongst the Turks maketh the vulgar soldier more base. Certainly wife and children are a kind of discipline of humanity; and single men, though they be many times more charitable, because their means are less exhaust, yet, on the other side, they are more cruel and hard hearted, (good to make severe inquisitors) because their tenderness is not so oft called upon. Grave natures, led by custom and therefore constant, are commonly loving husbands; as was said of Ulysses, *"Vetulam suam praetulit immortalitati."*[1] Chaste women are often proud and forward, as presuming upon the merit of their chastity. It is one of the best bonds, both of chastity and obedience, in the wife if she think her husband wise, which she will never do if she find him jealous. Wives are young men's mistresses, companions for middle age, and old men's nurses. So as a man may have a quarrel to marry when he will. But yet he was reputed one of the wise men, that made answer to the question, When a man should marry? "A young man not yet, an elder man not at all." It is often seen that bad husbands have very good wives; whether it be that it raiseth the price of their husbands' kindness when it comes, or that the wives take a pride in their patience. But this never fails, if the bad husbands were of their own choosing, against their friends' consent; for then they will be sure to make good their own folly.

(1613)

Note

1. "He preferred his old wife to immortality."

The Writer's Subject

1. At the beginning of this essay, Bacon seems to give the advantage to the single life. How does he go on to qualify this view?

2. What is the single man's view of marriage and family, according to Bacon?

3. Why are unmarried men "not always best subjects"?

4. Why does Bacon think that churchmen should be single, whereas soldiers should be married?

5. Why, in Bacon's view, do single men make good inquisitors?

6. What qualities does Bacon suggest are necessary in a good wife?

7. What advice does Bacon offer about the best time for a man to marry?

The Writer's Style and Strategy

1. Explain the metaphor in the first sentence.

2. This essay is a loosely constructed contrast between marriage and the single life. In what ways does Bacon impose order on what might otherwise seem a series of unconnected observations?

3. What does Bacon's comment about single men's views of "their girdles and garters" reveal about his attitude to the single life? (In the Renaissance, "girdles and garters" were belts and stocking fasteners worn by men.)

4. The sentence beginning, "grave natures, led by custom..." acts as a transition between Bacon's discussion of married or single men and his observations on good husbands and good wives. What is the function of the allusion to the Homeric story of Ulysses and Penelope in this sentence?

Suggested Topics for Writing and Discussion

1. Write a brief essay on marriage versus the single life, twentieth-century style.

2. In "Of Marriage and Single Life," Bacon writes about marriage and the single life, but only as it affects men. Write an essay in which you explain why a woman should or should not get married. Use appropriate examples to support your arguments in favour of marriage or the single life for women.

3. Is there, in your view, any "best time" to marry?

A Hearing

by Hugh Brody

In June, Joseph and his family set up their summer camp on the Reserve. Four small households camped together in a patch of woodland only a few hundred yards from Joseph's house. There Atsin and David stretched a small tarpaulin between the trees and a sloping ridge pole. This provided shelter from rain, but, being open-sided, was cool. Sam Crown and Jimmy Wolf, Joseph and Liza, and Reza, Shirley and Tommy all pitched tents around a central fireplace. Atsin had a fire in front of his camp, but he and David — along with everyone else who lived or visited there — spent much of their time sitting, chatting, and eating by Joseph's fire. 1

The hot days of summer had their own special mood. Every morning one or two of the younger men went to find the horses, following their tracks along the riverside or into the hay and oat fields where they liked to feed. Once they had chased them back to camp, the hunters tethered the ones they thought they might need during the day. But it was often too hot to hunt; days slipped by without much activity. The men lay for hours, a short distance from the fires, half asleep, getting up to eat, visit a neighbour, or play cards. Liza, Reza, and Shirley fried bannock on the campfire above which they carefully hung meat to smoke and to protect it from flies. On very still days they also built smoke fires to keep away the flies and wasps that persistently bit the horses. Children roamed the hillsides and river banks looking for berries, swimming, or hunting rabbits and grouse. 2

Thomas and Abe Fellow worked almost every day on the Reserve ranch, riding off to herd cattle, move a bull from one meadow to an- 3 other, or look for horses that had strayed into the surrounding woods. Some days Sam and Atsin suggested a hunt, and then we would ride down the Midden River valley or drive to promising areas within fifteen miles of the Reserve. In summer, bull moose and buck mule deer are in prime condition, and hunting spots were chosen with them in mind. But tracking in great heat and through thick undergrowth and clouds of mosquitoes is hard work. Although enough kills were made to maintain an adequate supply of fresh meat, we spent most days dozing in the shade of the campsite.

4   In early August, almost everyone on the Reserve went to the Fort St. John rodeo. In mid-August, Joseph's brother and sister-in-law visited for two weeks, camping with us in the small wood by Joseph's house. At this time berries were ripening in abundance — first strawberries, then gooseberries, blueberries, and saskatoon berries. Everyone picked them as they found them, the children sometimes returning to camp with hats or plastic bags full of blueberries. Thomas's sister-in-law stewed panfuls of them in fat; that way, everyone said, you can eat as much as you want without any risk of diarrhoea.

5   In August, the heat was often intense. During the middle of the day even the mosquitoes kept to the cool shade of the undergrowth. The stillness was broken only by groups of children who walked and rode to a deep swimming hole a mile from camp. There they splashed and swam, sometimes riding into the water until their horses were out of their depth and then clinging on as the animal swam, or plunging off when a horse lunged and bucked in protest. A few older men and women at times came and watched these games, but many people spent their days in almost total inactivity. Summer is a time for resting.

6   So July and August passed quickly, quietly, and pleasantly. We twice moved camp from one part of the woodland to another. A porcupine, one or two mule deer, and grouse contributed to the excellence of our diet. From time to time someone went fishing within a half mile of the camp and returned with a sucker or a few rainbow trout. But there were also mishaps. Joseph was stung on the face by a wasp and spent two days with a painfully swollen cheek. Jimmy Wolf cut himself on the leg when angrily swatting at a bee with his hunting knife. One of the horses developed sores on its back and could not be ridden. These and similar events lent small features to a hazy, undifferentiated passage of time.

7   Then, in early September, thoughts turned yet again to Quarry and Bluestone, and the need to build up stocks of meat. Joseph spoke of the marmot that would be easy to shoot as they basked, fat from a summer

of feeding, on rocks high in the foot hills. He also said they might now find caribou in the mountains. It was at this time that the Blueberry Reserve was evacuated. A pipe in a nearby gas-cleaning plant had fractured and the reserve had been enveloped in the middle of the night in a cloud of hydrogen-sulphide gas. Thanks to haste, nobody was killed; but the community was forced to live temporarily in summer tents a few miles east of the Alaska Highway. This alarming event caused much discussion. Joseph and others at the Reserve had relatives who lived at Blueberry, and there had long been rumours of impending drilling for oil or gas on the Reserve itself.

But as summer turned to another autumn, the events at Blueberry 8 were overshadowed by talk of the Alaska Highway Pipeline, and about a plan to hold hearings in each of the communities that might suffer some of the consequences of this enormous project. An employee of the Northern Pipeline Agency (an office set up by the federal government to prepare social and environmental conditions as well as to facilitate pipeline construction) visited the Reserve. He left a sheaf of papers at the house of the Chief. Then, some weeks later, a long and difficult document was also left, which set out, in provisional form, the terms and conditions that might govern the pipeline's construction. Finally, a notice was fixed to the door of the meeting hall that announced a date on which a public hearing into these terms and conditions would be held.

It is possible that a few people on the Reserve saw, or even tried to 9 read, the documents, although no one did at Joseph's camp. If they had tried, they would have made little sense of the tortured bureaucratese by which every idea in the documents was obscured. Perhaps agency officials had attempted to discuss the ideas that they were advancing. If so, the people's interest or understanding was too slight for such ideas to become topics of conversation in our camp. The Alaska Highway Pipeline was seen as a vast, unwelcome, and perplexing menace. But no one knew quite where it was supposed to go; few knew what it would carry; no one knew if its possible dangers had been considered. The construction project that developers had hailed, and environmentalists bewailed, as the largest and most significant in the history of free enterprise was little more than a vague and distant enigma to the people who were supposedly to be its first and absolute victims.

Some chiefs and other representatives of the Indians of northeast 10 British Columbia had visited Ottawa the year before to appear before a parliamentary subcommittee, where they had spoken out against the pipeline. But the connection between that visit and the papers left in the Chief's home was not clear. White officials were always saying that bits of paper were of special importance, but right now there were other important matters at hand: the beginning of the autumn hunt, marmot, caribou.

11   In September, Joseph's household, along with several others, returned to Quarry for the first autumn hunt; but the weather broke and for two weeks the hunters endured almost continuous rain, eventually returning to the Reserve. By this time the hearing had become a more pressing issue. Northern Pipeline Agency officials had drawn up a provisional timetable, and political anxieties about how the whole process was to be effected were becoming intense. Yet the many meetings and disputes about the hearing took place in offices in Vancouver, Calgary, and Ottawa, and did not bear in any direct way upon the people. In early October, however, the Indians were told that representatives of the company planning to construct the pipeline, officials of the Northern Pipeline Agency, political and legal workers from the Union of British Columbia Indian Chiefs, along with an independent presiding chairman, and the press would converge upon the Reserve in November. Then, they said, they would listen to the people. A schedule set out the dates on which a hearing would take place at each of the reserves and at several of the towns and white communities throughout the region.

12   These community hearings were characterized by the Northern Pipeline Agency as an opportunity for the Indians and others to respond to the terms and conditions which they, at the agency, had already drafted. This limitation would not be rigidly enforced, since it was bound to result either in endless misunderstandings or a reduction of the hearings to discussion that, for many people, might well be unintelligible. The preparation of terms and conditions — the rules that were supposed to reflect the Indian interest — had also taken place before any close attention had been given to the Indian point of view.

13   The people at the Reserve nonetheless anticipated their hearing with great interest. Doubts may have arisen in the minds of their political representatives. Reports and papers left in the reserves by various officials may have gone unread. But the people themselves insisted that the coming meeting was of great importance. There was an ever-growing sense of occasion. No one had taken much trouble to ask the Indians what they thought about pipelines or any other frontier activity, and a hearing seemed to many like the first real chance to express their long-neglected points of view. As the event came nearer, the Fort St. John

radio station repeatedly announced the days and times of different hearings. Everyone at the Reserve including Joseph began to look forward to the occasion.

The morning of the hearing was sunny and cold. No one was quite 14 sure when it as supposed to begin. The notice on the door of the Hall gave the time as 10 A. M., but some people insisted that nothing much was going to happen before noon. At Joseph's house there was some excitement. On the previous afternoon, Atsin and Sam had discovered the freshly prepared den of a black bear. Branches and earth had been piled up around the den's entrance: the bear was about to bed down for the winter. The way the branches had been pulled and heaped left the men sure that they would be able to force the animal from its den and kill it in the entranceway, where it could easily be dragged out. The sooner they went back to the new den, said Atsin, the better. At this time of year, after a whole summer of feeding and the early autumn cold, the meat and fur should both be in excellent condition and there would be plenty of fat. Joseph added that he could use some bear grease, the best thing for softening and protecting the leather of his saddles and bridles.

Joseph, Atsin, and Sam were adamant: we should go and get the bear 15 right away. Maybe we would be able to get back in time for the meeting; maybe the meeting should wait until later in the day; or maybe we could get the talking over with quickly, and be on our way to the den by early afternoon. It was a perfect day for hunting. Who could possibly want to spend it listening to talk? What was there to say about the pipeline anyway? After a long discussion, we finally agreed that the bear hunt could wait until first thing the following morning. Joseph and Atsin decided to stay for the hearing. Sam Wolf, however, said he would never listen to talk when he could be out hunting. He pointedly prepared his equipment and set off on foot to look for moose. Brian Akattah and I went to the hall to put up the maps the people of the Reserve had drawn to show the extent of their hunting and trapping territories. Everyone else patiently waited at home for the hearing to begin.

It was a long wait. The chairman came early, to be shown the Reserve, 16 but it was midday before a busload of officials drove up to the hall. Specialists on social and economic impacts, a secretary to oversee proceedings, people whose job it was to record every word that was spoken, all climbed out and began to assemble their equipment. In separate cars came the men from West Coast Transmission — the company that would build the British Columbian section of the line — with their diagrams of the pipeline, the press, and representatives of the Union of Chiefs.

17   Inside the hall, chairs and tables were arranged, maps pinned on the
walls. In the kitchen, beside the main meeting room, the women of the
Reserve were cooking. They had prepared two kinds of moose stew,
venison steaks, and a bountiful supply of bannock. Rich aromas filled
the hall and indicated that however numerous and alien the outsiders
and their technology might be, the Reserve was going to do its best to
turn the hearing into its own kind of occasion.

18   By the time the hall was finally ready for the hearing to begin, there
were at least as many outsiders to listen, report, or observe as there were
Indians prepared to speak. The visitors were talkative and jovial and
quickly chose their seats. The Indians were quiet and reluctant even to
enter the room. The chairman took his place at the altar-table on which,
just over a year ago, Stan had drawn his hunting map. The two transcribers sat among a tangle of equipment. The Reserve women stayed
in the kitchen, out of sight and busy with their work, but able to see and
hear through a hatch and doorway which opened into the hall. Joseph,
Jimmy Wolf, Abe Fellow, Robert Fellow, and Clare Akattah, with other
community elders and leaders, had been urged into sitting at a table to
one side of the chairman. They looked uncomfortable. No doubt they
were wondering what was expected of them and were puzzled by the
microphones an official kept rearranging in front of them — technology that hardly seemed necessary in so small a room.

19   In this unpromising way, the meeting at length began. The chairman
started by trying to explain its purpose. He spoke about the Alaska Highway Pipeline and sought to give some rudimentary history of the litiga-
tion by which it was being facilitated. Nervously, in an attempt to
overcome the problems of language and culture, and conscious of the
extreme lack of background information among the people who sat there
trying to make sense of it all, he laid out the reason for the hearing. He
talked about terms and conditions and explained what kinds of rules there
would be. He tried, also, to describe the differences between the roles of
the governments, agencies, and construction companies. And he emphasized his wish to hear all that the people of the Reserve might have to say
about the pipeline, or any of the other developments to which it related.

20   The elders at the table watched and listened. They quickly felt some
sympathy for the chairman, an elderly man with a quiet voice and gentle manner, who was wearing beaded moccasins. By keeping their focus on him, they lessened the disturbing effects of the other strangers
and could feel that they were able to talk and be listened to in a personal, human way.

But it was not easy for them. The chairman was followed by the   21
Northern Pipeline Agency's secretary and a representative of West Coast
Transmission who introduced their colleagues and said what each of
them did. The introductions were not translated into Beaver. At this time,
in any case, only a small number of the people had come to sit in the
hall. They continued to stand in the doorway, in the kitchen, or to wait
outside. When the chairman did at last ask the Indians to offer their points
of view, Joseph began to talk. His clarity and confidence filled the hall
and transformed its atmosphere. He spoke in Beaver, with an interpreter.
The unfamiliarity of the sounds and the richness of his tone cast a spell
over the proceedings. The absurdities and awkwardness of the event
faded away. Here, at last, was an Indian voice. After every few sentences,
Joseph paused and let the interpreter translate. In English, the words
were not easy to grasp, and its being rendered in the third person made
the sense no clearer. But the points were not lost:

> He was saying in our country there was no such thing as money before
> the white man came; our only way to make a living is to hunt and there
> is no such thing as money to get from one another and big bulldozers
> that come over, go across our country.

> He is saying as long as there is the sun that goes over, that he shall never
> stop hunting in this country and wherever he likes to do, as long as the
> sun is still there.

> He is saying that the white man pushed his way into our country, that he
> stakes up all the land and a long time ago there was no people and then
> now there is so many....

> He is saying if the pipeline goes through, the game will never be here
> and is there no way that we can stop this pipeline from going through
> and when the game goes away how would the people make their sur-
> vival for meat?

> He says if the white man makes more roads, what if they get on my
> trapline and if they cut all the trees down, where would I go for hunting
> and where would I get the fur?

Then another of the elders made his statement. Again the Beaver language filled the room. Again the translation was uncertain, but the hesitant and broken English combined with the resonance of the Beaver to
powerful effect.

One after the other the people spoke. Atsin tried to convey the impor-   22 tance of Quarry and, determined to speak in English, made a cryptic, struggling, but moving statement. Robert Fellow spoke in a mixture of Beaver and English about the progressive destruction of the timber on his trapline and tried to explain how this is driving away the squirrel, marten, and lynx. Clare Akattah talked about her ten-year-old son and the happiness he gets from trapping. Brian Akattah explained the significance of the people's hunting maps and pointed out that his family — like others on the Reserve — needed to have their trapline. His mother spoke in support of him and, in one sentence, encapsulated what everyone had been trying to say: "There is no way you can make paper into moccasins."

23   After the Reserve people had spoken, the representatives of West Coast Transmission explained their project. With the use of a pipeline map, they gave numbers, routes and scraps of history: 444 miles of 56-inch diameter pipe along a 125-foot right-of-way; nine construction camps at 50-mile intervals; four compressor stations, the nearest to be 46 miles away; at Mile 92 of the Highway there is already a compressor station. West Coast Transmission's other pipelines were built in the area in 1956, 1961, and 1964. Several gathering lines have been built around Fort St. John and Fort Nelson to connect the main lines with scattered gas fields. The proposed Alaska Highway pipeline, permissions granted, will be started in 1982 or 1983; the section on muskeg would be built in winter, the other parts in summer and fall; pipe would be brought into the area by the British Columbia Railroad, and off-loaded at Fort St. John, Beatton River, or Fort Nelson; this would be done in winter and the pipe then stored at compressor station sites to be distributed to construction points along the line.

24   Then the Northern Pipeline Agency representative spoke. Pipelines cause problems. There must be rules; the people here, and in all the other communities in the region, must say what rules they think they need. West Coast Transmission will have to follow the rules. Problems with traplines or any other issues can now be voiced. The job is to finalize rules, but there can be more discussion. "Our purpose in being here," he said, "is to listen to you so that we can set the best rules possible, but at the same time, recognizing that those rules have to be reasonable."

25   These men did not speak for long. Perhaps they sensed the impossibility of their task. Their statements were not translated. They may have been untranslatable. The divide between the details they offered and the people's voices was too enormous. West Coast Transmission and the Northern Pipeline Agency men came as employees of remote organizations to discuss a pipeline. They were on a business trip, doing a job.

The men and women of the Reserve spoke of their homes, their lives and, moved to do so by profound apprehensions about the future, they struggled against language barriers and nervousness.

By 2 P.M. everyone had spoken. Joseph and Abe Fellow made final   26 statements. The chairman expressed his thanks and admiration and adjourned the meeting. The West Coast Transmission men began packing up their map. Agency officials bantered cheerfully with one another. The transcribers coiled up their wires and packed away their machines. The Union of British Columbia Indian Chiefs' representatives and organizers exchanged the happy opinion that the hearing had been a success. Meanwhile, work in the kitchen continued. A few individuals had slipped in there to eat. Children crowded around their mothers, curious to glimpse the proceedings in the hall without being caught by the strangers' eyes. When the hearing adjourned, everyone was urged to help themselves to steaming dishes of stews, steaks, bannock. It was a lavish welcome, an invitation to share. If speeches and explanations had not captured the attention of the visitors, or had caused them to be at all uneasy, here was a feast to reassure everyone and, in its way, to give special emphasis to the importance of what the Indians had said.

It was all very convivial. The chairman and his associates, however,   27 were eager to be on their way. Tired and satisfied, they regarded the hearing as ended. Once the social niceties were over and done with, the visitors could return to their homes and hotels in town satisfied that a job had been well done. Another hearing was scheduled for the next day. The formal business of making statements and placing them on the record was over. Children now ran in and out, and the two worlds of kitchen and hall had become the combined setting for a feast.

But the people had more to say. The Whites may have completed   28 their work, but now that everyone was eating the Indians' food and talking to one another without agonizing and distorting formality, the hearing could get under way on the Indians' terms. Relaxed and scattered around the hall and kitchen in small groups, the visitors and officials failed to notice when Jimmy Wolf's brother Aggan and Aggan's wife Annie brought a moosehide bundle into the hall. Neither Aggan nor Annie had spoken earlier in the day, but they went directly to the table at which the elders had sat. There they untied the bundle's thongs and began very carefully to pull back the cover. At first sight the contents seemed to be a thick layer of hide, pressed tightly together. With great care, Aggan took this hide from its cover and began to open the layers. It was a magnificent dream map.

29   The dream map was as large as the table top, and had been folded tightly for many years. It was covered with thousands of short, firm, and variously coloured markings. The people urged the chairman and other white visitors to gather round the table. Abe Fellow and Aggan Wolf explained. Up here is heaven; this is the trail that must be followed; here is a wrong direction; this is where it would be worst of all to go; and over there are all the animals. They explained that all of this had been discovered in dreams.

30   Aggan also said that it was wrong to unpack a dream map except for very special reasons. But the Indians' needs had to be recognized; the hearing was important. Everyone must look at the map now. Those who wanted to might even take photographs. They should realize, however, that intricate routes and meanings of a dream map are not easy to follow. There was not time to explain them all. The visitors crowded around the table, amazed and confused. The centre of gravity had suddenly shifted away from procedural concerns, pipelines and terms and conditions, to the Indians' world.

31   A corner of the map was missing and one of the officials asked how it had come to be damaged. Aggan answered: someone had died who would not easily find his way to heaven, so the owner of the map had cut a piece of it and buried it with the body. With the aid of even a fragment, said Aggan, the dead man would probably find the correct trail, and when the owner of the map died, it would all be buried with him. His dreams of the trail to heaven would then serve him well.

32   Prompted by the map, the elders spoke again about the way their life is changing, and the extent to which frontier developments have damaged their lands. They complained, too, about the weakness of dreamers today: would the young people be able to use these essential skills? Some of these thoughts had been spoken into the microphones and, in inchoate form, had become part of the official record. But now there was no recording, nothing that made the words official. The people now spoke in their own ways, and with real confidence. Most important of all, they said what they wanted and needed. The officials and visitors expressed delight and interest, but it is difficult to know how much they understood. Did the dream map come from too remote a cultural domain? Did the fractured and hesitant English in which the Beaver people spoke too completely obscure their points? Or, taking place after the hearing had been adjourned, off the record, was the conversation around the map seen as no more than a further display of agreeable hospitality? It is never easy to judge the political significance of informal

events. Evoking a strange and distant world, the Indians who showed
the dream map could have failed to make their point simply because
they were now using their own, very unfamiliar idioms.

All the men and women who spoke, whether at the microphones, in   33
seemingly sociable conversations over plates of food, or while the dream
map was being shown, said that their lives depended on traplines. They
said that logging should be carried out in such a way as to leave enough
habitat for squirrels and marten. They said that sports hunters must be
kept out of the Indians' hunting territories. Many also insisted that the
Alaska Highway pipeline either should not be built at all, or should somehow be built in a way that would not drive away the region's moose.
They spoke of oppression in the past and disregard for their interests in
the present. The substance of their remarks, along with the gentle tones
they used, made it clear that the people had not given up hope, either of
being listened to or of leading the kind of life that strengthens their
economy and culture. They had tried to explain their concerns in many
different ways. They took part in the outsiders' hearing and used it to
explain their point of view, but they also prepared moose meat stew and
showed a dream map. Despite a century of experience that might urge
them to do otherwise, the Indians took the hearing seriously.

Many of the Whites who spent the day in the Reserve hall said they   34
were deeply moved. The chairman repeatedly thanked the people for
their words and generosity, and thanked the elders for sharing their wisdom. Yet discussion of the dream map soon petered out, and the officials hurried into their bus, anxious to drive back to town. The people
of the Reserve were puzzled. Where had their visitors gone? The meeting was just getting under way. Thinking that there must be some misunderstanding, they asked everyone to come back into the hall, though
representatives of the pipeline construction company had long since
driven away.

Inside the hall, the elders explained that whenever a dream map is   35
taken out, someone must play a drum and chant. The visitors would, of
course, want to share in this. And one of the elders made the room echo
with the soft but insistent rhythm of the drum, and sang. No one understood the words, and the singer was too shy to explain. He sat in a corner and relied on the power of the rhythm to hold everyone's attention.
At the end of the first song he stopped and looked up. Perhaps someone
else would now drum? The evening was just beginning.

But as soon as the drumming stopped the officials expressed their   36
thanks and escaped again to their bus. They were tired, they said, and it

really was time they were back in town. From their point of view the
meeting had ended more than an hour before. The people in the hall let
them go. Perhaps they were no longer surprised by this demonstration of
the white man's haste and incomprehension. No one criticized or complained. The drummer began another song. The sound of the bus driving
away broke into the music, but soon the noise of its engine faded into the
distance. When the second song ended, the men said that it was a pity there
had been no time to play the stick game. They had looked forward to it.

37   People lingered in the hall. A young man visiting from another village drummed and sang for a while. Others ate. The elders talked about
dreams and dreaming, and the maps of the Indians' hunting territories
were taken from the wall. The hall began to seem very empty. It was
still early. Outside a group of men talked about the meeting and the
weather. "Tomorrow will be fine and cold," said Joseph. "We'll go and
look for the bear early."

38   By the next morning it was hard to remember all that had happened
at the hearing. Atsin led us to the bear's den. He and Sam Crown judged
the lie of its interior by the shapes and textures of the ground, and then
they dug and pounded until the animal appeared at the entrance. Sam
shot it. Joseph and Robert Fellow skinned and butchered the bear while
the others set off on a moose hunt. The sports-hunting season was over.
The people again had the woods to themselves. No one said whether or
not they felt they had gained anything by all the talk of the previous
day. It is difficult to mix hunting with politics. But when they discovered a sports hunter's equipment cache and old campsite a few miles
from the bear kill, their expressions of indignation were nothing if not
political. As he uncovered cans of fuel, ropes, and tarpaulins, and looked
around to see if a kill had been made, Atsin declared over and over again
that white men had no right to hunt there, on the Indians' land. When
Joseph heard about the cache he said: "Pretty soon we'll fix it all up.
We've made maps and everyone will see where we have our land."

                                                                    (1981)

The Writer's Subject

1. Brody quotes Clare Akattah as saying "There is no way you can make
   paper into moccasins." (para. 22) How does this statement "encapsulate"
   what everyone had been trying to say at the hearing?

2. Brody describes what both the Indians and the white men say at the hearing. What differences are apparent in their ways of presenting their respective positions?

3. What details in the account show that the Indians take the hearing seriously?

4. What is the importance of the fractured pipe incident in Brody's narrative? (para. 7)

5. What details in the essay help us understand the Indians' sense of time? The white man's sense of time?

6. What is the importance of the Indians' debate about whether to attend the hearing or kill the bear? (paras. 14–15)

7. This essay is taken from a book entitled *Maps and Dreams*, and maps play an important part in this essay itself. What different significances do the Indians and the white men attach to maps at the hearing? What is the force of the concluding sentence of the essay?

The Writer's Style and Strategy

1. Why does Brody spend the first few pages of this essay giving a detailed account of Indian life in the summer months?

2. How does Brody make the reader aware of where his sympathies lie?

3. What use does Brody make of the *verbatim* rendering of the translation of Joseph's words at the hearing? Compare this translation with the explanation of their project by the representatives from West Coast Transmission.

4. What details of the hearing emphasize the contrasting attitudes and behaviours of the white men and the Indians?

Suggested Topics for Writing and Discussion

1. This essay centres on a clash of cultures. Discuss examples or instances of cultural conflicts that may exist within your own community.

2. Using your college library, find out what you can about the Alaska Pipeline Hearings and the outcome of the project.

3. Brody's essay is, in part, about the impact of technological change on a traditional way of life, a situation also common in other areas of the world (e.g., mining and logging operations in the Amazon, and hydroelectric projects such as the James Bay project in Quebec or the Aswan Dam project in Egypt). Choose an example of this kind of technological impact and discuss its effect on the way of life of a specific cultural group.

4. In his essay, "The Tyranny of the Clock," George Woodcock discusses modern industrial man's view of time as a "commodity." Compare this view of time with that of the Indians as described by Brody.

Re-hanging the National Wallpaper

The Group of Seven and the Public Mind

by Daniel Francis

1   When I lived in Ottawa in the 1970s, I used to enjoy passing lazy afternoons at the National Gallery looking at the pictures. I remember how
surprised I was when I first encountered the Group of Seven collection.
These paintings were completely familiar — I'd seen them in school-
books and on calendars, posters, t-shirts, everywhere — yet at the same
time they were completely unexpected. I realized that I had never really
seen them before. These were not the flat, insipid, washed-out images
of the reproduction factories. Instead they were luminous and bright and
spirited. In a word, they were beautiful — which was not a word I had
thought to associate with the Group of Seven before.

2   Most people who see the G7 for the first time in person must experience similar sensations of discovery and recognition. Our sense of them
has been so attenuated over the years by repeated exposure to whole-
sale reproduction — Robert Fulford has called them "our national wallpaper" — that only an encounter with the real thing can rehabilitate it.
Such an encounter becomes more probable this year because the National Gallery has mounted a major exhibition to celebrate the seventy-
fifth anniversary of the Group's formation. The show opened in Ottawa
last October and travels to Montreal, Toronto and Vancouver throughout 1996. It is supplemented by a handsome book-cum-catalogue, *The
Group of Seven: Art for a Nation*, by curator Charles Hill.

3   The new exhibition offers an excuse to think again about the place of
the G7 in our history, a task made necessary by the myths which have

A.Y. Jackson, *The Edge of the Maple Wood*

surrounded the Group since its inception. For quite some time history remembered the G7 as a group of radicals who were forced to endure the vicious abuse of ignorant critics for daring to break with European tradition and to paint Canada in a bold, new way. This was the Group's own story, parlayed into legend by themselves and their admirers. It was appealing because it offered posterity that most irresistible of all pleasures, the chance to condescend to the past. How could the critics have been so stupid, we wonder? Couldn't they recognize the future when they bumped into it?

More recently the myth of the misunderstood modernists has been exposed for the half-truth it always was. The G7, it turns out, was not the victim of malign critics suffering from a colonial mentality. In fact, they won success almost immediately. They had wealthy patrons, including the National Gallery; most of the reviews of their shows were encouraging; they were chosen to represent Canada in major exhibitions abroad. Within a decade of its formation the Group was being hailed as Canada's "national school" of painters.

In which case the more appropriate question becomes: Why? Why did Canadians embrace the Group so easily? The answer is that for all their radical rhetoric, the G7 was essentially conservative. They gave

Canadian art lovers a chance to dabble in what they thought was modernism while remaining comfortably anti-modern at the same time. In other words, the G7 are the Red Tories, the Progressive Conservatives, of Canadian art, taking new ideas and dressing them down to suit the stodgy cultural environment in which they found themselves.

6 The Group of Seven began to coalesce in the years leading up to World War One. Appropriately enough, the prehistory of the Group begins with a painting. In 1911, A.Y. Jackson, a young Montreal painter, exhibited a canvas called *At the Edge of the Maple Wood* at the annual showing of the Ontario Society of Artists in Toronto. The painting depicted a familiar sugaring-off scene in rural Quebec, but its vigorous colour and texture made a strong impression on several painters who saw it in Toronto. Together these artists were just beginning to articulate a new approach to interpreting the Canadian landscape. The reclusive genius Tom Thomson, working as a photo-engraver with the commercial art firm Grip Ltd., later said that *Maple Wood* opened his eyes to the Canadian landscape. Thomson's colleagues at Grip, J.E.H. MacDonald and Arthur Lismer, both praised its fresh approach to a familiar subject. "Jackson's contribution was the beginning of a kinship and a movement in Canada," Lismer said. Lawren Harris wrote later that "it stood out from all the other paintings as an authentic, new expression."

7 Lawren Harris, wealthy son of an Ontario farm machinery manufacturer, did not forget Jackson's painting, and two years later he bought it from Jackson, thereby inaugurating a friendship which would transform Canadian art. The painting was a turning point, not just for the Group but for the country. "*The Edge of the Maple Wood* was to Canadian art what *Le Déjeuner sur l'Herbe* or *Les Demoiselles d'Avignon* was to French art," Harold Town has written. "Its plangent colour and effortless virtuosity, its sense of absolute Canadian place, galvanized a grumble of dissatisfaction into the tumble of revolt."

8 The sale of the painting occurred at a crucial moment for A.Y. Jackson, who had been contemplating a life in exile south of the border. Instead, he was persuaded by Harris to visit Toronto first, which he did in May 1913. Immediately he was swept up in the energy of the new movement of artists centred on the Arts and Letters Club. He spent that summer and fall sketching on Georgian Bay where he met James MacCallum, a Toronto ophthalmologist and art enthusiast who was becoming the patron of the new movement. MacCallum invited Jackson to use his comfortable cottage on Go Home Bay, then offered

to pay all of his expenses if Jackson, instead of going to the States, remained in Toronto.

In Toronto Jackson, who was then thirty-one years old, found a group 9 of artists who were ardently committed to an idea: the idea of painting Canada. "We lived in a continuous blaze of enthusiasm," Lawren Harris wrote. "We were at times very serious and concerned, at other times, hilarious and carefree. Above all, we loved this country, and loved exploring and painting it." When the Studio Building opened on Severn Street near Bloor and Yonge early in 1914, it became the clubhouse for the new movement. Several of the commercial artists from Grip worked at the building. One of them, Fred Varley, wrote his sister that "we are all working to one big end. We are endeavouring to knock out of us all of the preconceived ideas, emptying ourselves of everything except that nature is here in all its greatness, and we are here to gather it and understand it if only we will be clean enough, healthy enough, and humble enough to go to it willing to be taught."

"Every day was an adventure," Jackson recalled of this period. He 10 shared a space with Thomson, another of Dr. MacCallum's protégés, and the two artists became friends. They painted together, went to the movies together, conspired to be famous together and began making sketching trips together to the bush country of Algonquin Park north of Toronto. Thomson had discovered this wilderness setting in the spring of 1912 and had spent the summer of 1913 camping out in the park at Canoe Lake. The following year two of Thomson's colleagues from Grip joined them: Fred Varley and Arthur Lismer. "The country is a revelation to me and completely bowled me over at first," Varley confided in a letter. Lismer was equally affected. "The first night spent in the north and the thrilling days after were turning points in my life," he wrote. A definite Algonquin School of painting was taking shape.

At this early stage Thomson provided the spark of inspiration. His 11 style, with its audacious use of vivid colour and blunt brush strokes, seemed to embody the raw energy of the northern landscape. All the better that he was self-taught and completely ignorant of modern painting. The others considered him the prototype of what the new Canadian artist should be: an untutored genius, whose art sprang from an intuitive understanding of the land. They all came from cities, but Thomson was a country boy, raised on a farm near Georgian Bay where he learned to handle a paddle, a hunting rifle and a fishing rod with equal facility. His familiarity with the outdoors impressed his clumsier, less robust painting companions.

Tom Thomson, *The West Wind*

12   Things were different when winter forced Thomson out of the woods back to Toronto, where he lived like a fish out of water. Low on funds, he camped out in a shack behind the Studio Building, where he lived with a minimum of creature comfort, staying in all day, venturing out at night to tramp the snow-filled ravines of the Don Valley on snowshoes. It was here that he completed some of the most famous paintings in Canadian history, paintings such as *The West Wind* and *The Jack Pine,* paintings which have become iconic images by which Canadians recognize themselves.

13   All the elements were present as early as 1914 for the formation of the Group of Seven, though at this point it probably would have been called The Algonquin School. It did not happen, only because World War One happened first. The war scattered the Algonquin painters in several directions. Some enlisted, others remained at home. They were all stunned in the summer of 1917 by the unexpected death of Tom Thomson. In those horrible war years death itself was no surprise; it was the way Thomson died which was so shocking. He was renowned as a woodsman, an expert canoeist, someone who could paddle all day without rest. Yet apparently, on one of his frequent fishing trips in Algonquin Park, he fell out of his canoe and drowned.

While his death left Thomson's colleagues profoundly saddened, it   14
seemed to stiffen their resolve to continue along the path they had chosen. World War One derailed the new movement temporarily, but it did
not fundamentally alter its direction. Unlike their European counterparts,
thrust by the spiritual crisis of the war into nihilistic experimentation,
most evident in Dada and Surrealism, the Canadians regrouped in Toronto more determined than ever to paint the native landscape.

There is no account by any of the participants of the decisive meeting   15
at Lawren Harris's house which led to the formation of the Group of
Seven in mid-March 1920. The name was probably borrowed from similar groups which existed in New York (The Eight, or Ashcan School,
organized the sensational Armory Show of 1913) and Berlin. The first
use of the name was in a letter dated March 21 from Arthur Lismer to
Eric Brown, director of the National Gallery in Ottawa. "Harris, Jackson,
MacD[onald], Johnston, [Franklin] Carmichael, Varley and myself,"
Lismer ticked off the names of the founding members. "'Group of Seven'
is the idea. There is to be no feeling of secession or antagonism in any
way, but we hope to get a show together that will demonstrate the 'spirit'
of painting in Canada." There was nothing like a formal vote or a decision to incorporate. The Group of Seven was a movement, not an organization. What bound the artists together was not membership in an
exclusive club but a shared commitment to certain ideas about painting.
   The first exhibition by the G7 opened at the Art Gallery of Toronto,   16
May 7, 1920. Subsequently the Group and its supporters invented the
legend that the new movement was besieged by adverse reviews and viciously negative criticism. According to Lawren Harris, they were "attacked from all sides." The initial exhibition created "an uproar," claimed
Jackson many years later. "There was plenty of adverse criticism, little
of it intelligent." In fact the response was favourable, if less enthusiastic than the painters had hoped for. Only about 100 people a day came
to see the show, but for the most part critics were polite. The National
Gallery purchased three of the canvases and helped to organize a smaller
touring exhibition in the United States. The 1920 show did not receive
the critical mugging which its participants claimed it did.
   This should come as no surprise. Members of the G7, while they liked   17
to see themselves as young rebels, were actually all established painters who by 1920 had been part of the Toronto art scene for a decade or
more. MacDonald, the eldest, was forty-seven years old; he had been
showing his paintings since before the war. So had Harris, Jackson and

Lismer, all of whom were approaching middle age. Both the Ontario government and the National Gallery had purchased their work. Several of the Group made their living as commercial artists and their illustrations appeared in such mainstream magazines as *Maclean's* and *Canadian Magazine*. Wealthy patrons were expressing interest. Still, despite all this evidence of support, the Group insisted throughout its life, and for many years after, that critical opinion was overwhelmingly against it.

18   The Group's persecution complex began developing back before the war. It took human shape in the portly figure of Toronto critic Hector Charlesworth, contributor to *Saturday Night* and a fixture on the city's art scene. While most reviewers approved, or at least tolerated, the Algonquin painters' riotous landscapes, Charlesworth conceived an enduring dislike for them which he expressed with vehemence. His first run-in with a future Group member occurred in 1916 when J.E.H. MacDonald exhibited several paintings at the annual Ontario Society of Artists show. "MacDonald certainly does throw his paint pots in the public's face," Charlesworth wrote. He went on to say that MacDonald's "crude" depictions of the Shield country could more aptly be titled "Hungarian Goulash and Drunkard's Stomach." MacDonald responded in a letter to the *Globe* newspaper in which he berated Charlesworth's ignorance and superficiality, and accused him of libel.

19   This skirmish has become one of the most celebrated incidents in Canadian art history, obscuring the fact that the Algonquin work actually received a pretty favourable reception. Charlesworth himself shied away from further confrontation for several years. He did not review the Group's inaugural show in 1920, nor did he take much notice of the flurry of exhibitions which followed over the next two years. But as public acceptance of the Group's work increased, he could not keep silent, bursting back into print in 1922 with an attack on the National Gallery for what he thought was its excessive patronage of the Group, "those theatrical scene painters." Charlesworth would never be reconciled to the new movement. He was particularly irritated by its claim to be the first painters to develop a distinctively "Canadian" approach to their art. He saw himself as the defender of an earlier generation of artists who were just as committed to "independent expression" as the Group, but got no credit for it. When British critics also praised the Group's work following a large exhibition of Canadian paintings in Wembley, England, in the spring of 1924, Charlesworth became even angrier. He had already gone on record as calling the Group's style

"freakish" and "violent." Following Wembley, invective took over completely. Members of the Group were a bunch of "paint slingers" devoted
to the "cult of ugliness."

In retrospect it is clear that the dustup with Charlesworth worked [20]
to the Group's advantage. The controversy kept the G7 in the public
eye, never a bad thing for artists struggling to find buyers for their
work. More important, it provided the Group with a narrative, a way
for the public to understand what was going on even when it did not
understand the artistic issues involved. According to this narrative,
members of the Group were young rebels fighting to establish a modern, "Canadian" outlook in the face of overwhelming opposition from
an ignorant press and a backward-looking Old Guard. In 1926, with
the appearance of Fred Housser's book, *A Canadian Art Movement:
The Story of the Group of Seven,* this interpretation of events was enshrined as history. Housser, a financial journalist, was an ardent supporter of the Group. His book described their break with European
traditions, their struggle to develop a new style through "direct contact with Nature herself," their disputes with the critics and "the entire
press of the country," and their ultimate emergence as the first important art movement to arise in Canada. The Group triumphed, wrote
Housser, because it was unafraid to express the native landscape in entirely new ways. No artists before the Group were mature enough to
take Canada as its own subject, he claimed, on its own terms. By
changing all that, wrote Housser, the Group represented the coming
of age of Canada as a culture.

Housser's book was a work of propaganda, not scholarship. Much of [21]
what he said about the G7 was simply not true. As he himself admitted,
the critical reception of their work actually was pretty favourable, Hector Charlesworth and a few others notwithstanding. The Group were
not the pariahs of the art world they made themselves out to be. Nor
were they the first to attempt to paint in a distinctively "Canadian" style.
Artists before them had chosen similar subject matter, although presented
in the manner of the civilized landscapes of Europe. Nor were members of the Group quite as innocent of European training and ideas as
Housser claimed. Jackson, Harris, Lismer, Varley and Carmichael all
studied abroad. Tom Thomson was the only one who was truly self-
taught, and he was not strictly speaking a member of the Group. Regardless, Housser's book went a long way to reconciling the public to
the new movement. Its publication roughly marks the transformation of
the Group from delinquent sons to patriarchs of the family. "No longer

Tom Thomson, *The Jack Pine*

can the Group enjoy the vilification that is the reward of the precocious few," observed playwright Merrill Denison in 1928, "because the many have now joined them and the calliope has become merely an over-crowded bandwagon."

22   The Group's success was due to other factors besides good public relations. Most importantly, of course, they were tremendously talented artists who produced some of the most beautiful and evocative paintings in the history of Canadian art. But the public usually requires something more than talent. It embraced the Group because the artists so successfully attached themselves to a nationalistic agenda. The Group claimed to be creating a new national consciousness. This was MacDonald's "big idea": the creation of a national purpose through an appreciation of the rugged Canadian landscape. "We believe wholeheartedly in the land," they declared. In this respect the Group perfectly matched the spirit of the times, in Canada at least. During the Twenties Canadians were seeking new ways of imagining themselves as a mature, independent nation. They were receptive, therefore, to a movement of artists which claimed to find in the local landscape a distinctive national identity, and claimed to have found a uniquely Canadian style for expressing it.

The Group's down-to-earth approach to painting also endeared them 23
to a broad public. G7 members were not tweakers of bourgeois noses.
They were painters who went into the wilderness to track down their
paintings, much like hunters after prey. They were "modern coureurs-
de-bois," not effete intellectuals starving in their garrets. They spoke of
art as an energetic, manly activity; they identified painting with adven-
turing and exploring. (The reality was somewhat different. Jackson, for
example, described J.E.H. MacDonald as "a quiet, unadventurous person, who could not swim, or paddle, or swing an axe, or find his way in
the bush.") They presented their work in simple, accessible language.
One of their pre-war exhibitions made no apology for offering "pictures
which were suitable for home use, such as one could live with and enjoy." Art was like "any other national Canadian industry," MacDonald
wrote: "when our people decide that Art had better be grown at home
than imported from Holland, they'll find that they'll get a better article
at a lower price." Spoken like a member of the Canadian Manufacturers' Association. These were all attitudes which appealed to Canadians
who wanted to feel proud of their youth and vitality and common sense,
not shamefaced at their lack of sophistication.

The Group was looking for a domestic audience where one had not 24
existed before. Charles Hill reveals that in 1924 only 2 percent of the
paintings purchased in Canada were by Canadian artists. There was virtually no demand for their work, so the G7 had to create one. They did
so by going down market. In an early version of the Art Bank, they made
their paintings available for rent; they toured them around to small towns;
they talked about their work in accessible language and presented themselves in non-threatening ways.

As Hill points out, the Group's relatively tame subject matter also 25
endeared it to the Canadian public. No one had to avert their eyes. There
were no nudes descending staircases, no Mona Lisas with moustaches.
Admirers could be modern, without being "modern," *au courant* without being immoral and nihilistic like those scandalous Europeans. This
was modern art that was clean and bracing and stood for something.
"There has not been the slightest attempt at degeneracy," declared Eric
Brown, sounding disappointingly conventional for the director of an
important art gallery.

Robert Fulford has said that the G7 was Canada's version of Modern- 26
ism. It is probably more accurate to say that, for better or for worse, the
Group was what Canada got *instead* of Modernism. Unlike members of

the Group, Modernist painters in other countries did not propagandize for nationalism. Quite the reverse, they despised nationalism as a root cause of the recent war. Nor did Modernists appeal to the comfortable classes. Quite the reverse, they were in revolt against the "botched civilization" of their elders. Merrill Denison could write in 1928 that the G7 was "as Canadian as the North West Mounted Police or an amateur hockey team." It is impossible to imagine the European avant-garde being compared to a police force.

27   Hill's survey of cultural life in Canada in the Twenties reveals that there was very little Modernism going on here. His point just as readily applies to the literary world where writers like Morley Callaghan, John Glassco, and even Robert Service (whose northern ballads make a kind of literary parallel to the work of the Group), had to go to Paris to find it. The experimental "isms" of Europe — Cubism, Surrealism, Futurism, Expressionism, Dadaism — gained no adherents in Canada. It is only in comparison to other Canadian artists that the G7 appeared modern. In comparison to European art, the Group was decidedly rearguard.

28   The Group succeeded in creating an audience for art in Canada, and for Canadian art. Wittingly or not, it also helped to create a very narrow vision of what constituted art. Under the Group's influence paintings came to be judged according to how Canadian they were, which tended to mean how many rocks, trees and totem poles they contained. The G7 became the country's official School because it was conservative, threatened no one, made almost no one uncomfortable, and appealed to a brand of nature worship masquerading as patriotism. With "modernists" like these, there was no need to be modern.

29 Eventually a new generation of artists and critics grew embarrassed by the G7, as Modernism somewhat belatedly began to find a following in this country. In the 1930s and 1940s, for example, abstraction took hold. In this new context, the Group's commitment to landscape seemed old-fashioned. And to a degree this view of the Group persists even in the epoch of Post-modernism in which we currently find ourselves.

30   The retrospective exhibition which the National Gallery has mounted would like to rescue the Group from such condescension, but evidently some of our cultural gatekeepers continue to feel uneasy in the presence of the west wind and the jackpine. When the show opened at the Art Gallery of Ontario in January, curators there felt obliged to mount a parallel show beside it. Titled The Oh!Canada Project, it aimed to provide an alternative "interactive" space for gallery visitors to express their

own feelings about Canada. When critic John Bentley Mays objected to this show on the grounds that it was a politically correct trivialization of the Group's work, he sparked a lively exchange of letters to the editor of the *Globe and Mail*. One side of the debate endorsed Mays's view; the other argued that he was a stuffy white guy who failed to recognize how relevant the AGO was marketing itself to new constituencies of gallery-goers.

If anything, the new show reveals that we have not found a way of being comfortable with our National School of Painters, whose work, whether Modernist or any other-ist, remains unique in the world of art. After all these years, some of us still feel the need to apologize for them. They continue to be an itch we cannot help scratching. Meanwhile, if you get a chance, do what I did. Go see the pictures. All the rest is complication. 31

(1996)

The Writer's Subject

1. Why did Robert Fulford call the works of the G7 "our national wallpaper"? (para. 2)

2. What are the myths about the G7 that the writer believes should be reexamined? What evidence does he cite to disprove those myths? (paras. 3, 16–17)

3. Why did the members of the G7 insist that they were the victims of hostile criticism, despite evidence to the contrary? (paras. 16–17)

4. How did the "dustup" with Hector Charlesworth work to the advantage of the G7? (para. 20)

5. Why does Francis call the book by Fred Housser "a work of propaganda, not scholarship" (para. 21)?

6. What political factors, in the writer's view, contributed to the success of the G7? (para. 22)

7. Explain the writer's assertion that "G7 members were not tweakers of bourgeois noses" (para. 23). How did this set them apart from painters in other countries?

8. Why, according to Francis, did experimental art such as Dadaism or Surrealism gain no adherents in Canada? Why does he call the G7 "rearguard" in comparison to their European contemporaries? (paras. 26–27)

9. How did the G7 painters set about creating a "domestic audience" for their work? (para. 24)

The Writer's Style and Strategy

1. What, in your view, is the prevailing tone of this article? How is it established? Is it well chosen for the writer's purpose?

2. What kind of audience would you imagine the writer has in mind for this article? Give specific evidence to support your view.

3. Francis describes the G7 as "the Red Tories, the Progressive Conservatives, of Canadian art" (para. 5). Explain the point of such a comparison.

4. What is meant by "a familiar sugaring-off scene in rural Quebec," and what is the writer's point in introducing this detail? (para. 5)

5. Explain the phrase "plangent colour." (para. 7)

6. Explain the distinction Francis draws between "movement" and "organization." (para. 15)

7. Francis describes claims and counterclaims concerning the work of the G7 and its importance. Is it possible to determine what his own views are? Point to any elements of the essay in content or style that in your view convey the writer's own opinions.

Suggested Topics for Writing and Discussion

1. The critic Harold Town is quoted as praising Jackson's painting "At the Edge of the Maple Wood" for "its sense of absolute Canadian place" (para. 7). What do you think this means? What might be the characteristics of a painting that conveys such an idea? Use as your example another painting by Jackson or any of the G7 painters.

2. Francis describes two paintings by Tom Thomson ("The West Wind" and "The Jack Pine") as "iconic images by which Canadians recognize themselves" (para. 12). Explain "iconic images," and say whether you would agree with this assessment of the paintings' impact.

3. Choose a work that is associated with a school or movement in painting, literature, music, or architecture produced in the last 50 years, and show how its features are characteristic or representative of the movement to which it belongs.

4. Francis argues that the work of the G7 was widely accepted in Canada "because it was conservative, threatened no one, made almost no one uncomfortable, and appealed to a brand of nature worship masquerading as patriotism" (para. 28). What, in your view, is the basis of the Group's continuing popularity across Canada today?

5. Choose any of the northern ballads by the poet Robert Service and demonstrate how it might be regarded as "a kind of literary parallel to the work of the Group." (para. 27)

6. Find the issues of the *Toronto Globe and Mail* carrying the article by John Bentley Mays on the National Gallery's G7 exhibition in October 1995, together with the correspondence that followed. Summarise the main points of the debate conducted in the newspaper, and offer your own views about the matter.

7. In his essay "Westward Oh!", Martin Walker examines the depiction by American artists of the old West. In what ways does his essay raise issues similar to those developed here by Daniel Francis?

De Mortuis

by J.H. Plumb

1   The British have hilarious fun over the quaint funerary habits of the Americans. The death of Hubert Eaton, the world's greatest entrepreneur of death, and the recent discovery of a funeral home for pets, by a wandering British journalist, released another gale of satirical laughter in the English press. The mockery was hearty and sustained; yet was it deserved? Well, certainly much of Mr. Eaton's Forest Lawn is hard to take — the wet, nursery language for the hard facts of dying ("the loved one" for the corpse, "leave taking" for burying, and "slumber" for death), the cosmetic treatment (the contortions of death waxed away, replaced by rouge and mascara and fashionably set hair) — all of this is good for a gruesome joke. The place names of Forest Lawn appall — Lullabyland, Babyland. The piped guff, the music that flows like oil, and the coy fig-leaved art give one goose flesh.

2   One turns, almost with relief, to a harsh fifteenth-century representation of the dance of death — livid corpses, jangling bones, and skulls that haunt. How wholesome, after Hubert Eaton, seem the savage depictions by Bonfigli of the ravages of plague, or even the nightmares of death painted by Hieronymus Bosch. And how salutary in our own age to turn from Forest Lawn to the screaming, dissolving bodies of a Francis Bacon painting, for surely this is how life ends for most of us, in pain, in agony.

3   And if Forest Lawn nauseates, what of the Pets Parlor? "Blackie" combed and brushed, stretched out on the hearth rug before a log fire, waits for his sorrowing owners. The budgerigar is wired to its perch. The Ming Room houses the Siamese cats, and if you want to do your

kitty proud, you can spend three hundred dollars or so on a stately laying out, a goodly coffin (if you're worried about its fun in the afterlife,
you can put an outsize rubber mouse in with it), and naturally a special
plot in Bide-A-Wee, the memorial park for pets. President Nixon's dog,
Checkers, had the treatment: he lies among the immortals in Bide-A-
Wee, like Hubert in Forest Lawn.

However, this will become a mere second-class death if deep-freez-   4
ing really catches on, as it shows every sign of doing. The Life Extension Society is spreading, and the entrepreneurs have smelled the profit
in immortality. As soon as the breath goes, get yourself encapsulated in
liquid nitrogen and stored in one of the specially constructed freezers
that are springing up all over America from Phoenix to New York. And
so wait for the day when they can cure what you died of, or replace
what gave way — the heart, the brain, the liver, or the guts — or reju-
venate your cells.

None of this is cheap: the capsule costs four thousand dollars, and then   5
there are the freezing costs and who knows what they may be in fifty
years, so it would be imprudent not to make ample provision. Forest
Lawn may be death for the rich; this is death for the richer, death for the
Big Time. But in America there are a lot of very rich, so maybe soon now,
outside all the large cities, there will be refrigerators as huge as pyramids,
full of the frozen dead. This surely must be a growth industry.

Perhaps by the year 2000 Hubert Eaton will seem but a modest pio-   6
neer of the death industry, for who does not crave to escape oblivion?
The rich have always tried to domesticate death, to make death seem
like life. The American way of death is not novel: seen in proper historical perspective it reaches back not only down the centuries but down
the millennia, for it is a response to a deep human need.

Some of the earliest graves of men, dating from paleolithic times,   7
contained corpses decked out with bits of personal finery and sprinkled
with red ocher, perhaps the symbol of blood and life, done in the hope
of a future resurrection. After the neolithic revolution, which created
much greater resources and considerable surplus wealth, men went in
for death in a very big way. Doubtless the poor were thrown away, burned
or exposed or pushed into obscurity, back to the anonymous mind from
which they came.

The rich and the powerful, high priests and kings, could not die; they   8
merely passed from one life to another. Because the life hereafter was
but a mirror image of life on earth, they took with them everything they
needed — jewels, furniture, food, and, of course, servants. In the Royal

Graves at Ur, some of the earliest and most sumptuous of tombs ever found, a row of handmaidens had been slaughtered at the burial — death's necessities were life's. No one, of course, carried this elaboration of funerary activity further than the Egyptians. And the tombs of Pharaohs and the high officials of the Egyptian kingdom make Forest Lawn seem like a cheap cemetery for the nation's down-and-outs.

9   What should we think of vast stone mausoleums outside Washington, stuffed with personal jewelry from Winston's, furniture from Sloane's, glassware by Steuben, food from Le Pavilion, etc., etc., and in the midst of it all the embalmed corpse of a Coolidge or a Dulles? We should roar with laughter. We should regard it as vulgar, ridiculous, absurd. Pushed back three millennia, such habits acquire not only decorum but also majesty, grandeur, awe.

10   The Egyptians were as portentous in death as in life, and their grave goods only occasionally give off the breath of life, unlike the Etruscans who domesticated death more completely and more joyously than any other society. A rich caste of princes built tombs of singular magnificence, filling them with amphorae, jewels, and silver. And they adorned their walls with all the gaiety that they had enjoyed alive. There was nothing solemn about their attitude to death. In their tombs they hunted, played games, performed acrobatics, danced, feasted; their amorous dalliance was both wanton and guiltless. Deliberately they banished death with the recollected gusto of life. No society has brought such eroticism, such open and natural behavior, to the charnel house. But in the annals of death, Etruscans are rare birds.

11   How different the grandiose tombs of medieval barons, with their splendid alabaster or marble effigies. There they lie, larger than life, grave, portentous, frozen in death, a wife, sometimes two, rigidly posed beside them, and beneath, sorrowing children, kneeling in filial piety, the whole structure made more pompous with heraldic quarterings. Yet these are but another attempt to cheat death, to keep alive in stone what was decaying and crumbling below. And even here a breath of life sometimes creeps in. The Earl and Countess of Arundel lie side by side, dogs beneath the feet, pillows under the head, he in armor, she in her long woolen gown. But, movingly enough, they are holding hands. The sons of Lord Teynham cannot be parted, even in death, with their hawk and hound. Nor were these tombs so cold, so marmoreal, when they were first built. They were painted, the faces as alive with color as the corpses in the parlors of Forest Lawn.

12   Seen in the context of history, Forest Lawn is neither very vulgar nor

very remarkable, and the refrigerators at Phoenix are no more surprising than a pyramid in Palenque or Cairo. If life has been good, we, like
the rich Etruscans, want it to go on and on and on, or at the very least to
be remembered. Only a few civilizations have evaded expensive funerary
habits for their illustrious rich, and these usually poverty stricken ones.
For all their austerity, the Hindus, burning bodies and throwing the ashes
into the Ganges, have maintained distinction in their pyres. Not only
were widows coaxed or thrown onto the flames, but rare and perfumed
woods were burned to sweeten the spirit of the rich Brahman as it escaped from its corrupt carapace. Cremation à la Chanel!

What is tasteless and vulgar in one age becomes tender and moving   13
in another. What should we say if we decorated our tombs with scenes
from baseball games, cocktail bars, and the circus, or boasted on the
side of our coffins of our amatory prowess, as erect and as unashamed
in death as in life. And yet when the Etruscans do just these things, we
are moved to a sense of delight that the force of life could be so strong
that men and women reveled in it in their graves.

So the next time you stroll through Forest Lawn, mildly repelled by   14
its silly sentimentality, think of those Etruscans; you will understand
far more easily why seven thousand marriages a year take place in this
California graveyard. After all, like those Arundels, Eros and Death have
gone hand in hand down the ages. The urge to obliterate death is the
urge to extend life, and what more natural than that the rich should expect renewal. How right, how proper, that Checkers should be waiting
in Slumberland.

(1967)

The Writer's Subject

1. What is Plumb's thesis, and where is it most clearly stated?

2. What aspects of American funerary practice provoked "satirical laughter"
   in the British press?

3. What is suggested about American attitudes to death in the first five paragraphs of the essay?

4. Why does Plumb seem to find the grim paintings of death described in
   paragraph 2 "wholesome" or "salutary" in comparison with the practices
   of Forest Lawn?

5. What parallels does Plumb draw between American burial practices and
   those of earlier civilizations? To what conclusions do these comparisons
   lead him, with respect to the apparent vulgarity of places like Forest Lawn?

6. How did the Etruscans banish death "with the recollected gusto of life"? (para. 10) What connection does Plumb draw between Etruscan burial practices in particular and those found in Forest Lawn? (paras. 13–14)

7. Why is Plumb not surprised that "seven thousand marriages a year take place in this California graveyard"? (para. 1)

The Writer's Style and Strategy

1. What examples of euphemism does Plumb include in the first paragraph?

2. What tone is established in the opening paragraph of the essay? Where is there a clear shift in tone, and what occasions that shift?

3. What is conveyed of the writer's attitude to American funerary practices by such statements as "the entrepreneurs have smelled the profit in immortality" (para. 4), or "This surely must be a growth industry?" (para. 5)

4. How does Plumb convey his sense of the absurdities involved in the burial of pets? (para. 3)

5. Show what use Plumb makes of comparison and contrast as a strategy to structure his argument. In this connection, what function is performed by paragraph 6?

6. In his use of historical evidence, Plumb alludes to the tombs of medieval barons and gives several examples. (para. 11) Discuss how the use of examples and descriptive details at this point develops Plumb's thesis.

7. Discuss the effectiveness of the essay's conclusion. How well does it round off Plumb's discussion? What does its tone reveal about his attitude?

8. Why does Plumb use a Latin title for this essay?

Suggested Topics for Writing and Discussion

1. Plumb describes some of the methods by which modern Americans try to "domesticate death." What aspects of funerary practice in your own community seem to you to have the same purpose?

2. Plumb treats cryogenics (a term to describe the deep-freezing of the dead, taken over from the branch of physics dealing with very low temperatures) somewhat sardonically; he focusses almost exclusively on its high costs. What is your own view of this process? Do you think that any ethical or religious considerations may be involved?

3. Many cemeteries in North America now forbid the erection of funerary monuments; they require instead that graves be marked only with a horizontal stone so that the effect of a park is achieved. What is your view of

this practice? Do you think cemeteries should be showplaces? Parks? Quiet places for the dead and their surviving family and friends?

4. Cemeteries are often fascinating places, especially as tourist attractions. Using travel guides from your local library or bookstore, find out what you can about some of the famous cemeteries of Europe and prepare your own "mini-guide to the best resting places." You may want to look up some of the following: Père-Lachaise in Paris — burial place of Frederick Chopin, Oscar Wilde, Jim Morrison and many other celebrated figures; the Protestant Cemetery in Rome — burial place of John Keats and Percy Bysshe Shelley's ashes; the Central Cemetery in Vienna — burial place of Mozart, Beethoven, Brahms, and Schubert; Highgate Cemetery in London — burial place of Karl Marx and George Eliot.

Nostalgia
by Witold Rybczynski

> *However, insofar as there is such reference to a historic past, the peculiarity of "invented" traditions is that the continuity with it is largely factitious.*
>
> Eric Hobsbawm
> The Invention of Tradition

1   We've all seen this comfortable man; his face looks out from the advertising pages of magazines. His graying hair, which is close-cropped, belies his age — he is only forty-three — just as his frayed shirt and faded Levi's belie his eight-figure income. The latter is barely hinted at by the silver Rolex discreetly half-hidden by the jacket sleeve, and by the hand-made cowboy boots. What he does for a living is not immediately clear. Well, we do know that despite his worn work clothes he doesn't pick lettuce; migrant workers don't wear muted wool-and-mohair sport jackets. He could be a professional athlete — a purveyor of light beer and deodorant — but his clothes are too low-key, and in any case he lacks a mustache. Still, whatever he does do, it seems to agree with him — a half-smile crosses his tanned face. But his glance is neither the vacuous stare of the professional clotheshorse nor the self-satisfied grin of the celebrity; this man looks content. "Look at me," he is saying, "I could dress any way I want, but I don't need to impress anyone, not even you. I feel good just like this." Since all ads, whether for cigarettes or for cancer research, are selling something, we can only conclude that what this man is selling is comfort.

2   Of course, this man is comfortable. Why shouldn't he be? He owns

90 percent of a business whose annual sales total a billion dollars. His personal after-tax income in 1982 was said to be fifteen million dollars. He has all the perks that success of this kind brings: an upper Fifth Avenue duplex (more about that later), an estate in Westchester, another on Jamaica, a beach house on Long Island, a ten-thousand-acre ranch in Colorado, and a private jet to travel among them.

What does he do, this business mogul, this multimillionaire, this comfortable man? He thinks up ways for people to dress. Fifty years ago he might have been a tailor or a dressmaker; if he had lived in France he would have been called a couturier. But to call Ralph Lauren a tailor is like calling the Bechtel Corporation a builder. The word does not convey the sheer size or the international scale of the operation. A tailor makes clothes; Lauren's corporation franchises manufacturers on four continents who turn out products that are sold in more than three hundred shops carrying his name, as well as in specialty boutiques in department stores in the United States, Canada, England, Italy, Switzerland, Scandinavia, Mexico, and Hong Kong. As it has grown, his business has also diversified. It started modestly, with neckties, but soon expanded to men's wear, then clothes for women, lately a special line for children. Now perfumes, soaps, cosmetics, shoes, luggage, belts, wallets, and eyeglasses all bear his imprimatur. Lauren's is that most modern of professions: he is the total fashion designer.

The first thing that strikes us about Lauren's clothes is how American they look. They are based on recognizable homegrown images: the western ranch, the prairie farm, the Newport mansion, the Ivy League college. The feeling of déjà vu is intentional: Lauren is an orchestrator of images. Although his clothes are not faithful replicas of period dress, their appearance does reflect popular ideas about various romantic periods of American history. We have seen them all before, in paintings, in photographs, on television, and, especially, in films.

Lauren understands films. One of his early designs for men's evening wear consisted of a black dinner suit, wing-collared shirt, white gloves, and a white silk muffler. Reporting on the show, *The New York Times* described this outfit as having "stepped out of a Leslie Howard movie"; Lauren himself appeared in black pinstripes and reminded the reporter of Douglas Fairbanks. The cinematic simile was appropriate, since Lauren had just designed the men's costumes for a film version of *The Great Gatsby*. For a brief time, Twenties-influenced fashion became popular; dress-for-success, Lauren called it. A few years later, many of his designs were featured in the film *Annie Hall*; the comfortable, relaxed clothes worn by its stars, Woody Allen and Diane Keaton, became the look of the year. This inclination to be a costumer, along with a career built as much on advertising as on fashion shows and *Vogue* magazine, has not assured Lauren a secure position in the fashion world. It is unlikely that there will ever be a Ralph Lauren retrospective of the Metropolitan Museum, as there was in 1984 for Yves Saint Laurent.

6   Whether or not fashion design is an art is arguable, but there is no doubt that today it is a very big business. It all started in 1967, when Yves Saint Laurent, the boy wonder of haute couture who had succeeded Christian Dior as Paris's leading dressmaker, opened Rive Gauche, a chain of shops that sold expensive but mass-produced clothes with the now-famous YSL label. Rive Gauche proved to be a great success (there are now more than 170 outlets around the world), and soon other couturiers such as Courrèges and Givenchy were lending — that is, selling — their talents to the *prêt a porter* trade. Even the conservative Chanel succumbed to this trend, although the house did so only after the death of its founder.

7   Haute couture had provided the fashion industry with glamour, but ready-to-wear clothing now became its bread and butter.[1] In the process many designers acquired a distinctly commercial relationship to the products that they endorsed; if you've seen athletes peddling golf clothes or tennis shoes you get the idea. It is difficult to believe that Pierre Cardin, for instance, would ever be caught dead wearing much of the perfume or the clothing (made in a Bombay sweatshop) that carries his cachet. It is obvious that the fashion pates often have little, if anything, to do with the design of "their" products; in any case, their reputations, like those of Arnold Palmer or Bjorn Borg, are made elsewhere. In that sense, at least, mass marketing, lucrative though it may be, is only a sideline.

8   Unlike Cardin and Saint Laurent, whose careers were founded in the exclusive dress salons, Lauren was never a couturier; from the beginning he was concerned with mass-produced clothing, and so he acquired an understanding of popular instead of elite tastes. His renown as a designer has been the result of his commercial success, not vice versa. His influence on the way that Americans dress is often overlooked, precisely because it has been indirect. Most of the women who copied Diane Keaton's loose tweed jackets or oversized men's shirts in 1977 were unaware that they were imitating Lauren originals. The 1980s fashion for Ivy League clothes — the so-called preppy look — was also Lauren-inspired.

9   What does this have to do with domestic comfort? In 1984, Ralph Lauren announced that he was entering the home furnishings field. The only surprise is that it took him so long. The relationship between cloth-

ing and interior decoration is venerable. Look at a Hogarth painting of
an early Georgian interior. The soft curves of the carved furniture were
a counterpart to the rich costumes of the time and complemented the
voluminous gowns of the women and the lace fronts and elaborate wigs
of the men. The slightly pompous interiors of the nineteenth century
also reflected clothing fashions; skirted chairs and gathered draperies
imitated the details of how cloth was used in skirts and gowns, and wallpaper copied the designs used in fabrics. The richness of Art Deco furniture mirrored its owners' luxurious costumes.

And how does Ralph Lauren intend to dress the modern home? The   10
line of furnishings — it is called a Collection — provides everything
needed to decorate the home. The Collection is meant to be, in the words
of Lauren's publicists, a total home environment. You can now put on a
Lauren dressing gown, slip on a pair of Lauren slippers, shower with
Lauren soap, dry with a Lauren towel, walk across a Lauren rug, glance
at the Lauren wallpaper, and slip between Lauren sheets, beneath a
Lauren comforter, to sip warm milk from a Lauren glass. You can now
be a part of the ad.

It is doubtful, however, that this is "the next plateau of life-style mar-   11
keting," as one enthusiastic distributor has called it. For one thing, the
Collection will have a limited clientele. The Lauren furnishings, which
are not mass-produced, are expensive, and are being sold only in fashionable department stores in major cities like Chicago, Dallas and Los
Angeles. For another, despite Lauren's long list of products the Collection is limited and does not include a full range of furniture — thus far
only a few wicker pieces are available. Nevertheless, it is worthwhile
examining how a corporation whose success is based on understanding
the public's taste for clothing interprets popular images of the home.

I go to Bloomingdale's, New York's store for the upper-middle-class   12
consumer, to witness this next plateau. "Fashion is a function of life-
style," a voice says as I get off the escalator. Startled, I turn. There he
is, the comfortable man, star of his own furnishings video. Across from
the television monitor is the entrance to the Ralph Lauren Home Furnishings boutique, which consists of a number of rooms displaying the
Lauren products. They remind me of the Shelburne Museum, in Vermont, where furnishings and objects are displayed in actual houses as
part of recreated room settings. This gives the historical rooms the impression of being inhabited. In Bloomingdale's, the Lauren rooms are
also fully recreated, with walls, ceilings, even windows, and look more
like movie sets than store displays.

13   It turns out that the Collection is not one line but four. The four have
names: "Log Cabin," "Thoroughbred," "New England," and "Jamaica."
The walls of the "Log Cabin" are chinked with white plaster, and the ceiling is supported by rough-hewn beams. Buffalo Check and Woodsman
Plaid blankets cover the massive pegged timber bed. The bedclothes are
soft brushed flannel with matching pillow shams, sheets, and bedskirts.
The rugged furniture is obviously handmade, and goes nicely with the
American Indian hearth rug on the floor. A pair of Bean boots stands by
the bed; on the side table is a copy of everyone's favorite summer-cot-
tage reading, the *National Geographic* magazine. The general effect is
one of moneyed rusticity, the furnishings equivalent of designer jeans.

14   "Jamaica" is across the aisle. It is obviously designed for the Sunbelt.
A giant bamboo four-poster bed, draped with what looks like voile but
could be mosquito netting, stands in the center of a cool white room.
The colors of the Italian linens, Swiss embroidery, and chambray com-
forters are feminine — pink and blue. The bedclothes and table linens
are trimmed with ruffles and embroidered with floral bouquet designs.
If the inhabitant of "Log Cabin" is out shooting moose, the owners of
this home must be on the verandah sipping Planter's Punch.

15   The decor of "Thoroughbred" is equally genteel — a country gentleman's room of dark colors highlighted by the polished brass of the bed-
stead and the gleaming mahogany wall paneling. Pheasant and hunting
motifs abound, as do paisley prints and tartans.[2] Wall coverings are
checks, tattersalls, and foulards. The effect is a bit overwhelming, like
being caught inside Rex Harrison's closet. At the foot of the bed are a
pair of riding boots. The publicity stills showed two beagle hounds dozing among the tweeds. I look for them in the cozy setting, but that must
be where Bloomingdale's drew the line. "Thoroughbred" includes a distinctly anglophile table setting: teapots, egg cups, and a covered muffin
dish, as well as plates ornamented with scenes of mounted polo players. "A dream England filtered through preppy America," an uncharitable British journalist called it.

16   "New England" contains staid Early American furniture; this could
be the bedroom of a restored Vermont country inn. The colors are muted,
the wall fabrics are solid and candy-striped to match the Oxford-cloth
bedclothes. It is the least theatrical of the four; Yankee sobriety doesn't
lend itself to dramatization.

17   The four themes have a lot in common. They are inspired by Lauren's
own homes — the Jamaican hideaway, the ranch, the New England farm.
They are aimed at the growing number of people who have second, and

even third homes — by the lake, next to the ski slope, or on the beach — and so they follow rural models. At the same time, the comfortable informality of these furnishings is likely to be just as appropriate to apartments and townhouses as to weekend retreats. The furnishings are also an extension of Lauren's clothing designs, which have been called "western and outdoorsy or conservative and tweedy." In that sense these are settings, for which the costumes have already been designed. This tendency to coordinate clothes and furnishings is to be continued in two other themes not featured in Bloomingdale's — "Mariner" and "Safari." The former is to establish an appropriately yachtsmanlike setting; the latter will convey, according to the designer, the feeling "of a hunter getting out of his Range Rover and aiming his elephant gun."

18   The settings have something else in common, something which has become the hallmark of the Lauren look. One of his early and more extravagant outfits for men consisted of a Donegal tweed jacket with black belt and bellows pockets, worn with white flannel trousers, and complete with collar pin and English shoes of saddle leather. "You just know that the gentleman wearing it belongs to a private club and drives a Rolls-Royce, or at least wants to give that impression," wrote a fashion reporter, who dubbed this the "Vanderbilt look." In much of his recent clothing designs, Lauren has managed to restrain a tendency to evoke the symbols and the style of turn-of-the-century wealth, but the major influence on the treatment of the furnishing themes continues to be what an associate calls the look of "old money."[3] Old, in most cases, means falling between 1890 and 1930. The log cabin setting, for instance, has the affected, cedar-stump rusticity that used to characterize rich men's hunting lodges at the end of the last century — although Lauren, a supporter of wildlife preservation, has carefully omitted the stuffed animal heads mounted on the wall. The "old world elegance and refinement" of the Jamaican furnishings brings to mind the relaxed pace of life in the white porticoed homes of the island during its colonial period. The country gentleman's retreat evoked by "Thoroughbred" could be Lord Sebastian Flyte's room in Evelyn Waugh's *Brideshead Revisited*. But this is not period decor in the conventional sense — it lacks the consistent and specific details of neo-Georgian or French Antique, to name two popular styles. Lauren is not so much interested in recalling the authentic appearance of a historical period as he is in evoking the atmosphere of traditional hominess and solid domesticity that is associated with the past.

19   This acute awareness of tradition is a modern phenomenon that reflects a desire for custom and routine in a world characterized by con-

stant change and innovation. Reverence for the past has become so strong
that when traditions do not exist, they are frequently invented. There
are other examples than the Scottish tartan. After England adopted a
national anthem in the mid-eighteenth century, most European nations
quickly followed suit. The results were sometimes curious. Denmark
and Germany, for instance, simply set their own words to the English
music. Switzerland still sings "Ruft die, mein Vaterland" to the strains
of "God Save the King," and until Congress adopted an official national
anthem — in 1931 — Americans sang "My Country 'Tis of Thee" to
the same regal music. The "Marseillaise" is original, and authentic; it
was written during the French Revolution. But Bastille Day was first
celebrated in 1880, a hundred years after the actual event.

20   Another example of invented tradition is the popular fashion for so-
called Early American or Colonial furniture. In most people's imagination it represents a link to the values of the Founding Fathers, the Spirit
of '76, an integral part of the national heritage. The truth is that the Colonial style owes its existence not to an unbroken continuity passed from
colonial father to republican son, but to the much more recent Centennial celebrations of 1876. The Centennial encouraged the founding of
many so-called patriotic societies, such as the Sons (now defunct) and
the Daughters (still active) of the American Revolution, the Colonial
Dames of America, and the Society of Mayflower Descendants. This new
interest in genealogy was due partly to the Centennial itself, and partly
to efforts by the established middle class to distance itself from the increasing number of new, predominantly non-British immigrants. This
process of cultural authentification was fortified by furnishing homes in
the so-called Colonial style, thus underlining the link to the past. Like
most invented traditions, the Colonial revival was also a reflection of its
own time — the nineteenth century. Its visual taste was influenced by the
then current English architectural fashion — Queen Anne — which had
nothing to do with the Pilgrim Fathers, but whose cozy hominess appealed to a public sated by the extravagances of the Gilded Age.

21   Lauren's invented traditions are derived from the literary and cinematic imagination. The English country life suggested by "Thoroughbred" was already in decline when Waugh wrote about it, forty years ago.
Today, where fox-hunting still exists, it is practiced almost in secret, to
avoid the attacks of various environmental and animal-welfare groups.
"Mariner" conjures up the Newport of F. Scott Fitzgerald, but although
his blazer-clad sailors lolled about on sixty-foot teak-decked ketches —
crewed by hired help — most of us have to be content with a car-topped

fiberglass dinghy. "Safari" recalls a time when wealthy Americans and
Europeans could go to Africa and shoot their hearts out; today, if they
go they are less likely to be carrying a Mannlicher — as Hemingway did
— than a Minolta. The real postindependence Jamaica is less old-world
charm than packaged tours, dope, and threatening Rastafarians. As for
the simple fireside pleasures implicit in "Log Cabin," these have been
replaced, or at least augmented, by hang gliders and mountain bikes.

What is also striking about these handsome interiors is the absence   22
of so many of the things that characterize modern life. We look in vain
for clock-radios, electric hair dryers, or video games. There are pipe
racks and humidors in the bedrooms, but no cordless telephones, no tel-
evisions. There may be snowshoes hanging on the cabin wall, but there
are no snowmobile boots by the door. In the tropical setting we glimpse
an overhead fan instead of an air-conditioning unit. The mechanical paraphernalia of contemporary living has been put away, and replaced by
brass-cornered gun boxes, silver bedside water carafes, and leather-
bound books.

Admittedly, these tableaux are not real interiors but only backdrops   23
designed to set off the fabrics, tableware, and bedclothes that form the
Furnishings Collection; it is unlikely that anyone would ever furnish
his or her home to look like the Lauren publicity brochures. But that is
beside the point; advertisements often represent a not altogether real,
stylized world, but one which does reflect society's view of how things
ought to be. These themes have been chosen to evoke popular images
that are informal and comfortable, reminiscent of wealth, stability, and
tradition. What they leave out is as revealing as what they include.

There is little doubt that these carefully arranged rooms would be   24
compromised by the introduction of modern objects. Like a director filming a costume epic who blanks out the telephone wires and the drone of
the overhead jet, Lauren has kept the twentieth century at bay. There is
no polypropylene thermal underwear drying in front of the stone fireplace, no electric toaster on the table, to intrude on the traditional
coziness of "Log Cabin," just as there is no personal computer on the
desk in "Thoroughbred." How do we fit reality into this dream world?
One way is to not even try. The headquarters of Estée Lauder Incorporated, a large cosmetics corporation, are located in the General Motors
Building in New York. The main offices are conventional; the chairman's
office is not — it resembles the small drawing room of a Loire château.
Estée Lauder's desk is Louis XVI, as are two of the side chairs. The
two wing chairs are Second Empire, the couch is Belle Epoque, and the

lamp holder is French Bouillotte (obviously, the candles have been re-placed by electrical bulbs). The only modern objects are two telephones. The office of Malcolm S. Forbes, owner of *Forbes* magazine, does not make even that compromise with modernity. No telephones disturb the top of his elegant Georgian partner's desk, which is flanked by a pair of Queen Anne corner chairs and a fine Chippendale-style wing chair. A chandelier hangs from the ceiling and illuminates the mahogany-paneled room, originally built in the nineteenth century and free from any re-minders of the twentieth. This is as much a place for drinking a glass of vintage port as for transacting business.

25   This sort of historical verisimilitude is difficult to achieve, and obvi-ously expensive. In any case, outside Mr. Forbes's and Mrs. Lauder's offices are the telex machines, flickering word processors, ergonomi-cally designed stenographer's chairs, steel file cabinets, and fluorescent strip lighting that are necessary for the proper functioning of a modern corporation. One reason that all this equipment is outside is that it is not easy to integrate it into a Louis XVI salon or a Georgian study. Only a few modern devices lend themselves to being camouflaged in period clothing. A Baume & Mercier carriage clock, for instance, has an oc-tagonal case of pearwood with brass fittings, that contains a quartz move-ment. A strictly modern device like a photocopier, on the other hand, has no precedents, it can only be disguised, and were this ever attempted the result would be about as satisfying as when television sets are made up to look like Colonial credenzas.

26   So the modern world is kept at bay. These office interiors, like the settings of the Lauren Collection, present the appearance of a way of life that no longer exists. Their reality is no deeper than the flocked covering on the wall; a cynic would point out that the lady in the Louis XVI office was actually born in Queens, and Mr. Forbes in Brooklyn (Lauren, that other anglophile, grew up in the Bronx). But whether the way of life is remembered, or simply imagined, it nevertheless signifies a widely held nostalgia. Is it simply a curious anachronism, this desire for tradition, or is it a reflection of a deeper dissatisfaction with the sur-roundings that our modern world has created? What are we missing that we look so hard for in the past?

                                                                                           (1986)

Notes

1. The dressmaker Charles Frédéric Worth invented the term "haute couture" in 1858. For a long time it could only be used by fashion houses that were recognized by the French gov-ernment Office pour Art et Création. Curiously, haute couture was *not* the highest accredita-tion; the work of the most select fashion houses was referred to as "couture création."

2. Lauren is certainly unaware, as are most people, of the recent origin of the "traditional" Scottish tartan. The idea of associating specific tartans with different families occurred during the first part of the nineteenth century — not in the mists of Celtic antiquity — and, like the kilt itself, was a modern invention. The introduction of tartans was the result of Queen Victoria's cult of the Highlands, as evidenced at Balmoral Castle, her Scottish country home, and of a sales campaign by cloth manufacturers who were seeking to develop larger markets for their products.

3. The friction between new and old money took a bizarre turn recently, when it was reported that Lauren had brought legal action for infringing on "his" corporate symbol against an organization that had the temerity to use the figure of a man on a horse swinging a mallet as its insignia. The object of his suit was the United States Polo Association, founded in 1900.

The Writer's Subject

1. Why does Rybczynski call Ralph Lauren a "total fashion designer"? (para. 3)

2. What is distinctly American about the look of Lauren's clothes? (para. 4)

3. In what respects, according to Rybczynski, does Lauren differ from such famous couturiers as Yves St. Laurent or Pierre Cardin? (paras. 5–8)

4. What does Rybczynski mean by calling the relationship between clothing and interior decoration "venerable"? (para. 9)

5. What do the different rooms in Lauren's "Collection" in Bloomingdale's have in common? What is the nature of their appeal, according to Rybczynski? (paras. 17–18)

6. What, according to Rybczynski, is Lauren's goal in making use of "period" designs? (paras. 18–23)

7. To what does Rybczynski attribute the modern awareness of and desire for tradition? (para. 19) What does he mean by "invented" traditions? (paras. 19–21)

8. What has been left out of Lauren's interiors? (paras. 22–24)

The Writer's Style and Strategy

1. Why does Rybczynski begin by describing Ralph Lauren as he appears in magazine advertisements?

2. What is Rybczynski's purpose in the repetition of "comfort" and "comfortable" in the first two paragraphs?

3. Discuss the meaning and the intended effect of the following statements, in their respective contexts:

   a) "Now perfumes, soaps, cosmetics, shoes, luggage, belts, wallets, and eyeglasses all bear his imprimatur" (para. 3);

   b) "The feeling of déjà vu is intentional: Lauren is an orchestrator of images" (para. 4);

   c) "You can now be a part of the ad" (para. 10).

4. Rybczynski gives detailed descriptions of the four Lauren rooms in Bloomingdale's. (paras. 12–18) What elements of diction or phrasing suggest the writer's attitude to those rooms?

5. What are the main stages of Rybczynski's discussion? How does he effect transitions from one stage to the next?

6. How does Rybczynski use contrast to drive home his point about "invented traditions" in paragraph 21?

7. Examine the last three paragraphs of the essay. Why does Rybczynski move away from a study of Ralph Lauren? Does the conclusion present us with a change of focus, or is another strategy involved?

8. While this essay is complete in itself, it is also the first chapter in Rybczynski's book, *Home: A Short History of an Idea*. What features of the essay suggest such a relationship? In this regard, look particularly at the last paragraph.

Suggested Topics for Writing and Discussion

1. Rybczynski says that Lauren's designs follow rural models. What, in your view, accounts for the appeal of the rural model, especially what Rybczynski calls "moneyed rusticity"?

2. Rybczynski says that "acute awareness of tradition is a modern phenomenon that reflects a desire for custom and routine in a world characterized by constant change and innovation" (para. 19). How important is tradition in your own family or community? Give examples to illustrate your view.

3. Rybczynski's essay is concerned with nostalgia as it is expressed in home furnishings. Write an essay in which you focus on two or three things that have nostalgic value for you and explain, if you can, the basis of their significance.

4. Analyze an ad for fashion — either in clothing or in home furnishings — and discuss what the ad suggests to the audience. Give attention to background as well as foreground details in the ad.

5. Analyze the current trends in fashion evident in the clothes of a particular group (e.g., college students, business executives, teenagers), and suggest what image the wearers seek to project.

To Our Valued Customers

In which Roger and Jan enable armchair shoppers to select a life

by Garry Trudeau

Dear Readers:

It's April again, which means Jan and I have just returned to Mill   1
Valley from another buying trek through the Annapurna, an ordeal that
has left us spent but elated. As always, you, our valued catalog customers, were never far from our thoughts — especially the evening we lingered over jasmine tea with a Mahayana Buddhist monk at the Four
Winds Monastery, perched precariously above a roaring tributary of the
Ganges. As we sipped to the rhythmic whirl of prayer wheels, I in my
all-cotton, breathable Sahib Gear™ Punting Pants, Jan in her wind-
resistant Amelia Earhart Aviator's Bra, we couldn't help noticing the
elegant saffron robe that enveloped our host. The rustic fabric, simple
and unfussy, draped beautifully — perfect, as Jan remarked to his holi-
ness, for curtains.

Well, one thing led to another, and before you knew it, we'd bought   2
the monastery and put the monks to work weaving our new Katmandu
Cottage Curtains (see page 32; also available in cranberry and moss).
We're proud to have brought a traditionally indolent people into the new
economy, giving them dignity and a chance to contribute to their country's nascent GNP. And because we've taught the monks to scrupulously
detoxify their dyes before dumping them upstream from the tiny, unspoiled Nepalese villages (whose honey-skinned children are so to die
for that Jan and I actually adopted one), your purchase of our hand-
stitched window dressing will help save the planet for future generations.

3   You can find this and other new offerings in our Simpler Times Furnishings Collection, which still features best sellers like our woven bamboo Margaret Mead Litter Chairs; our World War I Turkish Cavalry
Helmets (wonderful as planters); and our Lord Kitchener Lawn Furniture, made entirely of distressed, vintage cricket paddles. A new favorite
of Jan's dad, who's very particular when it comes to comfort, is our
hand-rubbed rhino-skin Royal Bengalese Club Chair. Sink into this
overstuffed beauty, and try not to imagine yourself in the highest ech-
elons of the Raj, ordering a vodka tonic or dispatching 1,000 Gurkhas
to certain death in the Khyber Pass.

4   The excitement over our new home furnishings spills over into the
latest additions to Sahib Gear™, our traditional themewear collection
for anyone born too late to experience colonial rule, steamer travel, first-
edition Fitzgerald, freshly ironed linen and servants who were like members of the family. Since you can't go back to Paris in the '20s or Havana
in the '40s or even Brooklyn in the '50s, we bring it to you, with all the
quality jodhpurs, dusters, spats, boaters, corsets, spurs, poodle skirts,
pince-nez and butcher's smocks you've come to expect from us — but
at a fraction of the price you might pay at an ordinary costume shop.

5   Why do we go to so much trouble? Because here at J. Entitlements
we believe that you, our valued customers, deserve a life — even if it's
not your own. Toward that goal, we now offer Enhanced Living®, a
total life-style ensemble inspired by the visual and sartorial motifs of
leading bygone eras. Simply choose a historical period or figure, and
one of our life-style engineers will refurbish your entire house and wardrobe with the corresponding furniture, objets, garments, fragrances and
bedding. We'll even panel your library with our famous Books-by-the-
Yard, with customized, hand-tooled leather spines of the classic works
with which you wish to be identified. (Call our 800 number for available titles.)

6   Finally, to complete your life-style package, we still offer our Papa
Hemingway Trophy Wife to preferred gentlemen customers. Exclusive
to us, each of our hand-picked replacement spouses has been raised under Jan's watchful eye at our own private boarding school, situated in
the rolling countryside of lovely Sonoma Valley. Why take a chance on
that stunning Lufthansa flight attendant who may or may not have a
prescription-drug problem? Choose from over 10 popular archetypes,
from Coquettish to Contemporary Bold. (Because of the normal cycles
of anorexia, Trophy Wives may vary slightly in size and appearance, so
please allow us to select one for you.)

Sometimes when Jan and I are raft-drifting down the languid Orinoco,   7
where the only sound is the mesh lining in Jan's flight vest wicking
moisture away from her skin, we'll gaze up into the indigo Venezuelan
night and thank the stars for our large, loyal customer base. Without
you, there wouldn't be a J. Entitlements — and we'd be just two more
lawyers without lives!

Well, that's all for now. See you in the Casbah or Key West or the   8
Côte d'Azur!

Best regards,

Roger and Jan

(1996)

The Writer's Subject

1. What kind of catalogue is being parodied here?

2. What kind of customer is being addressed by "Roger and Jan"?

3. What Western social attitudes does Trudeau hold up for inspection and ridicule in para. 2?

4. What kind of "simpler times" are being recalled in para. 3?

The Writer's Style and Strategy

1. How does the essay signal that it is a parody rather than the real thing?

2. One of Trudeau's goals in the essay is to point out the impact of the capitalist ethic on our social and moral values. How is this goal achieved?

3. Discuss the point of the references to clothes and fabrics in the first paragraph.

4. What kind of reader might be interested by the "Sahib Gear" collection? (paras. 1, 4) What assumptions do "Roger and Jan" make about such a reader?

5. Discuss the implications of the following names and phrases in para. 5: "J. Entitlements"; "Enhanced Living"; "one of our life-style engineers"; "our famous Books-by-the-Yard."

6. Why would "Roger and Jan" expect to "See you in the Casbah or Key West or the Côte d'Azur"? (para. 8)

Suggested Topics for Writing and Discussion

1. Look for advertisements or catalogues characterized by appeals to identifiable social groups, and analyze the language and images used by the advertiser.

2. What is the "Papa Hemingway Trophy Wife"? How would such a person appeal to the assumed audience for this advertisement? (para. 6) Would children be welcome in the world of Roger and Jan and their customers, and if so, how would they be described in the advertisement?

3. Compare this piece with the essay by Mike Royko, "Another Accolade for Charter Arms, Corp." What do the two pieces have in common?

4. What similarities do you find between Trudeau's essay and that by Witold Rybczynski, "Nostalgia"?

The Tyranny of the Clock

by George Woodcock

In no characteristic is existing society in the West so sharply distin- 1
guished from the earlier societies, whether of Europe or of the East, as
in its conception of time. To the ancient Chinese or Greek, to the Arab
herdsman or the Mexican peon of today, time is represented by the cyclic processes of nature, the alternation of day and night, the passage
from season to season. The nomads and the farmers measured and still
measure their day from sunrise to sunset, and their year in terms of seed-
time and harvest, of the falling leaf and ice thawing on the lakes and
rivers. The farmer worked according to the elements, the craftsman for
as long as he felt it necessary to perfect his product. Time was seen as a
process of natural change, and men were not concerned in its exact
measurement. For this reason civilizations highly developed in other
respects had the most primitive means of measuring time: the hourglass
with its trickling sand or dripping water, the sundial, useless on a dull
day, and the candle or lamp whose unburnt remnant of oil or wax indicated the hours. All these devices were approximate and inexact, and
were often rendered unreliable by the weather or the personal laziness
of the tender. Nowhere in the ancient or the mediaeval world were more
than a tiny minority of men concerned with time in the terms of mathematical exactitude.

Modern, western man, however, lives in a world which runs accord- 2
ing to the mechanical and mathematical symbols of clock time. The clock
dictates his movements and inhibits his actions. The clock turns time
from a process of nature into a commodity that can be measured and
bought and sold like soap or sultanas. And because, without some means

of exact timekeeping, industrial capitalism could never have developed and could not continue to exploit the workers, the clock represents an element of mechanical tyranny in the lives of modern men more potent than any individual exploiter or than any other machine. It is therefore valuable to trace the historical process by which the clock influenced the social development of modern European civilization.

3   It is a frequent circumstance of history that a culture or a civilization develops the device that will later be used for its destruction. The ancient Chinese, for example, invented gunpowder, which was developed by the military experts of the West and eventually led to the Chinese civilization itself being destroyed by the high explosives of modern warfare. Similarly, the super achievement of the craftsmen of the mediaeval cities of Europe was the invention of the clock, which, with its revolutionary alteration of the concept of time, materially assisted the growth of the Middle Ages.

4   There is a tradition that the clock appeared in the eleventh century, as a device for ringing bells at regular intervals in the monasteries, which, with the regimented life they imposed on their inmates, were the closest social approximation in the Middle Ages to the factory of today. The first authenticated clock, however, appeared in the thirteenth century, and it was not until the fourteenth century that clocks became common as ornaments of the public building in German cities.

5   These early clocks, operated by weights, were not particularly accurate, and it was not until the sixteenth century that any great reliability was attained. In England, for instance, the clock at Hampton Court, made in 1540, is said to have been the first accurate clock in the country. And even the accuracy of the sixteenth-century clocks is relative, for they were equipped only with hour-hands. The idea of measuring time in minutes and seconds had been thought out by the early mathematicians as far back as the fourteenth century, but it was not until the invention of the pendulum in 1657 that sufficient accuracy was attained to permit the addition of a minute-hand, and the second-hand did not appear until the eighteenth century. These two centuries, it should be observed, were those in which capitalism grew to such an extent that it was able to take advantage of the techniques of the Industrial Revolution to establish its economic domination over society.

6   The clock, as Lewis Mumford has pointed out, is the key machine of the machine age, both for its influence on technics and for its influence on the habits of men. Technically, the clock was the first really automatic machine that attained any importance in the life of man. Pre-

vious to its invention, the common machines were of such nature that their operation depended on some external and unreliable force, such as human or animal muscles, water, or wind. It is true that the Greeks had invented a number of primitive automatic machines, but these were used, like Héro's steam engine, either for obtaining "super-natural" effects in the temples or for amusing the tyrants of Levantine cities. But the clock was the first automatic machine that attained public importance and a social function. Clock-making became the industry from which men learnt the elements of machine-making and gained the technical skill that was to produce the complicated machinery of the Industrial Revolution.

Socially the clock had a more radical influence than any other ma- 7
chine, in that it was the means by which the regularization and regimentation of life necessary for an exploiting system of industry could be best assured. The clock provided a means by which time—a category so elusive that no philosophy has yet determined its nature—could be measured concretely in the more tangible terms of space provided by the circumference of a clock dial. Time as duration became disregarded, and men began to talk and think always of "lengths" of time, just as if they were talking of lengths of calico. And time, being now measurable in mathematical symbols, was regarded as a commodity that could be bought and sold in the same way as any other commodity.

The new capitalists, in particular, became rabidly time-conscious. 8
Time, here symbolizing the labour of the workers, was regarded by them almost as if it were the chief raw material of industry. "Time is money" was one of the key slogans of capitalist ideology, and the timekeeper was the most significant of the new types of official introduced by the capitalist dispensation.

In the early factories the employers went so far as to manipulate their 9
clocks or sound their factory whistles at the wrong times in order to defraud the workers of a little of this valuable new commodity. Later such practices became less frequent, but the influence of the clock imposed a regularity on the lives of the majority of men that had previously been known only in the monasteries. Men actually became like clocks, acting with a repetitive regularity which had no resemblance to the rhythmic life of a natural being. They became, as the Victorian phrase put it, "as regular as clockwork." Only in the country districts where the natural lives of animals and plants and the elements still dominated existence did any large proportion of the population fail to succumb to the deadly tick of monotony.

10   At first this new attitude to time, this new regularity of life, was imposed by the clock-owning masters on the unwilling poor. The factory slave reacted in his spare time by living with a chaotic irregularity which characterized the gin-sodden slums of early-nineteenth-century industrialism. Men fled to the timeless worlds of drink or Methodist inspiration. But gradually the idea of regularity spread downwards and among the workers. Nineteenth-century religion and morality played their part by proclaiming the sin of "wasting time." The introduction of mass-produced watches and clocks in the 1850s spread time-consciousness among those who had previously merely reacted to the stimulus of the knocker-up or the factory whistle. In the church and the school, in the office and the workshop, punctuality was held up as the greatest of the virtues.

11   Out of this slavish dependence on mechanical time which spread insidiously into every class in the nineteenth century, there grew up the demoralizing regimentation which today still characterizes factory life. The man who fails to conform faces social disapproval and economic ruin—unless he drops out into a non-conformist way of life in which time ceases to be of prime importance. Hurried meals, the regular morning and evening scramble for trains or buses, the strain of having to work to time schedules, all contribute, by digestive and nervous disturbance, to ruin health and shorten life.

12   Nor does the financial imposition of regularity tend, in the long run, to greater efficiency. Indeed, the quality of the product is usually much poorer, because the employer, regarding time as a commodity which he has to pay for, forces the operative to maintain such a speed that his work must necessarily be skimped. Quantity rather than quality becoming the criterion, the enjoyment is taken out of the work itself, and the worker in his turn becomes a "clock-watcher," concerned only with when he will be able to escape to the scanty and monotonous leisure of industrial society, in which he "kills time" by cramming in as much time-scheduled and mechanical enjoyment of cinema, radio, and newspaper as his wage packet and his tiredness will allow. Only if he is willing to accept the hazard of living by his faith or his wits can the man without money avoid living as a slave to the clock.

13   The problem of the clock is, in general, similar to that of the machine. Mechanized time is valuable as a means of co-ordinating activities in a highly developed society, just as the machine is valuable as a means of reducing unnecessary labour to a minimum. Both are valuable for the contribution they make to the smooth running of society, and should be used in so far as they assist men to co-operate efficiently

and to eliminate monotonous toil and social confusion. But neither
should be allowed to dominate men's lives as they do today.

Now the movement of the clock sets the tempo of men's lives—   14
they become the servants of the concept of time which they themselves
have made, and are held in fear, like Frankenstein by his own monster.
In a sane and free society such an arbitrary domination of man's functions by either clock or machine would obviously be out of the question. The domination of man by man-made machines is even more
ridiculous than the domination of man by man. Mechanical time would
be relegated to its true function of a means of reference and co-ordina-
tion, and men would return again to a balanced view of life no longer
dominated by time-regulation and the worship of the clock. Complete
liberty implies freedom from the tyranny of abstractions as well as from
the rule of men.

(1939)

The Writer's Subject

1. How did the concept of time in older societies differ from that in modern
   Western society? (para. 1)

2. How, according to Woodcock, did the development of the clock make possible the rise of industrial capitalism? (paras. 6–8)

3. What impact has the development of clock time had on the life of the modern worker, in Woodcock's view? (paras. 9–12)

4. At several points Woodcock uses the word "commodity" to describe the
   modern concept of time. What are the implications of this term, and how
   does its use further Woodcock's thesis?

5. What comparison does Woodcock make between the clock and the machine? (paras. 13–14)

The Writer's Style and Strategy

1. Discuss the appropriateness of Woodcock's choice of title.

2. Is there a rhetorical as well as an expository purpose behind Woodcock's
   explanation in paragraph 1 of how time was recorded by older societies?

3. Examine Woodcock's description of modern Western concepts of time in
   paragraph 2. How does his choice of words convey his attitude here? Does
   the diction seem "slanted" in any way?

4. Woodcock proposes to "trace the historical process by which the clock
   influenced the social development of modern European civilization." (para.

2) What principle seems to determine his choice of historical evidence? How does he use the history of the Industrial Revolution to further his argumentative purposes?

5. Discuss the ways in which Woodcock describes employers and workers throughout the essay. How does he make clear where his sympathies lie?

6. What use does Woodcock make of such clichés as "Time is money" or "as regular as clockwork" to further his argument?

7. Trace the stages by which Woodcock's argument moves from past to present, and from specific to general.

Suggested Topics for Writing and Discussion

1. Do you agree with Woodcock's view that we have become slaves to "mechanical time"? Draw on your own daily life to support your point of view.

2. Woodcock describes factory workers in the eighteenth and nineteenth centuries as slaves who were brutally exploited by ruthless capitalists. Find out what you can about conditions in factories, mills, or mines in the nineteenth century; using one or two particular examples, show whether or not Woodcock's assertions are justified.

3. Although Woodcock's essay is largely devoted to attacking "the tyranny of the clock," in paragraph 13 he acknowledges the importance of mechanical time in the smooth running of society. Write an essay on the beneficial aspects of mechanical time, illustrating your argument with specific examples.

4. Woodcock and Mumford argue that the clock is "the key machine of the machine age ... for its influence on the habits of men." (para. 6) Discuss the effects of one other machine upon our daily lives.

Politics and Morality

On Party-Lying

by Joseph Addison

Defendit numerus, junctaeque umbone phalanges.[1]

Juvenal

There is something very Sublime, tho' very Fanciful, in *Plato's* Descrip-   1
tion of the Supreme Being, that *Truth is his Body, and Light his Shadow*.
According to his Definition, there is nothing so contradictory to his
Nature as Error and Falshood. The Platonists have so just a Notion of
the Almighty's Aversion to every thing which is false and erroneous,
that they looked upon *Truth* as no less necessary than *Virtue*, to qualifie
an Human Soul for the Enjoyment of a separate State. For this Reason,
as they recommended Moral Duties to qualifie and season the Will for
a future Life, so they prescribed several Contemplations and Sciences
to rectifie the Understanding. Thus *Plato* has called Mathematical Demonstrations the Catharticks or Purgatives of the Soul, as being the most
proper Means to cleanse it from Error, and to give it a Relish of Truth,
which is the natural Food and Nourishment of the Understanding, as
Virtue is the Perfection and Happiness of the Will.

There are many Authors who have shewn wherein the Malignity of a   2
Lie consists, and set forth, in proper Colours, the Heinousness of the
Offence. I shall here consider one Particular Kind of this Crime, which
has not been so much spoken to: I mean, that abominable Practice of
Party-lying. This Vice is so very predominant among us at present, that
a Man is thought of no Principles, who does not propagate a certain
System of Lies. The Coffee-Houses are supported by them, the Press is
choaked with them, eminent Authors live upon them. Our Bottle-

Conversation is so infected with them, that a Party-Lie is grown as fashionable an Entertainment, as a lively Catch or a merry Story: The Truth of it is, half the great Talkers in the Nation would be struck dumb, were this Fountain of Discourse dryed up. There is, however, one Advantage resulting from this detestable Practice; the very Appearances of Truth are so little regarded, that Lies are at present discharged in the Air, and begin to hurt no Body. When we hear a Party-story from a Stranger, we consider whether he is a Whig or a Tory that relates it, and immediately conclude they are Words of Course, in which the honest Gentleman designs to recommend his Zeal, without any Concern for his Veracity. A Man is looked upon as bereft of common Sense, that gives Credit to the Relations of Party-Writers, nay his own Friends shake their Heads at him, and consider him in no other Light than as an officious Tool or a well-meaning Ideot. When it was formerly the Fashion to husband a Lie, and trump it up in some extraordinary Emergency, it generally did Execution, and was not a little serviceable to the Faction that made use of it; but at present every Man is upon his Guard; the Artifice has been too often repeated to take Effect.

3   I have frequently wondered to see Men of Probity, who would scorn to utter a Falshood for their own particular Advantage, give so readily into a Lie when it is become the Voice of their Faction, notwithstanding they are thoroughly sensible of it as such. How is it possible for those, who are Men of Honour in their Persons, thus to become Notorious Liars in their Party? If we look into the Bottom of this Matter, we may find, I think, three Reasons for it, and at the same time discover the Insufficiency of these Reasons to justifie so Criminal a Practice.

4   In the first place, Men are apt to think that the Guilt of a Lie, and consequently the Punishment, may be very much diminished, if not wholly worn out, by the Multitudes of those who partake in it. Though the Weight of a Falshood would be too heavy for *one* to bear, it grows light in their Imaginations, when it is shared among *many*. But in this Case a Man very much deceives himself; Guilt, when it spreads through Numbers, is not so properly divided as multiplied: Every one is criminal in proportion to the Offence which he commits, not to the Number of those who are his Companions in it. Both the Crime and the Penalty lie as heavy upon every Individual of an offending Multitude, as they would upon any single Person, had none shared with him in the Offence. In a Word, the Division of Guilt is like that of Matter; though it may be separated into infinite Portions, every Portion shall have the whole Essence of Matter in it, and consist of as many Parts as the whole did afore it was divided.

But in the second place, though Multitudes, who join in a Lie, can- 5
not exempt themselves from the Guilt, they may from the Shame of it.
The Scandal of a Lie is in a manner lost and annihilated, when diffused
among several Thousands; as a Drop of the blackest Tincture wears away
and vanishes, when mixed and confused in a considerable Body of Water: The Blot is still in it, but is not able to discover it self. This is certainly a very great Motive to several Party-Offenders, who avoid Crimes,
not as they are prejudicial to their Virtue, but to their Reputation. It is
enough to show the Weakness of this Reason, which palliates Guilt without removing it, that every Man, who is influenced by it, declares himself in effect an infamous Hypocrite, prefers the Appearance of Virtue
to its Reality, and is determined in his Conduct neither by the Dictates
of his own Conscience, the Suggestions of true Honour, nor the Principles of Religion.

The third and last great Motive for Mens joining in a popular 6
Falshood, or, as I have hitherto called it, a Party-Lie, notwithstanding
they are convinced of it as such, is the doing Good to a Cause which
every Party may be supposed to look upon as the most meritorious. The
Unsoundness of this Principle has been so often exposed, and is so universally acknowledged, that a Man must be an utter Stranger to the Principles, either of natural Religion or Christianity, who suffers himself to
be guided by it. If a Man might promote the supposed Good of his Country by the blackest Calumnies and Falshoods, our Nation abounds more
in Patriots than any other of the Christian World. When *Pompey* was
desired not to set Sail in a Tempest that would hazard his Life, *It is
necessary for me*, says he, *to Sail, but it is not necessary for me to Live*:
Every Man should say to himself, with the same Spirit, It is my Duty to
speak Truth, tho' it is not my Duty to be in an Office. One of the Fathers has carried this Point so high, as to declare *he would not tell a Lie
though he were sure to gain Heaven by it*: However extravagant such a
Protestation may appear, every one will own, that a Man may say very
reasonably *he would not tell a Lie, if he were sure to gain Hell by it*; or,
if you have a mind to soften the Expression, that he would not tell a Lie
to gain any Temporal Reward by it, when he should run the hazard of
losing much more than it was possible for him to gain.

(1712)

Note

1. *Motto.* Juvenal, *Satires*, 2. 46: They are protected by their numbers and the close shields of
   their phalanx.

The Writer's Subject

1. Comment on the appropriateness of the epigraph to the content of the essay.

2. While lamenting the prevalence of lying, Addison sees one advantage in its general acceptance; what is this advantage? (para. 2)

3. What are the reasons which Addison gives for the acceptance of party-lying by "Men of Probity"? (paras. 3–6)

4. What is Addison's own attitude to party-lying, and to lying in general? Where is this attitude given most explicit expression?

The Writer's Style and Strategy

1. What is the function of the opening paragraph? How does Addison effect a transition from this paragraph to his principal subject, party-lying?

2. In paragraph 2, Addison says "... a Man is thought of no Principles, who does not propagate a certain System of Lies." What is the figure of speech used here?

3. What is meant by the phrase "Our Bottle-Conversation" in paragraph 2?

4. Find an example of metaphor in paragraph 2 and explain its usefulness in emphasizing Addison's point.

5. Discuss the organization of paragraphs 3 through 6, and show how Addison deals with the arguments of those he is attacking.

6. Explain the analogy in the second sentence of paragraph 5, and discuss its effectiveness.

7. "If a Man might promote the supposed Good of his Country by the blackest Calumnies and Falshoods, our Nation abounds more in Patriots than any other of the Christian World" (para. 6). What is the tone of this statement?

Suggested Topics for Writing and Discussion

1. In what respects are Addison's views on politics similar to those expressed by George Orwell in his essay "Politics and the English Language"?

2. "Party-lying" is as common in our own time as in Addison's. Two notorious recent examples are the "Watergate Affair" during Richard Nixon's presidency and the "Iran arms deal" during that of Ronald Reagan. Find out what you can about one of these episodes in American politics, and offer your views about what the incident revealed concerning the morality of the political scene at the time.

3. Addison attacks those who lie for what they believe to be a good cause. (para. 6) Do you believe that there may in fact be any cause worth lying for? (You may wish to look at what Bronowski has to say in "The Real Responsibilities of the Scientist" concerning scientists who lie for what they consider to be good reasons.)

The Writer's Responsibility

by Margaret Atwood

1   The subject we have come together to address is one which increases in importance as the giants of this world move closer and closer to violent and fatal confrontation. Broadly put, it is: what is the writer's responsibility, if any, to the society in which he or she lives? The question is not a new one; it's been with us at least since the time of Plato; but more and more the answers of the world's governments have taken the form of amputation: of the tongue, of the soul, of the head.

2   We in Canada are ill-equipped to come to grips even with the problem, let alone the solution. We live in a society in which the main consensus seems to be that the artist's duty is to entertain and divert, nothing more. Occasionally our critics get a little heavy and start talking about the human condition, but on the whole the audience prefers art not to be a mirror held up to life but a Disneyland of the soul, containing Romanceland, Spyland, Pornoland and all the other Escapelands which are so much more agreeable than the complex truth. When we take an author seriously, we prefer to believe that her vision derives from her individual and subjective and neurotic tortured soul—we like artists to have tortured souls—not from the world she is looking at. Sometimes our artists believe this version too, and the ego takes over. *I, me* and *mine* are our favourite pronouns; *we, us* and *ours* are low on the list. The artist is not seen as a lens for focusing the world but as a solipsism. We are good at measuring an author's production in terms of his craft. We are not good at analyzing it in terms of his politics, and by and large we do not do so.

3   By "politics" I do not mean how you voted in the last election, al-

though that is included. I mean who is entitled to do what to whom, with impunity; who profits by it; and who therefore eats what. Such material enters a writer's work not because the writer is or is not consciously political but because a writer is an observer, a witness, and such observations are the air he breathes. They are the air all of us breathe; the only difference is that the author looks, and then writes down what he sees. What he sees will depend on how closely he looks and at what, but look he must.

In some countries, an author is censored not only for what he says   4
but for how he says it, and an unconventional style is therefore a declaration of artistic freedom. Here we are eclectic; we don't mind experimental styles, in fact we devote learned journals to their analysis; but our critics sneer somewhat at anything they consider "heavy social commentary" or—a worse word—"message." Stylistic heavy guns are dandy, as long as they aren't pointed anywhere in particular. We like the human condition as long as it is seen as personal and individual. Placing politics and poetics in two watertight compartments is a luxury, just as specialization of any kind is a luxury, and it is possible only in a society where luxuries abound. Most countries in the world cannot afford such luxuries, and this North American way of thinking is alien to them. It was even alien in North America, not long ago. We've already forgotten that in the 1950's many artists, both in the United States and here, were persecuted solely on the grounds of their presumed politics. Which leads us to another mistaken Canadian belief: the belief that it can't happen here.

It has happened here, many times. Although our country is one of   5
the most peaceful and prosperous on earth, although we do not shoot artists here, although we do not execute political opponents and although this is one of the few remaining countries in which we can have a gathering like this without expecting to be arrested or blown up, we should not overlook the fact that Canada's record on civil rights issues is less than pristine. Our treatment of our native peoples has been shameful. This is the country in which citizens of Japanese origin were interned during the Second World War and had their property stolen (when a government steals property it is called "confiscation"); it is also the country in which thousands of citizens were arrested, jailed and held without warrant or explanation, during the time of the War Measures Act, a scant eleven years ago. There was no general outcry in either case. Worse things have not happened not because we are genetically exempt but because we lead pampered lives.

6   Our methods of controlling artists are not violent, but they do exist. We control through the marketplace and through critical opinion. We are also controlled by the economics of culture, which in Canada still happen to be those of a colonial branch-plant. In 1960 the number of Canadian books published here was minute, and the numbers sold pathetic. Things have changed very much in twenty years, but Canadian books still account for a mere 25 percent of the overall book trade and paperback books for under 5 percent. Talking about this situation is still considered nationalistic chauvinism. Nevertheless, looked at in the context of the wider picture, I suppose we are lucky to have any percent at all; they haven't yet sent in the Marines and if they do it won't be over books, but over oil.

7   We in this country should use our privileged position not as a shelter from the world's realities but as a platform from which to speak. Many are denied their voices; we are not. A voice is a gift; it should be cherished and used, to utter fully human speech if possible. Powerlessness and silence go together; one of the first efforts made in any totalitarian takeover is to suppress the writers, the singers, the journalists, those who are the collective voice. Get rid of the union leaders and pervert the legal system and what you are left with is a reign of terror.

8   As we read the newspapers, we learn we are existing right now in a state of war. The individual wars may not be large and they are being fought far from here, but there is really only one war, that between those who would like the future to be, in the words of George Orwell, a boot grinding forever into a human face, and those who would like it to be a state of something we still dream of as freedom. The battle shifts according to the ground occupied by the enemy. Greek myth tells of a man called Procrustes, who was a great equalizer. He had a system for making all human beings the same size: if they were too small he stretched them, if they were too tall he cut off their feet or their heads. The Procrustes today are international operators, not confined to any one ideology or religion. The world is full of perversions of the notion of equality, just as it is full of perversions of the notion of freedom. True freedom is not being able to do whatever you like to whomever you want to do it to. Freedom that exists as a result of the servitude of others is not true freedom.

9   The most lethal weapon in the world's arsenals is not the neutron bomb or chemical warfare; but the human mind that devises such things and puts them to use. But it is the human mind also that can summon up the power to resist, that can imagine a better world than the one be-

fore it, that can retain memory and courage in the face of unspeakable suffering. Oppression involves a failure of the imagination: the failure to imagine the full humanity of other human beings. If the imagination were a negligible thing and the act of writing a mere frill, as many in this society would like to believe, regimes all over the world would not be at such pains to exterminate them. The ultimate desire of Procrustes is a population of lobotomized zombies. The writer, unless he is a mere word processor, retains three attributes that power-mad regimes cannot tolerate: a human imagination, in the many forms it may take; the power to communicate; and hope. It may seem odd for me to speak of hope in the midst of what many of my fellow Canadians will call a bleak vision, but as the American writer Flannery O'Connor once said, people without hope do not write novels.

(1981)

The Writer's Subject

1. Why is Atwood so critical of the attitudes of Canadians to art and artists?

2. What are the implications of the phrase "a Disneyland of the soul" (para. 2)?

3. What is Atwood's definition of "politics," and how does it bear on her view of the writer's responsibility? (para. 3)

4. Why does Atwood regard the separation of politics and poetics as a "luxury"? (para. 4)

5. After giving examples of Canadian violations of civil rights (para. 5), Atwood concludes that "Worse things have not happened not because we are genetically exempt but because we lead pampered lives." Discuss what Atwood means by this observation.

6. What does Atwood mean by describing the economics of Canadian culture as "those of a colonial branch-plant" (para. 6)?

7. Atwood asserts that "we are existing right now in a state of war" (para. 8). Who are the opponents in this war?

8. What answer does Atwood give to the question she raises in paragraph 1, "what is the writer's responsibility, if any, to the society in which he or she lives?" What qualities must the writer possess to fulfil that responsibility?

The Writer's Style and Strategy

1. Explain the significance of Atwood's use of "amputation" in the opening paragraph.

2. Is there any evidence in style, diction, or tone to indicate that this essay was originally prepared as a spoken address?

3. Why does Atwood first refer to the writer as "she" (para. 2), then shift to a masculine pronoun in subsequent paragraphs?

4. At several points Atwood uses irony as a means of underscoring her point of view. Pick out one or two examples of effective irony.

5. Examine the organization of paragraph 5. What means of development does Atwood employ? Why does she begin the second sentence with four subordinate clauses, each introduced by "although"?

6. Atwood defines "true freedom" negatively rather than positively in paragraph 8. Why does she employ this strategy of definition?

Suggested Topics for Writing and Discussion

1. Atwood provides several examples of the violations of civil rights in Canada. Investigate one of these and explain what climate of opinion or historical events led to the occurrence.

2. Atwood says that our society expects artists "to entertain and divert, nothing more." Is it possible, in your view, for artists to perform the duties which Atwood discusses and, at the same time, entertain and divert? Provide clear examples to support your view.

3. We regard our society as free. We are still subject, however, to various forms of censorship in the arts and in communication. Find and discuss one or two examples of censorship in any medium (books, movies, television, radio, newspapers, exhibitions, advertisements, etc.).

Shooting an Elephant
by George Orwell

In Moulmein, in Lower Burma, I was hated by large numbers of people 1
— the only time I have been important enough for this to happen to me.
I was subdivisional police officer of the town, and in an aimless, petty
kind of way anti-European feeling was very bitter. No one had the guts
to raise a riot, but if a European woman went through the bazaars alone
somebody would probably spit betel juice over her dress. As a police
officer I was an obvious target and was baited whenever it seemed safe
to do so. When a nimble Burman tripped me up on the football field
and the referee (another Burman) looked the other way, the crowd yelled
with hideous laughter. This happened more than once. In the end the
sneering yellow faces of young men that met me everywhere, the in-
sults hooted after me when I was at a safe distance, got badly on my
nerves. The young Buddhist priests were the worst of all. There were
several thousands of them in the town and none of them seemed to have
anything to do except stand on street corners and jeer at Europeans.

All this was perplexing and upsetting. For at that time I had already 2
made up my mind that imperialism was an evil thing and the sooner I
chucked up my job and got out of it the better. Theoretically — and
secretly, of course — I was all for the Burmese and all against their
oppressors, the British. As for the job I was doing, I hated it more bitterly than I can perhaps make clear. In a job like that you see the dirty
work of Empire at close quarters. The wretched prisoners huddling in
the stinking cages of the lock-ups, the grey, cowed faces of the long-
term convicts, the scarred buttocks of the men who had been flogged
with bamboos — all these oppressed me with an intolerable sense of

guilt. But I could get nothing into perspective. I was young and ill-educated and I had had to think out my problems in the utter silence that is imposed on every Englishman in the East. I did not even know that the British Empire is dying, still less did I know that it is a great deal better than the younger empires that are going to supplant it. All I knew was that I was stuck between my hatred of the empire I served and my rage against the evil-spirited little beasts who tried to make my job impossible. With one part of my mind I thought of the British Raj as an unbreakable tyranny, as something clamped down, in *saecula saeculorum*,[1] upon the will of prostrate peoples; with another part I thought that the greatest joy in the world would be to drive a bayonet into a Buddhist priest's guts. Feelings like these are the normal by-products of imperialism; ask any Anglo-Indian official, if you can catch him off duty.

3   One day something happened which in a roundabout way was enlightening. It was a tiny incident in itself, but it gave me a better glimpse than I had had before of the real nature of imperialism — the real motives for which despotic governments act. Early one morning the sub-inspector at a police station the other end of the town rang me up on the 'phone and said that an elephant was ravaging the bazaar. Would I please come and do something about it? I did not know what I could do, but I wanted to see what was happening and I got on to a pony and started out. I took my rifle, an old .44 Winchester and much too small to kill an elephant, but I thought the noise might be useful *in terrorem*. Various Burmans stopped me on the way and told me about the elephant's doings. It was not, of course, a wild elephant, but a tame one which had gone "must". It had been chained up, as tame elephants always are when their attack of "must" is due, but on the previous night it had broken its chain and escaped. Its mahout, the only person who could manage it when it was in that state, had set out in pursuit, but had taken the wrong direction and was now twelve hours' journey away, and in the morning the elephant had suddenly reappeared in the town. The Burmese population had no weapons and were quite helpless against it. It had already destroyed somebody's bamboo hut, killed a cow and raided some fruit-stalls and devoured the stock; also it had met the municipal rubbish van, and, when the driver jumped out and took to his heels, had turned the van over and inflicted violences upon it.

4   The Burmese sub-inspector and some Indian constables were waiting for me in the quarter where the elephant had been seen. It was a very poor quarter, a labyrinth of squalid bamboo huts, thatched with palm-leaf, winding all over a steep hillside. I remember that it was a

cloudy, stuffy morning at the beginning of the rains. We began questioning the people as to where the elephant had gone, and, as usual, failed to get any definite information. That is invariably the case in the East; a story always sounds clear enough at a distance, but the nearer you get to the scene of events the vaguer it becomes. Some of the people said that the elephant had gone in one direction, some said that he had gone in another, some professed not even to have heard of any elephant. I had almost made up my mind that the whole story was a pack of lies, when we heard yells a little distance away. There was a loud, scandalized cry of "Go away, child! Go away this instant!" and an old woman with a switch in her hand came round the corner of a hut, violently shooing away a crowd of naked children. Some more women followed, clicking their tongues and exclaiming; evidently there was something that the children ought not to have seen. I rounded the hut and saw a man's dead body sprawling in the mud. He was an Indian, a black Dravidian coolie, almost naked, and he could not have been dead many minutes. The people said that the elephant had come suddenly upon him round the corner of the hut, caught him with its trunk, put its foot on his back and ground him into the earth. This was the rainy season and the ground was soft, and his face had scored a trench a foot deep and a couple of yards long. He was lying on his belly with arms crucified and head sharply twisted to one side. His face was coated with mud, the eyes wide open, the teeth bared and grinning with an expression of unendurable agony. (Never tell me, by the way, that the dead look peaceful. Most of the corpses I have seen looked devilish.) The friction of the great beast's foot had stripped the skin from his back as neatly as one skins a rabbit. As soon as I saw the dead man I sent an orderly to a friend's house nearby to borrow an elephant rifle. I had already sent back the pony, not wanting it to go mad with fright and throw me if it smelt the elephant.

The orderly came back in a few minutes with a rifle and five cartridges, and meanwhile some Burmans had arrived and told us that the elephant was in the paddy fields below, only a few hundred yards away. As I started forward practically the whole population of the quarter flocked out of the houses and followed me. They had seen the rifle and were all shouting excitedly that I was going to shoot the elephant. They had not shown much interest in the elephant when he was merely ravaging their homes, but it was different now that he was going to be shot. It was a bit of fun to them, as it would be to an English crowd; besides they wanted the meat. It made me vaguely uneasy. I had no intention of

shooting the elephant — I had merely sent for the rifle to defend myself if necessary — and it is always unnerving to have a crowd following you. I marched down the hill, looking and feeling a fool, with the
rifle over my shoulder and an ever-growing army of people jostling at
my heels. At the bottom, when you got away from the huts, there was a
metalled road and beyond that a miry waste of paddy fields a thousand
yards across, not yet ploughed but soggy from the first rains and dotted
with coarse grass. The elephant was standing eight yards from the road,
his left side towards us. He took not the slightest notice of the crowd's
approach. He was tearing up bunches of grass, beating them against his
knees to clean them and stuffing them into his mouth.

6   I had halted on the road. As soon as I saw the elephant I knew with
perfect certainty that I ought not to shoot him. It is a serious matter to
shoot a working elephant — it is comparable to destroying a huge and
costly piece of machinery — and obviously one ought not to do it if it
can possibly be avoided. And at that distance, peacefully eating, the elephant looked no more dangerous than a cow. I thought then and I think
now that his attack of "must" was already passing off; in which case he
would merely wander harmlessly about until the mahout came back and
caught him. Moreover, I did not in the least want to shoot him. I decided that I would watch him for a little while to make sure that he did
not turn savage again, and then go home.

7   But at that moment I glanced round at the crowd that had followed
me. It was an immense crowd, two thousand at the least and growing
every minute. It blocked the road for a long distance on either side. I
looked at the sea of yellow faces above the garish clothes — faces all
happy and excited over this bit of fun, all certain that the elephant was
going to be shot. They were watching me as they would watch a con-
jurer about to perform a trick. They did not like me, but with the magical rifle in my hands I was momentarily worth watching. And suddenly
I realized that I should have to shoot the elephant after all. The people
expected it of me and I had got to do it; I could feel their two thousand
wills pressing me forward, irresistibly. And it was at this moment, as I
stood there with the rifle in my hands, that I first grasped the hollow-
ness, the futility of the white man's dominion in the East. Here was I,
the white man with his gun, standing in front of the unarmed native
crowd — seemingly the leading actor of the piece; but in reality I was
only an absurd puppet pushed to and fro by the will of those yellow
faces behind. I perceived in this moment that when the white man turns
tyrant it is his own freedom that he destroys. He becomes a sort of hol-

low, posing dummy, the conventionalized figure of a sahib. For it is the condition of his rule that he shall spend his life in trying to impress the "natives", and so in every crisis he has got to do what the "natives" expect of him. He wears a mask, and his face grows to fit it. I had got to shoot the elephant. I had committed myself to doing it when I sent for the rifle. A sahib has got to act like a sahib; he has got to appear resolute, to know his own mind and do definite things. To come all that way, rifle in hand, with two thousand people marching at my heels, and then to trail feebly away, having done nothing — no, that was impossible. The crowd would laugh at me. And my whole life, every white man's life in the East, was one long struggle not to be laughed at.

But I did not want to shoot the elephant. I watched him beating his 8 bunch of grass against his knees, with that preoccupied grandmotherly air that elephants have. It seemed to me that it would be murder to shoot him. At that age I was not squeamish about killing animals, but I had never shot an elephant and never wanted to. (Somehow it always seems worse to kill a large animal.) Besides, there was the beast's owner to he considered. Alive, the elephant was worth at least a hundred pounds; dead, he would only be worth the value of his tusks, five pounds, possibly. But I had got to act quickly. I turned to some experienced-looking Burmans who had been there when we arrived, and asked them how the elephant had been behaving. They all said the same thing: he took no notice of you if you left him alone, but he might charge if you went too close to him.

It was perfectly clear to me what I ought to do. I ought to walk up to 9 within, say, twenty-five yards of the elephant and test his behaviour. If he charged I could shoot, if he took no notice of me it would be safe to leave him until the mahout came back. But also I knew that I was going to do no such thing. I was a poor shot with a rifle and the ground was soft mud into which one would sink at every step. If the elephant charged and I missed him, I should have about as much chance as a toad under a steam-roller. But even then I was not thinking particularly of my own skin, only of the watchful yellow faces behind. For at that moment, with the crowd watching me, I was not afraid in the ordinary sense, as I would have been if I had been alone. A white man mustn't be frightened in front of "natives"; and so, in general, he isn't frightened. The sole thought in my mind was that if anything went wrong those two thousand Burmans would see me pursued, caught, trampled on and reduced to a grinning corpse like that Indian up the hill. And if that happened it was quite probable that some of them would laugh. That would never do.

There was only one alternative. I shoved the cartridges into the magazine and lay down on the road to get a better aim.

10   The crowd grew very still, and a deep, low, happy sigh, as of people who see the theatre curtain go up at last, breathed from innumerable throats. They were going to have their bit of fun after all. The rifle was a beautiful German thing with cross-hair sights. I did not then know that in shooting an elephant one would shoot to cut an imaginary bar running from ear-hole to ear-hole. I ought, therefore, as the elephant was sideways on, to have aimed straight at his ear-hole; actually I aimed several inches in front of this, thinking the brain would be further forward.

11   When I pulled the trigger I did not hear the bang or feel the kick — one never does when a shot goes home — but I heard the devilish roar of glee that went up from the crowd. In that instant, in too short a time, one would have thought, even for the bullet to get there, a mysterious, terrible change had come over the elephant. He neither stirred nor fell, but every line of his body had altered. He looked suddenly stricken, shrunken, immensely old, as though the frightful impact of the bullet had paralysed him without knocking him down. At last, after what seemed a long time — it might have been five seconds, I dare say — he sagged flabbily to his knees. His mouth slobbered. An enormous senility seemed to have settled upon him. One could have imagined him thousands of years old. I fired again into the same spot. At the second shot he did not collapse but climbed with desperate slowness to his feet and stood weakly upright, with legs sagging and head drooping. I fired a third time. That was the shot that did for him. You could see the agony of it jolt his whole body and knock the last remnant of strength from his legs. But in falling he seemed for a moment to rise, for as his hind legs collapsed beneath him he seemed to tower upwards like a huge rock toppling, his trunk reaching skywards like a tree. He trumpeted, for the first and only time. And then down he came, his belly towards me, with a crash that seemed to shake the ground even where I lay.

12   I got up. The Burmans were already racing past me across the mud. It was obvious that the elephant would never rise again, but he was not dead. He was breathing very rhythmically with long rattling gasps, his great mound of a side painfully rising and falling. His mouth was wide open — I could see far down into caverns of pale pink throat. I waited a long time for him to die, but his breathing did not weaken. Finally I fired my two remaining shots into the spot where I thought his heart must be. The thick blood welled out of him like red velvet, but still he did not die. His body did not even jerk when the shots hit him, the tor-

tured breathing continued without a pause. He was dying, very slowly and in great agony, but in some world remote from me where not even a bullet could damage him further. I felt that I had got to put an end to that dreadful noise. It seemed dreadful to see the great beast lying there, powerless to move and yet powerless to die, and not even to be able to finish him. I sent back for my small rifle and poured shot after shot into his heart and down his throat. They seemed to make no impression. The tortured gasps continued as steadily as the ticking of a clock.

In the end I could not stand it any longer and went away. I heard 13 later that it took him half an hour to die. Burmans were bringing dahs and baskets even before I left, and I was told they had stripped his body almost to the bones by the afternoon.

Afterwards, of course, there were endless discussions about the shoot- 14 ing of the elephant. The owner was furious, but he was only an Indian and could do nothing. Besides, legally I had done the right thing, for a mad elephant has to be killed, like a mad dog, if its owner fails to control it. Among the Europeans opinion was divided. The older men said I was right, the younger men said it was a damn shame to shoot an elephant for killing a coolie, because an elephant was worth more than any damn Coringhee coolie. And afterwards I was very glad that the coolie had been killed; it put me legally in the right and it gave me a sufficient pretext for shooting the elephant. I often wondered whether any of the others grasped that I had done it solely to avoid looking a fool.

(1936)

Note

1. Forever and ever.

The Writer's Subject

1. What were Orwell's feelings about his role as a representative of British imperialism in Burma? (paras. 1–2)

2. Orwell received his education at Eton, one of the finest schools in England; why, then, does he refer to himself as "ill-educated"? (para. 2)

3. What is Orwell's point in telling us at length about his initial difficulty in finding the elephant? (paras. 3–4)

4. Why did Orwell first take a rifle that he knew was too small to kill an elephant? What does this detail suggest about his state of mind at that point? (para. 3)

5. Why at first did Orwell not want to shoot the elephant? What considerations led him to change his mind? (paras. 6–9)

6. Why was Orwell concerned at the thought that the crowd might laugh if he were trampled to death? (para. 9)

7. Why did Orwell fail to kill the elephant with his first shot? Why did he leave the scene before the elephant finally expired? (paras. 10–13)

The Writer's Style and Strategy

1. What is Orwell's purpose in this essay?

2. Why does Orwell choose the form of autobiographical narrative to carry out his purpose?

3. Orwell provides many details of physical setting. Choose some of these and explain their importance in the narrative.

4. Besides setting the scene, how do the details in paragraph 1 prepare the reader for the central events in the narrative?

5. How does Orwell use concrete images to convey his inner conflict in paragraph 2?

6. Why does Orwell provide so many details about the elephant's destructiveness and the appearance of the dead Indian? (paras. 3–4) What relation do these details bear to the essay's conclusion?

7. How does Orwell convey the mood of the Burmans who witness his conduct in dealing with the elephant? Why does he place such emphasis on their forming a huge crowd? (paras. 5, 7, 9–10)

8. How does the final paragraph reinforce Orwell's earlier statement, "I had had to think out my problems in the utter silence that is imposed on every Englishman in the East"? (para. 2)

9. What is Orwell's purpose in providing such a vivid and detailed description of the elephant's death? (paras. 11–13)

10. How does Orwell's conclusion sum up and re-state the moral issues dramatized in the narrative?

Suggested Topics for Writing and Discussion

1. Orwell recounts a personal experience in "Shooting an Elephant." He begins his account of the experience by saying, "One day something happened which in a roundabout way was enlightening. It was a tiny incident in itself, but it gave me a better glimpse than I had had before of the real nature of...". Using Orwell's introduction, write a narrative in which you

discuss an enlightening personal experience and show how that experience has given you greater insight.

2. Orwell's essay demonstrates the powerful influence of social pressures on the individual. Have you ever found yourself in a situation in which you had to go against your own feelings or convictions in order to satisfy the rules or expectations of society? Recount this experience.

3. In our daily lives, we encounter many different kinds of authority. Choose one example of authority, describe the form it takes, and examine your own response to it.

Another Accolade for Charter Arms Corp.
by Mike Royko

1   I was pleased to see that the stories reporting the death of John Lennon were specific and accurate about the kind of gun that was used to murder the world-renowned musician.

2   It was a .38 calibre pistol made by Charter Arms Corp. of Bridgeport, Conn.

3   You might ask: What difference does it make what kind of gun was used?

4   It makes a great deal of difference. Especially to Charter Arms Corp.

5   There are guns and then there are guns. Cheap guns, ordinary guns, and finely crafted guns.

6   And when people become emotional about guns, as many do when somebody famous is killed, they tend to lump all guns together. They don't show proper respect for an excellent gun, such as the Charter .38.

7   It happens this is not the first time a famous person has been shot by this make of weapon. When former Alabama Gov. George C. Wallace was shot and paralyzed for life by another deranged person in 1974, the bullet that tore into his spine came from a Charter .38.

8   If I'm not mistaken, that makes the Charter .38 the first gun in modern times to have two famous people to its credit. The weapons used to blast President Kennedy, the Rev. Dr. Martin Luther King, Jr., and Sen. Robert F. Kennedy were all of different manufacture.

9   When Wallace was shot, a CBS reporter made it obvious that he didn't know a fine gun from a cheap gun.

10   The reporter went on network TV and said that Wallace had been wounded by a "cheap handgun." He obviously had in mind the kind of

Saturday Night Special that is so popular among the criminal riffraff who have no respect for quality and workmanship.

When the proud executives of Charter Arms Corp. heard the reporter, 11 they became indignant.

They contacted the CBS and demanded an apology. The incident was 12 described in an editorial in the company magazine of the Charter Corp.

The editorial, which was headlined "An Apology from CBS," said: 13

"We are too dedicated to high quality in American-made handguns and have poured too much of ourselves into our products to have one of them even casually referred to as a 'cheap handgun'.

"That was exactly the phrase used in a broadcast description of the handgun used by Arthur Bremer in his assassination attempt on Gov. Wallace, which happened to be one of our Undercover .38 Specials.

"The broadcast emanated from CBS ... and our public relations people were immediately instructed to bring the error to their attention."

The editorial went on to say that an apology was indeed received 14 from CBS network vice-president, who contritely told Charter Arms Corp., "I am sending a copy of your letter to all our TV producers. In the event that we make reference to the Undercover .38 special used by Arthur Bremer, we will certainly avoid characterizing it as a 'Saturday Night Special' or any other term which labels it as a 'cheap weapon'."

Presumably that soothed the wounded pride of the gunmakers at Char- 15 ter Arms Corp., since no further public protests were heard.

And you can't blame them for having felt hurt at such a slur on their 16 product. When Wallace was shot, a Charter .38 cost $105. Today, with rising prices, the gun costs about $180 or $190, depending on where you do your gun shopping.

That is not a cheap gun, especially when compared to the trashy weap- 17 ons that some gunmen, to whom quality is unimportant, arm themselves with.

Now I don't know if it was mere coincidence that both Bremer, who 18 shot Wallace, and Mark David Chapman, who apparently shot Lennon, used the same weapon. Or if it was that they both recognized quality when they saw it, and were willing to spend money to get the best.

But the fact is, both opted for quality and they got what they paid 19 for. There was no misfiring, no jamming, no bullet flying off line, and no gun exploding in their hands — all of which can happen when one uses a cheap gun.

True, Wallace wasn't killed. That was the fault of Bremer, not the 20 Charter gun. Bremer shot Wallace in the stomach, which isn't the best place to shoot a person if you want to kill him.

21   But even in that case, the gun did its job — blowing a terrible hole in Wallace's gut and putting him into a wheelchair for good.

22   In the case of Lennon, you couldn't ask for a better performance from a gun. Lennon was shot several times, but according to the doctor who pronounced him dead, the first bullet hit him in the chest and killed him on the spot. The other shots weren't even necessary.

23   You can never be sure of getting those kinds of results from a Saturday Night Special.

24   Now the Charter Arms Corp. has the unique distinction of having two famous people shot by one of their products, I wonder if they have considered using it in their advertising. Something simple and tasteful like: "The .38 that got George Wallace AND John Lennon. See it at your gun dealer now."

25   If so, they shouldn't wait. With so many handguns — both cheap and of high quality — easily available to Americans, it could be just a matter of time until another manufacturer moves into the lead in the famous-person derby. All it would take would be a few pop-pop-pops from say, a Colt — maybe a politician or two and another rock star or two — and they would have the lead.

26   On the other hand, maybe Charter Arms Corp. doesn't want recognition — just the kind of pride one feels in a job of fine craftsmanship.

27   If so, they have a right to feel proud.

28   Once again, your product really did the job, gents.

(1980)

The Writer's Subject

1. What precisely is Royko's target for satire here?

2. What concerns appear to be missing in Royko's references to the various victims of assassination? How do these omissions fit his purpose in the essay?

3. How does Royko apply the idea of quality and craftsmanship to the subject of guns?

4. Royko first describes the gunmen as "deranged." How does he subsequently treat them? How does this treatment fit his satiric purposes?

5. What is Royko's attitude to the Charter Arms Corp.? What does he imply about the company's values and possibly those of business in general?

6. What is Royko's attitude to handguns?

The Writer's Style and Strategy

1. What indications does the essay give that it was originally written for a newspaper audience?

2. What is the tone of Royko's essay? How is it established in the opening paragraph?

3. What persona does Royko create for the speaker of this essay?

4. Why does Royko constantly use "Corp." instead of "corporation" in referring to the gun company?

5. A method frequently employed by satirists is to reverse praise and blame, thus creating an ironic effect. Point out some specific examples of the praise/blame inversion and suggest Royko's real intent.

6. What use does Royko make of the editorial and the "Apology from CBS" published in the Charter Arms Corp. company magazine?

7. Why does Royko say that "Bremer shot Wallace in the stomach" but speak in the next paragraph of "blowing a hole in Wallace's gut"?

8. Discuss the intended effect of the last three sentences.

Suggested Topics for Writing and Discussion

1. Write an argument for or against the view that the individual citizen should have the right to possess a handgun.

2. Find some reports concerning the murder or attempted murder of a well-known public figure. Compare accounts of the incident and show how the attitudes and emphases of the reporters differ in their coverage of two or three particulars.

3. Write an essay in which you attack something you believe is wrong by ironically praising what you wish to criticize.

4. One target in Royko's essay is the marketing of guns. Choose another product with potential for harm (such as cigarettes, diet pills, instant formula for babies), and discuss the ways in which the product's manufacturer attempts to persuade consumers to buy it, despite its dangers.

Sport and Nationalism
by Alan Sillitoe

1   Sometime during February 1969 a certain person wrote to me from
Munich — I forget his name, because I destroyed the letter — asking
for my views on sport. His request was short, and put in rather general
terms, yet my mind immediately understood it in a particular way, as it
was meant to do, perhaps. For some reason I copied the body of my
reply into my notebook at the time, and this is what I told him:

2   'I have never practised any kind of sport. It has always seemed to me
that sport only serves to enslave the mind and to enslave the body. It is
the main "civilising" weapon of the western world ethos, a way of enforcing collective discipline which no self-respecting savage like myself could ever take to. Society was built on "competition", and "sport"
is a preliminary to this society and an accompaniment to it. It is a sort
of training ground for entering into the war of life. The Olympic torch
is a flame of enslavement — run from it as fast as you can, and that in
itself will give you plenty of exercise.'

3   In olden days sport was the king's pastime. Now, it can be everybody's. By sport I mean competitive sport, when one man or woman
matches himself or herself against another, either for so-called glory, or
for cash gain.

4   Even as late as the end of the nineteenth century a particularly vicious sport existed in a certain area of south-east England. Its name was
'kickshins' — which is as good a description of it as any. Two men would
stand facing, arms on each other's shoulders, and take it in turns to give
a kick at each other's shins. Matches were arranged between the kickshin
champions of various villages, and the local squires would bet on their
favourites.

Just as universal literacy was necessary to get people into the mod- 5
ern age, so mass competitive sport was used as further cement to enslave them. Like every such distraction offered to the people, the people
reached out to it with alacrity.

Why was this?   6

First of all, sport of big business and big propaganda was allied to 7
nationalism. If England lost a football match against Germany the people were made to feel as if the Battle of the Somme had just been
refought (and that maybe it would have been a better result if they'd
played cricket). If England won the game of football the Union Jack
was in blatant evidence, as a symbol of a national victory. It is no accident that the English say (a false claim in any case), that 'the Battle of
Waterloo was won on the playing fields of Eton.'

One might easily think that sport has taken the place of war. Not at 8
all. Sport is a means of keeping the national spirit alive during a time of
so-called peace. It prepares the national spirit for the eventuality of war.

The ceremony of the Olympic Games is initiated by shields and flags, 9
artillery salutes and fanfares of trumpets. The honour of each nation is
invoked and put at stake immediately the runner sets out with his flam-
ing torch.

It is almost as if sport is diplomacy carried on by other means. Sport 10
is encouraged in schools so that young boys won't masturbate. It is encouraged among the grown-ups, as participants or spectators, to take
their minds off urgent social problems, and the need to rebel when they
are not resolved quickly enough.

If England wins an international football match, or clears twenty gold- 11
plated tin medals at some games or other, then production goes up in
England's factories. Likewise when England lost at football in Mexico
in 1970, Mr. Harold Wilson, the Labour Party Prime Minister of the
day, lost the following general election to his Conservative opponent
Mr. Edward Heath.

Perhaps Mr. Heath is even looking for victories at the present Olym- 12
pic Games to increase his chances at the next election! Woe betide him
if England loses against Poland, or Brazil!

You might almost think that England's sporting prowess was linked 13
to the floating of the pound. One lost goal, and a few more cents are
chipped off it in the world's financial arenas. A few centimetres off the
high jump, and a left wing demonstration gets too close to the American Embassy in Grosvenor Square.

If England loses, faces are long for a week. Or they might be, if radio 14 and television had its way, for those media too pander to the lowest common denominator of nationalism when it comes to sport. They exult in what is known as victory, but hide as best they can so-called defeat.

15   True sport — I'm not sure that there is such a thing — but true sport, as I see it, is not to set people competing against each other both in deed and thought, but to work together as a team perhaps, against some arduous enterprise or obstacle. If a dozen people set out on foot to cross South America gathering scientific information on the way — that is good. But if two such groups set out in order to see who can do it quickest, or who can get to know most — that is demoralising.

16   If one man can jump sixteen feet, and another tries to jump seventeen in order to get a piece of gold with his name stamped on it — in smaller letters though than the name of his country — and so that he will become a national hero for a few weeks as well, that is both ludicrous and sinister.

17   He is surrounded by flags and partisan spectators while he performs his act, his national ritual, and all those people are getting some semi-sexual power-drive from the fact that his jump would be their jump if only they had trained for it, and hadn't eaten such big meals during their recent lives.

18   His power is their power. They see him or her, for a moment, as them, and them as him. And if at that moment a government minister or national general came into the stands and ordered them to jump to their feet, and then to jump sixteen feet the same as he — or she — they would no doubt all stand up fully confident that they could do it — or something close.

19   If some mechanism were fitted into every television set which, immediately after the big jump, put out a voice which said to all the watchers: 'Now YOU jump — for the good of your country, because those in every other country are doing the same to compete with you, and the honour of your country is at stake' — the nation would jump as one person. The nation in armchairs would become the nation in arms.

20   The Olympic Games cannot, therefore, be considered as anything other than a mass rally. Under the guise of international friendly competition the same old nationalist values and rivalries are fostered. It is not the thing to engender real friendship between countries, or between the people of these countries.

21   As soon as a man participates, either in body or spirit, either at the actual place or vicariously through the medium of the television set, or the radio, or the newspapers, he loses his individuality, and becomes

part of his nation — with unreasonable yearning in his heart.

We all know that in the totalitarian state sport is used to drill and 22 make the individual subservient to the totalitarian system. In a so-called democratic state, competitive sport is used for the same ends, in the same way, but so that the participants appear to be competing primarily for themselves and not their country. But as soon as they enter that stadium or arena they are just as much representatives of their country as are those who belong to a totalitarian system. The media sees to that and so do the people who take up the message of the media.

When that Olympic torch is lit we must see it for what it is. It is a 23 symbol of the oppression of the free human spirit. That flame is a burning torch being carried along the highway, and all sensible people would get out of its way, flee from it and take to the hills. When it gets to the stadium and the crowd roars, you know that that is the place to keep away from.

Gladitorial combats in Ancient Rome, chariot races in Constantino- 24 ple, bull-fights in modern Spain, and the Olympic Games in whatever place they are held — it means that the true and human spirit of man is being killed there, the body wrecked and abused, and the heart broken.

Just as all war supposes human weakness, and is directed against that 25 weakness, so all sport is a human way of arranging the survival of the fittest. Thus the arena is a sort of jungle concocted by so-called civilisation, wherein the fittest people are made to be the human measurement of nationalist aspirations.

It is a thing that the truly civilised must instinctively abominate, and 26 then with reason protest against. We must somehow make our sane voices heard — even while the crowd roars.

The voice of civilisation is not measured by the loudness of the roar- 27 ing. And civilisation itself must not be jeopardised by the contests in the arena. The Olympic torch lights up the hollow eyes of the dictator, and turns all eyes toward the national flag.

After the death of the Israelis the voices of commentators from the 28 Olympic Games in Munich have taken on tones of vile obscenity — real obscenity, the deepest obscenity of the spirit which henceforth will be represented by the Olympic Games.

The resumption of these so-called games in such indecent haste only 29 emphasised their true spirit — that of a host country unwilling to give up its pride, its financial investments; and of athletes who are in the grip of their physical investment at the expense of all human feeling.

That the 'games' should go on after the black-hearted murder of eleven 30 participants shows that true sporting spirit is so dead that one must doubt whether it ever existed. The continuation of the games is a victory for the Arab terrorists, for it is the quickest and most effective way of drawing a curtain on this atrocity.

(1972)

The Writer's Subject

1. Why does Sillitoe refer to himself in paragraph 2 as a "savage"?

2. What parallel does Sillitoe draw between the rise of literacy and the growth of competitive sport? (para. 5)

3. What is the connection, in Sillitoe's view, between sport and the spirit of nationalism? (paras. 7–9)

4. According to Sillitoe, what impact does sport have on the social or political climate of a nation? (paras. 10–14)

5. What contrast does Sillitoe draw between competitive sport and what he calls "true sport"? (para. 15)

6. How, in Sillitoe's opinion, are both athletes and spectators affected by competitive sport? What sinister influence does he imagine might be exerted over a television audience? (paras. 16–19)

7. On what grounds does Sillitoe maintain that the Olympic torch is "a symbol of the oppression of the free human spirit" (para. 23)? What parallels does he draw between the Olympics and totalitarianism?

8. This essay was written after the murder of eleven Israeli athletes at the Munich Olympics in 1972. Why is Sillitoe so outraged that the Games should have been resumed after this event? (paras. 28–30) How does that resumption seem to him a confirmation of his views on competitive sport?

The Writer's Style and Strategy

1. What is Sillitoe's strategy in beginning an essay written in 1972 with a brief anecdote and an excerpt from a notebook, both dating from 1969?

2. Sillitoe offers an argument against competitive sport based on assertion and appeals to emotion rather than on factual evidence and logical reasoning. Pick out passages in which you feel that the appeal to emotion is particularly evident.

3. Note the use of "loaded" language (e.g., "so-called glory," "gold-plated tin medals," "his national ritual"). Choose some examples of such language, and discuss the intended effect.

4. What is the purpose of the description in paragraph 4 of the game called "kickshins"? Does it add anything to Sillitoe's thesis?

5. On what does Sillitoe base his argument that there is a correlation between victory or defeat in sport and events on the English political scene? (paras. 11–13) How convincing is this argument?

6. Discuss how Sillitoe's paragraph structures, sentence lengths, and word choice suit his purpose. How do they serve to convey his tone?

7. How would you characterize the tone of this essay? Does the tone change as the essay progresses?

Suggested Topics for Writing and Discussion

1. At several points, Sillitoe attacks the media for helping to foster the spirit of nationalism in competitive sport. Argue for or against Sillitoe's position, bringing supporting evidence from radio, T.V., or the print media.

2. Sillitoe maintains that the Olympic Games promote an unhealthy, warlike nationalism among competitors. Do you agree? What elements of the Games, if any, do you think should be changed?

3. Like Ken Dryden, in his essay "The Game," Sillitoe sees sport as a function of "big business." To what extent, in your view, has commercialism helped or hindered the development of sport?

4. Sillitoe concludes his essay by asserting that "true sporting spirit" is dead. Write an essay in which you explain what you mean by "true sporting spirit," and indicate whether you agree with Sillitoe.

5. Does competition build a strong character? Explain your view.

A Modest Proposal

For Preventing The Children of Poor People in Ireland, From
Being a Burden to Their Parents or Country; and for Making
Them Beneficial to the Public

by Jonathan Swift

1   It is a melancholy object to those who walk through this great town or travel in the country, when they see the streets, the roads and cabin doors crowded with beggars of the female sex, followed by three, four, or six children, all in rags and importuning every passenger for an alms. These mothers, instead of being able to work for their honest livelihood, are forced to employ all their time in strolling to beg sustenance for their helpless infants; who as they grow up either turn thieves for want of work, or leave their dear native country to fight for the Pretender in Spain, or sell themselves to the Barbadoes.

2   I think it is agreed by all parties that this prodigious number of children in the arms, or on the backs, or at the heels of their mothers, and frequently of their fathers, is in the present deplorable state of the kingdom a very great additional grievance; and, therefore, whoever could find out a fair, cheap, and easy method of making these children sound and useful members of the Commonwealth, would deserve so well of the public as to have his statue set up for a preserver of the nation.

3   But my intention is very far from being confined to provide only for the children of professed beggars; it is of a much greater extent, and shall take in the whole number of infants at a certain age who are born of parents in effect as little able to support them as those who demand our charity in the streets.

As to my own part, having turned my thoughts for many years upon 4 this important subject, and maturely weighed the several schemes of other projectors, I have always found them grossly mistaken in their computation. It is true a child, just dropped from its dam, may be supported by her milk for a solar year, with little other nourishment; at most not above the value of two shillings, which the mother may certainly get, or the value in scraps, by her lawful occupation of begging; and it is exactly at one year old that I propose to provide for them in such a manner as instead of being a charge upon their parents or the parish, or wanting food and raiment for the rest of their lives, they shall on the contrary contribute to the feeding, and partly to the clothing, of many thousands.

There is likewise another great advantage in my scheme, that it will 5 prevent those voluntary abortions, and that horrid practice of women murdering their bastard children, alas! too frequent among us, sacrificing the poor innocent babes, I doubt, more to avoid the expense than the shame, which would move tears and pity in the most savage and inhuman breast.

The number of souls in Ireland being usually reckoned one million 6 and a half, of these I calculate there may be about two hundred thousand couples whose wives are breeders; from which number I subtract thirty thousand couples who are able to maintain their own children (although I apprehend there cannot be so many, under the present distresses of the kingdom); but this being granted, there will remain an hundred and seventy thousand breeders. I again subtract fifty thousand for those women who miscarry, or whose children die by accident or disease within the year. There only remain an hundred and twenty thousand children of poor parents annually born. The question therefore is, how this number shall be reared and provided for? which, as I have already said, under the present situation of affairs, is utterly impossible by all the methods hitherto proposed. For we can neither employ them in handicraft or agriculture; we neither build houses (I mean in the country) nor cultivate land; they can very seldom pick up a livelihood by stealing, till they arrive at six years old, except where they are of towardly parts; although I confess they learn the rudiments much earlier; during which time they can, however, be properly looked upon only as probationers; as I have been informed by a principal gentleman in the county of Cavan, who protested to me that he never knew above one or two instances under the age of six, even in a part of the kingdom so renowned for the quickest proficiency in that art.

7   I am assured by our merchants, that a boy or a girl before twelve
years old is no saleable commodity; and even when they come to this
age they will not yield above three pounds or three pounds and half a
crown at most on the Exchange; which cannot turn to account either to
the parents or the kingdom, the charge of nutriment and rags having
been at least four times that value.

8   I shall now therefore humbly propose my own thoughts, which I hope
will not be liable to the least objection.

9   I have been assured by a very knowing American of my acquaintance in London, that a young healthy child well nursed is, at year old, a
most delicious, nourishing, and wholesome food, whether stewed,
roasted, baked, or boiled; and I make no doubt that it will equally serve
in a fricassee or a ragout.

10   I do therefore humbly offer it to public consideration that of the hundred and twenty thousand children already computed, twenty thousand
may be reserved for breed, whereof only one-fourth part to be males;
which is more than we allow to sheep, black cattle, or swine; and my
reason is, that these children are seldom the fruits of marriage, a circumstance not much regarded by our savages; therefore one male will
be sufficient to serve four females. That the remaining hundred thousand may, at a year old, be offered in sale to the persons of quality and
fortune through the kingdom; always advising the mother to let them
suck plentifully in the last month, so as to render them plump and fat
for a good table. A child will make two dishes at an entertainment for
friends; and when the family dines alone, the fore or hind quarter will
make a reasonable dish, and seasoned with a little pepper or salt will be
very good boiled on the fourth day, especially in winter.

11   I have reckoned upon a medium that a child just born will weigh
twelve pounds, and in a solar year, if tolerably nursed, will increase to
twenty-eight pounds.

12   I grant this food will be somewhat dear, and therefore very proper
for landlords, who, as they have already devoured most of the parents,
seem to have the best title to the children.

13   Infant's flesh will be in season throughout the year, but more plentiful in March, and a little before and after: for we are told by a grave
author, an eminent French physician, that fish being a prolific diet, there
are more children born in Roman Catholic countries about nine months
after Lent than at any other season; therefore reckoning a year after
Lent, the markets will be more glutted than usual, because the number
of popish infants is at least three to one in this kingdom: and therefore

it will have one other collateral advantage, by lessening the number of Papists among us.

I have already computed the charge of nursing a beggar's child (in 14 which list I reckon all cottagers, laborers, and four-fifths of the farmers) to be about two shillings per annum, rags included; and I believe no gentleman would repine to give ten shillings for the carcass of a good fat child, which, as I have said, will make four dishes of excellent nutritive meat, when he has only some particular friend or his own family to dine with him. Thus the squire will learn to be a good landlord, and grow popular among his tenants; the mother will have eight shillings net profit, and be fit for work till she produces another child.

Those who are more thrifty (as I must confess the times require) may 15 flay the carcass; the skin of which artificially dressed will make admirable gloves for ladies, and summer boots for fine gentlemen.

As to our city of Dublin, shambles may be appointed for this purpose in the most convenient parts of it, and butchers we may be assured 16 will not be wanting: although I rather recommend buying the children alive, and dressing them hot from the knife as we do roasting pigs.

A very worthy person, a true lover of his country, and whose virtues 17 I highly esteem, was lately pleased in discoursing on this matter to offer a refinement upon my scheme. He said that many gentlemen of this kingdom, having of late destroyed their deer, he conceived that the want of venison might be well supplied by the bodies of young lads and maidens, not exceeding fourteen years of age nor under twelve; so great a number of both sexes in every county being now ready to starve for want of work and service; and these to be disposed of by their parents, if alive, or otherwise by their nearest relations. But with due deference to so excellent a friend and so deserving a patriot, I cannot be altogether in his sentiments. For as to the males, my American acquaintance assured me from frequent experience that their flesh was generally tough and lean, like that of our schoolboys by continual exercise, and their taste disagreeable; and to fatten them would not answer the charge. Then as to the females, it would, I think, with humble submission be a loss to the public, because they soon would become breeders themselves: and besides, it is not improbable that some scrupulous people might be apt to censure such a practice (although indeed very unjustly) as a little bordering upon cruelty; which, I confess, has always been with me the strongest objection against any project, how well soever intended.

But in order to justify my friend, he confessed that this expedient 18 was put into his head by the famous Salmanaazor, a native of the island

Formosa, who came from thence to London above twenty years ago: and in conversation told my friend, that in his country when any young person happened to be put to death, the executioner sold the carcass to persons of quality as a prime dainty; and that in his time the body of a plump girl of fifteen, who was crucified for an attempt to poison the emperor, was sold to his imperial majesty's prime minister of state, and other great mandarins of the court, in joints from the gibbet, at four hundred crowns. Neither indeed can I deny, that if the same use were made of several plump young girls in this town, who without one single groat to their fortunes cannot stir abroad without a chair, and appear at the playhouse and assemblies in foreign fineries which they never will pay for, the kingdom would not be the worse.

19   Some persons of a desponding spirit are in great concern about that vast number of poor people, who are aged, diseased, or maimed, and I have been desired to employ my thoughts what cause may be taken to ease the nation of so grievous an encumbrance. But I am not in the least pain upon that matter, because it is very well known that they are every day dying and rotting by cold and famine, and filth and vermin, as fast as can be reasonably expected. And as to the young, labourers, they are now in as hopeful a condition: they cannot get work, and consequently pine away for want of nourishment, to a degree that if at any time they are accidentally hired to common labour, they have not strength to perform it; and thus the country and themselves are in a fair way of being soon delivered from the evils to come.

20   I have too long digressed, and therefore shall return to my subject. I think the advantages by the proposal which I have made are obvious and many, as well as of the highest importance.

21   For first, as I have already observed, it would greatly lessen the number of Papists, with whom we are yearly overrun, being the principal breeders of the nation as well as our most dangerous enemies; and who stay at home on purpose with a design to deliver the kingdom to the Pretender, hoping to take their advantage by the absence of so many good Protestants, who have chosen rather to leave their country than stay at home and pay tithes against their conscience to an idolatrous Episcopal curate.

22   Secondly, the poor tenants will have something valuable of their own, which by law may be made liable to distress and help to pay their landlord's rent, their corn and cattle being already seized, and money a thing unknown.

23   Thirdly, whereas the maintenance of an hundred thousand children

from two years old and upwards, cannot be computed at less than ten shillings apiece per annum, the nation's stock will be thereby increased fifty thousand pounds per annum, beside the profit of a new dish introduced to the tables of all gentlemen of fortune in the kingdom who have any refinement in taste. And the money will circulate among ourselves, the goods being entirely of our own growth and manufacture.

Fourthly, the constant breeders besides the gain of eight shillings ster- 24 ling per annum by the sale of their children, will be rid of the charge of maintaining them after the first year.

Fifthly, this food would likewise bring great custom to taverns, where 25 the vintners will certainly be so prudent as to procure the best receipts for dressing it to perfection, and consequently have their houses frequented by all the fine gentlemen, who justly value themselves upon their knowledge in good eating; and a skilful cook who understands how to oblige his guests, will contrive to make it as expensive as they please.

Sixthly, this would be a great inducement to marriage, which all wise 26 nations have either encouraged by rewards or enforced by laws and penalties. It would increase the care and tenderness of mothers towards their children, when they were sure of a settlement for life to the poor babes, provided in some sort by the public, to their annual profit instead of expense. We should soon see an honest emulation among the married women, which of them could bring the fattest child to the market. Men would become as fond of their wives during the time of their pregnancy as they are now of their mares in foal, their cows in calf, their sows when they are ready to farrow; nor offer to beat or kick them (as is too frequent a practice) for fear of a miscarriage.

Many other advantages might be enumerated. For instance, the ad- 27 dition of some thousand carcasses in our exportation of barreled beef, the propagation of swine's flesh, and improvement in the art of making good bacon, so much wanted among us by the great destruction of pigs, too frequent at our tables, and which are no way comparable in taste or magnificence to a well-grown, fat, yearling child, which roasted whole will make a considerable figure at a Lord Mayor's feast or any other public entertainment. But this and many others I omit, being studious of brevity.

Supposing that one thousand families in this city would be constant 28 customers for infant's flesh, besides others who might have it at merry meetings, particularly weddings and christenings, I compute that Dublin would take off annually about twenty thousand carcasses; and the rest of the kingdom (where probably they will be sold somewhat cheaper) the remaining eighty thousand.

29   I can think of no one objection that will possibly be raised against
this proposal, unless it should be urged that the number of people will
be thereby much lessened in the kingdom. This I freely own, and it was
indeed one principal design in offering it to the world. I desire the reader
will observe, that I calculate my remedy for this one individual kingdom of Ireland and for no other that ever was, is, or I think ever can be
upon earth. Therefore let no man talk to me of other expedients: of tax-
ing our absentees at five shillings a pound: of using neither clothes nor
household furniture except what is of our own growth and manufacture: of utterly rejecting the materials and instruments that promote foreign luxury: of curing the expensiveness of pride, vanity, idleness, and
gaming in our women: of introducing a vein of parsimony, prudence,
and temperance: of learning to love our country, wherein we differ even
from Laplanders and the inhabitants of Topinamboo: of quitting our
animosities and factions, nor act any longer like the Jews, who were
murdering one another at the very moment their city was taken: of being a little cautious not to sell our country and conscience for nothing:
of teaching landlords to have at least one degree of mercy towards their
tenants. Lastly, of putting a spirit of honesty, industry, and skill into our
shopkeepers; who, if a resolution could now be taken to buy only our
native goods, would immediately unite to cheat and exact upon us in
the price, the measure, and the goodness, nor could ever yet be brought
to make one fair proposal of just dealing, though often and earnestly
invited to it.

30   Therefore, I repeat, let no man talk to me of these and the like expedients, till he has at least a glimpse of hope that there will ever be some
hearty and sincere attempt to put them in practice.

31   But as to myself, having been wearied out for many years with offering vain, idle, visionary thoughts, and at length utterly despairing of
success, I fortunately fell upon this proposal; which, as it is wholly new,
so it has something solid and real, of no expense and little trouble, full
in our own power, and whereby we can incur no danger in disobliging
England. For this kind of commodity will not bear exportation, the flesh
being of too tender a consistence to admit a long continuance in salt,
although perhaps I could name a country which would be glad to eat up
our whole nation without it.

32   After all, I am not so violently bent upon my own opinion as to reject any offer proposed by wise men, which shall be found equally innocent, cheap, easy, and effectual. But before something of that kind

shall be advanced in contradiction to my scheme, and offering a better, I desire the author or authors will be pleased maturely to consider two points. First, as things now stand, how they will be able to find food and raiment for a hundred thousand useless mouths and backs? And secondly, there being a round million of creatures in human figure throughout this kingdom, whose whole subsistence put into a common stock would leave them in debt two millions of pounds sterling, adding those who are beggars by profession to the bulk of farmers, cottagers, and labourers, with the wives and children who are beggars in effect; I desire those politicians who dislike my overture, and may perhaps be so bold to attempt an answer, that they will first ask the parents of these mortals, whether they would not at this day think it a great happiness to have been sold for food at a year old in the manner I prescribe, and thereby have avoided such a perpetual scene of misfortunes as they have since gone through by the oppression of landlords, the impossibility of paying rent without money or trade, the want of common sustenance, with neither house nor clothes to cover them from the inclemencies of weather, and the most inevitable prospect of entailing the like or greater miseries upon their breed for ever.

I profess, in the sincerity of my heart, that I have not the least personal 33 interest in endeavouring to promote this necessary work, having no other motive than the public good of my country, by advancing our trade, providing for infants, relieving the poor, and giving some pleasure to the rich. I have no children by which I can propose to get a single penny; the youngest being nine years old, and my wife past child-bearing.

(1729)

The Writer's Subject

1. How does the speaker demonstrate that the problems of poverty in Ireland have reached crisis proportions? (paras. 1–6)

2. What image of himself does the speaker project in the first six paragraphs of his Proposal? What clues are contained in the early paragraphs that might contradict that image?

3. What are the real values of the speaker, as revealed in paragraphs 7–9?

4. Why does the speaker propose to preserve only one male child to every four female children? (para. 10) How does this fit in with the speaker's general attitude to the poor of Ireland?

5. Who might be the speaker's "very knowing American acquaintance" in paragraph 9, and where is his identity made clearer?

6. At what points is the speaker's inhumanity most extreme?

7. What religious, economic, and social advantages does the speaker maintain would accrue to Ireland if his Proposal were to be implemented? (paras. 21–26)

8. What are the realities of life in Ireland, as these emerge from the Proposal? How are conditions in Ireland determined by its relation to England?

9. What is the function of the concluding paragraph? How does the final sentence undercut the speaker's intention?

The Writer's Style and Strategy

1. Why does Swift create a persona as the author of this Proposal? Would his intentions have been better served by a more direct attack on English policies in Ireland?

2. To what audience does the speaker address his Proposal, and what are its supposed values?

3. What effect is gained by delaying the revelation of the Proposal, with its details, until paragraph 10?

4. Discuss the speaker's use of statistics and his reference to authorities as ways of supporting his argument.

5. At what points in the essay does Swift's own voice seem to emerge from behind the mask? Why does Swift allow this to happen?

6. Irony consists in the reader's perception of a discrepancy between the appearance of things and their reality. Discuss the operation of irony in paragraph 17. What makes the speaker's references to his friend in that paragraph ironic?

7. How does Swift make the reader recognize that the inhumanity of the supposed writer is not so far removed from the real attitudes of the English rulers of Ireland?

8. Discuss the speaker's tone in this essay. Does the tone remain the same throughout, or does it change? Account for any shifts in tone.

Suggested Topics for Writing and Discussion

1. Choose an issue about which there has been some controversy (e.g. apartheid, the treatment of the indigenous peoples of North America, abortion, pornography) and offer a "Modest Proposal" to solve the problem.

2. Swift would have been horrified to see that the attitudes he burlesques through the speaker of "A Modest Proposal" have found grim expression

in the twentieth century (e.g., Hitler's "final solution," Stalin's "purges," South Africa's apartheid policy). Describe to Swift one or more of the horrors of modern history and the attitudes which gave rise to them.

3. Find one or two examples of writing that uses satire and/or humour in dealing with serious subjects. Do you think that humour is an appropriate means of dealing with topics of an horrific or disturbing nature? Are there any topics which you would consider a taboo subject, too sensitive to be treated in a humorous way?

Civil Disobedience
by Henry David Thoreau

1   I heartily accept the motto, — "That government is best which governs
'least;" and I should like to see it acted up to more rapidly and systematically. Carried out, it finally amounts to this, which also I believe, —
"That government is best which governs not at all;" and when men are
prepared for it, that will be the kind of government which they will have.
Government is at best but an expedient; but most governments are usually, and all governments are sometimes, inexpedient. The objections
which have been brought against a standing army, and they are many
and weighty, and deserve to prevail, may also at last be brought against
a standing government. The standing army is only an arm of the standing government. The government itself, which is only the mode which
the people have chosen to execute their will, is equally liable to be abused
and perverted before the people can act through it. Witness the present
Mexican war, the work of comparatively a few individuals using the
standing government as their tool; for, in the outset, the people would
not have consented to this measure.

2   This American government, — what is it but a tradition, though a
recent one, endeavoring to transmit itself unimpaired to posterity, but
each instant losing some of its integrity? It has not the vitality and force
of a single living man; for a single man can bend it to his will. It is a
sort of wooden gun to the people themselves. But is it not the less necessary for this; for the people must have some complicated machinery
or other, and hear its din, to satisfy that idea of government which they
have. Governments show thus how successfully men can be imposed
on, even impose on themselves, for their own advantage. It is excellent,

we must all allow. Yet this government never of itself furthered any enterprise, but by the alacrity with which it got out of its way. *It* does not
keep the country free. *It* does not settle the West. *It* does not educate.
The character inherent in the American people has done all that has been
accomplished; and it would have done somewhat more, if the government had not sometimes got in its way. For government is an expedient
by which men would fain succeed in letting one another alone; and, as
has been said, when it is most expedient, the governed are most let alone
by it. Trade and commerce, if they were not made of India-rubber, would
never manage to bounce over the obstacles which legislators are continually putting in their way; and, if one were to judge these men wholly
by the effects of their actions and not partly by their intentions, they
would deserve to be classed and punished with those mischievous persons who put obstructions on the railroads.

But, to speak practically and as a citizen, unlike those who call them-   3
selves no-government men, I ask for, not at once no government, but *at
once* a better government. Let every man make known what kind of
government would command his respect, and that will be one step toward obtaining it.

After all, the practical reason why, when the power is once in the   4
hands of the people, a majority are permitted, and for a long period continue, to rule is not because they are most likely to be in the right, nor
because this seems fairest to the minority, but because they are physically
the strongest. But a government in which the majority rule in all cases
cannot be based on justice, even as far as men understand it. Can there
not be a government in which majorities do not virtually decide right and
wrong, but conscience? — in which majorities decide only those questions to which the rule of expediency is applicable? Must the citizen ever
for a moment, or in the least degree, resign his conscience to the legislator? Why has every man a conscience, then? I think that we should be
men first, and subjects afterward. It is not desirable to cultivate a respect
for the law, so much as for the right. The only obligation which I have a
right to assume is to do at any time what I think right. It is truly enough
said, that a corporation has no conscience; but a corporation of conscientious men is a corporation *with* a conscience. Law never made men a
whit more just; and, by means of their respect for it, even the well-disposed are daily made the agents of injustice. A common and natural result of an undue respect for law is, that you may see a file of soldiers,
colonel, captain, corporal, privates, powder-monkeys, and all, marching
in admirable order over hill and dale to the wars, against their wills, ay,

against their common sense and consciences, which makes it very steep marching indeed, and produces a palpitation of the heart. They have no doubt that it is a damnable business in which they are concerned; they are all peaceably inclined. Now, what are they? Men at all? or small movable forts and magazines, at the service of some unscrupulous man in power? Visit the Navy-Yard, and behold a marine, such a man as an American government can make, or such as it can make a man with its black arts, — a mere shadow and reminiscence of humanity, a man laid out alive and standing, and already, as one may say, buried under arms with funeral accompaniments, though it may be, —

"Not a drum was heard, not a funeral note,
  As his corse to the rampart we hurried;
Not a soldier discharged his farewell shot
  O'er the grave where our hero we buried."

5   The mass of men serve the state thus, not as men mainly, but as machines, with their bodies. They are the standing army, and the militia, jailers, constables, posse comitatus, etc. In most cases there is no free exercise whatever of the judgment or of the moral sense; but they put themselves on a level with wood and earth and stones; and wooden men can perhaps be manufactured that will serve the purpose as well. Such command no more respect than men of straw or a lump of dirt. They have the same sort of worth only as horses and dogs. Yet such as these even are commonly esteemed good citizens. Others — as most legislators, politicians, lawyers, ministers, and office-holders — serve the state chiefly with their heads; and, as they rarely make any moral distinctions, they are as likely to serve the Devil, without *intending* it, as God. A very few, as heroes, patriots, martyrs, reformers in the great sense, and *men*, serve the state with their consciences also, and so necessarily resist it for the most part; and they are commonly treated as enemies by it. A wise man will only be useful as a man, and will not submit to be "clay," and "stop a hole to keep the wind away," but leave that office to his dust at least: —

"I am too high-born to be propertied,
  To be a secondary at control,
  Or useful serving-man and instrument
  To any sovereign state throughout the world."

6   He who gives himself entirely to his fellow-men appears to them useless and selfish; but he who gives himself partially to them is pronounced a benefactor and philanthropist.

How does it become a man to behave toward this American govern- 7
ment to-day? I answer, that he cannot without disgrace be associated
with it. I cannot for an instant recognize that political organization as
my government which is the *slave's* government also.

All men recognize the right of revolution; that is, the right to refuse 8
allegiance to, and to resist, the government, when its tyranny or its in-
efficiency are great and unendurable. But almost all say that such is not
the case now. But such was the case, they think, in the Revolution of
'75. If one were to tell me that this was a bad government because it
taxed certain foreign commodities brought to its ports, it is most probable that I should not make an ado about it, for I can do without them.
All machines have their friction; and possibly this does enough good to
counterbalance the evil. At any rate, it is a great evil to make a stir about
it. But when the friction comes to have its machine, and oppression and
robbery are organized, I say, let us not have such a machine any longer.
In other words, when a sixth of the population of a nation which has
undertaken to be the refuge of liberty are slaves, and a whole country is
unjustly overrun and conquered by a foreign army, and subjected to
military law, I think that it is not too soon for honest men to rebel and
revolutionize. What makes this duty the more urgent is the fact that the
country so overrun is not our own, but ours is the invading army.

Paley, a common authority with many on moral questions, in his chap- 9
ter on the "Duty of Submission to Civil Government," resolves all civil
obligation into expediency; and he proceeds to say, "that so long as the
interest of the whole society requires it, that is, so long as the established government cannot be resisted or changed without public
inconveniency, it is the will of God that the established government be
obeyed, and no longer.... This principle being admitted, the justice of
every particular case of resistance is reduced to a computation of the
quantity of the danger and grievance on the one side, and of the prob-
ability and expense of redressing it on the other." Of this, he says, every
man shall judge for himself. But Paley appears never to have contemplated those cases to which the rule of expediency does not apply, in
which a people, as well as an individual, must do justice, cost what it
may. If I have unjustly wrested a plank from a drowning man, I must
restore it to him though I drown myself. This, according to Paley, would
be inconvenient. But he that would save his life, in such a case, shall
lose it. This people must cease to hold slaves, and to make war on
Mexico, though it cost them their existence as a people.

In their practice, nations agree with Paley; but does any one think 10 that Massachusetts does exactly what is right at the present crisis?

   "A drab of state, a cloth-o'-silver slut,
    To have her train borne up, and her soul trail in the dirt."

Practically speaking, the opponents to a reform in Massachusetts are
not a hundred thousand politicians at the South, but a hundred thousand merchants and farmers here, who are more interested in commerce
and agriculture than they are in humanity, and are not prepared to do
justice to the slave and to Mexico, *cost what it may*. I quarrel not with
far-off foes, but with those who, near at home, co-operate with, and do
the bidding of, those far away, and without whom the latter would be
harmless. We are accustomed to say, that the mass of men are unprepared; but improvement is slow, because the few are not materially wiser
or better than the many. It is not so important that many should be as
good as you, as that there be some absolute goodness somewhere; for
that will leaven the whole lump. There are thousands who are *in opinion* opposed to slavery and to the war, who yet in effect do nothing to
put an end to them; who, esteeming themselves children of Washington
and Franklin, sit down with their hands in their pockets, and say that
they know not what to do, and do nothing; who even postpone the question of freedom to the question of free-trade, and quietly read the prices-
current along with the latest advices from Mexico, after dinner, and, it
may be, fall asleep over them both. What is the price-current of an honest man and patriot to-day? They hesitate, and they regret, and sometimes they petition; but they do nothing in earnest and with effect. They
will wait, well disposed, for others to remedy the evil, that they may no
longer have it to regret. At most, they give only a cheap vote, and a
feeble countenance and Godspeed, to the right, as it goes by them. There
are nine hundred and ninety-nine patrons of virtue to one virtuous man.
But it is easier to deal with the real possessor of a thing than with the
temporary guardian of it.

11   All voting is a sort of gaming, like checkers or backgammon, with a
slight moral tinge to it, a playing with right and wrong, with moral questions; and betting naturally accompanies it. The character of the voters
is not staked. I cast my vote, perchance, as I think right; but I am not
vitally concerned that that right should prevail. I am willing to leave it
to the majority. Its obligation, therefore, never exceeds that of expediency. Even voting *for the right* is *doing* nothing for it. It is only expressing to men feebly your desire that it should prevail. A wise man
will not leave the right to the mercy of chance, nor wish it to prevail

through the power of the majority. There is but little virtue in the action of masses of men. When the majority shall at length vote for the abolition of slavery, it will be because they are indifferent to slavery, or because there is but little slavery left to be abolished by their vote. *They* will then be the only slaves. Only *his* vote can hasten the abolition of slavery who asserts his own freedom by his vote.

I hear of a convention to be held in Baltimore, or elsewhere, for the   12
selection of a candidate for the Presidency, made up chiefly of editors, and men who are politicians by profession; but I think, what is it to any independent, intelligent, and respectable man what decision they may come to? Shall we not have the advantage of his wisdom and honesty, nevertheless? Can we not count upon some independent votes? Are there not many individuals in the country who do not attend conventions? But no: I find that the respectable man, so called, has immediately drifted from his position, and despairs of his country, when his country has more reason to despair of him. He forthwith adopts one of the candidates thus selected as the only *available* one, thus proving that he is himself *available* for any purposes of the demagogue. His vote is of no more worth than that of any unprincipled foreigner or hireling native, who may have been bought. O for a man who is a *man*, and, as my neighbor says, has a bone in his back which you cannot pass your hand through! Our statistics are at fault: the population has been returned too large. How many *men* are there to a square thousand miles in this country? Hardly one. Does not America offer any inducement for men to settle here? The American has dwindled into an Odd Fellow, — one who may be known by the development of his organ of gregariousness, and a manifest lack of intellect and cheerful self-reliance; whose first and chief concern, on coming into the world, is to see that the Almshouses are in good repair; and, before yet he has lawfully donned the virile garb, to collect a fund for the support of the widows and orphans that may be; who, in short, ventures to live only by the aid of the Mutual Insurance company, which has promised to bury him decently.

It is not a man's duty, as a matter of course, to devote himself to the   13
eradication of any, even the most enormous wrong; he may still properly have other concerns to engage him; but it is his duty, at least, to wash his hands of it, and, if he gives it no thought longer, not to give it practically his support. If I devote myself to other pursuits and contemplations, I must first see, at least, that I do not pursue them sitting upon another man's shoulders. I must get off him first, that he may pursue his contemplations too. See what gross inconsistency is tolerated. I have

heard some of my townsmen say, "I should like to have them order me out to help put down an insurrection of the slaves, or to march to Mexico; — see if I would go;" and yet these very men have each, directly by their allegiance, and so indirectly, at least, by their money, furnished a substitute. The soldier is applauded who refuses to serve in an unjust war by those who do not refuse to sustain the unjust government which makes the war; is applauded by those whose own act and authority he disregards and sets at naught; as if the state were penitent to that degree that it hired one to scourge it while it sinned, but not to that degree that it left off sinning for a moment. Thus, under the name of Order and Civil Government, we are all made at last to pay homage to and support our own meanness. After the first blush of sin comes its indifference; and from immoral it becomes, as it were, *un*moral, and not quite unnecessary to that life which we have made.

14   The broadest and most prevalent error requires the most disinterested virtue to sustain it. The slight reproach to which the virtue of patriotism is commonly liable, the noble are most likely to incur. Those who, while they disapprove of the character and measures of a government, yield to it their allegiance and support are undoubtedly its most conscientious supporters, and so frequently the most serious obstacles to reform. Some are petitioning the state to dissolve the Union, to disregard the requisitions of the President. Why do they not dissolve it themselves, — the union between themselves and the state, — and refuse to pay their quota into its treasury? Do not they stand in the same relation to the state that the state does to the Union? And have not the same reasons prevented the state from resisting the Union which have prevented them from resisting the state?

15   How can a man be satisfied to entertain an opinion merely, and enjoy *it*? Is there any enjoyment in it, if his opinion is that he is aggrieved? If you are cheated out of a single dollar by your neighbor, you do not rest satisfied with knowing that you are cheated, or with saying that you are cheated, or even with petitioning him to pay you your due; but you take effectual steps at once to obtain the full amount, and see that you are never cheated again. Action from principle, the perception and the performance of right, changes things and relations; it is essentially revolutionary, and does not consist wholly with anything which was. It not only divides states and churches, it divides families; ay, it divides the *individual*, separating the diabolical in him from the divine.

16   Unjust laws exist: shall we be content to obey them, or shall we endeavor to amend them, and obey them until we have succeeded, or

shall we transgress them at once? Men generally, under such a government as this, think that they ought to wait until they have persuaded the
majority to alter them. They think that, if they should resist, the remedy
would be worse than the evil. But it is the fault of the government itself
that the remedy *is* worse than the evil. *It* makes it worse. Why is it not
more apt to anticipate and provide for reform? Why does it not cherish
its wise minority? Why does it cry and resist before it is hurt? Why
does it not encourage its citizens to be on the alert to point out its faults,
and *do* better than it would have them? Why does it always crucify
Christ, and excommunicate Copernicus and Luther, and pronounce
Washington and Franklin rebels?

One would think, that a deliberate and practical denial of its author- 17
ity was the only offense never contemplated by government; else, why
has it not assigned its definite, its suitable and proportionate penalty? If
a man who has no property refuses but once to earn nine shillings for
the state, he is put in prison for a period unlimited by any law that I
know, and determined only by the discretion of those who placed him
there; but if he should steal ninety times nine shillings from the state,
he is soon permitted to go at large again.

If the injustice is part of the necessary friction of the machine of gov- 18
ernment, let it go: perchance it will wear smooth, — certainly the machine will wear out. If the injustice has a spring, or a pulley, or a rope,
or a crank, exclusively for itself, then perhaps you may consider whether
the remedy will not be worse than the evil; but if it is of such a nature
that it requires you to be the agent of injustice to another, then, I say,
break the law. Let your life be a counter friction to stop the machine.
What I have to do is to see, at any rate, that I do not lend myself to the
wrong which I condemn.

As for adopting the ways which the state has provided for remedy- 19
ing the evil, I know not of such ways. They take too much time, and a
man's life will be gone. I have other affairs to attend to. I came into this
world, not chiefly to make this a good place to live in, but to live in it,
be it good or bad. A man has not everything to do, but something; and
because he cannot do *everything*, it is not necessary that he should do
something wrong. It is not my business to be petitioning the Governor
or the Legislature any more than it is theirs to petition me; and if they
should not hear my petition, what should I do then? But in this case the
state has provided no way: its very Constitution is the evil. This may
seem to be harsh and stubborn and unconciliatory; but it is to treat with
the utmost kindness and consideration the only spirit that can appreci-

ate or deserves it. So is all change for the better, like birth and death, which convulse the body.

20   I do not hesitate to say, that those who call themselves Abolitionists should at once effectually withdraw their support, both in person and property, from the government of Massachusetts, and not wait till they constitute a majority of one, before they suffer the right to prevail through them. I think that it is enough if they have God on their side, without waiting for that other one. Moreover, any man more right than his neighbors constitutes a majority of one already.

21   I meet this American government, or its representative, the state government, directly, and face to face, once a year — no more — in the person of its tax-gatherer; this is the only mode in which a man situated as I am necessarily meets it; and it then says distinctly, Recognize me; and the simplest, the most effectual, and, in the present posture of affairs, the indispensablest mode of treating with it on this head, of expressing your little satisfaction with and love for it, is to deny it then. My civil neighbor, the tax-gatherer, is the very man I have to deal with, — for it is, after all, with men and not with parchment that I quarrel, — and he has voluntarily chosen to be an agent of the government. How shall he ever know well what he is and does as an officer of the government, or as a man, until he is obliged to consider whether he shall treat me, his neighbor, for whom he has respect, as a neighbor and well-disposed man, or as a maniac and disturber of the peace, and see if he can get over this obstruction to his neighborliness without a ruder and more impetuous thought or speech corresponding with his action. I know this well, that if one thousand, if one hundred, if ten men whom I could name, — if ten *honest* men only, — ay, if *one* HONEST man, in this State of Massachusetts, *ceasing to hold slaves*, were actually to withdraw from this copartnership, and be locked up in the county jail therefor, it would be the abolition of slavery in America. For it matters not how small the beginning may seem to be: what is once well done is done forever. But we love better to talk about it: that we say is our mission. Reform keeps many scores of newspapers in its service, but not one man. If my esteemed neighbor, the State's ambassador, who will devote his days to the settlement of the question of human rights in the Council Chamber, instead of being threatened with the prisons of Carolina, were to sit down the prisoner of Massachusetts, that State which is so anxious to foist the sin of slavery upon her sister, — though at present she can discover only an act of inhospitality to be the ground of a quarrel with her, — the Legislature would not wholly waive the subject the following winter.

Under a government which imprisons any unjustly, the true place for 22
a just man is also a prison. The proper place to-day, the only place which
Massachusetts has provided for her freer and less desponding spirits, is
in her prisons, to be put out and locked out of the State by her own act,
as they have already put themselves out by their principles. It is there
that the fugitive slave, and the Mexican prisoner on parole, and Indian
come to plead the wrongs of his race should find them; on that separate, but more free and honorable ground, where the State places those
who are not *with* her, but *against* her, — the only house in a slave State
in which a free man can abide with honor. If any think that their influence would be lost there, and their voices no longer afflict the ear of the
State, that they would not be as an enemy within its walls, they do not
know by how much truth is stronger than error, nor how much more
eloquently and effectively he can combat injustice who has experienced
a little in his own person. Cast your whole vote, not a strip of paper
merely, but your whole influence. A minority is powerless while it con-
forms to the majority; it is not even a minority then; but it is irresistible
when it clogs by its whole weight. If the alternative is to keep all just
men in prison, or give up war and slavery, the State will not hesitate
which to choose. If a thousand men were not to pay their tax-bills this
year, that would not be a violent and bloody measure, as it would be to
pay them, and enable the State to commit violence and shed innocent
blood. This is in fact, the definition of a peaceable revolution, if any
such is possible. If the tax-gatherer, or any other public officer, asks
me, as one has done, "But what shall I do?" my answer is, "If you really wish to do anything, resign your office." When the subject has refused allegiance, and the officer has resigned his office, then the
revolution is accomplished. But even suppose blood should flow. Is there
not a sort of blood shed when the conscience is wounded? Through this
wound a man's real manhood and immortality flow out, and he bleeds
to an everlasting death. I see this blood flowing now.

I have contemplated the imprisonment of the offender, rather than the 23
seizure of his goods, — though both will serve the same purpose, — because they who assert the purest right, and consequently are most dangerous to a corrupt State, commonly have not spent much time in
accumulating property. To such the State renders comparatively small
service, and a slight tax is wont to appear exorbitant, particularly if they
are obliged to earn it by special labor with their hands. If there were one
who lived wholly without the use of money, the State itself would hesitate to demand it of him. But the rich man — not to make any invidious

comparison — is always sold to the institution which makes him rich. Absolutely speaking, the more money, the less virtue; for money comes between a man and his objects, and obtains them for him; and it was certainly no great virtue to obtain it. It puts to rest many questions which he would otherwise be taxed to answer; while the only new question which it puts is the hard but superfluous one, how to spend it. Thus his moral ground is taken from under his feet. The opportunities of living are diminished in proportion as what are called the "means" are increased. The best thing a man can do for his culture when he is rich is to endeavor to carry out those schemes which he entertained when he was poor. Christ answered the Herodians according to their condition. "Show me the tribute-money," said he; — and one took a penny out of his pocket; — if you use money which has the image of Caesar on it, which he has made current and valuable, that is, *if you are men of the State*, and gladly enjoy the advantages of Caesar's government, then pay him back some of his own when he demands it. "Render therefore to Caesar that which is Caesar's, and to God those things which are God's," — leaving them no wiser than before as to which was which; for they did not wish to know.

24   When I converse with the freest of my neighbors, I perceive that, whatever they may say about the magnitude and seriousness of the question, and their regard for the public tranquillity, the long and the short of the matter is, that they cannot spare the protection of the existing government, and they dread the consequences to their property and families of disobedience to it. For my own part, I should not like to think that I ever rely on the protection of the State. But, if I deny the authority of the State when it presents its tax-bill, it will soon take and waste all my property, and so harass me and my children without end. This is hard. This makes it impossible for a man to live honestly, and at the same time comfortably, in outward respects. It will not be worth the while to accumulate property; that would be sure to go again. You must hire or squat somewhere, and raise but a small crop, and eat that soon. You must live within yourself, and depend upon yourself always tucked up and ready for a start, and not have many affairs. A man may grow rich in Turkey even, if he will be in all respects a good subject of the Turkish government. Confucius said: "If a state is governed by the principles of reason, poverty and misery are subjects of shame; if a state is not governed by the principles of reason, riches and honors are the subjects of shame." No: until I want the protection of Massachusetts to be extended to me in some distant Southern port, where my liberty is endangered, or until I am bent solely on building up an estate at home by

peaceful enterprise, I can afford to refuse allegiance to Massachusetts, and her right to my property and life. It costs me less in every sense to incur the penalty of disobedience to the State than it would to obey. I should feel as if I were worth less in that case.

Some years ago, the State met me in behalf of the Church, and com- 25 manded me to pay a certain sum toward the support of a clergyman whose preaching my father attended, but never I myself. "Pay," it said, "or be locked up in the jail." I declined to pay. But unfortunately, another man saw fit to pay it. I did not see why the schoolmaster should be taxed to support the priest, and not the priest the schoolmaster; for I was not the State's schoolmaster, but I supported myself by voluntary subscription. I did not see why the lyceum should not present its tax-bill, and have the State to back its demand, as well as the Church. However, at the request of the selectmen, I condescended to make some such statement as this in writing: — "Know all men by these presents, that I, Henry Thoreau, do not wish to be regarded as a member of any incorporated society which I have not joined." This I gave to the town clerk; and he has it. The State, having thus learned that I did not wish to be regarded as a member of that church, has never made a like demand on me since; though it said that it must adhere to its original presumption that time. If I had known how to name them, I should then have signed off in detail from all the societies which I never signed on to; but I did not know where to find a complete list.

I have paid no poll-tax for six years. I was put into a jail on this ac- 26 count, for one night; and, as I stood considering the walls of solid stone, two or three feet thick, the door of wood and iron, a foot thick, and the iron grating which strained the light, I could not help being struck with the foolishness of that institution which treated me as if I were mere flesh and blood and bones, to be locked up. I wondered that it should have concluded at length that this was the best use it could put me to, and had never thought to avail itself of my services in some way. I saw that, if there was a wall of stone between me and my townsmen, there was a still more difficult one to climb or break through before they could get to be as free as I was. I did not for a moment feel confined, and walls seemed a great waste of stone and mortar. I felt as if I alone of all my townsmen had paid my tax. They plainly did not know how to treat me, but behaved like persons who are underbred. In every threat and in every compliment there was a blunder; for they thought that my chief desire was to stand the other side of that stone wall. I could not but smile to see how industriously they locked the door on my meditations, which followed them out again without let or hindrance, and *they* were really all that was dangerous. As they could not reach me, they had resolved to punish my body; just as boys, if they cannot come at some person against whom they have a spite, will abuse his dog. I saw that the State was halfwitted, that it was timid as a lone woman with her silver spoons, and that it did not know its friends from its foes, and I lost all my remaining respect for it, and pitied it.

27   Thus the State never intentionally confronts a man's sense, intellectual or moral, but only his body, his senses. It is not armed with superior wit or honesty, but with superior physical strength. I was not born to be forced. I will breathe after my own fashion. Let us see who is the strongest. What force has a multitude? They only can force me who obey a higher law than I. They force me to become like themselves. I do not hear of *men* being *forced* to live this way or that by masses of men. What sort of life were that to live? When I meet a government which says to me, "Your money or your life," why should I be in haste to give it my money? It may be in a great strait, and not know what to do: I cannot help that. It must help itself; do as I do. It is not worth the while to snivel about it. I am not responsible for the successful working of the machinery of society. I am not the son of the engineer. I perceive that, when an acorn and a chestnut fall side by side, the one does not remain inert to make way for the other, but both obey their own laws, and spring and grow and flourish as best they can, till one, perchance, overshadows and destroys the other. If a plant cannot live according to its nature, it dies; and so a man.

28   The night in prison was novel and interesting enough. The prisoners in their shirt-sleeves were enjoying a chat and the evening air in the doorway, when I entered. But the jailer said, "Come, boys, it is time to lock up;" and so they dispersed, and I heard the sound of their steps returning into the hollow apartments. My room-mate was introduced to me by the jailer as "a first-rate fellow and a clever man." When the door was locked, he showed me where to hang my hat, and how he managed matters there. The rooms were whitewashed once a month, and this one, at least, was the whitest, most simply furnished, and probably the neatest apartment in the town. He naturally wanted to know where I came from, and what brought me there; and, when I had told him, I asked in my turn how he came there, presuming him to be an honest man, of course; and, as the world goes, I believe he was. "Why," said he, "they accuse me of burning a barn; but I never did it." As near as I could discover, he had probably gone to bed in a barn when drunk, and smoked

his pipe there; and so a barn was burnt. He had the reputation of being a clever man, and been there some three months waiting for his trial to come on, and would have to wait as much longer; but he was quite domesticated and contented, since he got his board for nothing, and thought that he was well treated.

He occupied one window, and I the other; and I saw that if one stayed 29 there long, his principal business would be to look out the window. I had soon read all the tracts that were left there, and examined where former prisoners had broken out, and where a grate had been sawed off, and heard the history of the various occupants of that room; for I found that even here there was a history and a gossip which never circulated beyond the walls of the jail. Probably this is the only house in the town where verses are composed, which are afterward printed in a circular form, but not published. I was shown quite a long list of verses which were composed by some young men who had been detected in an attempt to escape, who avenged themselves by singing them.

I pumped my fellow-prisoner as dry as I could, for fear I should never 30 see him again; but at length he showed me which was my bed, and left me to blow out the lamp.

It was like traveling into a far country, such as I had never expected 31 to behold, to lie there for one night. It seemed to me that I never had heard the town-clock strike before, nor the evening sounds of the village; for we slept with the windows open, which were inside the grating. It was to see my native village in the light of the Middle Ages, and our Concord was turned into a Rhine stream, and visions of knights and castles passed before me. They were the voices of old burghers that I heard in the streets. I was an involuntary spectator and auditor of whatever was done and said in the kitchen of the adjacent village-inn, — a wholly new and rare experience to me. It was a closer view of my native town. I was fairly inside of it. I never had seen its institutions before. This is one of its peculiar institutions; for it is a shire town. I began to comprehend what its inhabitants were about.

In the morning, our breakfasts were put through the hole in the door, 32 in small oblong-square tin pans, made to fit, and holding a pint of chocolate, with brown bread, and an iron spoon. When they called for the vessels again, I was green enough to return what bread I had left; but my comrade seized it, and said that I should lay that up for lunch or dinner. Soon after he was let out to work at haying in a neighboring field, whither he went every day, and would not be back till noon; so he bade me good-day, saying that he doubted if he should see me again.

33   When I came out of prison, — for some one interfered, and paid that
tax, — I did not perceive that great changes had taken place on the common, such as he observed who went in a youth and emerged a tottering
and gray-haired man; and yet a change had to my eyes come over the
scene, — the town, and State, and country, — greater than any that mere
time could effect. I saw yet more distinctly the State in which I lived. I
saw to what extent the people among whom I lived could be trusted as
good neighbors and friends; that their friendship was for summer weather
only; that they did not greatly propose to do right; that they were a distinct race from me by their prejudices and superstitions, as the Chinamen and Malays are; that in their sacrifices to humanity they ran no risks,
not even to their property; that after all they were not so noble but they
treated the thief as he had treated them, and hoped, by a certain outward
observance and a few prayers, and by walking in a particular straight
though useless path from time to time, to save their souls. This may be
to judge my neighbors harshly; for I believe that many of them are not
aware that they have such an institution as the jail in their village.

34   It was formerly the custom in our village, when a poor debtor came
out of jail, for his acquaintances to salute him, looking through their
fingers, which were crossed to represent the grating of a jail window,
"How do ye do?" My neighbors did not thus salute me, but first looked
at me, and then at one another, as if I had returned from a long journey.
I was put into jail as I was going to the shoemaker's to get a shoe which
was mended. When I was let out the next morning, I proceeded to finish my errand, and, having put on my mended shoe, joined a huckleberry
party, who were impatient to put themselves under my conduct; and in
half an hour, — for the horse was soon tackled, — was in the midst of a
huckleberry field, on one of our highest hills, two miles off, and then
the State was nowhere to be seen.

35   This is the whole history of "My Prisons."

36   I have never declined paying the highway tax, because I am as desirous
of being a good neighbor as I am of being a bad subject; and as for
supporting schools, I am doing my part to educate my fellow-countrymen now. It is for no particular item in the tax-bill that I refuse to pay
it. I simply wish to refuse allegiance to the State, to withdraw and stand
aloof from it effectually. I do not care to trace the course of my dollar,
if I could, till it buys a man or a musket to shoot one with, — the dollar
is innocent, — but I am concerned to trace the effects of my allegiance.
In fact, I quietly declare war with the State, after my fashion, though I

will still make what use and get what advantage of her I can, as is usual in such cases.

If others pay the tax which is demanded of me, from a sympathy **37** with the State, they do but what they have already done in their own case, or rather they abet injustice to a greater extent than the State requires. If they pay the tax from a mistaken interest in the individual taxed, to save his property, or prevent his going to jail, it is because they have not considered wisely how far they let their private feelings interfere with the public good.

This, then, is my position at present. But one cannot be too much on **38** his guard in such a case, lest his action be biased by obstinacy or an undue regard for the opinions of men. Let him see that he does only what belong to himself and to the hour.

I think sometimes, Why, this people mean well, they are only igno- **39** rant; they would do better if they knew how: why give your neighbors this pain to treat you as they are not inclined to? But I think again, This is no reason why I should do as they do, or permit others to suffer much greater pain of a different kind. Again I sometimes say to myself, When many millions of men, without heat, without ill will, without personal feeling of any kind, demand of you a few shillings only, without the possibility, such is their constitution, of retracting or altering their present demand, and without the possibility, on your side, of appeal to any other millions, why expose yourself to this overwhelming brute force? You do not resist cold and hunger, the winds and the waves, thus obstinately; you quietly submit to a thousand similar necessities. You do not put your head into the fire. But just in proportion as I regard this as not wholly a brute force, but partly a human force, and consider that I have relations to those millions as to so many millions of men, and not of mere brute or inanimate things, I see that appeal is possible, first and instantaneously, from them to the Maker of them, and, secondly, from them to themselves. But if I put my head deliberately into the fire, there is no appeal to fire or to the Maker of fire, and I have only myself to blame. If I could convince myself that I have any right to be satisfied with men as they are, and to treat them accordingly, and not according, in some respects, to my requisitions and expectations of what they and I ought to be, then, like a good Mussulman and fatalist, I should endeavor to be satisfied with things as they are, and say it is the will of God. And, above all, there is this difference between resisting this and a purely brute or natural force, that I can resist this with some effect; but I cannot expect, like Orpheus, to change the nature of the rocks and trees and beasts.

40   I do not wish to quarrel with any man or nation. I do not wish to split hairs, to made fine distinctions, or set myself up as better than my neighbors. I seek rather, I may say, even an excuse for conforming to the laws of the land. I am but too ready to conform to them. Indeed, I have reason to suspect myself on this head; and each year, as the tax-gatherer comes round, I find myself disposed to review the acts and position of the general and State governments, and the spirit of the people, to discover a pretext for conformity.

> "We must affect our country as our parents,
>   And if at any time we alienate
>   Our love or industry from doing it honor,
>   We must respect effects and teach the soul
>   Matter of conscience and religion,
>   And not desire of rule or benefit."

I believe that the State will soon be able to take all my work of this sort out of my hands, and then I shall be no better a patriot than my fellow-countrymen. Seen from a lower point of view, the Constitution, with all its faults, is very good; and the law and the courts are very respectable; even this State and this American government are, in many respects, very admirable, and rare things, to be thankful for, such as a great many have described them; but seen from a point of view a little higher, they are what I have described them; seen from a higher still, and the highest, who shall say what they are, or that they are worth looking at or thinking of at all?

41   However, the government does not concern me much, and I shall bestow the fewest possible thoughts on it. It is not many moments that I live under a government, even in this world. If a man is thought-free, fancy-free, imagination-free, that which *is not* never for a long time appearing *to be* to him, unwise rulers or reformers cannot fatally interrupt him.

42   I know that most men think differently from myself; but those whose lives are by profession devoted to the study of these or kindred subjects content me as little as any. Statesmen and legislators, standing so completely within the institution, never distinctly and nakedly behold it. They speak of moving society, but have no resting-place without it. They may be men of a certain experience and discrimination, and have no doubt invented ingenious and even useful systems, for which we sincerely thank them; but all their wit and usefulness lie within certain not very wide limits. They are wont to forget that the world is not governed by policy and expediency. Webster never goes behind government, and so cannot speak with authority about it. His words are wisdom to those legislators who contemplate no essential reform in the existing government; but for thinkers, and those who legislate for all time, he never once glances at the subject. I know of those whose serene and wise speculations on this theme would soon reveal the limits of his mind's range and hospitality. Yet compared with the cheap professions of most reformers, and the still cheaper wisdom and eloquence of politicians in general, his are almost the only sensible and valuable words, and we thank Heaven for him. Comparatively, he is always strong, original, and, above all, practical. Still, his quality is not wisdom, but prudence. The lawyer's truth is not Truth, but consistency or a consistent expediency. Truth is always in harmony with herself, and is not concerned chiefly to reveal the justice that may consist with wrong-doing. He well deserves to be called, as he has been called, the Defender of the Constitution. There are really no blows to be given by him but defensive ones. He is not a leader, but a follower. His leaders are the men of '87. "I have never made an effort," he says, "and never propose to make an effort; I have never countenanced an effort, and never mean to countenance an effort, to disturb the arrangement as originally made, by which the various States came into the union." Still thinking of the sanction which the Constitution gives to slavery, he says, "Because it was a part of the original compact, — let it stand." Notwithstanding his special acuteness and ability, he is unable to take a fact out of its merely political relations, and behold it as it lies absolutely to be disposed of by the intellect, — what, for instance, it behooves a man to do here in America to-day with regard to slavery, — but ventures, or is driven, to make some such desperate answer as the following, while professing to speak absolutely, and as a private man, — from which what new and singular code of social duties might be inferred? "The manner," says he, "in which the governments of those States where slavery exists are to regulate it is for their own consideration, under their responsibility to their constituents, to the general laws of propriety, humanity, and justice, and to God. Associations formed elsewhere, springing from a feeling of humanity, or any other cause, have nothing whatever to do with it. They have never received any encouragement from me, and they never will."

They who know of no purer sources of truth, who have traced up its 43 stream no higher, stand, and wisely stand, by the Bible and the Constitution, and drink at it there with reverence and humility; but they who behold where it comes trickling into this lake or that pool, gird up their loins once more, and continue their pilgrimage toward its fountain-head.

44   No man with a genius for legislation has appeared in America. They
are rare in the history of the world. There are orators, politicians, and
eloquent men, by the thousand; but the speaker has not yet opened his
mouth to speak who is capable of settling the much-vexed questions of
the day. We love eloquence for its own sake, and not for any truth which
it may utter, or any heroism it may inspire. Our legislators have not yet
learned the comparative value of free-trade and of freedom, of union, and
of rectitude, to a nation. They have no genius or talent for comparatively
humble questions of taxation and finance, commerce and manufactures
and agriculture. If we were left solely to the wordy wit of legislators in
Congress for our guidance, uncorrected by the seasonable experience and
the effectual complaints of the people, America would not long retain her
rank among the nations. For eighteen hundred years, though perchance
I have no right to say it, the New Testament has been written; yet where
is the legislator who has wisdom and practical talent enough to avail himself of the light which it sheds on the science of legislation?

45   The authority of government, even such as I am willing to submit to,
— for I will cheerfully obey those who know and can do better than I,
and in many things even those who neither know nor can do so well, —
is still an impure one: to be strictly just, it must have the sanctions and
consent of the governed. It can have no pure right over my person and
property but what I concede to it. The progress from an absolute to a
limited monarchy, from a limited monarchy to a democracy, is a progress
toward a true respect for the individual. Even the Chinese philosopher
was wise enough to regard the individual as the basis of the empire. Is a
democracy, such as we know it, the last improvement possible in government? Is it not possible to take a step further towards recognizing
and organizing the rights of man? There will never be a really free and
enlightened State until the State come to recognize the individual as a
higher and independent power, from which all its own power and authority are derived, and treats him accordingly. I please myself with
imagining a State at last which can afford to be just to all men, and to
treat the individual with respect as a neighbor; which even would not
think it inconsistent with its own repose if a few were to live aloof from
it, not meddling with it, nor embraced by it, who fulfilled all the duties
of neighbors and fellow-men. A State which bore this kind of fruit, and
suffered it to drop off as fast as it ripened, would prepare the way for a
still more perfect and glorious State, which also I have imagined, but
not yet anywhere seen.

                                                              (1849)

The Writer's Subject

1. What is the best kind of government, in Thoreau's view? (paras. 1–2)

2. Explain the distinction that Thoreau draws between "law" and "right." (para. 4)

3. On what grounds does Thoreau believe that "the mass of men serve the state as machines..."? (para. 4)

4. Why does Thoreau urge "honest men" to "rebel and revolutionize"? (paras. 7–8)

5. What is the difference, as Thoreau sees it, between "nine hundred and ninety-nine patrons of virtue" and "one virtuous man"? (para. 10)

6. Why does Thoreau regard patriots as "frequently the most serious obstacles to reform"? (para. 14)

7. Why in Thoreau's view is the constitution of the state an evil? (para. 19)

8. Explain Thoreau's statement that "Under a government which imprisons any unjustly, the true place for a just man is also a prison." (para. 22)

9. What does Thoreau mean by the assertion that the rich man "is always sold to the institution which makes him rich"? (para. 23)

10. How does Thoreau's experience in prison affect his view of his society? (paras. 31–33)

11. How does Thoreau regard those who have paid the taxes he owed to the state? (para. 37)

12. "Webster never goes behind government, and so cannot speak with authority about it" (para. 42). What does Thoreau mean by this?

13. What kind of relationship should there be between the individual and the state, in Thoreau's view?

The Writer's Style and Strategy

1. Discuss Thoreau's use of the rhetorical question in paras. 14–16.

2. Explain the analogy Thoreau draws between the workings of a machine and the workings of government in para. 18.

3. Find examples of Thoreau's use of literary allusions; analogy; metaphor; irony.

4. Discuss Thoreau's use of personal anecdote. What does it contribute to the development of his argument?

5. What is the predominant tone of Thoreau's essay? How is it established?

6. What kind of audience does Thoreau have in mind here? In what manner does he seek to establish a connection with that audience?

Suggested Topics for Writing and Discussion

1. Do you agree with Thoreau's view that "any man more right than his neighbours constitutes a majority of one already"? (para. 20)

2. Thoreau believes that the actions of "one HONEST man" can reform the evils in society (para. 21). Do you agree?

3. How would you respond to the refusal by a friend or neighbour to pay income tax on the grounds that the state is acting unjustly in some regard?

4. Thoreau argues for the superior claims of individual conscience over unthinking obedience to the laws of the state, even when the state is democratically governed. Choose an instance in recent history that might illustrate this principle in action.

5. Various bodies — governments, unions, student associations — often gather fees which are then sometimes put to uses that an individual might object to. Thus a union might support political action in a way opposed by one of its members. In such circumstances, does the individual have the right to put his or her own interests before those of the collective, and demand the reimbursement of fees or taxes?

6. Thoreau says, "Let every man make known what kind of government would command his respect, and that will be one step toward obtaining it" (para. 3). Write a brief essay in which you give your views about the kind of government that would command your respect.

Society and the Individual

The Game

by Ken Dryden

Once I used to wait in line like everyone else. Then one day a bank   1
teller motioned me out of the line, and I haven't been back in one since.
I feel no small guilt each time; nonetheless I continue to accept such
favours. For the tellers and me, it has become normal and routine. They
treat me the way they think people like me expect to be treated. And I
accept.

It is the kind of special treatment professional athletes have grown   2
accustomed to, and enjoy. It began with hockey, with teenage names
and faces in local papers, with hockey jackets that only the best players on the best teams wore, with parents who competed not so quietly
on the side; and it will end with hockey. In between, the longer and
better we play the more all-encompassing the treatment becomes. People give, easily and naturally. And we accept. Slippers, sweaters, plant
holders, mitts, baby blankets, baby clothes sent in the mail. Paintings,
carvings, etchings, sculptures in clay, metal, papier-mâché. Shirts,
slacks, coats, suits, ties, underwear; cars, carpets, sofas, chairs, refrigerators, beds, washers, dryers, stoves, TVs, stereos, at cost or no cost
at all. After all, a special person deserves a special price. A hundred
letters a week, more than 3,000 a year — "You're the best," all but a
few of them say. On the street, in restaurants and theatres, we're pointed
at, talked about like the weather. "There he is, the famous hockey
player," your own kids announce to their friends. In other homes, your
picture is on a boy's bedroom wall. Magazines, newspapers, radio, TV;
hockey cards, posters, T-shirts, and curios, anywhere, everywhere, name,
face, thousands of times.

3   And we love it. We say we don't, but we do. We hate the nuisance and inconvenience, the bother of untimely, unending autographs, hand-shakes, and smiles, living out an image of ourselves that isn't quite real, abused if we fail to, feeling encircled and trapped, never able to get away. But we also feel special — head-turning, chin-dropping, forget-your-name special. What others buy Rolls-Royces and votes and hockey teams for, what others take off their clothes for, what others kill for, we have. All we have to do is play.

4   If exposure is the vehicle of celebrity, attention is what separates one celebrity from another. Guy Lafleur and Yvon Lambert are both celeb-rities, yet on the same ice, the same screen, Lafleur is noticed, Lambert is not. Lambert, methodical and unspectacular, has nothing readily dis-tinctive about him. His image is passed over, his name unheard. Lafleur *is* distinctive. The way he skates, the sound of the crowd he carries with him, the goals he scores.

5   And so, too, others, for other reasons. Mario Tremblay, for his fiery, untamed spirit; Bob Gainey, for his relentless, almost palpable will; Ti-ger Williams, Eddie Shack, Ron Duguay, each colourful and exciting; and Dave Schultz, once king of the mountain. As sports coverage pro-liferates beyond games, as it becomes entertainment and moves to prime time, as we look for the story behind the story, off-ice performance be-comes important. And so personas are born, and sometimes made, and cameras and microphones are there as it happens. The crazies, the clowns, the "sports intellectuals," the anti-jock rebels (Jim Bouton, Bill "Spaceman" Lee), the playboys (Joe Namath, Derek Sanderson), each a distinctive personality, each a bigger celebrity because of what he does away from the game.

6   TV has given us a new minimum off-ice standard. The modern player must be articulate (or engagingly inarticulate, especially southern style). It's not enough to score a goal and have it picked apart by the all-seeing eyes of replay cameras. A player must be able to put it in his own elo-quent words. How did you do it? How did you feel? Live, on camera words that cannot be edited for the morning paper.

7   Celebrity is a full, integrated life, earned on-ice, performed, sustained, strengthened, re-earned off-ice. As Roger Angell once put it, we want our athletes to be "good at life." Role models for children, people we want to believe earned what they have, every bit as good at things off the ice as on. If they're inarticulate, harsh and pejorative, they're sud-denly just jocks. Merely lucky, less likable, less good at life, less cel-ebrated; finally, they even seem less good *on* the ice.

At its extreme, the process creates the category of professional ce- **8**
lebrity, people "famous for being famous," so accomplished at being
celebrities that their original source of deity is forgotten. At the least, it
encourages all celebrities to learn the *skills* of the public person. How
to look good, how to sound modest and intelligent, funny and self-dep-
recatory, anything you want. It's a celebrity's short-cut to the real thing,
but it works. Walter Cronkite *looks* trustworthy, Ronald Reagan *seems*
like a nice guy, Denis Potvin *sounds* intelligent; or is he only articulate? Good enough at something to be a public person, or simply a good
public person? You'll never get close enough long enough to know.

All around us are people anxious to help us look better. Not just flacks **9**
and PR types but a whole industry of journalists, commentators, biog-
raphers, award-givers. Ghost-writers who put well-paid words under our
names, then disappear; charity organizers, volunteers who give time and
effort so that "honorary presidents," and "honorary directors" may look
even better. Children in hospitals, old folks in old folks' homes — we
autograph their casts, shake their hands, make them props to our generosity and compassion. And never far away, photographers and camera-
men record the event. It is the bandwagon momentum of celebrityhood.

In the end, for us, is an image. After thousands of confused mes- **10**
sages, we cut through what is complex and render it simple. One image, concrete and disembodied. What agents call "Ken Dryden."

Recently, I asked an executive at an advertising agency to pretend he **11**
was trying to persuade a client to use me as a commercial spokesman
for his company. We'd met two or three times, several years before, so
he knew me mostly as others do. He wrote the following memo to his
client: "Historically I know you have had some concerns about using
an athlete ... either because of potential problems developing out of their
careers and public life, or due to simply their lack of availability. I think
Ken is quite different from the rest. He is known as a thoughtful, articulate and concerned individual. I think it would go without saying he
would not participate in any endorsation unless he was fully committed
to and satisfied with the product. (His Ralph Nader exposures would
assure that.) He is serious, respected and appears to be very much his
own man. I don't think we could ever consider using him in humorous
or light approaches (like Eddie Shack) unless it would be by juxtaposition with another ... actor or player. He has good media presence.... His
physical presence is also commanding. He is quite tall and impressive....
Other encouraging things would be his intelligence and educational back-

ground. He would be more in tune with our target audience with his credentials as a college graduate (Cornell) and a fledgling professional person (law). Also, during production, I think this intelligence and cool-ness would help in case of commercial production as well as helping to keep costs under control due to mental errors...."

12   So that's my image. Is it accurate? It doesn't matter. It's what people think, it presupposes how they'll react to me. And for the ad man and his client, how people will react is what matters.

13   If I don't like my image, I can do something about it. I can do things that are "good for my image." I can stop doing things that are "bad for my image." As actors remind us casually and often, I can do things to change my image. Is it too serious? If I run around the dressing room throwing water at the right moment, someone is bound to notice. A jour-nalist with a deadline to meet and space to fill, a new angle, news — "Dryden misunderstood."

14   Want to be known as an antique collector? Collect an antique. A theatre-goer? Go. Once is enough. Tell a journalist, sound enthusiastic, and, above all, play well. Then stand back and watch what happens. Clipped and filed, the news spreads like a chain letter, to other journal-ists who don't have time to check it out. Presto, it's part of your stand-ard bio. And your image.

15   If you substitute the word "reputation" for "image," as you might have done a few years ago, you'd have something quite different. A repu-tation is nothing so trifling or cynical. Like an old barge, it takes time to get going. It's slow and relentless, difficult to manoeuvre, even harder to stop. An image is nothing so solemn. It is merely a commercial as-set, a package of all the rights and good-will associated with "Ken Dryden" — something I can sell to whomever I want.

16   But it's a sticky matter. For the image I'm selling is *your* image of me. The good-will, though it relates to me, is your good-will. Whatever commercial value there is in my name, my image, it's you who puts it there. You like me or trust me, and any prospective buyer of my image, anxious to put my name alongside his product, knows that and counts on it to make you buy his product. And you might, even though it may not be in your best interest. So by selling my name, I have perhaps taken your trust and turned it against you.

17   I did a commercial once, six years ago. I'd decided I never would, but this one was different enough to start a web of rationalizations until I forgot the point and accepted. A fast-food chain was looking for a winter promotion; Hockey Canada, the advisory and promotional body,

wanted a fundraiser and a way to deliver the message to kids and their parents that minor hockey can be approached and played differently. The idea was a mini-book done by Hockey Canada, then sold through the restaurant chain. I was to be a collaborator on the book, and its public spokesman. But after doing the TV and radio ads (for the book, but with a corporate jingle at the end), and seeing the point-of-purchase cardboard likenesses of me in the restaurant, I realized my mistake.

Since then, I have turned down endorsements for, among other things,   18
a candy bar ("The way I see it, a full body shot of you in the net, mask up, talking, then we draw in tight on your catching glove, you open it, the bar's inside...."), a credit card company ("You may not know me without my mask, but..."), and a roll-on deodorant that would also be promoted by several other people whose names begin with the sound "dry."

It's a game — an ad game, an image game, a celebrity game — that   19
no one really loses. Everyone needs someone to talk about — why not about us? Everyone needs heroes and villains. We earn a little money, get some exposure. The commercials are going to be done anyway. Besides, it doesn't last long. A few years and images change, celebrity cools, it's over. It all evens out.

But it doesn't. We all lose, at least a little. We lose because you think   20
I'm better than I am. Brighter than I am, kinder, more compassionate, capable of more things, as good at life as I am at the game. I'm not. Off the ice I struggle as you do, but off the ice you never see me, even when you think you do. I appear good at other things because I'm good at being a goalie; because I'm a celebrity; because there's always someone around to say I'm good. Because in the cozy glow of success, of good news, you want me to be good. It's my angle, and so long as I play well the angle won't change. I appear bright and articulate because I'm an athlete, and many athletes are not bright and articulate. "Like a dog's walking on his hind legs," as Dr. Johnson once put it, "it is not done well; but you are surprised to find it done at all."

But you don't believe that, just as I don't believe it about celebrities   21
I don't know. They're taller, more talented, more compassionate. They glitter into cameras and microphones, give each other awards for talent and compassion, "great human beings" every one. Wet-eyed I applaud, and believe. And all of us lose. You, because you feel less worthy than you are. Me, because once, when I was twenty-three years old and trying to learn about myself, I wanted to believe I was, or soon would be, everything others said I was. Instead, having learned much and grown older, I feel co-conspirator to a fraud.

22   Professional athletes do exciting, sometimes courageous, sometimes ennobling things, as heroes do, but no more than you do. Blown up on a TV screen or a page, hyped by distance and imagination, we seem more heroic, but we're not. Our achievement seems grander, but it isn't. Our cause, our commitment, is no different from yours. We are no more than examples, metaphors, because we enter every home; we're models for the young because their world is small and we do what they do.

23   A few years ago, Joe McGinniss, author of *The Selling of the President, 1968*, wrote a book called *Heroes*. It sketches McGinniss's own tormented trail from being *the youngest*, to *the highly acclaimed*, to *the former* — all before he was thirty. At the same time, he ostensibly searches for the vanished American hero. He talks to George McGovern and Teddy Kennedy, General William Westmoreland, John Glenn, Eugene McCarthy, author William Styron, playwright Arthur Miller — some of them heroes of his, all of them heroes to many.

24   But it's like chasing a rainbow. He finds that, as he gets closer, his heroes disappear. In homes and bars, on campaign trails, they're distinctly, disappointingly normal. Not wonderfully, triumphantly, down-to-earth normal, but up-close, drinking-too-much, sweating, stinking, unheroically normal. And for heroes, normal isn't enough. We are allowed one image; everything must fit.

25   The Greeks gave their gods human imperfections. In the modern hero, however, every flaw is a fatal flaw. It has only to be found, and it *will* be. Moving from celebrity to hero is like moving from a city to a small town. In a city, the camera's eye, though always present, is distant. In a small town, there isn't that distance. There's no place to hide.

26   "Whom the gods would destroy," Wilfrid Sheed wrote in *Transatlantic Blues*, "they first oversell." Superficially created, superficially destroyed — for the hero, for the celebrity, it all evens out. Except a heavy price is paid along the way. We all lose again. You, because, saddened and hurt by heroes who turn out not to be heroes at all, you become cynical and stop believing. Me, because I'm in a box. What is my responsibility? Is it, as I'm often told, to be the hero that children think I am? Or is it to live what is real, to be something else.

27   Recently, a friend asked me to speak to his college seminar. Near the end of two hours, we began to talk about many of these questions. A girl raised her hand. She said that a year or two earlier, on the Academy Awards, she had seen Charlton Heston receive an award for his "humanitarian" work. Heston had made the point, the girl said, that thousands of volunteers had done far more than he, that they deserved the award.

I asked the class what that story told them about Charlton Heston. 28
That he's even modest, they decided. A few of the students laughed;
then, one by one, several others joined in.

(1983)

The Writer's Subject

1. In the opening paragraph Dryden describes the guilt he feels in accepting
   favours. What is the source of this feeling, and where is it most explicitly
   discussed in this essay?

2. Why, according to Dryden, is an athlete's "off-ice performance" so important if he achieves celebrity status? (paras. 5–7)

3. Dryden argues that "celebrity" is really an image, "one image, concrete
   and disembodied." Who or what creates this image, and for what reasons?
   Is the presumed reader involved in this process in any way? (paras. 8–10)

4. According to Dryden, how difficult is it for celebrities to change their images? (paras. 13–15)

5. Why, after making one commercial, did Dryden decline to be further involved in the advertising of products? (paras. 17–18)

6. What loss is involved in accepting the "image" of the celebrity at face
   value? (paras. 20–26)

7. What does Dryden mean when he says "In the modern hero ... every flaw
   is a fatal flaw" (para. 25)?

8. What is the dilemma of the professional athlete who attains celebrity? (para.
   26)

9. What point is Dryden making with his concluding anecdote about Charlton
   Heston?

The Writer's Style and Strategy

1. How does Dryden's opening sentence prepare the reader for what is to
   follow?

2. What method of development does Dryden employ in paragraph 2 to demonstrate his assertion that professional athletes have grown accustomed to
   special treatment?

3. What effect does Dryden achieve by italicising "looks," "seems," and
   "sounds" in paragraph 8? By putting his own name, "Ken Dryden," in quotation marks in paragraph 10?

4. Why does Dryden provide actual excerpts from the advertising agency's description of him? (para. 11)

5. Why does Dryden use so many short sentences and fragments in paragraph 14? How does this particular paragraph contribute to the overall tone of the essay?

6. What figure of speech does Dryden use to illustrate the difference between "reputation" and "image"? (para. 15)

7. Why does Dryden repeat "game" so many times in the opening sentence of paragraph 19?

8. How would you characterize Dryden's attitude to his own celebrity? How is this attitude revealed throughout the essay?

Suggested Topics for Writing and Discussion

1. Discuss the distinctions Dryden perceives between "jocks," sports celebrities, and professional celebrities, providing your own examples. Can you think of any professional athlete who might fit into all of these categories?

2. Examine Dryden's discussion of the modern hero (note especially paragraphs 23–26). He says, "… for heroes, normal isn't enough"; do you agree with this view? What is the role of the hero in our society? Is heroism possible in modern times?

3. Choose an advertisement in print or on television that makes use of a celebrity from the worlds of sport or entertainment. What is the image of the celebrity that the advertisement conveys? How is that image intended to influence our view of the product? Indicate whether, in your opinion, the advertisement affirms Dryden's views about "the ad game."

My Wood

by E.M. Forster

A few years ago I wrote a book which dealt in part with the difficulties   1
of the English in India. Feeling that they would have had no difficulties
in India themselves, the Americans read the book freely. The more they
read it the better it made them feel, and a cheque to the author was the
result. I bought a wood with the cheque. It is not a large wood — it
contains scarcely any trees, and it is intersected, blast it, by a public
footpath. Still, it is the first property that I have owned, so it is right
that other people should participate in my shame, and should ask themselves, in accents that will vary in horror, this very important question:
What is the effect of property upon the character? Don't let's touch economics; the effect of private ownership upon the community as a whole
is another question — a more important question, perhaps, but another
one. Let's keep to psychology. If you own things, what's their effect on
you? What's the effect on me of my wood?

    In the first place, it makes me feel heavy. Property does have this   2
effect. Property produces men of weight, and it was a man of weight
who failed to get into the Kingdom of Heaven. He was not wicked, that
unfortunate millionaire in the parable, he was only stout; he stuck out
in front, not to mention behind, and as he wedged himself this way and
that in the crystalline entrance and bruised his well-fed flanks, he saw
beneath him a comparatively slim camel passing through the eye of a
needle and being woven into the robe of God. The Gospels all through
couple stoutness and slowness. They point out what is perfectly obvious, yet seldom realized: that if you have a lot of things you cannot
move about a lot, that furniture requires dusting, dusters require serv-

ants, servants require insurance stamps, and the whole tangle of them makes you think twice before you accept an invitation to dinner or go for a bathe in the Jordan. Sometimes the Gospels proceed further and say with Tolstoy that property is sinful; they approach the difficult ground of asceticism here, where I cannot follow them. But as to the immediate effects of property on people, they just show straightforward logic. It produces men of weight. Men of weight cannot, by definition, move like the lightning from the East unto the West, and the ascent of a fourteen-stone bishop into a pulpit is thus the exact antithesis of the coming of the Son of Man. My wood makes me feel heavy.

3   In the second place, it makes me feel it ought to be larger.

4   The other day I heard a twig snap in it. I was annoyed at first, for I thought that someone was blackberrying, and depreciating the value of the undergrowth. On coming nearer, I saw it was not a man who had trodden on the twig and snapped it, but a bird, and I felt pleased. My bird. The bird was not equally pleased. Ignoring the relation between us, it took fright as soon as it saw the shape of my face, and flew straight over the boundary hedge into a field, the property of Mrs. Henessy, where it sat down with a loud squawk. It had become Mrs. Henessy's bird. Something seemed grossly amiss here, something that would not have occurred had the wood been larger. I could not afford to buy Mrs. Henessy out, I dared not murder her, and limitations of this sort beset me on every side. Ahab did not want that vineyard — he only needed it to round off his property, preparatory to plotting a new curve — and all the land around my wood has become necessary to me in order to round off the wood. A boundary protects. But — poor little thing — the boundary ought in its turn to be protected. Noises on the edge of it. Children throw stones. A little more, and then a little more, until we reach the sea. Happy Canute! Happier Alexander! And after all, why should even the world be the limit of possession? A rocket containing a Union Jack, will, it is hoped, be shortly fired at the moon. Mars. Sirius. Beyond which.... But these immensities ended by saddening me. I could not suppose that my wood was the destined nucleus of universal dominion — it is so very small and contains no mineral wealth beyond the blackberries. Nor was I comforted when Mrs. Henessy's bird took alarm for the second time and flew clean away from us all, under the belief that it belonged to itself.

5   In the third place, property makes its owner feel that he ought to do something to it. Yet he isn't sure what. A restlessness comes over him, a vague sense that he has a personality to express — the same sense which, without any vagueness, leads the artist to an act of creation. Some-

times I think I will cut down such trees as remain in the wood, at other times I want to fill up the gaps between them with new trees. Both impulses are pretentious and empty. They are not honest movements towards money-making or beauty. They spring from a foolish desire to express myself and from an inability to enjoy what I have got. Creation, property, enjoyment form a sinister trinity in the human mind. Creation and enjoyment are both very very good, yet they are often unattainable without a material basis, and at such moments property pushes itself in as a substitute, saying, 'Accept me instead — I'm good enough for all three.' It is not enough. It is, as Shakespeare said of lust, 'The expense of spirit in a waste of shame': it is 'Before a joy proposed; behind, a dream.' Yet we don't know how to shun it. It is forced on us by our economic system as the alternative to starvation. It is also forced on us by an internal defect in the soul, by the feeling that in property may lie the germs of self-development and of exquisite or heroic deeds. Our life on earth is, and ought to be, material and carnal. But we have not yet learned to manage our materialism and carnality properly; they are still entangled with the desire for ownership, where (in the words of Dante) 'Possession is one with loss'.

And this brings us to our fourth and final point: the blackberries. 6

Blackberries are not plentiful in this meagre grove, but they are easily seen from the public footpath which traverses it, and all too easily gathered. Foxgloves, too — people will pull up the foxgloves, and ladies of an educational tendency even grub for toadstools to show them on the Monday in class. Other ladies, less educated, roll down the bracken in the arms of their gentlemen friends. There is paper, there are tins. Pray, does my wood belong to me or doesn't it? And, if it does, should I not own it best by allowing no one else to walk there? There is a wood near Lyme Regis, also cursed by a public footpath, where the owner has not hesitated on this point. He has built high stone walls each side of the path, and has spanned it by bridges, so that the public circulate like termites while he gorges on the blackberries unseen. He really does own his wood, this able chap. Dives in Hell did pretty well, but the gulf dividing him from Lazarus could be traversed by vision, and nothing traverses it here. And perhaps I shall come to this in time. I shall wall in and fence out until I really taste the sweets of property. Enormously stout, endlessly avaricious, pseudo-creative, intensely selfish, I shall weave upon my forehead the quadruple crown of possession until those nasty Bolshies come and take it off again and thrust me aside into the outer darkness. 7

(1926)

The Writer's Subject

1. Why does Forster begin his essay with an oblique reference to his novel *Passage to India*?

2. What does Forster mean by the phrase "men of weight"? (para. 2)

3. Summarize the four points which Forster makes about the effect of property. Are these points all of the same kind?

4. How does Forster demonstrate the absurdity of the property owner's attempt to lay claim to property, and of his desire for expansion? (para. 4)

5. Why, according to Forster, are the desires to chop down or to plant trees "not honest movements towards money-making or beauty"? (para. 5)

6. Explain what Forster means by saying "creation, property, enjoyment form a sinister trinity in the human mind." (para. 5)

7. Why does Forster give such prominence to the public footpath in Lyme Regis? (para. 7)

8. Who are the "nasty Bolshies" that Forster refers to in his closing sentence? Why does he say that they will throw him "into the outer darkness"?

9. While Forster restricts his discussion to his wood, he may be commenting on broader issues. What might these be?

The Writer's Style and Strategy

1. What is Forster's tone in the opening paragraph, and how does he establish it? Is it maintained throughout the essay? Discuss the appropriateness of Forster's tone to his topic.

2. How does Forster narrow his discussion of the very large topic of property?

3. Forster uses many allusions in this brief essay. What use does he make of the allusions to the Gospels (to the Rich Man in *Matthew* 19:24; to the story of Dives and Lazarus in *Luke* 16:19–31)? To the story of Ahab (in *I Kings* 21:17–29)? To Canute and Alexander? To Tolstoy and Dante?

4. Trace Forster's references to the blackberries. What purpose do these references serve? Comment on his use of a single-sentence paragraph to introduce the subject of the blackberries.

5. Comment on Forster's final sentence, its meaning, structure and tone.

Suggested Topics for Writing and Discussion

1. What is the effect of ownership on you?

2. Forster says that he may one day "wall in and fence out." Discuss one or two examples of walls used to bound international "properties" (e.g., the Great Wall of China, Hadrian's Wall, the Berlin Wall), and say what the makers of the walls were hoping to wall in and fence out.

3. Forster uses very specific, concrete, and personal details to write on a highly abstract subject. Using Forster's method, write an essay on an abstraction which interests you (e.g., identity, loyalty, education, community, faith).

Child's Play 4?
by Patricia Highsmith

1   The rather odd title, *The Sleep of Reason*, comes from a phrase by Jean-Jacques Rousseau in *Emile*, and refers to Rousseau's belief that a child is in his own world, learning in his own way, often via childhood's apparent idleness, which Rousseau considers more beneficial than a strict schooling. The two child murderers in this case-history were playing truant from school on the day of the deed.

2   On February 12, 1993, two boys aged ten, Jon Venables and Bobby Thompson, lured James Bulger, then one month short of three, from a shopping centre in Bootle, Liverpool. They walked him some two-and-a-half miles across Liverpool, noticed by several passers-by, and their image had also been captured on the shopping centre's security video. The toddler was finally taken up on to a railway line, where the boys threw stones and bricks at his head and body and hit him with a fishplate, a heavy piece of metal used to fasten train rails. Some minutes after death, the body of James was placed across a rail so that the next train would sever it in half at the waist. The boys then made their way homeward, stopping in at their local video shop in Walton, a favourite hangout, and they ran an errand for the woman proprietor. One of the boys showed an interest in the television news that evening at home, but there was to be no discovery of the mangled corpse for a couple of days. During the long walk with James, the boys dropped in at a DIY shop, whose proprietor was more wary of the boys as possible shoplifters than as kidnappers. Here they stole or bought a tin of bright blue paint, a significant item as it transpired, an important colour for the scene they apparently had already in mind.

David James Smith, according to his publisher's blurb-writer, peels 3
away the outer layers of the story in search of an explanation. In fact he
does the opposite; his approach is to add fact upon fact — down to complete *Who's Who* entries for the judge and two barristers at the boy's trial
— and in order, presumably, to allow the reader to conclude that the two
young murderers were influenced by external factors. Both boys lived
in Walton, a working-class, run-down section of Liverpool. Truancy and
shoplifting among local children were commonplace. Social workers
who called sometimes at the two boys' school were greeted with a chorus of "Fuck off!" as likely as not, or silence and indifference. One has
the feeling that the teachers, like most of the parents burdened with too
many kids to manage properly, simply gave up in a quiet way.

It was the fuzzy security video images — enhanced as much as pos- 4
sible by the police — showing James in his grey trainer pants, holding
the hand of one boy and sometimes two, which gave the police unmistakable identification. Jon and Bobby were known to their mates and
teachers as "a pair" which was best kept separated. Bobby was said to
be the inventor of pranks, Jon the follower. When questioned apart, each
blamed the other for killing James Bulger. Jon insisted he had thrown
only pebbles at the toddler's head. It is easy to imagine that one stone
led to another as the two older boys stood over the fallen James on the
deserted railway line, impatient probably for James's death since they
had gone this far. James was unconscious for a while, and the boys threw
bricks, and finally the twenty-two-pound fishplate. One of the boys put
an ear against James's chest and pronounced him dead.

Though Smith makes no comment, he obviously deems the ITN in- 5
terview with Osty, Pitts and Stee, three kids who discovered the severed body, to be worth quoting verbatim, and it is eloquent in its way.
The TV crew are in a park.

Reporter: OK, so do you want to tell me how you came to find the body?
Stee: 'Cos we were walking along the railway and, erm ...
Pitts: (smiling) We was having a ciggie on the railway ...
Off camera children are gathering around, laughing. Osty says, pack it
in, laughing, all youse go away.
Stee: ... I just seen it there, just like in a coat, like an 'orse, with the
organs all coming out.
Osty: All the organs coming out, like big fat worms.
Stee: So like and then I said, 'ere, look at that, doesn't that look like a
baby.

They all laugh, except the reporter, and Stee falls away, cracking up.
Stee: Can we start it again?
Reporter: Yeah, we'll start it again. Just tell me how you came to dis-
cover the body.
Stee: Right, we were walking along the railway and er, like, we, erm
(laughing) and he dropped something, and he said, oiyo, come back 'ere,
I've lost me money ...
Reporter: Don't worry about the people behind you. Be sensible. It's not
funny.
Stee: He thought it was a dead cat wrapped up.
Pitts: Doll's legs ...
Reporter: Were you surprised that you found it?
Osty: No.

And so on. The interview lasted eight minutes. Understandably, only a
couple of lines were used.

6   The two boys' pre-trial interrogations were set down in detail, until
the breakdown of Jon ("I did kill him"), in the presence of his parents.
It is not until the second half of *The Sleep of Reason* that David James
Smith describes the boys' parents and the atmosphere in their homes.

7   Neil and Susan Venables were twenty-nine and twenty-five when Jon
was born, the third of their four children. Jon's brother Mark had been
born with a cleft palate, and required special care and speech therapy.
Neil was unemployed at the time of the Bulger tragedy, though he had
worked as a fork-lift truck driver. Neil and Susan separated in 1986, and
were later divorced, though they remained on good terms. Neil saw the
children on Saturdays, and minded them if Susan wanted an evening out.

8   In January 1991, a teacher reported odd behaviour on Jon's part: he
banged his head hard against furniture, gripped his desk and rocked back
and forth while making strange noises. He refused to do any written
work, stood on desks and threw chairs, and was spotted by a teacher
holding a 12-inch ruler against a boy's throat. The boy had become red-
faced. The teacher with difficulty managed to wrest the ruler away. With
the help of a social worker, Jon was put into Walton St Mary's Church
of England Primary School, headed by Irene Slack, whose credo was
do unto others, with emphasis on tolerance of races and religions. In
September 1991 Jon began in class 4D, and here he met Bobby
Thompson.

Some of their fellow pupils noticed that Jon and Bobby sulked and swore
behind the teachers' back. ... Bobby and Jon also had a reputation for

picking on people and bullying. ... Another boy thought [they] were weird.
They never talked to the others. They were like a little gang.

Bobby Thompson's older five brothers had all been through Irene   9
Slack's school, and Ms Slack had informed several child-care agencies
about the "hierarchy of bullying" among the Thompson brothers, each
picking on the brother just below him in age. The reader is apt to think
of James Bulger, smaller indeed, an easy mark.

Bobby's father, also called Bobby, was a bully even to his wife, if   10
he'd had a few drinks. Both of Walton families, he and Ann had married when they were eighteen. When Bobby had come to ask her father's consent to their marriage, Ann's father had given it, but the same
evening had taken his army belt to her, accusing her of being pregnant,
which was not the case. Ann married to escape a primitive and often
drunken household. Her husband Bobby was an apprentice electrician.
Ann had a job doing "wiring" at a local shop, but gave that up when the
first child, David, came along. In the next nine years, Ann had five children, all boys. While big Bobby drank at the pub, Ann stayed home and
minded the kids; there was no money for TV.

> She had a miscarriage after David, at three months, and was five months
> gone with the next pregnancy when they were all round his mother's ar-
> guing one Saturday night after going to the pub. Ann said she could keep
> her bloody son.... He and his brothers flung Ann down the hallway and
> jammed her in the door and she lost the baby not long after.

Social life picked up for Ann when they met a cheerful couple, here   11
called Barbara and Jack, with whom the Venables played cards. They
were all great friends until, to Ann's total surprise, Barbara ran off with
Bobby. The usual on-and-off behaviour followed, until October 1988
when Bobby disappeared for good. The family's general disorder was
worsened by little Bobby's brother Ian starting petty thievery and aero-
sol sniffing. Due to neurotic eating, Ann's weight grew to eighteen stone,
and she was grossly overweight at the time of the trial.

> Bobby had sat through seven hours ... of taped police interviews with-
> out making any admission of his participation in the abduction and kill-
> ing of James Bulger.... While Jon had said, "I did kill him", Jon was now
> blaming Bobby ... as were his parents, who would say that Jon had been
> led on by Bobby. Jon could not bring himself to talk about events on the
> railway line. It was an understandable way of trying to manage the un-
> manageable, but it was also a form of denial.

12   Apart from the security video photographs, the Crown had telling forensic evidence, including the tin of blue paint, which the boys had
thrown at James. Jon had managed to get some of the paint on his trousers and the sleeve of his jacket. James's blood was on the boys' shoes.
The imprint of one of Bobby's shoes with D lace-eyelets was clearly
defined on James's cheek giving the lie to Bobby's statement that he
hadn't done a thing to harm the little boy. When the boys were asked
about the video *Child's Play 3*, they squirmed and denied having seen it.

>   The last video rented from Videoscene on Neil Venables's membership
>   before the killing of James Bulger was *Child's Play 3*, which had been
>   taken out on January 18, 1993. *Child's Play 3* tells the story of a Good
>   Guy doll, Chucky, which comes to life possessed by the soul of a psy-
>   chopath, the Lakeside Strangler, and embarks on a series of murders:
>   "Don't fuck with Chuck". There are seven killings, played out in vivid
>   detail, including a long close-up of a man's face as he is being strangled,
>   a barber whose throat is cut by his own razor, and a youngster whose
>   body explodes when he jumps on a live grenade.
>   The film climaxes at a fun fair, inside the ghost train. The rail tracks
>   are wreathed in dry ice, and surrounded by various objects of gothic hor-
>   ror. Chucky's face is stained with blue paint from an earlier war game
>   battle with paint guns.... Chucky loses various limbs, before being shred-
>   ded in a wind machine.

13   The trial was set for November 1 at Preston Crown Court. In Liverpool Crown Court, both boys had entered a "not guilty" plea. They were
taken to the empty Preston Crown Court before the trial, so that its interior might not be intimidating to them. Jon was able to talk to Dr Bai-
ley, a woman psychiatrist, he could sit still and concentrate, but if she
turned the conversation toward the murder of James, Jon squirmed and
would say only that Bobby had suggested they sag (play truant) and go
to the Strand, which was the shopping centre. Still before the trial, Jon
was questioned directly: had he seen *Child's Play 3*? His feeble answer
was, "I don't like horror films". Bobby claimed to have seen only two
minutes of *Child's Play 2*, his mother having shooed him out of the
room where his older brothers had been watching it. As for the murder,
Bobby told his solicitor what he had told the police, that Jon had begun
by throwing the fishplate at James as he lay on the ground. Bobby said
Jon had removed James's grey pants and underpants and laid them over
James's face, "maybe because the blood coming out of his mouth looked
horrible".

David Turner, for Bobby's defence, contended that the "volume, na- 14
ture and quality" of the national publicity was so powerful as to make a
fair trial impossible. Jon's QC, Brian Walsh, supported his colleague.
The Crown counsel, Richard Henriques, said that no trial had ever been
stayed because of adverse publicity. And the judge, Sir Michael Morland,
while agreeing that "saturation" was the word for the media coverage,
still believed there could be a fair trial, and asked that the trial begin.
Henriques made an opening speech, alleging that the two defendants
acting together were responsible for James Bulger's death.

Not a word was addressed directly to either of the boys during the 15
trial. They sat a little distance apart on specially constructed platforms
that raised them to the visibility level of adults. Both had grown in the
months since the murder. Jon had put on weight, and was puffy-faced.
He wore a black jacket and black trousers. Bobby, with newly cropped
hair, wore his school tie under a grey sweater. They avoided looking at
each other.

> [Bobby's] face revealed no sign of distress, anxiety or any other emo-
> tional reaction. This was to be swiftly interpreted as the impassivity of
> an unfeeling psychopath, or the boredom of indifference....
>
> Bobby had earlier kicked off his shoes and removed his sweater. Now
> he fidgeted and sighed heavily. Jon had not previously been able to con-
> front what had happened. Now it was coming and he had no choice. He
> moved his hands restlessly and looked desperate.

Neil and Susan Venables were present, but Ann Thompson had not 16
come to court, because she couldn't face it. She was taking pills, and
seeing a psychiatric nurse. The Venables, Thompsons, and Denise and
Ralph Bulger had sought the help of Aftermath, a voluntary group created to help the families of those accused of serious crime. The judge
had issued an order about reporting: Bobby was to be called Child A
and Jon was Child B. The *Sun* had published pictures, though with the
boys' faces digitized to prevent recognition. Nothing said in court was
to be reported before a verdict was given. Neither could any witness or
member of the families concerned be interviewed until after the verdict. Ann Thompson did come to the court on the eighth day of the trial,
wet-eyed and shaken, accompanied by her nurse. She had wanted to
hear the teachers give evidence, as she felt they had failed her son in
some way.

David James Smith concedes that there are many unanswered ques- 17
tions in this case. There are also lies which remain unchallenged and

unrefuted. One wishes the author had ventured some analysis and opinion. Considering the stone-throwing of Jon and Bobby too, their togetherness throughout that long day of the murder, unto their walk homeward, one can only conclude, as did the jury, that each and both boys were guilty as charged.

18   After the verdict, Judge Morland made some remarks to the court, among them, "It is not for me to pass judgment on their upbringing, but I suspect that exposure to violent video films may in part be an explanation...." For this personal opinion the reader may feel like shouting "Hurrah!"

[Note: This essay was originally a review of *The Sleep of Reason: The Killing of James Bulger* by David James Smith, 1994.]

The Writer's Subject

1. Why did David James Smith call his book about the Bulger murder *The Sleep of Reason*? (para. 1)

2. What connection does Highsmith suggest between the death of James Bulger and the "hierarchy of bullying" in the Thompson family? (para. 9)

3. What domestic or social factors would appear to have caused or contributed to the tragedy of James Bulger's murder, as described in this essay?

4. What was the significance of the bright blue paint the boys bought during their walk with James Bulger? (paras. 2, 12)

5. What role in this story was played by the video of *Child's Play 3*? (paras. 12–13)

The Writer's Style and Strategy

1. Discuss the choice of title for this essay.

2. What is the tone of Highsmith's account of the murder in para. 2? How does the tone influence our response to the event being described?

3. Highsmith excerpts a television interview quoted verbatim in Smith's book, calling it "eloquent in its way" (para. 5). What does she mean? Is she being ironic?

4. What is the effect of Highsmith's description of the boys' appearance and behaviour at the trial? (para. 15)

5. At what points of this essay does the writer convey her own feelings about the incidents she describes?

Suggested Topics for Writing and Discussion

1. In your opinion, does violence on film or television contribute in any way to the violence in our society? Do you think any measures should be taken to deal with films like the *Child's Play* series?

2. Find another newspaper or magazine account of the murder of James Bulger, and compare it to Highsmith's version. Note any significant differences, and offer an explanation for them.

3. Compare Highsmith's attitude to the *Child's Play* films with the views expressed by Martin Amis in his essay "Blown Away."

4. Choose a recent book or article on a controversial topic that interests you, and write a review in which you both summarize the important aspects of the book and convey your opinion of the book's qualities.

Thoughts on a Shirtless Cyclist, Robin Hood and One or Two Other Things
by Russell Hoban

1   The other day when I was going to my office in the morning I saw a man without a shirt riding a bicycle in circles at a traffic light and shouting unintelligibly. It was a chilly morning, so he must have been uncomfortable without a shirt on, and he wasn't a hippy. He looked like a workman, and he didn't look drunk. So it seemed to me that he must be having a mental breakdown of some sort.

2   I thought about it for a while, and then it occurred to me that maybe the man's mind wasn't breaking down. Maybe what had broken down was the system of restraints and conventions inside him that ordinarily made him keep his shirt on and not shout. That system, I think, is part of what could be called an inner society. The inner society has its ballrooms and bedrooms and kitchens, its shops and offices, its narrow alleys and its open places, its figures of authority and rebellion, of usage and surprise, love and hate, should and should not, is and isn't. As in the outer society, some things are done and some are not.

3   When I had thought that far, my next thought was that on that particular day the man's inner society was rioting. The windows of the shops were being smashed, the offices were being deserted, and he was doing what he was doing.

4   My next thought was that the previous thought had been wrong: he was doing what he was doing because there were no rioters and no provision for riot in his inner society, and so there was no one for the job but him. His trouble, perhaps, was that his inner society was not suffi-

ciently different from the outer one: too many of the same things were done and not done. And having no interior colleague to whom he could assign the task or delegate the responsibility, he himself had to take off his shirt and ride in circles at a traffic light and shout. And it must have taken something out of him to do it.

Now my inner society, on the other hand, has always had that shirtless 5 shouting cyclist in it. I know him of old as I know myself, even though I hadn't given him much thought until I actually saw him in the outer world. So it isn't likely that I shall ever have to go out into the street and do that myself; he's always there to take care of it for me. There may, of course, come a day when I shall riotously put on a bowler hat and a neat black suit, buy a tightly furled umbrella, and mingle in wild silence with brokers in the city. One never knows what will come up.

Which brings me, by cobweb bridges perhaps invisible to the naked 6 eye, to a book I threw into an incinerator.

The book was *Robin Hood*. My edition, an American one, was bound 7 in what I think was Lincoln Green. I don't remember who it was that wrote that particular version of the story, but it had large black type and was illustrated by an artist named Edwin John Prittie with line drawings and paintings in full colour. I used to read that book up in an old wild-cherry tree, and it was the cosiest reading I can remember.

But there came a time when I got to be eighteen years old, and there 8 was a war, and I was going off to be a soldier, and it seemed to me that I had better stop being a child and be a man altogether. So I took *Robin Hood* and pitched it into the incinerator. It's a crime that I am driven to confess from time to time, as I do now.

When I came home from the war and found myself, surprisingly, alive 9 and having to go on with the business of growing up, I looked for that same edition that I had thrown away. Years later I found a copy. I haven't it with me now; it is gone again, lost in a removal. But I remember how it was when I held it in my hands again. There were all the pictures looking just as good as ever, and that whole dappled word-world of sun and shade with nothing lost whatever — Little John and Robin fighting on the plank bridge with their quarterstaves; the hateful Sheriff of Nottingham in his arrogance and his scarlet cloak; the beautiful Maid Marian and all the merry men in Lincoln Green; Robin in the *capul hide*, standing over the corpse of Guy of Gisborne. I've always liked the sound of the words *capul hide*: the skin of a horse, with the eyes of a man looking out through the eyeholes in the head — the skin of a dead beast hiding a live man, magical and murderous.

10   Obviously Robin Hood is a part of my inner society and has never stopped being in my thoughts, but it's only recently that I've become fully aware of how much he is to me, of how far the theme of that child's book has gone beyond childhood. Now as I think about him Robin Hood grows deeper and darker and stronger. Constantly he takes on new shadowy identities, and in his *capul hide* he sometimes evokes the dancing *Shaman* in the drawing on the cave wall at Les Trois Frères, sometimes Frazer's *Rex Nemorensis*, doomed King of the Wood, the killer waiting for his killer who will be next king.

11   In the absence of my found-and-lost-again edition I bought Roger Lancelyn Green's Puffin *Robin Hood*. On the title page was a stanza from the Alfred Noyes poem, *Sherwood*, and it gave me gooseflesh when I read it:

> Robin Hood is here again: all his merry thieves
> Hear a ghostly bugle-note shivering through the leaves ...
> The dead are coming back again, the years are rolled away
> In Sherwood, in Sherwood, about the break of day.

12   I wanted it to be Sherwood again, about the break of day. I turned the pages, reading with impatience. But it wasn't the same. This book started with Robin Hood's birth, and I didn't want that, I wanted the opening that had been in the cherry-tree book of childhood, and it wasn't there and I couldn't remember it.

13   Then, on page 19 I found it — the incident in which the Sheriff of Nottingham and his men capture a serf who had killed a royal deer. The beginning of my book came back to me then, just like Proust's Combray — all at once and clear and vivid. 'Saxon hind' was what my book called the serf, and I could see the scene again as it first came to me through the passing leaves, the prisoner trussed up on the sledge like meat, helpless, rolling his eyes in terror as the Sheriff's foresters drag him to his death. Robert Fitzooth, not yet Robin Hood the outlaw, encounters the group and questions the Sheriff's men. The Chief Forester taunts him about the power of the bow he carries, doubts that such a stripling can wield such a weapon. Fitzooth shows his strength and skill with a long shot that brings down one of the King's deer. And with that he has fallen into the forester's trap — like the prisoner, he has forfeited his life with that shot. The Sheriff's men attempt to take him, but he kills some of them and frees the 'Saxon hind.' They escape into the greenwood, and the outlaw life of Robin Hood begins.

14   The light and the air of that first encounter have never left my mind,

and the sounds of the forest, the hissing of the sledge runners over the grass, the rattle of weapons, the shouts, the whizzing arrows. It is the metaphorical value of that action that has made it so memorable for me: the free and active wild self of the forest, armed and strong, freed the bound and helpless captive self and so became the outlaw self I recognized within me — the self indwelling always, sometimes kept faith with, sometimes betrayed.

Free and savage, the Robin Hood who has always walked the path-   15
ways of my inner society has been exemplary — a standard and a reminder to the unfree and unsavage boy that I was, who lusted for that greenwood world: excellence was the price of Robin Hood's freedom, his untamedness, and his power. He was able to be what he was only because of his matchless skill; he was the archer who could shoot farther and truer than any other; he was a hero and a winner who had a thing that he could do better than anybody else.

Heroes who can do something well are still considered necessary for   16
children. And if many of today's books for grownups offer us a selection of the infirm and the awkward, the losers who lap up defeat like chicken soup ladled out by a Jewish-mother kind of fate, we need those too: the composite hero of the collective, cumulative, juvenile-adult imagination has got to have some antiheroism about him in order to be complete. Certainly anything that closes the gap between the real and the ideal makes the hero more useful for everyday reference — and here I can't help thinking about the god Krishna, who disported himself with fifty or sixty cowgirls at a wonderful party out on the meadow that lasted many nights, during which he made all the cowgirls think he was making love with each of them. But despite his divine powers — or because of them — he did it all with his mind, which I think is charming. A hero no better than the reader, however, will scarcely last a lifetime. And I think that heroes who excel and win all kinds of good things are the best kind. Myself, I can't use a mythology in which there is nothing to win and consequently nothing to lose. I have to have something to try for, and the more excellence I can manage the better I feel. In that respect Robin Hood has been a great help to me all my life.

Reading the Roger Lancelyn Green version, I realize that there was   17
a great deal more to the story and the archetypes than I had thought before. In my edition Marian was simply called Maid Marian, and nothing more was said about it. Once or twice as I grew older and more cynical I may have questioned the validity of her title. She was, after all, presumably sleeping rough like everyone else in the outlaw band,

and Robin being her lover, what could have been more natural than for them to sleep together? But Green spells it out and no mistake: Marian *was* a maid; she kept her virginity the whole time that she and Robin lived together in the forest. Although she had pledged herself to him the marriage was not to be consummated until the return of Richard the Lion-Hearted, the true and lawful king.

18   Robin Hood has no other woman that I ever heard of in any of the stories. So I have to think of him as celibate, as putting off the assumption of a full male role, as being less than a complete, grownup man. He is asexual and pure, mercurial, airy almost, Ariel-like — a natural innocent, murderous but sweet-natured, light and quick. And he shares with Marian that mystical virtue that chastity confers, so useful for catching unicorns. The male and the female elements, the *yang* and the *yin* of this legend, are allied but not conjoined at the peak of their vigour, and when later a legitimate union is formed, they decline.

19   Robin Hood is more often with Little John than with Maid Marian. He and his giant companion are like a clean-cut, somewhat prim ego and id. They continually test and prove themselves, tempting fate, daring all comers, looking for trouble, never content with safety and boredom. They fight with quarterstaves at their first meeting; they quarrel from time to time; they rescue each other from capture; they compete with each other against the terrible strong beggar with potent quarterstaff and the bag meal that blinds the usually cunning Robin. And so they stay young and jolly until King Richard, the lawful ruler, the inevitable mature authority, returns.

20   And with that return Robin Hood is absorbed into grownupness and legitimacy. He is pardoned, and no more an outlaw; he is married, and no more a child-man. His best men are called into the service of King Richard. Robin Hood's power is drained off into the lawful self; the puissant youth becomes the waning man.

21   I'm no scholar, and I have no idea of the origin of the legend that is Robin Hood. What is inescapable is that the stone of the legend is worn into shape by the sea of human perception and need that continually washes over it. Legends, myth and fantasy both ask and tell us how life is, and there seems to be a strong need in us to think about the theme that is in *Robin Hood*: the absorption into law and order of that mysterious, chthonic, demiurgic power that we vitally need but cannot socially tolerate. We regret the loss of it and we rationalize the necessity of that loss. We say to it, 'Yes, be there. But lose yourself in us at the proper time. Grow up.' But I wonder what the proper time is, and I won-

der if the loss is necessary. And I wonder what growing up is. And I wonder whether young people now are not validly reconsidering and reshaping that theme, reclassifying it as well, so that the values assigned are no longer the same as those agreed upon until now. Maybe what we've always called growing up is sometimes growing down. It bears thinking about.

Robin Hood is only one development of that theme; there must be 22 many others. In *Great Expectations*, for instance, Magwitch, the outlaw self, is content to subsidize anonymously Pip, the lawful self. And it is Magwitch the outlaw who refines what is base and shallow in the respectable youth. Pip thinks that Miss Havisham is financing him, but the money that makes it possible for him to cut a dash as a young gentleman does not come from her decaying beauty, wealth and gentility, but from the starveling and tenacious humanity of what in us is violent, inchoate, unshapen and fit only to be put in prison.

Again, in Conrad's *Secret Sharer*, a young captain, a young lawful 23 authority in his first command, is appealed to by a young man who closely resembles him, a fugitive fleeing trial for killing a mate on another vessel. With characteristic genius Conrad opens his story with the unfledged captain taking the anchor watch alone at night on his ship that is still unfamiliar to him. He looks over the side and sees looking up at him from the water a face like his own, the face of a desperate swimmer. The captain shelters his criminal *doppelganger* aboard his ship during a period of self doubt before putting to sea. But when the barque leaves port the fugitive must be put ashore to take his chances alone. A wide-brimmed hat, given him by the captain as protection against the sun, falls into the water and becomes a sea mark by which the young master gauges the current while negotiating a difficult offing under sail in light and baffling airs.

The fugitive's hat gets the lawful master safely out to sea, but the 24 fugitive cannot go with the ship. Magwitch gives Pip what he can and dies. Robin Hood is killed by the establishment that has no use for him. The predatory church that he has always fought will take him in, ailing and ageing, will bleed him to death at the end by the hand of the treacherous Prioress of Kirkleys Nunnery. Robin Hood, supported by Little John, will loose his last arrow from his deathbed and be buried where it falls. Marian, first magical maid and then magicless woman, will become a nun and Prioress in her turn. Robin in the earth and she in the nunnery will both regain their innocence and power.

After the first reading of the book, the death and the last arrow were 25 always there waiting for Robin Hood and me; he carried that death with him, carried that last arrow in his quiver always. He seems such a year-king! He seems, in his green and lightsome strength, always to hasten toward his sacrificial death that will bring forth from the winter earth another spring. And like a year-king, he must be given up, cannot be kept.

26   But I cannot give him up entirely. I think that we need our outlaw strength alive and brother to our lawful vigour. The one is not healthy without the other. I keep calling the elements outlaw self and lawful self, but that is unfair, really, to the essence of the thing. Society defines the terms of lawful and unlawful, because society makes the laws. And society is a retarded child with a loaded gun in its hands; I don't completely accept society's terms. Something in us makes us retell that myth; some drive there is in us to find and name the demon in us that is more real than laws and conventions that tell us what is right and what is wrong. And that demon is, I think, the radical spirit of life: it is the dark and unseen root system of our human tree whose visible branches are so carefully labelled and scientifically pruned by us. Maybe we think we don't need to know more about that nameless creative chaos, but we do, because in it we must find all real order. Polite gentlemen wearing suits and ties and with neat haircuts sit around tables with the death of the world in their briefcases, and they do not hesitate to tell us what is order. But to me it seems disorder. Other polite gentlemen some years ago sent up human smoke signals from the chimneys of crematoria, and they too defined order with great clarity. I think that fewer definitive definitions and many more tentative ones are needed now.

27   The fantasy of our legends, myths and stories helps with those definitions. It is as close as we can get to noumena through phenomena, as close as we can get to the thingness of things through the appearances of things. Fantasy isn't separate from reality; it is a vital approach to the essence of it. As to its importance, it is simply a matter of life and death. If we don't find out more about the truly essential thingness of things, then some future generation, if not this one, won't have anything left to find out about. So we must have fantasy constructed as scaffolding from which to work on actualities. And to work with fantasy is a risky business for the writer: it can change his whole world of actualities.

28   Which brings me back to the man on the bicycle, shirtless and shouting. I was sorry for that man. I know how he felt. I wish he had been able to do something better with the baffled demon in him. I think he might have found something better to do if he had had more workable material in his mind, more useful people in his inner society. Robin Hood

would have helped him, perhaps Captain Ahab too, and Lord Jim and Raskolnikov and goodness knows who else, functioning as surrogate actors-out of extreme and exaggerated degrees of the human condition. They might have taken on for him certain time-consuming and self-defeating tasks. They might have shown him other ways to be, might have freed him to do something more effective than what he was doing, might have helped him to find an identity in that wild surge of random creation that vanished into silence on the indulgent and indifferent air.

Well, you may say, perhaps that man wasn't a reader, and whatever 29 is in books won't help him. But books permeate both the outer and inner societies, moving through readers to non-readers with definitions and provision for societal roles, expectations and probabilities. Always more figures are needed to people our inner societies — personifications of all the subtly different modes of being, *avatars* of the sequential and often warring selves within us. Books in nameless categories are needed — books for children and adults together, books that can stand in an existential nowhere and find a centre that will hold.

(1971)

The Writer's Subject

1. What is the relevance of the opening anecdote of the shirtless cyclist to the essay as a whole?

2. Hoban gives prominence to the story of Robin Hood and his outlaws. What personal significance does he derive from the story? What meanings does he attach to it?

3. What connection is there between the outcome of the Robin Hood story and the growth of a child to adulthood? (paras. 19–21)

4. Why, according to Hoban, do we need a "composite hero" with anti-heroic as well as heroic qualities? (para. 16)

5. Why does Hoban think that "we need our outlaw strength alive and brother to our lawful vigour"? (para. 26)

6. Why does Hoban believe that fantasy is so important? (paras. 27–28)

7. Why does Hoban think that the shirtless cyclist might have done "something better with the baffled demon in him" if he had more experience of books? What importance does Hoban attach to books for the well-being of children and adults generally? (paras. 28–29)

The Writer's Style and Strategy

1. How does Hoban's title reflect the pattern of development of the essay?

2. Cornment on Hoban's use of "riotously" in his statement, "There may, of course, come a day when I shall riotously put on a bowler hat and a neat black suit, buy a tightly furled umbrella, and mingle in wild silence with brokers in the City." (para. 5)

3. How does Hoban signal the shift from the introductory material to the main body of his essay?

4. Hoban alludes to a number of examples from literature in addition to *Robin Hood*. How does he use these to advance his thesis?

5. What figure of speech is Hoban employing when he says, "Maybe we think we don't need to know more about that nameless creative chaos, but we do, because in it we must find all real order"? (para. 26)

6. What is the dominant tone of this essay and how does Hoban create it? Identify places where the tone seems to shift, and account for the shifts.

Suggested Topics for Writing and Discussion

1. Discuss a book that was important to you in your childhood.

2. Hoban says that Robin Hood, as a symbol of excellence, has been a great help to him all his life. Choose another literary hero or heroine. Identify and discuss those qualities that you think make the character a helpful model.

3. Hoban says, "we must have fantasy constructed as scaffolding from which to work on actualities." Choose a work of fantasy in any genre (film, drama, literature, painting) and discuss the ways in which the work helps us to a better understanding of reality. Make clear your definition of fantasy at the outset.

4. "Maybe what we've always called growing up is sometimes growing down." (para. 21) Apply Hoban's comment to your own experience; do you think that your growth into adulthood has involved losses as well as gains? (You may wish to read Wordsworth's poem "Ode: Intimations of Immortality" for another view of this subject.)

Bella Coola

by Edith Iglauer

This piece about Bella Coola was originally part of my book, *Fishing* 1
with John. My editor for the whole book was Bill Shawn, who had just
resigned from *The New Yorker*. It was a wonderful experience to work
with him so directly.

You can tell the difference right away between great editors and the 2
rest of them, because the great ones don't rewrite; they leave your
thoughts and phrasing intact, and just cleanup around them so that everything is very clear. Bill thought, and I agreed with him, that the Bella
Coola chapter carried a story of its own, but it broke the thread of the
narrative, so we removed it.

John and I went to Bella Coola because we had the time and were 3
more than halfway there when the 1975 fishermen's strike began. We
wanted to see whether we would like to move there. John believed Pender
Harbour, with its scenic beauty and proximity to Vancouver, was about
to become a tourist mecca and a place where retired people would want
to come to live, which is what has happened. He felt that many people
would be far more concerned with so-called "development" and the value
of their land, than with the quality of the life here. Areas of Pender Harbour could already be mistaken for a city suburb, houses side by side
with manicured lawns.

Fortunately for me, it rained almost the whole week we were in Bella 4
Coola: all kinds of rain, from cold drizzles to pelting rainstorms, and
once, a hailstorm. I say fortunately for me, because after I drove partway
up the only road into or out of Bella Coola, I knew I wasn't going to
live there. There are two other ways to depart from Bella Coola: by air,

and the weather can make it impossible to fly in or out for weeks; and by boat, and the Trudeau government eliminated the scheduled coastal passenger service that stopped regularly at Bella Coola.

5   I said to John, "If you want to live in Bella Coola, I will visit you from time to time, but I can't live here." After that week of rain, rain, rain, I never heard another word about moving there.

6   Our fishing life was put on hold while we were in Bella Coola, but our visit there was quite an experience. I was glad afterward that I had been there. Howard White liked what I wrote as an entity by itself, especially about the Bella Coola Road, and thought it should be part of *Raincoast Chronicles*.

7   Bella Coola. The name caught my eye on a map of Canada long before I ever dreamed of moving to British Columbia. I saw BELLA COOLA at the end of one section of a jagged waterway called North Bentinck Arm, part of a fjord that made a deep cut in the coastline. The words stood out because they were, I mistakenly thought, so Spanish, so romantic, in among a lot of Indian and Anglo-Saxon place names. I longed, for no logical reason, to go there some day.

8   When I came to British Columbia for the first time in 1969 with my two young sons, Jay and Richard, we flew out from New York, where we were living, and camped in provincial parks, following a route marked in heavy black ink on a worn road map that I clutched like a security blanket. Bella Coola was not one of the marked stops, but I figured we would make a side trip there if we possibly could.

9   Our route took us north on Vancouver Island, by ferry boat to Prince Rupert, along the Skeena River and down into the Chilcotin, to Williams Lake. At a crossroads there I saw a sign pointing west that said, BELLA COOLA.

10   We turned down a bumpy, dusty dirt road and stopped for gas. "How far is it to Bella Coola?" I asked.

11   The man selling the gas looked us up and down, stopped chewing tobacco long enough to spit accurately into a trash can and said, "How long you got?"

12   "Only today," I said. "I thought we'd go and take a look."

13   He shook his head. "It's a couple of hours just to get to the road," he said. "The Bella Coola Road. You driving?"

14   I said I was, and he shook his head again. "That's pretty rough road. You better come back when you got more time. Plenty of time."

15   In 1973 I met my second husband John Daly, a commercial salmon

fisherman, and went fishing with him on his forty-one-foot troller, the *MoreKelp*. One season we had to stop work suddenly for a whole month because the fishermen went on strike. We were in Namu, where B.C. Packers has an upcoast fish-buying installation in summer, when the strike started, so we decided to go on our boat to Eucott Bay and visit two elderly gentlemen, Frenchy and Simpson, who lived there on a rotting fish-camp float. On the way in I looked at the map and saw that we were now inside the same fjord-like waterway system as Bella Coola and said, "I wish we could go there!"

By coincidence, on our way out of Eucott we met Al Perkins, a big 16
man with a large black moustache, who was an old friend of John's. We stopped to admire his handsome new white troller, the *Salmon Stalker*, and he remarked, "I've just been to Bella Coola, where I've been looking for land. I live in Duncan, and that place is getting too crowded for me."

"I know what you mean," John replied. "I've been thinking of doing 17
the same thing myself."

The next morning John said, "I think we ought to explore the idea of 18
moving to Bella Coola ourselves," as he started the boat's motor. We were soon moving along back down from where we had come, and part way he turned left, and right, into new territory; I lost track of our direction in the winding passages. The channel had high rock borders, and as we proceeded, mile after mile, twisting and turning through a steep-sided corridor, snow-capped mountains appeared ahead, above and around us. We must have gone at least fifty miles, deeper and deeper into the fjord, until we were in the narrow reach of North Bentinck Arm.

While we were running, I plucked our reference book, *British Co-* 19
lumbia Coast Names, out from under the mattress on John's bunk and looked up Bella Coola. Spanish origin indeed! According to the book's author, Captain John Walbran, the name Bella Coola is "an adaptation of the name of a tribe of Indians residing in the neighbourhood," and Bella Coola is "the local spelling used by the postal authorities," and only one of several ways of spelling it; the others being Bela Kula; Bellaghchoolas; and Bel-houla. So much for Spain and romance!

After eight miles, we arrived at an area of mudflats and swamp grass 20
swathed in mist. Low red buildings marked CANADIAN FISH COMPANY were on our left, and to our right were a mass of floats crowded with the boats of other commercial fishermen on strike; plus the usual mix of sailboats and pleasure cruisers. Behind this picturesque jumble were the highest mountains I had yet seen on the mountainous B.C. coast, with

snowy tips and the white streaks of glaciers on their slopes. "It's like Switzerland here," I said. "These mountains have that same lofty beauty." I looked at the chart to reassure myself. "Bella Coola! What a surprise!" I exclaimed. "I didn't know it would be so lovely. I guess I didn't know anything about it at all."

21   John was busy looking for a place on the floats to tie up. He stopped beside a troller about the size of ours, the *Jan-Jac-Ann*. When our ropes were securely fastened to it, he came in and said, "Bella Coola has a big fishing fleet, and a strong union group. I've *always* thought I'd like to live in Bella Coola some day. When Al Perkins talked about moving here, I decided we'd take a look too. I don't know how much longer I can stand the noise of those airplanes flying in and out of Garden Bay, and the crowds. All the things I came to Pender Harbour to get away from are catching up with us. What I like about the people in Port Hardy and the Bella Coolaites is they don't want to increase the gross national product, they want to garden, and stay as they are. They do get tourists who fly in to hunt or fish, and a few drive in, but coming over that road is a long and hairy trip. I don't think Bella Coola is likely to get the hordes of tourists we get. At least, that's how it seems to me."

22   It had been raining, but now, at the end of the day, the sun took a notion to shine. I stood on our deck, dazzled by the scenery; fading rays of sun lit up the mountains, their glaciers and their valleys. "Is *this* Bella Coola?" I asked. "I don't see any houses."

23   "Oh, it's a two-mile walk to 'downtown' Bella Coola," John said. "I hope the telephone on the dock works. Last time I was here, the rain was *pouring* when I went up to phone you in New York, and most of the glass in the kiosk was smashed. All I got was a recorded voice, and I lost the money I had put in, besides. I walked into Bella Coola three or four times and tried to telephone. I reported the phone the first day, and when it wasn't fixed the second night, I put my foot through the last whole piece of glass and you know why? Because I kept getting that bloody recorded voice that said, 'The number you have reached is not in service.' It just enraged me. If I had a human answer I would have been far less mad. Those fiendish recorded voices are an atrocity against all who cannot afford a phone in their own houses; a non-humanity that causes real angry frustration. I certainly understand the violent vandalism that occurs in an inarticulate 'won't answer back' phone booth." With that, he turned and marched up the ramp to telephone.

24   The telephone must have worked, because he was back shortly to say we had been invited for supper by the local game warden, Tony

Karup. He arrived shortly in a yellow government truck; a greying, bald man in a khaki uniform. He drove us along a road bordered by the grassy flats of a river estuary that appeared to be a dumping ground for dilapidated and abandoned boats; and then we were in the main part of the town of Bella Coola. It consisted of a few rectangular streets, a United Church hospital, a library, several churches and stores. He pointed out a large store, famous for its excellent stock of books and handicrafts, that was owned and run by a local author, Cliff Kopas, whose book, *Bella Coola*, has become a standard historical reference. Driving along, it was clear that most of the Indian population in town lived on one side of the main intersection and the white people on the other.

We spent a pleasant evening at the neat, official house of the game 25
warden and his good-looking Danish wife, but our meal was interrupted several times by telephoned reports about a grizzly bear in the area. "It's been killing cattle right in town, and I don't want any vigilante action," Tony said, returning to the table looking concerned. "Everybody's complaining now about all kinds of bears since they heard about this one; about bears that show up at their back doors, or claw marks on the windows, or garbage bags ripped apart. I was talking to one of our best Indian guides this morning, and he said, 'If I want to attract a bear for my clients, I buy new bread and they can smell it for miles around.' He also told me, 'I was at the garbage dump yesterday and I felt the wind of a paw on the back of my neck, and I sure jumped into the cab of my truck in a hurry!'"

The next morning, John and I walked the two miles into town in driz- 26
zling rain that shortly turned into a downpour. When we were wandering around in the Cliff Kopas store, a tall, cheerful man greeted John. He was walking with the aid of two canes, and his name was Tom Gee. John called to me several counters away and I arrived in time to hear that Gee had jumped off a roof and landed on his heels, breaking them both. The last time John had seen him he was gillnetting.

Tom hustled us into his truck and for the several more days we stayed 27
in Bella Coola he was our guide and transportation. That was fortunate because it never stopped raining. The rain in Bella Coola had a special wetness that gave everything a damp aura, and soaked through my fairly waterproof red windbreaker. Even now, when I am asked my impression of Bella Coola, all I can remember is the rain and the friendliness of the people.

One morning when Tom arrived to pick us up he said, "I thought 28
we'd go up the Bella Coola Road, oh, just for an hour or so." He ex-

plained as we drove away that the local inhabitants had built the road themselves. It was a tremendous effort, over the mountain range that separated Bella Coola by land from any other community. It connected over the top of the range to the town of Anahim Lake, where my sons and I would have landed if we had been foolish enough to keep on driving from Williams Lake.

29   John said, "I've never been on that road. It's the only land route in and out of Bella Coola. The only other way to go is by boat or plane, and often the weather's so bad planes can't fly. The government wouldn't do anything about a road, so the Bella Coola people built their own. I think they got a little grant for dynamite. Constructing that road over that mountain range was an extraordinary achievement."

30   "What's the road like?" I asked.

31   John replied, "I once met the man in charge of roads for the government and he said to me, 'It's really embarrassing. When I make road inspections my wife and daughter sometimes come with me, but when I start down the Bella Coola road, they either insist on staying at Anahim or they drive in with me with a rug over their heads.'"

32   We turned and started up a gravel road through a valley. Tom stopped once to show us an old water wheel, and again to let cattle cross in front of us. We drove past Indian smokehouses, sheds with rows of deep red salmon hanging on lines, then a federal fisheries counting hut that looked like an outhouse perched over a stream, and then a house shaped like an ark. "Here's hippieville in Noah's Ark," Tom said, and then we were crossing a bridge over rushing water. "A truck went through here when the bridge collapsed, and a little boy drowned," he said. "The fellow driving found the boy pinned under a bunker." We passed a handsome farm. "That belongs to the biggest farmer around here; he also has a house in town," Tom said.

33   Somewhere along the way, near where Tom said the Bella Coola River joined with the white water of another river, I saw a sign that said, "Closed to bear hunting. Do not feed, tease or molest bears." The road was becoming steeper and below us was spread a vista of beautiful bare green hills and snow slides. Tom was driving in first gear now, very, very slowly. Rocks slid down, rolling around the fenders of the truck.

34   I saw Tom put his elbows on the wheel, steering with them while he lit a cigarette. It was a horrifying sight. "You'd be surprised at the number of people who come in and don't drive out again," he said casually. "They put their cars on a barge instead and fly home. The road was just a goat trail when I came over it in 1956, and pretty tough here in the begin-

ning; not the way it is now, with lots of turnbacks and turnarounds. Hello there!" he exclaimed, as a boulder hit the truck and rolled over the embankment.

I was sitting between the two men, so I had to stretch my neck to see   35
where the rock had gone. The boulder bounced along down until it disappeared into what looked to me like a bottomless chasm, at least two thousand feet down.

We stopped suddenly. A large truck was just ahead, which shocked   36
me. We could see such a short distance in front of us that I thought we had the road to ourselves. We sat and waited while the truck backed up over the edge. Its rear end hung out over space while it made the sharp turn in the road to go forward again.

Gee said, "Someone asked a trucker friend of mine how he did this in   37
winter, when it's a sheet of ice and he said, 'Nothin' to it. I just drink a gallon of goof at the top of the hill and it smoothes out like a prairie.'"

There was a general chuckle, which I joined in weakly. Then we went   38
through the same manoeuvre we had watched the truck make: backing over the edge in a switchback, to go forward. I tried not to think about the back end of our truck hanging out into space while we sat in the front end.

"There's never been a fatal accident on this road," Tom continued   39
cheerfully. "A fellow went over in a Toyota station wagon with a load of sewing machines 'way up past here, and dropped sixty feet onto a switchback below, hit a tree and hung up there. It wrecked the tree, and he was in the hospital for two or three days. That's all. People drive this road at a crawl because they know they have to, even if they are drunk."

We were grinding our way up the road again, catching up to the truck   40
ahead of us, then falling back to wait. We continued to stop and back up at each hairpin turn on what I now viewed as an insane road, admirable as the effort must have been to build it. I was not put at ease by Gee's steering with his elbows again as he lit another cigarette. John was silent, but I must have stirred nervously in my seat between them, because to ease the tension Gee said, "There were four bears on Main Street last night. One about four hundred pounds was seen in the telephone booth, probably phoning to find out where the garbage dump is, and when he came out someone saw him pick up a garbage can and walk off with it. A bear scattered a garbage pail on the back porch of the hotel, and another bear was seen by the beer hall, looking in store windows. I guess they're taking the path of least resistance and not picking berries any more. Tony finally shot one last night."

41   I was beyond conversation; just hoping, well praying, that Tom wouldn't light another cigarette. When I thought I couldn't stand looking over one more thousand or two thousand or whatever thousand-foot drop on another hairpin switchback turn, I saw a turn-around ahead. John glanced at his watch and cleared his throat. Tom said, "Do you think we'd better go back now? We're having supper with the matron of the hospital, who wants to meet you, and we shouldn't be late."

42   "I think we'd better," John said. We turned around and headed back. My relief was short-lived. Going down was worse. Looking through the windshield, the short span of road ahead extended only a few feet and disappeared in the vertical drop. Then, over the edge and down we went, to another vanishing point and another steep drop, prefaced by a switchback that left us teetering over the side of the mountain. I tried looking ahead. Glancing over the side, across John, was not a pleasing view either — just emptiness, nothing below as far as I could see from where I sat, except on the switchbacks, where I could unfortunately see exactly how far down it was into the canyons beneath us. I thought about the mother and daughter who drove with a blanket over their heads. I wished I had brought one with me. I would have used it, without shame.

43   John put his hand over mine. He said, "Tom, I heard you had some sort of an accident with your gillnetter. What happened?"

44   "It was off Egg Island, and the engine started to miss," Tom said, throwing his cigarette out the window. I took a stick of gum out of my purse and started chewing, bracing myself for the moment when he would light another cigarette. Mercifully, he didn't. "As soon as I turned off the switch she blew, and blew me right out over the drum into the water," he continued. "I think the fire caught in the fuel pump. I didn't have a skiff along, so I swam away from the boat and got mixed up in some kelp. Then I swam back to the boat, got a grip on the tail end of the net, and made a hand hold. With the stabilizer and poles and the mast coming down, I felt pretty small, I can tell you. Everything burning and no skiff; and a hundred and twenty dollars in my pocket that I couldn't use. I was sure I'd be picked up because I had seen the Air Rescue on Egg Island. Somebody finally *did* pick me up, but I've always taken a skiff with me since then. I don't know when I'll get back fishing though. Breaking all those little bones in your heels is *really* painful, and they take a long time to heal."

45   We were down in the woods, in the valley now, driving through lovely green forests. I sat back with an audible sigh of relief. "If we had gone the whole way to Anahim, how long is that road?" I asked.

"Two hundred and fifty miles," Tom said.   46
"And that's the *only* way out of Bella Coola by land?" I asked.   47
"That's right," John said.   48

Back on the boat that night I said to John, "If you move to Bella   49
Coola, I'll come and visit you. Maybe." He laughed and turned on the
news. A few minutes later, the fisherman on the *Jan-Jac-Ann* told us
that a strike vote had been called for the next day in Namu.

It was time to leave anyway. The continual rasp of our boat rocking   50
against its neighbour, the rumble of the Gardner being run to prevent
the chilly damp from overwhelming us, particularly in my quarters below, and the endless patter of raindrops on the pilothouse roof were getting on our nerves. For the first and only time on the *MoreKelp*, we
began to snap at one another.

I packed for travelling; stowing loose items in the sink, ramming a   51
knife in the cupboard door to keep it shut. The sun came out, casting a
lovely yellow-white light on the mountains as we moved slowly away
from the dock. I had seen Bella Coola, at last. It was beautiful, just as I
had imagined, but I had no regrets about leaving.

(1991)

The Writer's Subject

1. What drew the writer to Bella Coola in the first place?

2. What kind of community is Bella Coola, as drawn by Iglauer?

3. What do we learn about the way of life of the people Iglauer meets in
   Bella Coola?

4. What kind of man is Tom Gee?

The Writer's Style and Strategy

1. The essay, though obviously about Bella Coola and its infamous road, is
   also a piece of autobiography. What does Edith Iglauer tell us about herself, directly or indirectly?

2. What use does Iglauer make of dialogue?

3. What details does Iglauer select to emphasize the hazardous nature of the
   Bella Coola Road? How does she convey her own feelings during the drive?

4. How does Iglauer give the reader an insight into the character of her husband?

5. Discuss the last two paragraphs of the essay. Do they form an appropriate
   conclusion?

Suggestions for Writing and Discussion

1. Describe an occasion on which you were subjected to great stress (e.g., your acting debut; a mountain-climbing adventure; an athletic competition). Choose details that will help the reader understand your feelings on that occasion.

2. Describe a trip that turned out differently from your expectations, and convey your feelings about the experience.

3. Present a portrait of someone you know who seems unusual or special in some way. Focus on those details of character, appearance, or behaviour that bring out the particular qualities of the person you are describing.

The Shadow of Captain Bligh

by Hugh MacLennan

Not long ago, in the same evening, I listened to my gramophone re- 1
cording of Haydn's *Mass for St. Cecilia* and then went upstairs and began rereading the account of the mutiny on H.M.S. *Bounty* as written
by Nordhoff and Hall. The grand cadences of the Mass kept sounding
through my mind, and every now and then I stopped reading to let them
swell and subside. I was rereading the book for a purpose and I didn't
feel I could put it down. But the counterpoint made me realize with a
sensation of shock that Joseph Haydn and Captain Bligh were contemporaries, that the society that had produced and honoured the one was
the same society that had employed and respected the other.

Haydn's *Mass for St. Cecilia*, which was partially lost until Dr. Brand 2
recovered it little more than a decade ago, and which hardly anyone
had heard performed until it appeared recently in a recording of the
Haydn Society, is certainly one of the most sublime works the human
spirit has ever created. It seems to me worth all the music composed
since the death of Beethoven. Beethoven himself was never able to sustain the power that is manifest here, for his struggle with himself and
his medium was too great. Haydn's Mass, like the greatest work of
Shakespeare, is at once majestic and intimate. Above all it seems effortless, and its joy and triumph are so breath-taking that no one who is
moved by music can easily listen to it without reflecting that our modern world has produced no creative genius with his originality, his joy-
ousness, or his power.

Yet Haydn was not unique in his time. His career overlapped those 3
of Bach, Handel, Mozart, and Beethoven. Though his age acclaimed

him a master, it occurred to nobody in the eighteenth century to think it miraculous that he was able to compose those immensely complex works, some of great length, in so short a time. The best of his contemporaries were equally prolific and worked with equal speed. Handel composed *The Messiah* in a few weeks and Mozart wrote one of his most famous symphonies in a few days. Compared to these eighteenth-century masters, a modern creative artist moves at a snail's pace. Our most famous poets will die leaving behind only a slim body of published verse. The average modern novelist takes from two to three years to write a single good novel. Our musicians — men like Sibelius, Stravinsky, and Vaughan Williams — have together, in their long lives, equalled only a fraction of Haydn's output.

4   How lucky Haydn was to have lived before the radio and the telephone, before civic societies which would have made exorbitant and unavoidable demands on his time and energy, before publicity and interviewers and income tax and traffic horns and metropolitan dailies — to have lived, in short, before the age of distraction.

5   But *Mutiny on the Bounty* reminded me of the other side of the eighteenth century. The very fact of Captain Bligh implies that the forces which have made ours an age of distraction are far subtler and less avoidable than technical innovations like the telephone and the radio. *Mutiny on the Bounty* should be required reading for anyone who is apt, like myself, to be romantic about past ages and to decry his own. For Captain Bligh was just as typical of the eighteenth century as Haydn was. When I bow before Haydn I must remember that Haydn accepted without question and apparently without remorse the fact that he lived in a world that contained Captain Bligh.

6   Nothing Mickey Spillane has ever written can be compared in horror to some of the factual scenes in *Mutiny on the Bounty*. Few passages in literature describe more revolting episodes than those of the *Bounty* sailors being seized in the gangway and flogged until the flesh hung in strips from their backs. With our modern knowledge of neurology, we know that the agonies of these poor creatures did not end when the boatswain's mate ceased swinging the cat. Such beating damaged the nerve roots along the spine and condemned the victims to permanent suffering. What makes those scenes of torture so unbearable to think about is the added realization that they were not sporadic, were not the offshoots of a psychopathic movement like Nazism, but were standard practice in one of the most stable and reflective societies that ever existed. Captain Bligh's cruelty had the weight and approval of his entire society behind it. When

the mutineers were later court-martialled, the court had no interest in determining whether Bligh had been cruel or not. It was interested solely in whether the accused had obeyed to the letter the harsh laws of the British Navy.

Haydn, Bach, Handel, and Mozart, sublime spirits full of mercy, with 7 sensibilities exquisitely delicate, knew that men like Bligh were the mainstays of the societies they inhabited. Yet this knowledge, which to us would be a shame, felt personally, seldom if ever troubled their dreams or ruffled their serenity. The humanitarianism that disturbed Beethoven a generation later had not dawned when Haydn wrote the *Mass for St Cecilia.*

Haydn reached his prime in the last moments when it was possible 8 for a creative artist to mind his own business in the sense that his conscience could remain untroubled by the suffering of the unfortunate. If sailors were flogged to death and peasants had no rights, if a neighbouring country was ruined by famine or pestilence, if laws were unjust or princes cruel, none of it was Haydn's affair. He was compelled to no empathy in the suffering of others as modern artists are.

It is this awareness of personal responsibility for the welfare of stran- 9 gers that makes uneasy all men of imagination today, that troubles their work and makes much of it seem tortured, that frustrates it, too, for seldom can a modern man of creative imagination do anything concrete to change the world he lives in.

Responsible only to himself, to his family, and to his God, Haydn 10 enjoyed a freedom few artists have known since. The result was as glorious as it is inimitable. It is on most of his successors that the shadow of Captain Bligh has fallen and remained.

As Haydn represents the spiritual grandeur of the eighteenth-century 11 imagination, Bligh represents its irresponsibility. In Bligh's own words, it was only through fear and cruelty that the stupid, the weak, the incompetent, the ignorant, and the unfortunate could be ruled and compelled to do what their masters considered to be their duty. Unless they were so compelled, the supporters of the system argued, there could be no fineness, no spiritual grandeur, no great literature or beautiful buildings, no masses for St. Cecilia. Civilization, as men of Haydn's day conceived it, could not exist if it yielded to the prompting of a social conscience.

When we realize this it becomes easier to reconcile ourselves to the 12 fact that the world we live in is producing no more Haydns or Mozarts. In the nineteenth century men of imagination turned their attention to the miseries of the world they saw about them, accepted responsibility for it, and forever lost the peace and concentration of spirit which enabled the Haydns and Mozarts to devote the full force of their genius to the realization of the gifts God had given them.

13   Could a modern artist witness a public flogging and then go home and compose exquisite music? Could he even live quietly under a regime that permitted such atrocities and retain his own respect and that of others?

14   Merely to ask such questions is to answer them. Musicians who took no more active part in the Hitler regime than perform for a Nazi audience have had to spend years as outcasts before western society would accept them again. The social conscience of today demands the service of every artist alive, and does not forgive him if he refuses it.

15   On the other hand western society did not make outcasts of the physicists, chemists, and engineers who served Hitler. Until very recently science reserved for itself the same mental freedom that art enjoyed in Haydn's day. If politicians or monsters used the work of science for evil purposes, the scientists felt no personal responsibility. Enjoying such peace of mind, physicists and chemists have been able to devote the full force of their intellects to their work, and so their work has been more impressive than that of the artists who were their contemporaries. No wonder our age, when it looks for a genius to match Bach or Haydn, does not even stop to search among the ranks of the artists. It picks Einstein.

16   But when the atomic bomb fell on Hiroshima any number of scientists succumbed to a social conscience as the artists had done long ago. Einstein, Oppenheimer, and hundreds of others were overcome with a Hamlet-like self-questioning. If our world lasts long enough it will be interesting to see whether science in the next generation will be as original and productive as it has been in the last three. For a conscience, as Shakespeare knew when he created Hamlet, inhibits action and beclouds genius. Our collective conscience may not have made the modern artist a coward, but it has certainly made him a prisoner.

17   Consider in contrast to Haydn the life of Albert Schweitzer. Schweitzer began as a musician, and had he lived in the eighteenth century there is no knowing what masterpieces he might have composed. But his conscience would not permit him to devote his entire life to music, so he studied theology and became a minister of the Gospel. Then his conscience told him that preaching was not enough, so he studied medicine and became a doctor. His conscience then informed him that

it was self-indulgent to practise medicine in a comfortable European city while there were millions in the world without medical care of any kind. So Schweitzer took his gifts to one of the most primitive parts of Africa. There he has lived and worked ever since, among men so elemental that they can know nothing of Bach or Haydn and cannot even guess at the greatness of the strange healer who came to help them.

Albert Schweitzer will die leaving behind him no tangible or audible **18** monument, no record of objective achievement beyond a few books which are mere by-products of his life and interests. His enormous powers have been spread so widely in the service of others that neither as a musician, nor as a theologian, nor as a doctor-scientist, has his work, in itself, been such as to ensure his immortality. An earlier age would have said that Schweitzer had squandered his gifts on savages. But our age, rightly or wrongly, acclaims him as one of its noblest representatives because his life has translated into action, as hardly any other life has done, the highest aspirations of our social conscience.

No other modern artist I know of has made the total sacrifice of his **19** talents that Schweitzer made; yet no modern artist (musician or poet or even the great individualist, Picasso) has been undisturbed by the social conscience of our day.

Critics who argue that the subject-matter of modern art is proof of **20** the decadence of modern society don't really understand what they are talking about. Art has always been a reflection of the aspirations and obsessions of its time and the art of today is no exception. If it is haunted and distracted, if it is often ugly and even horrifying, it does not mean that the artists themselves are worse men than Haydn was. It means only that they have not refused, as Haydn did, to accept responsibility for Captain Bligh. For all its horrors, the twentieth century is better than the eighteenth; no politician or dictator who has tried to defy its conscience has been able, in the end, to succeed.

Some time in the future art may reflect the tranquillity that Haydn **21** knew. If it does so, it will not be because those artists of the future are likely to be abler men than artists of today. It will happen because, after this age of transition, the shadow of Captain Bligh has been removed from the whole world.

(1953)

The Writer's Subject

1. Why did MacLennan feel shock at the realization that the same society had produced both Haydn and Captain Bligh? (paras. 1–7)

2. What contrast does MacLennan draw between the productivity of eighteenth-century artists and that of modern artists? (para. 3)

3. What does MacLennan find most disturbing about the treatment of the sailors on the *Bounty*? (para. 6)

4. Why, in MacLennan's view, were artists such as Haydn not disturbed by the savagery of the world around them? What does MacLennan mean when he says that the shadow of Captain Bligh has fallen not on Haydn but on his successors? (para. 7–11)

5. Why does MacLennan think it is no longer possible for the world to produce any more Haydns or Mozarts? (paras. 12–14)

6. What contrast does MacLennan draw between the achievements of modern artists and those of modern scientists? (para. 15)

7. MacLennan says that today scientists, like artists, have become prisoners of conscience. How does he demonstrate this point? (para. 16)

8. What is MacLennan's attitude to Haydn?

The Writer's Style and Strategy

1. Explain the meaning of "counterpoint" as MacLennan uses it in the first paragraph.

2. How does MacLennan establish the contrast between the two sides of eighteenth-century life? How does MacLennan signal the shift in his discussion from the one to the other?

3. MacLennan's essay works, in part, on the principle of cause and effect. That is, because Haydn was not distracted by his society he could produce great works. What other instances of cause and effect are evident in this essay?

4. Despite the extensive use of detail and supporting examples, this essay relies heavily upon assertions or generalizations to convey a very personal impression of the relationship between art and life. Find one or two examples of such assertions or generalizations; examine the assumptions that underlie them; and comment on their persuasiveness, or lack of it.

Suggested Topics for Writing and Discussion

1. MacLennan suggests that modern artists can seldom do anything concrete to change the world they live in. Do you agree?

2. MacLennan chooses Haydn as representative of the great artists of the eighteenth century. Choose another artist (e.g., painter, writer, architect, composer) either from a past age or from our own time, and show why, in your view, this artist represents his or her age.

3. Do you agree with MacLennan's view that the development of a social conscience in modern times has made the production of great art an impossibility?

4. "Art has always been a reflection of the aspirations and obsessions of its time and the art of today is no exception." Choose a well-known work of twentieth-century art in any medium and explain how the work reflects the concerns of its time.

5. MacLennan uses Captain Bligh as a symbol of evil in the eighteenth century. Write an essay about the dark side of the twentieth century and focus on one individual as a symbol of the evil of the age.

St John's
by Jan Morris

1   *Of all the cities I have written about, anywhere in the world, none has given me more enjoyment than St John's, Newfoundland, the most entertaining town in North America.*

2   *It was as a historian of the British Empire that I first went there, thirty-odd years ago, Newfoundland having occupied a unique place in the imperial scheme of things, and St John's having remained until recent times an anachronistic curiosity among imperial towns. By the time I came to write this essay the Empire's effects had long faded, and there were different excitements that beguiled me, but I remembered with particular affection an incident from my original visit, in 1956, that said a lot about the continuing character of St John's.*

3   *In the Newfoundland of those days it was necessary to find a local guarantor before one could cash foreign money orders. Knowing nobody in town, and discovering that the public library had a copy of a book of mine about Venice, I introduced myself to the librarian and asked her to endorse a traveler's cheque. How could she confirm, she sensibly demanded, that I was who I said I was? By a simple literary test, said I; surely nobody else on earth could recite by heart the last line of my Venetian book, which she had upon her own shelves.*

4   *Solemnly she reached for the volume. Nervously I stood at her desk while she turned to the final page, and ran her eye down the paragraphs to the end of it. Well? she said. I cleared my throat. The concluding words of my book were not very stately. "No wonder," I mumbled them, feeling distinctly disadvantaged, "no wonder George Eliot's husband fell into the Grand Canal." Without a flicker that li-*

brarian of old St. John's closed the book, returned it to the shelf and authorized my money.

Thwack! Despite it all, the personality of St John's, Newfoundland, hits   5
you like a smack in the face with a dried cod, enthusiastically administered by its citizenry.

The moment you arrive they take you up Signal Hill, high above the   6
harbour, where winds howl, superannuated artillery lies morose in its
emplacements, and far below the ships come and go through the rock
gap of the Narrows. Within an hour or two they are feeding you seal-
flipper pie, roast caribou, partridgeberries, or salt cod lubricated with
pork fat. They introduce you to the mayor, John "Rags" Murphy. They
show you the grave of the last Beothuk Indian and the carcass of the
final Newfoundland wolf. They remind you that they, alone in continental North America, live three and a half hours behind Greenwich
Mean Time.

They chill you with tales of the corpses lying in Deadman's Pond.   7
They warm you up with Cabot Tower rum. They take you to the site of
the city's first (hand-operated) traffic signal. They show you the house
into which the prime minister of Newfoundland escaped from a lynch
mob in 1932, and the field from which the aviators Harry G. Hawker
and Kenneth Mackenzie-Grieve unfortunately failed to cross the Atlantic in 1919. They guide you down higgledy-piggledy streets of grey,
green, yellow, and purple clapboard. They explain to you in detail the
inequities of the 1948 Confederation referendums. They tell you repeatedly about their cousins in Boston, and involve you in spontaneous and
often incomprehensible conversations on street corners.

Such is the nature of this city; windy, fishy, anecdotal, proud, weather-   8
beaten, quirky, obliging, ornery, and fun.

I start with "despite it all" because St John's is undeniably a knocked-   9
about sort of town. Economic slumps and political hammerings, trag-
edies at sea, sectarian bigotries, riots, fires, poverty, and unemployment
— all have taken their toll, and make the little city feel a trifle punch-
drunk.

The very look of it is bruised. The outskirts of St John's are much   10
like the purlieus of many another North American city — malls, car
dealers, airport, duplexes, a big modern university — but its downtown
is bumpily unique. Set around the dramatically fjord-like harbour, overlooked by oil tanks and fort-crowned heights but dominated by the twin
towers of the Catholic basilica, its chunky wooden streets clamber up

and down the civic hills with a kind of throwaway picturesqueness, suggesting to me sometimes a primitive San Francisco, sometimes Bergen in Norway, occasionally China, and often an Ireland of long ago.

11   "Either it's the Fountain of Youth," said a dockyard worker when I asked him about a peculiarly bubbling sort of whirlpool in the harbour, "or it's the sewage outlet." St John's is nothing if not down-to-earth. The shambled slums I remember from twenty-five years ago have been miraculously abolished, but the best efforts of the conservationists have not deprived the town of its innate fishermen's fustian. The most enlightened restoration of its streets has not managed to make it self-conscious. The first dread fancy lampposts and ornamental bollards, the first whiff of novelty-shop sachets, the arrival on the waterfront of that most ludicrously architectural cliché, mirror-glass — even the presence of Peek-a-Boutique in the premises of the former Murray fishery depot — have so far failed to make St John's feel in the least chichi. It remains that rarity of the Age of Collectibles, an ancient seaport that seems more or less real.

12   I hear some expostulations, nevertheless. "Fishermen's fustian," indeed! For all their hospitality, I get the sensation that the inhabitants of St John's may prove prickly people to write about, and there is a prejudice I am told among some of the grander St John's persons (we can no longer, I suppose, call them St John's men) against the city's association with the fish trade.

13   Yet even the loftiest burghers' wives could hardly claim that this is a very sophisticated place. It is like a family city, meshed with internecine plot, but still somewhat reluctantly united by blood, history, and common experience. It is the poorest of the Canadian capitals; it has little industry and few great monuments; its responses are those of a permanently beleaguered seaport on a North Atlantic island — which is to say, responses altogether its own.

14   Actually within the city limits of St John's there are pockets of the probably spurious Arcadianism that Newfoundland picture postcards so love to show. Small wooden houses speckle seabluffs, dogs lie insensate in the middle of steep lanes, and here and there one may still see the fish stretched out to dry, as they have been stretched for 400 years, on the wooden flakes of tradition. Almost within sight of Peek-a-Boutique I met a hunter going off to the hills in search of partridge, buckling his cartridge belt around him, hoisting his gun on his shoulder, just like a pioneer in an old print. And immediately outside the windows of one of the city's fancier restaurants ("Step Back in Tyme to Dine") one

may contemplate over one's cods' tongues the whole rickety, stilted, bobbing, seabooted, genial muddle that is the classic image of maritime Newfoundland.

It really is a community of cousins, too. I happened to notice on a 15 monument one day that the now defunct police force called the Newfoundland Rangers numbered, among its Guzzwells, Stucklesses, and Snelgroves, a disproportionate number of Noseworthys. So I looked up that clan in the St John's telephone book: 305 are listed, by my count, including Randy Noseworthy, Ethel Noseworthy, Dwayne Noseworthy, Franklin Noseworthy, Major H. Noseworthy, and Noseworthy, Keating, Howard and Kung, Accountants — their names constituting in themselves, I thought, a proper register of St John's social consciousness.

It happened that while I was in town St John's was celebrating its 16 centenary as a municipality with what it called a Soiree — generally pronounced swarr-ee — and recalling a favourite old Newfoundland song:

There was a birch rine, tar twine,
Cherry wine and turpentine,
Jowls and cavalances, ginger beer and tea,
Pig's feet, cat's meat, dumplings boiled in a sheet,
Dandelion and crackies' teeth at the
Kelligrews's Soiree ...

The festivities closed with a public party at the St John's Memorial Stadium that powerfully reinforced the family illusion, and suggested to me indeed an enormous country wedding — everyone someone else's in-law, everyone ready to talk, with no pretence and no pretension either. Noseworthys were numerous, I do not doubt, and Kelligrews were certainly there in force, though content no longer with ginger beer and tea. Jigs and folk songs sounded from the stage, miscellaneous bigwigs sat stared-at in the middle like rich out-of-town relatives, and when people seemed slow to dance, jolly Mayor Murphy took the floor alone, offering free booze coupons to any who would join him — "You have to get them half-tight," he remarked to me as he handed out these inducements, jigging the while himself.

The pubs of St John's are mostly less than trendy. The downtown 17 corner store flourishes. The St John's *Telegram* carries not merely death announcements but long and sometimes extremely gloomy poems to go with them, such as:

He's gone, oh gone for ever,
The one we loved the best.
Our days of joy are ended
As the sun sets in the west.

"Your mouths are so big they could fit in a zoo," a member of the city
council told his colleagues in plenary session during my stay. "You're a
sook," responded the deputy mayor.

18   I puzzled, as every stranger must, about the mingled origins of this
pungent civic character, and the first strain I identified was undoubtedly the Irish. The simplicity of St John's is streaked, I came to sense,
with a particularly Irish reproach, wit, and irony — sometimes I felt
that Ireland itself was only just out of sight through that harbour entrance. The prickly pensioners and layabouts who hang around on Water Street, "The Oldest Continuously Occupied Street in North America,"
look pure Cork or Wexford. The instant response that one gets from
nearly everyone is Ireland all over. And the complex of buildings that
surrounds the Basilica of St John the Baptist, episcopal, conventual, didactic, societal buildings, is a reminder that here Irish values and memories, however dominant the British colonial establishment of the place,
proved always inextinguishable.

19   But that establishment too still flies its flags — literally, for at city
hall they flaunt not only the ensigns of the city, the province, and the
Confederation but actually the Union Jack too, for reasons defined for
me as "purely sentimental." This was a self-governing British possession within my own lifetime, after all (no school stamp collection of
my childhood was complete without the 1¢ Caribou of our oldest
colony), and within the city centre it is still easy enough to descry the
old power structure of the Pax Britannica. The governor's mansion is
recognizably the social fulcrum that it was in every British colony. The
garrison church is spick-and-span. The Anglican cathedral is authentically unfinished, like all the best Anglican cathedrals of the Empire.
The old colonial legislature is properly pillared and stately, and down
the hill is the Supreme Court building, smelling of warm wood and depo-
sitions in triplicate, which once also housed the prime minister's office,
responsible directly to the Crown in London.

20   Indeed, as a sign reminds us on the waterfront, The British Empire
Began Here — when Sir Humphrey Gilbert established the first permanent settlement of New Founde Land in 1583. The city is appropriately
rich in heroic memorials, commemorative plaques, royally planted trees
or dukely laid foundation stones (though as a matter of fact, St John's

being St John's, the stone laid by the Duke of Connaught in Bowring Park in 1914 turns out to be the thriftily recycled headstone of a dog's grave). Kipling himself worded the plaque at the site of Gilbert's landing, Field Marshal Earl Haig unveiled the Water Street war memorial. Nor are the imperial loyalties merely lapidary: one devoted monarchist drives around town with British flags stuck on her trunk and flying from her radio aerial, and another was not much pleased, I fear, when I suggested that in Britain itself royalism, like cigarette smoking, was primarily a lower-middle-class enthusiasm...

"Not that the British," even these zealots are quite likely to say, "ever   21
did much for Newfoundland." On the contrary, the general view seems to be that London behaved as negligently towards its oldest colony as Ottawa does to its youngest province. Most people I asked said that emotionally at least they would prefer to enjoy the independence signed away to Canada in 1949, but a good many told me that if they had the choice they would opt for union with the U.S.

This did not surprise me. In some ways St John's is very American.   22
It does not feel to me in the least like Canada, being altogether too uninhibited, but I can conceive of it as a half-Irish, half-Empire Loyalist backwater of New England. A century ago the Newfoundlanders were all for free trade with the Americans, at least, and would have got it if the British government had not intervened; today half the people I met seemed to have American connections of some kind or another, mostly in Boston. When I suggested to one elderly lady that closer links with the United States might in the end mean more corruption, exploitation, and general degradation, she seemed quite affronted. "That's only the *fringe* of things down there," she said.

But I looked her in the face as she said this, and I rather think I de-   23
tected in it, through the patina of the years, the bright eager features of a GI groupie of long ago. I know of nowhere in the world where the American soldiers of the Second World War are remembered with such affection, or where, perhaps as a result, the equivocal colossus of the south seems to be given the benefit of so many doubts. "I can assure you that at heart the Americans are very good people," my informant firmly added, and as we parted I swear I heard, as in historic echo, a giggle in the shadows of McMurdo's Lane, and a distant beat of "In the Mood."

These varied inheritances and associations save St John's from any   24
suggestion of provincialism. History does it, one might say. The fateful gap of the Narrows is like a door upon a world far wider than Canada

itself, while the city's particular kinds of expertise, to do with ships, and fish, and ice, and seals, and perilous navigations, make it a place beyond condescension. Memorial University of Newfoundland has a formidable reputation, the Marine Institute is world-famous, and ships of many nations and many kinds, perpetually coming and going through the harbour, give the town a cosmopolitan strength — rust-streaked fishing vessels from the deep Atlantic grounds, hulking coastguard ships, coastal freighters, ocean research vessels, container ships and warships and ships bringing salt for the winter roads — ships in such ceaseless progress that each morning of my stay, when I walked down to the waterfront before breakfast, I found that some new craft had come out of the night like a messenger while I slept.

25   The historical continuity of St John's, too, allows it a status beyond its size. The Grand Banks, which brought the first Europeans to these parts, still figure inescapably in its affairs, and the matter of the 200-mile fishing limit profoundly affects not only the economy of the port but its very style. Gone, like enemy aliens from a land at war, are the Iberian fishermen who used to bring a Latin emollient of wine and lantern light to this northern waterfront, but the statue of Our Lady of Fatima in the basilica, presented by grateful Portuguese mariners in 1955, pointedly remembers still the long Romance connection.

26   Then the matter of St Pierre-Miquelon, St John's own foreign-relations issue, is really a last irritant from the Seven Years' War, which ended in this very city 227 years ago. Though the islands are familiar enough to St John's people (university students go there for French-language immersion courses), their presence somewhere over the southern horizon queerly haunted my thoughts in the city — so resolutely foreign still out there, so utterly separate, a department of France behaving, so close to Mayor Murphy's homely bailiwick, with such absolute damned Frenchness.

27   The world has been passing through St John's certainly for a longer time, and perhaps with a greater intensity, than through any other Canadian city — from the Basques, Dutch, French, and English of the early years to the GIs of the Second World War and the Russian and Japanese seamen who are familiars of the place today. All their influences have been absorbed, in one degree or another, into the city's persona. To take two oppositely alcoholic examples (for St John's loves its drink): the rum called Newfoundland Screech, born out of the eighteenth-century Caribbean saltfish trade, is bottled in St John's to this day, while Newman's Celebrated Port Wine, originally sent here to mature because

the long sea voyage from Europe was said to have a beneficial effect upon it, is offered still under the antiseptic auspices of the Liquor Corporation.

Such range, for a city of 100,000 souls, longitude 52.43 W, latitude 28 47.34 N! No wonder St John's, though long reduced to the condition of a provincial capital, remains so defiantly itself. There is no false modesty here. "You're right, but it isn't true of St John's," a man told me when I remarked that the citizens of most Canadian cities wanted to talk about nothing but themselves — and he went on to rehearse in loving and elaborate detail all other superiorities of the civic character.

In fact the people of St John's are irresistible talkers about themselves, 29 and their peculiar accent, which strikes me as a cross between Irish, Devonian, and Atlantic Seal, makes the flow of their infatuation all the more unguent. Since everyone seems to know nearly everyone else, throughout my stay I felt myself encompassed within a web of overlapping reminiscence, amusement, and complaint. Gossip flows lively in St John's; images of scandal, joke, and mischief passed before me like figures on a wide and gaudy screen. The moneyed dynasties of the town, the Ayres, the Jobs, the Harveys, the Outerbridges, were dissected for me in richest idiom whether living or extinct; politicians suffered the sharp sting of Newfoundland iconoclasm; as I was guided around the streets one by one the pedigrees and peccadillos of their structures stood revealed. Here was the store which was all that was left of the Xs' fortunes, here the mansion where the wildly successful Ys resided. One of the less estimable of the lieutenant governors lived in this house, a whiz-kid entrepreneur had lately installed eight bathrooms in that, and down by the waterfront was the not very upmarket department store whose ownership had given Mayor Murphy his affectionate nickname.

All this makes life in the city feel remarkably *immediate*. There is no 30 lag, it seems, between introduction and confidence. By my second day in town I was being given under-the-counter comments on the local judiciary by a well-known politician. By my third day I was being treated to the lowdown about some spectacular financial goings-on. Hardly had I been introduced to a member of one of St John's oldest families, who has one house in town and another on its outskirts, in a kind of Newfoundland version of the transhumance system — hardly had I met this distinguished citizen and his wife before they were explaining why their cat is named after — well, I had better not say who it's named after, let alone why.

I was walking along a city street one day when a man sweeping leaves 31 launched upon me without warning an obviously political statement in such advanced Newfoundlandese that I can only reproduce it impressionistically, so to speak, with the help of a glossary of the dialect. It sounded something like: "Sish yarkin trapse John Murphy, tacker snarbucklerawny yok John Crosbie, glutch aninst Suzanne Duff." He looked at me expectantly for a response, so I simultaneously shook my head and nodded, to be on the safe side.

1　Extend Arm (*says a notice at a pedestrian crossing outside city hall*)
2　Place Foot on Street
3　Wait Until Cars Stop
4　Thank Driver

It struck me as a quintessentially St John's announcement, with its blend of the amiable, the unexpected, and the tongue-in-cheek. If reading this essay makes you too feel rather as though you are being slapped in the face with a dried codfish, that is because I was beguiled by almost everything about the city and its inhabitants (almost, because I do wish they wouldn't smoke so much ...). I dare say that if the long-promised oil bonanza ever happens the town will ruin itself with affluence, but I rather think not: it is too rooted in the satisfaction of being utterly unlike anywhere else.

32　　The standard history of St John's is a monumental two-volume work by Paul O'Neill. One might expect such a labour of municipal devotion to be heavy going; in fact it is one of the most consistently entertaining history books I have ever read, full of excellent stories, gamy characters, and surprising historical allusions. Similarly, every corner of old St John's offers its own intriguing details. At 100 Water Street there is the sweetly old-school china shop that the Steele family has run for more than a century, while not far away the Neyle-Soper Hardware Store displays in its windows, like *objets d'art* in a museum, grandly Newfoundland things like paraffin lamps, hatchets, scythes, and mousetraps that catch four mice at a time. There is a shop that sells nothing costing more than three dollars, and a shop that sells Young Seal Carcass at forty-nine cents a pound, and Kim Lee's Tailor Shop with tailoring visibly taking place inside. Above the old lovers' steps of McMurdo's Lane the starlings roost in their noisy thousands.

33　　See that object on the rooftop there? That's the periscope of a German U-boat, mounted triumphantly above the Crow's Nest Club, which was a famous haven of the convoy captains in the Second World War.

See those wagons beyond the dockyard? That's the rolling stock of the narrow-gauge Newfoundland Railway, forlornly immobilized here because the railroad no longer exists. Hear that bang? That's the gun on Signal Hill, fired each day at noon as it was in the days of the redcoats.

As for the concrete city hall, it is a very repository of the civic self- 34 esteem. Such banners and plaques and portraits and statues and old municipal photographs! Such ship models and armorial bearings and fraternal messages from admirals, mayors, and societies of merchant venturers! When I remarked how proper it was that the mayor's own office should look directly down upon the historic waterfront, somebody said yes, and directly down upon his own store, too — such is the organic frankness of this close-hauled sceptic town.

I was conscious always all the same, as I wandered so enjoyably 35 through the city, that life and history have never been easy here. Beneath the charm there lies a bitterness. St John's is full of disappointment, and is an exposed and isolated place in more senses than one. One afternoon, by driving the few miles out to Cape Spear, I made myself for a moment the easternmost person in North America, and was chilled to think, as I stood there in the wind, that while at my back there was nothing but the ocean, before me there extended, almost as far as the imagination could conceive, the awful immensity of Canadian rock, forest, prairie, and mountain. St John's is the edge of everywhere, the end and start of everything. The sign for Mile "0" of the Trans-Canada Highway stands immediately outside city hall; it was on Signal Hill that Marconi received the very first radio communication from across the ocean. Hawker and Grieve failed indeed to fly across the Atlantic from St John's, but Alcock and Brown succeeded, and here one evening in 1927 people hearing the drone of an aircraft ran outside to see Lindbergh's *Spirit of St Louis* disappear into the twilight for Paris.

And to this day, though much of the activity of St John's has moved 36 inland, everything in this city looks down, if only metaphorically, to the Narrows. Even the stolid Confederation Building, erected with a becoming diffidence well back from the bloody-minded seaport, peers cautiously from its distance towards that dramatic fissure. I found myself bewitched by it: repeatedly driving up to its headlands, or around the southern shore to the lighthouse at the end, or waving goodbye to the ships as they trod carefully between the buoys towards the open sea — a distant slow wave of an arm, from wheelhouse or forecastle, returning my farewell as seamen must have responded down all the centuries of Atlantic navigation.

37   Once I was contemplating that hypnotic view from the bar of the Hotel Newfoundland, which looks immediately out to the Narrows and the Atlantic beyond. It was evening, and the prospect was confused by the reflection, in the plate-glass windows, of the people, plants, and ever-shifting patterns of hotel life behind me. Beyond this insubstantial scene, though, I could see the stern outline of the cliffs, the floodlit Cabot Tower on Signal Hill, the white tossing of the ocean breakers, and the slowly moving masthead light of a ship sliding out to sea.

38   The hotel pianist was playing Chopin — and as he played, with the recondite inflections of Newfoundland conversation rising and falling around me, mingled with laughter and the clink of glasses, somehow the riding light of that ship, moving planet-like through the mirror images, brought home to me with a *frisson* the grand poignancy that lies beneath the vivacity of St John's. I thought it sad but exciting, there in the air-conditioned bar.

                                                                                     (1990)

The Writer's Subject

1. Given that the writer finds St. John's "knocked about," poor, and unsophisticated, why does she appear to like it so much?

2. Why does the city strike Morris as "a half-Irish, half-Empire Loyalist backwater of New England"? (para. 22) What attitudes does she detect among the citizens towards Britain and the U.S.?

3. What in Morris's view saves the city from the charge of provincialism? (para. 24)

4. In what ways, according to Morris, is St. John's a memorial to the British Empire? (paras. 19–20)

5. Why, according to Morris, is the "Narrows" such an important feature of St. John's? (para. 36)

6. What does Morris mean by "the grand poignancy that lies beneath the vivacity of St. John's"? (para. 38)

The Writer's Style and Strategy

1. Discuss the relevance of the introductory anecdote about the librarian in St. John's.

2. Why does Morris begin the main part of her essay with the word "Thwack!" (para. 5)? What is the point of her reference to dried cod?

3. Examine some of the terms with which Morris describes St. John's in the first six or seven paragraphs (e.g., "fishy," "quirky," "knocked-about," "punch-drunk," "bruised"), and discuss their appropriateness.

4. What sense does Morris give the reader of what the inhabitants of St. John's are like?

5. Discuss some of the methods that Morris employs to describe the city of St. John's. How does she avoid making her account a dull recital of facts and figures?

6. There is a marked shift in the mood of the essay over the last four paragraphs. Identify the nature of this change, and discuss the possible reasons behind it.

7. The essay sets out to describe a Canadian city. What, directly or indirectly, does it tell us about the writer herself?

Suggested Topics for Writing and Discussion

1. Morris introduces her description of St. John's with a personal anecdote about an encounter with one of the city's inhabitants. Construct your own version of this: write a brief personal account of an incident in which you meet someone who typifies the town or city in which you were brought up or in which you now live.

2. Point out those features (e.g., architecture, history, social institutions) that give the community or neighbourhood in which you live its distinctive character.

3. Choose one notable event in the history of your town or city, and prepare a ten-minute talk for a high school audience.

4. The writer speaks of the peculiarities of Newfoundland dialect. Are there any distinctive features in the vocabulary or idioms of your region?

Specifications for a Hero
by Wallace Stegner

1   In our town, as in most towns, everybody had two names — the one his parents had given him and the one the community chose to call him by. Our nicknames were an expression of the folk culture, and they were more descriptive than honorific. If you were underweight, you were called Skinny or Slim or Sliver; if overweight, Fat or Chubby; if left-handed, Lefty; if spectacled, Four Eyes. If your father was the minister, your name was Preacher Kid, and according to the condition and color of your hair you were Whitey, Blacky, Red, Rusty, Baldy, Fuzzy, or Pinky. If you had a habit of walking girls in the brush after dusk, you were known as Town Bull or T.B. If you were small for your age, as I was, your name was Runt or Peewee. The revelation of your shape at the town swimming hole by the footbridge could tag you for life with the label Birdlegs. The man who for a while ran one of our two grocery stores was universally known as Jew Meyer.

2   Like the lingo we spoke, our nicknames were at odds with the traditional and educational formalisms; along with them went a set of standard frontier attitudes. What was appropriate for Jimmy Craig in his home or in church or in school would have been shameful to Preacher Kid Craig down at the bare-naked hole. When we were digging a cave in the cutbank back of my house, and someone for a joke climbed up on top and jumped up and down, and the roof caved in on P.K. and he had to be dug out and revived by artificial respiration, even P.K. thought the hullabaloo excessive. He did not blame us, and he did not tattle on anyone. His notions of fortitude and propriety — which were at the other end of the scale from those of his parents — would not have let him.

When we first arrived in Whitemud the Lazy-S was still a working   3
ranch, with corrals, and calves, and a bunkhouse inhabited by heroes
named Big Horn, Little Horn, Slivers, Rusty, and Slippers. There was a
Chinese cook named Mah Li, who had been abused in imaginative ways
ever since he had arrived back at the turn of the century. In the first
district poll for a territorial election, in 1902, someone had taken Mah
Li to the polls and enfranchised him on the ground that, having been
born in Hong Kong, he could swear that he was a British subject and
was not an Indian, and was hence eligible to vote. When I knew him, he
was a jabbering, good-natured soul with a pigtail and a loose blue blouse,
and I don't suppose a single day of his life went by that he was not
victimized somehow. He couldn't pass anybody, indoors or out, without having his pigtail yanked or his shirt tails set on fire. Once I saw the
cowboys talk him into licking a frosty doorknob when the temperature
was fifteen or twenty below, and I saw the tears in his eyes, too, after he
tore himself loose. Another time a couple of Scandinavians tried to get
him onto a pair of skis on the North Bench hill. They demonstrated how
easy it was, climbed up and came zipping by, and then offered to help
his toes into the straps. But Mah Li was too many for them that time.
"Sssssssssss!" he said in scorn. "Walkee half a mile back!" When I
was ten or eleven Mah Li was a friend of mine. I gave him suckers I
caught in the river, and once he made me a present of a magpie he had
taught to talk. The only thing it could say was our laundry mark, the
number O Five, but it was more than any other magpie in town could
say, and I had a special feeling for Mah Li because of it. Nevertheless I
would have been ashamed not to take part in the teasing, baiting, and
candy-stealing that made his life miserable after the Lazy-S closed up
and Mah Li opened a restaurant. I helped tip over his backhouse on
Hallowe'en; I was part of a war party that sneaked to the crest of a knoll
and with .22 rifles potted two of his white ducks as they rode a mud
puddle near his shack in the east bend.

The folk culture sponsored every sort of crude practical joke, as it   4
permitted the cruelest and ugliest prejudices and percecutions. Any visible difference was enough to get an individual picked on. Impartially and
systematically we persecuted Mah Li and his brother Mah Jim, Jew
Meyer and his family, any Indians who came down into the valley in their
wobble-wheeled buckboards, anyone with a pronounced English accent
or fancy clothes or affected manners, any crybaby, any woman who kept
a poodle dog and put on airs, any child with glasses, anyone afflicted with
crossed eyes, St. Vitus's dance, feeble-mindedness, or a game leg. Sys-

tematically the strong bullied the weak, and the weak did their best to persuade their persecutors, by feats of courage or endurance or by picking on someone still weaker, that they were tough and strong.

5   Immune, because they conformed to what the folk culture valued, were people with Texas or Montana or merely Canadian accents, people who wore overalls and worked with their hands, people who snickered at Englishmen or joined the bedevilment of Chinamen, women who let their children grow up wild and unwashed. Indignation swept the school one fall day when the Carpenter kids were sent home by the new teacher from Ontario. She sent a note along with them saying they had pediculosis and should not return to school until they were cured. Their mother in bewildered alarm brought them in to the doctor, and when she discovered that pediculosis meant only the condition of being lousy, she had to be restrained from going over and pulling the smart-alec teacher's hair out. We sympathized completely. That teacher never did get our confidence, for she had convicted herself of being both over-cleanly and pompous.

6   Honored and imitated among us were those with special skills, so long as the skills were not too civilized. We admired good shots, good riders, tough fighters, dirty talkers, stoical endurers of pain. My mother won the whole town because once, riding our flighty mare Daisy up Main Street, she got piled hard in front of Christenson's pool hall with half a dozen men watching, and before they could recover from laughing and go to help her, had caught the mare and remounted and ridden off, tightly smiling. The fact that her hair was red did not hurt: among us, red hair was the sign of a sassy temper.

7   She was one of the immune, and so was my father, for both had been brought up on midwestern farms, had lived on the Dakota frontier, and accepted without question — though my mother would have supplemented it — the code of the stiff upper lip. She had sympathy for anyone's weakness except her own; he went strictly by the code.

8   I remember one Victoria Day when there was a baseball game between our town and Shaunavon. Alfie Carpenter, from a riverbottom ranch just west of town, was catching for the Whitemud team. He was a boy who had abused me and my kind for years, shoving us off the footbridge, tripping us unexpectedly, giving us the hip, breaking up our hideouts in the brush, stampeding the town herd that was in our charge, and generally making himself lovable. This day I looked up from something just in time to see the batter swing and a foul tip catch Alfie full in the face. For a second he stayed bent over with a hand over his mouth; I

saw the blood start in a quick stream through his fingers. My feelings were very badly mixed, for I had dreamed often enough of doing just that to Alfie Carpenter's face, but I was somewhat squeamish about human pain and I couldn't enjoy seeing the dream come true. Moreover I knew with a cold certainty that the ball had hit Alfie at least four times as hard as I had ever imagined hitting him, and there he stood, still on his feet and obviously conscious. A couple of players came up and took his arms and he shook them off, straightened up, spat out a splatter of blood and teeth and picked up his mitt as if to go on with the game. Of course they would not let him — but what a gesture! said my envious and appalled soul. There was a two-tooth hole when Alfie said something; he freed his elbows and swaggered to the side of the field. Watching him, my father broke out in a short, incredulous laugh. "Tough kid!" he said to the man next, and the tone of his voice goose-pimpled me like a breeze on a sweaty skin, for in all my life he had never spoken either to or of me in that voice of approval. Alfie Carpenter, with his broken nose and bloody mouth, was a boy I hated and feared, but most of all I envied his competence to be what his masculine and semi-barbarous world said a man should be.

As for me, I was a crybaby. My circulation was poor and my hands always got blue and white in the cold. I always had a runny nose. I was skinny and small, so that my mother anxiously doctored me with Scott's Emulsion, sulphur and molasses, calomel, and other doses. To compound my frail health, I was always getting hurt. Once I lost both big-toe nails in the same week, and from characteristically incompatible causes. The first one turned black and came off because I had accidentally shot myself through the big toe with a .22 short; the second because, sickly thing that I was, I had dropped a ten-pound bottle of Scott's Emulsion on it. 9

I grew up hating my weakness and despising my cowardice and trying to pretend that neither existed. The usual result of that kind of condition is bragging. I bragged, and sometimes I got called. Once in Sunday School I said that I was not afraid to jump off the high diving board that the editor of the Leader had projected out over the highest cutbank. The editor, who had been a soldier and a hero, was the only person in town who dared use it. It did not matter that the boys who called my bluff would not have dared to jump off it themselves. I was the one who had bragged, and so after Sunday School I found myself out on that thing, a mile above the water, with the wind very cold around my knees. The tea-brown whirlpools went spinning slowly around the deep water of the bend, looking as impossible to jump into as if they had been whorls 10 in cement. A half dozen times I sucked in my breath and grabbed my courage with both hands and inched out to the burlap pad on the end of the board. Every time, the vibrations of the board started such sympathetic vibrations in my knees that I had to creep back for fear of falling off. The crowd on the bank got scornful, and then ribald, and then insulting; I could not rouse even the courage to answer back, but went on creeping out, quaking back, creeping out again, until they finally all got tired and left for their Sunday dinners. Then at once I walked out to the end and jumped.

11   I think I must have come down through thirty or forty feet of air, bent over toward the water, with my eyes out on stems like a lobster's, and I hit the water just so, with my face and chest, a tremendous belly-flopper that drove my eyes out through the back of my head and flattened me out on the water to the thickness of an oil film. The air was full of colored lights; I came to enough to realize I was strangling on weed-tasting river water, and moved my arms and legs feebly toward shore. About four hours and twenty deaths later, I grounded on the mud and lay there gasping and retching, sick for the hero I was not, for the humiliation I had endured, for the mess I had made of the jump when I finally made it — even for the fact that no one had been around to see me, and that I would never be able to convince any of them that I really had, at the risk of drowning, done what I had bragged I would do.

12   Contempt is a hard thing to bear, especially one's own. Because I was what I was, and because the town went by the code it went by, I was never quite out of sight of self-contempt or the contempt of my father or Alfie Carpenter or some other whose right to contempt I had to grant. School, and success therein, never fully compensated for the lacks I felt in myself. I found early that I could shine in class, and I always had a piece to speak in school entertainments, and teachers found me reliable at cleaning blackboards, but teachers were women, and school was a woman's world, the booby prize for those not capable of being men. The worst of it was that I liked school, and liked a good many things about the womanish world, but I wouldn't have dared admit it, and I could not respect the praise of my teachers any more than I could that of my music teacher or my mother.

13   "He has the arteestic temperament," said Madame Dujardin while collecting her pay for my piano lessons. "He's sensitive," my mother would tell her friends, afternoons when they sat around drinking coffee and eating Norwegian coffee cake, and I hung around inside, partly for the sake of coffee cake and partly to hear them talk about me. The mo-

ment they did talk about me, I was enraged. *Women* speaking up for me, noticing my "sensitivity," observing me with that appraising female stare and remarking that I seemed to like songs such as "Sweet and Low" better than "Men of Harlech," which was *their* son's favorite — my mother interpolating half with pride and half with worry that sometimes she had to drive me out to play, I'd rather stay in and read Ridpath's *History of the World.* Women giving me the praise I would have liked to get from my father or Slivers or the Assiniboine halfbreed down at the Lazy-S. I wanted to be made of whang leather.

Little as I want to acknowledge them, the effects of those years re- 14
main in me like the beach terraces of a dead lake. Having been weak, and having hated my weakness, I am as impatient with the weakness of others as my father ever was. Pity embarrasses me for the person I am pitying, for I know how it feels to be pitied. Incompetence exasperates me, a big show of pain or grief or any other feeling makes me uneasy, affectations still inspire in me a mirth I have grown too mannerly to show. I cannot sympathize with the self-pitiers, for I have been there, or with the braggarts, for I have been there too. I even at times find myself reacting against conversation, that highest test of the civilized man, because where I came from it was unfashionable to be "mouthy."

An inhumane and limited code, the value system of a life more lim- 15
ited and cruder than in fact ours was. We got most of it by inheritance from the harsher frontiers that had preceded ours — got it, I suppose, mainly from our contacts with what was left of the cattle industry.

So far as the Cypress Hills were concerned, that industry began with 16
the Mounted Police beef herd at Fort Walsh, and was later amplified by herds brought in to feed treaty Indians during the starving winters after 1879. In practice, the Indians ate a good deal of beef that hadn't been intended for them; it took a while to teach them that the white man's spotted buffalo were not fair game when a man was hungry. The raiding of cattle and horse herds was never controlled until the Canadian Indians were moved to reservations far north of the Line after 1882. Nevertheless it was the Indians who first stimulated the raising of cattle on that range, and the departure of the Indians which left the Whitemud River country open to become the last great cattle country.

In some ways, the overlapping of the cattle and homesteading phases 17
of the plains frontier was similar to the overlapping of the horse and gun cultures earlier, and in each case the overlapping occurred latest around the Cypress Hills. Cattle came in from the south, homesteaders from the east and southeast. Among the homesteaders — Ontario men,

Scandinavians and Americans working up from the Dakotas, and Englishmen, Scots, and Ukrainians straight off the immigrant boats — there
was a heavy percentage of greenhorns and city men. Even the experienced dryland farmers from the States were a prosaic and law-abiding
lot by comparison with the cowboys they displaced. As it turned out,
the homesteaders, by appropriating and fencing and plowing the range,
squeezed out a way of life that was better adapted to the country than
their own, and came close to ruining both the cattlemen and themselves
in the process, but that is a later story. What succeeded the meeting and
overlapping of the two cultures was a long and difficult period of adaptation in which each would modify the other until a sort of amalgama-
tion could result. But while the adaptations were taking place, during
the years of uneasy meeting and mixture, it was the cowboy tradition,
the horseback culture, that impressed itself as image, as romance, and
as ethical system upon boys like me. There were both good and bad
reasons why that should have been true.

18   Read the history of the northern cattle ranges in such an anti-Ameri-
can historian as John Peter Turner and you hear that the "Texas men"
who brought the cattle industry to Canada were all bravos, rustlers,
murderers, gamblers, thugs, and highwaymen; that their life was divided
among monte, poker, six-guns, and dancehall girls; and that their law
was the gun-law that they made for themselves and enforced by hand.
Allow sixty or seventy per cent of error for patriotic fervor, and Mr.
Turner's generalizations may be accepted. But it is likewise true that
American cow outfits left their gun-law cheerfully behind them when
they found the country north of the Line well policed, that they cheerfully cooperated with the Mounted Police, took out Canadian brands,
paid for grazing leases, and generally conformed to the customs of the
country. They were indistinguishable from Canadian ranchers, to whom
they taught the whole business. Many Canadian ranches, among them
the 76, the Matador, the Turkey Track, and the T-Down-Bar, were simply Canadian extensions of cattle empires below the border.

19   So was the culture, in the anthropological sense, that accompanied the
cattle. It was an adaptation to the arid Plains that had begun along the Rio
Grande and had spread north, like gas expanding to fill a vacuum, as the
buffalo and Indians were destroyed or driven out in the years following
the Civil War. Like the patterns of hunting and war that had been adopted
by every plains tribe as soon as it acquired the horse, the cowboy culture
made itself at home all the way from the Rio Grande to the North Saskatchewan. The outfit, the costume, the practices, the terminology, the

state of mind, came into Canada ready-made, and nothing they encountered on the northern Plains enforced any real modifications. The Texas men made it certain that nobody would ever be thrown from a horse in Saskatchewan; he would be piled. They made it sure that no Canadian steer would ever be angry or stubborn; he would be o'nery or ringy or on the prod. Bull Durham was as native to the Whitemud range as to the Pecos, and it was used for the same purposes: smoking, eating, and spitting in the eye of a ringy steer. The Stetson was as useful north as south, could be used to fan the fire or dip up a drink from a stream, could shade a man's eyes or be clapped over the eyes of a bronc to gentle him down. Boots, bandanna, stock saddle, rope, the ways of busting broncs, the institution of the spring and fall roundup, the bowlegs in batwing or goatskin chaps — they all came north intact. About the only thing that changed was the name for the cowboy's favorite diversion, which down south they would have called a rodeo but which we called a stampede.

It was a nearly womanless culture, nomadic, harsh, dangerous, es- 20 sentially romantic. It had the same contempt for the dirtgrubbers that Scythian and Cossack had, and Canadian tillers of the soil tended to look upon it with the same suspicion and fear and envy that tillers of the soil have always expressed toward the herdsmen. As we knew it, it had a lot of Confederate prejudices left in it, and it had the callousness and recklessness that a masculine life full of activity and adventure is sure to produce. I got it in my eyes like stardust almost as soon as we arrived in Whitemud, when the town staged its first stampede down in the western bend. Reno Dodds, known as Slivers, won the saddle bronc competition and set me up a model for my life. I would grow up to be about five feet six and weigh about a hundred and thirty pounds. I would be bowlegged and taciturn, with deep creases in my cheeks and a hide like stained saddle leather. I would be the quietest and most dangerous man around, best rider, best shot, the one who couldn't be buffaloed. Men twice my size, beginning some brag or other, would catch my cold eye and begin to wilt, and when I had stared them into impotence I would turn my back contemptuous, hook onto my pony in one bowlegged arc, and ride off. I thought it tremendous that anyone as small and skinny as Slivers could be a top hand and a champion rider. I don't think I could have survived without his example, and he was still on my mind years later when, sixteen years old and six feet tall and weighing a hundred and twenty-five pounds, I went every afternoon to the university gym and worked out on the weights for an hour and ran wind sprints around the track. If I couldn't be big I could be *hard*.

21   We hung around the Lazy-S corrals a good deal that first year or two,
and the cowpunchers, when they had no one else to pester, would egg us
into what they called shit-fights, with green cow manure for snowballs;
or they would put a surcingle around a calf and set us aboard. After my
try I concluded that I would not do any more of it just at that time, and I
limped to the fence and sat on the top rail nursing my sprains and bruises
and smiling to keep from bawling out loud. From there I watched Spot
Orullian, a Syrian boy a couple of years older than I, ride a wildly pitch-
ing whiteface calf clear around the corral and halfway around again, and
get piled hard, and come up wiping the cow dung off himself, swearing
like a pirate. They cheered him, he was a favorite at once, perhaps all the
more because he had a big brown birthmark on his nose and so could be
kidded. And I sat on the corral rail hunching my winglike shoulder-
blades, smiling and smiling and smiling to conceal the black envy that I
knew was just under the skin of my face. It was always boys like Spot
Orullian who managed to be and do what I wanted to do and be.

22   Many things that those cowboys represented I would have done well
to get over quickly, or never catch: the prejudice, the callousness, the
destructive practical joking, the tendency to judge everyone by the same
raw standard. Nevertheless, what they themselves most respected, and
what as a boy I most yearned to grow up to, was as noble as it was
limited. They honored courage, competence, self-reliance, and they
honored them tacitly. They took them for granted. It was their absence,
not their presence, that was cause for remark. Practising comradeship
in a rough and dangerous job, they lived a life calculated to make a
man careless of everything except the few things he really valued.

23   In the fall of 1906 it must have seemed that the cowboy life was certain to last a good while, for the Canadian range still lay wide open,
and stockmen from the western states had prospected it and laid large
plans for moving bigger herds across the Line to escape the nesters and
sheepmen who had already broken up the Montana ranges. Probably
the entire country from Wood Mountain to the Alberta line would have
been leased for grazing, at the favorable Canadian rate of a few cents
an acre, if the winter of 1906–07 had not happened.

24   That winter has remained ever since, in the minds of all who went
through it, as the the measure of catastrophe. Some might cite the winter of 1886–87, the year of the Big Die-Up on the American range, but
that winter did not affect the Whitemud country, where cattle came in
numbers only after 1887. Some who had punched cows in Alberta in
the early days might cast a vote for the fatal Cochran drive of 1881,

when 8,000 out of 12,000 cattle died over by Lethbridge; and some
would certainly, just as weather, mention the April blizzard of 1892, or
the winter that followed it, or the big May blizzard of 1903. But after
1907 no one would seriously value those earlier disasters. The winter
of 1906–07 was the real one, the year of the blue snow. After it, the
leases that might have been taken up were allowed to lapse, the herds
that might have been augmented were sold for what they would bring
— fifteen to twenty dollars a head with suckling calves thrown in. Old
cattlemen who had ridden every range from Texas north took a good
long look around in the spring and decided to retire.

The ranches that survived were primarily the hill ranches with shel- 25
ter plus an access to bench or prairie hay land where winter feed could
be cut. The net effect of the winter of 1906–07 was to make stock farmers out of ranchers. Almost as suddenly as the disappearance of the buffalo, it changed the way of life of the region. A great event, it had the
force in the history of the Cypress Hills country that a defeat in war has
upon a nation. When it was over, the protected Hills might harbor a few
cowboys, and one or two of the big ranches such as the 76 might go on,
but most of the prairie would be laid open to homesteading and another
sort of frontier.

That new frontier, of which my family was a part, very soon squeezed 26
out the Lazy-S. The hay lands in the bottoms were broken up into town
lots, my father was growing potatoes where whitefaces had used to graze,
the punchers were drifting off to Alberta. But while we had them around,
we made the most of them, imitating their talk and their walk and their
songs and their rough-handed jokes; admiring them for the way they tormented Mah Li; hanging around in the shade of the bunkhouse listening
to Rusty, who was supposed to be the second son of an earl, play the
mouth organ; watching the halfbreed Assiniboine braid leather or horse-
hair into halter ropes and hackamores. I heard some stories about the
winter of 1906–07, but I never heard enough. Long afterward, digging
in the middens where historians customarily dig, I found and read some
more, some of them the reminiscences of men I knew. What they record
is an ordeal by weather. The manner of recording is laconic, deceptively
matter of fact. It does not give much idea of how it feels to ride sixty or
eighty miles on a freezing and exhausted pony, or how cold thirty below
is when a fifty-mile wind is driving it into your face, or how demoralizing it is to be lost in a freezing fog where north, south, east, west, even
up and down, swim and shift before the slitted and frost-stuck eyes.

They do not tell their stories in Technicolor; they would not want to 27 seem to adorn a tale or brag themselves up. The calluses of a life of hardship blunt their sensibilities to their own experience. If we want to know what it was like on the Whitemud River range during that winter when the hopes of a cattle empire died, we had better see it through the eyes of some tenderfoot, perhaps someone fresh from the old country, a boy without the wonder rubbed off him and with something to prove about himself. If in inventing this individual I put into him a little of Corky Jones, and some of the boy Rusty whose mouth organ used to sweeten the dusty summer shade of the Lazy-S bunkhouse, let it be admitted that I have also put into him something of myself, the me who sat on a corral bar wetting with spit my smarting skinned places, and wishing I was as tough as Spot Orullian.

(1955)

The Writer's Subject

1. On what principle were nicknames bestowed on the inhabitants of Stegner's town? (para. 1)

2. What does Stegner mean by "the standard frontier attitudes" shown by his companions? (para. 2)

3. Stegner says that the Chinese cook Mah Li was a friend of his, yet he still took part in the "persecution" of Mah Li; why did he do so? (paras. 3 and 4) Which of Stegner's townsfolk were immune from such persecution, and why? (paras. 5–7)

4. What is meant by "the code of the stiff upper lip"? (para. 7) How is this code related to the stories of Alfie Carpenter's accident (para. 8) and Spot Orullian's calf riding? (para. 21) Account for Stegner's feelings of envy.

5. What is the importance of Stegner's anecdote of his dive from the high diving board into the river? (paras. 10–11)

6. Why did the young Stegner find no satisfaction in his success at school, or in the praise of his mother's friends? (paras. 12–13)

7. What were the values of the "horseback culture" that impressed themselves so strongly on Stegner and boys like him? Which of these values does Stegner see as having been potentially damaging? (paras. 17–22)

8. What were the particularly romantic elements of the cattle culture? (para. 20)

9. Why did Stegner see Reno Dodds ("Slivers") as a model? (para. 20)

10. What was the impact of the winter of 1906–07 on the Cypress Hills country and the cattle culture? (paras. 23–26)

The Writer's Style and Strategy

1. Stegner's account forms a chapter of his book *Wolf Willow: A History, a Story and a Memory of the Last Plains Frontier*. What elements of this chapter reflect the book's subtitle?

2. Stegner is writing as an adult recalling his childhood. Choose one or two paragraphs which focus on Stegner's childhood experiences (e.g., paras. 10–11, or 21), and show how he manages to convey a sense of how he felt as a child.

3. How would you characterize the adult Stegner's attitude to the code of the frontier that he admired so much as a child? Where, and how, is that attitude revealed?

4. What function is performed by paragraph 14? How is it related to the preceding paragraphs?

5. What function is performed by paragraph 15?

6. What differences in diction are apparent in paragraphs 21 and 22? How does the style of each paragraph reflect its substance and purpose?

7. Stegner provides portraits of a number of characters, including Mah Li, Alfie Carpenter, Reno Dodds, and Spot Orullian. Choose one of these characters and explain how Stegner's description throws light on Stegner's childhood and the society he grew up in.

Suggested Topics for Writing and Discussion

1. Stegner describes a major change in the region of his childhood, from cattle-ranching and the cowboy culture to "homesteading and another sort of frontier." Find out what you can about the significant changes that have taken place in the neighbourhood or region in which you grew up. What gains or losses have the changes brought, in your view?

2. Stegner specifies the qualities that were demonstrated by the heroes of his childhood. Write an essay in which you use anecdote to describe the childhood heroes of your neighbourhood or region. In what ways are your "specifications" similar to or different from Stegner's?

3. Stegner describes at length his mortifying experience on the diving board. Re-create an event in your own childhood which caused you extreme embarrassment, fear, or humiliation. What feelings about the event do you have now as you look back on it?

4. What, in your view, are the qualities that constitute true heroism? What model would you offer for the admiration of children today?

Women in Society

How Many Feminists Does It Take to Change a Light Bulb?

Power, Politics, and Women's Humor

by Regina Barreca

Learning the Hard Way

When I started my first year as a student at Dartmouth College, there 1
were four men for every woman. I thought I had it made. Dartmouth
had only recently admitted women, and the administration thought it
best to get the alumni accustomed to the idea by sneaking us in a few at
a time. With such terrific odds in my favor socially, how could I lose?
I'd dated in high school and although I wasn't exactly Miss Budweiser,
I figured I'd have no problem getting a date every Saturday night. But I
noticed an unnerving pattern. I'd meet a cute guy at a party and talk for
a while. We would then be interrupted by some buddy of his who would
drag him off to another room to watch a friend of theirs "power-boot"
(the local vernacular for "projectile vomiting"), and I realized that the
social situation was not what I had expected.

Then somebody explained to me that on the Dartmouth campus 2
"They think you're a faggot if you like women more than beer." This
statement indicated by its very vocabulary the advanced nature of the
sentiment behind it. If a guy said he wanted to spend the weekend with
his girlfriend, for example, he'd be taunted by his pals, who would yell
in beery bass voices "Whatsa matter with you, Skip? We're gonna get
plowed, absolutely blind this weekend, then we're *all* gonna power-

boot. And you wanna see that broad again? Whaddayou, a faggot or something?"

3   It turned out that the male-female ratio did not prove to be the marvelous bonus I had anticipated. But still I figured that the school was good enough to justify spending the next few years getting down to studying and forgoing a wild social life. I thought it would all work out, that at least I would be accepted in my classes as a good student and get through the next couple of years without too much worry or trouble. Okay, I told myself, I could live with that and found in fact that dating guys from other schools was a healthy practice anyway.

4   But the real shock came in the classroom, where I was often one of two or three women. One professor, I remember, always prefaced calling on me or any other woman in the class by asking "Miss Barreca, *as a woman*, what is your reading of this text?" I was profoundly embarrassed to be asked my opinion as a woman, since it seemed somehow less authoritative than being asked my opinion as a student or as a "general" reader. At first, I jokingly replied that I would be happy to answer "as a person," but that it was hard for me to answer as a woman. When the professor didn't so much as smile, I knew that tactic wouldn't work. Every time I raised my hand to answer a question, I was asked my opinion *as a woman*. It frustrated and angered me, because I wanted to be treated as an individual and not as a representative of a group.

Just Like a Woman

5   It took months to understand that, in the eyes of this teacher, I'd always be a "miss" rather than just another, ordinary student. When I realized that there was no alternative, I figured I'd go with it, exaggerate the situation enough so that I could at least enjoy myself. So I started prefacing every answer with the phrase "As I woman, I think Shakespeare means ... ," "As a woman, it strikes me that Tennyson's point is ... " But then I figured, why stop at this? I started to say "As a woman, I think the weather's rather cold for June." "As a woman, I think I'll have the meatloaf for dinner." "As a woman, I think I'll go to bed early tonight." It started out as a joke, but as it caught on (a number of my friends started to use the same strategy to make the professors and guys in general hear how their remarks sounded), we started to examine further. Maybe we really were always speaking as a woman. Maybe there was no such thing as speaking as "just" a person. Maybe we always spoke as women whenever we spoke. Maybe this joke wasn't such a joke.

So that even as I stopped saying "As I woman, I believe such-and-   6
such," I started thinking it. It occurred to me that nothing was neuter or
neutral. I saw that my responses were in part determined by the fact of
my gender — as well as by other factors, like my class and ethnicity. I
didn't read novels about war in the same way a man would, for example, since I hadn't been brought up to consider going to war as a soldier
as a possible future for myself. I hadn't played war games as a kid, I didn't
find the idea of war engaging. It did not have "universal appeal," since it
didn't appeal to me, a narcissistic but nevertheless compelling argument.
In the same way that the male students complained that Jane Austen was
obviously a second-rate writer because all she was interested in was
marriage (Mark Twain once said that it was "a pity they let her die a
natural death"), so I decided to assert that Hemingway's concern for
bullfighting was no concern for an intelligent, insightful woman. Of what
interest is bullfighting to the contemporary female reader? Hemingway
was therefore second-rate, by their definition, since his subject matter had
limited appeal and seemed gender specific. I learned to answer "Of
course" when asked whether I responded to things as a female. I learned
to accept that and even enjoyed discovering the ways in which my viewpoint differed from the perspective offered by my male peers.

How Dare You Call Me a Feminist!

But even understanding that the world identified me first as a woman   7
and only secondly as anything else didn't stop me from being horrified
the first time somebody called me a "feminist." I thought being a feminist meant I couldn't wear lipstick or crave men with small behinds. I
thought that "feminist" meant I couldn't send Peanuts cards to guys who
I was afraid wouldn't call back, or buy stockings with seams. I thought
"feminist" meant no more steamy flirtations or prolonged shopping trips.
I thought it meant braided hair and short nails, maybe mandatory tofu. I
certainly associated feminism with humorless, dour, and — worst of all
— unblinkingly earnest women. That was because I was accepting the
male version of things, which was sort of like believing the mouse's
version of the cat, since it entailed being given access to a vision that
could see nothing besides teeth and claws.

I was warned about so-called feminists. I was told by boyfriends,   8
relatives, professors, and other disreputable sources that such women
were ambitious, sharp-tongued, a little too smart for their own good.
They told me that only women who couldn't get laid got political. They

told me what was perhaps the biggest and most interesting lie of all: that independence and ambition were unattractive in a woman. They also suggested, subtly but seriously, that too much of a sense of humor in a woman made her unattractive (a comment to which the comedian Elayne Boosler would reply "Comedy is very, very sexy when it's done right"). Luckily, during a moment that eclipsed all earlier illumination, I heard a female graduate student repeat a wonderful line from the writer Robin Morgan, "*We* are the women that men have warned us about." It was as if the little light bulb that appeared over Bugs Bunny's head when he got an idea suddenly appeared over mine. It seemed unnerving, actually, that I was gazing reprovingly at all those qualities that I myself possessed. I was certainly ambitious, ready to speak and eager to defend my position on a subject. I liked being a woman, was proud of my femininity, and believed myself to be equal to any task set before me by society — at least as well equipped to deal with it as any guy I sat next to in class (he could no more skin a bison than I could, and I could probably defend myself on Tenth Avenue more ably than he).

9   So, when I really thought about it, I was already a feminist no matter what I chose to call myself. When I looked around, I saw a lot of smart, funny women who also fit the bill. We were all feminists, whether or not we'd admitted it aloud before. It was sort of like admitting we were secretly Bad Girls, and for me the admission held the same sort of delightful relief. Oh, is *that* what I am? Is this what the word means, is this what the name names? Is this what a feminist is? Oh good!

This Is What a Feminist Looks Like

10 It's like when Gloria Steinem was told on her fortieth birthday "You don't look forty," to which she replied, "This is what forty looks like." When I was told after that moment of revelation, "You don't look/act/ speak like a feminist," I answered, "*This* is what a feminist looks/acts/ speaks like." These old narrow ideas of the feminist as a dour, sour-faced woman have got to go. Feminists are not a lonely tribe of women fenced off from the rest of society. Feminists read cookbooks and clip coupons from Sunday supplements. Feminists like to dance, flirt, and wear high heels, often doing all three at the same time. Feminists can like men — and enjoy the process of liking individual men for their own worth instead of valuing all men simply because they're male. Feminists enjoy the company of other women and value the company of other

women. Feminists don't wish they were men; they celebrate their womanhood.

Nicole Hollander had Sylvia's daughter pose the eternal question "Ma, 11 do you think I can be a feminist and still like men?" Sylvia replies, as she always does, in unequivocating terms: "Sure. Just like you can be a vegetarian and like fried chicken." While Hollander's example is wonderfully funny, it also indicates the way in which women struggle with the dos and don'ts of feminism. The point of feminism is not to alienate men, but for women to focus on our own concerns and needs, to establish our own values. These may or may not coincide with the already established values of our dominant culture, just as our concerns and needs may or may not fold neatly into a relationship. The point is to work on making decisions based on choices that are really choices instead of following a script — in other words, and in the terms of this book's central argument, it means learning to laugh at what we find funny instead of just following along with the laugh track.

I see, rather remarkably, my female students going through the same 12 sorts of trials and self-examinations today in spite of the fifteen years of feminism that have passed. Some of these women students are planning to go to medical school. Some are engineering majors. They are track stars or nationally ranked basketball players. These young women certainly work hard, compete fiercely, and are not embarrassed about admitting that their goals are high. They work to put themselves through school. Most of them aren't considering getting married until they're several years into their chosen professions. Most of them leave home after graduation to make their way in cities across the country and to find interesting, challenging jobs.

Yet when I ask how many of them consider themselves feminists, 13 only about a third in any one class will dare to raise their hands. These women may not be afraid of getting bad scores on the LSATs or GREs, but they're afraid of not getting a date. They can be independent, intelligent, and proud to be women. But a little word like "feminism" scares them. One girl, a student who'd taken two women-and-literature classes with me, said that she loved the material, that the books had changed how she thought about herself and her relationships with men. We were having coffee in my office, discussing the subversion of the marriage plot in the contemporary woman's novel, when I mentioned something about being pleased that her feminist perspective was being finely delineated by her careful work on the novel. "Oh, but I'm not a feminist," she said, surprising me. "I don't like that word." I gulped, and felt that, whatever work I'd done in class, I'd obviously left out a crucial discussion.

14   Why are so many women afraid to call themselves feminists?

The F Word

15   Catharine R. Stimpson wrote an article for *Ms.* in 1987 about how important it is for women to learn to say the "F Word" in public. Stimpson, who is the dean of the graduate school at Rutgers University, was of course referring to the word "feminism" when she used the term the "F Word." We know well enough that nobody's embarrassed to say the word "fuck" anymore, but a lot of women are still hesitant to say the word "feminism" in mixed company — as if saying "Yes, I'm a feminist" is much more unladylike than telling somebody, for example, to "fuck off."

16   The trouble is that, to a number of people, the two phrases are synonymous, which is a great pity. Stimpson suggests that if women continue to change in a positive way, then "people will be able to say 'feminist' as casually as they now say 'wife' or 'kid' or 'snack'"; she ends her article by calling for feminists to use "more audacity, more humor, when we speak of feminism." Stimpson once showed me how well and with what humor feminists deal with uncomfortable situations by having the good humor to joke me out of the horror I felt at having misspelled both her names — no easy trick when you think about it — in an article I'd published. She looked at me sternly, then laughed, and the laughter relieved me of the weight of my foolishness, because she obviously understood how bad I'd already made myself feel about it. It was a generous, welcoming gesture.

17   Most of feminism is made up of just such gestures. The last thing feminism is about is exclusion. Feminists can be defined as those women and men who recognize that the earth doesn't revolve around anybody's son — or around any one group. In a collection of essays on women's humor titled *Last Laughs: Perspectives on Women and Comedy*, Fay Weldon quotes this old joke: "Question: How many radical feminists does it take to change a light bulb? Answer: That's not funny!" Weldon then goes on to say that humor acts as a kind of shorthand; it "saves me from writing a long paragraph about how feminists get accused of not being able to make jokes, and a few of us certainly can't, which makes a few of us uneasy, which is why it's a joke in the first place."

18   When the radical feminist writer Andrea Dworkin writes "I'm a femi-

nist. Not the fun kind," I always feel apologetic about replying "I'm a feminist too, but actually I am the fun kind," because we sometimes have to worry about seeming too frivolous to be good feminists. (Apparently Dworkin is actually a warm, funny woman, someone who does use humor to make her point when she appears in public.) The writer Kate Clinton has come up with a compact word for feminist humorists — "fumerists" — because it captures the idea of being funny and wanting to burn the house down all at once.

Feminist humor, according to Clinton, "is about making light in this   19 land of reversals, where we are told as we are laughing, tears streaming down our faces, that we have no sense of humor." She goes on to say that "Men have used humor against women for so long — we know implicitly who is the butt of their jokes — that we do not trust humor. Masculine humor is deflective. It allows denial of responsibility, the oh-I-was-just-kidding disclaimer. It is escapist, something to gloss over and get through the hard times, without ever having to do any of the hard work of change. Masculine humor is essentially not about change."

The Difference Between Revolt and Revolution

The difference, in fact, between men's humor and women's humor seems   20 to be the difference between revolt and revolution. Masculine humor has of course included digs at the conventions of the world, poked fun at the institutions and establishments, but without the truly anarchic edge that characterizes feminine humor. Women's humor calls into question the largest issues, questions the way the world is put together. Granted, some humor by male writers does the same — Woody Allen comes to mind — but whereas such humor is not a hallmark of male humor, it is characteristic of women's humor.

Agnes Repplier, an American essayist born in 1855, argues, "Humor   21 distorts nothing, and only false gods are laughed off their earthly pedestals." In other words, an essentially sound target will not be damaged by humor; humor, as we've seen, depends on the perceived righting of an injustice. This is one reason women's humor does deal with the most fundamental concepts in our culture. Women's humor has a particular interest in challenging the most formidable structures, because they keep women from positions of power. Women's humor is about women speaking up. Women's humor takes subjects traditionally regarded as beyond joking for its subject matter. Repplier also said that "The worst in life, we are told, is compatible with the best in art. So, too, the worst in life is compatible with the best in humor." The poet Marianne Moore, born in 1887, wrote that "Humor saves a few steps; it saves years," and Katherine Mansfield, born in 1888, suggested in her journal that "To be wildly enthusiastic, or deadly serious — both are wrong. Both pass. One must keep ever present a sense of humor."

22   Professor Judy Little, whose scholarly book *Comedy and the Woman Writer* is one of the landmarks in the study of women and humor, suggests that a woman writer such as Virginia Woolf is, in fact, far more subversive than her male counterpart James Joyce, because Woolf calls into question not only the rules of religion but the need for religion at all. Little's argument suggests that, whereas a male writer might rave against the basic tenets of a system of beliefs, his female counterpart will be asking whether any belief system should be in power. Her question will be far more subversive than his because she's asking for the destruction of the system rather than for a change in it. Some male writers are, of course, subversive, and some women writers are conservative, but these examples do not render false the claim. Women's humor is irreverent, not only about one's self and about the details of life, but about the very "givens" of life itself. One could say, for example, that while some men do it — use humor that is truly subversive — some of the time, a great number of women do it most of the time. "The reason husbands and wives do not understand each other is because they belong to different sexes," said the early feminist Dorothy Dix. Putting the question of gender-specific perspectives into such simple terms makes the whole idea of a universal vision seem, well, funny.

23   Much male humor is aggressive and attempts to be controlling, but, for all its yelling and punching, ultimately masculine comedy reinforces generally held belief systems, leaving general rules and regulations untouched except at the most superficial level. Male comedy is directed toward and assumes a predominantly male audience.

24   While this is not surprising, it is still a shock to those people who would like to continue to see comedy as "universal" instead of gender specific. But, interestingly, even the male comics see their work in gender-specific terms, at least insofar as they see their success linked to their "dicks," seeing even the microphone they work with as a "dick substitute." According to Betsy Borns's book *Comic Lives*, they see their comedy in terms of virility and impotence. They see some essentially male quality as the element that allows them to control the audience.

25   Robin Tyler, a feminist stand-up comic, responds to this idea of see-

ing success in comedy in male-defined terms. "The mind is much more powerful than the prick," suggests Tyler, adding " — and the mind doesn't go down in two minutes." Tyler's point seems to be that women's power is not derived from the same sources as men's, but that the female sources might in fact be richer and more effective, especially with a predominantly female audience.

The Split Between the Real and the Ideal

When Nicole Hollander's cartoon suggested that the hallmark of wom-   26
en's humor is its focus on the split between the real and the ideal, she touched on what is a central distinction between women's comedy and men's comedy. Whereas men occasionally challenge the idea of reality or the conventions of society, women do it regularly. Whereas men occasionally seem to subvert the standing order, women make subversion their business. When I think of the subversive nature of women's humor, I think of Jane Wagner and Lily Tomlin creating the character of Trudy in their play *The Search for Signs of Intelligent Life in the Universe*. A bag lady in an umbrella hat, Trudy knows that she'd "got the kind of madness Socrates talked about, 'A divine release of the soul from the yoke of custom and convention.'" Trudy is a wonderful link between the hysterically funny woman and the one who's simply labeled "hysterical." Trudy says "Maybe I didn't have a breakdown — maybe I had a breakthrough." This character knows that consensus doesn't create truth, that just because everybody believes something doesn't make it true — think of the world being flat, or of women being told they have no sense of humor.

Whether you choose to call it feminist humor or feminine humor, or   27
"just" humor, if you're a woman, then you're making a woman's joke, laughing a woman's laugh. I would say that nearly all women's humor is in some way feminist humor (with the exception of those early, self-deprecating "I'm so ugly ... " jokes associated with the very earliest comedians). I'd say that women's humor is almost by definition feminist because, in the same way that we can't help but speak as women, we can't help but be funny as women. We're inevitably informed by our gender. If you're using any of the strategies of humor we've discussed earlier, then I'd say that you're using feminist humor, because you're offering some sort of challenge to the system. You're taking on a new perspective, offering your statement or question when the system would encourage you to be silent. When you make a joke, when you

laugh with your mouth open, or when you refuse to laugh at something you don't find funny even though you know you "should" laugh, then you're making a radical gesture. You're ignoring the script that tells you when to speak (almost never) and when to laugh (when someone else tells you to).

28   I'd say that anytime a woman breaks through a barrier set by society, she's making a feminist gesture of a sort, and every time a woman laughs, she's breaking through a barrier. Kate Clinton sees humor as a way into change. She writes, "Humor leads the way; it moves us past those in-bred, ingrained resistances." Clinton goes on to describe her version of feminist humor as being like lichen, "secreting tiny amounts of acid, year after year, eating into the rock. Making places for water to gather, to freeze and crack the rocks a bit. Making soil, making way for grasses to grow. ... It is the lichen which begins the splitting apart of the rocks, the changing of the shoreline, the shape of the earth. Feminist humor is serious, and it is about changing the world."

29   The comedian Joy Behar stated in an interview her belief that "It's important for a woman's point of view to be heard. People say to me, 'Do you speak as a woman?' No, I speak as a man. Of course I speak as a woman! What a stupid question that is. I'm a female. What? Am I supposed to speak as if I had a schlong? (That's Italian for 'facial hair')." Behars's point is that to ask someone if she "speaks as a woman" is as nonsensical as asking if someone speaks as "someone who lives in the twentieth century." There are certain assumptions that appear fairly basic. When women speak, we speak as women. We may not speak for all women, we're not necessarily representative of anyone besides ourselves, but when we speak it makes sense that we can't help but speak as who and what we are.

"It's So Hard to Be a Feminist If You Are a Woman"

30   Being a feminist raises complex issues even for those women who are committed to the cause of women's rights. Jane O'Reilly, in an essay reprinted in a collection of women's humor called *Pulling Our Own Strings*, writes, "I am often tired of being a feminist. I'm not even sure I am a feminist." O'Reilly wonders whether she can be a feminist and still be worried about her family, her appearance, her femininity, and with a sigh decides, "It's so hard to be a feminist if you are a woman."

31   But finally O'Reilly comes to the conclusion that it "helps to laugh. There is, after all, a certain inherent humor in being on the cutting edge

of a social revolution. It is funny, actually, to be unsure of what you feel more offended by: the guests ignoring your opinions or not complimenting you on your soufflé." In this sentence, O'Reilly offers a wonderful example of the bind that so many of us find ourselves in: we want to be congratulated equally on our "traditionally feminine" skills or attributes (being a terrific cook, having terrific legs) and our newly acquired achievements (being made a partner in the firm or being elected mayor). Since women have been continually adding on to the list of what we have to do without taking anything off the list (you're still supposed to be a terrific cook even after you've been made a partner), we're unsure what we want to have praised first.

This became clear to me when a group of friends and I were watch-   32
ing the 1989 Miss America pageant. We were applauding and eating even more popcorn and making more sundaes than usual, because the revised format included rather challenging questions for the contestants — such as asking that they discuss the level of responsibility of the government in providing equal access to the disabled. It wasn't exactly the same as watching Geraldine Ferraro get nominated, but after twenty-five years of being glued to these pageants (against all principles, of course) it seemed as if the criteria were being adapted to indicate the changing values of contemporary society. All of the young women gave intelligently reasoned, even well-researched answers, whereas in the past their predecessors had been asked only whether they thought world peace would be a good idea (acceptable answer: "Yes, I think so, honestly"). Hooray, we thought, they're not treating these women as body parts, but instead asking them to use their heads. Imagine our surprise when, as soon as the contestant answered the question, she had to walk across the floor and present her little behind to the judges so that they could grade her ass as well as her answer. "Great," my friend Wendy wailed, "now you're supposed to have an amazing rear and a good mind. I really thought if you had one you couldn't be expected to have the other. I surrender. I'm putting a white flag on my ass so they can tell." We broke out another bottle of Kahlua and opened another gallon of Breyer's in response. "If we were real feminists," said Bonnie through a mouthful of white Russian, "we wouldn't even be watching this, and we certainly wouldn't care what we looked like when we left the room because we'd be so sure that we made an overwhelmingly positive impression when we entered it." But then we were back to the funny, unnerving response "But this *is* what feminists act like — at least sometimes."

Toward a Funny Feminism?

33 Feminism, in fact, seems to be increasingly tied to humor. The leaders of the women's movement have historically harnessed humor for their purposes, as Professor Nancy Walker of Vanderbilt University has so carefully documented in her book *A Very Serious Thing*. Walker shows us that women's political and domestic humor has always been an effective challenge to long-held and oppressive ideas. Yet she is compelled to point out that, despite an underground tradition, women's humor "has been largely omitted from the official canon ... been allowed to go out of print, to disappear from all but the dusty reaches of library shelves." Walker gives us insights not only into the history of women's humor but also into the reasons that our humor is not often read as being as subversive as it really is. She suggests that what appears to be submission to the stereotypes of mother, housewife, or bimbo is often a thinly veiled indictment of the society that trivializes a woman's life.

34 Women's humor is often directed at the bizarre value systems that have been regarded as "normal" for so long that it is difficult to see how ridiculous they really are. When Gabrielle Burton, addressing the Symposium on Women's Mental Health in 1976, said that "We'll all be better off when word gets around that cleaning a toilet produces no more and no less than a clean toilet; it does not produce strength of character, nor is it interesting work," she pointed out that what is considered valuable work for a woman is not always genuinely valuable. Burton wasn't making a joke per se, but by simply emphasizing the sorts of situations women find themselves in, she was uncovering and therefore making humorous an unreasonable arrangement. Sometimes just the very act of naming something, saying something out loud, admitting something about how we view our lives is enough to make us laugh. It's so absurd, we realize as soon as we see it clearly, that it's funny.

35 There seems to be a growing awareness among feminists that, if the women's movement is going to survive, it has to gather the courage to laugh at itself and the world that made half the human race the "other" half. Also there is an awareness that feminism must embrace women who have, for whatever reasons, adopted the traditional script as well as the ones who have chosen more radical departures. A shared territory of humor can be one place where various groups of women can meet. When women laugh together, we underscore the ways in which our experiences of the world connect us rather than divide us.

36 Women are beginning to complain that men don't get the joke, that

they can't understand what's so funny. Elayne Boosler talks about the kind of humor that men can't get: "Men can say things in a department store that women can't say. When you're shopping with them and encourage them to try on a pair of trousers with some style, maybe a pair designed after 1978, men can say, 'But I already have a pair of black pants.' And men say things like, 'But you already own a pair of earrings just like the ones you're buying.'" Men, Boosler points out, will not understand about the need to save "nice" shopping bags from expensive stores and fold them neatly into exactly the right lines; the women in the audience laugh in recognition, whereas the men whisper "Why *do* you save those bags?" But, even concerning larger questions, women may laugh at issues men consider off limits — like the idea of men crying. Now, we know that men are "allowed" to cry, but it is like one of Jane Austen's truths universally acknowledged that women do not have contempt for men who cry but rather that women consider men who cry to be particularly dangerous, and so a fit subject for humor. Nora Ephron writes that we should " ... beware of the man who cries. It's true that men who cry are sensitive to and in touch with feelings, but the only feelings they tend to be sensitive to and in touch with are their own." Women may laugh at these passages because they have experienced the dangerous, vulnerable man; men usually react very badly to crying jokes and cannot see any humor in them. Boosler can count on the laughter of the women in the audience even at the expense of their male companions. There's no need, as there was for Anne Beatts ten years ago, to leave off the references that only women will get. In fact, when Boosler discusses shopping, she doesn't deprecate it as some trivial activity. She places it into a political framework. "For a woman who's spent her day making sixty-five cents on a man's dollar in some demeaning, low-level job, it's an amazing experience to walk into a place and have someone say to her 'How can *I* help *you*?'"

When women laugh together — like the hooker, socialite, and bag 37 lady at the end of *The Search for Signs of Intelligent Life in the Universe* — we recognize our similarities instead of focusing on our differences. The novelist and essayist Marilyn French in the afterword to *Intelligent Life* explains, "A major criticism leveled at feminist art by masculinists (male or female) is that it tends to belabor its points rather than simply assume them. But feminist art has to belabor its points — has to inform its audience that everything that exists is interconnected ... that body and emotion are as important as mind, and that these three are more important than domination — because these ideas diverge from the mainstream. [*Intelligent Life*] is the first work I know of that simply takes it as a given that a mass audience will accept feminist attitudes."

38   When we laugh at one of the characters' description of her favorite vibrator as "a sort of Hamburger Helper for the boudoir" and her argument for its positive benefits — "Ladies, it simply takes the guesswork out of making love. 'But doesn't it kill romance?' you say. And I say, 'What doesn't?'" — we find a moment during which we share a witty denial that women are romantic, unworldly, and easily pleased.

39   When a radical, separatist feminist from San Francisco can laugh at the same material that amuses a born-again homemaker from Iowa, we've located a nexus point where the concerns of women converge. In other words, is it possible for Gloria Steinem and Jeane Kirkpatrick to laugh at the same material? It is possible that, being successful in their own right, both Steinem and Kirkpatrick would laugh at Miss Manners's (Judith Martin's) advice to a reader whose concern was this: "As a businessman, how do I allow a businesswoman to pay for my lunch?" Miss Manners's typically impeccable reply: "With credit card or cash, as she prefers." Or they might agree with Jill Ruckelshaus's observation: "It occurred to me when I was thirteen and wearing white gloves and Mary Janes and going to dancing school, that no one should have to move backwards all their lives."

40   Is it possible, finally, for the Bad Girl and the Good Girl to laugh at the same time and at the same thing without one worrying about appearing nerdy and the other worrying about appearing degenerate? It appears that humor offers the possibility for the more conservative and the more radical among us to come to some agreement. We seem to be moving closer together in what we consider appropriate material for women's laughter.

41   Television has changed so much that in an episode of the highly successful program *Murphy Brown*, Candice Bergen can say that she's going to start her own country and describe it in the following terms: "Women only. Two men to do the electrical and the plumbing. Maybe one guy to open jars." Mainstream television programs can now employ humor that is cunningly close to the more outrageous humor used by people like Nicole Hollander. Hollander's character Sylvia responds to a man's apparently rhetorical question "What would you do without us?" with the statement "What would the world be like without men? Free of crime and full of fat, happy women." None of this is very far from the writings of the radical feminist writer Mary Daly, a professor at Boston College, whose treatise on theological and academic systems,

Gyn/Ecology, asks "Why has it seemed 'appropriate' in this culture that the plot of a popular book and film [*The Exorcist*] centers around a Jesuit who 'exorcises' a girl who is 'possessed'? Why is there no book or film about a woman who exorcises a Jesuit?"

At one point, Mary Daly addressed the question of women's humor   42 directly. "For example," writes Daly, "the cliché 'She lacks a sense of humor' — applied by men to every threatening woman — is one basic 'electrode' embedded ... deeply ... into the fearful foreground of women's psyches. ... The comment is urbane, insidious. It is ... devastating if believed. It is [a device] used especially against the wittiest women, who are dismissed as 'sharp-tongued.'" Daly's fiercely militant book is also extremely witty, undermining on every page the possible assertion that a radical feminist is necessarily humorless.

One intriguing aspect of the heightening feminist awareness of the   43 last few years is the way in which certain things that would have been perfectly acceptable a while back instantly become the subject not only of outrage but of humor — there are incidents that become comic just because they are no longer "naturally" acceptable. For example, Time Inc. ran a full-page ad on the back page of *The New York Times* that claimed "You don't build a company like this with lace on your underwear." Female executives, whether they sported lacy drawers or not, were at first horrified and then laughed hysterically over the mind-set that would produce such obviously outdated, inappropriate copy. The ad became an instant "inside" joke among the thousands of high-powered and ambitious women reading their copy of the *Times* before meeting their clients, workers, and colleagues. One highly placed executive told me that there were more conference calls made up of laughing women that morning than she imagined possible. Everybody was calling everybody else to share the moment that showed both how far we've come (at least it was clearly and obviously a bad, failed approach, so bad it was funny) and how far we have yet to go (enough people in a major corporation approved of that copy for it to go to press in the first place).

The same executive friend told me that the incident reminded her of   44 the uproar that occurred when, several years ago, a copy of the Sears Roebuck catalogue mistakenly included a photograph of a male underwear model whose penis was clearly visible through the flap of his Y front. "Only in this case," she said, referring to the *Times* ad, "they were only waving their penis around metaphorically." Time Inc. subsequently apologized for any possible offense caused by the ad. Since the company does have an excellent track record when it comes to employing

and promoting women, it seemed like a good idea to accept its apology
and carry on.

45   The important aspect of this story, however, is the idea that women
in positions of authority spontaneously and effectively manipulated into
humor what would once have been an ordinary sexist remark. These
women used the sexism of the ad against the perpetrators by laughing
them out of their sanctimonious self-assurance. Surely the folks who
placed the ad thought it was clubby and "only-boys-know-the-game" to
make a remark that equates economic power with jockey shorts. It took,
once again, a sort of emperor's-new-clothes mentality on the part of the
women in the business community to say "Nope, this is not going to
work, guys. It's actually *so* far off the mark that it's really funny." These
women had arrived at the point where they knew that their position was
unassailable, and they used humor to solidify their camaraderie while
at the same time turning their antagonists' attempt at humor against them.
"When you're in the head office, you can bet that you'll wear whatever
panties you please," said my executive friend with a laugh.

How Far Can We Go?

46   "How much fame, money, and power does a woman have to achieve
on her own before you can punch her in the face?" writes P. J.
O'Rourke, whose popular book *Modern Manners* was published in
1983. Is this funny? Are we still supposed to tolerate such a remark
because it's — ha ha, get it? — delivered as a joke? It is still considered funny, we must remind ourselves when we're starting to feel com-
placent about our strides forward, to debase women's accomplishments
and ambitions. The hidden anger of the supposedly sophisticated man
can be more damaging than the overt degradation of comics like Clay
and Kinison. The group that thinks it's okay to write advertising copy
about lacy underwear also thinks it's healthy to vent a little anger in
the manner of Ralph Kramden ("One of these days, right in the kisser")
toward women in power.

47   O'Rourke's implied question is "When is a woman accomplished
enough to be considered a man?" since fame, money, and power are all
identified as male characteristics. Any woman who has these, in other
words, should be prepared to step outside for a fistfight. Are women
trying to be men? As one piece of popular graffiti has answered this
question, "Women who aspire to be as good as men lack ambition." One
appropriate response to such a question was the one given by Charlotte

Whitten, a Canadian politician. Whitten, former mayor of Ottawa, coined the now widely quoted statement that posits "Whatever women do they must do twice as well as men to be thought half as good. Luckily, this is not difficult." Nicole Hollander has Sylvia listening to a television commentator explaining that "Man is the hunter and woman is the civilizing influence, and when women abandon that role, men become ...," and Sylvia supplies the ending to that sentence by chiming in, " ... cranky, and start wars." But perhaps one of Hollander's most astute comments on the topic of the world's perceptions of women's roles is the one where a commentator says that "Women with names like Dawn and Cheryl have less of a chance for success in business than women with names like ... ," and Sylvia fills in, " ... Roger and Bill."

In such a cartoon, Hollander shows us through her humor that when women are refused power, it has more to do with the system than with the women. The political nature of so much women's humor supports Elayne Boosler's assertion that "the best who stand up, stand up for something." A generation earlier, Dorothy Parker made a distinction between wit and wisecracking: "Wit has truth in it; wisecracking is simply calisthenics with words." 48

(1991)

The Writer's Subject

1. What is the relevance to Barreca's topic of her anecdote about the male students on the Dartmouth campus? (paras. 1–3)

2. Why was Barreca frustrated and angered to be asked her opinion "as a woman"? (para. 4) What strategy did she use to ridicule such an attitude?

3. What did Barreca learn about the conditioning of her responses? (paras. 5–7)

4. Why was Barreca so horrified at the thought of being labelled a feminist? (paras. 7–8) What helped her to view the term in a positive light?

5. What, according to Barreca, is "the point of feminism"? (para. 11) Do you agree with the definitions she provides?

6. Why, in Barreca's view, is good humour so important to feminism? (paras. 16–19)

7. What are the chief differences between men's humour and women's humour, as noted by Barreca? (paras. 20–26) How are these differences manifested?

8. Why, according to the writer, is women's humour almost always feminist humour? (para. 27)

9. What is Barreca's point in describing the 1989 Miss America pageant? (para. 32)

10. Why do women consider men who cry to be "particularly dangerous"? (para. 36)

11. How does humour help to bring together the conservative woman and the radical woman, according to Barreca? (paras. 35–40)

12. Why were female executives so amused by the ad placed in the *New York Times* by Time Inc.? What did the ad reveal about the male-dominated world of business? (paras. 43–45)

The Writer's Style and Strategy

1. Comment on Barreca's title.

2. What are the implications of Barreca's statement "I thought I had it made" in the opening paragraph? What does the statement reflect about a single woman's expectations at the time Barreca went to college?

3. How does Barreca's use of slang in paras. 1 and 2 contribute to her construction of the environment at Dartmouth?

4. Discuss Barreca's use of writings by other feminist authors as a means of strengthening her own arguments.

5. Discuss Barreca's different levels of tone. What effects does she aim for by shifts in tone? What kind of audience would she seem to be addressing?

6. Explain the analogy in para. 28, between feminist humour and lichen.

7. Discuss Barreca's use of example and illustration to support her arguments.

Suggested Topics for Discussion and Writing

1. Using whatever sources are available to you, compare male and female humour in light of Barreca's arguments, and indicate whether your findings agree with hers.

2. Do you agree with Barreca that, despite the great strides women have made, it is "still considered funny ... to debase women's accomplishments and ambitions"? (para. 45) Can you provide examples of such attitudes?

3. Barreca suggests that the differences between men and women are such that they call into question "the whole idea of a universal vision" (para. 21). Do you agree?

4. Do you agree with Barreca's view that humour is gender-specific? Support your argument with specific examples.

5. Do you agree with Barreca that women's humour tends to be more subversive than men's? Give examples to support your opinion.

6. Barreca cites an episode from the comedy show *Murphy Brown* to show how television has embraced feminist humour. Find other examples from movies or television that would reinforce Barreca's claim. Compare an early TV sit-com (e.g., *I Love Lucy*, *The Dick van Dyke Show*) with a show of the '90s (e.g., *Roseanne*, *Ellen*) and discuss the roles assigned to women in each.

Dangerous Determination
by Moira Farr

"When I found so astonishing a power placed within my hands, I hesitated a long time concerning the manner in which I should employ it."
Doctor Victor Frankenstein, from *Frankenstein*, by Mary Shelley

1   In an Angus Reid poll on new reproductive technologies conducted last June, Canadians were asked, "Are you aware of anything that can he done to human sperm in a lab to improve the chances of having a boy or a girl?" Seventy-two percent answered no.

2   The pollsters stated in their report that "Canadians are not yet aware of the application of new reproductive technologies in the area of genetic screening. During the focus groups, it was discussion of sex preselection and genetic engineering that produced the most future shock in the minds of participants."

3   I hate to break it to 72 percent of Canadians, but future shock is not an appropriate response to something that has been around for a long time now. While we weren't paying much attention, sex determination (followed by abortion of the wrong-sex fetus) and sex preselection — through new reproductive technologies such as sperm separation, ultrasound, amniocentesis and chorionic villi sampling — have moved steadily from the realm of sci-fi imagining to concrete reality. That makes it harder to deal with, and more crucial that we do; the way old ideology allies with, and thoroughly informs, new technology is nowhere more evident than in the practice of gender preselection and determination, which has mostly been advanced through strong cultural

biases against females and, in the name of population control, by way of eliminating them.

It's easy and obvious to express repugnance, and apparently most 4 Canadians do, at the thought of any technology being used to rid the population of people with traits society happens to devalue, now or in the future (femaleness, red hair, myopia, where would it end?). But the question of how to stop this from happening once we've said "Isn't it awful?" seems so fraught with ethical dilemmas that until recently, most of us, including feminists, haven't wanted to touch it with a ten-foot speculum.

Discussion of sex selection within the National Action Committee 5 on the Status of Women (NAC) proved so contentious, only a passing reference to it appeared in the initial draft brief to the Royal Commission on New Reproductive Technologies (though the final document states that NAC is against sex selection and the licencing of clinics offering sex determination and preselection services). The brief presented by the Ontario Advisory Council on Women's Issues had 38 recommendations on new reproductive technologies, but not one of them dealt specifically with sex selection. The Toronto Women's Health Network, which also presented a brief, was under the impression that NAC would address it. In a newsletter, the network admitted it "heaved a mighty sigh of relief that someone else was including this issue in their written submission."

As NAC ultimately recognized, it is time for Canadian feminists to 6 face the unpleasant and paradoxical aspects of this issue: is there a way to regulate sex-selection technology without infringing on abortion rights? Do laws emanating from patriarchal governments have any place in the realm of women's health? Some feminists would answer no to both those questions, opting in the case of sex selection for an ignore/disapprove-in-theory strategy. "No encouragement should be given to the uses of [sex selection] while recognizing that there is no way of enforcing a prohibition," argues sociologist Thelma McCormack in her 1988 article, "Public Policies and Reproductive Technology: A Feminist Critique."

Banning the technologies outright may not be the answer — they are 7 capable of use for less sinister purposes than weeding out women, such as giving couples the choice of whether to bear children with sex-linked disorders, or allowing families to "balance" the sexes of their offspring — though ethical arguments against both of these uses have been advanced by disabled activists and feminists; and it should also be noted that these uses have never been, and aren't now, the chief focus for research and development of sex-selection techniques.

8   Nor can we stop people who want to determine the sex of their children from employing methods that include everything from intercourse positions to vaginal douches. But we can start to examine the implications of the whole concept as it gains ground in Canada; a completely hands-off approach, in my view, amounts to encouragement. At the very least, restrictions on the proliferation of high-tech commercial clinics offering sex preselection and determination services should be considered. India and Denmark have enacted legislation that limits the use of sex-selection techniques. Germany, understandably sensitive about the eugenic capabilities of new reproductive technologies, is working on such legislation. One thing is certain; ignoring the problem won't make it go away. And misogyny, in the service of a patriarchal status quo, has a banal way of insinuating itself until we accept it as just part of life.

9   I first became aware of the notion of sex selection a couple of years ago, through a television documentary about the uses of ultrasound and amniocentesis in India for determining gender and, in virtually all cases, aborting fetuses that show up female. After swearing loudly at the TV (an ineffective form of protest that is nevertheless therapeutic in the short-term), I did what I usually do when confronted with horrible things happening *out there*; felt gloomy and helpless, discussed it with a few friends and gradually let it slip from my consciousness.

10   But last July, I was reactivated while perusing, of all things, Rosemary Sexton's society column in *The Globe and Mail*. Covering a benefit ball in aid of The Canadian Hemophilia Society, Sexton quoted a Toronto woman named Susan Bernstein, the mother of a hemophiliac boy (the disorder affects only males), who had gone to a gender preselection clinic in order to better the chances that her second child would be female. Of those using the clinic, Bernstein said, "I'm one of the few who wants a girl."

11   I called Bernstein. Yes, she had contacted a Toronto clinic (there is also one in Calgary), a franchise of a U.S. outfit, operated by urologist Alan Abramovitch. Susan Cole wrote an article in the Toronto weekly *NOW* when this clinic opened in 1987. She reported in detail on the sex-preselection techniques offered: the Ericsson method, perfected and patented by American biologist Ronald Ericsson, involves separating sperm into those containing male and those containing female chromosomes (when being inseminated with female sperm, the woman must take the fertility drug Clomid); and for selecting girls, the

Sephadex method (by now gathering cobwebs), which filters female sperm through a tube.

Bernstein hadn't decided whether to go through with the procedure, 12 which would cost about $1,800; she wasn't yet sure if the increased odds claimed for having the gender of choice were accurate. She was discussing her concerns with a geneticist at North York Hospital (in the end, she concluded that the clinic wasn't for her). She said that clients had to sign a consent form saying they would accept either gender, but she also came away with the impression that the majority of Abramovitch's clients wanted boys. (Unfortunately, I was unable to verify this with Abramovitch, who did not return repeated phone calls. However, I subsequently learned that Ericsson's clinics operate in 46 countries in Europe, the U.S., Asia and Latin America; Ericsson himself has stated that in one study, 248 of 263 couples selected boys.)

I began doing further research, and found that feminists throughout 13 the world have done their homework on this one. In articles with titles like "Sex Selection: From Here to Fraternity," and "The Endangered Sex," they point to the overwhelming preference for sons evident in the folklore and customs of virtually all cultures. They show how the new sex selection technologies researched and developed in the past three decades have served that preference, in the most dramatic cases (in some areas of China, for instance), very clearly being seen as a "humane" alternative to female infanticide and neglect (sort of like the difference between public hanging and the electric chair, I guess).

Even in Europe and North America, where son preference is gener- 14 ally less pronounced than in some Third World countries, study after study indicates that the majority of people who use sex-preselection and determination techniques do so to ensure the birth of males — if not exclusively, then at least as their first child, which leads feminists to speculate on the psychological and social ramifications of entire nations filled with first-born sons and second-born daughters. In India, where sex selection has been so rampant that males have begun outnumbering females in the population, women have rallied and won (as of 1989) acts of parliament that seek to control prenatal sex determination.

Feminists have also revealed the repulsive ideas about global popu- 15 lation control that have driven research into sex selection and other new reproductive technologies: Gena Corea, in *The Mother Machine*, outlines the ideas of a doctor in the seventies who gained widespread coverage for his proposal that a "boy-pill" be developed; no less a personage than Clare Booth Luce endorsed this notion in the *Washington Star*.

Corea also writes about an organization called The Good Parents Group of Nutley, New Jersey (I don't make these things up, I just report them), which "supports the practice of aborting the female fetuses of the poor in India (it calls this 'Therabort') and has offered to help finance a model therapeutic termination clinic. Women found to be carrying male fetuses would not be permitted abortions at the clinics unless the fetus were defective."

16   Rationales for the development of artificial wombs have also been based on ideas about the expendability of women. A man named Edward Grossman argued in a 1971 article entitled "The Obsolescent Mother," that with this technology "geneticists could program-in some superior trait; sex preselection would be simple; women could be permanently sterilized." When this astonishing article was cited by Robin Rowland, in a chapter she wrote in the book *Man-Made Women*, I thought at first, why highlight loony ideas from some grimy, marginal tract? Then I looked up the bibliography: Grossman's piece had appeared in *The Atlantic*. It's no wonder feminist writers have begun speaking about the unspeakable: femicide.

17   Absorbing all this stuff about the threat of female extermination, I thought I might perhaps be getting a little overwrought; other feminists I spoke to didn't seem that concerned. And when I polled several hospitals, I was heartened to find that most Canadian doctors, such as Philip Wyatt, head of the clinical genetics centre at North York General Hospital, find the idea of gender selection "extremely distasteful." In other words, if you were to present yourself at a hospital ultrasound clinic today, and say "tell me the sex of my fetus so I can abort it if it's female," you probably would not be accommodated.

18   But that "distaste," Wyatt makes clear, isn't part of some formal, written code of ethics. It's just a matter of how most individual Canadian doctors happen to feel. And one night last October, I heard an item on *As It Happens*, in which Dale Goldhawk interviewed a doctor, John Stevens of California, who had patented an ultrasound technique he said could determine the sex of a fetus at nine weeks. Stevens spoke obnoxiously about protecting his "intellectual property;" he whined about unfair treatment in Canada. He had advertised his services in the Vancouver community newspaper, *The Link*, aimed at the South Asian community in that city. There had been an uproar; Goldhawk also interviewed a member of a South Asian women's group, whose protest to the newspaper had caused the ads to be withdrawn by the publisher. And a doctor from Vancouver's Grace Hospital expressed disapproval and

skepticism about Stevens' technique, and said that the American doctor had not been granted hospital privileges (he wouldn't reveal why) and so would not be able to set up a clinic in Vancouver.

I tuned in the next night, wondering if the "Talk Back" segment of 19 the show, where listeners phone in responses to what they've heard, would include some reaction to the Stevens item. It did, but not of the kind I'd anticipated. No outraged female voices that night. Both callers featured were men; one basically said: So what if this guy wants to operate in Canada, let him. The other seemed to have totally missed the point, harshly criticizing the piece for being biased because it didn't include an interview with a male member of the South Asian community.

Stevens got a lot of ink and air-time across Canada after that initial 20 *As It Happens* item. He thought it "authoritarian" of Canadians not to welcome him with open arms; it wasn't his responsibility, he argued, if clients went on to abort female fetuses his ultrasound technique revealed. In fact, he presented himself as a kind of hero, saving South Asian women from the shame of bearing daughters, which could result in violent reactions from angry husbands.

Charges of racist stereotyping ensued, and I wanted to find out what 21 the situation really was in Canada's South Asian communities. I phoned Aruna Papp, director of a Toronto organization called South Asian Family Services, and asked her if it was true that some South Asian women were so pressured to bear sons that they would seek out sex-preselection and determination services, and abort female fetuses. "Yes!" She replied as though she'd been waiting a long time for someone to ask her that question. Could she cite examples? "Well, I've lived with it," she replied, with a mirthless laugh, and proceeded to tell me some very painful details of her life.

She was born in Pakistan, the first of six daughters in her family. 22 (Her parents finally got a boy on try number seven.) "All my life, I tried to be the son I wasn't," she says, explaining that Hindu cultural and religious beliefs hinge salvation on the birth of sons. "It's only in middle age that I've been able to feel it's okay to be a woman." Now divorced, she says some South Asian women in Canada do suffer abuse at the hands of their husbands when they bear daughters. (She herself had two daughters, then "eventually" a son.) According to Papp, pregnant women in these communities in Canada often go "for a holiday" to India and Pakistan, where despite legislation, it is still easier to obtain access to sex-determination services and subsequent abortions, and return to Canada, female-fetus free.

23   Some feminists and doctors I've interviewed (including Philip Wyatt, who has referred people to the Abramovitch clinic, and says he has witnessed an East Indian woman having a "complete mental breakdown" when told she was carrying a female fetus) have argued that the pressure on South Asian women in Canada to bear sons, and the abuse that can result when they don't, is reason enough to allow, however warily, sex-preselection clinics to operate here.

24   But Aruna Papp is not the only woman of South Asian descent who doesn't want to see these clinics, or the kind Stevens proposes, starting up in Canada. Sharmini Peries, a board member of the South Asian Women's Group in Toronto, argues strongly against them. While she makes it clear that not *all* South Asian families value sons above daughters (she herself was never so pressured, and she and her husband have "two beautiful daughters"), she doesn't deny the existence of such bias. But she is adamant in her denunciation of Stevens and his ilk. "Doctor Stevens has a gun to our heads as surely as Marc Lepine did," she states, in no uncertain terms. The same position is held by South Asian women's groups in Vancouver.

25   John Stevens may for now be thwarted from coming to Canada to "make a buck," as he puts it (though he is setting up a clinic in Buffalo, in hopes that residents of southern Ontario will make the trip across the border). But it isn't any law, or even the cry of outrage from South Asian women's groups that is keeping him out; he simply hasn't yet been able to persuade a Canadian hospital, for reasons that haven't been made public, to affiliate with him (a licensing requirement of provincial colleges of physicians and surgeons).

26   Are the medical profession's rules, regulations and codes of moral conduct enough to safeguard against the future use of technologies in ways that are injurious to the status of women? Medical licensing bodies in Alberta and Ontario have apparently had no problem giving the go-ahead to clinics offering sex-preselection services. Wouldn't it have been more appropriate to have had some form of public debate about whether commercial operators of American franchises should be allowed to offer such services in Canada *before* they were up and running? (I realize this is a time-honoured approach to women's health matters: barrel ahead, then say "oops, we goofed" when the casualties roll in.)

27   The Canadian Medical Association has stated to the commission that it does not consider gender preselection or determination an ethical practice, except in cases where there is a family history of a sex-linked disorder, and CMA ethics-committee director Eike Kluge told me he'd like

to see gender clinics shut down. But the CMA is not a regulating body; it provides guidelines, but can't enforce them.

I'm dismayed when feminists downplay the current availability and 28 appeal of sex-selection techniques in Canada, and make statements like "This isn't India," as CARAL did in its brief to the royal commission. What exactly is that supposed to mean? Regardless of their ethnic origin, the people using sex-preselection clinics here are Canadians, availing themselves of services open to all in the great, free capitalist marketplace.

Beyond the issue of whether we should support the commercializa- 29 tion of reproductive health services, we are dealing with a trend primarily fuelled by the insidious power of hate-filled ideas; in this case, a patriarchal bias that utterly negates the value of daughters, blames females giving birth to females for overpopulation, and suggests that beyond their reproductive capacities — which we may soon be able to wholly duplicate in labs anyway — women have nothing of worth to contribute to the world. It shouldn't matter what group such ideas are aimed at, or how widespread we perceive their present influence to be. When James Keegstra taught high school students that the world was run by a Jewish conspiracy, did we say "What's the big deal? This isn't Nazi Germany. And it's only a few kids in rural Alberta anyway." No. Media klieg lights shone on Keegstra until he was brought before a human-rights commission and then lost his job. When Philippe Rushton of the University of Western Ontario came forward with claims of a connection between race and intelligence, did we say, "Oh well, he's just one professor. Who cares?" No. People like David Suzuki denounced Rushton in public; CBC Radio's *Quirks and Quarks* won at least one award for a show that completely discredited his research.

As far as I know, neither Keegstra nor Rushton ever secured a plat- 30 form for their views on the op/ed page of *The Globe and Mail*; but a Vancouver freelance writer named Graeme Matheson did, to argue in favour of eliminating women. In case you missed "What's Wrong With Choosing Your Baby's Sex?" here's one highlight: "Following the laws of supply and demand, as the numbers of available women fell, their value would go up ... grooms [in India] could eventually expect to pay for brides, raising the value of girls...."

Fortunately, a rebuttal to both the racism and sexism of Matheson's 31 Nutleyite views appeared four days later, written jointly by NAC president Judy Rebick, Sharmini Peries, and Judy Vashti Persad of Women Working With Immigrant Women. Their response was stinging and eloquent, but I couldn't help thinking that if feminists had been more vigilant on this issue, it would have been their view that appeared first, and Matheson who would have been forced, if so moved, to write a letter to the editor.

32   In wading through the ethical dilemmas posed by sex selection, I've been torn between the stance of feminists such as Thelma McCormack who, though personally offended by the notion of sex selection, do not support *ad hoc* legislation on this or any other technology and the more interventionist approach favoured by some members of NAC and South Asian women's groups, who feel most threatened by sex-selection technology right now. Ultimately, all feminists want the same thing: holistic, woman-centred, woman-run health centres accessible to all, where care does not revolve around drugs and high-tech gizmos. We are a long way from such Utopian setups right now, but my feeling (and just like a woman, I'm trusting my intuition on this one) is that the existence of boy factories in Canada does nothing to further such a goal, especially when they appear to be aiding and abetting the victimization of women of a particular cultural group. At the very least, we should stand alongside these women and denounce such practices; call for government support services (shelters, education) to be channelled towards women who are physically and emotionally abused when they give birth to daughters (ditto for the daughters themselves); monitor and study legislation in other countries (which regulates the use of sex-selection techniques, *not* access to abortion) and think about how it might be applied in Canada; finally, seriously consider the virulently sexist legacy of this use of technology, and its potential contribution to the future of humanity, before standing aside in good liberal fashion and watching it flourish.

33   It beats swearing at the TV.

(1991)

The Writer's Subject

1. Discuss the relevance to the essay of the epigraph from *Frankenstein*.

2. What evidence does Farr bring in support of her contention that the practice of gender preselection and determination "has mostly been advanced through strong cultural biases against females"? (para. 3)

3. What dilemmas face feminist groups in dealing with the issue of sex selection? (paras. 4–6)

4. What controls on sex preselection presently exist? Does Farr believe such controls should be introduced in Canada?

5. How, according to Farr, is research into reproductive technologies linked to "repulsive ideas about global population control"? (para. 15)

6. Farr observes that women of South Asian descent in Canada face certain pressures created by gender bias. What are these pressures?

7. What measures does Farr believe are needed to counter the threat to women posed by current sex-selection technology?

The Writer's Style and Strategy

1. Why does Farr begin her essay with an account of an opinion poll on new reproductive technologies?

2. Where does Farr make her own position on sex selection clear? How does her choice of language indicate her attitude to this technology and its advocates?

3. In the course of her essay Farr mentions James Keegstra and Philippe Rushton, neither of whom has anything to do with reproductive technology. (paras. 29–30) What effect does she hope to create by alluding to these men?

4. Who is Farr addressing in her article? Point out details of diction and tone that suggest the kind of audience she has in mind.

5. How effective is the essay's closing sentence?

Suggestions for Writing and Discussion

1. In 1990 the Canadian government established a federal Royal Commission on New Reproductive Technologies. Find out what you can about the goals of the Commission, and about its reception by feminist groups.

2. Farr argues for regulation and control of sex-selection technology, and calls for the study of legislation governing such technology in other countries. Do you think that sex selection should be subject to government regulation?

3. What is your response to Farr's accusations of misogyny in current official handling of women's health issues?

Murder Among the Lovebirds
by Janet Flanner

1   Maybe our grandmothers were right and female standards are, on all sides, not so high as they used to be. Certainly an eclectic comparison between the mediocre murder recently committed by the nineteen-year-old Parisian flapper Mlle. Violette Nozière and the stylish assassination achieved by the consummate Mme. Germaine d'Anglemont, aged forty-eight, indicates a deplorable decline in the younger generation. Mme. d'Anglemont shot her lover like a lady, because she was jealous; Violette Nozière killed her father like a cannibal, because she wanted to eat and drink up the savings that were his French life and blood.

2   Even in their private lives — or as private as could be, considering that both females lived on love for sale — Germaine d'Anglemont cut the grander figure, since, though an uneducated foundling, in her long life she had learned to dine with royalty, own a smart house, accept diamonds, and take such an intelligent interest in politics that senators and deputies had been her slaves. And even the gentleman she finally shot was a chief magistrate.

3   Though her doting parents had educated her over their heads and means in a Paris private school, in her brief career Violette Nozière had learned merely how to drink bad cocktails with penniless collegiates, was at home only on the Boul' Mich', gave her mother's engagement ring to a lover rather than received any gem from him, and certainly never met any member of the government until, on trial for parricide, she made the acquaintance of her judge.

4   Germain d'Anglemont was the last of the silk-ruffled, scented, hard-lipped, handsome prewar courtesans, and she made a fortune. Violette

was, one fears, not the last of the fake-silver-foxed, hard-toothed, modern young monsters of mediocre looks and without any sense of the business of life. Being up to date, her crime cruelly lacked the grand manner.

Since she was faintly intellectual, Violette Nozière characteristically 5 chose poison and patience as her weapons. Though she did not succeed till August 1934 in putting her father into his grave and her mother into the hospital, she practised up on murdering them in March by giving them, "as a nice new tonic" with their evening coffee, six and three tablets of veronal, respectively, which they hungrily swallowed, since both were passionate patent-medicine gourmets

At shortly past midnight after the March evening, contented with their 6 coma, their daughter set fire to the flat's modest parlor curtains, walked across the hall, roused a neighbor with a scream of "Fire!" and a brainy afterscream of, "I think the electricity must have short-circuited." The local fire brigade was called, and the next day M. and Mme. Nozière made the second page of the Parisian newspapers for the first and last time — thereafter they were unfortunately to be front-page stuff — for being unconscious from suffocation in what was called "A Bizarre Conflagration." Murder in an odd form was on its way to the Rue de Madagascar, where the three Nozières dwelt till they started on their separate paths toward cemetery, clinic and prison.

In the five months which followed, the immodest Violette did noth- 7 ing unusual — for her. She continued her afternoon and evening life on the large sidewalks and in the small hotels of the Boulevard Saint-Michel where, from the age of fifteen, she had been playing hooky from the costly female seminary for which her parents had scrimped so that she might star in mathematics. But though majoring in geometry, Vi knew less about Euclid than about a lot of other men. At her trial, it was brought out that she was not only a nympho- — but also a mythomaniac — or a natural tart plus a born liar.

On the Café d'Harcourt terrace, she picked up men with a dual pur- 8 pose, the second being to tell them fantastic fibs — that she was an heiress, that her grandmother owned a château, that an aunt had millions, an uncle billions, that she herself was noble, that she was a trigonometry professor, and that her father was a director in the French railways. He was, in a way. He was the locomotive engineer on the Paris-Vichy fast train; her grandmother's country place was a cottage where, after her granddaughter's arrest, the old peasant humbly died of shame among her cabbages. Indeed, only two things unusual were performed by Vi during those fatal five months. She continued to try to kill her mother occasionally: at any rate, whenever the girl prepared breakfast for her, *maman* was deathly sick after, so Vi must have been putting something into the coffee — besides the chicory, that is. (Her father, having just fallen out of his engine cab onto his head, was momentarily in the hospital and so drank his bad coffee without ill results.)

9   Violette's second odd act was to fall in love: the emotion was great, since she eventually killed for it; the object was slight — an eighteen-year-old gigolo law student with sleek hair, slack morals, and American horn-rimmed spectacles, worn like a foolish foreign trade-mark on his French phiz. His name was Jean Dabin; his father, in Vi's mythology, was also probably a railway director — i.e., in reality, a whistle-blowing petty station-master on the Paris belt railroad.

10   Violette's love for Jean was the only true passion in her life, except that for murder. To him she gave all she had — herself plus one hundred francs a day, which she got from other men by night. She also promised to give him a secondhand Bugatti and a first-rate September holiday, for, as she said, she was shortly expecting to inherit one hundred and eighty thousand francs, or the exact sum her father had saved up from a lifetime of driving the Paris-Vichy express.

11   On August 23, her patience and poison and passion finally focused. Violette Nozière repeated what she had tried out in March, except that she increased her father's dose to twenty powdered veronal tablets and her mother's to six. This time she also gave herself a small dose of milk of magnesia, as she was feeling liverish. Then she curled up in a chair for a nap by her parent's couch while they died — she hoped. At two a.m. when she called the same neighbor, she this time screamed — since she had turned on the kitchen range without lighting it — "Gas!" and, as a new addition, "I think the pipe has burst."

12   The neighbor was, of all men to call in twice, an electrician and gas fitter by trades. Whatever he had failed to smell in March, this time he smelled not only gas but a rat. So did Vi, at dawn in the city hospital, sitting tenderly by her mother's bedside; the authorities had refused to let her sit tenderly by her father's slabside in the morgue. Sensing danger, she calmly rose and walked out into the new Paris day and what for one week seemed limbo, since no one could find her. By dinner, her news photo as "Wanted for Parricide" was posted all over Paris. Police hunted her everywhere, except at the Bal Tabarin (where she spent the first night after her crime gracefully waltzing) and on the Boulevard de la Madeleine, where a white-faced, neurotic, not very pretty young creature plied her trade while whispering crazily to her customers that her

father was a railway director, her grandmother owned a château, and that she herself was an heiress...to one hundred and eighty thousand francs...oh, yes, she was surely an heiress by now.... On the sixth day she was trapped into a second rendezvous by a gallant young male who had recognized her face on the pillow from the newspaper he'd tossed on the chair. Arrested, she told the truth, probably for the first time in her life. At any rate she said she was glad she'd killed her father, who, she claimed, was a satyr, though her relief at hearing that her mother was yawning back from the jaws of death may have been a lie.

Her trial for murder in the autumn of 1934 was melodramatic. It 13 opened in the Paris Assizes with a five-minute silence for King Alexander of Yugoslavia, who had also just been murdered in Marseilles. In the three days which followed, Violette fainted frequently, was occasionally nearly lynched by angry crowds, and was constantly hectored in court by her mother, who was sentimentally suing her for damages for having robbed her of the sweetest husband woman ever knew.

In addition to other details, the jury was swayed by the fact that 14 Violette had also robbed what she thought was her mother's corpse of a thousand francs pinned to the maternal corset. With lust for money to spend on her lover in cafés (for bad Martinis) accredited as her miserable motive, the jury judged her guilty of the uncivilized crime of parricide, whereupon the judge read what remains the most medieval death sentence preserved in modern French law: "She is to have her head cut off in death upon a public place in Paris. She shall be taken there barefooted, clad only in her chemise and with her head covered by a black veil. Before the execution shall be done, let the clerk in a clear voice read aloud this Judgment." Though women are no longer guillotined in France, and if they were, no matter whom they had killed, they would be allowed to die dressed and with their boots on, the rare sentence was followed by unusual silence in court, suddenly broken by Violette's vulgarly shouting, "Curse my father, curse my mother!"

To the outraged gendarme who dragged her away, she shouted in 15 one of her illuminating afterthoughts, "Fetch my handbag with my powder, rouge, money. I must have dropped it in the prisoner's box." What was most precious she had clearly left behind her in court. Thus passed from youth into lifelong imprisonment the best-educated, worst-mannered young murderess in French annals. But it was the fact of the girl's having rudely slept in the intimate presence of the dead and dying that caused the French jury to cut her off from civilized society as long as she might live.

16   The jury in the same Paris court which had just tried Germaine
d'Anglemont for having shot her late love, Causeret, had only cut her off
from civilized society for eleven months. And even that period of seques-
tration was a cultivated *passetemps*, since she spent it as prison librarian;
both before and after murdering, dear Germaine was ever the bookworm.
Her crime, trial, sentence, were all as cynical and sociable as her origin.
Born a love child humbly named Huot, whose father only made her acquaintance when she was aged eleven, at twelve Germaine had won the
catechism prize in her orphan asylum, at fourteen had her first flirtation,
at fifteen her first carriage and pair and the stylish name of D'Anglemont,
which she picked out of a dime novel. The week before Mlle. Huot became Mme. d'Anglemont, she had been noted — pretty and shabby —
in the then famous Jardin de Paris Café, the noting being done by a ta-
bleful which included Catulle Mendès, the poet; Henry Bernstein, the
playwright; Prince Fouad, now King of Egypt; and other gentlemen of
the 1905 *belle époque*, one of whom asked her how she got there.

17   She said she had run away from home penniless and had got into the
café by pawning her umbrella for three francs with the *vestiaire*. The
gentlemen handed her five hundred francs (one hundred dollars in those
lovely days) to get some decent clothes, three francs to get her umbrella,
and invited her to dine. Her second lover, according to the list the Paris
judge indelicately read out at her murder trial thirty-four years later,
was a Dutch millionaire named Van Horschoot; the third was an Argen-
tine tutor the Dutchman had hired to complete the girl's education —
though she seemed to know a great deal already; the fourth love was
the Prince Franz Josef of the royal house of Bavaria, who died of a broken heart because she wouldn't marry him.

18   Among the innumerable others she did not marry were the Polish
Count Wielsinski, who, instead of a wedding ring, could give her only
diamonds and pearls; the Agha Khan, who merely gave her a diamond
(though it was eighteen karats); Camille Picard, today Deputy from the
Vosges; a M. France, who was seventy and in sugar; a M. Astruc, at
whom she once threw an expensive Gothic statue of the Virgin; and a
Dr. Morgilewski (whom she never saw again for thirteen years, till the
fatal day when she telephoned him to come round professionally as she
seemed to have shot one of his successors). The mass of Parliamentar-
ians she also enmeshed finally dwindled down, in her forties, to the late-
lamented Chief Magistrate Causeret, young, promising politician, fickle,
married, father of children — and what was worse, son of the prime
Rector Causeret of Clermont University.

"If I've omitted any of your lovers, pray excuse me, Madame," the   19
Judge said ironically at her trial. "The list is already so long. You were
a *courtisane de haut vol* — a highflier; you are also, alas, a good shot."
It was her custom to practise in the shooting gallery near the Rond-
Point where Ivar Kreuger bought his fatal suicide gun: she kept two
pistols in her boudoir alongside the statue of Sainte Thérèse — all three
useful as weapons to a woman in a jealous rage. For it was for jealousy
that she murdered Causeret. She had him followed through the streets
of Paris by a hunchback female detective (a masseuse, when spying was
scarce), who reported that he had gone to a department store to buy
suspicious silk pajamas, instead of going, as he had announced, to talk
politics with an old gentleman.

At noon, five minutes after Causeret had returned to her smart Place   20
Beauvais flat to lunch, there was still nothing to eat on the dining-room
table, but there was a corpse with only a bullet in its stomach in the
boudoir. As Germaine later admitted to the jury, she'd been a little hasty
— the handsomest apology a murderess ever made.

At her trial the jury also was hasty; in one minute they saw it would   21
be useless to condemn her, since they also saw, all around the court, the
visiting politicos who would demand and obtain her pardon. The jury
therefore judged her guilty but with a cynically strong recommendation
for mercy, which to the judge's mind meant a sentence of eleven months.
Thus the quality of mercy was for once strained, since six years is a
normal clement "stretch" for French female killers. Along with her
eleven months, Germaine d'Anglemont also got bouquets of flowers in
court, and her male friends shook hands, kissing hers.

In her trial, justice was not done. Yet injustice would have been ac-   22
complished had not a D'Anglemont's punishment been infinitely less
than a Nozière's. For in a way these two were test cases, illustrating the
modern French attitude toward murder, which can be summed up thus:
the manner of killing is as important as the manner of living.

(1936)

The Writer's Subject

1. What were the principal differences in character and background of the
   two women described by Flanner? (paras. 1–4)

2. Why, according to Flanner, did Violette Nozière want to murder her parents? (paras. 7–10)

3. How was Violette eventually captured? (para. 12)

4. What was Germaine d'Anglemont's motive for murdering her lover? (para. 19)

5. Why was Germaine's sentence so much lighter than Violette's, even though both women were convicted of murder? (para. 21)

6. Why does Flanner believe that an injustice would have been done "had not a D'Anglemont's punishment been infinitely less than a Nozière's"? (para. 22)

The Writer's Style and Strategy

1. A writer, particularly a journalist, will often choose an "angle" from which to approach a subject. What "angle" is established in the opening paragraph? How does it determine the shape of the account that follows?

2. Flanner's essay first appeared in the *New Yorker*, a weekly magazine. Judging by Flanner's treatment of her subject, what conclusions might you draw about the *New Yorker*'s readership?

3. The tone of Flanner's essay is ironic throughout. What does the tone reveal about Flanner's attitude to the two women she describes, and to the society which condemned them?

4. Why does Flanner refer to Violette as "Vi" at many points in her essay? (paras. 7–12)

5. Flanner uses a variety of devices in her prose, including parallel or contrasting sentence elements, nouns or noun clauses in series, parenthetical comments, unexpected juxtapositions, colloquialisms, and alliteration. Pick out examples of each of these in paragraphs 6–11, and indicate how their use contributes to the ironic effect sought by Flanner.

6. Why does Flanner describe some of Germaine d'Anglemont's innumerable lovers? (paras. 17–18) How does that description prepare the reader for the essay's concluding paragraphs?

7. How does Flanner's title reflect the tone of the essay as a whole?

Suggested Topics for Writing and Discussion

1. Germaine d'Anglemont served a sentence of only eleven months before she was released. Today in North America, though murderers must generally serve much longer sentences, many become eligible for early release through parole. Do you think that a murderer should ever be released from jail?

2. Find two or three published accounts of a recent murder trial in local newspapers and national magazines. What differences are apparent in the vari-

ous accounts of the proceedings? How is the character of the murderer drawn in each of your sources?

3. In discussing the sentencing of two murderers, Flanner demonstrates the application, a rather extreme one, of a double standard. Using an instance from public or private life, discuss another situation in which a double standard seems to apply.

Women's Clothes — Towards Emancipation

by Alison Lurie

The Superficially Liberated Woman

1   The more conventional late-Victorian and Edwardian woman, though she was no longer supposed to be childish and frail, was far from liberated by modern standards. Though her appearance was queenly, like most queens of recent years her freedom was hedged round with duties and restrictions. She was often called "divine" — and, as is the custom with goddesses, stood on a pedestal, which is an inconvenient place to stand if you want to do anything other than be worshipped. If you move at all, you are in danger of falling off — of becoming, in the popular phrase of the time, a "fallen woman."

2   The first wave of feminism, as historians of costume have pointed out, did not liberate most women from the bulky and elaborate clothes of the period. Indeed in many ways the female fashions of the time were more oppressive than those of midcentury. The corset had previously ended at or just below the waist, accommodating the many pregnancies of the early-Victorian woman. Now advances in medical science had decreased infant mortality, and it was no longer necessary or fashionable to have many children. The late-Victorian corset lengthened to midthigh, severely restricting locomotion. Gradually it began to push the chest forward and the hips back, creating the S-bend figure with its low-slung monobosom and protruding monorump. Over the corset were worn a corset cover, a camisole, several petticoats, and dresses with trail-

ing skirts and trains. All these garments were richly trimmed with lace, ruffles, tucks, ribbons and embroidery; they were in constant danger of being rumpled or soiled, often giving a literal meaning to the current euphemism "soiled dove."

The ordinary woman who held a job or emancipated opinions might   3 wear, instead of a lace-trimmed gown, a more plainly cut wool or linen suit (the "tailor-made") with a shirtwaist, tie and straw boater that imitated those of men. But this imitation was superficial. Beneath her clothes her corset was as uncomfortable and confining as ever, and when she lifted her heavy floor-length skirt she showed a froth of delicate petticoats and lacy stockings. The message of this costume was clear: the masculine efficiency or intellectual force were only external; underneath she was still a member of the frailer sex. To wear such clothes, however, did not necessarily mean acceptance of the status quo. Some feminists wore them deliberately in order to confuse or disarm their opponents: indeed, several of the leaders of the Emancipation Movement were famous for their stylishness. This stratagem was also used during the second wave of women's liberation, by Gloria Steinem among others.

The Modern Girl

In the early twentieth century substantial gains in dress reform were   4 achieved. Slowly, women began to liberate themselves from the duty of acting as walking advertisements of their own helplessness and their male relatives' wealth. (The struggle was an uphill one, however, and it is by no means over.) There was also a gradual relaxation of the corset and a rise in the skirt, which cleared the ground by 1905, and by 1912 was above the ankle. Once women could breathe a little more easily and had no trains to trip over they were better able to take part in sports. Some, though to our eyes still absurdly handicapped, joined in professional competition. By the end of World War I women's clothes had become relatively unconfining, but they were still sex-typed, and by no means as comfortable as those of men. Various counterrevolutionary efforts were made — notably, the introduction of the hobble skirt in 1910 — but these were generally unsuccessful. As in all transitional periods, however, they provided a useful guide to the political and social views of the women who wore them.

The clothes of the 1920s were thought at the time to represent an   5 extreme of freedom for women, and certainly they were a relief to anyone old enough to have worn the styles of twenty years earlier. For one

Portrait of Mr. and Mrs. I.N. Phelps-Stokes, John Singer Sargent 1897
Reprinted by permission of the Metropolitan Museum of Art,
Bequest of Edith Mintern Phelps Stokes, 1938

thing, they drastically reduced the time spent in washing, ironing and mending, and also in simply getting dressed and undressed. The woman who bobbed her waist-length hair, for instance, saved several hours a week that had previously been employed in brushing it out, washing and drying it, braiding it at night and putting it up in a pompadour over pads of wire mesh and false hair every morning.

Twenties' dresses often had little-boy collars or ties, but these were   6
no more than piquant additions to a recognizably feminine costume; they declared that their wearer was charmingly boyish, but not that she was a boy. The fulminations of contemporary critics against mannish women and womanish men seem exaggerated today. In photographs of the twenties men and women do look more alike; but this is because they both look more like children, and the difference between the sexes is less pronounced in childhood. Even in her Buster Brown or Peter Pan collar the flapper of the 1920s (like the Gibson Girl of a generation earlier in her mannish shirt and tie) is only male from the waist up. Below it, her skirt, silk stockings and pumps proclaim that basically she is a female.

Wearing the Pants

Reform of the bottom half of women's costume got seriously underway   7
in the 1890s, when the introduction of the bicycle was followed by the introduction of the divided skirt for female bicyclists. Though at first it was called unfeminine and even shocking, the divided skirt was in fact voluminously modest. Eventually it was generally accepted — possibly because no one could mistake it for masculine dress.

Real trousers took much longer to become standard female wear. It   8
was not until the 1920s that women and girls began to wear slacks and even shorts for sports and lounging. The new style was greeted with disapproval and ridicule. Women were told that they looked very ugly in trousers, and that wanting to wear The Pants — in our culture, for centuries, the symbolic badge of male authority — was unnatural and sexually unattractive. Nevertheless the fashion spread, and by the mid-1930s a woman could go on a picnic, play tennis or dig in the garden in clothes that did not handicap her. This freedom, however, was limited to the private and informal side of life. Wearing slacks to the office or to a party was out of the question, and any female who appeared on a formal occasion in a trouser suit was assumed to be a bohemian eccentric and probably a lesbian. Most schools and colleges insisted on skirts for classes and in the library until the 1960s; and even today this cus-

tom occasionally survives. At the Frick Collection Library in New York women may not be admitted unless they are wearing skirts; a particularly ancient and unattractive skirt is kept at the desk for the use of readers ignorant of this rule.

9   The woman who wore slacks or shorts before 1960, too, was only outwardly liberated. Underneath her clothes she was more pinched and squeezed and trussed-up than she had been in the twenties. Her bra hauled her breasts up toward the shoulders and forced them into the currently fashionable shape, often with the help of wires or deceptive padding. The straps of this bra usually cut into the flesh, leaving sore red lines on her shoulders and around her body to match the sore red lines left lower down by her tight elastic girdle. Even slim women wore girdles, since the fashionable figure had almost no hips or derrière, and a bouncy rear end was thought vulgar. There was also no other decent way to hold up the obligatory stockings: unless your skirt was very full, any garter belt would show an embarrassing outline beneath it.

To Freedom and Partway Back

10   The fifties and early sixties were the years of the baby boom, togetherness and the feminine mystique; and, as usually happens in patriarchal periods, female and male clothes were sharply distinguished. The New Look Woman and the Man in the Gray Flannel Suit were almost as distinct in silhouette as their grandparents. Nevertheless it was in this period that trousers for women began to edge their way into respectability. At first they took rather peculiar and unbecoming forms. The popular "toreador" or "Capri" pants, for instance, came in odd, glaring colors and ended a tight, awkward six inches above the ankle as if they had shrunk in the wash. They were often worn under maternity or mock-maternity smocks, producing a costume that resembled that of a medieval page. It was accompanied by shoes as narrow and sharply pointed — and no doubt as uncomfortable — as those fashionable in the fourteenth and fifteenth centuries. This outfit was appropriate, since the harassed, untrained middle-class mother of the baby-boom years — unlike her own parents — had no servants, and was reduced to waiting hand and foot on her husband and too many children.

11   In the late 1960s trousers for women finally became elegant as well as respectable, and underwear vanished or mutated into harmless forms. Even before the second wave of women's liberation got underway, the long struggle for comfort and freedom in female dress seemed to have been won at last. The introduction of panty hose freed women from the

ugly and often painful rubber and metal and plastic hardwear they had been using to hold up their stockings. It was again permissible to have curves below the waist as well as above; and millions of girdles went into the trash can, where they were soon joined by millions of padded and wired bras. During the 1970s pants suits and slacks were worn to work, to parties, to the theater, in elegant restaurants and on international planes, by women of all ages. They were usually accompanied by comfortable low-heeled shoes or boots. Fashion editors asserted, and women believed, that the bad old days were over forever.

In the last few years, however, there have been ominous signs of re-   12
trenchment and a counterrevolutionary movement seems to be gaining force. If one is pessimistic it is possible to see the sixties and seventies as merely a period of temporary victory. Indeed, the entire history of female fashion from 1910 to the present can be viewed as a series of more or less successful campaigns to force, flatter or bribe women back into uncomfortable and awkward styles, not only for purposes of Vicarious Ostentation and security of sexual ownership, but also and increasingly in order to handicap them in professional competition with men. The hobble skirt, the girdle, the top-heavy hats of the teens and the forties, the embarrassingly short dresses of the twenties and the sixties, all have aided this war effort. Today its most effective strategic devices are fashionable footwear and the demand for slimness.

The Shoe as a Strategic Weapon

Attempts to limit female mobility by hampering locomotion are ancient   13
and almost universal. The foot-binding of upper-class Chinese girls and the Nigerian custom of loading women's legs with pounds of heavy brass wire are extreme examples, but all over the world similar stratagems have been employed to make sure that once you have caught a woman she cannot run away, and even if she stays around she cannot keep up with you. What seems odd is that all these devices have been perceived as beautiful, not only by men but by women. The lotus foot, which seems to us a deformity, was passionately admired in China for centuries, and today most people in Western society see nothing ugly in the severely compressed toes produced by modern footwear. The high-heeled, narrow-toed shoes that for most of this century have been an essential part of woman's costume are considered sexually attractive, partly because they make the legs look longer — an extended leg is the biological sign of sexual availability in several animal species — and because they produce what anthropologists call a "courtship strut." They also make stand-

ing for any length of time painful, walking exhausting and running impossible. The halting, tiptoe gait they produce is thought provocative — perhaps because it guarantees that no woman wearing them can outrun a man who is chasing her. Worst of all, if they are worn continually from adolescence on, they deform the muscles of the feet and legs so that it becomes even more painful and difficult to walk in flat soles.

14   Literally as well as figuratively modern women's shoes are what keep Samantha from running as fast as Sammy. As anyone who has worn them can testify, it is hard to concentrate on your job when your feet are killing you — especially if you are faint with hunger because you had only half a grapefruit and coffee for breakfast so as to stay a glamorous ten pounds below your natural healthy weight. For a while in the sixties and seventies it was not necessary to be handicapped in this way unless you chose to be. During the last few years, however, women have begun wearing tight high-heeled shoes again, even with pants, and the most fashionable styles are those that, like clogs and ankle-strap sandals, give least support to the feet and make walking most difficult.

Counterrevolution and Ambiguity

15   There have been other signs recently that all is not well with the independent woman. One is the gradual demotion of the pants suit for both daytime and evening wear. By now it has become a low-status indicator, especially when made of polyester, and is seldom seen in middle-class circumstances. It has been replaced by the "skirted suit" recommended as the proper costume for white-collar success, which must of course be worn with panty hose and heels. Another ominous sign is the narrowing of the skirt to the point where ordinary gestures like sitting on a low sofa or stepping over a puddle become difficult.

16   Prudence Glynn, a former fashion editor of the London *Times*, was one of the first to point out the internal contradictions of much postfeminist fashion. The platform shoes and clogs that became popular during the seventies, for instance, are usually made on a wide last which does not compress the foot; however, they produce a clumping, awkward gait and are not only hard to manage but dangerous, often leading to serious injury. As Prudence Glynn puts it, "By their height they cater to an instinct in women to be taller and thus of more consequence vis-à-vis men. By their construction, which makes walking extremely difficult, they cater to an instinct to remain vulnerable."

17   Another popular style of the time, known as the Annie Hall Look after the clothes worn by Diane Keaton in the film of the same name,

was ambiguous in a more complex way. Essentially it involved the wearing of actual men's clothing: elegant three-piece suits, vests, shirts, ties and hats in pale colors — beige, off-white, tan and gray — often with a twenties look. Everything was worn very large and loose — collars open, shirts ballooning out, sleeves and trouser legs rolled up. These clothes were accompanied by huge handbags and kooky, childish costume jewelry: ceramic and wood and painted-tin ice cream cones and rainbows and Mickey Mice.

The wearing of men's clothes can mean many different things. In the   18
thirties, sophisticated actresses such as Marlene Dietrich in top hat and tails and elegantly cut suits projected sophistication, power and a dangerous eroticism. The slacks and sweaters of the war period, and the jeans and pants outfits of the sixties and early seventies, were serious gestures toward sexual equality.

The Annie Hall style is a double message. It announces that its wearer   19
is a good sport, a pal: not mysteriously and delicately female, but an easy-going, ready-for-anything tomboy type, almost like one of the guys. She will not demand to be protected from the rain or make a fuss about having to stand up at a football game. She probably enjoys active sports and is good at them (though not annoyingly, competitively good). Besides, you can see from her Snoopy pin that she has a sense of humor and is just a kid at heart.

At the same time, however, these clothes convey an ironic antifeminist   20
message. Because they are worn several sizes too large, they suggest a child dressed up in her daddy's or older brother's things for fun, and imply "I'm only playing; I'm not really big enough to wear a man's pants, or do a man's job." This is a look of helpless cuteness, not one of authority; it invites the man to take charge, even when he is as incompetent himself as the characters played by Woody Allen.

(1981)

The Writer's Subject

1. What connection does Lurie make between women's clothes and the degree of female emancipation in late-Victorian society? (paras. 1–3)

2. To what extent did dress reform in the 1920s close the gap between the sexes? (paras. 4–6)

3. What, according to Lurie, was the early reaction to the wearing of slacks or shorts by women? (paras. 7–9) How far did this trend in women's clothes really represent liberation?

4. Lurie notes that in the sixties women's trousers were often worn with smocks, "producing a costume that resembled that of a medieval page". (para. 10) Why does she call such an outfit "appropriate"?

5. Why, according to Lurie, was the introduction of pantyhose so important to women's clothing styles? (para. 11)

6. What contrast does Lurie draw between the fashions of the sixties and seventies, and those of the last few years? What does she mean by the statement that "a counterrevolutionary movement seems to be gaining force"? (para. 12)

7. How does Lurie interpret the styles of footwear customarily worn by women? Why is she disturbed by the modern fashion for high-heeled shoes? (paras. 13–14)

8. In the last four paragraphs of the essay, Lurie discusses the wearing of men's clothes by women. Why does this fashion seem to her to "convey an ironic antifeminist message"?

The Writer's Style and Strategy

1. Lurie's account is a mixture of social history, sociological commentary, and polemic. Where does Lurie move away from history and analysis to make her own position clear? How does she do so?

2. Discuss the language of paragraph 12. What is the extended metaphor through which Lurie presents the history of changes in women's fashions?

3. Discuss the structure and development of Lurie's paragraphs. Where does she usually place the topic sentence? (See, for example, paras. 8–11.)

4. From time to time Lurie shifts from the impersonality of the third person to "you." Discuss the purpose and effectiveness of this shift in point of view in paragraphs 13 and 14.

5. How does Lurie demonstrate that women have been handicapped by fashion? (paras. 13–15)

6. Examine Lurie's description of the "Annie Hall look" in paragraphs 17–20. What is Lurie's attitude to this fashion, and how is it conveyed?

Suggested Topics for Writing and Discussion

1. Lurie sees a direct connection between women's clothes and the degree of women's independence in a male-dominated society. To what extent do you agree with her findings? Are the current fashions, as were those in 1981 when this essay was written, a sign that "all is not well with the independent woman"?

2. Lurie's analysis focuses on women's fashions. What might a similar study of men's clothes tell us about the status of men in modern society?

3. Lurie discusses ways in which women's clothing "sex-types" them. Discuss other ways in which society encourages boys or girls (or both) to fix their sexual identities.

4. When *Dress for Success*, a book on women's clothing, appeared in 1976, it soon established a "dress code" for professional women. A spate of such books followed and, in fact, even became a target for satire — as in 1984's collection of Garry Trudeau's cartoons entitled *Dressed for Failure, I See. Dressing Thin* (1981), *Dressing Rich: A Guide to Classic Chic for Women with More Taste than Money* (1984), and *Dressing Up: How to Look and Feel Absolutely Perfect for Any Social Occasion* (1984) were included in the books for women; *Dressing Right* (1976) and *Dressing to Win: How to Have More Money, Romance, and Power in Your Life* (1984) were among those for men. Using your local library or bookstore, locate one such book and analyze its appeal. Write an essay outlining the book's assumptions about the audience's interests.

Are Feminists Alienating Women from the Sciences?

by Noretta Koertge

1   Why are there still so few women in the natural sciences? Thanks to the women's movement and other social changes, women are now entering the legal and medical professions in record numbers, and the percentage of female graduate students and professors in most disciplines is climbing steadily. Yet at my university (which is all too typical of research institutions) only 7 per cent of the tenure-track positions in the natural and mathematical sciences are occupied by women. There are no female faculty members of any rank in computer science, only one each in chemistry and geology, and a grand total of two each in our large physics and mathematics departments.

2   Why? Are the hard sciences really the last bastions of male chauvinism, or is something more complex going on? Could certain feminist stances be part of the problem?

3   The traditional feminist analysis of the factors that made science an unlikely career choice for women began by documenting the long history of discrimination faced by women scientists. The analysis then focused on socialization and gender stereotypes — how little girls were encouraged to play with dolls and were deprived of such toys as Erector or Meccano sets. In high-school science laboratories, feminists noted, the girls were the ones who recorded data and wrote up the lab reports while the boys dissected frogs and wired up circuits with capacitors and galvanometers.

4   In recent years, feminist sociologists of science have added other

factors to the analysis. Female science students are less apt to have supportive faculty mentors, they found, and are less likely to be well integrated into the informal peer networks. Since some scientists, especially those working in universities, are expected to spend 80 hours a week in the lab, it is especially difficult for young women to combine a career in science with family life. Some sociologists also pointed out that in any extremely competitive situation, be it the Olympics or the quest for scientific discoveries, very small advantages could make a big difference in the outcome. One need not posit gross acts of sexism — which have become much less frequent, thanks to the feminist movement — to explain why so few women have wound up with successful scientific careers.

The moral of all this was clear, but daunting for reformers: For women   5
to feel at home in science, special initiatives to make it accessible and interesting to girls would have to begin as early as in pre-school and would have to be systematically reinforced all the way through graduate school and the early years of postdoctoral training. It was taken for granted that more women should become scientists. It also was assumed that once the barriers of overt sexism and gender stereotyping were removed, no intrinsic reasons would exist for women not to value and enjoy science as much as men do.

After all, what nobler cause could anyone wish for than to under-   6
stand the innermost workings of the universe and make discoveries that could help alleviate pain and drudgery? How ignorant and unjust to assume that women might be better suited to deal only with matters of "*Kinder, Kuche* and *Kirche*"! Yet theorists who now try to base feminist epistemology and ethics on the mother-child relationship come perilously close to saying just that.

According to traditional feminist analysis, the problem was to dis-   7
cover how to remove the distorting factors so that women could fit comfortably into science. The new feminist agenda is quite different: Science must be changed so that it fits women's special talents and thus becomes a suitable occupation for a feminist to pursue.

Although feminists themselves often understate the conflict, the tra-   8
ditional and new imperatives for feminist reform are diametrically opposed: Traditional feminists wanted little girls to overcome their anxiety about math and learn statistics, while the new feminists want science to become less quantitative, to accommodate the qualitative methods of inquiry at which women are alleged to excel. Whereas traditional feminists believed that science should be an equal-opportunity career, their successors argue that science, like football, is intrinsically ori-

ented toward males and saturated with patriarchal male values.

9   Thus, they believe, science will have to be revolutionized before it will be an acceptable calling for women. Any feminist who wants to pursue a scientific career will have to think of herself as a missionary and exercise vigilance to keep from going native! By implication, the feminist credentials of any woman who does manage to succeed in science today are open to question.

10   Why are these feminists so opposed to science? Perhaps most fundamental is their belief that the very methods of science predispose it to be more useful for evil than for good. For example, some feminist philosophers argue that the agenda of the "hard" sciences has always been to dominate nature and to penetrate her secrets. The very process of analyzing the workings of natural systems is seen as intrinsically destructive.

11   In their view, the much-vaunted scientific goals of objectivity, controlled experiments, isolation of variables, precise measurements, quantitative analyses, and abstract theoretical models are all seen as potentially destructive to both the natural system being studied and the psyche of the researcher. Accordingly, if little girls haven't the stomach for dissections or the patience to work out vector representations of the stresses in a beautiful spider web, we should congratulate them, not try to socialize them into the narrow and often life-destroying habits of white male scientists.

12   In part, this critique stems from the ecological and pacifist concerns that many of us share today; feminists have joined other intellectuals in raising urgent and legitimate questions about the misuses of science and technology. But what the new feminists add to the call for a more inclusive and socially responsible science is the conviction that all problems are the fault of patriarchal males and that women are constitutionally more revolted by the loss of human life and the annihilation of species than men are, a speculation that is self-serving and unsubstantiated.

13   Such criticism of science seems so extreme that one might imagine — or hope — that it would have little effect outside the hothouse environment of feminist theorizing. Unfortunately, though, it is gaining credibility. In researching our new book, Daphne Patai, professor of women's studies at the University of Massachusetts at Amherst, and I learned how strong the anti-science element in feminism had become. A young research biologist at a government agency told us that she hesitated to tell feminist acquaintances what she did because of their antipathy to science. (So much for the efficacy of the role models.)

A senior sociologist, highly regarded as a scholar and a founding 14
member of the National Organization for Women, described to us the
hostility of feminist graduate students toward courses on statistics and
quantitative methods. She also noted their resistance to any sort of critical
scrutiny of the numbers they eagerly quoted about rape, harassment,
and other mistreatment of women. She was dismayed further by feminist colleagues' out-of-hand dismissal of any research that included biological perspectives on social issues. We concluded that the ethos of
contemporary women's studies not only would discourage young women
from seeking a career in science, but also would make them feel morally and politically enlightened in remaining ignorant about science.

As C.P. Snow so eloquently described in his writings about the gap 15
between the "two cultures" of the sciences and humanities, many otherwise well-educated people feel intimidated by science and mathematics. Because of old sexist stereotypes, females disproportionately feel this
way. But it hardly helps to replace the old "two cultures" split with one
between the sexes, by claiming that "women's ways of knowing" are
incompatible with the allegedly masculine substance and method of science. What young women really need is special encouragement and equal
opportunity to learn science, not a feminist rationalization for failure.

Groups such as the Association for Women in Science are sincerely 16
attempting to dismantle the barriers that women still face. But others,
in which I am sorry to include all too many of my fellow feminist philosophers of science, are really more interested in undermining the epis-
temological authority of science and making it subservient to their own
political agenda than in making science a truly inclusive discipline. It
would be tragic if the educators, administrators, and legislators who have
ignored the problems of women in science for so long should now, in a
paroxysm of liberal guilt, uncritically swallow every nostrum prescribed
in the name of feminism.

For example, it obviously is a good idea to include more pictures of 17
great woman scientists in school textbooks, but it distorts both the history and integral values of science to claim that women who were herb-
alists, wild-flower painters, and midwives also were scientists, whose
contributions have been stolen or denied. And although it is surely wise
for science educators to accommodate as many learning styles and cognitive preferences as possible, it is a real disservice to students if we
pretend that the heavy reliance on mathematical reasoning in the physical sciences is a patriarchal plot. We all need to expand our cognitive
repertoires instead of tailoring them to the service of identity politics.

18   Science has already profited from responsible feminist critiques and should continue to do so. And, just as the influx of refugees changed American science during World War II, we can expect that as more women and members of minority groups enter science, they too will influence both the research priorities and the ethos of science. Science *can* be improved in many ways, but I have no doubt that past scientific discoveries — ranging from better contraceptives to computers — have already played a crucial role in the liberation of women. What a tragedy if feminists were to alienate women from such a powerful — and beautiful — repository of knowledge about the natural world.

(1994)

The Writer's Subject

1. What are some of the chief factors that feminist analysts have identified as having kept women from becoming successful scientists? (paras. 3–4)

2. What, according to Koertge, is the "new feminist agenda" with respect to science? (paras. 7–9)

3. Explain the reference to *"Kinder, Kuche,* and *Kirche."* (para. 6)

4. According to Koertge, how does the new feminism differ from traditional feminism in its view of science as a career for women? (paras. 8–9)

5. Why do the new feminists reject the methods of science? How does this rejection manifest itself in the attitudes of young women graduate students? (paras. 10–13)

6. What, according to the writer, would be the consequences of accepting the feminist claim that "woman's ways of knowing" are incompatible with modern scientific method? (paras. 15–16)

The Writer's Style and Strategy

1. What is the effect of phrasing the title as a question?

2. Comment on the use the writer makes of "little girls" and "women" in para. 8.

3. Explain the medical metaphor in the last sentence of para. 16.

4. How does the writer attempt to persuade us that the anti-science arguments of the new feminists are wrong-headed? Examine the ways in which she describes the views of the new feminist philosophers of science, paying particular attention to diction and tone. (See paras. 10–12, 14–17.)

5. What sort of audience does the writer have in mind here? Would it include the kind of feminist scientists she describes?

Suggested Topics for Writing and Discussion

1. In your opinion, do women still face the traditional barriers of sexism and gender stereotyping in such fields as science or engineering?

2. Koertge alludes to the split between the sciences and the humanities described by the English writer C.P. Snow in a famous essay on "The Two Cultures." Snow was describing the situation in the 1960s. Would you say that the sciences and the humanities are separate "cultures" today? How do humanists and scientists look at the world? If you do see differences, how might the gap between them be narrowed?

3. The writer alludes (para. 12) to the concerns shared by many intellectuals, including feminist thinkers, about "the misuses of science and technology." What kinds of misuse might she have in mind? In what areas do you think science and scientists need to be made more socially responsible?

4. Koertge discusses the efforts of textbook writers to include more women scientists in science texts to raise the profile of women in science (para. 17). Examine one or two textbooks with which you are familiar to determine whether they have been, or should be, revised or updated to take more account of the contributions by women in any particular field.

Marilyn Monroe: The Woman
Who Died Too Soon

by Gloria Steinem

1   Saturday afternoon movies — no matter how poorly made or incredible the plot, they were a refuge from my neighborhood and all my teenage miseries. Serials that never ended, Doris Day, who never capitulated, cheap travelogues, sci-fi features with zippers in the monster suits: I loved them all, believed them all, and never dreamed of leaving until the screen went sickeningly blank.

2   But I walked out on Marilyn Monroe. I remember her on the screen, huge as a colossus doll, mincing and whispering and simply hoping her way into total vulnerability. Watching her, I felt angry, even humiliated, but I didn't understand why.

3   After all, Jane Russell was in the movie, too (a very bad-taste version of *Gentlemen Prefer Blondes*), so it wasn't just the vulnerability that all big-breasted women seem to share. (If women viewers prefer actresses who are smaller, neater — the Audrey Hepburns of the world — it is not because we're jealous of the *zoftig* ones as men suppose. It's just that we would rather identify with a woman we don't have to worry about, someone who doesn't seem in constant danger.) Compared to Marilyn, Jane Russell seemed in control of her body and even of the absurd situations in this movie.

4   Perhaps it was the uncertainty in the eyes of this big, blond child-woman; the terrible desire for approval that made her different from Jane Russell. How dare she express the neediness that so many women feel, but try so hard to hide? How dare she, a movie star, be just as unconfident as I was?

So I disliked her and avoided her movies, as we avoid that which 5 reflects our fears about ourselves. If there were jokes made on her name and image when I was around, I joined in. I contributed to the laughing, the ridicule, the put-downs, thus proving that I was nothing like her. Nothing at all.

I, too, got out of my neighborhood in later years, just as she had es- 6 caped from a much worse life of lovelessness, child abuse, and foster homes. I didn't do it, as she did, through nude calendar photographs and starlet bits. (Even had there been such opportunities for mildly pretty girls in Toledo, Ohio, I would never have had the courage to make myself so vulnerable.) Yes, I was American enough to have show-business dreams. The boys in my neighborhood hoped to get out of a lifetime in the factories through sports; the girls, if we imagined anything other than marrying a few steps up in the world, always dreamed of show-business careers. But after high-school years as a dancer on the Toledo show-business circuit, or what passed for show business there, it seemed hopeless even to me. In the end, it was luck and an encouraging mother and a facility with words that got me out; a facility that helped me fake my way through the college entrance exams for which I was totally unprepared.

But there's not much more confidence in girls who scrape past col- 7 lege boards than there is in those who, like Marilyn, parade past beauty-contest judges. By the time I saw her again, I was a respectful student watching the celebrated members of the Actors Studio do scenes from what seemed to me very impressive and highbrow plays (Arthur Miller and Eugene O'Neill were to be served up that day). She was a student, too, a pupil of Lee Strasberg, leader of the Actors Studio and American guru of the Stanislavski method, but her status as a movie star and sex symbol seemed to keep her from being taken seriously even there. She was allowed to observe, but not to do scenes with her colleagues.

So the two of us sat there, mutually awed, I think, in the presence of 8 such theater people as Ben Gazzara and Rip Torn, mutually insecure in the masculine world of High Culture, mutually trying to fade into the woodwork.

I remember thinking that Strasberg and his actors seemed to take 9 positive pleasure in their power to ignore this great and powerful movie star who had come to learn. Their greetings to her were a little too studiously casual, their whispers to each other about her being there a little too self-conscious and condescending. Though she stayed in the back of the room, her blond head swathed in a black scarf and her body hidden in a shapeless black sweater and slacks, she gradually became a presence, if only because the group was trying so hard *not* to look, to remain oblivious and cool.

10   As we filed slowly out of the shabby room after the session was over, Marilyn listened eagerly to the professional postmortem being carried on by Ben Gazzara and others who walked ahead of us, her fingers nervously tracing a face that was luminous and without makeup, as if she were trying to hide herself, to apologize for being there. I was suddenly glad she hadn't participated and hadn't been subjected to the criticisms of this rather vulturous group. (Perhaps it was an unschooled reaction, but I hadn't enjoyed watching Strasberg encourage an intimate love scene between an actor and actress, and then pick them apart with humiliating authority.) Summoning my nerve, I did ask the shy, blond woman in front of me if she could imagine playing a scene for this group.

11   "Oh, no," Marilyn said, her voice childish, but much less whispery than on the screen, "I admire all these people so much. I'm just not good enough." Then, after a few beats of silence: "Lee Strasberg is a genius, you know. I plan to do what he says."

12   Her marriage to Arthur Miller seemed quite understandable to me and to other women, even those who were threatened by Miller's casting off of a middle-aged wife to take a younger, far more glamorous one. If you can't be taken seriously in your work, if you have an emotional and intellectual insecurity complex, then marry a man who has the seriousness you've been denied. It's a traditional female option far more acceptable than trying to achieve that identity on one's own.

13   Of course, Marilyn's image didn't really gain seriousness and intellectuality. Women don't gain serious status by sexual association any more easily than they do by hard work. (At least, not unless the serious man dies and we confine ourselves to being keepers of the flame. As Margaret Mead has pointed out, widows are almost the only women this country honors in authority.) Even Marilyn's brave refusal to be intimidated by threats that she would never work in films again if she married Miller, who was then a "subversive" called to testify before the House Un-American Activities Committee, was considered less brave than Miller's refusal to testify. Indeed, it was barely reported at all.

14   Perhaps she didn't take her own bravery seriously either. She might be giving up her livelihood, the work that meant so much to her, but she was about to give that up for marriage anyway. As Mrs. Arthur Miller, she retired to a Connecticut farm and tried to limit her life to his solitary work habits, his friends, and his two children. Only when they badly needed money did she come out of retirement again, and

that was to act in *The Misfits*, a film written by her husband.

On the other hand, the public interpretation was very different. She 15
was an egocentric actress forcing one of America's most important playwrights to tailor a screenplay to her inferior talents: that was the gos-
sip-column story here and in Europe. But her own pattern argues the
case for her. In two previous marriages, to an aircraft factory worker at
the age of sixteen and later to Joe Di Maggio, she had cut herself off
from the world and put all her energies into being a housewife. When it
didn't work out, she blamed herself, not the role, and added one more
failure to her list of insecurities. "I have too many fantasies to be a housewife," she told a woman friend sadly. And finally, to an interviewer: "I
guess I *am* a fantasy."

The Misfits seemed to convey some facets of the real Marilyn: hon- 16
esty, an innocence and belief that survived all experience to the contrary, kindness toward other women, a respect for the life of plants and
animals. Because for the first time she wasn't only a sex object and victim, I also was unembarrassed enough to notice her acting ability. I began to see her earlier movies — those in which, unlike *Gentlemen Prefer
Blondes*, she wasn't called upon to act the female impersonator.

For me as for so many people, she was a presence in the world, a life 17
force.

Over the years, I heard other clues to her character. When Ella 18
Fitzgerald, a black artist and perhaps the greatest singer of popular songs,
hadn't been able to get a booking at an important Los Angeles night-
club in the fifties, it was Marilyn who called the owner and promised to
sit at a front table every night while she sang. The owner hired Ella,
Marilyn was faithful to her promise each night, the press went wild,
and, as Ella remembers with gratitude, "After that, I never had to play a
small jazz club again."

Even more movingly, there was her last interview. She pleaded with 19
the reporter to end with "What I really want to say: That what the world
really needs is a real feeling of kinship. Everybody: stars, laborers, Ne-
groes, Jews, Arabs. We are all brothers.... Please don't make me a joke.
End the interview with what I believe."

And then she was gone. I remember being told, in the middle of a 20
chaotic student meeting in Europe, that she was dead. I remember that
precise moment on August 5, 1962 — the people around me, what the
room looked like — and I've discovered that many other people remember that moment of hearing the news, too. It's a phenomenon usually
reserved for the death of family and presidents.

21   She was an actress, a person on whom no one's fate depended, and
yet her energy and terrible openness to life had made a connection to
strangers. Within days after her body was discovered, eight young and
beautiful women took their lives in individual incidents clearly patterned
after Marilyn Monroe's death. Some of them left notes to make that
connection clear.

22   Two years later, Arthur Miller's autobiographical play, *After The Fall*,
brought Marilyn back to life in the character of Maggie. But somehow
that Maggie didn't seem the same. She had Marilyn's pathetic insecurity, the same need to use her sexual self as her only way of getting
recognition and feeling alive. But, perhaps naturally, the play was about
Miller's suffering, not Marilyn's. He seemed honestly to include some
of his own destructive acts. (He had kept a writer's diary of his movie-
star wife, for instance, and Marilyn's discovery of it was an emotional
blow, the beginning of the end for that marriage. It made her wonder:
Was her husband exploiting her, as most men had done, but in a more
intellectual way?) Nonetheless, the message of the play was mostly
Miller's view of his attempts to shore up a creature of almost endless
insecurities; someone doomed beyond his helping by a mysterious lack
of confidence.

23   To women, that lack was less mysterious. Writer Diana Trilling, who
had never met Marilyn, wrote an essay just after her death that some of
Marilyn's friends praised as a more accurate portrayal than Miller's. She
described the public's "mockery of [Marilyn's] wish to be educated";
the sexual awareness that came only from outside, from men's reactions, "leaving a great emptiness where a true sexuality would have supplied her with a sense of herself as a person with connection and content."
She questioned whether Marilyn had really wanted to die, or only to be
asleep, not to be conscious through the loneliness of that particular Saturday night.

24   Trilling also recorded that feeling of connection to Marilyn's loneliness felt by so many strangers ("especially women to whose protective-
ness her extreme vulnerability spoke so directly"), so much so that we
fantasized our ability to save her, if only we had been there. "But we were
the friends," as Trilling wrote sadly, "of whom she knew nothing."

25   "She was an unusual woman — a little ahead of her times," said Ella
Fitzgerald. "And she didn't know it."

26   Now that women's self-vision is changing, we are thinking again
about the life of Marilyn Monroe. Might our new confidence in wom-
en's existence with or without the approval of men have helped a thirty-

six-year-old woman of talent to stand on her own? To resist the insecurity and ridicule? To stop depending on sexual attractiveness as the only
proof that she was alive — and therefore to face aging with confidence?
Because the ability to bear a child was denied to her, could these new
ideas have helped her to know that being a woman included much more?
Could she have challenged the Freudian analysts to whom she turned
in her suffering?

Most of all, we wonder if the support and friendship of other women   27
could have helped. Her early experiences of men were not good. She
was the illegitimate daughter of a man who would not even contribute
for her baby clothes; her mother's earliest memory of her own father,
Marilyn's grandfather, was his smashing a pet kitten against the fireplace in a fit of anger; Marilyn herself said she was sexually attacked
by a foster father while still a child; and she was married off at sixteen
because another foster family could not take care of her. Yet she was
forced always to depend for her security on the goodwill and recognition of men; even to be interpreted by them in writing because she feared
that sexual competition made women dislike her. Even if they had wanted
to, the women in her life did not have the power to protect her. In films,
photographs, and books, even after her death as well as before, she has
been mainly seen through men's eyes.

We are too late. We cannot know whether we could have helped   28
Norma Jean Baker or the Marilyn Monroe she became. But we are not
too late to do as she asked. At last, we can take her seriously.

(1972)

The Writer's Subject

1. Why was Steinem's first response to Marilyn Monroe one of anger and
   humiliation? (paras. 2–5)

2. In what ways was Steinem's early life like Monroe's? (para. 6)

3. How was Monroe treated by members of the Actors Studio? How did this
   episode affect Steinem's view of Monroe? (paras. 7–10)

4. Why, according to Steinem, did Monroe marry the celebrated American
   playwright, Arthur Miller? (para. 12)

5. What qualities in Monroe's character does Steinem find admirable? How
   are those qualities illustrated?

6. What is the importance of Marilyn's last interview described in paragraph
   19?

7. Why, according to Steinem, did the news of Monroe's death have an impact on so many people? (paras. 20–21, 24)

8. Steinem suggests that Miller may have exploited his marriage to Monroe. How? (para. 22)

9. What, according to Steinem's account, was missing in Monroe's life?

10. Why, in Steinem's view, was Marilyn Monroe "the woman who died too soon"? (paras. 25–28)

The Writer's Style and Strategy

1. Steinem's essay presents an initially hostile view which is re-evaluated and then altered. Analyze the stages of the essay to show how Steinem presents this shift in view.

2. What use does Steinem make of her own experiences in her attempt to explain the mysterious appeal of Marilyn Monroe?

3. What tone does Steinem create by means of the transition from paragraph 5 into paragraph 6?

4. What is Steinem's purpose in repeating "mutually" in paragraph 8?

5. What use does Steinem make of the Actors Studio anecdote to illustrate Monroe's character? Why does she quote directly Monroe's comments about Lee Strasberg? (para. 11)

6. This essay was originally published in *Ms.* magazine. What features of Steinem's style or approach suggest that she was writing specifically for a feminist audience?

Suggested Topics for Writing and Discussion

1. Marilyn Monroe achieved considerable fame as the sex symbol for her generation. Who in your view, among today's male and female stars, has attained the status of a sex symbol? Explain this person's appeal for the present generation.

2. Steinem alludes to the American dreams of escape from an ordinary life to fame and fortune, chiefly through sports for the boys and show business for the girls. Are these, in your view, still the stuff of escape dreams for American — and Canadian — youth?

3. Steinem says that a traditional option for a woman has been to marry a man in order to gain an identity rather than achieve that identity on her own. Do you think that is still the case?

Women and Criticism
by Helen Taylor

Few things are more interesting to an observer of mankind than the end-   1
less variety and absolutely contradictory nature of the objections raised,
in society and contemporary literature, to every possible proposal for
altering anything. It seems to be in the nature of the human mind to
hold that no reason can be necessary for doing nothing; this is so natural a thing to do, apparently, that the inducements and the justification
for it are, at all times, self-evident to all the world. But, when any one
proposes to break in upon any established order whatever, by any plan
which is actually intended to be carried into practical operation, then
there arises a multitudinous host of objections, not from one side only
but from every side, a tumult of clashing arguments, of opposing difficulties, a cross-fire which sometimes reminds us of Falconbridge —

"From north to south
   Austria and France shoot in each other's mouth,"

when those who fancy themselves allies unintentionally destroy one
another's position, by blows aimed at an intermediate enemy.

It is this variety and inconsistency in the objections raised to all re-   2
forms which is one of the chief elements in the priceless value, for human progress, of free discussion. If the truth had to do battle alone against
all its adversaries the task would be a much harder one than it is at
present, and the result, if not more uncertain, would certainly be much
longer deferred. But, where discussion is free, the *mêlée* is generally so
confused that whoever will consent to fight at all can hardly help dealing some blows at error. He who strikes at random may fight against

truth too, but, if there is one distinguishing mark of truth as opposed to error, it is its vital power, its strength to endure, the ineradicable energy with which it revives from apparent annihilation. A much weaker blow will kill falsehood, and, as a general rule, the same weakness of mind which makes people hold an opinion on insufficient grounds makes them find very insufficient arguments strong enough to overthrow it. Thus, while it is true that error is manifold, yet its opponents are manifold also. A consistent reasoner will often be surprised at the weapons with which a victory may be gained for his own side; yet a logical intellect is not so hard and dry a thing but that some of the most humorous scenes of the comedy of human life may receive their keenest relish from the sense of incongruity between cause and effect.

3   But, of all the battle-fields of confused and diverse opinion, none is more strangely and chaotically intermingled than the perennial dispute, which all the world loves to join in, as to the comparative merits, duties, faults, and virtues of men and women. Feelings, passions, fancies, sentiments, resentments, hopes, dreams, fears, come pouring in, all eager to do their part in settling the matter, so that, in this particular contest, prejudice and ignorance seem calm and rational in comparison with the rest of the combatants. Nor is this abundance of personal feeling astonishing when we come to consider the subject, since every one is personally concerned in it; no one can help being a man or a woman at some time if he lives long enough. The cattle plague may be discussed among sailors, or fine art with Quakers, in which case it might be possible to secure judges who possess the qualification, so essential in the eyes of many critics, for fitness to judge — that, however little they know of the subject, they care less. But, however little a woman may know of physiology, or psychology, or history, or politics, or social science, or mental science, or difficult subjects of that sort, she is not likely to doubt that she knows woman's nature, which, after all, is only a form of that which all these sciences put together are intended to investigate. What gentle, timid, home-keeping lady will hesitate to pronounce (firm in the consciousness of her own incapacity) what nature destined for all time to be the lot of one half the human race? Is she not a woman herself, and, being so, must she not understand women? Do we not all know ourselves? And, knowing ourselves, as we all do, so well, does it not of necessity follow that we know all who resemble us in any important respect? And, knowing ourselves, is it not evident that we must know what is good for us? And, knowing these things by nature, it cannot be going out of a woman's sphere, nor need any strength of mind,

to pronounce what ought to be the relative position of men, women, and children, in politics, arts, sciences, and domestic life. It is, indeed, so difficult to find a woman unprejudiced about women, that those who think least of their own capacities are more confident as to the absence of capacity in women, than those ladies (if any there are) who lay claim to strength of mind can be as to the presence of it. For the women who profess to be in some degree competent to consider the subject, generally only hazard the suggestion that women might possibly prove equal to men if they were placed in the same circumstances, and they propose only that the law shall make no distinctions, and so leave things to adjust themselves. But those who think they know woman's proper place from their own internal consciousness, want laws to keep her there. Not content to remain in that vague state of mind which only suits scientific accuracy, and requires experiment and test before considering any fact as certain; content still less with that impartiality which may do well enough for the lawgiver or statesman, but which does not become an ignorant woman; they demand a positive recognition by law and institutions of the difference between two things, of which difference these ladies are perfectly sure, because they know one of the two quite well.

When all women, strong or weak-minded, have given in their contribution to this universally-interesting subject, it is far from being exhausted. If women naturally have an opinion upon it because they are women, men have one because they are not. Even those who think the only suitable relations between the two are those of superiority and subordination cannot deny this. The question of where the lamb was entitled to drink from, was not less interesting to the wolf than to the lamb. It would be taking a very narrow view of the matter to deny that the wolf had, at least, a right to be heard, in support of claims on which so much of his comfort in life depended. The fact is, that the nearer we could come to a complete equality between men and women in the laws and institutions under which they live, the better chance would there be of getting at something like impartial opinion on the subject. The nearer it could be brought to being nobody's interest to think one way or another about it, the nearer we should be to arriving at some cool and unbiased judgment. No observer can help seeing at present that the interests at stake are too important to permit much impartiality. People are either, consciously or unconsciously, blinded by their personal wishes and experience, or else, making a strenuous effort to be magnanimous, they endeavour to secure themselves against being selfish by an entire

4

renunciation of all personal claims. The common opinion that women are more enthusiastic and less reasoning than men, and that men are more deliberate, and know better what they mean when they say a thing, than women, may perhaps explain why, on the whole, most women decide against, and most men in favour of themselves. But, if women were really entitled in justice to any rights and privileges which most of them disclaim, it may be doubted whether the fact of their renouncing such rights from pure although mistaken motives of duty would be any evidence of unfitness for their exercise.

5   Yet, among the many answers commonly given when the question is asked, Why women should not have all occupations and privileges open to them, and be free to adopt or renounce masculine, as men are feminine, pursuits? none reappears more frequently than the assertion that women themselves do not wish for any such freedom. With many persons it is a received axiom that women do not like liberty. There is nothing, it would seem, that a woman more dislikes than being permitted to do what she likes. Husbands and fathers know by experience that women never wish to have their own way. One reason for this appears to be that women are endowed by nature with so strong and peculiar an idiosyncrasy that they must necessarily run counter to it if they are let alone. The laws of nature are so powerful in women that it is essential to make human laws in aid of them. The instincts of their sex so imperiously demand of women to do what is feminine, that it is necessary for men to forbid them to do anything masculine. Therefore it stands to reason that women who wish to be guided by womanly instinct must place themselves under the guidance of men. Possessed by an innate sense of feminine propriety, women feel that if the law did not protect them against themselves they would be inclined to do many unsuitable things. With men it is different; no laws are needed to define what men may or may not do, for men, with their less acute moral perceptions, are not likely to do what is unsuited to them. But legislative enactments can alone keep women from leaving their firesides to plunge into the fierce contentions and angry passions of the political world; were they free to choose for themselves it is to be feared they would desert their infants in order to command armies; their love of beauty and their physical weakness would induce them to apply themselves to the most repulsive and laborious occupations, such as no man would like to see a woman employed in, and from which they would naturally, but perhaps very unfairly, drive out their more robust masculine competitors. Then, too, being gentle, docile, and retiring, naturally fitted to obey, is it not likely

that if left to their own guidance, they would show themselves quarrel-
some, self-willed, and altogether unmanageable?

Leaving those who will to unravel these very curious series of logi-   6
cal sequences, or perhaps leaving these contradictory propositions to
neutralize one another, it may be worth while to go on a few steps further, and consider the question on the ground of general principles, which
cover a much larger space than the mere distinction between men and
women: for, the moment we step beyond the charmed circle which shuts
in women in most people's imagination, we find ourselves on ground
where it is comparatively usual to appeal to reason, and to expect that
reasons shall have some sort of consistency in them. On no other subject is it commonly held that so small an amount of experimental evidence is sufficient to build up such a wide induction as on this. It is the
commonest thing in the world to hear even educated people, who, on
other topics, pride themselves on having some foundation for what they
say, confound together in one group millions of women, of different
races and different religions, brought up in different climates, and under different institutions, and predict, with quiet security, how all these
would act under utterly untried conditions — such as perfect political
and social freedom — of which the history of the world has never yet
furnished even a single instance whereon to ground a sober judgment.
How utterly this whole way of treating such a subject is opposed to all
the scientific tendencies of our time, it is hardly worth while to stop to
point out.

The growing habit of studying history from a philosophical point of   7
view, and drawing generalizations from its teaching in a scientific spirit,
will, no doubt, do much to induce men (and women too) to consider the
destinies, the duties, and the rights of women in a serious and logical
manner, and to lay aside the jokes and the sentimental preferences which
at present encumber and entangle all discussion on the subject. It may
even be presumed, that, fortified with such studies, some women may
no longer shrink from being called "strong-minded," as from an abusive epithet, and that men may only hesitate to apply it to them, as being more complimentary than they are often likely to deserve.

But, when rational habits of thought, and a comparatively widely   8
extended acquaintance with scientific methods of observation and experiment, have done much good work on the public mind, still we cannot expect a thorough cure in the fanciful method of treating women's
rights, until legislation, by loosening a little the tightness of its bonds,
opens the door to observation, and permits a few, however timid, ex-

periments to be made. At present it is hard to complain of those who appeal to their own imagination as warrant for their highly imaginative assertions of what would happen if any changes were introduced into the condition of women, for to what else can they appeal? The truth is, as we take it, that the law is a great deal too minute in its legislation on this subject; for, if we come to consider it, we find that it is marked in the highest degree by the characteristic of early and antiquated legislation: it protects the interests of both men and women a great deal too much, and, by taking too much care of them, will not allow them to take care of themselves. It is this same meddlesome spirit which in former times produced sumptuary laws, and fixed the rate of interest and of wages; which forbade the exportation of gold and other valuable commodities from the realm, and gave rise to the whole system of commercial protection.

9   But the striking and brilliant success of free trade principles has happily had a powerful effect in opening the eyes of every civilized people to the mischievous effects of over-legislation. The benefit of the promulgation of such principles ought not to stop even at this result, great as it is. For the philosophical principles, and the whole train of reasoning which lead to free trade, not merely indicate that over-legislation is a check upon individual energy and enterprise, but point to the direction which all the legislation should take, viz. — to development, and not to the repression, of the faculties of those who have to obey it. That the law is made for man, not man for the law, is the spirit of modern legislation, and we recognise the working of this spirit where we see the law removing hindrances to human energy, not where we see it imposing them. The hindrances that we are willing to see imposed by the law are only those that prevent people from hindering one another, not such as are imagined to be beneficial to themselves. We are willing to see a man hindered from stealing another man's goods, but we murmur if he is not allowed to sell his own at as low a price as he pleases. The application of any such principle will show at once how very defective is our present legislation as regards women, and how antiquated is the train of reasoning by which such legislation is defended. Indeed, the only logical defence of our present legislation would be that it considers only the interests of men, and looks upon women as a subject, and even as an antagonistic class, whose hands are to be bound for the benefit of those whom the law really intends to protect. It is not impossible that some such point of view was that which really actuated those who originated our present system, many parts of which have come down to us

from times when men had not, even in thought, got beyond the idea
that —

> "Those should take who have the power,
>   And those should keep who can."

But the most violent assertor of the sacred rights of sex would shrink
now from making such a notion the ground either of his own claims or
her own abnegation. Agreeing, therefore, as most disputants would probably do, that no one wants to oppress and enslave women for other people's benefit, we are thrown back upon the theory, that, solely for their
own good, they are excluded from all the professions, from all political
rights, from a share in the great national institutions for education, and
from every other privilege possessed only by men. The energy and the
enterprise women might show in any or all these departments is checked
by the law, only in order to protect them, just as our traders and manufacturers used to be protected against foreign competition. The development of their faculties is forbidden to take place in these directions,
only in order that they may be turned into more healthy and natural channels, just as particular industries used to be encouraged by law because
it used to be thought that our island possessed peculiar facilities for those,
and just as particular methods of manufacture used to be enjoined because it was supposed that our people would employ wrong methods if
the law did not restrict them to right ones. Now, on the supposition
(which lies at the root of the Protective system) that our lawgivers know
the true interest of every individual of the nation better than he can know
it for himself, there can be no objection to all this as a whole, and, if we
think we see reason to object to the working of any particular portion
of the system, we must set ourselves to show what are its specially inconvenient results, and what good might be expected to come from the
relaxation of particular restraints. Just as, under a system of commercial protection, it would be necessary to show that some particular trade
is an exceptional one in order to get it freed from the general rule, so,
on such a supposition, we must show that some particular profession or
occupation is (unlike the majority of others) suited for women, before
we can get it opened to them.

It is precisely this necessity, arising, as we have endeavoured to show,   10
from ignoring the fundamental principles of modern government, that
opens the door to the flood of peculiarly contradictory and imaginative
discussion which characterises every attempt at carrying out some little
modification of the highly "protected" condition of women. For how

can discussion on this subject be otherwise than imaginative? By the nature of the case those who are urging change are asking to be allowed to try experiments. Until experiments have been tried, we can only imagine what would be their practical results. When we are reduced to imagination one man's imagination is as good as another's, and the Irishman in the story would perhaps have said that a conservative's imagination is "better too." The reformer imagines great benefits, the conservative imagines dire disaster, to be the consequences of most change. What can decide between the two, except that invincible "logic of facts" to which protective law sternly forbids a hearing? Deprived of this impartial umpire, people disport themselves in all the wide regions of fanciful conjecture; analogy is put forward for sober argument; figurative phrases as logical proof; a single example as conclusive evidence; personal taste as the law of nature; accidental circumstances as the immutable condition of the universe. And it is the natural consequence of such discussion's being fanciful that it should also be contradictory. For no two men's imagination depicts a thing exactly in the same light. No two reformers desire, and no two conservatives dread, a change for precisely the same reasons. One man wishes a thing because it does what another man deprecates it for not doing. Thus many persons at the present moment shrink from opening the medical profession to women, because they think it might make them less delicate; others fear that such a movement, by enabling women always to consult physicians of their own sex might foster a morbid degree of delicacy. Thus two different descriptions of imagination may figure the results of the same change as making women too delicate and not delicate enough. In this particular instance, as in many others of the same sort, it is not difficult to detect that the fancy of the objectors has seized hold of different parts of the same subject, and exaggerated a part into the whole. One class persists in regarding exclusively the probable effect upon the physicians, the other that on the patients; and both are apt to forget that, in so very extensive a portion of humanity as the whole female sex, there may easily be room for such varieties of character as would be healthily affected by both sets of influences.

11   From all these workings of the imagination there is no final appeal but to facts. Experiments must be tried before we can hope to arrive at trustworthy conclusions. They can be tried cautiously if we fancy, as many people do fancy, that, in dealing with women, we are dealing with very explosive materials. But, until we are willing to try them in some way we cannot deny that those who are willing to appeal to facts are

more candid, and those who desire to have recourse to experiment are more practical, than those who are content to defend the present state of things by vague predictions of possible evil, while they refuse to put their own predictions to even the most gentle test.

Just such predictions of national ruin were made arguments against 12 free trade, and against such arguments no reply could be so effectual as the national prosperity which free trade has produced. But, until free trade had actually been tried, this argument was not available for its supporters. Having been tried, and having succeeded, free trade, however, remains an example of how human energy can find the best and easiest channels for itself when relieved from all restrictive legislation; an example likely in time to modify old opinions on many topics, and perhaps on none more than on the freedom that can safely be allowed to women.

(1866)

The Writer's Subject

1. Why does the author seem undisturbed at the "variety and inconsistency in the objections raised to all reforms"? (para. 2) How is this observation connected with other parts of the essay?

2. To what is Taylor referring when she speaks of "the sense of incongruity between cause and effect" at the end of para. 2?

3. What are the views of the "gentle, timid, home-keeping lady" described in para. 3? What is Taylor's response to such views?

4. Why should some women want laws to keep all women in their "proper place"? (para. 3)

5. Why, in Taylor's opinion, do "most women decide against, and most men in favour of themselves" in the matter of rights and privileges in society? (para. 4)

6. How does Taylor handle the argument that "women do not like liberty" and are themselves opposed to being given freedom of choice in all pursuits? (para. 5)

7. On what basis, in Taylor's opinion, do most people form their opinions about women's readiness for political and social freedom? (para. 6)

8. Why does Taylor regard the laws pertaining to women's rights as "meddlesome" and "defective"? Why does she compare these laws to earlier legislation that placed restraints on trade and manufacturing? (paras. 8–9, 12)

The Writer's Style and Strategy

1. Discuss Taylor's use of figurative language in the first two sentences of para. 3.

2. Identify those points in para. 3 where Taylor advances her argument through irony.

3. What is the point of the contrast Taylor draws between sailors and Quakers on one hand, and women on the other? (para. 3)

4. Taylor's paragraphs are lengthy, a characteristic of late 19th-century prose. Consider the organization of paras. 3, 6, and 9. How does the writer structure and control the flow of ideas to maintain coherence and continuity?

Suggested Topics for Writing and Discussion

1. Taylor shows how proposals for change can produce opposition on a wide variety of grounds, often contradictory in nature. Choose a controversial topic on which there has been public debate — e.g., a proposal to build a new airport, proposals to lower the voting age or restrict driving licenses — and compare some of the arguments offered by *either* supporters *or* opponents.

2. Taylor's essay describes the condition of women and the restrictions upon their activities in England in 1866. Compare the situation of women in Taylor's time with their position in our own society. Are there still any restrictions placed on what women may do?

3. Find out what you can about the platform of a feminist organization such as NAC or LEAF, and outline the major goals of the organization.

Feeding, Feasts, and Females

by Margaret Visser

It has for most of history been common for men and women to eat apart, 1
especially in public. Often taboos ensure that they eat different foods,
women typically being forbidden various edible substances judged dangerous either to their morality or to their reproductive powers. Eating
together in private often both entails and "means" marriage: it involves
sharing the same house. Ceasing to eat together is tantamount to divorce — or ceasing to "sleep together," as we still put it. Our euphemism is not merely coy; it contains the suggestion of sharing the same
private space. Cooking, like digesting, is a common metaphor for pregnancy. The woman offers cooking in exchange for sex; the man offers
sex in exchange for cooking. It follows that women "receive" sex as
men "are fed" food. Eating can be spoken of as synonymous with the
sex act itself. In the languages of the Ghanaian LoDagaa and Gonja,
the verb "to eat" is frequently used for sex, covering a semantic field
very similar to that of the English word "enjoy."

The conjunction of the opposite poles of femaleness and maleness in 2
the married couple is very commonly made to stand for socially and
culturally vital oppositions, including one or more of the following: private and public, inside and outside, domesticity and "work," down and
up, left and right, dark and light, cold and hot, back and front, curved
and straight, soft and hard, still (female) and moving (male), and so forth.
Being made to "stand for" these in turn enforces conformity with the
expectations. If "a woman's place is in the home," her place implies all
the "female" characteristics: interiority, quietness, a longing to nurture,
unwillingness to stand forth, and renunciation of the "male" claims to

authority, publicity, loudness, brightness, sharpness. These qualities have a multitude of practical applications; for example, they either make a woman altogether unfit and unwilling to attend feasts, or they influence the way she behaves while participating in them.

3   An ancient Greek wife would not have been seen dead at a symposium. She was thought — and considered herself to be — the embodiment of purity in the family. Her honour was, and had at all costs to remain, unassailable: the legitimacy of her offspring, and the honour of her menfolk, depended upon it. It was all right for *betairai* (courtesans) to mix with revelling and orgiastic males; they were shameless women, outrageous in their freedom and lack of *tenue*. A dining room was called an *andron*, "a room for men": a woman eating there was a woman out of place, marginalized and unworthy of respect. Unphilosophically minded ancient Greeks apparently thought, as many people nowadays still do, that important ideas should never be discussed at table. Plutarch has one such symposiast put it like this: "Philosophy should no more have a part in conversation over wine than should the matron of the house." According to this view, the Persians got it right when they drank and danced with their mistresses, but never with their wives. Wives were serious, but *betairai* and mistresses could be taken lightly. When men, therefore, were asked to a party, they left their wives at home. But a wedding feast was a crowded affair, Plutarch makes his sympotic conversationalists say elsewhere, because women were responsible for a lot of the activities at a wedding — and an invited woman must invariably come accompanied by her husband.

4   Formality at public events is almost invariably a male affair, because it involves social rank (which has often been denied to all but the very top women) and publicity. Formality has always been contrasted with relaxation and intimacy, which are enjoyed at home, where the women have their place. (Men inhabit both spheres, public and private, whereas women have rarely done so; this one-sided overlap is one of the important inconsistencies in the scheme.) It follows that at a banquet in many traditional societies, men observe rank and precedence at table, while women serve the diners, or sit and eat in a separate place where far less ceremony is observed; they might sit in a crowd in the middle of the room, for example, while the men are ranged in order round the walls. At a Winnebago Indian feast, the men sat observing strict precedence round the periphery of the meeting house, with plenty of room between them; the women and children crowded together in a tiny space behind a screen at the back. The women have generally cooked such feasts,

though occasionally men will have insisted on handling the meat (a pres-
tigious, "masculine" food) themselves. The women may even think of
being permitted to serve the food as a tremendous, and jealously guarded,
privilege. Women, say the Javanese who practise the *slametan* feast, are
mburi, "behind" (that is, in the kitchen; during the feast they peep
through the bamboo partitions at the men as they eat), whereas men are
ngarepan, "in front," consuming the food prepared by the women.

In nineteenth-century Japan, women were seldom invited to dinner,   5
but if they were they were expected to sit apart, in one corner of the
room. In China, they feasted separately from the men, as women do in
societies where there is a very strong division between the sexes. In
the Ming period, the imperial women, dowagers, wives, daughters, and
sisters of their men would host the wives of ministers and officials in
the Inner Quarters of the Palace of Female Tranquillity. Their banquets
were accompanied by female musicians. Hostesses were required, however, to offer fewer courses at dinner than the men, and to offer wine
less often. It is assumed that in private, on ordinary occasions, male
and female members of the imperial family ate together, as the com-
moners did. In the United Arab Emirates today, as in other Arab countries, women often meet and dine together, with complex and
sophisticated civility.

It is with a great sense of superiority that a male host may "feed" his   6
guests but not himself partake of the meal; and a woman who cooks
and serves a dinner without eating much of it herself may do so with a
real sense of the power conferred by the bestowal of food. (Guests always feel uncomfortable eating in front of an abstemious host.) But it
is necessary for the giver to be present during the meal to enjoy this
particular kind of ego enhancement, for prestige is personal: it is non-
existent where there is no knowledge of the person being honoured. As
late as the nineteenth century in French peasant households, the women
would serve the men at table, but themselves eat standing, or draw up
stools by the fire and hold their dishes on their laps; the old and the
children might be expected to join them there. It is possible, but unlikely, that such an arrangement expressed appreciation and respect for
women.

Young boys in strictly sex-segregated societies must one day make   7
the transition from living as children with the women to joining the men.
The initiation, whether accompanied or not by ceremonial rites, is effected in large part by the young male taking his predestined place in
public life, among the men at dinner. Girls do not take this step; they

remain, in this sense, children. (To "stay where you are," even metaphorically, is of course to cleave to the principle of stillness and cen-
trality which has hitherto been so important in the symbolism of being
female.) A man often prefers a woman to keep the status of dependent
child: he may reward her for accepting this position by finding her sexually attractive if she does so.

8   A woman maintains her role as mother by feeding her family; some
African societies are said to think of the wife as "mother of her husband" for this reason. Food is a female concern, and often one of the
main sources of a woman's power in the household. Women gather food,
shop, choose what is to be eaten, and cook it. Social anthropologists
have long called women the "gatekeepers" of food supplies in the house.
However, since they choose food which they know their husbands and
children like and demand, the "gatekeeper" role is often merely executive. Women are reported to make their cooking expressive of their feelings: they "reward" men by producing a special dish, with particular
care; they show disapproval by not having dinner ready on time, or by
refusing to put effort into the meal. Gertrude Stein tells the story of her
French cook Hélène, who disapproved of Matisse because a Frenchman "should not stay unexpectedly to a meal particularly if he asked
the servant beforehand what there was for dinner." One could expect
such behaviour from foreigners, but in a Frenchman it was unacceptable. When Matisse was invited to dinner she would, for example, serve
him fried eggs, never an omelette. "It takes the same number of eggs,"
she coldly asserted, "and the same amount of butter, but it shows less
respect." Monsieur Matisse would understand.

9   If an African wife refuses to cook at all, her husband cannot make
her do it; men are often not only incapable of cooking but forbidden to
cook. In some Nigerian tribes they are not allowed even to discuss food
or express directly a desire to eat: a Jukun male will say, "I am going to
eat," when he means he is thirsty, and use a phrase like "I shall go into
my hut" (the *kunguni*, where Jukun males eat alone) for "I want some
dinner." Eating, for him, requires the kind of euphemism which in our
society is reserved for sex or excretion. This attitude towards eating is
part of the allocation of roles, and again it goes back to the sexual model:
"giving food" for women corresponds to "giving sex" for men; it would
be extremely confusing to do things the other way round. It is fairly
common for a man to refuse to eat what his wife has cooked, as a sign
of his displeasure; he is protected, of course, from having to do without
food altogether if he has several wives. A further connection between

food and sex is suggested by the fact that a polygamous male usually eats food prepared by the wife he is currently sleeping with.

Brewing beer is an ancient female preserve; and where beer is cen- 10 tral to the economy and nutrition of a society — as it often still is in Africa, among South American Indians, and elsewhere — control over it naturally becomes a source of female power. It may link up with another commonly traditional female skill and responsibility: that of making and controlling the use of clay pots. (The ancient Greek god Dionysus — feminine is so much of his nature — had power both over wine and over the area of Athens called Ceramicus, where pots were made.) The Newar women of Nepal must personally serve the beer they have made, even at a public feast. Among the LoDagaa of Ghana, a woman's good beer can turn her home into a beer house, a place where people gather to exchange news and gossip. She sells her product, and pours it out for her clients, always setting aside a calabash of it for herself to show she has not poisoned the batch. She plays a role rather like that of European society hostesses who used to keep "open house" or a "salon" on certain days of the week where people could collect together and socialize. The hostess of a tea party, like the LoDagaa breweress, must pour the tea.

Because food and drink usually reach the family through the wom- 11 en's hands, fear of women frequently translates into suspicion that they are poisoners. Knives, in the traditional view, are "male" weapons. They are wielded aggressively, and they pertain to the masculine realm of fighting, war, and the hunt; they are essential for carving meat. From a symbolic point of view, knives are phallic. We have seen how in medieval Europe, men were supposed to cut for their womenfolk at table. Poison, on the other hand, is a secretive, sneaky way of killing anyone, in addition to which it is often liquid, and administered in food — all of which makes poison a peculiarly "female" weapon, certainly in the folklore and mythology of all races, and possibly in fact as well. Fear of poison can strengthen the pressure upon men not to rove, but stay with their families: they might eat only what is prepared for them by their wives or mothers, or by women otherwise in their control.

Alcoholic drinks, like knives, have always been thought especially 12 dangerous in the hands of women, and men have taken great care to prevent their own partiality for alcohol from infecting "the fair sex." Their solicitude has, until recently, been effective: the percentage of female heavy drinkers has usually been comparatively very low. (It is now rising alarmingly, according to Noel and McCrady for example.) Women must take responsibility for their unborn children, and it is certain that heavy drinking during pregnancy can have ill effects. In any case, what was disgraceful behaviour in a man was always far worse if seen in a woman. During the nineteenth century in Europe, women at table were not to ask for wine; the men were expected to keep them supplied. A man would serve himself and his female partner simultaneously: he would bow, then drink with her. Women were expected not to accept wine every time they were offered it. In France it was correct for a man to offer a woman water at the same time as wine, for a woman, says the Baronne Staffe, never drinks wine neat except at the dessert: she always insists that it be *trempé*, mixed with water.

13   Women in the Mediterranean countries, from the sixteenth century until recent times, appear to have astonished visitors by their sobriety. In France, in particular, men "cut" their wine with water, but "honourable" French women, if they touched wine at all, "used it merely to redden their water slightly." Wine, these days, has become an object of awe and reverence; the only people who add water to it are those who can obtain it cheaply and drink it regularly, and who pay comparatively little regard to its quality. Women drink it at table as much as men do — but even the most recent of etiquette manuals cling to the idea that men should really serve women with the dangerous liquid, "regardless of the symbolism," as Miss Manners puts it. If the host (not the hostess) does not get up and refill glasses when necessary, then "each man should pour wine for the woman on his left."

14   "Young ladies do not eat cheese, nor game, nor savouries," states a late Victorian etiquette book. The reason was almost certainly the same as that occasionally suggested for women not drinking: their breath would cease to be pleasing to men. Women still conform to expectations about eating less than men do, and preferring lighter, paler foods — chicken and lettuce, for example, over beef and potatoes. In Japan, women were actually given smaller rice bowls and shorter, slimmer chopsticks. In the Kagoro tribe of northern Nigeria, men use spoons, but women are not allowed this privilege. Among the Pedi of South Africa, in the 1950s, women and children used the special men's porridge dishes, but only when they were cracked and "no longer sufficiently respectable" for male use. Cooking and serving food to the men as they do, women are accustomed all over the world to eating what is left over from dinner; they are often able, of course, to look out for themselves while preparing the meal. In Assam, where pollution rules mean that lower castes may accept food from higher castes but not the other

way round, a woman eats from the same plates as her husband, after the men have finished their meal: nothing could make the pair more intimate, and nothing could more clearly demonstrate that she is lower than he.

In Europe, families have often eaten all together at home, though 15 where several families lived in one dwelling and dinners fed a lot of people, it was probably most common for the men to be fed first, served by the women. It was the nobility who took part in most of the formal banquets, and among them women were sometimes admitted, sometimes allowed on sufferance, and sometimes excluded altogether. During the Middle Ages, women might sit in a gallery or balcony especially pro- vided so that they could watch the men at dinner. But noblemen could at certain places and times sit each with a female partner beside him — "promiscuous seating," as the Victorians were to call this arrangement. Another possibility was for all the women to sit at one end of the table, apparently as meticulously ranked as were the men at their end. At very big banquets there might be ladies' tables, apart from the men's. We are told that Louis XIV would invite particular women whose company he fancied to join him at high table, or have the noblest and most beautiful women seated at his table for him; his wife the queen, who might be present, or obliged to preside over a separate, all-female dinner else- where, did not have the equivalent privilege.

From Elizabethan times women seem to have carved meat at British 16 tables; this is a marked departure from the outlook which insisted that knives were the perquisites of males. In the early eighteenth century the hostess often did all the carving and serving of meat at table. Lady Mary Wortley Montagu as a young girl took carving lessons; on the days when she presided over her widowed father's table, "she ate her own dinner earlier in order to perform without distraction." As the cen- tury progressed, men would offer to help their wives or daughters in this task. But by the end of the eighteenth century, servants increasingly carved for the diners; and with the arrival of dinner à la russe in the mid-nineteenth century, carving at formal meals was invariably done by servants, away from the dining table itself. At family dinners, the tradition has survived in Britain of the chief male portioning out the roast before the assembled group.

At the end of dinner, wrote Emily Post in 1922, the hostess, having 17 decided that the moment has come, "looks across the table, and catch- ing the eye of one of the ladies, slowly stands up. The one who happens to be observing also stands up, and in a moment everybody is standing." The choreography is strict: the gentlemen give their partners their arms and conduct them out of the dining room into the drawing room. They bow slightly, then follow the host to the smoking room for coffee, cigars, and liqueurs. If there is no smoking room, the women leave the dining room alone. The host sits at his place at the table, and the men all move up towards his end.

18   Where port is served, the bottle on its coaster stands before the host, the tablecloth having been removed before the ritual begins. He pours for whoever is on his right — to save this person, seated in the honourable place, from having to wait until last to be served. Then the bottle is slid reverently along the polished wooden tabletop (originally so that the dregs might be disturbed as little as possible, though all good ports should be decanted before they are drunk); or it is rolled along in a wheeled silver chariot; or it is handed with special ceremonial gestures from male to male, as drinking cups were handed at ancient Greek symposia. But port is passed clockwise (to the left), not as drinks circulated in ancient Greece, to the right. "Beg your pardon, sir," says Jingle in *The Pickwick Papers*, after the waiter has left the men to themselves, "bottle stands — pass it round — way of the sun — through the button-hole [both these expressions are ways of saying "to the left": men's buttonholes are traditionally placed on the left] — no heeltaps [meaning "leave no wine at the bottom of the glass"]." At the British Factory House dinners in Oporto, the men move into a second dining room in order to enjoy vintage port, for fear of any smell of food interfering with the drink's aroma.

19   The men discuss politics, and sit with whomever they like; hierarchical seating is often suspended at this time. It is even correct for a man "to talk to any other who happens to be sitting near him, whether he knows him or not," wrote Emily Post in 1922: the men are at last among themselves, and rules can be relaxed. The women, meanwhile, are served coffee, cigarettes, and liqueurs in the library or the drawing room. The hostess sees to it that no one is left out of the conversations which take place. By the 1920s, all of this lasted no longer than fifteen to twenty minutes. The host "takes the opportunity of the first lull in the conversation" to shepherd the men to join the ladies" in the drawing room. When the men arrive, they must cease talking to each other and find a woman with whom to converse.

20   This ritual performance was commonly carried out at formal dinner parties in Britain at least into the 1960s; it probably still occurs. Americans were told by Emily Post exactly how it was done into the middle

of this century, even though at least one American etiquette book a hundred years earlier had professed disgust for the idea. Several foreign visitors to Britain in the eighteenth century had found the custom exotic and distasteful. On the Continent, the company and conversation of women had become essential to the makings of a good dinner party; there was no question of doing without them at any point in the proceedings. Men of polished manners were not supposed to hanker after the kind of behaviour, associated with male company, which could not stand the scrutiny of women.

For the point of the ceremony of women "leaving the table" and men being left alone until they "joined the ladies" was not only that men wanted to discuss matters which could not be expected to interest their wives or be understood by them. The origin of it lay in the heavy drinking and toasting, the coarse jokes and laughter among men which the presence of women might inhibit. The ladies would leave the men to it, and perhaps eventually have to go home alone, as drinking and roistering continued into the night. In eighteenth-century Scotland, according to Lord Cockburn's *Memorials* "saving the ladies" meant that the men would take their womenfolk home, then return to the scene of the dinner party to drink competitive healths to them. They paired off to see who could imbibe more in honour of his true love, "each combatant persisting till one of the two fell upon the floor ... These drinking competitions were regarded with interest by gentlewomen, who next morning inquired as to the prowess of their champions." 21

Heavy toasting died out during the nineteenth century, but a new reason for the men staying on alone came in with the advent of smoking, which at first respectable women would not dream of trying. By the time the ceremony of the ladies' withdrawal was described by Emily Post, it had been firmly contained within constricted time limits. There had been significant changes: for example, it had previously been necessary for the women to send a servant in to call the men to them — in Thomas Love Peacock's novel *Headlong Hall* (1816), "the little butler now waddled in with a summons from the ladies to tea and coffee." At a later date, coffee would be sent in to the men to remind them soon to adjourn. Later still, the men were expected to curtail their own gathering and show at least ritual eagerness to rejoin the women. Both men and women, Post is careful to insist in 1922, now smoked; women must be supplied with cigarettes too, and the thought of anyone getting drunk does not even arise. 22

Another idea behind the ceremony was that when men and women 23

were together, they felt constrained to behave very formally; only when
the sexes were segregated could they relax and "be themselves." The
dinner party, with its newly necessary "promiscuous" seating (men and
women alternating at the table), had been an exhausting performance;
it had actually been quite difficult, because of the seating, to speak to
people of the same sex as oneself. The after-dinner time among men at
the table or women in the drawing room was conceived as a relief from
having too strictly to "behave." English nineteenth-century novelists
often use the separation of the sexes after dinner as a chance to further
the plot by means of free conversation, and a male character's arrival
from the dining room, his choice of a female partner for conversation,
became dramatic expressions of the women's interest in him, and of his
preferences.

24   All through history, women have been segregated from men and from
public power, and "shielded" from the public view; they have been put
down, put upon, and put "in their place" — a place defined by males.
Yet this is not the whole story; and in the long run it may not be the
most important story. For women — and men have very often admitted
it, in their behaviour if not always in words or in kindness — have been
an enormous civilizing influence in the history of humankind. It is not
only that the way women are treated in any specific society is an infallible test of the health of that society. Women have also played the role
— and it has been with the connivance of men — of consciousness-
raisers in the domain of manners, comfort, and consideration for others. And the more men prized civilized manners, the more they
"behaved" in the presence of women. The ideal claimed by Americans
in the nineteenth century, when the custom of the ladies leaving the men
after dinner was found distasteful, was in fact a sign that grown men
were ready to think it normal to behave decently even when there were
no women present.

25   Women certainly felt more immediately the advantages of courtesy
— "la courtoisie généreuse," the Baronne Staffe called it — and accepted the ceremonial artificiality which saw them as "weaker" than
men, but also "finer." Women had to be bowed to, have hats lifted to
them, doors opened for them, seats offered to them; they were served
first at dinner. Theirs was, ritually speaking, the higher place, in spite
of the underlying realities of their social and economic position. Women
in "polite society" consequently became sticklers for etiquette — conservative perhaps, but also protective of the gains conquered. The etiquette manuals, many of them written by women in the nineteenth

century, are filled with comments about male difficulties with correct behaviour, and bristling with advice about how men might improve themselves. They always assume that women find it far easier to manage all the skills and nuances required.

And in fact it has come to pass that in many important respects women 26 have won. Men who succeed and are admired in our culture must demonstrate that they have opted for finesse, sympathetic awareness, and self-control. "Male" vices which men forbade in women, such as alcohol abuse and smoking, have become disreputable in men also — although many women are now claiming the "right" at last to indulge in them. Fighting, swaggering, overeating have all gone out of style; one result of the technological revolution has been to remove the requirement that "real men" should show themselves to be rough, and overbearing: one does not need to be physically powerful in order to control the instruments of technology. The gap between the sexes has closed not only because women have increasingly entered what has until now been the men's public sphere of operations, but because men have gradually been made to feel that they should attain the level of behaviour which previously they expected only from the opposite sex. In short, they have become more like women.

(1991)

The Writer's Subject

1. What connection does Visser draw between gender and eating customs?

2. Why would a married woman in ancient Greece not wish to be present at a public banquet? (para. 3)

3. In what ways, according to Visser, is food "one of the main sources of a woman's power in the household"? (para. 8)

4. Why has poison been viewed as a singularly "female" weapon? (para. 11)

5. Why, according to Visser, have women traditionally eaten and drunk less than men? (paras. 12–14)

6. Why, until quite recently, have men and women separated at the conclusion of a meal? (paras. 17–23)

7. In what ways, in Visser's view, have women exerted a great civilizing influence in society? (paras. 24–26)

The Writer's Style and Strategy

1. At what points does Visser's essay move beyond a historical survey of customs and rituals associated with eating?

2. Discuss Visser's use of contrast as a means of structuring her paragraphs.

3. Discuss Visser's use of examples to support her general observations, and comment on the range of her references.

4. Why does Visser refer on a number of occasions to Emily Post?

5. Explain the relevance to Visser's argument of her anecdote about Gertrude Stein's cook, Hélène. (para. 8)

Suggested Topics for Writing and Discussion

1. Visser argues that women have traditionally attained a higher level of social behaviour than men, and that men, in becoming more socially adept, "have become more like women." Do you agree?

2. Visser's essay deals extensively with the rituals of dining in different societies through history, and with the roles of women in those rituals. To what extent do women still perform the roles traditionally assigned to them in matters relating to food?

3. Visser maintains that "the way women are treated in any specific society is an infallible test of the health of that society" (para. 24). Test this assertion by comparing the way women are treated in two or three different nations or cultures.

4. Do you think that the concept of "courtesy," whereby men treat women with special politeness, still has any place in our society?

Ethnicity and Culture

Ethnicity and Culture

I Am Canadian

by Neil Bissoondath

In the West Indies, where I grew up, long and boisterous parties, on the   1
whole, inconvenience no-one. They are held at houses, both inside and
outside. Neighbours tend to be invited; children sleep where they fall.
Food and drink are in plentiful supply, music is loud and lively, meant
not as background filler but as foreground incentive to dance. There is
nothing sedate about the archetypal West Indian party. So central is "a
good time" to the West Indian sense of self that someone — not a West
Indian — once wryly commented that she had the impression that parties, and not calypso or reggae, were the great West Indian contribution
to world culture. Booming music, the yelp and rumble of excited voices,
the tramp of dancing feet are accepted as an integral part of the region's
cultural life.

Transfer this to, say, Toronto or Vancouver — not to a house sur-   2
rounded by an extensive yard but to an apartment hemmed in by other
apartments. Transfer the music, the dancing, the shouting — everything
but invitation to the neighbours, who in this case are likely to be unknown and uncommunicative. It takes little imagination to appreciate
the tensions that may, and do, arise.

A simple lack of consideration for the rights of others? Yes — but it   3
may be, as some claim, that everything is political.

*3. (1) It is hereby declared to be the policy of the Government of Canada
to (a) recognize and promote the understanding that multiculturalism reflects the cultural and racial diversity of Canadian society and acknowledges the freedom of all members of Canadian society to preserve,
enhance and share their cultural heritage.*

— Canadian Multiculturalism Act

The view has frequently been expressed to me that, in light of the importance of parties in West Indian culture, and considering the official policy of multicultural preservation in Canada, complaints about noise or demands that stereo volumes be lowered can be justifiably viewed as a form of cultural aggression. Changing the tone of the party, the argument goes, results in a lessening of its Caribbean character — and is therefore a sign of cultural intolerance. Implicit in this view is the idea that everything deemed cultural is sacred — as well as the idea that the surrounding society must fully accommodate itself to displays, no matter how disruptive, of cultural life. In this atmosphere, a party is no longer just a party; it becomes a form of cultural expression and therefore subject to political and legal protection.

4   This is an admittedly aggressive interpretation of multicultural philosophy, but it is neither far-fetched nor fully indefensible. Open-ended political policy is, almost without exception, subject to an endless stretching of the envelope: there will always be someone — or some group — attempting to go further than anyone has gone before. Because we have failed to establish the limits of diversity, because we have so blithely accepted the mentality of division, we find ourselves lost in a confusion of values. Multiculturalism has made us fearful of defining acceptable boundaries; it has caused us to confuse the establishment of circumscription with a lack of respect. And so we find ourselves in danger of accepting, in its name, a slide into ethical chaos.

5   In 1992, the Ontario College of Physicians and Surgeons expressed concern over a rise, unexplained and unexpected, in the number of requests for infibulation, otherwise known as female circumcision. The procedure, long viewed in Western culture as a kind of mutilation, involves, according to a doctor quoted in *The Toronto Star*, "cutting off a young girl's external genital parts, including the clitoris. In some countries, it includes stitching closed the vulva until marriage, leaving a small opening for urination and menstrual flow.... Various health risks have been linked to it, including immediate serious bleeding, recurring infections, pain during intercourse, hemorrhaging during childbirth and infertility.... Charles Kyazze, head of Ottawa's African Resource Centre, believes it is being performed here by members of the community. In some cases, he says, families are sending their children to Africa to have it done." The result is the reduction of the woman to the status of machine, capable of production but mechanically, with no pleasure in the process. This, however, is an unabashedly "Eurocentric" view of infibulation.

A more culturally sensitive view is presented in an article for *The Globe* 6 *and Mail* by Christine Hodge, a Canadian working for the United Nations World Food Program in Chad. She tells of a woman named Khadidja Ahmat Rahmasaleh, head of nutritional services in the Chadean ministry of social affairs and promotion of the family. Ms. Rahmasaleh, a Muslim, is an intelligent, educated, and "forward-thinking" woman dedicated to the traditions of her tribe, her family, and her God. But this is not all she is. She has spent five years at university in Italy. She is familiar with the ways of the West, and seeks to "incorporate the ways of two worlds that often seem at loggerheads." Her experiences and studies in Italy convinced her that circumcision "was neither necessary nor right."

And yet, to Ms. Hodge's disappointment, Ms. Rahmasaleh's two 7 daughters, aged seven and nine, had undergone the procedure — at the daughters' own request: "Because they were not circumcised, they were not considered to be women. Their friends refused to let them join in games and conversations." Cut off from the life of the community, the girls grew sullen and depressed — and to be cut off from the community in Chad is to risk more than a social life, it is to risk life itself.

It was the community that had raised the funds to send Ms. 8 Rahmasaleh to Italy; the community that would provide sustenance in time of inevitable famine; the community that would tend to the children in the event of their mother's death.

For any mother, but particularly for a Chadean mother cognizant of 9 her family's uncertain circumstances, it was an intolerable situation. Ms. Rahmasaleh decided the girls would undergo neither of the two traditional procedures — infibulation, in which the entire external genitalia are cut off and the wound sewn up, or the less radical excision of the clitoris and labia major, which would remove sexual pleasure but diminish health risks. She devised instead a method — a pinprick to the clitoris — that would satisfy the ceremonial need to draw blood while leaving her children intact — unpleasant, no doubt, but not mutilating.

Despite opposition — her own mother and aunts insisted the girls' 10 clitorises be removed — her method was employed, as it was again later on for her ten-year-old niece.

Ms. Hodge, although not present, was yet able to witness the proce- 11 dure and the ensuing celebrations through the miracle of technology: everything had been videotaped. She ends her article still opposed to female circumcision — she does not flinch from the word "barbaric" — but with a greater appreciation of the context that prompts its continuance.

12   And that, in the end, is the point: context is everything. How far, in
the Canadian context, do we go in accommodation? Female circumcision is clearly a vital, traditional rite of passage to womanhood for these
Chadean women. Do we, in rejecting it, impose an uncontextualized,
"Eurocentric" value system on certain ethnic groups? Should we, in certain circumstances (a sterile operating room, trained medical person-
nel), respect the right of certain women to undergo what we see as
mutilation? And what of those cultures in which male offspring are vital? Do we permit the use of the available technology to permit sex-
selection? But multiculturalism ends where our notions of human rights
and dignity begin — and therein lies the thorny question of limits.

13   The Multiculturalism Act suggests no limits to the accommodation
offered to different cultural practices, so that a few years ago a Muslim
group in Toronto demanded, in the name of respect for its culture, the
right to opt out of the Canadian judicial system in favour of Islamic
law, a body of thought fundamental to the life and cultural outlook of
its practising members. In the opinion of its spokesmen, this right should
be a given in a truly multicultural society. It is not an argument without
philosophical merit — on practical grounds, it's a different matter. Can
Canada accommodate citizens whose loyalties do not encompass its
long-established legal system? It is a sensitive topic.

14   On January 18, 1994, talk-show host Jane Hawtin of CFRB Radio in
Toronto posed the following question: "Should Canada relax its rules
and laws to accommodate the Muslim culture?" The question arose from
the Montreal case in which a girl had been sodomized by her stepfather
and also from a case in Edmonton in which a judge permitted the marriage of a fourteen-year-old pregnant girl. In both cases the judges "cited
Muslim values for their leniency." (The Montreal man, according to the
judge, "… did not have … vaginal sexual relations [with the victim] …
so that he could preserve her virginity, which seems to be a very important value in their religion.") The question — based, as one man said,
on "certain preconceived notions about Islam" — prompted protest from
some Toronto Muslims. And yet, it is precisely because those "preconceived notions" exist that the question should be asked, the notions de-
bated and cleared up, limits established.

15   The same could be said about a proposal from a group of women's
organizations that sought to overturn a policy that directed police to always lay charges in wife-assault cases. One of the great victories in the
battle against violence against women, the policy had come to be seen
as inadequate, or even counter-productive, in helping to protect immi-

grant women and women from visible minorities. The principal reason given for the proposed change was that, because police and the courts seem to deal more harshly with minority groups, assaulted women who call the authorities face ostracization from their own communities. Moreover, it was reported in *The Globe and Mail*, "women, especially from the black community, just simply don't call the police because they are afraid of the consequences for their partner." The answer, the women's groups suggested, was in establishing "tailor-made charging policies by ethnic or racial group, municipality by municipality."

The proposal is one of divisiveness fraught with complexity and rich 16 with racist possibilities. It does not address the inadequacies of the present approach but simply attempts to sidestep them in unwieldy fashion with a show of essentially meaningless cultural and racial sensitivity.

While the acceptance of female circumcision and sex-selection, and 17 the establishment of a separate legal system for Muslims, are virtual impossibilities — they take the right to "opt out" to unacceptable extremes — the racial segregation of schools apparently is not. This is an idea that writer Cecil Foster has described in *The Globe and Mail* as "sweeping through the Canadian black community. It calls for black-focused public schools, where the curriculum, teachers and emphasis would be primarily black, or 'Afrocentric,' to use the current buzzword."

The drive to segregation is a deep-seated one, prompted by the al- 18 ienation of black students from the school system. "The textbooks exclude them," Foster writes, "and the teachers and principals are usually white and uncaring. The entire attitude of the public education system makes them feel set apart by negative stereotypes that black students, for example, are more fulfilled on the basketball court than in the physics lab."

While this view ignores the role of the family — the black American 19 novelist Leon Forrest once pointed out that there is "a problem in Afro-American society these days: if a woman has a niece and a nephew, she'll give the niece a copy of a Toni Morrison book and take the nephew to the Bulls game" — the consequence is a drop-out rate for black students two or three times higher than for the general student population. It is, by any stretch of the imagination, a worrisome trend, and the temptation to establish schools where a black staff would provide positive role models, "living proof in the classrooms, playgrounds and principals' offices that blacks are capable of achieving great things," must be seductive. Foster quotes the words of Vernon Farrell, chairman of the

African-Heritage Educators Network: "Black-focused schools will cause students to reflect on shared history, social relationships, belief systems, social practices and collective responses to political and economic realities. Above all, students will develop a sense of identity, critical consciousness and belonging." All the things, in other words, that multiculturalism was supposed to provide and has not.

20 This construction of a safer world, the withdrawal into it, is a sign of despair. It indicates dissatisfactions with the world as it is and a lack of faith that the system can ever acquire legitimacy. The despair is not difficult to understand. It comes from the evisceration that follows years of anger and fatigue — both of which emerge from living constantly with society's stereotypical brushings. A black youth commits a crime and all black youths must suffer the suspicion of the streets: the wary eyes, the tensed bodies, the wide berths. How many people react in similar fashion to white or Asian youths in the aftermath of a crime committed by one of their number? The dream of flight, of retreat, is a plea for security, an urge that is understandable but also, by its very nature, self-defeating, even when it is presented as principle, clothed in buzzwords.

21 Buzzwords are dangerous creatures. They disguise with quasi-intellectual terminology the true nature of the topic they pretend to describe; they lend a respectability, an apparent complexity, to essentially simplistic ideas. An "Afrocentric" or "black-focused" school system, racially segregated, racially staffed, would simply be a return to the past: to the racial separations of the American south; to the separate but (un)equal approaches of apartheid. It might produce higher grades — and even that is debatable — but would it prepare students for the wider world? It might facilitate the acquisition of knowledge, but would it facilitate the socialization necessary to life beyond the comforting confines of its walls?

22 A separate education system is an illusory answer to the problems faced by black youth in our society. It would solve nothing, and when students graduate they would inevitably feel the falling away of its racial comforts. It would merely provide a context for withdrawal from society, while the racial problems can be solved only by engagement with it. It is, in the end, as Foster points out, simply a recipe for self-ghettoization.

23 Unlike infibulation and sex-selection, a racially segregated school system is a topic of serious and prolonged discussion. It is an idea that, to many, has great merit. Not to me. Racial segregation has never been

a pretty thing; it has betrayed more than it has aided. Moreover, if we give black parents the right to send their children to all-black schools, do we also give the right to white parents to send their children to all-white schools? And does not such an approach spell the death of any ideal of a multi-racial, multi-ethnic society?

One does not surrender to problems; one grapples with them. Prob- 24 lems exist in the public-school system; the needs of many of its students are not being met. It is in that arena, then, and not in the artificial creation of a separate one, that the solutions must be found.

How selectively, in our confusion, we judge our evils. And how eas- 25 ily the instinct of sensitivity leads to a loss of perspective. How easily it betrays the urge to do what's right.

The public face of Canadian multiculturalism is flashy and attractive; it 26 emerges with verve and gaiety from the bland stereotype of traditional Canada at "ethnic" festivals around the country. At Toronto's "Caravan," for instance, various ethnic groups rent halls in churches or community centres to create "pavilions" to which access is gained through a purchased "passport." Once admitted — passport duly stamped at the door with a "visa" — you consume a plate of Old World food at distinctly New World prices, take a quick tour of the "craft" and "historical" displays, and then find a seat for the "cultural" show, traditional songs (often about love in the wheat fields) and traditional dances (often about harvesting wheat) performed by youths resplendent in their traditional costumes.

After the show, positively glowing with your exposure to yet another 27 tile of our multicultural mosaic, you make your way to the next pavilion, to the next line-up for food, the next display, the next bout of cultural edification. And at the end of the day, you may be forgiven if you feel, guiltily to be sure, that you have just sat through a folksy, Canadian-mosaic version of the Jungle Cruise at Walt Disney World in Florida.

But cultural heritage, as we have seen, is not always a pretty thing. 28 Ethnicity (the classification of human beings by race, religion, language, cultural traditions, and other traits held in common) can be like a futon mattress; it can cushion and comfort, it can provide a safe and warm place — but the stuffing sometimes shifts, becomes lumpy and irksome, and the lumps must be either accepted or pounded out. Accepting the lumps makes for uneasy sleep. Too often, ethnic communities accept the uneasy sleep. Or, as the novelist Joy Kogawa more elegantly put it:

"In an age when loneliness, malaise and an overwhelming bigness assail us, our ethnic communities are sometimes no more than bits of driftwood to which a few people cling in the midst of a typhoon. What we need are lifeboats. What we need is Noah's ark."

29   At the heart of multiculturalism bob these "bits of driftwood": communities shaped by notions of ethnicity; more particularly, by a heightened sense of ethnicity; most particularly, by a heightened sense of their own ethnicity. They are, many of them, what the poet and professor Roy Miki, a Canadian of Japanese descent and a man with a powerful sense of historical grievance, has termed "racialized."

30   To be "racialized" is to have acquired a racial vision of life, to have learnt to see oneself, one's past, present and future, through the colour of one's skin. It is not new — *Mein Kampf* hinges on a racial vision; apartheid could not have existed without a racial vision — but it is, in certain circles, acquiring a new respectability as old enemies grow to resemble each other. Nor is this as simple or as agreeable a proposition as it may appear. Ethnicity, race, and their permutations are peculiarly conducive to the spinning of fantasy, so that Christopher Columbus becomes merely the evil European who enslaves and massacres noble natives by conquering Paradise; so that the Toronto writer and social activist June Callwood is transformed into a racist.

31   A sense of one's racial and cultural background, like a sense of one's personal likes and dislikes, is essential to an individual sense of self. But neither history nor race nor culture is destiny: human beings are saved from that by intelligence and the gift of irony. And it is the ironic eye, questioning, judging, that ultimately refuses to simplify.

32   Samuel Selvon, Bharati Mukherjee, Rohinton Mistry, Hanif Kureishi, and I are all writers, all of the same "ethnicity" to a certain extent, all ethnically "South Asians," all "Indians." Yet I suspect that, as a group, we are at least as dissimilar as similar. When any of us meet, there is no gravitation around an ethnic bonfire. I feel a greater affinity for the work of Timothy Mo — a British novelist born of an English mother and a Chinese father — than I do for that of Salman Rushdie, with whom I share an ethnicity.

33   My point is simple, but it is one usually ignored by multiculturalism and its purveyors — for to recognize the complexity of ethnicity, to acknowledge the wild variance within ethnic groups, would be to render multiculturalism and its aims absurd. The individuals who form a group, the "ethnics" who create a community, are frequently people of vastly varying composition. Shared ethnicity does not entail unanimity of vi-

sion. If the individual is not to be betrayed, a larger humanity must prevail over the narrowness of ethnicity.

I have lived in Canada for more than twenty years, longer than I have 34
lived anywhere else. I have built a life and a career here. I know who I
am, am at ease with it. But I also know that the specifics of my personality did not freeze, upon my arrival in Toronto, into a form suitable for
multicultural display. Migration — the act of leaving, the act of re-establishment — creates its own experience, effects its own change. One
is no longer simply what one was in the first part of one's life. To pretend that one has not evolved, as official multiculturalism so often seems
to demand of us, is to stultify the personality, creating stereotypes, stripping the individual of uniqueness: you are not yourself, you are your
group. It is not really a mosaic that one joins — the parts of a mosaic fit
neatly together, creating a harmonious whole — but rather a zoo of exoticism that one enters. Some are scandalized to speechlessness when I
mention that the Trinidad Carnival leaves me unmoved, that I never pine
for sandy beaches. Stereotype comforts; its demise disorients. But how
wearying it can become.

The struggle against stereotype, the basis of all racism, is, in the end, 35
a profoundly personal one. Government programmes are essential, but
no bureaucratic regime can ever be as effective a stop to stereotype and
racist typecasting as an immediate challenge by those who object.

At the same time, to accept the assigned role of multiculturalism — 36
to play the ethnic deracinated and costumed — is to play to stereotype.
It is to abdicate one's full humanity in favour of one of its exotic features, ethnicity.

Multiculturalism is ethnicity as public policy: it is society's view of 37
the individual's assigned place within its construct. And yet I would
suggest that ethnicity's true value lies in the opposite point of view: as
one of the many elements that inform the way the individual views the
world.

In the spring of 1994, the Montreal *Mirror* ran a short article detail- 38
ing some of my hesitations about multiculturalism. A printed response
came from a man suspicious of my hesitations. He explained that, before multiculturalism, he had had no sense of self, no sense of what he
was and where he had come from; he had known nothing of his cultural
background, and had never been taught his ancestral language.
Multiculturalism, he felt, had rectified all that. This echoes a remark
Myrna Kostash once made to me; she felt that multiculturalism, by of-

ficially recognizing the experience and particularities of "Ukrainian-Canadians," had validated her own existence in Canada: such explicit recognition of her exoticism, her otherness, was clearly a comfort to her.

39   This is understandable, and yet unsettling: that we have in this country people who depend on government policy to shore up, to validate, at times even to create their sense of self and of community. It speaks of a startling dependence on government and public policy. I couldn't help wondering about the upbringing of the young man who, before multiculturalism, held himself to be culturally deprived: where, I wondered, were his parents and family through all of this? Was it the role of the state to provide him with a knowledge of his familial past and his ancestral language? It was, it seemed to me, a question of responsibilities — and how much easier it is to point the finger at a distant state than at loved ones.

40   Perhaps encouraged by the Charter of Rights and Freedoms, we are increasingly jealous of our individual rights. We insist that the state keep its hands out of our personal affairs: my sex life is my own, we say, for instance. Yet so many of us seem to depend on the state for the sense of self that comes from official recognition of our cultural background. Is this not a kind of psychic surrender?

41   It may be that one of the unstated desires behind the institution of multiculturalism was a wish to mark ourselves as different from the United States: if they have a melting pot, then we'll have a mosaic. If they ask immigrants to shrug off their past and assume a new identity, we'll ask immigrants to conserve their past and make it their only identity.

42   Both approaches are essentially illusory, it seems to me, each an exercise in the falsifying of the self. Pretending to continue being simply what one has been in the past, or what one's parents have been, inevitably entails a betrayal of the self — just as pretending, under the assimilative U.S. model, that one is no longer what one has been, that one has completely remade oneself, is also a betrayal of the self. The human personality is not static; it is altered fundamentally, but not wholly, by circumstance and experience. And while the U.S. approach is untrue to the individual, the Canadian approach is untrue to both the individual and the state. For if many who emigrate to the United States eventually come to think of themselves as simply "American," strengthening the social fabric, too few who come to Canada end up accepting themselves — and one another — as simply "Canadian," thereby weakening the social fabric. (If Canada, as a historical, social, legal, and cultural con-

cept, does not demand respect for itself and its ideals, why should any respect be expected?)

A middle way must be found, a route that establishes certain basic 43
social parameters to which all must dedicate themselves and within which one is free to live as one wishes. The view is not alien to us. It was expressed over two decades ago by the Royal Commission on Bilingualism and Biculturalism: "The process of integration goes hand in hand with what anthropologists call 'acculturation.' Anyone who chooses Canada as his adopted country adopts a new style of life, a particular kind of existence.... Acculturation is the process of adapatation to the environment in which an individual is compelled to live as he adjusts his behaviour to that of the community." We have managed to lose that early and essential view, and in so doing lose ourselves.

It is time we removed personal culture and ethnicity from the ma- 44
nipulative realm of public policy and returned it to individuals and their families, the only sphere where they have any true and lasting value. As a young television producer of Indian background once remarked: "I don't need some bureaucrat in Ottawa to tell me who I am." Society has sufficient reasonable expectations of its citizens. Let us cease adding to them unreasonable ones.

In his book *The New Canada*, Preston Manning offers an excerpt from 45
a presentation made to the Reform Party (of which, let it be clear, I am not a supporter) by Professor Rais Khan, chair of the political-science department at the University of Winnipeg. It is a statement that lays bare the creed of the immigrant and points the way to what Bharati Mukherjee has termed the exuberance of immigration:

> "People, regardless of their origin, do not emigrate to preserve their culture and nurture their ethnic distinctiveness. If they wished to do that, they would stay where they were because the environment is more conducive to the perpetuation of one's culture and ethnicity. Immigrants come here to become Canadians; to be productive and contributing members of their chosen society. I am one of them. I did not come here to be labelled as an ethnic or a member of the multicultural community, or to be coddled with preferential treatment, nurtured with special grants, and then to sit on the sidelines and watch the world go by. I came here to be a member of the mainstream of the Canadian society. I do not need paternalism; I need opportunity. I do not want affirmative action; I expect fairness. I do not desire special consideration; I wish to be treated equally.... Whether or not I preserve my cultural background is my personal choice;

whether or not an ethnic group preserves its cultural background is the group's choice. The state has no business in either."

46   Heritage belongs first and foremost to the individual. It seems to me possible to instruct an individual child in his or her cultural heritage without erecting ghetto walls by engaging in communal endeavour. Emphasizing the "I" and de-emphasizing the "we" may be the only way to avoid the development of cultural chauvinism — the idea that "we" are superior to "them," and the chasms that result.

47   My own daughter will grow up knowing her families, seeing the photos of those now dead, hearing the stories of a distant past. She will know of her Québécois great-grandfather who went to war and returned damaged. She will know of her Trinidadian great-grandfather who began life in poverty and ended it in wealth. She will hear of the grandmothers she never knew. She will be acquainted with the varied streams of history that have come together to create her, at this particular time, in this particular place. She will be acquainted, then, with her heritage: that body of knowledge that firmly plants the individual; the body of knowledge that requires no particular soil, no particular air; the body of knowledge that is like freedom because it can be carried safely through time and space in the capacious pocket of the mind, as orienting as a compass; the body of knowledge, then, that no-one can ever steal or play with or manipulate into the service of social engineering. Personal knowledge and sensitivities are media for growth. They are not the basis for public policy.

(1994)

The Writer's Subject

1. What is Bissoondath's point in placing an "archetypal West Indian party" in Toronto or Vancouver? (paras. 1–3)

2. What does Bissoondath mean by the phrase "the mentality of division"? (para. 4)

3. What dangers does Bissoondath see in official multicultural acceptance of different cultural practices?

4. What use does Bissoondath make of the experience of a mother and her daughters from the republic of Chad? (paras. 5–12)

5. How does Bissoondath illustrate his point that official Multiculturalism may promote legal uncertainties and some degree of cultural confusion? (paras. 13–15)

6. Why does the writer oppose the idea of racial segregation in Canadian schools? (paras. 17–24)

7. What are the writer's views on ethnic festivals? (paras. 26–27)

8. How does Bissoondath react to the term "racialized"? (paras. 29–31)

9. What role does Bissoondath assign to "the ironic eye" (para. 31)?

10. On what grounds does the writer reject the idea that ethnicity acts as a unifying force? (paras. 31–37)

11. Why is Bissoondath critical of those who argue that multiculturalism has helped them to develop a sense of self that was lacking before? (paras. 38–40)

12. What is the process of "acculturation" referred to in a Royal Commission report cited by Bissoondath? (para. 43)

13. What does Bissoondath mean by "cultural heritage"? In what way does it differ from the concept of multiculturalism as described in this essay? (paras. 46–47)

The Writer's Style and Strategy

1. How does Bissoondath draw on the views of other writers to support his arguments?

2. What audience is Bissoondath addressing in this essay?

3. To what extent does Bissoondath present opposing views? Is he fair to those who hold views differing from his own?

4. What is the tone in which Bissoondath describes ethnic festivals in paras. 26 and 27? How is that tone established? What is the writer's goal here?

5. Examine the use of figurative language in para. 28. How effective is its use here?

6. Discuss the meaning and effect of the phrase " — to play the ethnic deracinated and costumed — " (para. 36).

Suggested Topics for Writing and Discussion

1. Do you agree with Bissoondath that multiculturalism reduces people of different races to stereotypes? (para. 34)

2. Bissoondath calls for a "middle way," a balance between the claims of the state and the right of individuals to live as they wish. (para. 43) How might this be accomplished? How can we ensure that a policy of cultural tolerance does not undermine the values of the larger community?

3. How has a consciousness of racial or "ethnic" heritage shaped or influenced your own life or that of other members of your family?

4. Canada has become home to people from a wide variety of cultural backgrounds. Do you think the people of Canada are well served by official policies of multiculturalism, or do you think we should adopt the assimilative "melting-pot" approach taken by the United States?

5. Bissoondath asks, "And what of those cultures in which male offspring are vital? Do we permit the use of the available technology to permit sex-selection?" (para. 12) Read Moira Farr's essay, "Dangerous Determination," then offer your own views on this question.

Taking the Missionary Position
by Susan Crean

When *Into the Heart of Africa* opened at the Royal Ontario Museum in   1
November 1989, it was with a dull, deceptive thump. The controversy
that shattered the museum's polite facade, earning it the title Racist
Ontario Museum, simmered in private for almost three months before
it erupted; but, by the end of the exhibition's nine month run, both curator and institution had been thoroughly discredited.

I had been aware that an exhibition of the African collection was in   2
the offing for some time, as someone from the museum had contacted
my father about displaying Great Uncle John's pith helmet, a family
relic he'd donated to the museum to accompany the small collection of
African artifacts Great Uncle had himself deposited with the Royal Military Institute before he died in 1907. Born in 1858, this older brother of
my grandfather became a professional soldier at 18, fought with the
Queen's Own Rifles and, by the mid-eighteen-nineties, was in west
Africa with the British forces of occupation in what is now Ghana, leading a battalion of Hausa men of the Gold Coast Regiment with whom
he would fight in the fabled Asante wars of 1900.

To be blunt about it, Great Uncle John spent his entire adult life in   3
one part or another of the globe killing native people on behalf of God,
Queen and Empire. His job was to provide the brute force necessary to
keep *"Pax" Britannica* operating in the interests of the British merchant
class. In Africa this involved participating in the vainglorious "cause"
of bringing European civilization, Christianity and commerce to the
continent, though it was, of course, experienced by the African people
as the hostile aggression by a race of foreigners it actually was.

4   It is easy enough to grasp the political and ideological dynamics of the world that produced Captain Crean and put him in Africa. What his presence does in the here and now — specifically his presence in *Into the Heart of Africa* — is provoke the ultimate (and unanswerable) question about his personal role in the imperial scheme. Did he pillage and loot? Did he rape women or brutalize children? Did he kill in anger or just in the line of duty? We are talking here of the ugly macho underside of the war; the secret part we are never asked to remember on Remembrance Day, the part veterans and generals keep to themselves.

5   The truth is, though, that none of us get to choose our ancestors, and none of us can claim any singular moral authority for condemning their exploits. Even if they can individually be a source of eternal shame, it's a shame that ultimately has to be shared; in Great Uncle's case, by the white community as a whole. Still, it must be said that it is one thing to have an ancestor who took part in deplorable events a century ago and quite another to have a major cultural institution use his story in your own time to perpetuate misunderstanding.

6   Which brings me back to the ROM show. Because of Great Uncle I had some inkling about its origin and, indeed, guest curator Jeanne Cannizzo has said the project grew around her desire to exhibit the African collection that had been languishing in storerooms for almost a century. Even the exhibition brochure introduces it as "an historical journey through the world of sub-Saharan Africa, illustrated by the ROM's outstanding collections."

7   So I wasn't at all prepared for what I found: Great Uncle elevated to the status of a quaint Canadian Rambo dressed in original Tilley Endurables. He is treated as a historical figure; an entire case of "his" collection of Hausa weaponry and Asante objects (drum, quran pouch, stool and tobacco pipe) is displayed, his life is illustrated with newspaper accounts from the battle-front and his 1902 photograph of the Hausa battalion is mounted on a wall nearby.

8   Most disconcerting, however, is the appearance of the old pith helmet, reverently displayed in the very first room, in hushed lighting and a glass box of its own. Spruced up with a new red band and brass spike atop, it floats in timelessness, reminding me, curiously, of a similar sight I saw years ago at Saint Joseph's Oratory in Montreal on my first visit there in 1957, age 12. I'd never been inside a Roman Catholic church before, and I was astonished by the make-believe setting of that enormous stone basilica, the inside walls festooned with the discarded

crutches and braces of the cured, the heavy scent of incense combined with the sounds of Latin.

And then I saw it, something I had never seen in my life before — a 9 real human heart. In this case, the preserved heart of the sainted Brother André. It was all quite fantastic to me, but most fantastic of all was that pickled heart, which I approached with a mixture of horror and wonder, my own heart thumping.

Thirty years later I am assaulted by the same combination of revul- 10 sion and fascination in front of Great Uncle's bloody dress helmet. Only the embalming fluid is missing.

The official guide explains that *Into the Heart of Africa* is divided 11 thematically into four areas; the Imperial Connection, the Military Hall, the Missionary Hall and the Africa Room. The first three of these and more than half the exhibition space, then, is devoted to the history of a small band of white Canadians, missionaries and militia men, who brought artifacts back with them as souvenirs and trophies.

As I walk along I find myself growing increasingly disturbed by 12 the roll-call of former owners, the detailed label explanations of whose estate gave what and how it passed along from one person to another and eventually to the museum. The names parade along like a nag- ging subtext, casting the artifacts as misappropriated byproducts of all that religious and military fervour. The lives of the white folks are fea- tured, their stories personalized and connected to the larger stream of history while beside them, in photos and in absentia, the Africans with whom they lived remain silent. And, with a couple of rare exceptions, nameless.

The imbalance bothers me, as does the presentation of the objects as 13 the possessions of people who in reality traded, seized and otherwise made off with them as spoils of war. It strikes me as bad karma not to mention bad form. And a good example of how contemporary art his- tory and ethnography, ruled as they are by linear academic techniques, are at the mercy of whatever documentation is available.

As I go along I am also thinking of the headlines I am going to read, 14 taking off on the title — *Into the Heart of Controversy, Into the Heart of Racist Canada, Into the Belly of Bigotry.* Take your pick. I say this not because the exhibition denies Canada's colonialist past (although I think it more accurate to call it imperialist past, as the activity of Brit- ish colonials was very unambiguous as to who were the colonizers and who was being colonized in Africa), nor because it whitewashes the role of Canadians in it. Nor is it because the curator and organizers condone the white supremacist rhetoric the exhibit depicts. But they are awfully quiet and oblique in their disapproval, never directly condemning or examining its legacy.

15   There is a sense that it all happened so long ago, explanations aren't necessary. Says the brochure: "The rich cultural heritage of African religious, social and economic life is celebrated through objects brought back by Canadian missionaries and military men over one hundred years ago. The exhibition examines this turbulent but little-known period in history when Canadians participated in Britain's efforts to colonize and convert the African nations." For whom, I wonder, was this period merely turbulent, and to whom is the period so little-known?

16   And there I think, lies the error. By presenting the African collection through the history of its donors, by giving pride of place to the personal stories of the white Canadians who happened to bring them to Canada, Cannizzo creates a context in which that history is claimed rather than criticized and rejected, showcased even while she tut-tuts from between the lines. "Well, Great Uncle certainly was a scoundrel, and who knows what he got up to in Africa; but, well, you can't blame the old boy for being a product of his time." That seems to be the sentiment.

17   Cannizzo does try to dissociate herself by putting ironic quotes around phrases like "barbarous people" and "savage customs." But such subtle irony is not only lost on those who can't (or don't) read the explanatory texts, it is also a pretty limp way to examine a subject as grave as racially motivated genocide. And, occasionally, she slips up, for example on one plaque: "Canadian missionaries were often inspired by the exploits of the British hero, missionary explorer Dr. David Livingstone. They followed him into the heart of Africa." The absence of ironic quotes around the word hero beside "Livingstone" is telling, implying that unlike "savage customs" it is not an idea under suspicion, much less one up for retirement.

18   The most curious of all the curatorial decisions that undermined Cannizzo's good intentions was undoubtedly the audio-visual lantern slide show called, "In Livingstone's Footsteps." This was a re-creation of the kind of fundraising lecture missionaries would have given in church halls in the early part of this century to awe-struck Torontonians. At the beginning and end of the presentation (and in writing on a panel at the entrance to the viewing room) is the disclaimer, "The sense of cultural superiority and paternalism that you will hear in this fictional narrative was characteristic of the missionary world view at the time.

So was the genuine spirit of adventure and the sincere belief that missionaries were bringing 'light' to the 'Dark Continent.'" Now, if you have ever watched people in a museum you'll know the vast majority tend to drift in and out of such presentations; relatively few pay strict attention all the way through. To make matters worse, the day I was there, the soundtrack could be heard throughout the first part of the exhibition, and detached phrases kept wafting through my consciousness. The unctuous voice delivering highly derogatory commentary could have been that of the ROM's director on the intercom for all I knew. By the time I reached the end of the section and realized the voice was an actor's and the opinions not those of anyone living (presumably), I had been assailed with this semi-subliminal commentary for over an hour.

With a similar weird disregard for the sensibilities of visitors, especially black children, the installation made use of some extremely graphic and violent images. At the end of the first set of rooms a wall-sized sketch from the *Illustrated London News* shows a British soldier on horseback plunging his sword into the chest of a Zulu warrior. Further on, in the missionary section a photograph shows four African women kneeling on the ground doing laundry in tubs while a white woman in voluminous skirts looks on, smiling approvingly. This, the caption tells us, is "Mrs. Thomas Titcombe offering 'a lesson in how to wash clothes' to Yagba women in Northern Nigeria in 1915." (Tell me this is how you would explain the cultural bias and racial arrogance of that image to school children.)

And whatever is one to make of the old-fashioned decorative display of captured spears and shields arranged with gemsbok and hartebeest horn, a typical "trophy-wall" of a Toronto home circa 1900? Why this compulsion to humanize the white experience of imperialism, I wonder. And likewise, why the decision to let the soundtrack of the slide show dominate the environment when African music (which is piped into headsets in the last room) could have been?

I left the show feeling nervous and slightly ill. The final section, featuring a glorious display of textiles and musical instruments where, at last, the African pieces were left to speak on their own behalf, was worth the wait. And it seemed to me they stole the show. But they couldn't save the show from itself or prevent the unintended response some people had to it. (I can't help thinking of the anonymous visitor who wrote in the comment book at the exhibit exit, "A good display of life in primitive Africa.") By last February, members of the black community had begun to organize. The Coalition for the Truth about Africa, some 30

19

20

21

community groups strong, was formed and charges were levelled that the show was conceptually and structurally racist.

22   This, incidentally, was not the first hint there were going to be people who did not see *Into the Heart of Africa* the way the ROM or the curator did; people who were going to be offended, even angered by it. Six months before the exhibit opened, initial contact with the community brought back complaints about the brochure, which described the show in tired, stereotypical language. Under pressure, it was withdrawn and another produced. A consultant was also hired to hold focus groups and smooth community relations.

23   In June 1989, an informal reception for members of the black community was held. But this preview may have done more harm than good, as several of those invited left with the distinct impression they were being presented with a *fait accompli*, their views not seriously solicited, only their support. In curator Hazel A. da Breo's interview for *Fuse* magazine, Cannizzo said as much herself. "There is not a large number of Black Canadians who are specialists in art," she said. "There is a wider issue in how museums choose curators but that's a policy. ... I also think that the generation of scholarly aspects of the exhibition must be done by experts, however those experts are defined. For me it's not a race issue, it's a question of expertise. Scholarly issues should be left in the hands of scholars."

24   Admittedly Cannizzo does flash occasional warnings to visitors that everything is relative and objects change their meaning with context. One text says "The context in which an object is used, found, or viewed can significantly alter its meaning and function. What was once an African spear or shield became a trophy when collected by a Canadian soldier campaigning in Africa. It then appeared as a piece of decorative art when displayed in that soldier's home. Later in a museum collection it was catalogued as an ethnographic object. Now when viewed by you it takes on another meaning as a museum exhibit." And again: "[I]t is impossible actually to reconstruct another cultural reality in a museum. The artifacts you see here are displayed according to their 'function' or 'form' in a way that would be quite familiar to late nineteenth century museum-goers, but not the people who made them. The things are theirs, the arrangement is not."

25   That says a lot, actually, and Cannizzo is right. The traditions of the institution and its constituent "departments" (academic disciplines) are derived from European, not African, culture. The coalition was making roughly the same point when it reminded the museum that the white

point of view was still telling the story and presenting the information while African voices and interpretations were absent or invisible. As the show's nine-month run progressed, the coalition pressed the case that the exhibition was biased and misleading. "The exhibit depicts a colonialist, imperialist, racist interpretation of Africa's historical past," it stated in a letter to *Contrast* magazine in May of that year. "The curators have effectively disguised the destruction that was brought upon African society and have deliberately neglected the tremendous contribution Africans made to World Science, Technology and Culture."

There were criticisms of some facts and interpretations and several 26 writers, teachers and scholars — notably Molefe Kete Asante, chairman of African Studies at Temple University in the U.S. — denounced the show in its entirety. After viewing the exhibition, Asante told reporters, "They have reinforced that same kind of arrogance the missionaries had. The presentation of Africa this way is not only fragmentary, it is limited and gives a very, very negative impression."

Indeed, young children were reported to have had nightmares after 27 seeing the show, and the Toronto Board of Education commissioned a review, which recommended the exhibition was unsuitable for elementary school children and suitable for high school students only if significant classroom preparation was provided beforehand. Poet Ayanna Black gives this analysis of what went wrong. "They used the propaganda of the period without proper explanation or preamble. [The curator] did not want to manipulate the material, but she ended up implanting racist images because the critique of 'intellectual arrogance' did not come through. People missed it. I watched when they came upon that picture of the Zulu warrior. It was such a shock, some just froze and couldn't go on."

For others — writer and broadcaster Robert Payne, for instance — 28 the disclaimers were adequate. In a *Share* editorial, he wrote, "In so many words they tell us that *Into the Heart of Africa* is very narrow in its perspective. So I look at the various stringed instruments on display, and tell myself that they are the great grandfathers and great grandmothers of today's guitar. I see colourful, intricately woven fabric, and they hint at the great contribution which Africans have made to today's fashions ... The links are obvious — or should be to anyone in touch with history." All the same, Payne allows that the ROM was insensitive and probably stupid to mount such an exhibit, "because the glorification of colonialism in so multicultural a city as Toronto is colossally bad judgement."

29   Too true. In her various calculations about context and the shifting
meanings of things, Cannizzo would seem to have missed something;
namely the context in which her own creation was going to happen, in
which it was, in fact, transformed from an academic event into a *cause
célèbre*. While she could never have predicted the exhibit would coincide with the bloodiest year on record for the shooting of black youths
by Toronto police, much less with the release of Nelson Mandela, she
might still have thought about how African descendants would feel about
reliving those brutal nineteenth century attitudes. As Payne put it, "Given
our druthers, most of us are a touch reluctant to celebrate the men who
raped our grandmothers." (Ditto, I'd say, about celebrating our grandfathers who were rapists.) But if Cannizzo's research was closed to present
time (she did not consider consulting with contemporary artists and
teachers relevant), one still might have expected the ROM to bring a
little savvy and street-smarts to the party.

30   For example, in anthropological circles, cultural appropriation is a
very live and exceedingly touchy issue at the moment. More than one
anthropologist has been asked to leave town and more than one museum has found itself confronted by native people contesting its use of
collections that are part of their heritage. (I think of the Lubicon in
Calgary three years ago protesting *The Spirit Sings*.) And more than once
white artists, ethnologists and writers have been asked to respect native
ownership of images and not to usurp their right to tell their own stories. Although this has been raised primarily in connection with native
communities, the same sensitivities clearly come into play with an exhibition like *Into the Heart of Africa*.

31   So why did the ROM stand so resolute and inflexible behind the terse
assertion that the show was historically accurate? "It's a historical examination of Canada's involvement in Africa," said the museum's director, Cuyler Young, in response to Asante's remarks. "It has to tell a
story that's historically true. The essence of this exhibition was to demonstrate what was wrong with Canadians' attitudes as missionaries."
(And even on that score, the ROM managed to outrage people. An irate
William Samarin, professor of linguistic anthropology at the University
of Toronto, wrote in *Christian Week*, "It is deplorable ... that a public
institution should exploit what should be a tribute to Africans as an opportunity to reinforce the stereotype of the missionary as an ethnocen-
tric, bigoted and insensitive person.")

32   The shame of it is that the ROM dug in its heels and refused to take
any criticism whatsoever. In this they were helped by white journalists

like Michael Valpy in *The Globe & Mail* and Christopher Hume in the *Toronto Star*, who declared that negative responses to the exhibition were simply unfounded and suggested, by implication, that the protestors were disingenuous.

Yet, surely the point is not whether those who missed the cues and 33
were offended by the show had any right to be, or whether they ought to have had the grace to give the ROM benefit of their doubt. (Concludes Hume in a tone of insufferable superiority, "If Coalition members were better informed, they would have realized that the organizers of *Into the Heart of Africa* are on their side. There may be plenty of instances of racism in Canadian museums, but this isn't one of them.") The ROM is, after all, in the business of education and communication, and whatever else you want to say about the rights and wrongs of *Into the Heart of Africa*, the museum has to assume some responsibility for the fact people felt demeaned and misrepresented by it. It doesn't do to claim purity of purpose for yourself while casting aspersions on all objections, especially when they come in such number and with such unanimity from the very community whose past you are displaying. It begins to sound like arrogance, like an invocation of a divine right of expertise. But the ROM persisted and, instead of listening or learning why and how it was that the exhibit had such a negative impact, took the position that the show was historically accurate and that was all that mattered.

With no room to maneuver, the coalition began insisting that the ex- 34
hibit be closed. A mini Oka developed as the two sides failed to meet, and in the end, the museum let the worst of all possible situations happen. Groups of mostly black protestors gathered outside on the sidewalk voicing their objection to an exhibition representing their own cultural heritage while inside, mostly white staff busied themselves calling the police. Predictably, there were arrests, and the museum went to court to get an injunction to keep the protestors at bay, threatening them with lawsuits. A dreadfully symbolic replay of the clash of attitudes depicted inside in *Into the Heart of Africa*.

Ironically and very unexpectedly, the last word came from two other 35
Canadian museums that had booked the show. Both announced early last September they were cancelling out. Sylvie Morel, director of exhibitions for the Museum of Civilization, says the decision was made in the face of evidence the exhibit was failing to communicate what it had set out to. The Vancouver Art Gallery took a look at the Toronto troubles and read the same message. (And eventually, in November, the

two American museums that had also taken the show followed suit.)

36   Even while we can enjoy the sight of the ROM being forced to eat crow, questions remain. Such as, how well was Jeanne Cannizzo served by her partner in the project? Sure museum officials came to her defence — by standing up behind her and saying nothing. But did they improve matters or provoke them by resorting to the old routine of pulling rank on critics and depicting them as extremists? Why could they not move an inch or two to meet what were perfectly legitimate complaints? Was there really no way to introduce an authentic African voice in the exhibition; no better way to deconstruct toxic images from the past; no way of accommodating a different perspective or of redesigning the show so the collection could remain on view instead of being hustled back into storage?

37   *Into the Heart of Africa* was above all a spoiled opportunity. The ROM walked straight into the controversy with its eyes open and its heart closed; a classic case of a cultural institution unable to see its own bias and unprepared to examine its own cultural assumptions. What the situation called for was some generosity and a bit of ordinary humility; what we got was a stone wall and that, in my book, was adding insult to the original injury.

                                                                            (1991)

The Writer's Subject

1. What was the "Pax Britannica"? (para. 3) Why does Crean put extra emphasis on the word "Pax"?

2. Why does Crean compare her great-uncle's "old pith helmet" to the preserved heart of a saint in Montreal? (paras. 8–10)

3. What exactly is the "imbalance" that Crean finds disturbing? (para. 13)

4. What in Crean's view was the prime error committed by the exhibition's curator, Jeanne Cannizzo, and how was this error reflected in the selection and presentation of the objects in the exhibition?

5. What efforts did the Royal Ontario Museum make to distance itself from the colonialist and racist attitudes shown by the British in Africa in the 19th century?

The Writer's Style and Subject

1. Discuss the implications of Crean's title.

2. Why does Crean begin her essay with the story of her great-uncle John?

3. Discuss Crean's description of her great-uncle as "a quaint Canadian Rambo dressed in original Tilley Endurables." (para. 7)

4. Where does Crean first make her personal views apparent? In what ways, in your opinion, do those views affect Crean's account of the exhibition she describes?

5. In what ways does Crean convey public reaction to the ROM exhibition?

6. Do you think that Crean is fair in her presentation of Jeanne Cannizzo (curator of the exhibition) and the Royal Ontario Museum?

Suggested Topics for Writing and Discussion

1. In what respects did the exhibition "Into the Heart of Africa" raise the issue of "cultural appropriation"? (para. 30) For other discussions of this issue, see the essays by Giangrande and Keeshig-Tobias elsewhere in this anthology.

2. Crean points out that removing objects from their usual context and placing them in a museum changes their meaning and function, so that we look at them in a new way. Imagine a museum exhibition a hundred years from now, the purpose of which is to "explain" how people in Canada lived in the 1990s. Which objects would you choose to represent the domestic side of Canadian life? Write the accompanying catalogue commentary.

3. In financially troubled times, should museums be subsidized by public funds?

4. Visit an exhibition at a museum or art gallery, and write a review for your local newspaper, in which you offer your opinion about the value and importance of the exhibition.

Matata

by *Kildare Dobbs*

1   Although his face was not less brown than other faces of his tribe, it had a sort of pallor, as if the blood under the skin were thinner, less warm and confident as it moved in his veins than that of his fellows. Yet you didn't feel any repellent coldness about him. You felt he had been sadly hurt, outraged in some catastrophic way which had caused him to withdraw into himself, to close the damper upon his vital fires. He was now plainly at the nadir of his life, like a tree in the depth of winter from whose twigs and branches the sap has retreated, so that it seems dead beyond all hope of recovery. I saw that he walked with a limp, but that alone did not account for the weariness of his movements. And though there were a few white hairs tangled in his wooly poll, I could see that he was not an old man.

2   He had come to ask for a job as a clerk; he told me his name was Matata. We talked in English, which he spoke very well — I sensed that it helped his self-esteem to address me in my own language. I asked what experience he had. After a momentary pause he said in a flat tone, 'For fifteen years I was treasury clerk of this district.' I looked up in surprise. The post was one of considerable responsibility involving the management of large sums of money, and I had not seen Matata before. I had prided myself on knowing all the better-educated men in the tribe.

3   'But where have you been since you left?'

4   'In prison,' said Matata.

5   It was not hard to find him a job. Men of his ability were too rare in the territory to be discarded merely because of a criminal record, and I was able to give Matata a desk in my own office where he could not

have offended even if he had wanted to. The arrangement suited both of us. He had a measure of privacy which he needed and could not otherwise have found. I for my part was able to answer for his good conduct without having to make tedious enquiries. Moreover, I was able to draw on his experience and have the benefit of his advice in many affairs where a knowledge of tribal custom and local history was useful. In time we came to trust one another, and even to be friends. At first his confidences came reluctantly (I never pressed for them), but as the months went by he began to put forth his leaves and be himself again without fear, to tell what he had hoped for from his life, how he had pursued it, and how come to grief. Like most colonial relations, ours was imperfect. I became Matata's patron, and we both knew it. But if he sought my favour (and so, in a sense, was degraded) and sometimes resorted to guile, I myself, for less obvious and even more devious reasons, needed and invited his confidence. The proof of my corruptness is that I am now coldly moralizing upon our relation, whereas true friendship, like true love, is a secret we hug to ourselves and do not speak of aloud, even to hidden listeners.

Matata had been convicted of stealing about four hundred shillings   6 from the funds for which he was responsible. His story was that he had borrowed it to meet the needs of some relatives he was bound by custom to support. He had intended to replace the cash and had not falsified his accounts in any way. Unfortunately his books were checked before he had a chance to put the matter straight. The District Commissioner immediately had him arrested and charged, and in due course he was tried in the High Court and sentenced by an impartial judge to three years' imprisonment. 'You have abused a position of public trust,' said the judge. 'It is men like you who hold your country back in its progress towards self-government. There has been too much of this sort of thing recently, and I propose to make an example of you. I take into account your long service and previous good character.' Poor Matata heard all this twice over, once in English and again in his own tongue from the interpreter. He thought over it in prison.

Though he had been educated at government schools and so touched   7 with Western knowledge and ideas, his upbringing had been little different from that of his fellow tribesmen. He had been born into a large family. While yet a small child he had learnt to address them all correctly, to distinguish between those with whom he could speak freely and those with whom his relations were governed by tabu. He learnt to call his father *Dada* and his mother *Yuva*. That was simple enough.

But he had to call all his father's brothers *Dada* too, and all his mother's sisters *Yuva*. So he had six fathers and four mothers to start with. But that was not all, for his proper father had two other wives who were also called *Yuva*, and not only they, but their sisters as well. The daughters of all these so-called mothers and fathers were considered his sisters, and their sons his brothers. This army of siblings all had claims on him.

8   It was not surprising that Matata's first confused thoughts in the early months of his imprisonment were to believe himself completely innocent. This is commonly the reaction of a normally law-abiding man who finds himself convicted of a crime. The impersonality of the legal machine which crushes him in its cogs, the remoteness of formal evidence from the inner realities of motive and intention, the brusque efficiency of police and clerks, the patient obtuseness of judges — all these combine to put the whole situation from him as utterly unreal. At the same time the ground of his faith in himself and in other people is sprung like the trap from under the condemned. He has thought of himself as a middling decent person. Now it seems he was mistaken. He is a monster so dangerous that he must be locked away for years.

9   Matata felt all this and more. For the better part of his adult life he had been working hard at the business of civilizing himself and his people. He believed in civilization. He believed in roads and schools and penicillin and septic tanks. He was not bored, as I was, by the apostles of hygiene, the health officer and his team of sanitary inspectors. It is true that he, like the rest of his tribe, always referred to the health officer as Bwana Mavi, or Mister Excrement, but he intended no disrespect. Mr. Excrement was as much a limb of civilization as Matata's gold watch, which he loved very much and at which, in idle moments, he used to stare raptly like a man in a trance. Since Matata loved civilization so well, it went very hard with him to discover that he was not loved equally in return. In his heart, too, he looked at the world as a man of his tribe. Working with the white men in the days of their power was like working with powerful spirits; it conferred wealth and prestige. But these spirits exacted a price. So long as you walked carefully they smiled on you and showed you their secrets. The moment you made a mistake they turned on you without mercy and tore out your heart.

10   It was the prison superintendent, a severe but good-hearted Afrikaner, who helped Matata recover some of his faith in himself. He gave him a responsible job and cheered him when he felt sorry for himself. Matata was grateful to this rough good man.

Though Matata became once more a useful and happy member of   11
his tribe, I could not console myself with any notion that his sufferings
had turned out for the best, or that others would profit by his example.
Failure teaches a man nothing except compassion for the failure of others. I am still haunted, shall perhaps always be haunted, by the image
of Matata as I first saw him, halting towards my desk, his dark eyes full
of a pain I did not then understand, but which is now as familiar as a
guilty secret.

(1962)

The Writer's Subject

1. Why was Matata a man of rare ability in the territory? (paras. 2–5)

2. What benefits accrued to both Dobbs and Matata through their working
   together in the same office? (para. 5)

3. Why does Dobbs accuse himself of deviousness and corruptness? (para.
   5)

4. How does Matata's theft of money throw light on the clash between his
   own culture and that of the white man he served?

5. What are Matata's reactions to his arrest and subsequent imprisonment?

6. What did civilization mean to Matata? (para. 9)

7. Why does Dobbs say that he is still haunted by the image of Matata as he
   first saw him? (para. 11)

The Writer's Style and Strategy

1. Why does Dobbs devote the first paragraph to a physical description of
   Matata? How does this prepare us for the essay's conclusion?

2. Discuss the use Dobbs makes of the metaphor of the tree in paragraphs 1
   and 5.

3. Why does Dobbs give the words of the "impartial" judge in direct speech
   rather than merely reporting his judgment? (para. 6)

4. What does Dobbs's reference to the health officer and his team as "the
   apostles of hygiene" convey about his attitude to them? (para. 9)

Suggested Topics for Writing and Discussion

1. Compare this essay with Orwell's "Shooting an Elephant." In what respects
   did the writers react in similar fashion to their experiences as colonial administrators?

2. To Matata his gold watch is a symbol of civilization. Choose this or some other object or artifact and discuss it as a symbol of civilization (i.e., civilizations in general, or a particular civilization).

3. Describe a person from a culture other than your own and indicate what you have learned about this person's culture and cultural values. What has this contact taught you about your *own* culture and its values?

Black Like Me

by Fil Fraser

When I was a careful boy growing up in Montreal, Canada was a coun-   1
try in which blacks like me developed an instinct about where we were
welcome. Unlike the U.S., where racism was direct, Canada was, in its
unsung way, more subtle. Here "discriminating" restaurants gave off a
palpable hostility that seeped into your system as you sat at table, ig
nored. No one asked you to leave or told you to stay out, you were just
not served. Across the border you could still see "No niggers" billboards,
hand-lettered, which struck with a force that a new generation cannot
understand.

We Frasers were in some ways more vulnerable since we didn't run   2
with the pack — the pack being the black community centred on St.
Antoine Street, not far from Windsor station where most heads of households worked as "red-caps" and conductors. My father, a student at
McGill when he came to Canada in the 1920s, decided we should live
away from what a later generation would describe as a ghetto. We went
down to St. Antoine Street for haircuts and for semiannual visits to hear
Reverend Este preach at the Negro church. But we lived in St. Leonard
de Port Maurice, a farming community abutting refinery row on the island's east end. The St. Antoine Street kids knew their turf and stuck to
it. We experimented, and in the process developed sharp and useful reflexes.

The Montreal of my growing up was just as harsh on its majority   3
culture, Francophones. English-speaking westenders, who saw no virtue in bilingualism, called them Frenchmen, usually with an alliterative
expletive, or pea-soupers, or pepsis, the latter term making no sense to

me, since I liked Pepsi too. The French kids also developed a sense about where they were welcome — west of the Ontario streetcar line, behind Morgan's department store, was territory to be careful in.

4   Those of us who belonged to minorities, visible or otherwise, knew what we were up against, put our heads down, and did the best we could. A boy in my class at Montreal High told me he couldn't get into McGill's medical school, even with first-class marks, because the quota for Jewish students that year had been filled. Amazingly (why would anyone want to go where he wasn't wanted?), there was a waiting list for Jews. Today, I hear, the man is a prominent politician, not a doctor.

5   In the early years of World War II, when I was not quite a teenager, marauding bands of English-Canadian soldiers roamed east-end Montreal, looking for Frenchies to beat up. That was after Mackenzie King capitulated and it was no longer "Not necessarily conscription, but conscription if necessary," and Mayor Camillien Houde was interned for heaping profanity on the idea of French Canadians' fighting the English war. Every so often an English-Canadian soldier was caught offbase by a French gang. That was bad. But no one had it worse than the handful of French Canadians who had enlisted voluntarily.

6   Later, when the war was over and Montreal became "the Paris of North America," many of the displaced persons, "D.P.s" who had come to reinvent their lives, were doing well with new, anglicized names. But Eartha Kitt, the toast of Paris and New York, couldn't get into the Ritz. And the Caughnawaga Indians, rich in their ancient traditions, were just another local tourist attraction.

7   There were variations on the theme as you crossed the country. We had heard, without great surprise, about the internment of Japanese Canadians in the west. After all, we had Germans locked up along with Camillien Houde. Every now and then some of the scandal sheets would flash headlines about the Ku Klux Klan somewhere out near Moose Jaw going after Catholics, and the better-informed French Canadians, almost always Catholic, knew about Ontario's Orangemen. Ukrainians were *out* in Edmonton, Germans were *out* in Winnipeg. Across the country who was out varied from place to place. Who was *in* never changed. To be of British descent was to have access to the corridors of power and prestige. Everybody else tried to join in. We all sang "God Save the King" and saluted the Union Jack.

8   Canada was a "white man's country" — as Mackenzie King put it in 1908, when he was deputy minister of labour. The phrase became the title of a book by Ted Ferguson. "That Canada should remain a white

man's country," Ferguson quotes the future prime minister as saying, "is ... not only desirable for economic and social reasons but highly necessary on political and national grounds." That meant a white, Anglo-Saxon, Protestant, man's country. It never occurred to us, then, what that meant to women. Our immigration policy, pragmatic since "les filles du roi," was to bring in Chinese to do the dirty work of building the railroad, and central and eastern Europeans with their sheepskins to fill up the Prairies and create business for the railroad. The policy did not include giving the immigrants any real piece of the Canadian action.

And yet, astonishingly, Canada today is unique in the world, embrac-   9
ing and encouraging more diversity than any other country. We are officially, and by degrees viscerally, a multicultural country. The British are a minority, and beginning to act like it. Multiculturalism is enshrined in the Canadian Charter of Rights and Freedoms, is reflected in our institutions, and is seeping, far more rapidly than we realize, into our collective psyche. Canada has become a country that says its citizens are equal, regardless of race, or religion, or origin, or age, or physical or mental status, or sex. The courts back up that idea, it seems, almost weekly.

How did this happen? I don't remember any politician running a cam-   10
paign on the virtues of multiculturalism — at least not until the very recent past. No government has been elected on the promise of settling the debt with the natives, or making the country safe for boat people. And yet the mould is made, and set. No politician, no government, can now dismantle the charter, the institutions, the labour agreements, the judicial precedents that make us the only truly open, multicultural country in the world.

I suppose I'm as typically Canadian as anyone. I was born in   11
Montreal. My father came from Trinidad, a scholarship student who chose not to go back to help his country; my mother was born on a Canadian ship, inbound from Barbados, about to dock in Montreal. That puts me in roughly the same situation as a third of Canadians, belonging to neither of the so-called founding peoples.

I think the ferment began as we entered the 1960s. Diefenbaker was   12
in Ottawa, having been given considerable assistance by a waning but still potent Maurice Duplessis. Jean Lesage, following hard on Duplessis' heels with the same objectives but a different style, set the Quiet Revolution in motion, with spectacular success. No one now disputes whether Francophones can claim to be *maîtres chez nous*. Tommy Douglas was in Regina running the first socialist government in North America.

13   For reasons that had nothing to do with politics, I moved from
Montreal to Regina in 1958. The next year a local firm, Queen City
Real Estate, refused to rent an apartment to me. Not many years earlier,
in Montreal, I would have shrugged, told myself that my reflexes were
getting rusty, and moved on to the next listing. But there was something different now about the Canadian atmosphere, and about me. I
found out quickly and easily from an embarrassed clerk that Queen City
had a "whites only" rental policy. My reaction was interesting — not
anger, or fear, or shame. Rather it was a welcome opportunity to right a
wrong, summed up simply as "You can't do that in this country." Any
more. Saskatchewan had passed a bill of rights, and "The Queen vs.
Queen City Real Estate" was the first case of discrimination tried under
the legislation. The attorney general insisted that the crown, not the com-
plainant, lay the charge; and with little fanfare, Queen City was found
guilty and fined. It offered me an apartment, which I declined.

14   I met John Diefenbaker in the early 1960s, mainstreeting in Prince
Albert. How easily politicians moved about in those days! Dief, full of
righteous vitality, was out for a walk down a road that was really called
Main Street, shaking hands and talking to the people with no entourage
and no bodyguards. When he shook my hand I felt genuine warmth,
which I returned. As a reporter, I had covered the 1958 election for radio station CFCF in Montreal with appropriate cynicism, nearly getting
punched by George Hees when I asked him about the Diefenbaker-
Duplessis axis which delivered the Tory landslide in Quebec.

15   But I felt that Diefenbaker's 1960 Canadian Bill of Rights had been
a mile-stone for Canada. It redeemed him in my mind for the alliance
with Duplessis, who these days is being given a revised place in history
as a defender of Quebec autonomy. But in my time in Montreal he was
known, among other things, as the author of the Padlock Law, used as a
legal bludgeon against Jehovah's Witnesses in Quebec under the guise
of fighting communism.

16   I had argued in favour of the Bill of Rights, with all its limitations. It
was not entrenched in the constitution and it applied only to federal law.
It could be dismissed, as it was by J.D. Morton in *Saturday Night* in
September, 1960, as "a lawyer's tool." I remember well the arguments
that the bill would limit rather than enlarge human rights already, opponents said, effectively guaranteed under British common law. The bill
would open loopholes, it was full of escape clauses. It could even be
superseded by the War Measures Act. And so on. With the passage of
the bill, Canadians, for the first time, could not be discriminated against

on the basis of race, colour, or creed. The bill moved individual rights out of British common law and into hard legislation.

The Royal Commission on Bilingualism and Biculturalism came officially face to face, for the first time in our history, with the fact that there was an important minority in Canada of neither British nor French descent. In the commission's report the term "multiculturalism" first assumed the status of hard currency. The other day I came across a brochure I had saved announcing a conference on multiculturalism for Canada in August 1970, at the University of Alberta. The conference was opened by Senator Paul Yuzyk, and I, wearing as one of my hats the programme directorship of Canada's first educational television station, got a half hour to talk about multiculturalism in broadcasting. The back of the programme listed the sixteen recommendations in book four of the B & B Commission, "The Cultural Contribution of the Other Ethnic Groups." 17

Jean Lesage's clarion call to an awakening French Canada did much more than give Francophones a new sense of themselves. It stirred the aspirations of minorities in other provinces. If Francophones in Quebec could get out from under the British hegemony, what about Ukrainians in Alberta, Italians in Toronto, Chinese in Vancouver, and Indians everywhere? 18

And there were the thousands who, when they encountered discrimination, began slowly to realize, as I did, that "You can't do that in this country, any more" — and found the laws backed them up. Many who had come in waves of postwar immigration — from Hungary and Czechoslovakia and Poland, from Bangladesh and Uganda, from the United States during the Vietnam war, from the East and West Indies, and later from southeast Asia — didn't come here to be second-class citizens or part of a melting pot. They came to what they perceived as a compassionate country. Few other nations had opened their doors as Canada did. And the remnant of racism and discrimination they found, now with no legal, institutional, or moral base, was ripe for attack. 19

In many parts of Canada the attack is now in full flood. But even though the outcome of the war seems inevitable, no one should believe that all the battles have been won. While those of us who have been here for a generation or more usually find a comfortable niche, it's still tough to be a new immigrant in Canada. And while there are some who see a future in which we double our present population with new immigration, there are also those who continue to fight the rearguard action. For all the usual reasons: they'll take our jobs — they won't adapt to 20 our system — they'll only bring another country's problems to our shores — they'll spoil our way of life.

21   In a series of articles under the heading "A Minority Report," the *Toronto Star* illustrated "the Metro mosaic." More than 100 minority groups, who make up a majority of the population, still face prejudice, hidden and unhidden. Some kids today, as I did in the 1930s and 1940s, have to fight their way home from school. Still, we've come a long way from the days when immigrants were greeted with signs that proclaimed "no dogs or Jews allowed."

22   In 1986 the minister of justice, John Crosbie, told the House of Commons that the government was committed to ending discrimination that keeps individuals in Canada from fully realizing their potential, and embraced its duty to take the lead in making sure that federal laws and policies met the high standards of the charter and that individuals were not forced unnecessarily into court.

23   In a speech last April in Toronto, the then minister of state for multiculturalism, Otto Jelinek, was able to say, "Our society has become *irreversibly* multicultural and multiracial," even though he has still not resolved the question of an apology and honourable compensation for the wartime insult to Japanese Canadians. And the prime minister, speaking to the same gathering, issued what might well have been the slogan for multiculturalism in the 1980s. "Tokenism is over," he said. "Fairness is in."

24   Our record, in the years after World War II, stands in stark contrast to a long and shameful series of events culminating with the internment of Japanese and German Canadians in the 1940s. In 1903 the government of Canada raised the head tax on Chinese immigrants originally established at $50 in 1885, to $500. In 1914, a boatload of 376 Indian refugees was refused permission to land in Vancouver, and suffered incredible privation because we were stingy, to put it kindly, about giving them food and water. In 1939, 907 Jews escaping Nazi Germany aboard the *St. Louis* were refused entry to Canada. At the time, Hitler's attempted genocide was in full flood.

25   Canada's postwar immigrants landed with a painful awareness of war and racism. After they found their feet in this new land, they weren't about to put up with more. There was little to be done about private prejudice but, as the law developed, in provincial and federal jurisdictions it said that public services were equally available to all.

26   It was, ironically, Pierre Trudeau who finished the legal transformation that John Diefenbaker, for whom he had only disdain, had started.

The full-bodied reverberations from the act of patriation and the enshrinement of the charter in the Canadian constitution will be felt beyond the next generation. Canada's first ombudsman, George McClelland, a former commissioner of the RCMP, was appointed by the government of Alberta in 1967. By 1986 all provinces except Prince Edward Island had established such an office. Now, not only did human-rights legislation have teeth, but a publicly funded defender. Individual rights in Canada no longer depend upon some vaguely defined and unevenly interpreted "common law." Our most "uncommon" laws (if you look around the world) are meeting the tests of the courts, as precedent upon precedent builds a legal and moral base.

It's somehow typical that we Canadians have difficulty recognizing 27 our uniqueness. We see ourselves as a not very powerful, not very innovative, not very exciting land that is nevertheless safe. We look to other countries with envy, wishing we had their strength, their depth of culture and character, their creativity.

But look more closely. Our first motherland, France, is culturally stag- 28 nant, lurching from political to economic to social crisis. Britain, once the home of empire, is in danger of losing its role as leader of the Commonwealth. Its immigration policy is a shambles; its class society still flourishes; its problems with Ireland defy solution. And when we look, nervously, at our continental neighbour, our desire to buy into the American dream becomes highly selective. The melting pot never really worked — yet in the United States multiculturalism is a very recent notion. Everyone — the Puerto Ricans, the Indians, the Mexicans, the various other Latinos — is "American," whether they like it or not.

In the Middle East, the cradle of civilization, even brothers can't get 29 along. Beirut, once one of the world's most sophisticated cities, is a war zone. In Israel, Jews attack Jews, desecrating synagogues. India is still trying to grapple with racial and religious strife, even though untouchability is officially dead. China is working at being homogeneous. In the Soviet Union some are more equal than others. The Swiss are multicultural, but only for the four official groups. Most of the world's countries are either unicultural, uniracial, and religiously homogeneous, or else caught up in internal strife.

It's not hard to understand why the notion of multiculturalism is so 30 difficult, and why so few countries have contemplated adopting the ideal as policy. It is, first of all, risky. When you allow people to emigrate from other countries and keep their cultures, their ties to former countries, you invite ancient rivalries and hatreds to settle into the land. The hope is that old hurts and fears will mellow as those people find a measure of security in a benign environment — and the Canadian experience has, by and large, borne this out.

31   But multiculturalism, with its implicit ties to other cultures, also obviates narrow nationalism. In a way, you ride the fine line between being an open, free, and tolerant society, and not really being a country at all, at least in the "My country right or wrong" sense. The gamble is that in the end there is pride in tolerance; that a new kind of nationhood, safer in a tinderbox world, can be built on the open international communication that comes with multiculturalism. As Eric Hoffer noted of the "true believer," those who most loudly protest, defend, and propagate the faith are those who are the least secure in it. Nations that feel threatened, uncertain of their morality, become aggressive and dangerous.

32   How then to explain Canada's behaviour? Does the moral authority flowing from our compassionate immigration policy, from our record in foreign aid, from Pearson's Nobel Peace Prize or Trudeau's international stardom, give a kind of courage? Is there some special serenity, some security that stems from knowing that multiculturalism, while not easy, works? Not only are we comfortable with the extraordinary diversity of our peoples, we plan expansion on the same basis. Major political parties are now arguing not about where new immigrants will come from, or what their colour or creed will be, but about how many we can absorb, and how soon.

33   Canadians have yet to discover the creativity of their social order. If we can solve the problems of making it possible for people of every kind to live together in reasonable harmony, we have a message for the world. The problems of this shrinking planet are problems we're solving in Canada.

34   When I was invited to a mainstream event in the 1950s it was because I was exotic. In the sixties and seventies I was often the token black. But in the eighties when they call, I know it's really me they want. Not bad for a kid who grew up in east-end Montreal thinking someone had put him on the wrong planet.

(1987)

The Writer's Subject

1. What differences does Fraser perceive between racist attitudes in Canada and those in the U.S.A.?

2. How were immigrants and members of minorities treated in Canada in the first half of the 20th century?

3. What changes came about to improve the situation of minorities starting in the 1960s?

4. Why does Fraser consider himself to be "as typically Canadian as anyone"? (para. 11)

5. How does Fraser back up his claim that Canada is "the only truly open, multicultural country in the world"? (para.10)

6. What does Fraser mean by stating that "multiculturalism, with its implicit ties to other cultures ... obviates narrow nationalism"? (para. 31)

The Writer's Style and Strategy

1. Discuss Fraser's choice of title.

2. How does Fraser make use of personal experience to strengthen his argument?

3. What does Fraser mean by the statement "We are officially, and by degrees viscerally, a multicultural country"? (para. 9)

4. Though this is a short essay, Fraser makes many specific references to Canadian politics and history. Where do you find the use of such details particularly effective?

Suggested Topics for Writing and Discussion

1. Find out what you can about some of the political figures mentioned by Fraser, such as Mackenzie King, Camillien Houde, John Diefenbaker, Jean Lesage, or Tommy Douglas. What part did they play, directly or indirectly, in the development of multicultural policies in Canada?

2. Fraser states that, despite many improvements in the area of human rights, "it's still tough to be a new immigrant in Canada." (para. 20) Do you agree with this opinion?

3. Would you agree with Fraser's claim that the Canadian experience has shown that multiculturalism works? Compare his view with the view expressed by Neil Bissoondath.

4. Find out what you can about one or two of the racist incidents alluded to by Fraser in paragraph 24.

Allowing the Mind to Wander

by Carole Giangrande

1   A few years ago, I travelled through a cluster of isolated hamlets in north-western Saskatchewan, home to Cree and Metis trappers, some of whom I was lucky enough to interview. A timid but curious big-city writer, I drove, trudged and flew my way through this huge expanse of bush and snow with notebooks, tape recorder and absolutely no first-hand experience of either wilderness life or native issues.

2   Through the introductions of a local Cree (who was kind enough to act as interpreter), I had come to document the loss of trapping lands that the federal government had expropriated in the late 1950s for the Air Weapons Testing Range that straddles the provinces of Alberta and Saskatchewan.

3   One of the trappers, a lively talker who spoke in Cree, told his story with such immediacy that it felt as if it had been only the day before that he was tricked out of his trapping lands for small change and false promises that the land would be returned. As he spoke he grew more animated and he took the pen out of my hand and marked an X on my pad to show me how he — lacking English but not trust — innocently signed the deal.

4   Without his language or his particular experience, I had only the journalist's sense of the person before me who gave the story meaning, a vital and sympathetic individual whose suffering and forbearance were as evident as his unexplainable good nature in the face of so much injustice. Even more remarkable was the fact that the man still had it in him to trust another stranger, this time one who promised to tell his story. His faith felt mysterious to me, the kind of small, unnoticed gift

that so often slips between words as easily as light through the slats of a blind. It was not something a writer with conscience would dismiss lightly, let alone betray.

Anyone who works with the one-on-one intimacy of print and radio 5 has to start by assuming that such revelations are possible, and that the experiences of a single human being have the power to resonate with all the silent emotions of those who are reading or listening. Never mind that the trapper grew up a native in the bush while I, a Canadian of Italian descent, lived my early years in New York City's Bronx. Common humanity is supposed to turn a babble of voices into a dialogue whatever our race or culture, a fact as fundamental to an interviewer as tapes and mikes and recording gear.

Or so I thought. My old perceptions of common ground appear al- 6 most simple-minded these days, a smokescreen hiding the differences between privileged and oppressed of all races, a way of denying the power relationship that exists between those of my (white) race and every other. At the annual meeting of the Writers' Union in Kingston, Ontario, last spring, a number of writers, shamed by the complaint of white dominance over native culture, promised to abstain from handling native subject matter of any kind.

However well-intentioned, their pledge left me grateful to have 7 published my work back in 1983. It also left me wondering how many publishers today would touch an account of that same native trapper's experience as perceived, however insightfully, by a non-native. Without forgetting that "cultural appropriation" is a painful and sensitive issue for many, we're also in real danger of denying what is most human in us by cluttering our psychic landscape with "No Trespassing" signs.

Glutted as we are with politics, we keep forgetting that there are other, 8 equally profound dimensions of human understanding and reality. Telling writers and artists of one culture that they are no longer welcome to imagine and enter into the heart of another is a denial of the miraculous and the unexpected, of the hope we place in new insight and its power to reach out and heal old wounds. We end up saying that there is little more to life than the particulars: nation, gender, politics, ethnic group and the color of our mortal human skin.

What we are really talking about is our lack of belief in capital-H 9 Humanity, that very old idea now getting a rough ride through the byways of the global village. Common human ground is out of fashion politically. Some see it as a crude form of Western dominance, a euphemism for a world-view imposed by white, male humanity. Instead, we're moving into a New Babel of what theologian Gregory Baum calls "a multitude of small narratives," a cluster of exclusively cultural and racial understandings of the world, empty of any "larger story" of collective human purpose or destiny.

10   This new form of tribalism has some good things to offer; a sense of heritage and place is far better than the emptiness of life on a bland, "globalized" MacPlanet where the only "big picture" gets bounced off a satellite dish. Yet we Canadians, dispossessed and alienated, "distinct" and "sovereign," have been pushing our luck. Right about now we could do with a Gandhi or a Martin Luther King to speak to ideals that are universal and above the tribe before our near-violent obsession with cultural differences puts an end to us as a country.

11   And those of us who write can have faith in the power of the imagination where we transcend ourselves, where we enter into and become the people of all races — real or fictitious — that we write. In this way we understand and cherish them as deeply and with as much courtesy as we would our loved ones.

12   Rather than avoid writing outside our cultural experience, our hope of defying the curse of racism lies in doing just the opposite. The gift of words and language then becomes our common ground, symbolic of the human mystery that defies race and includes us all. For such creative acts, the appropriate metaphor is not "theft" but love. Simplistic? No more so than guns or the rhetoric of death.

                                                                                        (1990)

The Writer's Subject

1. What did Giangrande learn from her interview with a Cree trapper in northwestern Saskatchewan?

2. What has led the writer to view her earlier perceptions as "almost simpleminded these days"? (para. 6)

3. Explain the meaning of Giangrande's statement that we are "in real danger of denying what is most human in us by cluttering our psychic landscape with 'No Trespassing' signs." (para. 7)

4. What does the writer mean by the phrase "our lack of belief in capital-H Humanity"? (para. 9)

5. What, as Giangrande sees it, are the advantages and the disadvantages of what she calls a "new form of tribalism"? (para. 10)

6. What in Giangrande's view is the importance of the imagination in countering racism?

The Writer's Style and Strategy

1. Why does the writer give such prominence to the anecdote about her interview with the Cree trapper?

2. What does Giangrande choose to tell us about herself? Is it relevant to her purpose in the essay?

3. Why does the writer invoke the names of Gandhi and Martin Luther King? (para. 10)

4. Comment on Giangrande's phrase, "the emptiness of life on a bland, 'globalized,' MacPlanet." (para. 10)

5. What is the tone of the concluding paragraph? How does the writer's choice of words help to create that tone?

Suggested Topics for Writing and Discussion

1. Giangrande remarks that "'cultural appropriation' is a painful and sensitive issue for many." (para. 7) Explain what she means, and compare the position she takes on this issue with the views of Lenore Keeshig-Tobias.

2. Do you agree or disagree with the writer's contention that one need not have been born into a culture in order to write about it?

3. Giangrande fears that "our near-violent obsession with cultural differences" may put an end to Canada as a country. What are your views on this subject?

Is That All There Is?

Tribal Literature

by Basil H. Johnston

1   In the early 60's Kahn-Tineta Horn, a young Mohawk model, got the attention of the Canadian press (media) not only by her beauty but by her articulation of Indian grievances and her demands for justice. Soon after Red Power was organized threatening to use force. Academics and scholars, anxious and curious to know what provoked the Indians, organized a series of conferences and teach-ins to explore the issues. Even children wanted to know. So for their enlightenment experts wrote dozens of books. Universities and colleges began native studies courses. Ministries of Education, advised by a battery of consultants, adjusted their Curriculum Guidelines to allow units of study on the native peoples of this continent. And school projects were conducted for the benefit of children between ten and thirteen years of age.

2   One such project at the Churchill Avenue Public School in North York, Ontario lasted six weeks and the staff and students who had taken part mounted a display as a grand finale to their studies. And a fine display it was in the school's library.

3   In front of a canvas tent that looked like a teepee stood a grim chief, face painted in war-like colours and arms folded. On his head he wore a head-dress made of construction paper. A label pinned to his vest bore the name, Blackfoot. I made straight for the chief.

4   "How!" I greeted the chief, holding up my hand at the same time as a gesture of friendship.

5   Instead of returning the greeting, the chief looked at me quizzically.

"How come you look so unhappy?" I asked him. 6

"Sir! I'm bored," the chief replied. 7

"How so, chief?" 8

"Sir, don't tell anybody, but I'm bored. I'm tired of Indians. That's 9
all we've studied for six weeks. I thought they'd be interesting when
we started, because I always thought that Indians were neat. At the start
of the course we had to choose to do a special project from food preparation, transportation, dwellings, social organization, clothing, and hunting and fishing. I chose dwellings" and here the chief exhaled in
exasperation "... and that's all me and my team studied for six weeks;
teepees, wigwams, longhouses, igloos. We read books, encyclopedias,
went to the library to do research, looked at pictures, drew pictures. Then
we had to make one. Sir, I'm bored."

"Didn't you learn anything else about Indians, chief?" 10

"No sir, there was nothing else...Sir?...Is that all there is to Indians?" 11

Little has changed since that evening in 1973. Books still present 12
native peoples in terms of their physical existence as if Indians were
incapable of meditating upon or grasping the abstract. Courses of study
in the public school system, without other sources of information, had
to adhere to the format, pattern, and content set down in books. Students studied Kaw-lijas, wooden Indians, who were incapable of love
or laughter; or Tontos, if you will, whose sole skill was to make fires
and to perform other servile duties for the Lone Ranger; an inarticulate
Tonto, his speech limited to "Ugh!," "Kimo Sabi," and "How."

Despite all the research and the field work conducted by anthropolo- 13
gists, ethnologists and linguists, Indians remain "The Unknown Peoples" as Professor George F. Tait of the University of Toronto so aptly
titled his book written in 1973.

Not even Indian Affairs of Canada, with its more than two centuries 14
of experience with natives, with its array of experts and consultants,
with its unlimited funds, seems to have learned anything about its constituents, if we are to assess their latest publication titled *The Canadian Indian*. One would think that the Honourable William McKnight,
then Minister of Indian and Northern Affairs, under whose authority
the book was published in 1986 should know by now the Indians who
often come to Ottawa, do not arrive on horseback, do not slay one of
the RCMP mounts and cook it on the steps of the Parliament Buildings. Moreover, most Indians he has seen and met were not dressed in
loincloths, nor did they sleep in teepees. Yet he authorized the publication of a book bereft of any originality or imagination, a book that per-

petuated the notion and the image that the Indians had not advanced one step since contact, but are still living as they had one hundred and fifty, even three hundred years ago. There was not a word about native thought, literature, institutions, contributions in music, art, theatre. But that's to be expected of Indian Affairs; to know next to nothing of their constituents.

15   Where did the author or authors this latest publication by Indian Affairs get their information? The selected readings listed at the back of the book provide a clue; Frances Densmore, Harold Driver, Philip Drucker, Frederick W. Hodge, Diamond Jenness, Reginald and Gladys Laubin, Frank G. Speck, Bruce G. Trigger, George Woodcock, Harold A. Innis, Calvin Martin, E. Palmer Patterson, eminent scholars, none of whom spoke or attempted to learn the language of any of the Indian nations about whom they were writing. Modern scholars because they are not required by their universities to learn, are no more proficient in a native language than were their predecessors.

16   Herein, I submit, is the nub and the rub. Without the benefit of knowing the language of the Indian nation that they are investigating, scholars can never get into their mind, the heart and soul and the spirit and still understand the native's perceptions and interpretations. The scholar must confine his research and studies to the material, physical culture, subsistence patterns and family relationships.

17   Without knowing the spiritual and the intellectual, aesthetic side of Indian culture, the scholar cannot furnish what that little grade five youngster and others like him wanted to know about Indians.

18   Admitting his boredom was that grade five youngster's way of expressing his disappointment with the substance of the course that he and his colleagues had been made to endure. In another sense, it was a plea for other knowledge that would quench his curiosity and challenge his intellect.

19   Students such as he, as well as adults, are interested in the character, intellect, soul, spirit, heart of people of other races and cultures. They want to know what other people believe in, what they understand, what they expect and hope for in this life and in the next, how they keep law and order and harmony within the family and community, how and why they celebrated ceremonies, what made them proud, ashamed, what made them happy, what sad. Whether the young understand what they want to know and learn does not matter much, they still want to know in order to enrich their own insights and broaden their outlooks.

20   But unless scholars and writers know the literature of the peoples

that they are studying or writing about they cannot provide what their students and readers are seeking and deserving of.

There is, fortunately, enough literature, both oral and written, avail- 21 able for scholarly study, but it has for the most part been neglected. Myths, legends, and songs have not been regenerated and set in modern terms to earn immortalization in poetry, dramatization in plays, or romanticization in novels.

What has prevented the acceptance of Indian literature as a serious 22 and legitimate expression of native thought and experience has been indifferent and inferior translation, a lack of understanding and interest in the culture and a notion that it has little of importance to offer to the larger white culture.

In offering you a brief sketch, no more than a glimpse, as it were, of 23 my tribe's culture, I am doing no more than what anyone of you would do were you to be asked "What is your culture? Would you explain it?" I would expect you to reply, "Read my literature, and you will get to know something of my thoughts, my convictions, my aspirations, my feelings, sentiments, expectations, whatever I cherish or abominate."

First, let me offer you an observation about my language for the sim- 24 ple reason that language and literature are inseparable, though they are too often taught as separate entities. They belong together.

In my tribal language, all words have three levels of meaning; there 25 is the surface meaning that everyone instantly understands. Beneath this meaning is a more fundamental meaning derived from the prefixes and their combinations with other terms. Underlying both is the philosophical meaning.

Take the word "Anishinaubae." That is what the members of the na- 26 tion, now known as Chippewa in the United States or Ojibway in Canada, called themselves. It referred to a member of the tribe. It was given to the question "What are you?" But it was more than just a term of identification. It meant, "I am a person of good intent, a person of worth" and it reflected what the people thought of themselves, and of human nature; that all humans are essentially, fundamentally good. Let's separate that one word into its two terms. The first, "Onishishih" meaning good, fine, beautiful, excellent: and the second "naubae" meaning being, male, human species. Even together they do not yield the meaning "good intention." It is only by examining the stories of Nanabush, the tribes' central and principal mythical figure who represents all men and all women, that the term Anishinaubae begins to make sense. Nanabush was always full of good intentions, ergo the people of the tribe. The

Anishinaubae perceive themselves as people who intended good and therefore of merit and worth. From this perception they drew a strong sense of pride as well as a firm sense of place in the community. This influenced their notion of independence.

27   Let's take another word, the word for truth. When we say "w'daeb-awae" we mean he or she is telling the truth, is correct, is right. But the expression is not merely an affirmation of a speaker's veracity. It is as well a philosophical proposition that in saying a speaker casts his words and his voice as far as his perception and his vocabulary will enable him or her, it is a denial that there is such a thing as absolute truth; that the best and most the speaker can achieve and a listener expect is the highest degree of accuracy. Somehow that one expression, "w'daeb-awae," sets the limits to a single statement as well as setting limits to truth and the scope and exercise of speech.

28   One other word: "to know." We say "w'kikaendaun" to convey the idea that he or she "knows." Without going into the etymological deri-vations, suffice it to say that when the speaker assures someone that he knows it, that person is saying that the notion, image, idea, fact that that person has in mind corresponds and is similar to what he or she has already seen, heard, touched, tasted or smelled. That person's knowl-edge may not be exact, but similar to that which has been instilled and impressed in his or her mind and recalled from memory.

29   The stories that make up our tribal literature are no different from the words in our language. Both have many meanings and applications, as well as bearing tribal perceptions, values and outlooks.

30   Let us begin at the beginning with the tribe's story of creation which precedes all other stories in the natural order. Creation stories provide insights into what races and nations understand of human nature; ours is no different in this respect.

31   This is our creation story. Kitchi-manitou beheld a vision. From this vision, The Great Mystery, for that is the essential and fundamental meaning of Kitchi-manitou and not spirit as is often understood, were created the sun and the stars, the land and the waters, and all the crea-tures and beings, seen and unseen, that inhabit the earth, the seas and the skies. The creation was desolated by a flood. Only the manitous, creatures and beings who dwelt in the waters were spared. All others perished.

32   In the heavens dwelt a manitou, Geezhigo-quae (Sky-woman). Dur-ing the cataclysm upon the earth, Geezhigo-quae became pregnant. The creatures adrift upon the seas prevailed upon the giant turtle to offer his

back as a haven for Geezhigo-quae. They then invited her to come down.

Resting on the giant turtle's back Geezhigo-quae asked for soil. 33

One after another water creatures dove into the depths to retrieve a 34 morsel of soil. Not one returned with a particle of soil. They all offered an excuse; too deep, too dark, too cold, there are evil manitous keeping watch. Last to descend was the muskrat. He returned with a small knot of earth.

With the particle of mud retrieved by the muskrat Geezhigo-quae 35 recreated an island and the world as we know it. On the island she created over the giant turtle's shell, Geezhigo-quae gave birth to twins who begot the tribe called the Anishinaubaeg.

Millenia later the tribe dreamed Nanabush into being. Nanabush 36 represented themselves and what they understood of human nature. One day his world too was flooded. Like Geezhigo-quae, Nanabush recreated his world from a morsel of soil retrieved from the depths of the sea.

As a factual account of the origin of the world and of being, the story 37 has no more basis than the biblical story of creation and the flood. But the story represents a belief in God, the creator, a Kitchi-manitou, the Great Mystery. It also represents a belief that Kitchi-manitou sought within himself, his own being, a vision. Or perhaps it came from within his being and that Kitchi-manitou created what was beheld and set it into motion. Even the lesser manitous, such as Geezhigo-quae and Nanabush, must seek a morsel of soil with which to create and recreate their world, their spheres. So men and women must seek within themselves the talent or the potential and afterward create their own worlds and their own spheres and a purpose to give meaning to their lives.

The people begotten by Geezhigo-quae on that mythological island 38 called themselves Anishinaubaeg, the good beings who meant well and were human beings, therefore fundamentally good. But they also knew that men and women were often deflected from fulfilling their good intentions and prevented from living up to their dreams and visions, not out of any inherent evil, but rather from something outside of themselves. Nanabush also represented this aspect of human nature. Many times Nanabush or the Anishinaubaeg fail to carry out a noble purpose. Despite this, he is not rendered evil or wicked but remains fundamentally and essentially good.

Men and women intend what is good, but they forget. The story called 39 "The Man, The Snake and The Fox" exemplifies this aspect of human nature.

40   In its abbreviated form the story is as follows. The hunter leaves his lodge and his family at daybreak to go in search of game to feed his wife and his children. As he proceeds through the forest, the hunter sees deer, but each time they are out of range of his weapon.

41   Late in the afternoon, discouraged and weary, he hears faint cries in the distance. Forgetting his low spirits and fatigue he sets out with renewed optimism and vigour in the direction of the cries. Yet the nearer he draws to the source of the cries, the more daunted is the hunter by the dreadful screams. Only the thought of his family's needs drove him forward, otherwise he might have turned away.

42   At last he came to a glade. The screams came from a thicket on the opposite side. The hunter, bow and arrow drawn and ready, made his way forward cautiously.

43   To his horror, the hunter saw an immense serpent tangled fast in a thicket as a fish is caught in the webbing of a net. The monster writhed and roared and twisted. He struggled to break free.

44   The man recoiled in horror. Before he could back away, the snake saw him.

45   "Friend!" the snake addressed the man.

46   The man fell in a heap on the ground the moment that the snake spoke. When he came to much later the snake pleaded with the man to set him free. For some time the man refused but eventually he relented. He was persuaded by the monster's plea that he too, though a serpent, had no less right to life than did the man. And the serpent promised not to injure the man on his release. The hunter was convinced.

47   The snake sprang on his deliverer the moment the last vine was cut away.

48   It was like thunder as the man and the snake struggled. Nearby a little fox heard the uproar. Never having seen such a spectacle the fox settled down to watch. Immediately he realized that the man was about to be killed.

49   Why were the snake and the man locked in mortal struggle? The little fox shouted for an explanation. The man and the snake stopped.

50   The hunter gasped out his story, then the snake gave his version. Pretending not to understand the snake's explanation the fox beguiled the aggressor into returning to the thicket to act out his side of the story.

51   The snake entangled himself once more.

52   Realizing that he had been delivered from the edge of death by the fox, the man was greatly moved. He felt bound to show his gratitude in some tangible way. The fox assured him that no requital was required.

Nevertheless the hunter persisted. How might he, the hunter, perform some favour on behalf of the fox?

Not only was there no need, the fox explained, there was nothing 53 that the man could do for the fox; there was not a thing that the fox needed or desired of human beings. However, if it would make the man happier, the fox suggested that the man might feed him should he ever have need.

Nothing would please the man more than to perform some good for 54 his deliverer; it was the least that he could do for a friend who had done so much.

Some years later the hunter shot a little fox who had been helping 55 himself to the family storage. As the man drew his knife to finish off the thief, the little fox gasped, "Don't you remember?"

That no snakes as monstrous as the one in the story are to be found 56 on this continent makes no difference to the youngsters' sense of outrage over the treachery of the snake and the forgetfulness of the man; nor does the exercise of speech which enables the snake and the fox to communicate with the hunter and each other prevent the young from being moved to compassion for the fox. Their sense of justice and fairness bears them over the anomalies in the story.

Before the last words "Don't you remember?" have echoed away, 57 the young begin to ask questions. "Why? Why did the man not recognize the fox? Why did he forget? How did the man feel afterwards? Why did the snake attack the man? Why did the snake break his promise? Why didn't the man leave the snake where he was? Do animals really have as much right to live as human beings do?"

Indians cared, loved as passionately as other people. 58

The story called "The Weeping Pine" raises the same questions about 59 love and marriage and the span of either that have been asked by philosophers, poets, and lovers of every race and generation. It does not pretend to give answers to these age old questions beyond suggesting that love may bloom even in circumstances where it is least expected to flower and endure. But owing to shoddy translation, the story has been presented as an explanation for the origin of pine trees.

According to the story, the elders of a village came to a certain young 60 woman's home where she lived with her parents, brothers and sisters. They had come to let her family know that they had chosen her to be the new wife to an old man. This particular man had been without a friend since the death of his first wife some years before. The old man was described as good-natured and kind. As one who had done much to benefit the tribe in his youth, the old man deserved something in return from his neighbours. In the opinion of the elders the most fitting reward the old man could have was a wife. In their judgement the young woman they had chosen would be a suitable companion for the old man.

61   They assured her that the tribe would see to it that they never had need.

62   Because this sort of marriage was a matter that the young woman had not considered, it was unexpected. The delegation understood this. They did not demand an immediate answer but allowed the young woman a few days in which to make up her mind.

63   The young woman cried when the delegation left. She didn't want to marry that man. That old man whose days were all but over and who could never look after her. She had, like every young girl her age, hoped to marry someone young, full of promise, someone she would love and who would love her in return. Besides, it was too soon. How could she, not yet eighteen, be a companion to an old man of seventy or more? The disparity was too great.

64   At first her parents too were aggrieved. But soon after they prevailed upon her to defer to the wishes of the elders, and her father delivered word of their daughter's consent to the elders.

65   But neither the disparity in age nor the disposition of the young girl to enter into a loveless marriage was too great; in the years that followed she came to love this old man. And they had many children.

66   Thirty years later the old man died.

67   On the final day of the four-day watch, the mourners went home but the widow made no move to rise. She continued to keen and rock back and forth in great sorrow.

68   "Come mother, let us go home," her children urged, offering to assist her to her feet and to support her on their way home.

69   "No! No! Leave me. Go," she said.

70   "Mother! Please. Come home with us," her children pleaded. Nothing they said could persuade their mother to leave.

71   "No. You go home. This is where I belong. Leave me."

72   Her children prayed she would relent; give in to the cold and hunger. They went home, but they did not leave their mother alone. During the next few days a son or daughter was always at her side, watching with her and entreating her to come home. They tried to comfort her with their own love and care, assuring her that her wound would pass and heal. They even brought her food and drink to sustain her. She refused everything.

As their mother grew weaker with each passing day, the children be- 73
sought the elders to intercede on their behalf. Perhaps the elders could
prevail on their mother.

But the elders shook their heads and said, "If that is what she wants, 74
there is nothing that you can do to change her mind. Leave her be. She
wants to be with him. Leave her. It's better that way."

And so the family ceased to press their mother to come home, though 75
they still kept watch with her. They watched until she too died by the
graveside of her husband, their father.

Using the term "grandchild" that all elders used in referring to the 76
young, the elder who presided over the woman's wake said, "Our granddaughter's love did not cease with death, but continues into the next
life."

The next spring a small plant grew out of the grave of the woman. Many 77
years later, as the sons, daughters and grandchildren gathered at the
graveside of their parents, they felt a mist fall upon their faces and their
arms. "It is mother shedding tears of love for dad," cried her daughter.

And it is so. On certain days, spruces and pines shed a mist of tears 78
of love.

By remaining at her husband's graveside until she too died, the woman 79
fulfilled the implied promise, "whither thou goest, there too will I go"
contained in the term "weedjeewaugun," companion in life, our word
for spouse.

As she wept for her love she must have wept for the love of her chil- 80
dren. Their love threatened to break that bond that held her to her husband. No! She would not let even death part her from the man to whom
she had given her heart, her soul, her spirit forever.

It is unlikely that the woman ever uttered more than "K'zaugin" (I 81
love you) during her marriage. In this respect she was no different from
most other women, or men for that matter, who are not endowed with
the poetic gift, though they feel and love with equal passion and depth.
K'zaugin said everything. I love you, today, tomorrow, forever. It expressed everything that the finest poets ever wrote and everything that
the unpoetic ever thought and felt but could not put into rhyme or rhythm.

(1991)

The Writer's Subject

1. What is the point of the anecdote about the school project Johnston describes in the first section of the essay?

2. Why is Johnston so critical of the book entitled *The Canadian Indian*, published in 1986 by the Department of Indian Affairs? (para. 14)

3. What, in Johnston's view, is lacking in scholarly studies of Indian life and culture?

4. Why does Johnston attach such significance to tribal language?

5. Johnston states that creation stories "provide insights into what races and nations understand of human nature." (para. 30) What insight is embodied in the creation story that Johnston then presents in paragraphs 31–38?

6. What do the other stories related by Johnston tell us about the beliefs or values of North American Indians?

The Writer's Style and Strategy

1. Discuss the way Johnston organizes the essay. Why is the larger part devoted to tribal narratives?

2. What relation does the title bear to Johnston's thesis?

3. What is the writer's attitude towards the school display he describes in paragraphs 2–11? How does he make this attitude plain?

4. What is the point Johnston wishes to emphasize by his allusion to the figure of Tonto in paragraph 12?

5. Johnston observes that "language and literature are inseparable." (para. 24) How is this illustrated in his retelling of Indian stories?

Suggested Topics for Writing and Discussion

1. Johnston is highly critical of modern scholars for their inadequate understanding of Native Indian languages and culture. Examine one of the books or articles on Canadian Indians by any of the writers listed by Johnston in paragraph 15, and discuss the work's strengths and/or weaknesses. Provide specific examples to support your view.

2. According to Johnston, "Creation stories provide insights into what races and nations understand of human nature". (para. 30) Find examples of creation myths from other cultures, and discuss how these stories reflect a particular understanding of human nature.

3. What aspects of First Nations' literature and culture do you think should be included in the high-school curriculum?

Stop Stealing Native Stories
by Lenore Keeshig-Tobias

> *AAA-IIII-EEE Y-AAh!*
> *Clear the way.*
> *In a sacred manner I come.*
> *The stories are mine!*
> — Ojibway war song

Critics of non-native writers who borrow from the native experience have 1
been dismissed as advocates of censorship and accused of trying to
shackle artistic imagination, but their objections are prompted by something much more.

Where The Spirit Lives may be a bad film. *Bone Bird* by Calgary 2
novelist Darlene Barry Quaife may oversimplify native spirituality. W.P.
Kinsella's Hobbema stories may be insulting. But the real problem is
that they amount to culture theft, the theft of voice.

Canada's Francophones have a strong and unique voice in North 3
America. Why? Because they have fought to ensure that their language
remains intact. Language is the conveyor of culture. It carries the ideas
by which a nation defines itself as a people. It gives voice to a nation's
stories, its *mythos*.

How do Canadians feel about the U.S. mythos defining them and their 4
country? This is quickly becoming a reality, I fear, because Canadians
have been too quick to hand over their voice and their stories to Americans.

Stories, you see, are not just entertainment. Stories are power. They 5
reflect the deepest, the most intimate perceptions, relationships and
attitudes of a people. Stories show how a people, a culture, thinks. Such
wonderful offerings are seldom reproduced by outsiders.

6   This is the root of the problem with *Where The Spirit Lives*, which deals with the treatment of native students in government-sponsored residential schools during the 1930s. The film has been shown on the CBC and TVOntario and as part of Canada Day at the recent festival in Palm Springs, California.

7   So what is it all about, anyway? In the end, a little Indian girl and her brother ride off into the vast, uninhabited wilderness. (Anne Shirley goes west?) They ride right out of the sentimentalized Canadian consciousness — stoic child warriors noble in defeat, marching home with Bible in hand. (A book of truth, perhaps, but whose?)

8   Native people were not involved in any creative aspect of the film. Their voice was heard only through cultural consultants hired to provide the nuances and insights lacked by the movie's writer and producers.

9   Cultural insight, nuance, metaphor and symbols give a book or film the ring of truth, but their essence — the thing that gives stories universal appeal, that allows true empathy and shared emotion — is missing from *Where The Spirit Lives*, as it is from most "native" writing by non-natives.

10   Canadians all too often use native stories, symbols and history to sell things — cars, tobacco or movies. But why hasn't Basil Johnston's *Indian School Days* become a best-seller? Why hasn't *Half Breed* by Marie Campbell been reprinted? (Why, for that matter, has Ms. Campbell, as one of Canada's "celebrated" authors, never received a writer's grant?)

11   *Where The Spirit Lives*, after having squeezed out the native version of what happened in the residential schools, turns around and tells natives to make their own movies. How can we? Even if we had access to financial backers, they would say: "Residential schools? It's been done."

12   With native people struggling for justice with land claims and in education, what makes Canadians think they have equality in the film industry? In publishing? With agencies that make arts grants? In the arts themselves?

13   Instead, the Canadian cultural industry is stealing — unconsciously, perhaps, but with the same devastating results — native stories as surely as the missionaries stole our religion and the politicians stole our land and the residential schools stole our language. As Leslie Marmon Silko writes in *Ceremony*, stories "are all we have, you see — all we have to fight off illness and death."As a storyteller I was once advised by an elder that there is a season for storytelling — winter. "Blackflies, mosquitoes and other creatures like those stories," she cautioned.

14   How quaint, I thought. Nonetheless, I respected her advice and as

time went on, I began to understand it. If storytellers sit around all summer telling stories, then surely they'll become the feast of blackflies
and mosquitoes. My elder was telling me that these stories are meant
for certain ears only — and native ears.

So potent are stories that, in native culture, one storyteller cannot tell   15
another's story without permission.

But why are Canadians so obsessed with native stories anyway? Why   16
the urge to "write Indian?" Have Canadians run out of stories of their
own? Or are their renderings just nostalgia for a simpler, more "at one
with nature" stage of human development? There's a cliché for you.

Maybe Canadian stories about native people are some form of exor-   17
cism. Are they trying to atone for the horrible reality of native-Cana-
dian relations? Or maybe they just know a good story when they find
one and are willing to take it, without permission, just as archaeologists
used to rob our graves for museums.

What about the quest for native spirituality? It is mostly escapist, and   18
people such as Quaife would rather look to an ideal native living in never-
never land than confront the reality of what being native means in Canadian society.

For example, residential-school survivors tell of children being forced   19
to eat their own vomit when their stomachs could no longer hold down
the sour porridge. They tell of broken knuckles from fingers being
rapped. Some even tell of having pins stuck through their tongues as
punishment for speaking their own language. (Now, that's censorship.)

And what about the teacher who was removed from one residential   20
school for abusing children? He was simply sent to another, more remote school.

It's not that these stories have never been told; Canadians just haven't   21
heard them. Nor does it mean that writers and storytellers are incompetent and inexperienced, as Mr. Kinsella seemed to suggest.

It means our voices have been marginalized. Imagine, Canadians tell-   22
ing native stories because their government outlawed native languages,
native culture.

However, as Ms. Campbell said on CBC Radio's Morningside, "If   23
you want to write our stories, then be prepared to live with us." And not
just for a few months.

Hear the voices of the wilderness. Be there with the Lubicon, the Innu.   24
Be there with Teme-Augama Anishnabai on the Red Squirrel Road. The
Saugeen Ojibway. If you like these stories, fight for them. I dare you.

(1990)

The Writer's Subject

1. What does the writer mean by "the theft of voice"? (para. 2)

2. What is the relevance of the writer's observations about French and English Canada in paragraphs 3 and 4?

3. What are Keeshig-Tobias's objections to *Where The Spirit Lives*, a film about the treatment of Native students in residential schools? How do these objections fit into the argument as a whole?

4. Why, according to Keeshig-Tobias, are Canadians "obsessed" with Native stories? (para. 16)

5. Why does the writer object to non-Native Canadians telling stories about Native people?

6. According to the writer, how has Native experience been dealt with in stories by non-Natives?

The Writer's Style and Strategy

1. What is the prevailing tone of this essay?

2. Examine paragraph 7. What details convey the writer's attitude to the story she is describing?

3. Discuss the references in this essay to particular Native and non-Native writers. How does Keeshig-Tobias use such references to advance her argument?

4. The writer frequently asks questions (see, for example, paragraphs 10, 12, 16). What is the effect she is aiming at through this technique?

5. Discuss the effectiveness of the essay's ending.

Suggested Topics for Writing and Discussion

1. Keeshig-Tobias argues that non-Natives have "marginalized" Native voices and stolen Native stories. Compare her view with the position taken by Carole Giangrande in her essay "Allowing the Mind to Wander."

2. What is your view of the argument that a people's mythos, the stories that embody their history and culture, should not be appropriated by outsiders?

3. Do you think that Canadians are, as the writer argues in paragraph 16, nostalgic for "a simpler, more 'at one with nature' stage of human development"?

4. Find out what you can about the Native Indian residential schools described in the books referred to in paragraph 10 of the essay.

In the Canon,
For All the Wrong Reasons
Amy Tan

Several years ago I learned that I had passed a new literary milestone. I had made it to the Halls of Education under the rubric of "Multicultural Literature," also known in many schools as "Required Reading." 1

Thanks to this development, I now meet students who proudly tell me they're doing their essays, term papers, or master's theses on me. By that they mean that they are analyzing not just my books but me — my grade-school achievements, youthful indiscretions, marital status, as well as the movies I watched as a child, the slings and arrows I suffered as a minority, and so forth — all of which, with the hindsight of classroom literary investigation, prove to contain many Chinese omens that made it inevitable that I would become a writer. 2

Once I read a master's thesis on feminist writings, which included examples from *The Joy Luck Club*. The student noted that I had often used the number four, something on the order of thirty-two or thirty-six times — in any case, a number divisible by four. She pointed out that there were four mothers, four daughters, four sections of the book, four stories per section. Furthermore, there were four sides to a mah jong table, four directions of the wind, four players. More important, she postulated, my use of the number four was a symbol for the four stages of psychological development, which corresponded in uncanny ways to the four stages of some type of Buddhist philosophy I had never heard of before. The student recalled that the story contained a character called Fourth Wife, symbolizing death, and a four-year-old girl with a feisty spirit, symbolizing regeneration. 3

4   In short, her literary sleuthing went on to reveal a mystical and rather Byzantine puzzle, which, once explained, proved to be completely brilliant and precisely logical. She wrote me a letter and asked if her analysis had been correct. How I longed to say "absolutely."

5   The truth is, if there are symbols in my work they exist largely by accident or through someone else's interpretive design. If I wrote of "an orange moon rising on a dark night," I would more likely ask myself later if the image was a cliché, not whether it was a symbol for the feminine force rising in anger, as one master's thesis postulated. To plant symbols like that, you need a plan, good organizational skills, and a prescient understanding of the story you are about to write. Sadly, I lack those traits.

6   All this is by way of saying that I don't claim my use of the number four to be a brilliant symbolic device. In fact, now that it's been pointed out to me in rather astonishing ways, I consider my overuse of the number to be a flaw.

7   Reviewers and students have enlightened me about not only how I write but why I write. Apparently, I am driven to capture the immigrant experience, to demystify Chinese culture, to point out the differences between Chinese and American culture, even to pave the way for other Asian American writers.

8   If only I were that noble. Contrary to what is assumed by some students, reporters, and community organizations wishing to bestow honors on me, I am not an expert on China, Chinese culture, mah jong, the psychology of mothers and daughters, generation gaps, immigration, illegal aliens, assimilation, acculturation, racial tension, Tiananmen Square, the Most Favored Nation trade agreements, human rights, Pacific Rim economics, the purported one million missing baby girls of China, the future of Hong Kong after 1997, or, I am sorry to say, Chinese cooking. Certainly I have personal opinions on many of these topics, but by no means do my sentiments and my world of make-believe make me an expert.

9   So I am alarmed when reviewers and educators assume that my very personal, specific, and fictional stories are meant to be representative down to the nth detail not just of Chinese Americans but, sometimes, of all Asian culture. Is Jane Smiley's *A Thousand Acres* supposed to be taken as representative of all of American culture? If so, in what ways? Are all American fathers tyrannical? Do all American sisters betray one another? Are all American conscientious objectors flaky in love relationships?

Over the years my editor has received hundreds of permissions re- 10
quests from publishers of college textbooks and multicultural anthologies, all of them wishing to reprint my work for "educational purposes."
One publisher wanted to include an excerpt from *The Joy Luck Club*, a
scene in which a Chinese woman invites her non-Chinese boyfriend to
her parents' house for dinner. The boyfriend brings a bottle of wine as a
gift and commits a number of social gaffes at the dinner table. Students
were supposed to read this excerpt, then answer the following question:
"If you are invited to a Chinese family's house for dinner, should you
bring a bottle of wine?"

In many respects, I am proud to be on the reading lists for courses such 11
as Ethnic Studies, Asian American Studies, Asian American Literature,
Asian American History, Women's Literature, Feminist Studies, Feminist Writers of Color, and so forth. What writer wouldn't want her work
to be read? I also take a certain perverse glee in imagining countless
students, sleepless at three in the morning, trying to read *The Joy Luck
Club* for the next day's midterm. Yet I'm also not altogether comfortable about my book's status as required reading.

Let me relate a conversation I had with a professor at a school in 12
southern California. He told me he uses my books in his literature class
but he makes it a point to lambast those passages that depict China as
backward or unattractive. He objects to any descriptions that have to do
with spitting, filth, poverty, or superstitions. I asked him if China in the
1930s and 1940s was free of these elements. He said, No, such descriptions are true; but he still believes it is "the obligation of the writer of
ethnic literature to create positive, progressive images."

I secretly shuddered and thought, Oh well, that's southern California 13
for you. But then, a short time later, I met a student from UC Berkeley,
a school that I myself attended. The student was standing in line at a
book signing. When his turn came, he swaggered up to me, then took
two steps back and said in a loud voice, "Don't you think you have a
responsibility to write about Chinese men as positive role models?"

In the past, I've tried to ignore the potshots. A *Washington Post* re- 14
porter once asked me what I thought of another Asian American writer
calling me something on the order of "a running dog whore sucking on
the tit of the imperialist white pigs."

"Well," I said, "you can't please everyone, can you?" I pointed out 15
that readers are free to interpret a book as they please, and that they are
free to appreciate or not appreciate the result. Besides, reacting to your

critics makes a writer look defensive, petulant, and like an all-around bad sport.

16   But lately I've started thinking it's wrong to take such a laissez-faire attitude. Lately I've come to think that I must say something, not so much to defend myself and my work but to express my hopes for American literature, for what it has the potential to become in the twenty-first century — that is, a truly American literature, democratic in the way it includes many colorful voices.

17   Until recently, I didn't think it was important for writers to express their private intentions in order for their work to be appreciated; I believed that any analysis of my intentions belonged behind the closed doors of literature classes. But I've come to realize that the study of literature does have its effect on how books are being read, and thus on what might be read, published, and written in the future. For that reason, I do believe writers today must talk about their intentions — if for no other reason than to serve as an antidote to what others say our intentions should be.

18   For the record, I don't write to dig a hole and fill it with symbols. I don't write stories as ethnic themes. I don't write to represent life in general. And I certainly don't write because I have answers. If I knew everything there is to know about mothers and daughters, Chinese and Americans, I wouldn't have any stories left to imagine. If I had to write about only positive role models, I wouldn't have enough imagination left to finish the first story. If I knew what to do about immigration, I would be a sociologist or a politician and not a long-winded storyteller.

19   So why do I write?

20   Because my childhood disturbed me, pained me, made me ask foolish questions. And the questions still echo. Why does my mother always talk about killing herself? Why did my father and brother have to die? If I die, can I be reborn into a happy family? Those early obsessions led to a belief that writing could be my salvation, providing me with the sort of freedom and danger, satisfaction and discomfort, truth and contradiction I can't find in anything else in life.

21   I write to discover the past for myself. I don't write to change the future for others. And if others are moved by my work — if they love their mothers more, scold their daughters less, or divorce their husbands who were not positive role models — I'm often surprised, usually grateful to hear from kind readers. But I don't take either credit or blame for changing their lives for better or for worse.

Writing, for me, is an act of faith, a hope that I will discover what I   22
mean by "truth." I also think of reading as an act of faith, a hope that I
will discover something remarkable about ordinary life, about myself.
And if the writer and the reader discover the same thing, if they have
that connection, the act of faith has resulted in an act of magic. To me,
that's the mystery and the wonder of both life and fiction — the connection between two individuals who discover in the end that they are
more the same than they are different.

And if that doesn't happen, it's nobody's fault. There are still plenty   23
of other books on the shelf. Choose what you like.

(1996)

The Writer's Subject

1. Why is Tan uncomfortable about the fact that *The Joy Luck Club* is "required reading" in a number of fields? (paras. 1–2, 11) How does she convey her discomfort?

2. How does Tan respond to the notion that her work is full of brilliant symbolic devices? (paras. 5–6)

3. Why is Tan disturbed that some readers take her fictional stories to be representative of Asian culture? (paras. 8–10)

4. What expectation is placed upon the "ethnic" writer, in Tan's experience?
   (paras. 12–13)

5. Why does Tan think that a writer must speak publicly about her intentions? (paras. 15–17)

6. What "early obsessions" led Tan into writing? (para. 20)

The Writer's Style and Strategy

1. Discuss the list in para. 8 of topics on which Tan claims not to be an expert. What effect is Tan aiming at by presenting these topics in this way?

2. Why does Tan present the reader with a series of questions in para. 9?

3. What kind of reader does Tan seem to be addressing? Refer to details of
   tone and vocabulary, as well as to content, to support your opinion.

4. An autobiographical piece such as this creates a picture of the writer in
   our minds through not only *what* is said, but also *how* it is said. What kind
   of personality is projected through this essay? Support your conclusions
   with specific references to the text.

Suggested Topics for Writing and Discussion

1. Do you think that Tan is being fair to critics who find meanings or symbols in her work that she herself was not aware of? Is it possible to have a valid interpretation of a work that differs from the author's? (A useful exercise here might be to compare two or three critical interpretations of a short poem.)

2. Tan describes the view of the California professor who insisted that it is "the obligation of the writer of ethnic literature to create positive, progressive images" (para. 12). What argument might be made in support of such a view?

3. What is "the canon" alluded to in Tan's title? Why has it been such a source of contention in recent years? (For one critic's view, see Harold Bloom's *The Western Canon: The Books and School of the Ages*, 1994.)

4. Tan states that "I do believe writers today must talk about their intentions — if for no other reason than to serve as an antidote to what others say our intentions should be" (para. 17). Do you, as a reader, welcome authors' discussion of their intentions? Do you agree with Tan that such explanations are necessary?

Westward Oh!
by Martin Walker

The American Western artist Irving Couse painted *The Captive* in 1892, 1
when he was in Paris. It depicts an event which had taken place nearly 50
years earlier, and which became a highly symbolic archetype for the perils inherent in the white man's thrusting advance across Indian country.

The capture of 17-year-old Lorinda Bewly by the Cayuse chief, Five 2
Crows, in 1847 became a celebrated "atrocity," a key moment in the
process which changed American perceptions of the Indians who stood
in the way of their expansion; the transformation from noble Red Man
to murderous savage within a single generation. The painting has now
become once more a highly-charged political symbol in an extraordinary row which is convulsing the American art establishment.

"Couse's lurid treatment unconsciously expresses his culture's fears 3
of miscegenation," says the catalogue commentary on *The Captive*. "This
is evident first in the network of intimations that thinly repress an actual sexual encounter. Bewly's skewed and foreshortened body suggests
as much as the blood on her wrist a violent physical confrontation with
Five Crows. The array of phallic objects pointing in her direction, together with the tepee's open entry, further imply a sexual encounter.

"Yet at odds with its violent racial drama, the picture develops an- 4
other, quieter erotic relationship. If Bewly's body is skewed and foreshortened, cut and cutoff, it is at the same time almost gently displayed
for the viewer. Against the logic of the narrative, Bewly's figure is ori-
ented more to the picture plane than to her Indian captor. It is the viewer
who sees her face, hair, and covering gesture. Through the fiction of
the scene, what is denied to Five Crows becomes available to the (white)

audience who would see Couse's painting."

5 Grand and formal exhibitions of art in a national gallery occasionally and sometimes deliberately provoke an aesthetic furore. But an entirely political row over a retrospective of 19th century American painting, in a city dedicated to the U.S. Constitution and its inalienable right to free speech, is something remarkable.

6 Senators are threatening budgetary retaliation against the Smithsonian, the complex of national museums which receives some $300 million a year in public funds. The public is flocking to the show, and engaging in furious debate in the large comment books thoughtfully provided for the purpose. Galleries in the Western cities of St. Louis and Denver have now cancelled their plans to show the exhibition. And angry editorials in the national press are trumpeting accusations of something close to treason. "Only in the land of the free is it possible to mount an entirely hostile ideological assault on the nation's founding and history; to recast that history in the most distorted terms — and have the taxpayers foot the bill," says the *Wall Street Journal*.

7 On this occasion, the usually more liberal *Washington Post* led the charge with a political commentary disguised as an art review: "With the sort of tortured revisionism now so stridently de rigueur in academia, it effectively trashes not only the integrity of the art it presents but most of our national history as well, reducing the saga of America's Western pioneers to little more than victimization, disillusion and environmental rape."

8 The exhibition — *The West As America: Reinterpreting Images Of The Frontier* — contains 164 paintings, sculptures and engravings of the way American artists between 1820 and 1920 portrayed the nation's expansion across the prairies and to the Pacific. The fuss has arisen because of the interpretation placed on their vision by the exhibition's curator and organizer, William Treuttner, and the scholars he recruited.

9 "Images from Christopher Columbus to Kit Carson show the discovery and settlement of the West as a heroic undertaking," says the plaque at the exhibition's entrance. "A more recent approach argues that these images are carefully staged fiction, constructed from both supposition and fact. Their role was to justify the hardship and conflict of nationbuilding. Western scenes extolled progress, but rarely noted damaging social and environmental change. Looking beneath the surface of these images gives us a better understanding of why national problems created during the westward expansion still affect us today."

10 The exhibition begins with a photograph, taken on the rooftop of a building just across the river from bustling New York in 1903. The West-

ern artist Charles Schreyvogel, who painted the famous *Defending The Stockade*, stands at his easel, painting from life a fully dressed U.S. cavalryman who is kneeling and aiming his revolver at some Indian attacker who is at least 2,000 miles and probably 40 years away.

Defending The Stockade, or an event very like it, is a scene that almost 11 certainly did take place in the brutal decade after the end of the U.S. Civil War when the Army was despatched to win and hold the frontier for settlers, railroads and Western civilization. And the exhibition documents the way the railroad companies became patrons of the painters they sent out to record the West in a suitable way. The point the exhibition seeks to make is that by the time Schreyvogel painted it, the Indians were history, and his art has a more contemporary cultural resonance, as a metaphor of patriotic and Anglo-Saxon America holding the gates against a flood of immigrants from southern and eastern Europe. "The paintings reveal far more about the urban culture in which they were made and showed. For it was according to the culture's attitudes — about race, class and history — that artists such as Schreyvogel and Remington created the place we know as the 'Old West'," says the plaque.

Just across the hall is the photograph, taken at about the same time, 12 of another U.S. cavalryman who is riding a wooden horse and managing to look extremely heroic. He is a model for Frederic Remington, most famous of the artists of the Old West. Remington's classic *Fight For The Water Hole* depicts five cowboys, their horses huddled in the hollow around the dwindling pond, grimly fighting off the encircling Indians in an implacable desert heat.

"This painting is about fear of the impending industrial era. These 13 'last stand' paintings were popular with the wealthy patrons who bought them. They had a lot to lose with social change," says the exhibition organizer, William Treuttner, in an interpretation which has infuriated the press, the politicians and much of the American public who were flooding into Washington for their Desert Storm victory parade. But Treuttner quotes Remington himself to sustain his argument that the 20th century creators of the myth of the Old West were working within a political context attuned to their own times. The unashamedly racist Remington himself was deeply opposed to more immigration and diluting the Anglo-Saxon stock, and thoroughly disapproving of the new politicized working class which the immigrants manned.

"You can't glorify a Jew — coin-lovin' puds — nasty humans," 14 Remington wrote to a publisher friend. "I've got some Winchesters and when the massacring begins which you speak of, I can get my share of 'em and what's more I will." He went on to attack "Jews, injuns, Chinamen, Italians, Huns, the rubbish of the earth I hate."

15   Sent to Chicago by *Harpers' Weekly* to cover and illustrate the famous Pullman strike, Remington described the strikers as "a malodorous crowd of anarchistic foreign trash ... vicious wretches with no blood circulating above the ears ... will follow readily any demagogue with revolutionary tendencies."

16   One of his illustrations is called *Giving The Butt*, and portrays a squad of clean-cut soldiers smashing their rifle butts into the faces of brutish strikers armed with sticks and their bare hands. For Remington, the soldiers were "pure and simple of speech, honest and no man can be one who can't pass the most rigid physical examination imaginable."

17   Remington was aware of the gap between the reality of the West during the Indian wars and his own much later painting. "I sometimes feel that I am trying to do the impossible in my pictures in not having a chance to work direct but as there are no people such as I paint, it's 'studio' or nothing," Remington wrote. And he was conscious of the wider artistic movement, which he defined as "we fellows who are doing the 'Old America' which is so fast passing."

18   In this carefully documented context, the deconstruction of the icons of the American frontier myth becomes more plausible. The commentary on the plaque alongside *Fight For The Water Hole* says the painting is a metaphor for "the plight of an embattled capitalist elite in an era of strikes, violence and widespread immigration. ... Does it borrow its imagery — a group of outnumbered whites desperately defending against the 'strike' of a racial enemy — from the urban world where Remington lived?"

19   Reading the catalogue and knowing what Remington wrote and thought, the commentary makes sense. But many of the attacks upon this exhibition have been made on a more casual basis. Senator Ted Stevens of Alaska, who has warned the gallery's administrators that when they next apply for government funds, "You're in for a battle," had not at that point visited the exhibition at all.

20   And yet the senator went on to demand of the curators, in an inquisition which reminded *Newsweek* magazine of McCarthy's Un-American Activities Committee witch-hunting in the 1950s: "Why should people come to your institution and see a history that is so perverted? I don't think the Smithsonian has any business, or has ever had any business, developing a political agenda."

21   The senators perceive a political agenda in the way the exhibition

Carson's Men, Charles Russell, 1913

Defending the Stockade, Charles Schreyvogle, 1905

Fight for the Waterhole, Frederic Remington, 1903

The Captive, Irving Couse, 1892

argues that the Western artists were "propagandists for the dominant and aggressive white culture." And they have been infuriated by the commentaries on the gallery's walls which set each group of paintings in context. The one they cite most reads: "Artistic representation of Indians developed simultaneously with white interest in taking their lands. At first, Indians were seen as possessing a natural nobility and innocence. This assessment gave way gradually to a far more violent view that stressed hostile savagery."

The attack by Senator Stevens has been taken up by other Western 22 senators, their regional patriotism excited by his charge that "We from the West live here in the East really under attack all the time — to see that exhibit, I'll tell you, it really set me off."

Remember, he had not seen it. But Senator Alan Simpson of Wyo- 23 ming has been twice, and professes himself "shocked." Senator Slade Gorton of Washington State toured the show and was "appalled."

The attendance of the Chief Justice of the Supreme Court, and Vice- 24 President Dan Quayle (who are both by virtue of office on the gallery's Board of Regents) has been demanded to see "what abuse is being perpetrated in the nation's name."

This would be so much knockabout for a quiet month in politics ex- 25 cept for two things. The first is that America's intellectual great and good have entered the debate. The renowned historian and former Librarian of Congress, Daniel Boorstin, visited the exhibition and wrote in the Commentary book: "Perverse, historically inaccurate, destructive exhibit. No credit to the Smithsonian."

The second striking development is the way this revisionist treat- 26 ment of the Old West has been taken as symptomatic of an alleged penetration of a broadly leftist ideology into the nation's cultural institutions. The way the exhibition compares the concept of "Manifest Destiny" in America's conquest of the West to its quasi-imperial role in Asia, culminating in the disaster of the Vietnam War, has reopened old wounds.

"Ever since the 1960s, the one-time campus radicals of the Baby 27 Boom generation have sought repeatedly and noisily to rewrite the rules of American society in ways large and small," ran a furious denunciation of the exhibition in the *Washington Post*.

"On the campuses they seized by force in the 1960s and 1970s they 28 have moved from early demands as students for such things as black studies programmes to efforts as tenured professors to reshape not only the core curriculum of American higher education but its value system as well ... aging radicals now as teachers and curators increasingly in charge of the nation's cultural patrimony," it went on.

29   The curators have tried to fend off the attacks by toning down the commentaries alongside the paintings, removing phrases like: "This predominance of violent and negative views was a manifestation of Indian-hating, a largely manufactured, calculated reversal of the basic facts of white encroachment and deceit."

30   But the fuss goes on, a new round in the war of attrition between politicians and the art establishment which follows the decision last year by Washington's Corcoran Gallery to withdraw an exhibition of Robert Mapplethorpe's homo-erotic photographs. This year's debate has been heightened by the success of the movie *Dances With Wolves*, Kevin Costner's Oscar-winning portrayal of the Oglala Sioux Indians and their fate at the hands of the white settlers and the U.S. Army.

31   But the America that flocked to see the Costner movie is also an America newly invigorated by the simplistic flag-waving patriotism of George Bush's election campaign, by the war against Iraq and "the end of the Vietnam syndrome." In this context, an artistic and academic re-interpretation of the myth of the frontier becomes a subversive attack upon the quasi-divine American mission of winning the West.

32   Take Charles Russell's *Carson's Men*, which the exhibition argues to be a powerful religious allegory, from the Golgotha-like skull of the dead cow at Kit Carson's feet to the cross made by his figure and the rifle across his saddle-bow.

33   "Other details, the halo-like hats, the twilight sky that recalls the time of day of the Deposition (from the Cross), and above all the remarkably symmetical arrangement of Carson and the two men, with the central-ized Carson higher against the sky and closer to the viewer, intensify the picture's allusions to the Crucifixion," suggests the catalogue.

34   It is an argument which portrays the visceral and mystic power of the Western myth which the exhibition has set out to challenge. And in the process, it has exposed the raw nerves beneath the fragile new patriotism, and the old guilts about the price the Indians paid for the imposition of the new white empire upon the West.

(1991)

The Writer's Subject

1. Walker's essay focuses on an exhibition entitled "The West As America," held in Washington, D.C. in 1991. According to the exhibition catalogue cited by Walker, what does Couse's painting "The Captive" reveal about the fears of America in the late 19th century?

2. What evidence did the exhibition provide that many images of the heroic settlement of the West were "carefully staged fiction"? (para. 9)

3. Walker cites the attacks made on the exhibition by a number of Western senators. What appear to be the chief grounds of their criticism?

4. What connection do the exhibition's critics see between "this revisionist treatment of the Old West" and current developments in American cultural institutions? (paras. 26–28)

5. Why does it seem to Walker that the America that "flocked" to see *Dances With Wolves* may be offended by the attitudes conveyed in the Washington exhibition? (paras. 30–31)

6. In what ways, according to Walker, did the racism of the artist Frederick Remington inform his paintings? (paras. 13–18)

The Writer's Style and Strategy

1. How does Walker present the conflicting viewpoints in the "furious debate" created by the Washington exhibition? Is he fair to both sides of the argument?

2. Where does Walker allow his own views to be seen? Pick out words or phrases which may indicate the writer's position.

3. Why does Walker begin his account of the exhibition with a discussion of Couse's painting "The Captive," rather than with a general description of the exhibition as a whole?

4. Discuss the last three paragraphs. Do they provide a satisfactory conclusion to the article?

5. What do such matters as level of diction, allusion, or historical or political reference tell us about the kind of audience Walker is addressing here?

Suggested Topics for Writing and Discussion

1. Walker sees the furore concerning "The West As America" exhibition as part of a broader conflict between art and the state. What are some of the issues in this conflict, as stated or implied in Walker's article?

2. Walker describes the angry reaction of some Western senators to the "revisionist" interpretation of the old West presented by the Washington exhibition. Political hostility to the arts is not uncommon, whether at the local or the national level; find one or two other examples of attacks on artists or writers by political figures, and identify the issues in contention.

3. Walker cites a number of passages from the exhibition catalogue and plaques that "deconstruct" the American frontier myth and its icons. Choose an image that makes a statement about Canada's past and offer your own interpretation of what that image reveals. Examples might include the famous photograph of "The Last Spike," Benjamin West's painting of the death of General Wolfe, or the painting by Rex Woods of the Fathers of Confederation.

4. Choose a well-known painter or photographer, and find out what you can about the artist's work as a whole. Then select a representative work by that artist, and say what it tells us about the time (and place) in which it was created. What does it reveal about the cultural or political assumptions of the artist or of the artist's time?

5. Do you think that public funding of museums or art galleries should depend on public approval of the kinds of works collected and exhibited?

Women in the Shadows

Reclaiming a Métis Heritage

by Christine Welsh

When I was invited to speak at the "Feminisms in the Cinema" confer- 1
ence at York University in November 1990, I very regretfully declined
as I was in the final throes of completing the script for my documentary
film *Women in the Shadows,* and I felt unable to step back from that
process and to speak about it with any kind of clarity or objectivity.
Happily, that is no longer the case. What follows is the story of the film
— and of how I came to make it — as well as my thoughts about the
role such films are playing in giving voice to the rich and multifaceted
experience of aboriginal women in Canada.

Women in the Shadows is a very personal film. It tells the story of 2
my search for my Native identity and my ongoing struggle to reclaim
my past and my heritage — an odyssey into the past and a process of
discovery in which the making of the film ultimately played an integral
part. It reaches back across time to examine the lives of my own
foremothers, Native women who were remarkably representative of the
time and place and society in which they lived and whose lives illustrate the sometimes painful choices that confronted Native women
throughout the turbulent history of the Métis in western Canada. The
film records my struggle to understand the choices my grandmothers
made — to recognize that, for many Native people, denial of their Native heritage and assimilation to the "white ideal" was largely a matter
of survival — and to accept them for who and what they were: Native
women who struggled to make a better life for themselves and their chil-

dren and whose strength, courage, and resilience were fundamental to the evolution of a people and a nation.

3   *Women in the Shadows* is my/their story. As a film it is but an extension of an enduring oral story-telling tradition that is both ancient and contemporary and which, in its totality, encompasses the entire story of a people, both past and present. It is not a story which presumes to speak for all Native women, for we come from many nations and we have many different stories, many different voices. I can tell only my own story, in my own voice. Leslie Marmon Silko, the Laguna poet and storyteller, puts it this way:

> As with any generation
> the oral tradition depends upon each person
> listening and remembering a portion
> and it is together —
> all of us remembering what we have heard together —
> that creates the whole story
> the long story of the people.
> I remember only a small part.
> But this is what I remember.

4   From the air, the Qu'Appelle Valley of southern Saskatchewan is an aberration — a great green gash that slices crookedly across a precise geometric patchwork of yellow wheat fields and brown summer fallow. The muddy stream that snakes across its flat bottom widens here and there to form broad, shallow lakes, creating an oasis of cool greenery in an otherwise arid and treeless plain. Before the coming of the Europeans, the valley provided a welcome haven for the Plains Indians and the wildlife upon which they depended, and at the height of the fur trade in the old Northwest it formed an important link in the system of waterways and cart trails that began at the forks of the Red and Assiniboine Rivers and ran west and north to Fort Edmonton and south to the Cypress Hills and Montana. And it was here, in the late 1860s, that Métis buffalo hunters from Red River, in pursuit of the great herds that were being pushed farther and farther west, established temporary winter camps that would eventually become the permanent settlement of Lebret.[1]

5   My great-grandparents were among the first Métis families to set up camp down on the flats beside Mission Lake where the village of Lebret now stands. As long as the buffalo were plentiful they continued to live from the hunt, wintering in the Cypress Hills and returning to Lebret each summer to sell their buffalo robes, meat, and pemmican at the

Hudson's Bay Company post at Fort Qu'Appelle. With the disappearance of the buffalo they no longer wintered out on the plains, choosing
to remain at Lebret and earn their living by trading, freighting, farming,
and ranching. They are buried there beside the lake among their kinfolk,
and the names on the headstones in that little cemetery — Blondeau,
Delorme, Desjarlais, Ouellette, Pelletier, Welsh, and many more — bear
silent witness to the diaspora of the Red River Métis.

Of course the word *Métis* meant nothing to me when, as a child, I   6
accompanied my parents and grandparents and brother and sisters on
our annual midsummer pilgrimage to Lebret. We all piled into my father's car and made the trip out to the valley in a state of high spirits
that was nonetheless leavened with a note of solemn observance. The
saskatoons would be ripe, and there would be plenty of berries to pick
in the deep gullies of the valley — not to mention the milkshakes to be
had at the Valley Café in Fort Qu'Appelle before we started back to the
city. But first there would be the obligatory climb to the little white
chapel that perched high above Lebret — a hot, dusty trek up a narrow
trail cut straight into the side of the hill and marked at intervals by tow-
ering white crosses signifying the Stations of the Cross that could be
seen for miles up and down the valley. The chapel was invariably locked
in a futile attempt to discourage vandals, so after catching our breath
we would make our descent, sliding and scrambling, grabbing tufts of
sagebrush to break our fall. After that there would be a visit to the big
stone church down on the flats beside the lake and then a tour of the
adjacent graveyard during which my grandmother would pray for all
our relatives, both living and dead. I still remember the taste of the berries and the milkshakes, and the smell of dust, sagebrush, and incense.
And I still remember those headstones with all the strange-sounding
names. "French," my grandmother said. "French." That was all.

I don't know when I first realized that among those ghostly relatives   7
there was Indian blood. It was something that just seemed to seep into
my consciousness through my pores. I remember my bewilderment when
the other children in my predominantly white, middle-class school began to call me "nichi" on the playground. I had never heard the word
before and was blissfully ignorant of its meaning, but it wasn't long
before I understood that to them it meant "dirty Indian." Snippets of
family mythology reinforced my growing sense that this was something
to be ashamed of — especially the story of how my other, Eastern European grandmother had not wanted my mother to marry my father because he was part-Indian. By the time I was in high school I had invented

an exotic ethnicity to explain my black hair and brown skin and I successfully masqueraded [as] French or even Hawaiian, depending on who asked. But I lived in mortal terror that the truth would get out because, no matter how hard I tried to hide it, my native background seemed to be written all over me.

8   The 1960s gave rise to a new pride in Native identity among Native people across Canada, and even though I had no contact with other Native people I was swept up by the spirit of the times and began to feel that it was no longer necessary to try to hide who I was. But who was I? By the time I reached university in the early 1970s, denial of my Native ancestry had given way to a burning need to know. My curiosity was fueled by the discovery of a much-worn volume entitled *The Last Buffalo Hunter,* a biography of my great-grandfather, Norbert Welsh, which had been written in the 1930s and rescued by my mother from a secondhand bookshop. I reveled in the references to Norbert's Indian mother and his part-Indian wife, but they were shadowy figures — half-formed, incomplete — who seemed to inhabit only the margins of Norbert's story. And even though I was clearly interested in tearing away the shroud of mystery that seemed to surround them, my attempts were largely futile. Whenever I tried to raise the subject, strenuous attempts were made, especially by my grandmother, to diminish and deny any connection we might have to Native people. She actively discouraged my burgeoning interest in and involvement with "things Indian": "we" were very different from "them," she implied, and such associations would only bring me grief.

9   In spite of my grandmother's dire predictions, I spent much of the next fifteen years traveling to Indian communities across Canada and making documentary films on issues of concern to Native people. The work was enormously satisfying and rewarding, but my personal goal — to find out who I was and where I belonged — remained elusive. I soon realized that, while I might have Indian blood in my veins, I had no natural claim to understanding or participating in Indian culture: my family's rejection and denial of its Native heritage and my own "white," middle-class upbringing had seen to that. I was naive enough to think that I could bridge the gulf by sustained effort and sheer force of will, but no matter how hard I tried to fit into Indian society I always had the sense that here, too, I was an outsider — this time because I was "too white." I learned the hard way that one who swims between cultures can get stranded from either shore: I found myself adrift in a treacherous current of confusion, self-loathing, and despair, and I began to wonder if perhaps my grandmother had been right after all.

I saw very little of my grandmother during those years. I was living   10
in Toronto, she was in Regina, and our contact consisted of occasional
letters and brief visits once or twice a year. But the passage of time and
my own lonely struggle to try to understand and come to terms with my
Native heritage gradually led me to see her in a whole new light. Whereas
in my youth I had felt nothing but contempt for the values that had led
her to deny her Native heritage, I now began to feel a genuine bond of
compassion and respect for this formidable old woman who seemed to
visibly shrink and grow more fragile with each passing season. I was
acutely aware that, just as we were getting to know each other, we would
soon be separated for good. She was my only living connection with
the past, my only hope of finding out who I really was, so even though
she was still reluctant to talk about the past I kept on asking my questions. While she continued to steadfastly maintain the distinctions between our family and other Native people, she must have had some sense
of how important this was for me because she began to try to give me
some answers. And so began a series of long afternoons, often separated by intervals of several months, during which she told me about
her parents and grandparents, about growing up in Lebret and being sent
to school at the convent in St. Charles, about raising her family during
the Great Depression and sending two of her sons to fight in World War
II, never to see them return. We spent hours poring over old family photographs, putting names and faces to those ghostly ancestors who had
haunted my childhood. And then, quite suddenly, she died.

I was uncomfortably pregnant with my first child and was unable to   11
undertake the journey from Toronto to Regina for my grandmother's
funeral, but I was there in spirit as she made the trip out to the valley
for the last time and was laid to rest in the little cemetery on the flats
down by the lake. She never saw my son, Daniel; he was born a few
months after she died. Somehow those two events marked a turning point
for me. I was determined that my child was not going to grow up as I
had, cut off from his past. But how could I give him a sense of who he
was and where he came from if I didn't know myself? And with my
grandmother gone, how would I ever find out? The only thing she left
me was a child's sampler, mounted in a faded gilt frame, that had been
embroidered by my great-grandmother and that bore her name: Maggie
Hogue. It seemed like such an insignificant thing at the time, but in fact
my grandmother had bequeathed to me the very thing she had been unable to give me while she was alive — the key to unlocking the mystery
of my past.

12   . I put my great-grandmother's sampler up on the wall in my kitchen,
but with the demands of being a new mother I scarcely gave it a moment's thought during the months that followed. I had returned to university and was pursuing my deepening interest in Native history by
studying the recent work that had been done on the role of Native women
in the North American fur trade. For almost 200 years, beginning with
the founding of the Hudson's Bay Company in 1670, the fur trade dominated the history of what is now western Canada. From it there emerged
a unique society which drew upon both Indian and European customs
and technology. Though it has been traditionally regarded as an exclusively male pursuit, I learned that women — Native women — in fact
played an essential economic, social, and political role in the fur trade.
Initially, very few white women were permitted to brave the perils of
the "Indian country," so most fur traders took Indian (and later mixed-
blood) women as "country wives." These "marriages à la façon du pays"
were socially sanctioned unions, even though they were not formalized
according to the laws of church or state. But with the establishment of
the first settlements in the early 1800s white women began to go west,
and it soon became fashionable for the traders to legally marry white
women and to try to sever their ties with their Native country wives.

13   In the forefront of this trend was Sir George Simpson, governor of
Rupert's Land[2] and, by all accounts, the most important personage in
the Canadian fur trade, who had taken as his country wife a mixed-blood
woman named Margaret Taylor. Though she bore him two sons, Margaret
Taylor was abandoned by Simpson when he married his English cousin,
a move which signaled the widespread rejection of Native women as
marriage partners by "men of station" in fur-trade society and reflected
the increasing racial and social prejudice against Native women throughout pre-Confederation Canada. Clearly, Margaret Taylor's story epitomized a crucial chapter in the history of Native women in Canada, but I
was equally intrigued by its epilogue — her hastily arranged marriage
to a French Canadian voyageur whose name was startlingly familiar:
Amable Hogue.

14   On the basis of my great-grandmother's faded sampler and a rather
incidental footnote in a history book, I began a search that eventually
verified my connection to my great-great-great-grandmother, Margaret
Taylor — a search which culminated in the making of *Women in the
Shadows*. For me, finding Margaret was the beginning of a journey of
self-discovery — of unraveling the thick web of denial, shame, bitterness, and silence that had obscured my past and picking up the fragile

threads that extended back across time, connecting me to the grandmothers I had never known and to a larger collective experience that is
uniquely and undeniably Métis.

My search for my Native grandmothers was hampered both by the   15
inadequacies of traditional historical sources with respect to women and
by the code of silence that existed in my own family with respect to our
Native heritage. But, after venturing down a couple of blind alleys, I
finally called my great-aunt Jeanne, who is my grandmother's youngest
sister and the only surviving female relative on that side of my family.
When I was growing up, Aunt Jeanne hovered on the edge of the family and her infrequent visits were characterized by an atmosphere of
tension that you could cut with a knife. When I called Aunt Jeanne I
hadn't seen or spoken to her in more than twenty years, yet she was
surprised and touched that I remembered her and seemed eager to help
me in any way she could. Aunt Jeanne knew about Margaret Taylor,
and knew that she had some connection to Governor Simpson, but said
that this had never been discussed because, in the words of Jeanne's
mother, it had brought shame on the family. Nevertheless, Aunt Jeanne
was able to tell me the names of Margaret Taylor's daughters and
granddaughters, and in the act of naming them I finally had the sense of
reaching back and grasping hands with all my grandmothers and great-
grandmothers — right back to Margaret Taylor.

Like most Native women of her time, Margaret Taylor left no dia-   16
ries, no letters, no wills — no written record that might have helped me
reconstruct her life as *she* perceived it. Her voice is not heard in the
historical record, and so I was forced to rely on the logs, journals, letters, and account books that form the written history of the fur trade for
the few maddening snippets of factual information to be found about
her life. For it was the men of the fur trade — our European forefathers
— who wrote the story of the historic encounter between Indian and
European on this continent. And because they wrote it, the history that
has been passed down to their descendants — the history that has been
taught to generations of half-breed children, including me — is their
story, from their point of view. In the absence of any other version of
the story, we have identified with them — with their struggle, their courage, their triumph. But what about our Indian foremothers? What about
their struggle and their courage? The fur traders wrote almost nothing
about the Indian women who shared their lives. And thus the voices of
our grandmothers remain silent, leaving us to wonder about the story
they would have told if they had been able to write it down.

17   The existing records show that my great-great-great-grandmother, Margaret Taylor, was born on Hudson's Bay in 1805. Her mother was an Indian woman who was known only as Jane. Jane is almost nameless, certainly faceless, but I can make some reasonably well-informed assumptions about what her life might have been like. She was probably one of the Homeguard Cree — the "Great House people" who, by the late 1700s, had forged close ties with the traders who lived in the isolated trading posts on the shores of Hudson's Bay. In exchange for the European goods that had revolutionized their lives — guns, knives, axes, kettles, cloth, beads, and brandy — the Cree traded their furs and supplied the posts with country provisions to help the traders survive the long, cold winter months.

18   It was incomprehensible to these people that the fur traders had brought no women with them, for women were the strength and backbone of aboriginal society — those with the power to give life and the wisdom to sustain it. In offering their women as wives for the newcomers, the Cree were making a remarkable gesture of friendship and goodwill, one that drew the white men into the heart of aboriginal society in a way that nothing else could and established bonds of kinship, understanding, and trust that formed the very foundation of the fur trade. For it was the women who taught their new husbands the skills needed to survive in the wilderness, and it was their comfort and companionship that made life bearable for the fur traders in this strange new land. As guides, teachers, helpmates, and wives they occupied an important and privileged position as "women in between" two worlds, and it was they who bridged the gulf between the old ways and the new.[3]

19   Margaret Taylor's mother, Jane, was one of these women. I do not know when or where she was born, but I do know that sometime in the late 1790s she became the "country wife" of one George Taylor, the Hudson's Bay Company's sloopmaster at York Factory on Hudson's Bay. But what did she feel, my Indian grandmother, at the prospect of marrying a white man? Was it enthusiasm, indifference, dread? I'll never know for sure. All I know is that their union produced at least eight children, including Margaret, and that when George Taylor retired from service with the Hudson's Bay Company in 1815 he returned to England, leaving Jane and their children behind.[4]

20   It seems that Jane remained at York Factory, at least for a time, for the post journal indicates that she continued to receive provisions during the following winter — some damaged salt pork, a little flour, a few biscuits. But after that, nothing — no record of where she went or

how she managed. Most likely she returned to live with her own people, taking her daughters with her. There they would have learned to live according to her ways — to know the animals and birds, and to recognize the voices of their ancestors. Yet they carried within them the spirit of two peoples: they remembered other voices, other ways, and they must have known that they were different. Not Cree like their mother, though they spoke her language; not English like their father, though they bore his name; but something else, something unique — a new people.

It must have been Jane who taught her children to make the best of 21 who and what they were — to take from two cultures the things they would need to make their way in a world that was shifting and changing before their very eyes. No longer could her daughters rely on those skills that had made her so indispensable to her husband — those things that had been passed from mother to daughter among her people for as long as anyone could remember. The fur traders no longer needed Indian wives to help them survive in the wilderness: they now looked with pleasure on the light-skinned, mixed-blood daughters of their own kind for the womanly qualities they sought in a wife. With no father to look to their future and pave the way for a suitable marriage, it must have been Jane who painstakingly groomed her daughters to survive in the only way that seemed possible — by becoming all that the traders most desired, shining examples of European ideals of beauty, modesty, and virtue. And in time her diligence paid off, for it was *her* daughter who eventually caught the eye of the governor himself, George Simpson.

Margaret Taylor was just twenty-one years old when she became the 22 "country wife" of the governor of Rupert's Land. Her brother Thomas was George Simpson's personal servant, and it was probably through him that Margaret first came to the governor's attention. Though George Simpson was notorious for indulging in short-lived liaisons with young Native women, his relationship with Margaret Taylor appeared to be different. He relied on her companionship to an unusual degree, insisting that she accompany him on his historic cross-continental canoe journey from Hudson's Bay to the Pacific in 1828. Not only did Simpson recognize and assume responsibility for their two sons, but he also provided financial support for Margaret's mother and referred to Thomas Taylor as his brother-in-law, thus giving Margaret and the rest of fur-trade society every reason to believe that their relationship constituted a legitimate "country marriage" (H.B.C.A. fo. 10, 346). Nevertheless, while on furlough in England in 1830 — and with Margaret and their two sons anxiously awaiting his return at Fort Alexander at the mouth of the Winnipeg River — Simpson married his English cousin, Frances Simpson.

23   It is not hard to imagine Margaret's shock when she learned that the governor was returning with a new wife. No doubt she and her children were kept well out of sight when Simpson and his new bride stopped at Fort Alexander during their triumphant journey west from Montreal to Red River. Once the Simpsons were installed at Red River the governor lost no time in arranging for Margaret's "disposal," and a few months later she was married to Amable Hogue, an event which drew this comment from one contemporary observer: "The Governor's little tit Bit Peggy Taylor is also Married to Amable Hog what a down fall is here … from a Governess to Sow."[5]

24   Amable Hogue, who had been among Simpson's elite crew of voyageurs, was hired as a stonemason on the construction of Simpson's new headquarters at Lower Fort Garry. From her vantage point in the Métis laborers' camp just outside the walls, Margaret would have been able to watch the governor and his bride take up residence in their magnificent new home. For his service, the Hudson's Bay Company gave Hogue a riverfront lot on the Assiniboine River just west of its juncture with the Red — a piece of prime real estate that now lies in the heart of downtown Winnipeg. And it was there that Margaret Taylor spent the rest of her life, raising her family, working beside her husband on their riverfront farm, and joining with her neighbors in the buffalo hunts that were the lifeblood of Red River Métis.

25   My great-great-great-grandmother's life spanned the rise and fall of the Métis nation. By the time she died in December 1885 — just a few weeks after the hanging of Louis Riel — the world that she and other Métis women had known had changed irrevocably. Rupert's Land had become part of the emerging Canadian nation, and immigrants from eastern Canada and Europe were pouring into the old Northwest to lay claim to homesteads on land that had been the home of Indian and Métis people for generations. The buffalo were gone, the fur trade was no more, the Indians were confined to reserves, and the Métis had lost their land and their way of life. The Métis resistance that had begun at Red River in 1870 and that ended at Batoche in 1885 resulted in the final dispossession and marginalization of the Métis people. In the dark years that followed, very few Métis people spoke about being Métis and there was widespread denial of Métis identity among the generations of Métis who survived that troubled time and who grew up in its aftermath.

It is impossible to know when the process of denial and assimilation 26
began in my own family, but I feel in my heart that it goes right back to
what happened to Margaret Taylor. Here, I believe, are the roots of our
denial — denial of that fact of blood that was the cause of so much
pain and suffering and uncertainty about the future. Is it such a surprise
that, many years later, Margaret's own son would choose to describe
his mother as "a sturdy Scotswoman" rather than the half-breed that
she really was?[6] Perhaps Margaret herself perpetrated this myth, if not
for her sons' sake then certainly for her daughters', to try to spare them
a fate similar to her own and that of her mother. I'll never know. But I
do know that the denial of our Native heritage, which has been passed
on from generation to generation of my family, is explicable in light of
those events that took place so long ago, and I am finally able to see it
not as a betrayal but as the survival mechanism that it most certainly
was. For we *did* survive — even though, for a time, we were cut off
from our past and our people — and we did so largely because of the
resourcefulness, adaptability, and courage of my grandmothers.

Unlike Alex Haley, whose search for "roots" was prompted by obscure 27
snatches of stories passed from generation to generation of his family
and pumped into him like plasma from the time he could remember,
my search for my Native grandmothers was prompted by silence — the
silence that is the legacy of assimilation. When I began, I assumed that
no such fragments, no messages from the past, had survived in my family. Yet in my Aunt Jeanne I found incontrovertible evidence that this
was not the case. For Aunt Jeanne, the answer to the question "Do you
remember?" was like coming up from very deep water, giving voice to
things which had not been forgotten but which had been deliberately
submerged in a process of alienation from her Native heritage and assimilation into the dominant society which had become more firmly
entrenched with each new generation. Yet for me, for Aunt Jeanne, and
for all the other Native women who participated in the making of *Women
in the Shadows,* the act of remembering — of reclaiming that which
had been lost to us — was a process of affirmation: affirmation of the
importance of Native women's experience; affirmation of the strength,
courage, and resilience of our grandmothers, affirmation of our ability
to speak both our past and our present, and to make our voices heard.

Thus, in the end, *Women in the Shadows* is about one Native wom- 28
an's reconciliation with her past, her people, and herself. It is both a
coming-to-terms with loss — the price that has been paid for assimila-

tion by countless numbers of indigenous people in Canada and indeed throughout the world — and a celebration of survival. Yet, as Métis poet and historian Emma LaRocque pointed out during the making of the film, our survival carries with it certain responsibilities:

29

> You and I are survivors. We're here because the generations that came before us survived, and maybe generations a hundred years from now will be there because we survived. We have to go on, and part of going on is that we are creating and re-creating and freshly creating. That's our role right now. But unlike Margaret and your grandmothers and my grand-mothers, the challenge for us today is to survive — to be who we are — without paying the price of hating ourselves and rejecting a part of our-selves. That's the big issue — not just that we survive, but that we sur-vive well and healthily without having to abandon anything that is of us.

30

Contemporary aboriginal women are responding to that challenge. Our stories, poems, songs, and films have a recurring theme — that of survival, continuance. It is a theme born of what Emma describes as "a haunting and hounding sense of loss" that is unique to a people dispos-sessed and that compels us to keep saying over and over again: "I re-member" (LaRocque, xxviii). For our words and music and images are testaments to the remarkable fact that *we are still here* — that we have survived near-annihilation, and that we continue to resist — and though they necessarily give voice to our pain, they also express our vision for the future, and in so doing they become tools for healing, for empower-

31 ment, and for change.

As we continue to raise our voices — to write, to sing, to teach, to make films — we do so with the certainty that we are speaking not only for ourselves but for those who came before us whom history has made mute. We have a responsibility to our children and our people to ensure that the voices of our grandmothers are no longer silent. And so the voices of my grandmothers are alive today, for they speak through me.

(1995)

Notes

1. Métis: In Canada, the name given to the mixed blood population that resulted from the inter-mingling and intermarriage between Indians and Europeans that followed the European in-vasion and colonization of the Americas. Written with a small "m," métis is a racial term for anyone of mixed Indian and European ancestry. Written with a capital "M," Métis is a socio-cultural or political term for those originally of mixed ancestry who evolved into a distinct indigenous people during a certain historical period in western Canada. This latter group includes the Métis to whom this paper refers — the descendants of Hudson's Bay Company men and the predominantly Cree women with whom they founded families in the decades following the coming of the HBC traders to Hudson's Bay in the 1670s.

2. Rupert's Land: The vast drainage basin of Hudson's Bay given by royal charter to the Hudson's Bay Company in 1670.

3. For a thorough discussion of the role of Native women in the Canadian fur trade, see Sylvia Van Kirk, *"Many Tender Ties": Women in Fur-Trade Society, 1670–1870* (Winnipeg: Watson and Dwyer Publishing Ltd., 1980).

4. For information on the family of George Taylor, see Hudson's Bay Company Archives (H.B.C.A.) biographical file on George Taylor; also H.B.C.A. D4/113, fo. 146-d.

5. This is what W. Sinclair says to E. Ermatinger, August 15, 1831; quoted in John Galbraith, *The Little Emperor: Governor Simpson of the Hudson's Bay Company* (Toronto: Macmillan of Canada, 1976), p. 109.

6. Article in the *Winnipeg Free Press*, January 11, 1919: "Mr. and Mrs. Joseph Hogue, Both Born in Manitoba, Wedded 60 Years Ago Today."

The Writer's Subject

1. What personal significance does Christine Welsh attach to the making of her film *Women in the Shadows*? (paras. 1, 27–28)

2. How does the writer view her grandmothers' denial of Native ancestry? (para. 2)

3. What is the connection, in Welsh's view, between her film and Native tradition? (para. 3)

4. Why does the writer call the Qu'Appelle Valley of southern Saskatchewan an "aberration"? (para. 4)

5. Why did Welsh feel the need as a child to invent an "exotic ethnicity"? (para. 7)

6. What was it in Welsh's experience that led her to develop a strong interest in her Native ancestry? (para. 8)

7. Welsh states that "one who swims between cultures can get stranded from either shore" (para. 9). In what way does this reflect her own situation?

8. What proved to be "the key to unlocking the mystery" of the writer's past? (para. 11)

9. According to Welsh, what was the role played by Native women in the fur trade of western Canada? (paras. 12, 18)

10. How did Welsh's Cree ancestor Jane teach her daughters to adapt to the changes taking place in the world around them? (para. 21)

11. What connection does Welsh draw between the fate of the Riel rebellion in 1885 and the life experience of her relative Margaret Taylor? (paras. 25–26)

The Writer's Style and Strategy

1. Explain the difference between "métis" and "Métis," as Welsh uses these terms.

2. Explain Welsh's use of the phrase, "the diaspora of the Red River Métis" at the end of para. 5. In what other context does one usually find the word "diaspora," and why has the writer chosen to use it here?

3. Examine para. 6, in which Welsh describes her family's "annual midsummer pilgrimage to Lebret" during her childhood. What effect is she trying to achieve here? What techniques does she employ?

4. Explain the term "voyageur" in para. 13.

5. Explain the allusion to Alex Haley's search for "roots" in para. 27. What is the relevance of this allusion?

6. Discuss the effectiveness of the closing paragraph. To what extent is it a suitable conclusion to Welsh's essay?

7. What tone does Welsh employ in describing the experiences of her forebears? Do you detect any bitterness or anger, or is the tone restrained?

8. Welsh employs a variety of modes — autobiographical reminiscence, history, narrative, argument. Identify instances of these modes in the essay. In your opinion, does the writer succeed in harmonizing them to achieve her purpose?

Suggested Topics for Writing and Discussion

1. Welsh describes her feelings as an "outsider." Drawing on your own experience or observation, discuss the treatment accorded to "outsiders" by the community in which you live.

2. Welsh observes that, because the historical records were written by men, "the voices of our grandmothers remain silent ..." (para. 16). Can you reconstruct an account of your own family history that includes records (diaries, letters, photographs) provided by the female members of your family?

3. In what ways, do you think, historical accounts written by women might differ from those written by men? Notable women historians include C.V. Wedgewood, Barbara Tuchman, and Antonia Fraser. Select a chapter from any work by one of these or other women historians and say whether it is possible to detect the influence of gender in style, content, or approach.

4. Has your life been touched in some significant way by the experience of a relation, male or female?

The World of Science

The body of Tollund Man.

The Body in the Bog
by Geoffrey Bibby

The business of the archaeologist is the digging up of the past, the re- 1
construction of remote history. He does his best to find out what our
remote ancestors did and thought and felt from the material remains
they left in the ground. A distinguished archaeologist has unflatteringly
described himself and his colleagues as surgeons probing into the workings of the human brain with picks, shovels, and builders' trowels. "Fortunately," he adds "our patients are already dead."

This comparison must not be taken too literally. When Sir Mortimer 2
Wheeler describes the archaeologist as investigating people who are
dead, he means, I am afraid, that we are trying to find out about these
dead-and-gone people by studying the things they left behind them, their
implements and weapons and coins and pots and pans. The nearest we
normally get to the people themselves is their skeletons, and there is a
limit to what can be deduced from dry bones.

I wish to tell an archaeological detective story that is different — a 3
detective story that begins with a body and no artifacts.

My part in the story began on Monday, April 28, 1952, when I arrived 4
at the Prehistoric Museum of Aarhus, in mid- Denmark, to find a dead
body on the floor of my office. On an iron sheet stood a large block of
peat, and at one end of it the head and right arm of a man protruded,
while one leg and foot stuck out from the other end. His skin was dark
brown, almost chocolate colored, and his hair was a brownish red.

He had been found on Saturday afternoon by workers cutting peat in 5
a little bog near Grauballe, about twenty miles away. He lay a yard below the surface, but peat had been dug for generations there so that the

"surface" had lain much higher, even within living memory. The finders had informed the local doctor of their discovery, not so much because he was a doctor but because he was known to be an antiquary of repute. And he had informed Professor Peter Glob, who was the director of our museum.

6   This was not Professor Glob's first "bog body"; he knew what to expect and made preparations accordingly. The next day he drove out to the bog, cut a section through the peat exposing the lie of the body, drew and photographed that section, took samples of the peat surrounding the body, and then cut out the whole block in which the body lay and brought it in to the museum in a truck.

7   That Monday we carefully dug away the peat covering the body, taking samples every two inches. The body lay face down, with one leg drawn up and the arms twisted somewhat behind it. It was completely naked. When we removed the peat from below the body (after turning it over in a plaster cast to preserve its original position), we still found nothing, no trace of clothing, no artifacts — nothing except the naked body.

8   At this point we turned for help to the professor of forensic medicine at Aarhus University, who carried out a thorough autopsy and presented us with a lengthy and detailed report:

9   "This most unusually well-preserved body has, as a result of the particular composition of the earth in which it has lain, undergone a process of conservation which appears to resemble most closely a tanning. This has made the skin firm and resistant, and has to a high degree counteracted the various processes of decay which normally commence soon after death ... the subject is an adult male, and the condition of the teeth suggests that he was of somewhat advanced age.... On the front of the throat was found a large wound stretching from ear to ear.... This wound may with certainty be interpreted as an incised lesion, probably caused by several cuts inflicted by a second person. The direction of the wound and its general appearance make it unlikely that it could be self-inflicted or accidentally inflicted after death.... The investigation of the hair suggests that the subject was dark-haired. The reddish coloration is presumably accounted for by the body having lain in peat."

10   So the man from Grauballe had had his throat cut, and we had a murder mystery on our hands.

11   The investigation went on. The police expert reported: "There is nothing unusual about the fingerprints obtained. I myself possess the same type of pattern on the right thumb and middle finger — without therefore claiming any direct descent from Grauballe Man. Among the

present-day Danish population the two patterns occur with a frequency of, respectively, 11.2 and 68.3 per cent."

More important were the results we got from the peat samples and 12 from a portion of the liver region that we had excised and sent to the radioactive-carbon laboratory.

It happens that the botanists of Scandinavia have worked out in great 13 detail the changing composition of the vegetation of the region since the last ice age ended more than ten thousand years ago. They do this by means of the thousands of infinitesimal grains of pollen to be found in any cubic centimeter of peat. The time within this sequence when any particular specimen of peat was formed is shown by the proportion of certain types of pollen grains, particularly of tree pollen. And the pollen analysts could tell us that the peat immediately below Grauballe Man had been formed early in the period the Danes call the Roman Iron Age, a period extending from the beginning of the Christian Era to about A.D. 300.

But they could tell us more. The peat *above* the body was of *earlier* 14 date than that directly below and around the body, and the peat at a little distance to either side of the body was earlier still. The body had clearly been buried in a hole cut in the peat — but not in a hole cut to receive it. The only explanation to fit the facts was that a hole had been cut, probably to obtain peat for fuel, had stood open for some years (long enough for new peat to form in the water at the bottom of the hole), and then Grauballe Man had been thrown into this new peat and the hole had been filled in with peat from the surface layers.

The radio-carbon laboratory — which determines the age of organic 15 substances by measuring the residual carbon-14 in the specimen — could tell us that this had occurred and that Grauballe Man had died in A.D. 310, with a possible error of a hundred years in either direction. This did not surprise us; for, though local newspapers and gossip had made much of a certain "Red Christian," a drunkard farmhand who was said to have disappeared one night some sixty years before, not far from the Grauballe peat bog, we should have been very surprised indeed if the pollen laboratory and the radio-carbon laboratory had *not* given us a date in the region of 100 B.C.–A.D. 300.

For Grauballe Man was far from being an isolated example. Bodies 16 have always been turning up in the peat bogs of Denmark — and not only in Denmark. They are frequently found in northwest Germany and even as far south as Holland. In that area there are records of something like two hundred bog bodies. Since the earlier records are not very detailed, sometimes merely an entry in a parish registry of the "body of a poor man drowned in such and such a bog," the statistics are far from exact. The earliest doubtful record of this nature is from 1450, at Bonstorf in Germany. And the first detailed report is from 1773, when a completely preserved body of a man was found three feet deep in the peat at Ravnholt on the Danish island of Fünen. The body lay on its back with its arms crossed behind it — "as though they had been bound," says the parish clerk. Apart from a sheepskin around the head, it was naked. When the sheepskin was removed, it could be seen that the man had had his throat cut.

17   In 1797, in southwest Jutland, another well-preserved male body was found, naked save for one oxhide moccasin but covered with two calfskin cloaks. The cause of death is not recorded, and the body was hurriedly buried in a nearby churchyard when it began to dry out and decompose.

18   And so it went. Every few years a body would be found, would be a nine-day wonder in its immediate locality because of its surprising state of preservation, and would be buried again when it began to smell.

19   A few of the bodies achieved more than local fame. In 1853, about fifty miles south of Copenhagen a body was found, probably that of a woman, though there was little left besides the skeleton and the long, fair hair. The body was noteworthy because it was accompanied by a bronze brooch and seven glass beads, which even then could be dated to the Iron Age and which we can now date to about A.D. 300.

20   Eight years earlier a much more complete female body had been found at Haraldskaer, in south Jutland, not far from the burial mounds of Gorm, the last heathen king of Denmark and his queen, nor from the site of the first Christian church in Denmark, built about A.D. 950 by Gorm's son, Harald Bluetooth. The body lay in the peat with its hands and feet held down by forked sticks, and it achieved some notoriety in Denmark because some learned antiquaries claimed that it was Queen Gunhild of Norway, who, according to legend, had been enticed to Denmark by Harald Bluetooth and drowned by him in a morass. Even at the time of discovery, though, the evidence for this identification was regarded as too slender.

21   The first photograph of a peat-bog body dates from 1873 and is of a body found near Kiel. It was a man's body with a triangular hole in the forehead. He was naked except for a piece of leather bound around the left shin, but his head was covered with a large square woollen blanket and a sewn skin cape. An attempt was made to preserve him for exhibition by smoking, and several photographs were taken, some extrava-

gantly posed. The first photograph of a body *in situ* was taken in 1892. The body was found not many miles away from the place where Grauballe Man was discovered sixty years later, and very close indeed to another recent find, the Tollund Man.

The list could be continued almost indefinitely. But it is only within 22 recent years that pollen analysis has been developed to a stage where the bodies can be accurately dated. And all the bodies found since have proved to date to the same restricted period of Danish prehistory, the first three centuries of the Christian Era. This fact makes it possible — indeed essential — to regard them as a single "case."

Apart from Grauballe Man, four bodies have been found in the peat 23 bogs of Denmark since World War II, and all have been subjected to the same thorough analysis that we gave Grauballe Man. Three came from the same bog, the large peat area of Borremose in north Jutland. The first was a man, naked like so many of the others but with two cloaks of skin beside him. Around his neck was a rope noose, which may have been the cause of death, although the body was too badly preserved to be certain. There were odd features about the noose; it had been knotted at the neck, and both of the fairly short ends had been bent over and lashed with leather thongs to prevent them from unraveling, surely an unduly elaborate treatment for an ordinary hangman's noose.

The second body was that of a woman, again poorly preserved. The 24 upper part of the body appeared to have been naked, while the lower part was covered with a blanket, a shawl, and other bits of clothing. There was a leather cord around the neck, but the cause of death was apparently a crushing blow on the skull.

The third body was also a woman's, a rather stout lady who lay face 25 downward in the peat with only a blanket wrapped around her middle and held in place by a leather strap. She was no sight for squeamish archaeologists — she had been scalped and her face battered to pieces, though perhaps after death.

It is with quite unjustified relief that one turns from the rather maca- 26 bre Borremose bodies to the well-known Tollund Man whose portrait has been in the press of the world and who has had the honor of appearing on British television. Tollund Man was discovered in 1950, two years before Grauballe Man and under the same circumstances, by farmers cutting peat. The discovery was reported to the police, and they called in Professor Glob, who described what he saw:

"In the peat cut, nearly seven feet down, lay a human figure in a 27 crouched position, still half-buried. A foot and a shoulder protruded, perfectly preserved but dark-brown in color like the surrounding peat which had dyed the skin. Carefully we removed more peat, and a bowed head came into view.

28   "As dusk fell, we saw in the fading light a man take shape before us. He was curled up, with legs drawn under him and arms bent, resting on his side as if asleep. His eyes were peacefully shut; his brows were fur-rowed, and his mouth showed a slightly irritated quirk as if he were not overpleased by this unexpected disturbance...."

29   Tollund Man was found to be naked except for a leather belt around his waist and a leather cap upon his head, a cap made of eight triangu-lar gussets of leather sewn together. There was one other item. Around his neck was the elaborately braided leather rope with which they had hanged him.

30   It is clear, I think, that we have a case of mass murder. There are too many points of similarity between the killings for it to be possible to consider each independently of the others. I should point out, though, that their generally fantastic state of preservation is not one of these points of similarity. It is merely our good fortune The preservation is due the fact that the peat bogs contain sufficient humic acid and tannic acid to halt the processes of decay and start a tanning process that can preserve the body. (This process, incidentally, we have carried to its logi-cal conclusion with Grauballe Man. Eighteen months in an oak vat in a concentrated solution based on oak shavings has completed the tanning process that nature commenced some eighteen hundred years ago. Grauballe Man, on exhibition at the Prehistoric Museum in Aarhus, needs only a little linseed oil now and then in order to last indefinitely.)

31   There is one condition for preservation, however, for otherwise the peat bogs would be full of the bodies of every animal that falls into them. The body must be *buried* in the peat, deep enough down to be below the oxygen-containing surface levels. And this — the fact that all these bodies were disposed of in old cuttings in the peat — *is* one of the

32 common factors that cause us to regard all the killings as a single phe-nomenon.

33   Another is the fact that all the bodies are naked. Though it is the rule rather than the exception for articles of clothing to be found with the bodies, and sometimes wrapped around the bodies, they are never regu-larly clothed in the garments. But the most obvious similarity is that all have died violent deaths and that all are found in bogs.

34   And that leads to the next step in the inquiry: the question of motive. Why are these bodies there at all?

These are not ordinary burials. Archaeologists are very well ac-   35
quainted with the burials of this period of Danish prehistory. They were
elaborate, clearly showing evidence of belief in an afterlife in which
the dead would have need of material things. The graves are large and
edged with stones. The body lies carefully arranged on its side, together
with a whole set of pottery vessels, or in the case of the wealthy, with
glass and silver ware imported from the Roman Empire. The vessels
must have held provisions for the journey to the afterworld, for there is
often a leg of pork or of mutton with the rest of the provisions, and
even a knife to carve the joint.

It is clear that whatever it was that resulted in the deaths of the bod-   36
ies in the bogs also deprived them of regular, ritual burial.

We must dismiss the most obvious explanation — that the bodies   37
were victims of robbery with violence. All are dated to the comparatively short period of three hundred years at the beginning of our era. It
may have been a lawless time — though farther south it is the period of
the Pax Romana — but certainly it was no more lawless than many other
periods: the period before, of the great Celtic and Germanic wander-
ings; or the period after, when the Roman Empire was breaking up and
all the vultures flocked to the kill; or the Viking period; or much of the
Middle Ages. We should expect a much greater spread in date if the
bodies are to be explained as the victims of robber bands.

We must widen our scope and look not so much at the bodies as at   38
the bogs. What do we find there?

Any Danish archaeologist can answer that question at length. And   39
he can illustrate his answer at the Danish National Museum in Copenhagen, where room after room is full of things found in bogs. More
than half of the best treasures of Danish prehistory have been found in
bogs, and the archaeologist will tell you that these treasures were offerings to the gods.

Now, archaeologists have often been accused of calling in hypotheti-   40
cal gods and cult practices whenever they find anything they cannot
explain by obvious mundane means. A theory of offerings in the peat
bogs must not be accepted uncritically. But how else is one to explain
why a Stone Age farmer, some four thousand years ago, very carefully
laid seven large, new, unused stone axes side by side in a row in a peat
bog? How is one to explain why several pairs of the big bronze trumpets known as lurs, the finest known products of the Danish Bronze Age,
have been found in the bogs in good working order?

It begins to look as though anything of prehistoric date found in the   41 bogs of Denmark is a priori likely to be an offering to the gods. If we move forward to the actual period of the bog bodies, we find the offerings in the bogs getting more numerous and more varied and richer. In the early 1950's I spent three years a few miles south of our museum, helping to dig out an immense offering of weapons — several thousand iron swords and spearheads and arrowheads and shield bosses — all of them burned, bent, hacked to pieces, and then deposited in a lake in the middle of a peat bog. They had been deposited at various times — it was a regular place of offering — but all during the period A.D. 150–300. Among the weapons lay the skeletons of two horses — and here perhaps we approach quite close in spirit to the bog bodies, for the horses had been beheaded before they were offered, and marks on the bones showed quite clearly where spears had been stuck into the carcasses, before or after death.

42   We are entering a dark region. Our probings into the minds of our distant ancestors are lifting a corner of a veil that seems to cover an area of deep superstition, a time when the peat bogs were the abodes of gods and spirits, who demanded sacrifice. When we look now at the bodies in the bogs it seems by no means impossible that they, too, were offerings; that the sacrifices to the gods also included human sacrifices.

43   We must ask ourselves what we know about the gods and goddesses of this period.

44   At the northern end of that very bog at Borremose in which three of the bodies were found, there was discovered in 1897 a large caldron of solid silver. In itself the Gundestrup caldron is far and away the most intrinsically valuable of all the bog offerings. But it is more than that; it is a picture book of European religion around the beginning of the Christian Era. Its sides are decorated, inside and out, with a series of panels bearing pictures, in relief, of gods and goddesses, of mythical animals, and of ritual scenes. Admittedly the caldron is believed to have been manufactured in southeast Europe and to have been brought to Denmark as booty, but the deities portrayed are like the native Danish gods of the period.

45   It is particularly noteworthy that each one of these deities, although otherwise naked, bears a torque, or broad necklet, at the throat, which appears to have been a symbol of kingship and of divinity. It has even been suggested — perhaps not entirely fancifully — that the oddly elaborate nooses around the necks of Tollund and Borremose Man in some way set them apart as consecrated to the gods. We know from the sagas, not many hundreds of years later, that in Viking times hanged men

were sacred to Odin, the chief god of the Viking pantheon.

One of the interior caldron panels shows clearly that the idea of hu- 46
man sacrifice was not alien to the religion of the time. It is admittedly a
different ceremony of sacrifice, with the victim dropped headfirst into,
or perhaps slaughtered above, a caldron, perhaps the Gundestrup caldron itself. The cutting of the throats of animal victims and the draining of their blood into a caldron was not unknown even among the
civilized Greeks and Romans — and Grauballe Man, like many of the
victims in the Danish bogs, had had his throat cut.

Speculation concerning details of ritual, though fascinating, can hardly 47
be justified by the slender evidence at our disposal. But the general picture cannot be questioned: the Danes of the early Christian centuries
worshipped torque-bearing gods and goddesses; they were not averse to
human sacrifice; and the holy places of the divinities were the peat bogs.

There is one source of information that we have not yet tapped. The 48
historians and geographers of the Roman Empire wrote books, some of
which describe the manners and customs of peoples beyond the imperial frontiers. The books must be used with caution; few of the authors
had visited the regions they describe, and their accounts may well be as
full of misunderstandings and fanciful explanations as anything the
modern archaeologist can invent to explain what he finds.

But there is a passage in Tacitus's *Germania*, an account of the peo- 49
ples beyond the Rhine written in A.D. 98, that bears on our study of the
Danish bog bodies. Tacitus names seven tribes to the north of Germany,
including the Angles, who are known to have lived in south Jutland before they invaded England in the fifth century together with the Saxons
and Jutes. And he says: "these people ... are distinguished by a common worship of Nerthus, or Mother Earth. They believe that she interests herself in human affairs and rides through their peoples. In an island
of Ocean stands a sacred grove, and in the grove stands a car draped
with a cloth which none but the priest may touch. The priest can feel
the presence of the goddess in this holy of holies, and attends her, in
deepest reverence, as her car is drawn by oxen. Then follow days of
rejoicing and merrymaking in every place that she honors with her advent and stay. No-one goes to war, no-one takes up arms; every object
of iron is locked away; then, and only then, are peace and quiet known
and prized, until the goddess is again restored to her temple by the priest,
when she has had her fill of the society of men. After that, the car, the
cloth and, believe it if you will, the goddess herself are washed clean in
a secluded lake. This service is performed by slaves who are immedi-

ately afterwards drowned in the lake. Thus mystery begets terror and a pious reluctance to ask what that sight can be which is allowed only to dying eyes."

50   Here we may be getting close to an answer. Nerthus — Mother Earth — is clearly a goddess of fertility; she may be the "goddess with the torque." And the time of peace and rejoicing when the goddess is driven around the countryside in her draped carriage will be the time of sowing, the vernal equinox. Pagan survivals of this spring festival still exist in many parts of Europe, in mummers' plays and Maypole dancing and Queens of the May. And in the National Museum in Copenhagen may be seen one of the ox-drawn carriages that almost certainly was used to carry the image of the fertility goddess around the fields. It was found — inevitably — in a peat bog, Dejbjerg in east Jutland, in the 1880's. Richly carved and decorated with ornaments of bronze, it is far too fine a wagon to have been used for mundane purposes. Upon it stands a palanquin, a carrying chair with a canopy, within which the image of the goddess must have rested.

51   A final point brings the evidence full circle to the bodies in the bogs. Microscopic examination of the stomach contents of the men from Borremose, Tollund, and Grauballe shows that their food for several days before death had been vegetarian. It seems to have consisted of some sort of porridge or mash composed of various kinds of corn, or sorrel and heart's ease (both cultivated during the Iron Age), and of the seeds of such weeds as were accidentally harvested along with the corn. It has been suggested that this was a ritual diet, part of the ceremony needed to make the corn grow. Be that as it may, it is significant that there was no trace of any of the edible plants or fruits of summer in the stomach contents. So whatever our uncertainty about the precise year of death, we can say with confidence that the season of the year was winter or early spring.

52   Further we cannot go. We have been probing, with our picks and shovels and builders' trowels, not merely into the brains but perhaps also into the souls of men, and we must be content if our diagnosis is imprecise and inconclusive. But it does take us a little way beyond the conventional archaeological picture of the material lives of the simple peasants of barbarian Europe. Behind the material life, interleaved with it and perhaps dominating it, was the world of taboos and magic and superstition, the spirits of the earth and of the heavens, who had to be bribed or placated or bought off. One of the occupational risks of Iron Age Europe, right up to the end of the Viking period scarcely a thou-

sand years ago, was that of being chosen as victim, as the price to be paid for prosperity in the next harvest or victory in the next war. It was only with the coming of Christianity that human sacrifice ceased in Europe; looking on the bodies from the Danish bogs we should do well to realize that there, but for the grace of God, lie we.

(1968)

The Writer's Subject

1. How did Bibby and his colleagues first come to realize that they had a murder mystery on their hands?

2. What part did the Scandinavian botanists play in the investigation? (paras. 12–15)

3. Bibby describes the characteristics of a number of bog bodies. What features did these have in common that led him to conclude that these bodies represented "a case of mass murder"? (para. 29)

4. Why did the archaeologists dismiss "the most obvious explanation — that the bodies were victims of robbery with violence"? (para. 35)

5. What led Bibby and his colleagues to conclude that these bodies were ritual offerings?

6. What was the significance of the Gundestrup cauldron in the unravelling of the mystery of the bog bodies? (paras. 42–44)

7. How does Tacitus's account of the goddess Nerthus throw light on the circumstances of the ritual murders? (paras. 47–48)

8. How does Bibby's conclusion demonstrate that the archaeologist's interests are not restricted to a study of material remains?

The Writer's Style and Strategy

1. Bibby speaks of his intention to tell "an archaeological detective story." In what ways does the essay follow the pattern implied by such a description?

2. Is this essay intended for a specialist or a generalist audience? Pick out details of content, style, or diction that support your opinion.

3. Was the reasoning employed in Bibby's investigation primarily deductive or inductive?

4. Discuss the uses that Bibby makes of paragraphs of one or two sentences.

5. What features of Bibby's approach lead the reader to have confidence in the plausibility of his conclusions?

Suggestions for Writing and Discussion

1. ˙ Find out what you can about archaeological excavations in your region or community. What conclusions have been reached about the history of your region through such investigations? (A good place to begin your study is your local museum.)

2 Bibby speaks of the part played by scientific experts in his investigation (e.g., pollen analysis, carbon dating). With the help of a librarian, locate an account of a fairly recent archaeological "dig" or underwater expedition (e.g., in the Mediterranean, in China). Show what part science and technology have played in helping the archaeologists understand their finds.

3. Bibby points to the importance of ritual in pre-Christian Danish society. Though we no longer subscribe to rituals of the kind Bibby describes, we do practise other kinds of rituals. Discuss one or two rituals still practised in your community in connection with such occasions as births, deaths, marriages, harvest, etc.

The Real Responsibilities of the Scientist
by Jacob Bronowski

We live in times of very difficult decisions for scientists, for statesmen, 1
and for the lay public. Many of these decisions are forced on us by new
scientific discoveries, and the difficulties in making them are created
by the distance between the scientist and the public. (Indeed, there is a
frightening distance even between scientists in one field and those in
another.) This sense of distance is, I think, a grave threat to the survival
of the kind of society in which science can flourish at all.

People hate scientists. There is no use in beating about the bush here. 2
The scientist is in danger of becoming the scapegoat for the helplessness which the public feels. And if an immense revulsion of public feeling does lead to the destruction of the scientific tradition, then the world
may again enter a dark age as it did after the Goths destroyed Rome. It
is not impossible that the whole mechanical and intellectual society
which we know could be abolished by a great wave of fanaticism.

That is the danger which faces us, because people hate scientists. But 3
even if this danger does not materialize, something as terrible can happen — and is happening. This is that the scientist is forced, by the hatred of public opinion, to side with established authority and government.
He becomes a prisoner of the hatred of the lay public, and by that becomes the tool of authority.

My purpose is not to underline these obvious dangers, which we may 4
hide from ourselves but which in our hearts we all know to exist. My
purpose is to try to give a picture, as I see it, of the real responsibilities
of scientists, government, and public, in order that, beginning from this
diagnosis, we may begin to cure the great and threatening division between them.

The Abuse of Science

5 What the lay public does when it hates the scientist is what it does also when it hates policemen and ministers of state and all symbols of authority. It tries to shift the responsibility for decisions from its own shoulders to the shoulders of other people. "They have done this," it says. And "They" is always the law, the government — or in this case, the scientist.

6   You must allow me here to make a digression which is not strictly part of my theme, but which I think needs saying. It is this: that we must not forget that scientists do bear a heavy responsibility. I am of course about to explain that really the public and governments bear the main responsibility. But this does not shift from us, the scientists, the grave onus of having acquiesced in the abuse of science. We have contrived weapons and policies with our public conscience, which each of us individually would never have undertaken with his private conscience. Men are only murderers in large groups. They do not individually go out and strangle their neighbor. And scientists are only murderers in large groups — collectively. For scientists are very ordinary human beings. Any collection of people in any laboratory contains good and bad, people with consciences and without, and what we have allowed to happen is the conquest of science by the minority without conscience which exists in every group.

7   It is sad that scientists have been exceptionally corruptible. Look into your own experience. Most of us have come from poor parents. We have worked our own way up. The practice of science has enabled us to earn salaries which would be unthinkable to us if we had stayed peddling whatever our fathers peddled. Quite suddenly, the possession of a special skill has opened to us a blue door in the antechambers of prime ministers. We sit at conference tables, we have become important people, because we happen to be able to be murderers. And therefore scientists have been bought with large salaries and fellowships and rewards quite inappropriate to their merits, because a policy was furthered by their techniques. The scientist has proved to be the easiest of all men to blind with the attractions of public life.

8   Having said this I now propose to stop abusing the scientist. I think it is right that we should all make this confession of guilt — I have been as guilty as anyone else — but this is all spilt milk, this is all water over the dam. We must now look toward what we can do to remedy what has happened. And it cannot be remedied by a gigantic strike of

scientists, who will suddenly refuse to have anything to do with commercial or war research, because the society of scientists contains too many fallible human beings to make this practicable.

When the public dreams of such a strike, when it says: "scientists 9 ought not to have invented this or disclosed that secret," it is already demanding something of the individual scientist which lies beyond his personal responsibility.

The voters of Great Britain elect for the purpose of making their policy 10 six hundred and thirty members of Parliament. They do not elect the people who go to Harwell or the people who go to my own research laboratory. That is: we have already deputed to those whom we elect the responsibility for framing policy in peace and war, and it is quite wrong to ask a body of professional experts like the scientists to take this responsibility from the men whom our society has named.

The individual scientist is not the keeper of the public conscience, 11 because that is not what he was chosen for. The population at large, through its deputed ministers, has chosen scientists to execute certain public orders which are thought to represent the public will. And you cannot ask the scientist to be executioner of this will, and judge as well. If you have given a body of scientists this particular hangman's task, you cannot ask them also to form a collective opposition to it. The collective responsibility belongs to the lay public and through that, to those who were elected by that public to carry it out.

Thus when Einstein on August 2, 1939, wrote a letter to President 12 Roosevelt in order to draw his attention to the possibility of an atomic bomb, he was acting with exemplary correctness. He was disclosing to the elected head of government a matter of public importance on which the decision was not his, the writer's, but was the President's to make.

We must explain to people that they are asking of scientists quite the 13 wrong collective decision when they say, "you should not have invented this," or "you should not have disclosed that." This is asking us all to betray the public in the same way as Dr. Klaus Fuchs did, by asking scientists to make decisions which are for the nation to make. The only man who ever, on his own responsibility, was willing to shoulder public responsibility in this way, was Dr. Fuchs. But so far from being hailed as the only sane scientist, he was treated as quite the opposite — as of course he was, since scientists have no right to betray the will of the nation. Yet Fuchs did just what the public asks of every scientist — he decided what to do with a scientific invention.

The Private Conscience

14 Very well. We will agree that the scientist is not the keeper of the nation's policy. Then what is he the keeper of? He is the keeper of his own private conscience. His responsibility is not to be seduced as a person. He has the right to act individually as a conscientious objector. Indeed, I believe he has the duty to act as a conscientious objector. I would like to repeat this point. It is in this country an offense to betray the armed forces or to seduce their members from their allegiance. It is not an offense to refuse to be a soldier. And I believe that this is exactly like the position of the scientist. He has no business to act as if he commands the army, but he has a business to settle with his own conscience: the serious business whether he personally will engage in forms of research of which he does not morally approve.

15 My claim then is that the individual scientist should exercise his own personal conscience. This is his duty. What is the duty of governments in this respect? It is to make it possible for him to exercise his conscience. The responsibility of governments in this is to create the conditions in which a scientist can say: No! to projects in which he does not want to take part. He must even be able to give advice which is distasteful to those in authority, and still must not be hounded out of public life or prevented from making a living.

16 In all countries the serious threat to scientists who have once touched the fringes of secret subjects is that they are then caught in something from which they can never escape again. They do not get a passport, in case somebody captures them. They cannot get a job because, if they do not want to do this, then they are too dangerous or awkward to be trusted with anything else. This is what we must prevent governments from doing, and this can only be prevented by the opinion of quite ordinary citizens. This is the duty which citizens owe to scientists, to insist that governments shall make it possible for scientists to be conscientious objectors if they wish.

17 I have explored this subject in general terms, and I would now like to be specific. I would like to tell you precisely what I think is the responsibility of the public, of the scientists, and of governments.

18 The responsibility of the public is to make the decisions of policy on which their future depends, and to make them themselves. And in a democracy the apparatus for this is to elect those people in whose judgment you have confidence — and to elect them on the issues which in fact face the world. Now you can only elect such people, you can only put pressure on them about public issues, if you are well informed. The

greatest lack of public opinion today is lack of information about what is possible and not possible in science. This sets my teeth on edge every time I read a scientific newsflash. I will quote one of many instances which I find distasteful: the use of the phrase "cobalt bomb." This is a technical term for a piece of medical equipment, but has suddenly become transformed into something to describe how a hydrogen bomb might be clothed. As a result, of the fifty million people in this country, forty-nine million and nine hundred odd thousand have heard the words "cobalt bomb," but are helplessly confused between radio-active treatment and something that you blow people up with. The public must be well informed; and the public gets not only the government it deserves, but the newspapers it deserves.

19 If this is once granted, the next step I think is simple. If it is once granted that we believe in democratic election, and that in our generation this can only be carried out by a public informed on the scientific issues on which the fate of nations hangs, then the duty of the scientist is clear. The duty of the scientist is to create the public opinion for right policies, and this he can only create if the public shares his knowledge.

20 My generation has a heavy task here, because it ought to spend the bulk of its time — alas — not in laboratories at all, but in explaining to the voting public what is going on in the laboratories. What are the choices which face us? What could be done with antibiotics, with new materials, with coal (if you like), and with alternative forms of energy? These are urgent questions and yet, however many times we raise them, the layman still does not understand the scale of the changes which our work is making, and on which the answers must hang.

21 There is a slightly irreverent story about this. At the time the Smyth Report was published in America there was published in this country a White Paper on the British contribution to atomic energy. One of the documents in it is the directive which Mr. Winston Churchill, as he then was, gave about the setting up of an atomic energy project. This directive begins with the words, "Though personally satisfied with the power of existing explosives...." This bland phrase is a monument to a nonscientific education. For it could only have been written by a man, an intelligent man, who simply does not understand how big a million is. The difference between atomic explosives and ordinary explosives is the difference between the length of a nuclear bond and a molecular bond; and this is a factor of more than a million. To suppose somehow that in multiplying the energy of an explosive by a million, you are doing nothing very different from multiplying it by two, or five, or ten —

this is simply not to grasp the scale of the world.

22   And the public does not grasp it. To say "ten to the sixth" to anybody, however educated, is still to invite the reproof today that one is stressing mere numerical details. One of our tasks, as scientists, must be to educate people in the scale of things.

23   While I am telling improper stories — improper only in the amusing sense — I will tell you that everybody who works in industrial research has this trouble all the time, when he discusses the economics of new processes. We put forward the result of research, or we simply estimate what would happen if a piece of research proved successful. And at once we get back a balance sheet from the finance department which says: The current process makes a profit of 2/2d a ton, and what you have in mind might make a loss of 8d a ton; it is therefore not worth pursuing. This, if you please, is the comment on a piece of research which, if it works on the full scale, might cut costs by a factor of five. But no accountant understands a factor of five; he budgets in shillings and pence, and what is liable to loss is to him as good as lost. One cannot explain a factor of five, or a factor of a million, to people who have not been brought up in a scientific tradition. This is what I mean when I say that the scientist has a duty to become a teacher to the public in understanding the pace, the nature, the scale of the changes which are possible in our lifetime.

Government and Opportunity

24   I have detailed the duties of the public and of the scientist. What are the duties of government? The duties of government are to give its public the opportunity to learn, and therefore to give scientists the opportunity to teach. And I have already suggested that these duties are twofold. One is to give scientists freedom to live their own lives if they do not want to go on with research projects which seem to them without conscience. The other is the duty to allow scientists to speak freely on subjects of world importance.

25   As for the second, everyone who has ever been connected with the atomic energy projects knows how it is met today. We spend our time waiting for some American journalist to publish some piece of information which we know to be accurate, so that we may then quote it as being the opinion of the *New York Times*. I am being frank about this: I do it all the time. I read what the greatest indiscreet senator said to the small indiscreet reporters, and I know that nine statements are nonsense and one statement is accurate. Then I quote the one that is accurate — but not as my opinion.

Of course it is natural that governments resist the explosive opinions   26
of scientists. All governments, all societies are resistant to change. Rather
over two thousand years ago, Plato was anxious to exile poets from his
society; and in our lifetime, for the same reason, governments are, in effect, anxious to exile or at least silence scientists. They are anxious to exile
all dissidents, because dissidents are the people who will change society.

There is a simple difference between governments and scientists.   27
Governments believe that society ought to stay the way it is for good —
and particularly, that there ought to be no more elections. Scientists believe that society ought to be stable, but this does not mean the same thing
to them as being static. We scientists want to see an *evolving* society,
because when the physical world is evolving (and we are helping to
evolve it) the forms of society and government cannot be kept the same.

The Moral Contract

Having described the duties of the public, of scientists, and of govern-   28
ments, let me now underline what I have said by describing what happens in all three cases if these duties are not kept. If governments do
not allow scientists freedom of conscience, to work at what they like
and to refuse to work at what they do not like, and to speak freely about
why they do so, then you get the gravest of all disasters — the disaster
of state intolerance. This is a disaster because it saps both sides of the
moral contract. For there is a moral contract between society and its
individuals which allows the individual to be a dissident; and if the state
breaks this moral contract, then it leaves the individual no alternative
but to become a terrorist. I do not know whether the great state trials in
Russia were just or were false. But I know that if they were just, if men
like Radek and Trotsky and Zinoviev really committed those enormi-
ties, then this in itself condemns the system of government which does
not allow any other form of protest than such a form. The grave danger
to our society too is that this becomes the only choice which is left open
to scientists, if state intolerance imprisons them and tries to turn them
into a secret Egyptian priestcraft.

The great sin of the public is acquiescence in this secrecy. I am hor-   29
rified by the feeling that I get, from such trifling things as American
advertisements, that people really enjoy the sense that they are not to
be trusted. There is an advertisement running in the *New Yorker* at the
moment (I think for a clothing firm) which shows a man who has just
got out of an airplane. He has a face like a prizefighter, he is well-dressed
and wears what in New York is called a sharp hat, and he carries a bag

in one hand which is chained to his wrist. He is carrying secret documents. This is the holy of holies. This is what we are to admire — the man with his mouth shut tight who is not trusting you and me, because of course you and I are not to be trusted. When people come to believe this, when they themselves believe that it is better for them not to know, then totalitarianism is on the doorstep. Then you are ready for Hitler to get up and say: "I am the man who will take your communal responsibilities. I will make your decisions for you."

30   And the third in our scheme, the scientist, must preserve the tradition of quarrelling, of questioning, and of dissent on which science (and I believe all post-Renaissance civilization) has been built. He must do this for two reasons. First, there is the mundane reason which is obvious in the failure of German research after Hitler took power. It is this: that you do not get good science as soon as you have reduced the scientists to yes-men. It is the nature of scientists to be thoroughly contrary people — let us own up to that. It is the nature of science as an activity to doubt your word and mine. As soon as you get a science, such as atomic energy research in totalitarian Germany, in which the young men are no longer allowed to question what the great men have said, then that science is dead. You can find in the files of the German Atomic Energy Commission that several young men made what I suppose must be called very good suggestions, but they were not followed because (such is the influence of totalitarianism) Heisenberg already knew the answers.

31   This does not happen in English laboratories yet. Mr. Churchill begins by saying that he is satisfied with existing explosives, but after the comma he does give scientists the opportunity to be dissatisfied. This tradition, this independence and tolerance, is I believe the base of all our values; and this is what we as scientists must preserve.

The Duty of Heresy

32 I have given you the simple practical grounds for allowing scientists to be awkward, but I believe also that imaginatively and intellectually this is equally important. The sense of intellectual heresy is the lifeblood of our civilization. And the heresy of scientists cannot be confined to their science. Newton was thoroughly and rightly contrary in science, and he was also a thorough heretic in religious matters. For the same reason, people like Oppenheimer and Einstein are found to associate with such unreliable characters. You cannot say to scientists: "When you get into the laboratory at nine in the morning you are going to become a dissenter; and when you go out at five-thirty you are going to become a

citizen who touches his cap and who is politically sound." The intellect is not divided into these simple categories.

I have said that the duty of the scientist is today publicly to become a 33 teacher. Let me end by saying something of what he is to teach. There is, of course, the scientific method. There are things about the scale and order of size, of which I have spoken. There are the possibilities which are open to us in controlling nature and ourselves. Above all, he can teach men to ask whether the distance between promise and achievement in our age need be quite so large; whether there must be such a gap between what society is capable of doing and what it does. All this, every scientist can teach.

But every scientist can also teach something deeper. He can teach 34 men to resist all forms of acquiescence, of indifference, and all imposition of secrecy and denial. We must resist the attitude of officials, that there ought to be a good reason why something should be published before you allow it. We must teach even officials that there will have to be a very good reason indeed before anyone is silenced by secrecy.

Mr. Gordon Dean, former chairman of the American Atomic Energy 35 Commission, has just been complaining against secrecy on practical grounds. He says that the commercial reactors which are being built in America are still on the secret list and that this is handicapping American business in its competition with English business for world reactor markets. God works in a mysterious way and it may be that by this anxiety to sell atomic power, science will be liberated. At any rate, let us not look askance at any ally in the drive against silence. My message, in this and in all else, has been the scientist's duty to speak. There is one thing above all others that the scientist has a duty to teach to the public and to governments: it is the duty of heresy.

(1956)

The Writer's Subject

1. What is the chief responsibility of the scientist, as Bronowski sees it?

2. Why, according to Bronowski, do people regard scientists in the same way that they regard other symbols of authority? (para. 5)

3. How, in Bronowski's view, have scientists contributed to the abuse of science? (para. 7)

4. How does Bronowski answer those who think that scientists should oppose government policy on such matters as war research? (paras. 8–13)

5. How does Bronowski illustrate the danger of allowing a scientist rather than a government to make the decision about what to do with a scientific invention? (para. 13)

6. Why does Bronowski say the scientist "has the duty to act as a conscientious objector"? (para. 14)

7. Why is it so important for the public to be well informed, and what are the responsibilities of the scientist in this regard? (paras. 18–22)

8. What are the consequences of governments' not allowing scientists freedom of conscience? (para. 28)

The Writer's Style and Strategy

1. How does Bronowski make clear that his audience is made up of scientists?

2. What evidence in the style of this essay indicates that it was also intended to reach a wider audience?

3. "The Real Responsibilities of the Scientist" is a good example of a public address. Bronowski skilfully identifies himself with his audience and employs direct appeals to his listeners, anecdotes, clear transitions between the stages of his argument, and restatements of central ideas for clarity. Find examples of these and other techniques which demonstrate Bronowski's command as a public speaker.

4. What use does Bronowski make of anecdote and historical example?

Suggested Topics for Writing and Discussion

1. Bronowski is opposed to "all imposition of secrecy and denial." Do you think there are ever circumstances in which a scientist should observe total secrecy in connection with his or her research?

2. Bronowski speaks of the importance of educating the public on matters of science. What does an educated citizen need to know about science in order to perform his or her duties as a responsible member of a democratic society?

3. In recent times several fields of science have led to controversy (e.g., *in vitro* fertilization, organ transplants, genetic engineering, irradiation of food, nuclear energy). Focusing on one area of scientific research, discuss the extent to which you think governmental controls should be exercised.

4. Should governments continue to supply power needs through the development of atomic energy, or should they make greater use of other resources, such as fossil fuels, hydro-electric power, or solar energy?

The Aggressive Egg
by David H. Freedman

Ah, fertilization — that miraculous process to which we all owe our   1
existence. Let's review: first, a wastefully huge swarm of sperm weakly
flops along, its members bumping into walls and flailing aimlessly
through thick strands of mucus. Eventually, through sheer odds of pin-
ball-like bouncing more than anything else, a few sperm end up close
to an egg. As they mill around, the egg selects one and reels it in, pin-
ning it down in spite of its efforts to escape. It's no contest, really. The
gigantic, hardy egg yanks this tiny sperm inside, distills out the chromosomes, and sets out to become an embryo. Or would you have put it
differently? Until very recently, so would most biologists. For decades
they've been portraying sperm as intrepid warriors battling their way to
an aging, passive egg that can do little but await the sturdy victor's final, bold plunge. But the first description is closer to the truth, insists
Emily Martin, a 47-year-old researcher at Johns Hopkins who has spent
the past seven years examining the metaphors used to describe fertilization. Martin is not a biologist; she's a cultural anthropologist. But her
efforts to spotlight the male-skewed imagery that permeates our views
of reproduction have placed her at the center of a growing debate about
how cultural myths can turn into scientific myths, and vice versa.

Martin didn't set out to skewer biologists. Actually she was studying   2
biology, among other things, at the University of Michigan in 1965 when
a course on Japanese music hooked her on investigating other cultures.
After picking up a Ph.D. in cultural anthropology from Cornell in 1971,
she spent nine years traveling back and forth between the United States,
Taiwan, and China, where she was studying Chinese rituals and social

organization. Then, having done the study of a foreign culture that's traditionally expected of anthropologists, and being pregnant with her first child, she started casting about for a new project closer to home. "Studying your own culture is harder," she says, "because everything seems so normal to you."

3   Not until 1982, while attending a class for expectant parents before the birth of her second child, did Martin stumble on her topic. "It suddenly hit me that the way everyone was talking about their bodies was really weird," she recalls. "It was *the* body, *the* uterus, and *the* contraction — as if these things weren't a part of us. I realized that medical science was in need of some sort of interpretation, and my wedge would be reproductive issues." Martin started off by interviewing dozens of women on their feelings about every aspect of reproduction, from menstruation to menopause. Her book *The Woman in the Body,* published in 1987, explored the relation between images of the body and ideas about oneself. But by 1985 Martin realized that she had been looking at these issues from only one point of view. "I decided to do an ethnographic study in a scientific setting, to see how biologists thought about some of these questions," she says. "Also, I thought I should be including male reproductive processes as well." Fertilization research, she realized, would allow her to cover all the bases.

4   As she began her background studies, Martin was surprised to find that popular literature, textbooks, and even medical journals were crammed with descriptions of warrior sperm and damsel-in-distress eggs. Martin found that classic biology texts, for example, enthused about the human male's "amazing" productivity — some 200 million sperm every hour — while practically complaining over the "waste" of the 2 million immature eggs present in the human female at birth, only some 400 of which the ovaries ever "shed" for possible fertilization, with the rest destined to "degenerate" over the woman's lifetime. "The real mystery," says Martin, "is why the male's vast production of sperm is not seen as wasteful."

5   Less mysterious, in Martin's opinion, was the motivation for such biased language. "Men link potency to strong sperm," she says. "You'd like your sperm to be like you; no wonder everyone believed sperm were torpedoes." In all her searching, Martin came up with only a single depiction of less-than-mighty sperm: Woody Allen's portrayal of a neurotic sperm nervous about his imminent ejaculation in the movie *Everything You Always Wanted to Know About Sex But Were Afraid to Ask.*

6   Woody Allen aside, the durability of the masterful sperm imagery astonished Martin. It continued to dominate the contemporary technical and

popular literature despite a growing body of evidence that the egg plays anything but a passive role. From the early 1970s on, studies of the sperm and eggs of many species have revealed that molecules released by the egg are critical to guiding and "activating" the sperm — that is, triggering the sperm to release proteins that help it adhere to the egg. In fact, the egg might just as well be called eager as passive. Among many species of lizards, insects, some crustaceans, and even turkeys, the egg doesn't always wait for the sperm's arrival. It can begin dividing without fertilization, and females can reproduce without sperm at all.

Yet none of this had made a dent in biologists' language. "When I asked them about it, they told me I had a point," says Martin. "They claimed the imagery came up only when they needed to explain their research, and not in the lab. But I wanted to know what was really going on." 7

By 1986 Martin had begun hanging out with a team of researchers at Johns Hopkins who were observing sperm mobility in hopes of coming up with a strategy for a new contraceptive. They had started the year before with a simple experiment — measuring human sperm's ability to escape and swim away from a tiny suction pipet placed against the side of the sperm cell's head. To the team's great surprise, the sperm turned out to be feeble swimmers; their heads thrashed from side to side ten times more vigorously than their bodies pushed forward. "It makes sense," says Martin. "The last thing you'd want a sperm to be is a highly effective burrower, because it would end up burrowing into the first obstacle it encountered. You want a sperm that's good at getting away from things." 8

The team went on to determine that the sperm tries to pull its getaway act even on the egg itself, but is held down against its struggles by molecules on the surface of the egg that hook together with counterparts on the sperm's surface, fastening the sperm until the egg can absorb it. Yet even after having revealed the sperm to be an escape artist and the egg to be a chemically active sperm catcher, even after discussing the egg's role in "tethering" the sperm, the research team continued for another three years to describe the sperm's role as actively "penetrating" the egg. 9

Meanwhile, Martin was keeping an eye on two other fertilization groups. They too seemed at times to disregard their own observations when writing about fertilization. Researchers at the University of Wisconsin, for example, described the way sea urchin sperm first make contact with an egg by quickly stringing together protein molecules into a filament that extends out until it reaches the egg. But instead of describ- 10 ing this as an innocuous process of assembly and attachment, the group wrote — in a pioneering paper that otherwise points out the egg's ability to actively "clasp" and "entwine" — that the sperm's filament "shoots out and harpoons" the egg. Likewise, when a researcher at the Roche Institute of Molecular Biology in Nutley, New Jersey, wrote in 1987 of his discovery that mouse eggs carry a molecular structure on their coating that fits inside a complementary structure on the sperm, helping bind the two together, he described the two structures, naturally enough, as a lock and key — but he called the egg's protruding structure the lock and the sperm's engulfing structure the key.

11   Martin doesn't suggest that these researchers willfully distorted their imagery. In fact, she notes that one of the investigators at Johns Hopkins was her politically correct husband, Richard Cone. What's more, Martin concedes that she herself was slow to recognize the disparity between the discoveries at Johns Hopkins and the way the findings were written up. "It didn't strike me for a few years," she says. But innocent or not, she adds, the cultural conditioning these biologists had absorbed early in their careers influenced more than their writing: it skewed their research. "I believe, and my husband believes, and the lab believes, that they would have seen these results sooner if they hadn't had these male-oriented images of sperm. In fact, biologists could have figured out a hundred years ago that sperm are weak forward-propulsion units, but it's hard for men to accept the idea that sperm are best at escaping. The imagery you employ guides you to ask certain questions and to not ask certain others."

12   People preparing to dismiss Emily Martin as a humorless feminist have their work cut out for them. At once animated and easygoing in her cramped, cactus-strewn office, Martin chuckles as she goes through an inch-thick file of hapless-egg and macho-sperm imagery clipped from magazines. (In one Gary Larson cartoon, a housewife egg fends off a swarm of sperm trying to get past her by posing as phone repairmen, insurance salesmen, and UPS deliverymen.) "I just think this stuff is a riot," she says. In fact, it's the biologists who seem a little stuffy. Though she usually lectures to students, Martin recalls one lecture she gave to biologists at the Woods Hole Oceanographic Institution in 1990. "It was one of the most painful experiences of my life," she says. "I had gotten to the point where the audience is usually rolling in the aisles, and all I got was stony silence. I could see they were furious. On the other hand, I can understand their feelings; I get defensive when someone criticizes cultural anthropology."

One researcher who doesn't bristle at Martin's jabs is Scott Gilbert, 13
a developmental biologist at Swarthmore College. Though he suggests
Martin may go a little overboard in stressing the egg's aggressiveness
— for example, he prefers to think of the egg as "engaging in a dialog"
with the sperm rather than gluing it down — he does believe her views
are a vast improvement over the conventional explanation. "Most studies clearly show that the sperm is attracted by the egg and activated by
it," says Gilbert. "But if you don't have an interpretation of fertilization
that allows you to look at the egg as active, you won't look for the molecules that can prove it. You simply won't find activities that you don't
visualize."

Now that the discrepancy between experiment and interpretation is 14
being brought out into the open, the professional literature seems to be
coming around — although a recent issue of the biology journal *Cell
Differentiation and Development* placed on its cover a Prince Charming sperm delivering a wake-up kiss to a long-eyelashed Sleeping Beauty
egg. As for the popular press, Gilbert and Martin cite the same recent
example as particularly egregious: an article titled "Sperm Wars" that
appeared as a cover story in a national science magazine whose name
you'd recognize in a minute, which referred to the sperm cell as "a formidable .00024-inch weapon, tipped with a chemical warhead" (see
DISCOVER, July 1991). On the other hand, *Developmental Biology,*
the most popular college textbook in its subject area, takes great pains
to point out the new, equal opportunity view of fertilization. No wonder: Gilbert wrote it.

One reason the older interpretation is dying hard is that it tends to be 15
self-reinforcing, not only in suggesting ready-made imagery that can
skew observations but also in subtly determining who becomes a biologist in the first place. "This business has stopped certain people from
entering the field," says Gilbert. "Why would a woman want to continue if people are telling her she's passive?"

Nevertheless, as Martin points out, a growing number of women *are* 16
continuing in biology. But that won't guarantee more evenhanded interpretations. "Scientific training involves a rigorous socialization process that doesn't allow for different perspectives," she says. "It's hard to
say that women biologists are any less guilty of these things than men."

Even if biologists do move away from the passive-egg myth, other 17
images are waiting in the wings. These days, says Martin, researchers
seem ready to confer a "spider woman" aspect on the egg. "Men have
always turned to spider imagery when they are confronted with women

who acquire power," she charges. Indeed, her file of magazine clippings contains several images in support of her claim. One striking example: the cartoonish silhouette employed as the emblem of the once-popular *Charlie's Angels* television series, which depicts the three starring female characters, guns and all, unmistakably merged into the eight-limbed shape of a spider.

18   Though Martin is the first to insist that much of the fertilization imagery is good for a laugh, she doesn't mean to let scientists dismiss it all as a big joke. "People say, 'Oh, what difference does it make?' as if this stuff doesn't affect anyone," she says. "But our culture *is* affected by these powerful visual images. We all put so much faith in science, and so much of the negative load lands on women."

19   She notes, as another example, that it's been known since the 1960s that women exposed to toxic chemicals bear children who run a higher risk of serious medical problems. Those findings reinforced the cultural notion that women should be sheltered, and some companies have rules to prevent women of reproductive age from working at jobs that might involve exposure to these chemicals. But only in the past few years have comparable studies shown that men exposed to high levels of lead, vinyl chloride, and about a dozen other chemicals also have children who are at higher risk. "It's the notion of invulnerable sperm," she claims, "that made it take so long for scientists and the public to accept the male role in birth defects and infertility."

20   Martin has recently shifted her focus to metaphors used in other areas of medical research. For example, she says, "when AIDS was seen as affecting only the 'dregs' of society, scientists described it as a monkey virus. Now that well-to-do white women are getting it, all of a sudden researchers are talking about AIDS being an autoimmune disease." There are, of course, other reasons that researchers' language might change, including a growing knowledge of how the AIDS virus in fact wreaks havoc on the host's immune system. Martin is still studying the literature and observing researchers in immunology labs. For now, she concedes, "all you can do is raise a question. It's often impossible to prove causality."

21   Although she is no longer studying fertilization imagery, Martin still lectures on the topic because, she contends, "the work shows that science can have social effects. When we anthropomorphize the egg and sperm, when we turn them into a miniature bride and groom complete with personalities, what effect does this have on abortion legislation? These effects aren't intended by scientists, but they happen. They blend

moral and scientific issues together in a way that makes me want to stand up and say something."

There's further irony in the traditional metaphors. The notion of 22 fiercely battling, competitive sperm suggests that they're battling each other in a "race" to the egg. In fact, says Cone, they have a hard time making their way through the mucus glop, and like a team of bicyclists they "take turns" up front parting strands of mucus. So in a sense sperm are cooperative. The egg, on the other hand, is the real competitive loner. Only one matures each month, and the one out in front suppresses the maturation of all the others. The macho image of sperm not only obscures this reality; it actually reverses what's been observed.

Can biased metaphors be eliminated from science? Martin doesn't 23 think so. Even if they could be, she doesn't think that antiseptically neutral language would be desirable. Metaphor is, after all, a powerful vehicle for creative thinking. "The goal shouldn't be to clean the imagery out," she says, "but to be aware that it's there." It also helps, she adds, to be able to take a joke. "Humor takes away the sting," she says, "along with the potential for inculcating harmful ideas."

(1992)

The Writer's Subject

1. What are the two descriptions of the fertilization process in the opening paragraph of the essay? What use does the writer make of metaphor in these descriptions?

2. What thesis does the opening paragraph set out to demonstrate?

3. What did the researcher Emily Martin find unusual about expectant mothers' references to their bodies? (para. 3)

4. What was it in the language of the reproductive sciences that made Martin feel that biological science was biased in favour of males? (paras. 4–5)

5. How, according to Emily Martin, have the findings of biological researchers been skewed by cultural conditioning? (para. 11) How might this affect what they see? (paras. 13, 19)

6. Why is Martin disturbed by the spider-image associated with the TV series *Charlie's Angels*? (para. 17) How is this relevant to her concerns with reproductive science?

7. How, in Martin's view, can biased language in science have significant social effects? (paras. 20–21)

The Writer's Style and Strategy

1. This essay is for the most part an account by one person of the research and opinions of others. In your opinion, does the writer succeed in giving full play to the ideas of the scientists he interviewed, without getting himself in the way? Does the reader get any sense of the personality or views of the writer of this piece?

2. Explain the reference in para. 4 to "warrior sperm and damsel-in-distress eggs." What figure of speech is involved here? How does it reflect the conclusions reached by Emily Martin?

3. What specific evidence does the essay provide that traditional views of the roles of sperm and egg need to be revised? (paras. 6–10, 22)

4. How does the writer support his assertion at the beginning of para. 12 that Emily Martin is not "a humorless feminist"?

5. What use does Freedman make of other scientific authorities to support Martin's point of view?

Suggested Topics for Writing and Discussion

1. Martin notes (para. 20) other areas of medical research in which metaphors reflect cultural biases. Choose a text in any branch of the sciences and examine its use of language. Are there any points at which the supposedly neutral tone of scientific writing gives way to more subjective — even biased — language?

2. Freedman's article was published in 1992. Find another recent discussion of the human reproductive cycle, and examine the terms used to describe the roles of the egg and the sperm. Do they reflect a more up-to-date understanding of the process?

3. Martin notes the importance of humour in dealing with potentially controversial scientific ideas. At one point she cites Woody Allen's film *Everything You Always Wanted to Know About Sex But Were Afraid to Ask*. Can you find any instances in any medium — film, television, radio, print, cartoons, advertising, etc. — of the humorous treatment of a scientific concept?

4. One scientist cited in the essay thinks that women might be dissuaded from becoming biologists by the older interpretation of the reproductive process (para. 15). Do you think that this viewpoint is valid? What other factors may still be at work in determining who, or who does not, enter a career in the sciences?

5. Martin is quoted as saying, "Studying your own culture is harder ... because everything seems so normal to you" (para. 2). Draw upon your own experience to describe an instance or instances when you have become aware that what appears "normal" in your own culture is odd or strange to someone from another culture.

Posture Maketh the Man

by Stephen Jay Gould

1   No event did more to establish the fame and prestige of The American
Museum of Natural History than the Gobi Desert expeditions of the
1920s. The discoveries, including the first dinosaur eggs, were exciting
and abundant, and the sheer romance fit Hollywood's most heroic mold.
It is still hard to find a better adventure story than Roy Chapman An-
drews's book (with its chauvinistic title): *The New Conquest of Central
Asia*. Nonetheless, the expeditions utterly failed to achieve their stated
purpose: to find in Central Asia the ancestors of man. And they failed
for the most elementary of reasons — we evolved in Africa, as Darwin
had surmised fifty years earlier.

2   Our African ancestors (or at least our nearest cousins) were discovered in cave deposits during the 1920s. But these australopithecines failed
to fit preconceived notions of what a "missing link" should look like,
and many scientists refused to accept them as bona fide members of
our lineage. Most anthropologists had imagined a fairly harmonious
transformation from ape to human, propelled by increasing intelligence.
A missing link should be intermediate in both body and brain — Alley
Oop or the old (and false) representations of stoopshouldered
Neanderthals. But the australopithecines refused to conform. To be sure,
their brains were bigger than those of any ape with comparable body
size, but not much bigger. Most of our evolutionary increase in brain
size occurred after we reached the australopithecine level. Yet these
small-brained australopithecines walked as erect as you or I. How could
this be? If our evolution was propelled by an enlarging brain, how could
upright posture — another "hallmark of hominization," not just an inci-

dental feature — originate first? In a 1963 essay, George Gaylord Simpson used this dilemma to illustrate

the sometimes spectacular failure to predict discoveries even when there is a sound basis for such prediction. An evolutionary example is the failure to predict discovery of a "missing link," now known [*Australopithecus*], that was upright and tool-making but had the physiognomy and cranial capacity of an ape.

We must ascribe this "spectacular failure" primarily to a subtle prejudice that led to the following, invalid extrapolation: We dominate other animals by brain power (and little else); therefore, an increasing brain must have propelled our own evolution at all stages. The tradition for subordinating upright posture to an enlarging brain can be traced throughout the history of anthropology. Karl Ernst von Baer, the greatest embryologist of the nineteenth century (and second only to Darwin in my personal pantheon of scientific heroes) wrote in 1828: "Upright posture is only the consequence of the higher development of the brain ... all differences between men and other animals depend upon construction of the brain." One hundred years later, the English anthropologist G. E. Smith wrote: "It was not the adoption of the erect attitude or the invention of articulate language that made man from an ape, but the gradual perfecting of a brain and the slow building of the mental structure, of which erectness of carriage and speech are some of the incidental manifestations." 3

Against this chorus of emphasis upon the brain, a very few scientists upheld the primacy of upright posture. Sigmund Freud based much of his highly idiosyncratic theory for the origin of civilization upon it. Beginning in his letters to Wilhelm Fliess in the 1890s and culminating in his 1930 essay on *Civilization and Its Discontents*, Freud argued that our assumption of upright posture had reoriented our primary sensation from smell to vision. This devaluation of olfaction shifted the object of sexual stimulation in males from cyclic odors of estrus to the continual visibility of female genitalia. Continual desire of males led to the evolution of continual receptivity in females. Most mammals copulate only around periods of ovulation; humans are sexually active at all times (a favorite theme of writers on sexuality). Continual sexuality has cemented the human family and made civilization possible; animals with strongly cyclic copulation have no strong impetus for stable family structure. "The fateful process of civilization," Freud concludes, "would thus have set in with man's adoption of an erect posture." 4

5   Although Freud's ideas gained no following among anthropologists, another minor tradition did arise to stress the primacy of upright posture. (It is, by the way, the argument we tend to accept today in explaining the morphology of australopithecines and the path of human evolution.) The brain cannot begin to increase in a vacuum. A primary impetus must be provided by an altered mode of life that would place a strong, selective premium upon intelligence. Upright posture frees the hands from locomotion and for manipulation (literally, from *manus* = "hand"). For the first time, tools and weapons can be fashioned and used with ease. Increased intelligence is largely a response to the enormous potential inherent in free hands for manufacture — again, literally. (Needless to say, no anthropologist has ever been so naive as to argue that brain and posture are completely independent in evolution, that one reached its fully human status before the other began to change at all. We are dealing with interaction and mutual reinforcement. Nevertheless, our early evolution did involve a more rapid change in posture than in brain size; complete freeing of our hands for using tools preceded most of the evolutionary enlargement of our brain.)

6   In another proof that sobriety does not make right, von Baer's mystical and oracular colleague Lorenz Oken hit upon the "correct" argument in 1809, while von Baer was led astray a few years later. "Man by the upright walk obtains his character," writes Oken, "the hands become free and can achieve all other offices. ... With the freedom of the body has been granted also the freedom of the mind." But the champion of upright posture during the nineteenth century was Darwin's German bulldog Ernst Haeckel. Without a scrap of direct evidence, Haeckel reconstructed our ancestor and even gave it a scientific name, *Pithecanthropus alalus*, the upright, speechless, small-brained ape-man. (*Pithecanthropus*, by the way, is probably the only scientific name ever given to an animal before it was discovered. When Du Bois discovered Java Man in the 1890s, he adopted Haeckel's generic name but he gave it the new specific designation *Pithecanthropus erectus*. We now usually include this creature in our own genus as *Homo erectus*.)

7   But why, despite Oken and Haeckel's demurral, did the idea of cerebral primacy become so strongly entrenched? One thing is sure; it had nothing to do with direct evidence — for there was none for any position. With the exception of Neanderthal (a geographic variant of our own species according to most anthropologists), no fossil humans were discovered until the closing years of the nineteenth century, long after the dogma of cerebral primacy was established. But debates based on

no evidence are among the most revealing in the history of science, for in the absence of factual constraints, the cultural biases that affect all thought (and which scientists try so assiduously to deny) lie nakedly exposed.

Indeed, the nineteenth century produced a brilliant exposé from a 8 source that will no doubt surprise most readers — Friedrich Engels. (A bit of reflection should diminish surprise. Engels had a keen interest in the natural sciences and sought to base his general philosophy of dialectical materialism upon a "positive" foundation. He did not live to complete his "dialectics of nature," but he included long commentaries on science in such treatises as the *Anti-Dühring*.) In 1876, Engels wrote an essay entitled, *The Part Played by Labor in the Transition from Ape to Man*. It was published posthumously in 1896 and, unfortunately, had no visible impact upon Western science.

Engels considers three essential features of human evolution: speech, 9 a large brain, and upright posture. He argues that the first step must have been a descent from the trees with subsequent evolution to upright posture by our ground-dwelling ancestors. "These apes when moving on level ground began to drop the habit of using their hands and to adopt a more and more erect gait. This was the decisive step in the transition from ape to man." Upright posture freed the hand for using tools (labor, in Engels's terminology); increased intelligence and speech came later.

> Thus the hand is not only the organ of labor, it is also the product of labor. Only by labor, by adaptation to ever new operations ... by the ever-renewed employment of these inherited improvements in new, more and more complicated operations, has the human hand attained the high degree of perfection that has enabled it to conjure into being the pictures of Raphael, the statues of Thorwaldsen, the music of Paganini.

Engels presents his conclusions as though they followed deductively 10 from the premises of his materialist philosophy, but I am confident that he cribbed them from Haeckel. The two formulations are almost identical, and Engels cites the relevant pages of Haeckel's work for other purposes in an earlier essay written in 1874. But no matter. The importance of Engels's essay lies, not in its substantive conclusions, but in its trenchant political analysis of why Western science was so hung up on the a priori assertion of cerebral primacy.

As humans learned to master their material surroundings, Engels ar- 11 gues, other skills were added to primitive hunting — agriculture, spinning, pottery, navigation, arts and sciences, law and politics, and finally,

"the fantastic reflection of human things in the human mind: religion."
As wealth accumulated, small groups of men seized power and forced
others to work for them. Labor, the source of all wealth and the primary
impetus for human evolution, assumed the same low status of those who
labored for the rulers. Since rulers governed by their will (that is, by
feats of mind), actions of the brain appeared to have a motive power of
their own. The profession of philosophy followed no unsullied ideal of
truth. Philosophers relied on state or religious patronage. Even if Plato
did not consciously conspire to bolster the privileges of rulers with a
supposedly abstract philosophy, his own class position encouraged an
emphasis on thought as primary, dominating, and altogether more noble and important than the labor it supervised. This idealistic tradition
dominated philosophy right through to Darwin's day. Its influence was
so subtle and pervasive that even scientific, but apolitical, materialists
like Darwin fell under its sway. A bias must be recognized before it can
be challenged. Cerebral primacy seemed so obvious and natural that it
was accepted as given, rather than recognized as a deep-seated social
prejudice related to the class position of professional thinkers and their
patrons. Engels writes:

> All merit for the swift advance of civilization was ascribed to the mind,
> to the development and activity of the brain. Men became accustomed to
> explain their actions from their thoughts, instead of from their needs ...
> And so there arose in the course of time that idealistic outlook on the
> world which, especially since the downfall of the ancient world, has domi-
> nated men's minds. It still rules them to such a degree that even the most
> materialistic natural scientists of the Darwinian school are still unable to
> form any clear idea of the origin of man, because under that ideological
> influence they do not recognize the part that has been played therein by
> labor.

12   The importance of Engels's essay does not lie in the happy result
that *Australopithecus* confirmed a specific theory proposed by him —
via Haeckel — but rather in his perceptive analysis of the political role
of science and of the social biases that must affect all thought.

13   Indeed, Engels's theme of the separation of head and hand has done
much to set and limit the course of science throughout history. Academic science, in particular, has been constrained by an ideal of "pure"
research, which in former days barred a scientist from extensive experimentation and empirical testing. Ancient Greek science labored under
the restriction that patrician thinkers could not perform the manual work

of plebeian artisans. Medieval barber-surgeons who had to deal with battlefield casualties did more to advance the practice of medicine than academic physicians who rarely examined patients and who based their treatment on a knowledge of Galen and other learned texts. Even today, "pure" researchers tend to disparage the practical, and terms such as "aggie school" and "cow college" are heard with distressing frequency in academic circles. If we took Engels's message to heart and recognized our belief in the inherent superiority of pure research for what it is — namely social prejudice — then we might forge among scientists the union between theory and practice that a world teetering dangerously near the brink so desperately needs.

(1973)

The Writer's Subject

1. Why did anthropologists formerly believe that growth of the brain must have preceded upright posture in the evolution of man? (para. 3)

2. What effect did the discovery of australopithecine man have upon older theories of the brain in the evolution of man?

3. What is the modern view regarding the relationship between brain size and posture as summarized by Gould in paragraph 5?

4. Why does Gould give so much prominence to the essay on evolution by the nineteenth-century political philosopher Engels, when, as Gould himself says, the scientific aspects of the essay were probably derived from the work of Ernst Haeckel? (paras. 8–13)

5. What is the particular class bias which Gould cites as operative in western society (i.e., from Plato's time onward)? How has this bias affected attitudes towards scientific research? (para. 11)

6. What is Gould's concluding plea concerning attitudes towards scientific research? (para. 13)

The Writer's Style and Strategy

1. What is the function of the opening paragraph of the essay?

2. Much of Gould's argument is conducted by reference to nineteenth and twentieth century authorities. How does Gould use these authorities to develop his thesis?

3. What use does Gould make of asides and parenthetical comments?

4. Why does Gould put the word "pure" in quotations in paragraph 13?

5. Gould is a scientist writing for non-scientists. What features of his style reflect his awareness of his intended audience? Where might he be addressing his arguments to his fellow scientists, too?

6. Comment on Gould's title. What phrase is it meant to echo?

Suggested Topics for Writing and Discussion

1. Gould says, "Debates based on no evidence are among the most revealing in the history of science, for in the absence of factual constraints, the cultural biases that affect all thought ... lie nakedly exposed." Consider one controversial topic (e.g., creationism vs. Darwinism, whether life exists on other planets, whether God exists, at what moment human life begins), and discuss the "cultural biases" that seem to underlie one side or other of the debate.

2. Gould is critical of what he calls "pure" research and implies an irresponsibility on the part of the scientific community. What do you think are the primary considerations that should govern scientific research? (Compare Gould's comments about the scientist's relationship to the society to those made by Bronowski in "The Real Responsibilities of the Scientist.")

3. Gould speaks of the class attitude, which he says prevailed until Darwin's day, that thought was "more noble and important than the labour it supervised." What attitudes does our own society have toward labour today?

Some Enemies of Science
by J.B.S. Haldane

Last week my wife successfully poisoned a number of rats. They were 1
eating the food of our chickens, and would have eaten the smaller of
the birds if they had got the chance. Owing to the failure of a more
humane poison she found herself compelled to use phosphorous; which
is a slow and, to judge from the experience of the human beings who
commit suicide by eating matches, often rather painful means of death.

During the same period I killed two rats in the course of experimen- 2
tal work intended to advance medical science. One of them, if we can
judge from human experience (and we have no more direct means of
evaluating the consciousness of animals), died after a period of rather
pleasant delirium like that of alcoholic intoxication. The other had con-
vulsions, and may have been in pain for three or four minutes. I should
be very thankful if I knew that I should suffer no more than it did before my death. It therefore seems to me somewhat ridiculous that,
whereas my wife is encouraged by the Government and the Press, I
should be compelled to apply to the President of the Royal Society and
another eminent man of science for signatures to an application to the
already overworked Home Secretary, before I can even kill a mouse in
a slightly novel manner.

It is probably right that some control should be kept over experiments 3
likely to involve severe and prolonged pain to animals; but it is monstrous
that with regard to wholly or nearly painless procedures the scientific man
should be worse treated than any other member of the community. 4

Under the present law, or, at any rate, under the law as at present
interpreted, a license is required for a large number of absolutely pain-

less experiments, and, what is more serious, they can only be performed in a limited number of laboratories. In consequence, the isolated amateur worker, who has played so great a part in the development of British science, is debarred from wide fields of physiology. The sportsman may go out and shoot as many rabbits as he pleases; and if some of them are wounded and escape to die a lingering death in their holes, no blame attaches to him. But if he anaesthetizes one of his own rabbits at home, and opens its abdomen to observe the effect of a drug on its intestines, killing it before it recovers consciousness, he will be lucky if he escapes with a fine.

5   Nor may the doctor, after his day's shooting of unanaesthetized partridges, acquire surgical skill by an operation on an anaesthetized animal, even in a licensed laboratory. He has to practise on human patients. There are, of course, a few operations of human surgery for which animals would furnish relatively little guidance. In the majority of cases, however, they would be of very real value, and have been proved to be so in America. Not only is medical science already greatly hampered by the law, but a constant fight has to be kept up to preserve what possibilities are left it. It is worth while enquiring into the reasons which have led to this state of affairs.

6   There are a few honest anti-vivisectionists. They are, of course, vegetarians; for the painless killing of animals for physiology is no more reprehensible than their killing for meat. They wear canvas shoes, cotton or woollen gloves, and artificial pearls if any. They refuse to sit on leather-covered chairs, or to wear horn-rimmed spectacles. They do not spray their roses, or employ Keating's powder even under the gravest provocation. I have not met any of them, but I am quite prepared to believe that they exist. No one who does not come up to this rather exacting standard can logically demand the total abolition of vivisection. But logic is not the strongest point of the enemies of science

7   All others who demand the prohibition of experiments on anaesthetized animals are quite definitely hypocrites, engaged in the familiar pursuit of

> 'Compounding sins they are inclined to
> By damning those they have no mind to.'

There are few more disgusting spectacles in our public life than that of the two or three sporting peers who habitually introduce or support Bills to prohibit such experiments. Each of them has caused more pain to animals in a single day's sport than the average physiologist inflicts in a lifetime, and usually for no end except his personal pleasure. For it seems to me that from the ethical point of view a fairly sharp distinction can be drawn between the killing of animals bred for this purpose at considerable expense, which would produce far more food if applied to agriculture; and that of rabbits, hares, and pigeons which must be kept down in the interest of crops and livestock. Personally, since I have realized from my own experience with shell splinters that it is no fun to carry bits of metal about one's person, I would no more shoot a rabbit than kill my bacon for breakfast. But I certainly do not condemn those who do so.

We must next consider the relatively small number of anti-vivisection- 8 ists who would merely prohibit all painful or possibly painful experiments. Now, the world is so constituted that we cannot avoid inflicting pain on others. I cannot dig in my garden without bisecting a number of earthworms, or drive a car for any time without running over a few of the various animals whose flattened corpses decorate our country roads. But it is our duty, as far as possible, to diminish the amount of pain in the world. The question therefore is whether medical research does this or not.

Now, anti-vivisectionist literature distorts both sides of the account. 9 It states that a great deal of severe suffering is inflicted on animals in the name of science, and that there is little or no return for this in the diminution of human and animal suffering. With regard to the first of these assertions I can speak with a certain degree of experience. I have seen numerous experiments on animals, but I have never seen an animal undergoing pain which I would not have been willing to undergo myself for the same object. Why, then, it may be asked, should not all painful experiments be done on human volunteers?

There are several reasons why not. One is the very simple fact that 10 many of these experiments possibly or necessarily involve the death of the animal. For example, rats are frequently inoculated under the skin of their sides with transplantable cancers. These are not painful, for the rat does not wince or squeak when the lump is pressed. If it were allowed to die of cancer it would often suffer; for the original tumour or its metastases elsewhere would press on nerves, and one of them would probably start to ulcerate. But before either of these events occurs, all such rats in the laboratory in which I work are killed, and the tumours used for chemical study of inoculation. A man, even if he could legally be used for such a purpose and chloroformed before pain began, would presumably suffer from the anticipation of an early death.

11   Just the same applies to deformity. A rickety child suffers mainly because it cannot take part in the activities of its comrades and is made to realize that it is deformed. A rickety rat has none of these disadvantages, not only because it is probably not self-conscious, but because under laboratory conditions all its acquaintances are rickety too. Finally, there is the question of expense. Human beings cost a lot in board and lodging, and must be compensated for loss of time. If, as in experiments on the effects of small changes in the diet, hundreds of individuals and years of time are needed, this consideration is generally final.

12   However, if we are to believe anti-vivisectionists, animals constantly undergo tortures which no human being would voluntarily endure. I recently received an illustrated pamphlet, which I should think is fairly typical, describing the sufferings of laboratory animals. There was a picture of an oven in which dogs were slowly heated till they died, while a physiologist watched their agonies through a window. The thought of such cruelty would have made my blood boil, if it had not already been partially boiled in such a chamber on several occasions. Under such circumstances one becomes dizzy long before there is any definite pain, and death, if it occurs, is from heat stroke, not from burning. Personally, I prefer being overheated in a bath. Immersion of all but the head in water kept hot enough just not to be painful, causes loss of consciousness, after a good deal of panting, in about twenty minutes. Hence there is reason to think that a lobster, if put into cold water and heated fairly slowly, feels no pain, which it must certainly do if dropped into boiling water. Probably, however, it would suffer still less if about 2½ per cent of salt were added to the cold water.

13   Then came a picture of a dog's mouth held open by a somewhat brutal-looking contrivance. This was said to be taken from a scientific periodical called the 'Transactions of the Physiological Society.' There is, unfortunately, no such journal, nor could I find the picture in the Proceedings of that body for the date given. Perhaps, therefore, it was the anti-visectionist's idea of what an instrument of scientific torture ought to look like. But if I had been a maiden lady with a pet dog and no knowledge either of the facts or the literature of physiology, I might have sent a cheque to one of the ladies and gentlemen who make a living by compiling documents of this kind.

14   In some cases experiments are supposed to be painful out of ignorance rather than malice. A group of experiments by Sir John Bradford, in which parts of the kidneys of dogs were removed under an anaesthetic, are constantly described in parliament as torture. Some of these

dogs recovered completely, others died with the symptoms of chronic kidney disease, which in human beings seldom causes any pain worse than a headache. Stone in the kidney can, of course, be very painful, but the dogs were not so treated as to cause them pain of this type, nor did they show any signs of suffering it. As a matter of fact, too, dogs can stand a good deal of wounding without much suffering, so far as one can judge. I know this, not from laboratory experience, but because I have owned a dog whose courage and love affairs constantly led him into fights with larger dogs.

A large part of the unhappiness of dogs in English laboratories is 15 directly due to the anti-vivisectionists. In the laboratory where I work there are a number of dogs, each of which, for two or three months in the year, eats certain organic compounds which it transforms in its body. The newly formed compounds are excreted in the urine. To facilitate the collection of urine an operation has been performed on them analogous to circumcision, and not nearly so severe as tail-docking. Of course, an anaesthetic was used. But because the operation has been performed in the cause of science rather than fashion, these dogs are forbidden by law to leave the laboratory. They are exercised in the grounds twice daily, but may not go into the street, and must lead a rather dull life. This regulation is typical of the present law, which is designed quite as much to hamper research as to protect animals.

While the large majority of experiments performed annually are nearly 16 painless, a few dozen, which attempt to reproduce a painful human disease, and thus to discover its cause or cure, are as painful as the disease which they imitate, except that when the animal's condition is clearly hopeless it can be killed.

I do not think it will be necessary to convince any reader of this book 17 of the value of medical research. It has been the principal cause which renders the worst slum of to-day healthier than the palace of a century ago. If that result had been reached by the infliction of appalling torture on millions of animals the ethical justification of this torture would certainly be a matter for discussion. Actually the fate of experimental rats, for example, is no worse than that of pet rats, which generally die from deficient diet or epidemic disease.

It remains to consider the psychology of anti-vivisectionists. I think 18 that their most important motive is a hatred of science, which they attack at its weakest point. They hate science partly because they do not understand it, and will not take the trouble to; partly because it is ethically neutral. Many of them feel that disease must be a punishment for

sin, and that it could be avoided if we lived according to their own particular prejudices. This view has been taken by most religions, though,
of course, Jesus did not share it (John, chap. 9, v. 3). Almost all believe
that there is some short cut to health. So a great many simple-lifers,
vegetarians, faith-healers, Christian scientists, and so forth, are opposed
to medical research, and say that its results are worthless.

19   In some cases anti-vivisection goes with pacifism. The fallacy involved in this association is rather interesting. Non-resistance of human
evil is sometimes effective. A certain percentage of human smiters are
seriously disconcerted if one turns the other cheek to them. But this
kind of method does not work on bacteria, which have no finer feelings. We cannot find out how they behave, and thus acquire power over
them, except by experiments on men or animals. This is a very unfortunate fact, but then the universe differs in a great many ways from what
we should wish it to be. Medicine continued on non-experimental lines
(with a very few exceptions) from the dawn of history till the seven-
teenth century. And in consequence it remained stationary during thousands of years. If its enemies get their way it will begin to stagnate again.

20   But there is a less respectable side to the anti-vivisectionist mind.
During the recent agitation against experiments on dogs I made an offer of £100 (published in the *Daily Mail*) to the National Canine Defence League, if they would produce any evidence for certain libels on
the medical profession which they were circulating in order to obtain
signatures for a petition. I got no answer from the league, but a number
of abusive and most instructive letters.

21   One of them, from E. Hough of Hammersmith, objected to experiments 'on the dear, faithful doggies for the benefit of worthless human
beings.' 'I like to think,' she wrote (for I picture the writer as an elderly
and soured spinster) 'that God will torture physiologists in a future life.
I would not lift a finger to save one of them if he were writhing in agony.'
There is, then, a group of anti-vivisectionists who like to think about
torture. As they can no longer attend the burning of atheists and witches,
they gloat over imaginary stories of animal torture till their blood boils;
and then cool it with the thought of physiologists in hell fire. Thanks
largely to the psychological mutilation to which our society subjects
adults, and more particularly children, the world is over-full of

'Ceux dont le rêve obscur salit tout ce qu'il touche,'[1]

and I suspect that a fair number of them become anti-vivisectionists.

22   Those who have benefited by the results of medical research and wish

it to continue might do worse than support the Research Defence Society, which carries on a lonely fight against a vast flood of lies. And they should urge the following alterations in the law, none of which would increase animal suffering in the faintest degree. Stray dogs impounded by the police should be used for experiment. This would abolish dog stealing for laboratories, and save the lives of some thousand dogs per year. No licence should be required for experiments on fully anaesthetized animals which are killed under the anaesthetic. Surgeons should be allowed to practise their art under the same conditions. Animals should not be condemned to imprisonment for life because an experiment has been done on them. And in the interests of national economy the number of officials and of Government forms used in the supervision of research should be cut down.

At present biological and medical research workers are enormously 23
handicapped by the law and by public opinion. Several hospitals, out of deference to subscribers, do not allow animal experiments. They thus render the rapid diagnosis of various diseases impossible, and kill a certain number of patients annually. And medical teaching is seriously handicapped in the same way. These are some of the reasons why England is less healthy than a number of other European countries. Antivivisectionists are responsible for far more deaths per year in England than motor vehicles, smallpox, or typhoid fever.

(1928)

Note

1. "Those whose dark dream dirties all that it touches."

The Writer's Subject

1. What is Haldane's point in contrasting his wife's use of rat poison and his own experiments? (paras. 1–2)

2. What, in Haldane's view, distinguishes the "honest anti-vivisectionists" from those he calls hypocrites? (paras. 6–7)

3. What are Haldane's reasons for rejecting the idea that all painful experiments should be carried out on human volunteers? (paras. 9–11)

4. On what grounds does Haldane blame the anti-vivisectionists for "a large part of the unhappiness of dogs in English laboratories"? (para. 15)

5. What motives does Haldane attribute to the anti-vivisectionists? (paras. 18–19)

6. What does he fear may happen to medical research if the anti-vivisection-ists get their way? (para. 19)

7. Why, according to Haldane, is England "less healthy than a number of European countries"? (para. 23)

The Writer's Style and Strategy

1. How does Haldane seek to convince his reader that animals used in ex-periments suffer little or no pain? (paras. 10, 12, 14)

2. What picture does Haldane draw of his opponents, the anti-vivisection-ists? What tone does he generally adopt in his description of them? Does he make use of any loaded terms in his references to them? (See, for ex-ample, paras. 6, 7 and 18.)

3. For what reason does Haldane allude to his own experience with shell splin-ters? (para. 7)

4. How does Haldane deal with the charges in the anti-vivisectionists' pam-phlet described in paragraphs 12 and 13? What does he imply about its authors at the end of paragraph 13?

5. How does Haldane make use of irony to answer his opponents in para-graph 19?

6. Why does Haldane give prominence to the letter from E. Hough in para-graph 21? Why does he picture the writer as "an elderly and soured spin-ster"?

7. Explain the function of paragraph 22.

Suggested Topics for Writing and Discussion

1. Haldane argues against the restrictions placed on scientists who wish to use animals for medical research. What is your view of this issue? Do you believe that scientists should be free to experiment with animals in the interests of reducing human suffering? Are there any restrictions which you think should be imposed?

2. Haldane complains that a hunter, unlike the scientist, may kill or maim animals without penalty. Write an argument for or against recreational hunting, addressing your argument to an audience opposed to your own views.

3. Choose one area of modern medical research (e.g., artificial organs or limbs, drug therapy, disease control, plastic surgery) and show the contribution it has made to the quality of life, either of the individual or of the society at large.

4. Haldane's essay originally appeared in 1928, but the issue which he addresses is still widely discussed. One present-day spokesman for those opposing the use of animals in experiments is Peter Singer, the author of *Animal Liberation*. Consult Singer's work and shape a response to Haldane's arguments.

5. Compare Haldane's views on the scientific use of animals with the views expressed by David Suzuki in "The Pain of Animals".

The Cathedral Square
by Jay Ingram

1   The cathedral square, the Piazza del Duomo, is the living heart of the northern Italian city of Milan. The square is dominated at the east end by the great cathedral, begun in 1386 but not completed until 1965, when the last of five bronze doors was installed. The cathedral impresses by size and complexity if not by elegance: made entirely from white and pink Italian marble, it's one of the biggest churches in the world, capable of accommodating up to 40,000 people (although full houses are said to be rare). Tourist books play up the numbers: 135 marble spires, 2,245 marble statues, and inside, 52 eighty-foot pillars, each bearing a crown of statues. D.H. Lawrence called it "an imitation hedgehog of a cathedral," but others have been a little more generous: Bill Bryson, in *Neither Here Nor There* thought it was "quite splendid in a murky sort of way."

2   In front of the cathedral is an open space about the size of a football field, and in the middle stands a statue of King Victor Emmanuel urging his troops on in battle. All the buildings which border the square are known intimately to the Milanese, but the most important is the Galleria, the great glassed-in nineteenth-century shopping mall. It opens out onto the square on the left side as you stand facing the cathedral, and is *the* place to meet, eat, drink and converse. It is also the way to La Scala, the great opera house. Imagine — a mall with history and class. Further along that same side of the square are the well-known restaurant/bar Motta (where you can prepare your own spaghetti dish from either regular or "gourmet" ingredients), the Duomo hotel and Rinascente, the department store. On the right side of the square as you face the cathedral

1. Cathedral
2. Galleria
3. The way to La Scala
4. Motta
5. Rinascente
6. Royal Palace
7. Arengario
8. Galtrucco
9. Statue of Victor Emmanuel

Cathedral square — aerial view.

are the outwardly unassuming Royal Palace at the far end, a small building called the Arengario (home these days for the tourist offices) and then
finally at the near corner the long-established Galtrucco, for expensive
made-to-measure men's suits. The tenants, shops and restaurants come
and go, but the buildings of the Piazza del Duomo remain unchanged,
and everyone who lives in Milan knows them intimately.

3   In 1978 neuropsychologist Edoardo Bisiach chose the Piazza del
Duomo as the site for an unusual experiment. Not actually the piazza
itself, but the mental representation of it. Bisiach had at the time two
stroke patients who had suffered damage to the right side of the brain.
One was an eighty-six-year-old woman, a retired manager, the other a
seventy-two-year-old male lawyer. Because most of the stroke damage
was on the right, and the brain's language centres are almost always on
the left, these two patients had escaped aphasia, the loss of speech that
is the most obvious result of a stroke. But what disability did they have?

4   Bisiach asked both of them to picture the Piazza del Duomo in their
mind's eye, and then list as many of the buildings as they could remember. The trick was that they were to imagine two different perspectives:
first standing at the end of the square looking towards the cathedral,
then standing on the cathedral steps and looking back towards where
they had previously imagined themselves to be. The results of this simple test cast a dramatic new light on one of the strangest phenomena in
the neuropsychologist's case book: unilateral neglect.

5   The eighty-six-year-old retired manager, when imagining herself looking towards the cathedral, listed the Royal Palace, the set of stairs just
in front of the Palace, the Arengario and further away (and not actually
visible to someone standing in the square) the Via delle Ore. All of these
are on the right side of the square as you look towards the cathedral.
She named nothing on the left at all. But when asked to describe the
vista from the cathedral steps, she came up with an entirely different
list of buildings, including jewellers' shops, a shirt shop, Motta and the
Via Dante — all of them on the right as you look from the cathedral
steps back down the square.

6   The lawyer did the same. Imagining the square with the cathedral in
front of him, he listed the cathedral itself, the corner of the Royal Palace, the Arengario, and Galtrucco (the men's wear shop at the extreme
right of this perspective). After mentally switching to the cathedral steps
and looking back, he listed a whole new set of buildings, streets, shops
and restaurants, including Motta and Rinascente. Again these are all on
the right side if you are standing in front of the cathedral.

This bias towards the right side of things (and lack of awareness of 7 the left) is called neglect. It usually happens after damage to the right part of the brain, especially in the parietal lobe, above and behind the right ear. Neglect patients act as if the left side of space doesn't exist. They eat only from the right side of the plate. If the plate is rotated so that the remaining food is now on the right side, the patient usually claims that the food somehow mysteriously appeared out of nowhere. (They're right: for them the left side *is* nowhere.) They may read only the right-hand words in a newspaper column, or even the right side of each word, or shave only the right side of the face (which of course is on the right in the mirror). Neglect is most severe immediately after a stroke, usually fading as the weeks pass.

This little sketch of neglect suggests that these patients might just 8 have a strange form of tunnel-vision, with the tunnel skewed to the left. But that is not true — it has been demonstrated over and over that damaged vision, although it might appear together with neglect as a result of the same stroke, doesn't necessarily lead to neglect, nor does neglect depend upon visual defects. Neglect is something beyond vision.

Edoardo Bisiach's experiment turned neglect into something much 9 more dramatic — and curious — than it had been before. He showed that patients suffering from neglect have a bias towards the right, not just when they're looking at something, but even when they are *imagining* it. Neglect can't be dependent on vision, because their mind's-eye world is skewed to the right as well. The lawyer in this experiment was also asked to describe the office he had worked in for decades, again from two perspectives, coming in the door and sitting at his desk. Again he was only aware, or could only report, objects that were on his right.

This experiment also underlines just how profound this right-handed 10 bias, or neglect of the left, is. The second description of the square and the office followed almost immediately upon the first, yet each contained a completely different set of landmarks. Yet at no time did these patients — or do most neglect patients — remark on the inconsistency or even absurdity of the situation. Where had the first set of buildings gone when each was reporting from the cathedral steps? Who knows? When prodded both were able to add to their list, even in one case mentioning a building on the left side, but fundamentally these two patients, although each obviously had a complete set of buildings in memory, were able to scan the right side of that mental layout only.

This is a little more complicated than it might seem at first glance, 11 because a typical resident of Milan probably has in his head both a list of buildings in the piazza and their location relative to each other. These might be two independent stores of information or the list of buildings might be inseparable from the imagined map of the square; either way, both the lay-out and the memory are disturbed in neglect.

12   The idea that you can neglect half of the world around you is difficult to understand. You might think that the obvious therapy for such patients would be to encourage them to train themselves to look at the left side of the plate, or to work harder to imagine the left side of the square. But although neurologist and author Oliver Sacks described a neglect patient who did learn to turn all the way around to her right (close to 360 degrees) to view things on the left (and even requested a rotating wheelchair to make it easier), most of the time this isn't feasible. People who are aware they have a blind spot obscuring the left side do learn to move their head to compensate. But people with neglect are usually unaware they have a problem. They literally don't know what they're missing. They don't see their mental image of the Piazza del Duomo as full and clear on the right and somehow fuzzy and/or abbreviated on the left. What they imagine, or perceive, is what there is. It is not that they have lost the concept of "left" — the patients in Bisiach's experiment knew the left-to-right distribution of the buildings they were aware of — it is that there is much less "left" than you or I would see or imagine. You can't convince someone who doesn't believe there's any more "left" out there to turn farther in that direction. Can one who is not experiencing neglect envision this experience? Not directly, but I think it is possible to get a feel for this peculiar alteration of personal space by adopting a completely different point of view.

13   In a book called *Flatland,* published more than a hundred years ago, author Edwin Abbott described what life would be like in two dimensions. Flatlanders, an assortment of circles, triangles, squares and straight lines, live in a world with no vertical dimension, no up and down. They are entirely unaware — and cannot even conceive — of a third dimension. They glide about in a surface film of a world, identifying each other by the reflection of light from their sides: a circle presents an image that is bright in the centre and fades gradually away on both sides, a square may be uniformly bright if seen side-on, but will appear as a bright point if presented corner first.

14   The hero of the story, a Flatlander named A. Square, is confronted by a stranger from a three-dimensional world called Spaceland. The stranger is a sphere, something that is completely alien to A. Square. As long as the sphere hovers over Flatland, he remains invisible (though

audible) to A. Square. A. Square can't look up, nor could he even understand what "looking up" would mean. When the sphere descends and pushes his way partly through Flatland, all that A. Square can see is a circle, the slice of the sphere that is at that moment in the plane of Flatland. To prove that he is more than just a circle, the sphere leaves Flatland by floating slowly upward. But to A. Square, this is no proof of an extra dimension, merely the demonstration that this particular circle was some kind of "extremely clever juggler" who had the unusual ability of being able to shrink to a point and even disappear completely, only to reappear unpredictably wherever he chose.

A. Square was completely incapable of imagining that this circle   15 whose size changed with time could be a single intact three-dimensional object. A patient suffering from neglect is equally unaware of the full dimensions of space, and the cathedral square experiment suggests that they would have great difficulty remembering a time when they were aware of the spatial world in its entirety. Edoardo Bisiach's experiment established that neglect affects not just the scene a patient may be viewing, but also the mental representation of that scene in the brain. It's an experiment that has served as the theme for many variations, each of which has yielded new insights into neglect.

One of the most startling twists was reported in 1993, again by Ital-   16 ian researchers, this time at the University of Rome. Their patient, a stroke victim, showed no signs of neglect in any of the standard psychological tests. These include putting a mark in the exact centre of a horizontal line (neglect patients put their mark far to the right of centre, as if the left side of the line doesn't exist), or drawing a clock face (neglect patients either pack all twelve numbers onto the right side of the face or simply leave out the numbers 7 through 11). Unlike this patient, Bisiach's two subjects had shown clear signs of neglect on such tests. This man apparently had a normal sense of the space he was viewing at any moment, yet when asked to describe from memory the layout of a famous square in Rome, the Piazza dei Cinquecento, he consistently missed buildings on the left, no matter which direction he imagined himself to be facing. (It's reassuring that most of these experiments have been done in Italy with Italian piazzas. You can imagine what subjects' testimony will be when and if these experiments are replicated in North America: "There's the McDonald's on the right just past the Taco Bell. The entrance to the mall is just behind the Wal-Mart with the six-decker parking lot behind that ...")

Whereas Bisiach showed that neglect affects the mental landscape as   17 well as the one being viewed, this man illustrates that the two can be separated, and that it is possible to be unable to pay attention to the left side of a mental scene, even though you might be perfectly capable of seeing, or attending to all of an actual scene you are viewing. This raises all kinds of interesting questions. If this man were actually standing in the Piazza del Cinquecento, and looking at the buildings on all sides, then was asked to close his eyes and name them, could he do it? If he could, would a half-minute to clear his short-term or "working" memory mean that he would lose that recently remembered picture of the square and, having to rely on a mental image, revert to neglecting the left? What if he were standing at one end, with his eyes open, and was asked to imagine standing at the other end looking back at himself — what would he describe?

18   This particular case was even more interesting because the damage to the brain was not in the area that is almost always affected in neglect: high up on the right side in what's called the parietal lobe. This man had suffered damage to the right frontal lobe — much farther forward, and practically on the other side of the country as far as the brain is concerned. It's not clear what the significance of this is. There are also patients who exhibit the reverse set of symptoms: severe neglect on all the standard tests, but an unimpaired ability to list from memory the buildings around a square, or describe what can be seen when driving in either direction on the same road. The bottom line is that in neglect the mental landscape can be intact while the visual is impaired, or vice-versa.

19   It's difficult to know what, if anything, these patients think about their situation. Most of the time they seem unaware of it, like Flatlanders accepting the dimensions of the space they know. One German patient attributed his near-collisions with cars as he was out walking to the "rude behaviour of the Berliners." Another would go to the local bakery every day, which was a short walk and a right turn from his home. On coming out of the bakery he would often turn right again (because of his neglect), find he'd gone too far, turn back and walk right past his house (now on his left), realize again he'd made a mistake, make an about-face and finally get home. He attributed his inability to walk directly home from the bakery to "absentmindedness," and came up with the classic neglect patient's view of the whole matter: "Your idea that I cannot see the whole space is one of the typical inventions of a scientist."

20   The more clinical reports of neglect patients you read, the more struck you are, not only by the strange symptoms but also by the listlessness of these patients. They just don't seem to care. Some of that could be

attributed to a kind of shock reaction to the terrible blow of a stroke, but even when neglect patients recover from the immediate effects of the stroke, and the neglect fades, they rarely offer any profound glimpses into the condition. So we are left wondering what it is like to inhabit the distorted landscape of the neglect patient and what it might tell us about the brain.

(1994)

The Writer's Subject

1. What is implied by the statement "Imagine — a mall with history and class"? (para. 2)

2. Why does the writer emphasize that the people of Milan are "intimately" familiar with the buildings in the Piazza del Duomo"? (para. 2)

3. Why did the psychologist Edoardo Bisiach choose the Piazza del Duomo as the site for his experiment?

4. What did the experiment reveal about the workings of the human brain?

5. Explain the term "neglect" as applied to the condition described in the essay.

6. What is the difference between impaired vision and "neglect"? (paras. 8–9)

7. In what way do patients suffering from "neglect" experience a "peculiar alteration of personal space"? (para. 12)

8. Why is it "reassuring" to the writer that many of the neglect experiments he describes have been done in Italy rather than in North America? (para. 16)

9. What was learned from the 1993 experiment described in paras. 16–18?

10. How do neglect patients typically react to their condition? (paras. 19–20)

The Writer's Style and Strategy

1. What sort of reader is Ingram writing for? How does this determine the way he explains the concept of "neglect"?

2. By what means does Ingram convey to the reader the experience of viewing the world from the perspective of a patient suffering from neglect?

3. How would this essay be affected if there were no diagram of the Piazza del Duomo?

4. What use does Ingram make of Edwin Abbott's book *Flatland*?

Suggested Topics for Writing and Discussion

1. Jay Ingram refers to the neurologist and author Oliver Sacks (para. 12). Choose an episode or chapter in one of Sacks' books, and compare the ways in which he and Ingram convey the complexities of the human brain to non-specialist readers.

2. Choose a scientific or technical journal that includes articles for the intelligent non-specialist. Comment on the article's effectiveness in conveying complex ideas to the non-specialist reader.

3. Write a short essay on a medical, scientific or a technological topic (e.g., the human heart, the piston engine, the computer chip, the unborn child) in which you provide the non-technical reader with a clear explanation in everyday language of the object or process involved.

4. If you have a friend or relative who has suffered a stroke, describe what you have observed about any changes in the way that person seems to see or experience the world.

The Discus Thrower
by Richard Selzer

"Do not go gentle"

I spy on my patients. Ought not a doctor to observe his patients by any 1
means and from any stance, that he might the more fully assemble evidence? So I stand in the doorways of hospital rooms and gaze. Oh, it is
not all that furtive an act. Those in bed need only look up to discover
me. But they never do.

From the doorway of Room 542 the man in the bed seems deeply 2
tanned. Blue eyes and close-cropped white hair give him the appearance of vigor and good health. But I know that his skin is not brown
from the sun. It is rusted, rather, in the last stage of containing the vile
repose within. And the blue eyes are frosted, looking inward like the
windows of a snowbound cottage. This man is blind. This man is also
legless — the right leg missing from midthigh down, the left from just
below the knee. It gives him the look of a bonsai, roots and branches
pruned into the dwarfed facsimile of a great tree.

Propped on pillows, he cups his right thigh in both hands. Now and 3
then he shakes his head as though acknowledging the intensity of his
suffering. In all of this he makes no sound. Is he mute as well as blind?

The room in which he dwells is empty of all possessions — no get- 4
well cards, small, private caches of food, day-old flowers, slippers, all
the usual kickshaws of a sickroom. There is only the bed, a chair, a
nightstand, and a tray on wheels that can be swung across his lap for
meals.

"What time is it?" he asks.   5

6   "Three o'clock."

7   "Morning or afternoon?"

8   "Afternoon."

9   He is silent. There is nothing else he wants to know. "How are you?"
I say.

10   "Who is it?" he asks.

11   "It's the doctor. How do you feel?" He does not answer right away.

12   "Feel?" he says.

13   "I hope you feel better," I say.

14   I press the button at the side of the bed.

15   "Down you go," I say.

16   "Yes, down," he says.

17   He falls back upon the bed awkwardly. His stumps, unweighted by
legs and feet, rise in the air, presenting themselves. I unwrap the band-
ages from the stumps, and begin to cut away the black scabs and the dead,
glazed fat with scissors and forceps. A shard of white bone comes loose.
I pick it away. I wash the wounds with disinfectant and redress the
stumps. All this while, he does not speak. What is he thinking behind
those lids that do not blink? Is he remembering a time when he was
whole? Does he dream of feet? Of when his body was not a rotting log?

18   He lies solid and inert. In spite of everything, he remains impressive,
as though he were a sailor standing athwart a slanting deck.

19   "Anything more I can do for you?" I ask.

20   For a long moment he is silent.

21   "Yes," he says at last and without the least irony. "You can bring me
a pair of shoes."

22   In the corridor, the head nurse is waiting for me.

23   "We have to do something about him," she says. "Every morning he
24   orders scrambled eggs for breakfast and, instead of eating them, he picks
up the plate and throws it against the wall."

25   "Throws his plate?"

26   "Nasty. That's what he is. No wonder his family doesn't come to visit.
They probably can't stand him any more than we can."

27   She is waiting for me to do something.

27   "Well?"

29   "We'll see," I say.

30   The next morning I am waiting in the corridor when the kitchen delivers his breakfast. I watch the aide place the tray on the stand and
swing it across his lap. She presses the button to raise the head of the
bed. Then she leaves.

In time the man reaches to find the rim of the tray, then on to find the 31
dome of the covered dish. He lifts off the cover and places it on the
stand. He fingers across the plate until he probes the eggs. He lifts the
plate in both hands, sets it on the palm of his right hand, centers it, balances it. He hefts it up and down slightly, getting the feel of it. Abruptly,
he draws back his right arm as far as he can.

There is the crack of the plate breaking against the wall at the foot of 32
his bed and the small wet sound of the scrambled eggs dropping to the
floor.

And then he laughs. It is a sound you have never heard. It is some- 33
thing new under the sun. It could cure cancer.

Out in the corridor, the eyes of the head nurse narrow. 34

"Laughed, did he?" 35

She writes something down on her clipboard. 36

A second aide arrives, brings a second breakfast tray, puts it on the 37
nightstand, out of his reach. She looks over at me shaking her head and
making her mouth go. I see that we are to be accomplices.

"I've got to feed you," she says to the man. 38

"Oh, no you don't" the man says. 39

"Oh, yes I do," the aide says, "after the way you just did. Nurse says 40
so."

"Get me my shoes," the man says. 41

"Here's oatmeal," the aide says. "Open." And she touches the spoon 42
to his lower lip.

"I ordered scrambled eggs," says the man. 43

"That's right," the aide says. 44

I step forward. 45

"Is there anything I can do?" I say. 46

"Who are you?" the man asks. 47

In the evening I go once more to that ward to make my rounds. The 48
head nurse reports to me that Room 542 is deceased. She has discovered this quite by accident, she says. No, there has been no sound. Nothing. It's a blessing, she says.

I go into his room, a spy looking for secrets. He is still there in his 49
bed. His face is relaxed, grave, dignified. After a while, I turn to leave.
My gaze sweeps the wall at the foot of the bed, and I see the place where
it has been repeatedly washed, where the wall looks very clean and very
white.

(1977)

The Writer's Subject

1. This essay takes the form of narration, with the usual elements of a story: character, plot, setting. The focus is on the central action, and there is no "thesis" in the sense of an explicit statement of meaning or intention. What, then, is the point of the essay? What meaning, or meanings, may be derived from the story Selzer tells?

2. Why does the doctor compare himself to a spy in the first and last paragraphs?

3. What is suggested about the doctor's patients by the last two sentences of the first paragraph?

4. What details reveal the doctor's feelings about the patient in Room 542? In what ways are the nurses' feelings different from the doctor's?

5. Suggest why the patient laughs as he breaks the plate of eggs. Why does it seem to the doctor that this laugh is "something new under the sun. It could cure cancer"?

6. Why does the patient ask for his shoes? What is Selzer's point in noting that the patient does so "without the least irony"?

The Writer's Style and Strategy

1. Discuss the purpose and the effectiveness of the comparisons of the patient to a snowbound cottage and a bonsai.

2. What is the effect of the phrase "vile repose"?

3. Discuss Selzer's use of dialogue as a means of revealing elements of character in the patient, the doctor, and the two nurses.

4. Why does Selzer choose not to give names to any of the people in his narrative?

5. How does Selzer use details of setting to enhance the mood of his narrative?

6. What is the effect of the phrase "Room 542 is deceased" in the conclusion?

7. How has the reader been prepared for the ending? How is it related to the essay's opening?

8. What are the connotations of the phrase, "The Discus Thrower"? Why is this title so effective (as compared with "The Plate Thrower," "A Difficult Patient," "The Dying Man," or some such title)?

Suggested Topics for Writing and Discussion

1. Offer an argument for or against the view that the terminally ill should be cared for, and allowed to die, at home rather than in a hospital.

2. Write a narrative describing an experience in which you have found yourself an involved observer (e.g., visiting a hospital patient, witnessing an accident).

3. Read Dylan Thomas's poem "Do not go gentle into that good night," and discuss Selzer's reasons for alluding to that poem in the epigraph to his essay. How does your reading of the poem enrich your understanding of Selzer's essay?

The Pain of Animals

by David Suzuki

1   Medical technology has taken us beyond the normal barriers of life and death and thereby created unprecedented choices in *human* lives. Until recently, we have taken for granted our right to use other species in any way we see fit. Food, clothing, muscle power have been a few of the benefits we've derived from this exploitation. This tradition has continued into scientific research where animals are studied and "sacrificed" for human benefit. Now serious questions are being asked about our right to do this.

2   Modern biological research is based on a shared evolutionary history of organisms that enables us to extrapolate from one organism to another. Thus, most fundamental concepts in heredity were first shown in fruit flies, molecular genetics began using bacteria and viruses and much of physiology and psychology has been based on studies in mice and rats. But today, as extinction rates have multiplied as a result of human activity, we have begun to ask what right we have to use all other animate forms simply to increase human knowledge or for profit or entertainment. Underlying the "animal rights" movement is the troubling question of where we fit in the rest of the natural world.

3   When I was young, one of my prized possessions was a BB gun. Dad taught me how to use it safely and I spent many hours wandering through the woods in search of prey. It's not easy to get close enough to a wild animal to kill it with a BB gun, but I did hit a few pigeons and starlings. I ate everything I shot. Then as a teenager, I graduated to a .22 rifle and with it, I killed rabbits and even shot a pheasant once.

4   One year I saw an ad for a metal slingshot in a comic book. I ordered

it, and when it arrived, I practised for weeks shooting marbles at a target. I got to be a pretty good shot and decided to go after something live. Off I went to the woods and soon spotted a squirrel minding its own business doing whatever squirrels do. I gave chase and began peppering marbles at it until finally it jumped onto a tree, ran to the top and found itself trapped. I kept blasting away and grazed it a couple of times so it was only a matter of time before I would knock it down. Suddenly, the squirrel began to cry — a piercing shriek of terror and anguish. That animal's wail shook me to the core and I was overwhelmed with horror and shame at what I was doing — for no other reason than conceit with my prowess with a slingshot, I was going to *kill* another being. I threw away the slingshot and my guns and have never hunted again.

All my life, I have been an avid fisherman. Fish have always been 5 the main source of meat protein in my family, and I have never considered fishing a sport. But there is no denying that it is exciting to reel in a struggling fish. We call it "playing" the fish, as if the wild animal's desperate struggle for survival is some kind of game.

I did "pleasure-fish" once while filming for a television report on the 6 science of fly fishing. We fished a famous trout stream in the Catskill Mountains of New York state where all fish had to be caught and released. The fish I caught had mouths gouged and pocked by previous encounters with hooks. I found no pleasure in it because to me fish are to be caught for consumption. Today, I continue to fish for food, but I do so with a profound awareness that I am a predator of animals possessing well-developed nervous systems that detect pain. Fishing and hunting have forced me to confront the way we exploit other animals.

I studied the genetics of fruit flies for twenty-five years and during 7 that time probably raised and killed tens of millions of them without a thought. In the early seventies, my lab discovered a series of mutations affecting behaviour of flies, and this find led us into an investigation of nerves and muscles. I applied for and received research funds to study behaviour in flies on the basis of the *similarity* of their neuromuscular systems to ours. In fact, psychologists and neurobiologists analyse behaviour, physiology and neuroanatomy of guinea pigs, rats, mice and other animals as *models* for human behaviour. So our nervous systems must closely resemble those of other mammals.

These personal anecdotes raise uncomfortable questions. What gives 8 us the right to exploit other living organisms as we see fit? How do we know that these other creatures don't feel pain or anguish just as we do? Perhaps there's no problem with fruit flies, but where do we draw the line? I used to rationalize angling because fish are cold-blooded, as if warm-bloodedness indicates some kind of demarcation of brain development or greater sensitivity to pain. But anyone who has watched a fish's frantic fight to escape knows that it exhibits all the manifestations of pain and fear.

9   I've been thinking about these questions again after spending a weekend in the Queen Charlotte Islands watching grey whales close up. The majesty and freedom of these magnificent mammals contrasted strikingly with the appearance of whales imprisoned in aquariums. Currently, the Vancouver Public Aquarium is building a bigger pool for some of its whales. In a radio interview, an aquarium representative was asked whether even the biggest pool can be adequate for animals that normally have the entire ocean to rove. Part of her answer was that if we watched porpoises in the pool, we'd see that "they are quite happy."

10   That woman was projecting human perceptions and emotions on the porpoises. Our ability to empathize with other people and living things is one of our endearing qualities. Just watch someone with a beloved pet, an avid gardener with plants or, for that matter, even an owner of a new car and you will see how readily we can personalize and identify with another living organism or an object. But are we justified in our inferences about captive animals in their cages?

11   Most wild animals have evolved with a built-in need to move freely over vast distances, fly in the air or swim through the ocean. Can a wild animal imprisoned in a small cage or pool, removed from its habitat and forced to conform to the impositions of our demands, ever be considered "happy"?

12   Animal rights activists are questioning our right to exploit animals, especially in scientific research. Scientists are understandably defensive, especially after labs have been broken into, experiments ruined and animals "liberated." But just as I have had to question my hunting and fishing, scientists cannot avoid confronting the issues raised, especially in relation to our closest relatives, the primates.

13   People love to watch monkeys in a circus or zoo and a great deal of the amusement comes from the recognition of ourselves in them. But our relationship with them is closer than just superficial similarities. When doctors at Loma Linda hospital in California implanted the heart of a baboon into the chest of Baby Fae, they were exploiting our close *biological* relationship.

14   Any reports on experimentation with familiar mammals like cats and dogs are sure to raise alarm among the lay public. But the use of primates

is most controversial. In September 1987, at the Wildlife Film Festival in Bath, England, I watched a film shot on December 7, 1986, by a group of animal liberationists who had broken into SEMA, a biomedical research facility in Maryland. It was such a horrifying document that many in the audience rushed out after a few minutes. There were many scenes that I could not watch. As the intruders entered the facility, the camera followed to peer past cage doors, opened to reveal the animals inside. I am not ashamed to admit that I wept as baby monkeys deprived of any contact with other animals seized the fingers of their liberators and clung to them as our babies would to us. Older animals cowered in their tiny prisons, shaking from fear at the sudden appearance of people.

The famous chimpanzee expert, Jane Goodall, also screened the same 15 film and as a result asked for permission to visit the SEMA facility. This is what she saw (*American Scientist*, November–December 1987):

> Room after room was lined with small, bare cages, stacked one above 16 the other, in which monkeys circled round and round and chimpanzees sat huddled, far gone in depression and despair.
>
> Young chimpanzees, three or four years old, were crammed, two to- 17 gether into tiny cages measuring 57 cm by 57 cm and only 61 cm high. They could hardly turn around. Not yet part of any experiment, they had been confined to these cages for more than three months.
>
> The chimps had each other for comfort, but they would not remain 18 together for long. Once they are infected, probably with hepatitis, they will be separated and placed in another cage. And there they will remain, living in conditions of severe sensory deprivation, for the next several years. During that time they will become insane.

Goodall's horror sprang from an intimate knowledge of chimpanzees 19 in their native habitat. There, she has learned, chimps are nothing like the captive animals that we know. In the wild, they are highly social, requiring constant interaction and physical contact. They travel long distances, and they rest in soft beds they make in the trees. Laboratory cages do not provide the conditions needed to fulfill the needs of these social, emotional and highly intelligent animals.

Ian Redmond (*BBC Wildlife*, April 1988) gives us a way to under- 20 stand the horror of what lab conditions do to chimps:

> Imagine locking a two- or three-year-old child in a metal box the size of 21 an isolette — solid walls, floor and ceiling, and a glass door that clamps shut, blotting out most external sounds — and then leaving him or her for

months, the only contact, apart from feeding, being when the door swings open and masked figures reach in and take samples of blood or tissue before shoving him back and clamping the door shut again. Over the past 10 years, 94 young chimps at SEMA have endured this procedure.

22   Chimpanzees, along with the gorilla, are our closest relatives, sharing ninety-nine per cent of our genes. And it's that biological proximity that makes them so useful for research — we can try out experiments, study infections and test vaccines on them as models for people. And although there are only about 40,000 chimps left in the wild, compared to millions a few decades ago, the scientific demand for more has increased with the discovery of AIDS.

23   No chimpanzee has ever contracted AIDS, but the virus grows in them, so scientists argue that chimps will be invaluable for testing vaccines. On February 19, 1988, the National Institute of Health in the U.S. cosponsored a meeting to discuss the use of chimpanzees in research. Dr. Maurice Hilleman, Director of the Merck Institute for Therapeutic Research, reported:

24   We need more chimps.... The chimpanzee is certainly a threatened species and there have been bans on importing the animal into the United States and into other countries, even though ... the chimpanzee is considered to be an agricultural pest in many parts of the world where it exists. And secondly, it's being destroyed by virtue of environmental encroachment — that is, destroying the natural habitat. So these chimpanzees are being eliminated by virtue of their being an agricultural pest and by the fact that their habitat is being destroyed. So why not rescue them? The number of chimpanzees for AIDS research in the United States [is] somewhere in the hundreds and certainly, we need thousands.

25   Our capacity to rationalize our behaviour and needs is remarkable. Chimpanzees have occupied their niche over tens of millennia of biological evolution. *We* are newcomers who have encroached on *their* territory, yet by defining them as *pests* we render them expendable. As Redmond says, "The fact that the chimpanzee is our nearest zoological relative makes it perhaps the unluckiest animal on earth, because what the kinship has come to mean is that we feel free to do most of the things to a chimp that we mercifully refrain from doing to each other."

26   And so the impending epidemic of AIDS confronts us not only with our inhumanity to each other but to other species.

(1989)

The Writer's Subject

1. Why has modern biological research depended so heavily on the use of animals?

2. Why did the squirrel-hunting experience described in paragraph 4 have such an effect on the young Suzuki?

3. Suzuki, himself a geneticist of note, is troubled by thoughts of the work he did on fruit flies (paras. 7–8). Why?

4. Why is Suzuki critical of the practice of keeping whales in aquariums?

5. Why, according to Suzuki, is the use of primates in research so controversial?

6. What role do chimpanzees play in the research on AIDS?

The Writer's Style and Strategy

1. How does Suzuki draw on personal experience to advance his argument?

2. Discuss the ways in which Suzuki appeals to the reader's emotions.

3. What use does Suzuki make of quotations from other sources?

4. How does Suzuki convey his own horror at some of the practices of research on animals? In this regard, comment on his use of connotative language, particularly in paragraphs 4 and 14.

Suggested Topics for Writing and Discussion

1. What are the arguments for and against keeping wild animals in zoos or aquariums?

2. Should scientists be permitted to make unrestricted use of animals in biological research?

3. Is it fair to animals to keep them as household pets for our own pleasure?

4. Suzuki gives particular prominence to the work of the chimpanzee expert Jane Goodall. Find out what you can about the significance of her studies of chimpanzee behaviour in the wild.

Humanities and Science
by Lewis Thomas

1 Lord Kelvin was one of the great British physicists of the late nine-teenth century, an extraordinarily influential figure in his time, and in some ways a paradigm of conventional, established scientific leader-ship. He did a lot of good and useful things, but once or twice he, like Homer, nodded. The instances are worth recalling today, for we have nodders among our scientific eminences still, from time to time, need-ing to have their elbows shaken.

2 On one occasion, Kelvin made a speech on the overarching impor-tance of numbers. He maintained that no observation of nature was worth paying serious attention to unless it could be stated in precisely quanti-tative terms. The numbers were the final and only test, not only of truth but about meaning as well. He said, "When you can measure what you are speaking about, and express it in numbers, you know something about it. But when you cannot — your knowledge is of a meagre and unsatisfactory kind."

3 But, as at least one subsequent event showed, Kelvin may have had things exactly the wrong way round. The task of converting observa-tions into numbers is the hardest of all, the last task rather than the first thing to be done, and it can be done only when you have learned, be-forehand, a great deal about the observations themselves. You can, to be sure, achieve a very deep understanding of nature by quantitative measurement, but you must know what you are talking about before you can begin applying the numbers for making predictions. In Kel-vin's case, the problem at hand was the age of the earth and solar sys-tem. Using what was then known about the sources of energy and the

loss of energy from the physics of that day, he calculated that neither the earth nor the sun were older than several hundred million years. This caused a considerable stir in biological and geological circles, especially among the evolutionists. Darwin himself was distressed by the numbers; the time was much too short for the theory of evolution. Kelvin's figures were described by Darwin as one of his "sorest troubles."

T.H. Huxley had long been aware of the risks involved in premature 4 extrapolations from mathematical treatment of biological problems. He said, in an 1869 speech to the Geological Society concerning numbers, "This seems to be one of the many cases in which the admitted accuracy of mathematical processes is allowed to throw a wholly inadmissible appearance of authority over the results obtained by them.... As the grandest mill in the world will not extract wheat flour from peascods, so pages of formulas will not get a definite result out of loose data."

The trouble was that the world of physics had not moved fast enough 5 to allow for Kelvin's assumptions. Nuclear fusion and fission had not yet been dreamed of, and the true age of the earth could not even be guessed from the data in hand. It was not yet the time for mathematics in this subject.

There have been other examples, since those days, of the folly of 6 using numbers and calculations uncritically. Kelvin's own strong conviction that science could not be genuine science without measuring things was catching. People in other fields of endeavor, hankering to turn their disciplines into exact sciences, beset by what has since been called "physics envy," set about converting whatever they knew into numbers and thence into equations with predictive pretensions. We have it with us still, in economics, sociology, psychology, history, even, I fear, in English-literature criticism and linguistics, and it frequently works, when it works at all, with indifferent success. The risks of untoward social consequences in work of this kind are considerable. It is as important — and as hard — to learn when to use mathematics as how to use it, and this matter should remain high on the agenda of consideration for education in the social and behavioral sciences.

Of course, Kelvin's difficulty with the age of the earth was an excep- 7 tional, almost isolated instance of failure in quantitative measurement in nineteenth-century physics. The instruments devised for approaching nature by way of physics became increasingly precise and powerful, carrying the field through electromagnetic theory, triumph after triumph, and setting the stage for the great revolution of twentieth-century physics. There is no doubt about it: measurement works when the instruments work, and when you have a fairly clear idea of what it is that is being measured, and when you know what to do with the numbers when they tumble out. The system for gaining information and comprehension about nature works so well, indeed, that it carries another hazard: the risk of convincing yourself that you know everything.

8   Kelvin himself fell into this trap toward the end of the century. (I don't mean to keep picking on Kelvin, who was a very great scientist; it is just that he happened to say a couple of things I find useful for this discussion.) He stated, in a summary of the achievements of nineteenth-century physics, that it was an almost completed science; virtually everything that needed knowing about the material universe had been learned; there were still a few anomalies and inconsistencies in electromagnetic theory, a few loose ends to be tidied up, but this would be done within the next several years. Physics, in these terms, was not a field any longer likely to attract, as it previously had, the brightest and most imaginative young brains. The most interesting part of the work had already been done. Then, within the next decade, came radiation, Planck, the quantum, Einstein, Rutherford, Bohr, and all the rest — quantum mechanics — and the whole field turned over and became a brand new sort of human endeavor, still now, in the view of many physicists, almost a full century later, a field only at its beginnings.

9   But even today, despite the amazements that are turning up in physics each year, despite the jumps taken from the smallest parts of nature — particle physics — to the largest of all — the cosmos itself — the impression of science that the public gains is rather like the impression left in the nineteenth-century public mind by Kelvin. Science, in this view, is first of all a matter of simply getting all the numbers together. The numbers are sitting out there in nature, waiting to be found, sorted and totted up. If only they had enough robots and enough computers, the scientists could go off to the beach and wait for their papers to be written for them. Second of all, what we know about nature today is pretty much the whole story: we are very nearly home and dry. From here on, it is largely a problem of tying up loose ends, tidying nature up, getting the files in order. The only real surprises for the future — and it is about those that the public is becoming more concerned and apprehensive — are the technological applications that the scientists may be cooking up from today's knowledge.

10   I suggest that the scientific community is to blame. If there are disagreements between the world of the humanities and the scientific enterprise as to the place and importance of science in a liberal-arts education,

and the role of science in twentieth-century culture, I believe that the scientists are themselves responsible for a general misunderstanding of what they are really up to.

Over the past half century, we have been teaching the sciences as **11** though they were the same academic collection of cut-and-dried subjects as always, and — here is what has really gone wrong — as though they would always be the same. The teaching of today's biology, for example, is pretty much the same kind of exercise as the teaching of Latin was when I was in high school long ago. First of all, the fundamentals, the underlying laws, the essential grammar, and then the reading of texts. Once mastered, that is that: Latin is Latin and forever after will be Latin. And biology is precisely biology, a vast array of hard facts to be learned as fundamentals, followed by a reading of the texts.

Moreover, we have been teaching science as though its facts were **12** somehow superior to the facts in all other scholarly disciplines, more fundamental, more solid, less subject to subjectivism, immutable. English literature is not just one way of thinking, it is all sorts of ways. Poetry is a moving target. The facts that underlie art, architecture, and music are not really hard facts, and you can change them any way you like by arguing about them, but science is treated as an altogether different kind of learning: an unambiguous, unalterable, and endlessly useful display of data needing only to be packaged and installed somewhere in one's temporal lobe in order to achieve a full understanding of the natural world.

And it is, of course, not like this at all. In real life, every field of **13** science that I can think of is incomplete, and most of them — whatever the record of accomplishment over the past two hundred years — are still in the earliest stage of their starting point. In the fields I know best, among the life sciences, it is required that the most expert and sophisticated minds be capable of changing those minds, often with a great lurch, every few years. In some branches of biology the mind-changing is occurring with accelerating velocities. The next week's issue of any scientific journal can turn a whole field upside down, shaking out any number of immutable ideas and installing new bodies of dogma, and this is happening all the time. It is an almost everyday event in physics, in chemistry, in materials research, in neurobiology, in genetics, in immunology. The hard facts tend to soften overnight, melt away, and vanish under the pressure of new hard facts, and the interpretations of what appear to be the most solid aspects of nature are subject to change, now more than at any other time in history. The conclusions reached in science are always, when looked at closely, far more provisional and tentative than are most of the assumptions arrived at by our colleagues in the humanities.

14 The running battle now in progress between the sociobiologists and the antisociobiologists is a marvel for students to behold, close up. To observe, in open-mouthed astonishment, the polarized extremes, one group of highly intelligent, beautifully trained, knowledgeable, and imaginative scientists maintaining that all sorts of behavior, animal and human, are governed exclusively by genes, and another group of equally talented scientists saying precisely the opposite and asserting that all behavior is set and determined by the environment, or by culture, and both sides brawling in the pages of periodicals such as *The New York Review of Books*, is an educational experience that no college student should be allowed to miss. The essential lesson to be learned has nothing to do with the relative validity of the facts underlying the argument, it is the argument itself that is the education: we do not yet know enough to settle such questions.

15 It is true that at any given moment there is the appearance of satisfaction, even self-satisfaction, within every scientific discipline. On any Tuesday morning, if asked, a good working scientist will gladly tell you that the affairs of the field are nicely in order, that things are finally looking clear and making sense, and all is well. But come back again, on another Tuesday, and he may let you know that the roof has just fallen in on his life's work, that all the old ideas — last week's ideas in some cases — are no longer good ideas, that something strange has happened.

16 It is the very strangeness of nature that makes science engrossing. That ought to be at the center of science teaching. There are more than seven-times-seven types of ambiguity in science, awaiting analysis. The poetry of Wallace Stevens is crystal-clear alongside the genetic code.

17 I prefer to turn things around in order to make precisely the opposite case. Science, especially twentieth-century science, has provided us with a glimpse of something we never really knew before, the revelation of human ignorance. We have been used to the belief, down one century after another, that we more or less comprehend everything bar one or two mysteries like the mental processes of our gods. Every age, not just the eighteenth century, regarded itself as the Age of Reason, and we have never lacked for explanations of the world and its ways. Now, we are being brought up short, and this has been the work of science. We have a wilderness of mystery to make our way through in the centuries ahead, and we will need science for this but not science alone. Science

will, in its own time, produce the data and some of the meaning in the data, but never the full meaning. For getting a full grasp, for perceiving real significance when significance is at hand, we shall need minds at work from all sorts of brains outside the fields of science, most of all the brains of poets, of course, but also those of artists, musicians, philosophers, historians, writers in general.

It is primarily because of this need that I would press for changes in 18 the way science is taught. There is a need to teach the young people who will be doing the science themselves, but this will always be a small minority among us. There is a deeper need to teach science to those who will be needed for thinking about it, and this means pretty nearly everyone else, in hopes that a few of these people — a much smaller minority than the scientific community and probably a lot harder to find — will, in the thinking, be able to imagine new levels of meaning that are likely to be lost on the rest of us.

In addition, it is time to develop a new group of professional think- 19 ers, perhaps a somewhat larger group than the working scientists, who can create a discipline of scientific criticism. We have had good luck so far in the emergence of a few people ranking as philosophers of science and historians and journalists of science, and I hope more of these will be coming along, but we have not yet seen a Ruskin or a Leavis or an Edmund Wilson. Science needs critics of this sort, but the public at large needs them more urgently.

I suggest that the introductory courses in science, at all levels from 20 grade school through college, be radically revised. Leave the fundamentals, the so-called basics, aside for a while, and concentrate the attention of all students on the things that are *not* known. You cannot possibly teach quantum mechanics without mathematics, to be sure, but you can describe the strangeness of the world opened up by quantum theory. Let it be known, early on, that there are deep mysteries, and profound paradoxes, revealed in their distant outlines, by the quantum. Let it be known that these can be approached more closely, and puzzled over, once the language of mathematics has been sufficiently mastered.

Teach at the outset, before any of the fundamentals, the still impon- 21 derable puzzles of cosmology. Let it be known, as clearly as possible, by the youngest minds, that there are some things going on in the universe that lie beyond comprehension, and make it plain how little is known.

Do not teach that biology is a useful and perhaps profitable science; 22 that can come later. Teach instead that there are structures squirming inside all our cells, providing all the energy for living, that are essentially foreign creatures, brought in for symbiotic living a billion or so years ago, the lineal descendants of bacteria. Teach that we do not have the ghost of an idea how they got there, where they came from, or how they evolved to their present structure and function. The details of oxidative phosphorylation and photosynthesis can come later.

23   Teach ecology early on. Let it be understood that the earth's life is a system of interliving, interdependent creatures, and that we do not understand at all how it works. The earth's environment, from the range of atmospheric gases to the chemical constituents of the sea, has been held in an almost unbelievably improbable state of regulated balance since life began, and the regulation of stability and balance is accomplished solely by the life itself, like the internal environment of an immense organism, and we do not know how that one works, even less what it means. Teach that.

24   Go easy, I suggest, on the promises sometimes freely offered by science. Technology relies and depends on science these days, more than ever before, but technology is nothing like the first justification for doing research, nor is it necessarily an essential product to be expected from science. Public decisions about what to have in the way of technology are totally different problems from decisions about science, and the two enterprises should not be tangled together. The central task of science is to arrive, stage by stage, at a clearer comprehension of nature, but this does not mean, as it is sometimes claimed to mean, a search for mastery over nature. Science may provide us, one day, with a better understanding of ourselves, but never, I hope, with a set of technologies for doing something or other to improve ourselves. I am made nervous by assertions that human consciousness will someday be unraveled by research, laid out for close scrutiny like the workings of a computer, and then, *and then!* I hope with some fervor that we can learn a lot more than we now know about the human mind, and I see no reason why this strange puzzle should remain forever and entirely beyond us. But I would be deeply disturbed by any prospect that we might use the new knowledge in order to begin doing something about it, to improve it, say. This is a different matter from searching for information to use against schizophrenia or dementia, where we are badly in need of technologies, indeed likely one day to be sunk without them. But the ordinary, everyday, more or less normal human mind is too marvelous an instrument ever to be tampered with by anyone, science or no science.

25   The education of humanists cannot be regarded as complete, or even adequate, without exposure in some depth to where things stand in the

various branches of science, and particularly, as I have said, in the areas of our ignorance. This does not mean that I know how to go about doing it, nor am I unaware of the difficulties involved. Physics professors, most of them, look with revulsion on assignments to teach their subject to poets. Biologists, caught up by the enchantment of their new power, armed with flawless instruments to tell the nucleotide sequences of the entire human genome, nearly matching the physicists in the precision of their measurements of living processes, will resist the prospect of broad survey courses; each biology professor will demand that any student in his path must master every fine detail within that professor's research program. The liberal-arts faculties, for their part, will continue to view the scientists with suspicion and apprehension. "What do the scientists want?" asked a Cambridge professor in Francis Cornford's wonderful *Microcosmographia Academica*. "Everything that's going," was the quick answer. That was back in 1912, and universities haven't much changed.

26   The worst thing that has happened to science education is that the great fun has gone out of it. A very large number of good students look at it as slogging work to be got through on the way to medical school. Others look closely at the premedical students themselves, embattled and bleeding for grades and class standing, and are turned off. Very few see science as the high adventure it really is, the wildest of all explorations ever undertaken by human beings, the chance to catch close views of things never seen before, the shrewdest maneuver for discovering how the world works. Instead, they become baffled early on, and they are misled into thinking that bafflement is simply the result of not having learned all the facts. They are not told, as they should be told, that everyone else — from the professor in his endowed chair down to the platoons of post doctoral students in the laboratory all night — is baffled as well. Every important scientific advance that has come in looking like an answer has turned, sooner or later — usually sooner — into a question. And the game is just beginning.

27   An appreciation of what is happening in science today, and of how great a distance lies ahead for exploring, ought to be one of the rewards of a liberal-arts education. It ought to be a good in itself, not something to be acquired on the way to a professional career but part of the cast of thought needed for getting into the kind of century that is now just down the road. Part of the intellectual equipment of an educated person, however his or her time is to be spent, ought to be a feel for the queernesses of nature, the inexplicable things.

28   And maybe, just maybe, a new set of courses dealing systematically with ignorance in science might take hold. The scientists might discover in it a new and subversive technique for catching the attention of students driven by curiosity, delighted and surprised to learn that science is exactly as Bush described it: an "endless frontier." The humanists, for their part, might take considerable satisfaction watching their scientific colleagues confess openly to not knowing everything about everything. And the poets, on whose shoulders the future rests, might, late nights, thinking things over, begin to see some meanings that elude the rest of us. It is worth a try.

(1983)

The Writer's Subject

1. What, according to Thomas, was the nineteenth-century view of the importance of numbers and quantitative measurement? What showed the limitations of this view? (paras. 1–5)

2. How does the uncritical use of numbers and calculations persist into our own day? (para. 6)

3. What "trap" did Lord Kelvin fall into? (paras. 7–8)

4. According to Thomas, what is the impression of science held by the general public? Who does he maintain is primarily responsible for creating this impression? (paras. 9–10)

5. What point is Thomas making when he compares the current teaching of science with the teaching of Latin? (para. 11)

6. How does Thomas counter the view that scientific facts are "more solid, less subject to subjectivism" than facts in other disciplines? (paras. 12–13)

7. What "essential lesson" is to be learned from following the public controversy between sociobiologists and their opponents? (para. 14)

8. What does Thomas mean by his assertion that "The poetry of Wallace Stevens is crystal-clear alongside the genetic code"? (para. 16)

9. Why does Thomas attach importance to the scientific education of nonscientists? What role does he foresee for poets, historians, and philosophers? (paras. 17–19)

10. What changes does Thomas suggest in the teaching of science? What does he think such teaching should emphasize? (paras. 20–24)

11. What are Thomas's objections to specialization in education? (para. 25)

The Writer's Style and Strategy

1. What is Thomas's purpose?

2. What kind of audience does Thomas have in mind for this essay? Support your view with specific references.

3. What are the general characteristics of Thomas's diction and sentence style? How appropriate are they to his purpose and audience?

4. Why does Thomas begin his essay by recounting the errors of the famous nineteenth-century English scientist, Lord Kelvin?

5. At what point does Thomas shift from an attack on erroneous ways of thinking about science to proposals for change? How is this shift signalled?

6. What patterns of diction and sentence structure does Thomas employ to add force to his arguments in paragraphs 20–23?

Suggested Topics for Writing and Discussion

1. Thomas argues that a knowledge of science should be "part of the intellectual equipment of an educated person, however his or her time is spent." What aspects of modern science do you think an educated person should know something about? Provide examples to support your view.

2. Thomas believes that it is vital for humanists to acquire some understanding of science. Discuss the corollary of this view: that courses in the humanities should be included in the education of scientists.

3. In the course of his essay, Thomas rejects the view that the task of science is to seek "mastery over nature," and expresses concern at the possibility that technology may be misapplied to achieve such a goal. Is there any evidence that Thomas's fears may be justified? What developments in modern science or medicine do you think should be regarded with concern?

4. Thomas says, "The worst thing that has happened to science education is that the great fun has gone out of it." Do you agree? To support your view, use examples from a particular area of science education (e.g., a programme in college or university, the curriculum for children in a particular stage of school).

5. Lewis Thomas, Rachel Carson, and David Suzuki all point to the dangers and problems of living in, as Carson says, "an era of specialists, each of whom sees his own problem and is unaware of the larger frame into which it fits." Argue for or against the training of specialists in our society.

Unexpected Vistas
by James Trefil

1   One of the great rewards of hiking or backpacking is to follow a trail and, suddenly and without warning, top a hill or come to a break in the trees and see the panorama of the countryside laid out before you. The view of the distant waterfall or rolling hills is often remembered as the high point of the entire excursion.

2   Such experiences occur in intellectual life, too. The moment of the "Aha!" — which cartoonists usually render by showing a light bulb coming on above someone's head — is an analogous happening. So too is the unexpected discovery that two things seemingly unconnected with each other are in fact intimately related. But while every hiker on a given trail will see the same view, the intellectual vista has the property that each person who comes to it can see something entirely different.

3   For example, imagine a line of motorists at a traffic light. Each of them is looking at the same thing, a rectangular yellow box with three colored lights in it. But it is possible, even likely, that each of them *sees* something very different from the others. Suppose that the first person in line is an electrical engineer. To him, the traffic light is just one appendage of a large computer-operated grid that regulates the movement of vehicles throughout the downtown area. If you pressed him to go on — to describe the far reaches of his view — he might start musing about the light as one example of control systems and eventually wind up talking about the best-designed control system of them all, the human brain.

4   The driver of the second car in line is the representative of a large manufacturing firm. He sees the traffic light as an item that is built in a factory and sold to the city. After thinking for a while, he might go on

to talk about the vast interconnecting web of economic activity, from mining to maintenance work, that has to be in place before something like a traffic signal is possible. He might even end with some general speculations about human beings as tool-making animals.

In the third car is an attorney. To him the traffic light might symbol- 5
ize the set of laws human beings have developed. The mechanical or economic aspect of the device would be much less important than the rules of conduct it symbolizes. After all, at any given moment there are thousands of cars being driven in a city, and almost every driver obeys the traffic signals. Behind this display of mass obedience, our attorney may see the vast structure of the modern legal system, from legislators to courts to police officers. If pressed, he might go on to speculate about those aspects of the human character that require such a system to al-low large groups of people to live together in relative harmony.

Each of our motorists sees the traffic light as part of a large intercon- 6
nected network. The simple apparatus is seen to be just one aspect of an important system that governs some aspect of our lives. In a sense, the traffic light is like an object in the foreground of some marvelous medieval landscape painting, a device the artist uses to induce us to look further and see the rich tapestry of nature and civilization that lies be-hind it. I will call each driver's view of the traffic light a vista, a term that carries with it the connotation of wide-ranging view.

So the traffic light teaches us several important lessons. It tells us 7
that the breadth and scope of the vista really have very little to do with the object that starts us looking. Whether the traffic light is seen as just a self-contained mechanical device or as part of a much larger system is primarily a function of the individual looking at it, and, more impor-tantly, of that individual's training and habits of thought.

The traffic light also teaches us that two individuals looking at the 8
same thing need not see the same vista. It's almost as if two hikers reach the same point in a trail, from which one sees a waterfall while the other sees a shady forest. We can often get an entirely different view of the world just by talking to people whose backgrounds lead them to see vistas different from our own.

Like other professionals, scientists have their unique vistas. It would 9
be a mistake, however, to assume that all scientists share a common view of things. I was frequently surprised during the several years I spent as part of an interdisciplinary team in cancer research by just how much the training of the other team members affected the way they looked at our work. To a biologist a cell is part of an evolving, growing, living

system; to a physicist it is a "black box" that processes energy and produces an ordered system; to a statistician it is one more bit of data to put into a computer program. Clearly, there is no such thing as a single, monolithic "scientific" vista.

(1983)

The Writer's Subject

1. How does Trefil's use of the word "vista" unite the ideas in paragraphs 1 and 2?

2. Trefil says in paragraph 2 that "every hiker on a given trail will see the same view," but he goes on to say in paragraph 8 that "two individuals looking at the same thing need not see the same vista." Is this simply a contradiction?

3. What principle is Trefil demonstrating by his example of the motorists and the traffic light?

4. Why does Trefil state that "there is no such thing as a single, monolithic 'scientific' vista" (para. 9)?

The Writer's Style and Strategy

1. In discussing the nature of perception and the "intellectual vista," Trefil is dealing with abstract, intangible ideas. How does he help the reader to grasp these ideas?

2. What is Trefil's general pattern of reasoning: inductive or deductive?

3. Examine the concluding paragraph. How does its development reflect the pattern of discussion that precedes it?

Suggested Topics for Writing and Discussion

1. Trefil makes the point that "two individuals looking at the same thing need not see the same vista." With this in mind, put yourself into the place of two different persons and write brief descriptions on one of the topics below. Or, choose two "vistas" of another subject which interests you.

    (a) A prison, from the viewpoint of an inmate and of a guard.

    (b) A college or university from the viewpoint of a student and of a worker in the campus cafeteria.

    (c) An alpine meadow from the point of view of a hiker and of a real estate developer.

    (d) A funeral from the point of view of a child and of an adult.

2. Choose a process or concept which you have recently been introduced to in one of the subjects which you are studying. Put yourself in the position of a tutor and use an extended analogy to explain the matter in everyday, simple, or familiar terms.

3. Write a well-developed paragraph using an analogy. You may wish to use one of the topics which follow.

   (a) A university or college education as a savings account.

   (b) A selling technique as a method for catching fish.

   (c) A freshman at registration as a mouse in a maze.

   (d) The university or college curriculum as a smorgasbord.

4. Using one of the following topics as a starting point, develop an essay of explanation by means of an analogy.

   (a) Falling in love.

   (b) Writing an essay.

   (c) Stopping trade in drugs.

   (d) Listening to music.

Biographical Notes

ADDISON, Joseph (1672–1719)

English playwright, essayist, and critic; celebrated for his style, particularly in his contributions to the periodicals *The Spectator, Tatler,* and *The Guardian.*

ALLEN, Woody (b. 1935)

Pseudonym of Heywood Allen Konigsberg; American film director, writer, actor, and comedian; widely acclaimed for such films as *Annie Hall* (1977; Academy Award) and *Hannah and Her Sisters* (1986); author of *Getting Even* (1971), *Without Feathers* (1975), and *Side Effects* (1981), and *Three Films: Broadway Danny Rose, Zelig, and The Purple Rose of Cairo* (1987).

AMIS, Martin (b. 1949)

Oxford-born critic and editor, frequent contributor to such periodicals as the *Times Literary Supplement, New Statesman,* and *New Yorker;* author of many novels, including *Time's Arrow* (1991) and *The Information* (1995).

ANDERSEN, Kurt (b. 1954)

U.S.-born writer and editor; he has worked for NBC Television and *Time Magazine,* and was editor of *Harvard Lampoon.* Co-author of *Tools of Power* (1980).

ANDERSON-DARGATZ, Gail (b. 1963)

British Columbia-born author of *The Miss Hereford Stories* (1994) and the award-winning *The Cure for Death by Lightning* (1996).

ATWOOD, Margaret (b. 1939)

Canadian poet, critic, novelist; winner of Governor General's awards for poetry (*The Circle Game,* 1966), and for fiction (*The Handmaid's Tale,* 1985). Her most recent novel is *Alias Grace* (1996).

BACON, Francis (1561–1626)

English statesman and philosopher; writer on learning and scientific method (*The Advancement of Learning,* 1605; *Novum Organum,* 1620).

BAKER, Russell (b. 1925)

American journalist and humourist, long-time columnist for the *New York Times,* and winner of two Pulitzer Prizes.

BARRECA, Regina (b. 1957)

A native of Brooklyn, New York; educated at Dartmouth, Cambridge, and CUNY. An English professor at the University of Connecticut, author and editor of many books, including *Sex and Death in Victorian Literature* (1990), *The Penguin Book of Women's Humor* (1994), and *The Erotics of Instruction* (1997).

BETTELHEIM, Bruno (1903–1990)

Austrian-born American professor of educational psychology, author of studies on emotionally-disturbed children and child rearing, including *The Empty Fortress* (1967), *The Children of the Dream* (1969), and *The Uses of Enchantment: The Meaning and Importance of Fairy Tales* (1976).

BIBBY, Geoffrey (b. 1917)

British archaeologist, author of *Testimony of the Spade* (1956) and *Four Thousand Years Ago: A World Panorama of Life in the Second Millenium B.C.* (1961).

BISSOONDATH, Neil (b. 1955)

Canadian novelist and short story writer, born in Trinidad. Author of *Digging Up the Mountains: Selected Stories* (1985), *On the Eve of Uncertain Tomorrows* (1990), and *Selling Illusions: The Cult of Multiculturalism in Canada* (1994).

BRODY, Hugh (b. 1943)

British anthropologist; participant in research on Inuit and Indian language and customs in Canada, and author of a number of studies, including *The People's Land* (1975), *Maps and Dreams: Indians and the British Columbia Frontier* (1981), and *The Living Arctic* (1987).

BRONOWSKI, Jacob (1903–1974)

Polish-born English scientist, critic, essayist; concerned for much of his life with the relationship between art, science, and human values, examined in such books as *The Common Sense of Science* (1951), *Science and Human Values* (1956), and *The Ascent of Man* (1973).

CARSON, Rachel (1907–1964)

Biologist for U.S. Fish and Wildlife Service from 1936–1952; author of *The Sea Around Us* (1951), *The Edge of the Sea* (1955), *Silent Spring* (1962).

CASTILLO, Edward D.

Chair of Native American Studies at Sonoma State University; a California Cahuilla Indian. Editor of *Native American Perspectives on the Hispanic Colonization of Alta California* (1992).

CREAN, Susan (b. 1945)

Art critic and observer of Canadian culture. She is the author of *Who's Afraid of Canadian Culture?* (1973), *Two Nations: An Essay on the Culture and Politics of Canada and Quebec* (1983), and *Newsworthy: The Lives of Media Women* (1985). More recently, she was the editor of *Twist and Shout: A Decade of Feminist Writing in This Magazine* (1991).

DE QUINCEY, Thomas (1785–1859)

An Oxford-educated writer and critic, friend of the poets Wordsworth and Coleridge, and best known for his *Confessions of an English Opium-Eater* (1822).

DOBBS, Kildare (b. 1923)

Canadian journalist; born in India, served in British colonial service in Tanganyika 1948–52; author of *Running to Paradise* (1962; Governor General's Award).

DRYDEN, Ken (b. 1947)

Canadian lawyer, formerly star goaltender for the Montreal Canadiens; author of *The Game* (1984), a study of professional hockey, and *In School: Our Kids, Our Teachers, Our Classrooms* (1995).

EISELEY, Loren (1907–1977)

Anthropologist, historian, and philosopher of science, author of many books and articles explaining science to the lay reader (*Darwin's Century*, 1958; *Firmament of Time*, 1960; *The Star Thrower*, 1978).

FARR, Moira

A Canadian freelance writer based in Toronto. A contributing editor of *This Magazine*.

FLANNER, Janet (1892–1978)

Regular contributor to the *New Yorker* from 1925–75, with her "Letter from Paris." under the pseudonym "Genet."

FORSTER, E.M. (1879–1970)

Novelist, essayist, writer of short stories; best known for *A Room with a View* (1908), *Howard's End* (1910), and *A Passage to India* (1924).

FRANCIS, Daniel (b. 1947)

A native of British Columbia, Francis has worked as a journalist in Medicine Hat and Ottawa. Author of *Battle for the West: Fur Traders and the Birth of Western Canada* (1982), and *Discovery of the North: Exploration in Canada's Arctic* (1986).

FRASER, Fil

A journalist born and raised in Montreal's East End; formerly with AC-CESS, Alberta's educational television network, he is now President of Vision TV.

FREEDMAN, David H. (b. 1954)

Journalist and science writer.

FRYE, Northrop (1912–1991)

Critic, editor, professor of English at University of Toronto; one of the most influential literary theorists of his time; author of many books, including *Anatomy of Criticism* (1957); *The Bush Garden: Essays on the Canadian Imagination* (1971); *The Great Code: The Bible and Literature* (1982); and *The Double Vision: Language and Meaning in Religion* (1991).

GIANGRANDE, Carole (b. 1945)

Canadian author of *The Nuclear North: The People, the Regions and the Arms Race* (1983), *Down to Earth: The Crisis in Canadian Farming* (1985), and *Missing Persons* (1994).

GOULD, Stephen Jay
Harvard paleontologist and geology professor, author of award-winning books on evolution and biological determinism, including *Ever Since Darwin* (1977), *The Mismeasure of Man* (1981), *The Flamingo's Smile: Reflections in Natural History* (1985), *Wonderful Life: The Burgess Shale and the Nature of History* (1990), and *Questioning the Millennium* (1997).

HALDANE, J.B.S. (1892–1964)
Controversial English geneticist and biochemist, known for his eccentric scientific methods, and for his work on heredity; author of many books and essays on science and society.

HIGHSMITH, Patricia (1921–1995)
A native of Texas, Highsmith spent much of her life writing and travelling in Europe. A prolific novelist and short-story writer, she is perhaps best known for her first novel, *Strangers on a Train* (1950), adapted for the screen by Alfred Hitchcock in 1951.

HIMMELFARB, Gertrude (b. 1922)
Born in New York, professor of history at Brooklyn College and the Graduate School of the City University of New York 1965–78; Fellow of the British Academy and the American Academy of Arts and Sciences. Author of many books and articles, including *Darwin and the Darwinian Revolution* (1959) and *The Idea of Poverty: England in the Industrial Age* (1984).

HOBAN, Russell (b. 1925)
American author of books for children, including *The Mouse and His Child* (1967), and for adults, including *Turtle Diary* (1975) and *Riddley Walker* (1980).

HOGGART, Richard (b. 1918)
British academic, critic, and educator. Contributor to many collections of critical essays; author of the influential study *The Uses of Literacy* (1957) and numerous other books, including *Only Connect* (The Reith Lectures, 1972) and *The Future of Broadcasting* (1982).

IGLAUER, Edith
American-born writer who has written about Canada's North in such books as *Denison's Ice Road* (1975) and *Inuit Journey* (1979); married commercial fisherman John Daly, about whom she wrote in *Fishing with John* (1988); a frequent contributor to major national magazines such as the *New Yorker* and *Maclean's*.

INGRAM, Jay
Canadian broadcaster and writer on science; host of CBC's science program *Quirks and Quarks* for many years. He has written non-fiction for children (*Twins: An Amazing Investigation*, 1988), as well as adults (*The Science of Everyday Life*, 1990, and *The Burning House: Unlocking the Mysteries of the Brain*, 1994).

JOHNSON, Samuel (1709–1784)
English essayist, poet, critic, editor, and lexicographer (*A Dictionary of the English Language*, 1755).

JOHNSTON, Basil H. (b. 1929)
An Ojibway writer born on Parry Island Indian Reserve, Ontario; member of the Ethnology Department at the Royal Ontario Museum; author of many short stories, essays and books on First Nations' culture and history, including *Ojibway Heritage* (1976), *How the Birds Got Their Colours* (1978), *Indian School Days* (1988), and *The Manitous: The Spiritual World of the Ojibway* (1995).

KAEL, Pauline (b. 1919)
Controversial film critic for the *New Yorker* from 1968–1991; many of her reviews are collected in book form (*Kiss Kiss, Bang Bang*, 1968; *Deeper into the Movies*, 1973; *When the Lights Go Down*, 1980; *Movie Love*, 1991). Received a National Book Award in 1974 for *Deeper into the Movies*.

KEESHIG-TOBIAS, Lenore
Toronto-based Ojibway poet, storyteller and cultural activist; past editor of *Ontario Indian*; writer of a number of children's tales, editor of *Into the Moon: Heart, Mind, Body, Soul: The Native Women's Writing Circle* (1996).

KENNEDY, X.J. (b. 1929)
Pseudonym of Joseph Charles Kennedy, poet, professor of English, editor of literary anthologies; author of *An Introduction to Poetry* (1990) and *Dark Horses: New Poems* (1992).

KOERTGE, Noretta (b. 1935)
American-born professor of history and philosophy of science at Indiana University, editor of *Philosophy and Homosexuality* (1985), author of several novels, including *Valley of the Amazons* (1984), and co-author (with Daphne Patai) of *Professing Feminism: Cautionary Tales from the Strange World of Women's Studies* (1994).

LAURENCE, Margaret (1926–1987)
Canadian writer best known for her novels of prairie life, including *A Jest of God* (1966) and *The Diviners* (1974), both of which received a Governor General's Award. Her memoir, *Dance on the Earth*, appeared posthumously in 1989.

LEACOCK, Stephen (1869–1944)
Economics professor at McGill, and a prolific writer of humorous books, including *Literary Lapses* (1910), *Sunshine Sketches of a Little Town* (1912), and *Arcadian Adventures with the Idle Rich* (1914).

LURIE, Alison (b. 1926)
English professor and novelist; Pulitzer Prize in fiction for *Foreign Affairs* (1984). Recent works include *Don't tell the Grown-ups: Subversive Children's Literature* (1990) and *Women and Ghosts* (1994).

MacLENNAN, Hugh (1907–1990)
Canadian novelist, essayist, and former English professor at McGill University; winner of five Governor General's Awards; his novels include *Two Solitudes* (1945), *The Watch That Ends the Night* (1959), and *Voices in Time* (1980).

MORRIS, Jan (b. 1926)
British writer, born James Morris, name changed to Jan after sex change in 1972. A distinguished journalist for the London *Times* and the *Manchester Guardian*; fellow of the Royal Society of Literature; author of many books on travel and history, including *Venice* (1960, 1974), *Oxford* (1965, 1978), *Among the Cities* (1985), and *City to City* (1990).

MOWAT, Farley (b. 1921)
Born in Ontario; a fierce and controversial defender of life in the Canadian Arctic (*People of the Deer*, 1952) and of animals threatened by humans(*Never Cry Wolf*, 1963, *A Whale for the Killing*, 1972, and *Sea of Slaughter*, 1982). Recent work includes *Aftermath: Travel in a Post-War World* (1995).

NATOLI, Joseph (b. 1943)
A native New Yorker, Natoli is a writer and critic, has taught English and the humanities, and has worked as a bibliographer and librarian. He has written on literary theory, psychological perspectives on literature, and film theory. Books include *A Postmodern Reader* (1993), co-edited with Linda Hutcheon.

ORWELL, George (1903–1950)
Pseudonym of English political journalist and satirist Eric Blair; served with the Indian Imperial Police in Burma, 1922–27; fought with the Republicans in Spain, describing the experience in *Homage to Catalonia* (1938); author of *Animal Farm* (1945) and *Nineteen Eighty-Four* (1949).

PLUMB, John Harold (b. 1911)
Cambridge historian, broadcaster, contributor to journals; author of many books on cultural and political history, and of a work on the nature of history, *The Death of the Past* (1969).

RICHLER, Mordecai (b. 1931)
Canadian satirist, author of essays and novels, including *The Apprenticeship of Duddy Kravitz* (1959), *St. Urbain's Horseman* (1971; Governor General's Award), and *Solomon Gursky Was Here* (1990). His most recent work of fiction is *Barney's Version*, winner of the 1997 Giller Prize.

ROYKO, Mike (1932–1997)
Reporter and columnist for Chicago newspapers since 1959, winner of Pulitzer Prize in 1972.

RYBCZYNSKI, Witold Marian (b. 1943)
Scottish-born architect and planner. Author of several books, including

Home: A Short History of an Idea (1986), *The Most Beautiful House in the World* (1989), *Waiting for the Weekend* (1991), and *City Life: Urban Expectations in a New World* (1995).

SALUTIN, Rick (b. 1942)

A critic, playwright, novelist, journalist, and contributing editor of *This Magazine*. His works include the plays *1837: The Farmer's Revolt* (1976) and *Les Canadiens* (1977), the novel *A Man of Little Faith* (1988), and two works of non-fiction, *Waiting for Democracy: A Citizen's Journal* (1989) and *Living in a Dark Age* (1992).

SELZER, Richard (b. 1928)

Surgeon, essayist, writer of short stories. Collections of his essays include *Confessions of a Knife* (1979) and *Rituals of Surgery* (1987).

SILLITOE, Alan (b. 1928)

Self-educated English novelist and short-story writer, author of such anti-establishment works as *Saturday Night and Sunday Morning* (1958) and *The Loneliness of the Long-Distance Runner* (1959).

STEGNER, Wallace (1909–1993)

Formerly professor of English at Stanford; writer about the American and Canadian West (*The American West as Living Space*, 1987); writer of short stories and novels, winning a Pulitzer Prize for *Angle of Repose* (1971), and author of *On the Teaching of Creative Writing* (1988).

STEINEM, Gloria (b. 1934)

Journalist; a leading figure in the American feminist movement; founded *Ms.* magazine in 1972. Author of *Marilyn* (1986), a book on Marilyn Monroe, and an autobiographical work, *Revolution from Within* (1992).

SUZUKI, David (b. 1936)

Canadian scientist, academic, and broadcaster, renowned for his work in genetics; the host of the CBC television programme *The Nature of Things*. Among his books are *Genethics: The Clash Between the New Genetics and Human Values* (1989), *The Wisdom of the Elders* (1992), and *Time to Change: Essays* (1994).

SWIFT, Jonathan (1667–1745)

Irish satirist and pamphleteer; dean of St. Patrick's in Dublin; critic of English policy in Ireland; author of *Gulliver's Travels* (1726).

TAN, Amy (b. 1952)

Award-winning Chinese-American author of novels, essays, and short stories. Her best-known work is *The Joy Luck Club* (1989), for which she also wrote the screenplay. Tan has also worked as a reporter and a free-lance technical writer.

TAYLOR, Helen (1831–1907)

An advocate of political and legal rights for women, and daughter of the English feminist Harriet Taylor Mill, Taylor spent several years on the stage before becoming devoted secretary to her stepfather John Stuart Mill, whose *Autobiography* she edited in 1873.

THOMAS, Lewis (1913–1993)

Formerly professor of pathology; head of Sloan-Kettering Cancer Center; contributor of many articles to medical and scientific journals, some cllected in the National Book Award-winning *Lives of a Cell: Notes of a Biology Watcher* (1974) and in *Late Night Thoughts on Listening to Mahler's Ninth Symphony* (1983). His most recent work is *Et Cetera, Et Cetera: Notes of a Language Watcher* (1990).

THOREAU, Henry David (1817–1862)

American essayist, naturalist, and poet. He taught school in Concord, Massachusetts and there wrote *Walden, or, Life in the Woods* (1854), an account of the two years he spent living alone in a hut by Walden Pond, near Concord. He is perhaps best known for his essay on civil disobedience, written after his brief imprisonment for failing to pay a state poll tax in 1845.

TREFIL, James (b. 1938)

Professor and author of works explaining developments in science to the general public (*From Atoms to Quarks*, 1980; *The Unexpected Vista*, 1983). His other works include *Space, Time, Infinity: The Smithsonian Views the Universe* (1985), and *Science Matters: Achieving Scientific Literacy*, coauthored with Robert M. Hazen (1991).

TRUDEAU, Garry B. (b. 1948)

American cartoonist and writer, best known for his "Doonesbury" comic strip, and winner of a Pulitzer Prize in 1975 for editorial cartooning. He is a distant relative of former Prime Minister Pierre Trudeau.

TUCHMAN, Barbara (1912–1989)

Journalist, historian, winner of Pulitzer Prizes for *The Guns of August* (1962) and *Stillwell and the American Experience in China, 1911–1945* (1971).

TWAIN, Mark (1835–1910)

Pseudonym of Samuel Langhorne Clemens, steamboat pilot, prospector, journalist; celebrated as a lecturer and humorist; author of *The Adventures of Tom Sawyer* (1876), *Life on the Mississippi* (1883), *The Adventures of Huckleberry Finn* (1884).

VANDERHAEGHE, Guy (b. 1951)

Canadian novelist and short story writer; author of collection *Man Descending* (1982; Governor General's Award). Longer works of fiction include *My Present Age* (1984), *Homesick* (1989), and *The Englishman's Boy* (Governor General's Award, 1996).

VISSER, Margaret (b. 1940)

South-African born professor of Classics; author of *Much Depends on*

Dinner: The Extraordinary History and Mythology, Allure and Obsessions, Perils and Taboos, of an Ordinary Meal (1986), The Rituals of Dinner (1991), and The Way We Are (1994).

WALKER, Martin (b. 1947)

English journalist, novelist, and social commentator who has reported on international affairs for the *Manchester Guardian* for many years. Books include *The National Front* (1977), *Daily Sketches* (a history of political cartoons) (1978), *The Waking Giant: The Soviet Union under Gorbachev* (1986), and *The Cold War: A History* (1994).

WELSH, Christine

Saskatchewan-born Métis writer and film-maker with a particular interest in the experience of aboriginal women in Canada. Writer and producer of the National Film Board documentary film *Women in the Shadows* (1991); writer and director of *Keepers of the Fire* (National Film Board, 1994).

WHITE, E.B. (1899–1985)

Journalist, essayist, contributor to the *New Yorker* for over half a century; author of renowned children's books *Stuart Little* (1945) and *Charlotte's Web* (1952).

WILSON, Edward O. (b. 1929)

Harvard professor of zoology, one of the world's leading experts on the insect world, whose book *Sociobiology: The New Synthesis* (1975) put forward controversial theories about genetic determinism and human behaviour. His book *On Human Nature* (1978) was awarded the 1979 Pulitzer Prize in general non-fiction. Recent publications include *The Diversity of Life* (1992).

WOODCOCK, George (1912–1995)

Canadian critic; friend and biographer of George Orwell (*The Crystal Spirit*, 1966); prolific writer of travel books, critical studies, literary and social histories. In 1959 founded *Canadian Literature*, which he edited until 1977.

WOOLF, Virginia (1882–1941)

Innovative and influential English novelist (*To the Lighthouse*, 1927; *The Waves*, 1931), a literary critic, and an early advocate of feminism (*A Room of One's Own*, 1929).

Glossary

Abstract   This is used in two ways: first, to mean general as opposed to specific or particular; second, to mean general as distinguished from concrete, a physical embodiment (e.g., *home* is abstract; a *wooden-frame house* is concrete). While writers may rely upon abstractions to some extent, they usually introduce **concrete** or specific details to give the abstraction matter, body, and meaning.

Allusion   A fleeting or casual reference to a well known person, place, thing, event, or phrase. These may be real or fictional. Allusions are generally drawn from history, literature, mythology, the *Bible,* or other such sources. Examples: Cleopatra, the shot heard around the world (the assassination of the Archduke Ferdinand), Tom Sawyer, Athena, Eve. Allusions are an economical way for writers to enlarge upon a statement.

Analogy   A comparison of some length; analogy is usually employed to explain something new in terms of something familiar, something unknown in terms of the known. (See Trefil's "Unexpected Vistas.") Analogy is frequently employed in argument, usually to dramatize the writer's position, but it is often open to question because the two things compared, though they may be alike in many points, may not be alike in all essential points.

Analysis   A method of exposition which employs logical division. The writer uses analysis to break the topic into component parts as a means of organizing the discussion.

Argument   A prose form which, in presenting a particular view, assumes that there are two sides to the issue under discussion; the writer of argument aims to influence readers to see the matter from the writer's point of view, to change their beliefs and opinions. The writer usually employs one or more of the other prose forms — exposition, narration, description — to present an argument. In trying to prove a point, the argumentative writer employs **logic** by appealing to reason with various kinds of proofs. The writer of argument usually defines terms and explains facts and ideas. Logical argument usually proceeds by **inductive reasoning** (from specific examples to a general conclusion) or **deductive reasoning** (from premises to a logical conclusion).

Another element of argument which has some importance is the demonstration of the speaker's good character in the establishing of the line of argument. Look, for example, at the closing paragraphs of Swift's "Modest Proposal" to see how the speaker seeks to demonstrate his disinterestedness in the cause he advances.

A distinction is usually made between **argument** and **persuasion**. The argumentative writer employs *logic* to appeal to the reader's intellect with the aim to change the reader's mind whereas the persuasive writer employs various devices of *pathos* to appeal to the reader's feelings or emotions with the aim to instigate action. While the proof in argument rests upon the presentation of objective evidence, that in persuasion derives in large part from the writer's use of controlled language, particularly **diction** with powerful connotations. Whatever the technique used, the writer aims to convince readers to share the writer's own values and opinions (and, in the case of persuasion, possibly to take action to change a situation). Whether an author chooses to emphasize logic or pathos depends on the subject and the audience.

Assumption That part of an argument which is not stated because the writer takes for granted the clarity of the position or the sympathy of the audience. (A good example is the belief of the Proposer in Swift's "A Modest Proposal" that his audience will share his view that any solution proposed for Ireland's problems will be acceptable.)

Burlesque A form of comedy in which people, actions, or literary works are made ridiculous by incongruous imitation and by exaggeration. The sublime may be made ridiculous, a serious subject approached with considerable silliness, or a frivolous subject treated with high seriousness. Style is important (e.g., a style which is usually reserved for serious matters is used to treat trivial matters, or the reverse). **Parody** and **caricature** are species of burlesque. Generally, burlesque makes fun of a literary *form*, whereas **parody** makes fun of a particular *work*. (See Woody Allen's "Slang Origins.")

Caricature A type of portrait which makes its subject ridiculous by exaggerating or distorting prominent features without losing the general likeness. In visual art, the cartoon — especially the political cartoon — is the commonest form.

Classification A strategy of expository writing used to break a subject into categories or classes. Once the subject is placed in classes, the writer discusses the characteristics which distinguish the members of the class one from another.

Cliché An over-used expression that has lost its original power. Clichés are entirely predictable (e.g., "as old as the hills," "as innocent as a newborn babe," "as fresh as a daisy").

Coherence Logical connection or congruity of thought within writing. When the various parts of an essay fit together and the flow of thought from section to section is clear and easy to follow, the essay has coherence. This quality is also achieved when the essay develops a single, central idea, since it is difficult to separate coherence from **unity**.

Colloquialism A word used chiefly in conversation. Appropriate to informal writing, but not to formal writing.

Comparison and Contrast A strategy of expository writing used to explore similarities and differences between two subjects. In strict terms, **comparison** is used to present a subject by means of showing similarities between two or more things. To be comparable, the components of the comparison should be members of the same class. In common practice, however, comparison often includes differences or elements of **contrast** as well, for the writer may be striving to emphasize only general similarities rather than point-by-point similarities (as, for example, the strict comparisons required for effective **analogy**).

Conclusion The closing of an essay, that part which gives the reader a sense of resolution of ideas, and a sense of an ending. The conclusion may be brief — a line or two — or it may be a section of the essay on its own. There are many strategies for conclusions, from the signals of transitional phrases such as "finally" and "in conclusion" to a reiteration of the opening stance with a variation. Writers may conclude with such techniques as an answer to an opening question, with echoes of the instruction, with a plea for action, with an allusion, a quotation, an ironic statement, or an illustrative anecdote.

Concrete Definite, particular, capable of being seen and understood directly; the opposite of **abstract**. *Rain* and *Tokyo* are concrete, *weather* and *city* are abstract.

Connotation The associative meanings of a word; implications and overtones that may be added to the dictionary meaning of a word. While the denotation of "mother" is "a female who has borne offspring," its connotation is emotionally charged with associations of love, security, nurture, protection, warmth, etc. Connotations of "mother" are so powerful, for example, that we speak of issues not readily open to attack as "motherhood" issues.

Contrast The presentation of a subject by means of showing differences between two or more things. To be contrasted, the subjects discussed should be members of the same class. See **comparison**.

Deductive Reasoning The process of reasoning from premises to a logical conclusion. Deduction is often presented in the form of a logical syllogism. The classic example is: "All men are mortal; Socrates is a man; therefore, Socrates is mortal" (inference or conclusion). If the syllogism is correctly constructed, then the inference is *logically* valid. Logical *fallacies* occur when the conclusion does not follow from the premises (e.g., "Some students are radical; John is a student; therefore, John is a radical"). Even if the logic is sound, however, the conclusion will not be true if one of the premises is false (e.g., "All students are radicals; John is a student; therefore, John is a radical").

Definition The act of stating what a word, term, phrase or set of terms signifies, usually by means of placing it in a class and demonstrating how it differs from other members of the class. The essay of definition generally extends a definition by means of details, anecdotes, examples, and metaphorical language (e.g., Forster employs definition in part to answer the central question of his essay, "My Wood"; Allen parodies the essay of definition in "Slang Origins").

Denotation The dictionary meaning of a word. "Mother," for example, denotes "a female who has borne offspring; a female parent." (See also **connotation**.)

Description A type of writing which uses details or images appealing to the five senses to create a mental picture. A descriptive essay or passage of description in an essay employs specific details and concrete diction to explain a person, place, scene, thing, or sensory experience.

Diction Choice of words. Diction will depend upon the writer's intended audience, purpose, and the stylistic effect aimed at. The writer may choose many different levels of diction: simple or colloquial rather than Latinate diction in order to address a school-aged audience; words with strong connotations rather than words relatively free of associations in order to persuade; archaic or foreign words and phrases in order to impress, or to give a false seriousness to the topic. A writer may draw from formal or standard language, informal or colloquial language, slang, or dialect (e.g., old man, old coot, eighty-year-old, octogenarian).

Emphasis The arrangement of the components of a composition to ensure that the important points are prominent (in an essay as a whole, in an argument, in a paragraph, in a sentence). Emphasis may be achieved through order of increasing importance, proportion of evidence, repetition of elements, transitional markers (e.g., "the single most important factor is ..."), metaphorical language, rhetorical questions, and mechanical devices such as underlinings, exclamation marks, or the highlighting of material in obvious ways (headings, indentations).

Epigraph A quotation or motto which prefaces a work. Epigraphs are often in foreign languages. (See Addison's "On Party-lying," Selzer's "The Discus Thrower.")

Euphemism The substitution of a mild or roundabout expression for another felt to be distasteful, blunt, or painful (e.g., "pass away" for "die").

Exposition A prose form which explains or informs. Definition, classification, illustration and example, analysis, and comparison and contrast are some of the common means of developing an expository piece.

Figures of Speech A form of expression in which the usual, literal meanings of words are extended. Figures of speech are based upon comparisons of unlike things which have some point of similarity. See this glossary for some of the common figures of speech: **metaphor, simile, personification, allusion, analogy, irony, paradox.**

Inductive Reasoning   The process of reasoning from specific examples or illustrations to a general principle. Inductive reasoning, the method of the scientist, is generally more common in argumentation than deductive reasoning. A writer may, in practice, state the conclusion first and then proceed to show the specifics which lead to the general principle. An inductive argument is only as valid as its supporting evidence; this evidence must be relevant, representative, accurate, and complete; the writer who employs induction must be certain that the evidence will bear close scrutiny.

Introduction   The opening of an essay. Introductions are remarkably variable, but they do have some functions in common: they establish the **tone** of the essay; and they often show the plan of the essay as a whole. A writer may try to "grab" readers by means of rhetorical questions, surprising statements or statistics, engaging anecdotes, allusions, paradoxes, quotations, or a particular claim about the importance of the subject.

Irony   A reality that differs significantly from appearance. In its broadest terms, *verbal irony* is a sarcastic or humorous means of discourse in which what is expressed literally means the opposite, as for example, when "I had an absolutely great day" means "I had a terrible day." *Irony of situation* presents a discrepancy between what is expected to happen and what actually does happen. To sustain irony, authors often employ a naive narrator or expositor; the well-intentioned but simplistic Proposer in Swift's "A Modest Proposal" is a striking example (see also *Persona*).

Jargon   A specialized vocabulary used by a particular group; the language of "insiders" intended for a particular audience within a profession or special-interest group (pilots, psychoanalysts, skiers, motorcycle gangs).

Metaphor   A figure of speech which compares two unlike things without using "like" or "as," and which asserts the identity of the two terms of comparison: e.g., "The road was a ribbon of light." (See also **simile**.) A metaphor's effectiveness is dependent upon its power of association. Dead metaphors are those in such frequent use that their metaphorical nature is hardly ever thought of (e.g., "a head of state" or "the hands of a clock" no longer recall the parts of the body they refer to). See Orwell's "Politics and the English Language" for a discussion of dying metaphors.

Narration   The telling of a story which may be real or fictional. When a story is told for the sake of the story itself, it may be said to be "pure" narration. Narration is, however, commonly employed to support an argument or to illustrate an exposition.

Objective   The detached way in which a writer sees the material, characterized by an impersonal, fact-based and unbiased approach. In contrast, **subjective** writing is characterized by an individual, opinion-based, and judgmental approach (e.g., "The douglas fir is a conifer" is a fact; "the douglas fir is the noblest of the conifers" is an opinion.) Total objectivity is not possible, of course, since the writer is an individual with individual perceptions and a unique consciousness. (See also **Point of view**.)

Paradox A statement that seems self-contradictory or absurd but which actually contains some truth in it. This rhetorical device is used to attract attention. An example taken from Wordsworth: "The child is father of the man."

Parallel Structures or Constructions Elements with similar rhetorical importance (e.g., words, phrases, clauses) used in similar patterns. A writer will use two or more words from the same grammatical category, and relate them in the same way in order to achieve a particular effect. Virginia Woolf's "How Should One Read a Book?" has many examples: "It may be one letter — but what a vision it gives! It may be a few sentences — but what vistas they suggest!" See also Samuel Johnson, an author celebrated for his use of parallel structures.

Parody A composition which mimicks the language and style of another work. Parody is generally intended to ridicule an author or a particular work — one which is usually serious. The parody has been used as a powerful means of satire by authors from ancient Greece to modern times. (See also **Burlesque**.)

Persona The Latin word for the mask worn by actors in classical drama. A persona is a character, "second self," or voice created by an author for a specific audience. An author might, for various reasons, be able to speak more freely through a persona than in his own voice. Often, a persona is used for satiric purposes as, for example, in Swift's "A Modest Proposal" and Royko's "Another Accolade for Charter Arms Corp."

Personification A figure of speech which endows an inanimate object or abstraction with human qualities (e.g., "the heavens wept").

Persuasion A writing approach used to convince an audience to do something or to share the writer's beliefs. The writer employs various devices of *pathos* to move the reader to action. An important part of persuasive writing is the establishment of the author's credibility or *ethos* — the writer's ethical stance, fairness, knowledge, honesty. (See **Argument**.)

Point of View Literally, the point from which something is seen, the angle from which a writer tells a story. Writers use the first-person point of view (characterized by "I") to establish a familiar tone and to emphasize personal involvement; the third-person point of view (characterized by "he," "she," and "it") to maintain distance; and the second-person point of view (characterized by "you") to establish an immediate one-to-one relationship with the reader. Writers often shift point of view for a particular purpose. (See Gloria Steinem's "Marilyn Monroe: The Woman Who Died Too Soon.") In a loose way, point of view may refer to the writer's closeness to or distance from the subject. (See also **objective/subjective**.)

Pun   A humorous play on the meaning of words, or on their sound (e.g., "How big is this bookstore?" "Oh — about two stories"). An author may also pun upon a well known phrase (e.g., Lewis Thomas's "physics envy," a pun on "penis envy").

Refutation   A technique in argument in which the writer recognizes and then counters the arguments or objections of those opposed him; sometimes called rebuttal.

Rhetorical Question   Often used to suggest only questions which do not require an answer. In practice, a rhetorical question may also be the starting point for a discussion which does, in fact, provide the answer (e.g., Virginia Woolf's "How Should One Read a Book?").

Rhythm   Patterned emphasis in language through the use of light and heavy stresses, long or short syllables, or repetitions of phrase or clause. Rhythm is a characteristic feature of good prose, but it does not have the regularity of rhythm in poetry.

Sarcasm   The blatant and caustic use of apparent praise for actual disapproval or criticism. It is the commonest form of irony.

Satire   The literary art of diminishing a subject by making it ridiculous and creating in the reader attitudes of amusement, contempt, or scorn. The laughter arising from satire is not laughter for the fun of laughter; rather the laughter is a weapon, usually directed against a particular target (e.g., a particular individual, a character type, an institution, a class, a nation, or perhaps mankind itself). Satire is usually employed with the aim of correcting human vice and folly.

Simile   A figure of speech which, using "like" or "as," compares two distinctly different things or actions (e.g., Orwell's "The friction of the great beast's foot had stripped the skin from his back as neatly as one skins a rabbit").

Slang   A level of language associated with conversation and informal writing. It is characterized by liveliness of expression employed for effect, and it is considered to be at the "low" end of colloquial expression. Slang tends to date quickly (e.g., "tin lizzie" for automobile). In general, it should be avoided, but an isolated example or two may create a special effect.

Style   The appropriate use of language or, in the words of Swift, "proper words in proper places." But style is more than the fitting of language with context, for it is highly individualistic — as the old adage "the style is the man" suggests; style is *how* the writer says what he says. Writers establish a personal style and create a sense of life in written work by many different means. Among these are choice of diction, figures of speech, sentence structure (length and variety), particular rhetorical patterns, tonal variations, and rhythm.

Subjective   An attitude of personal involvement with the topic discussed. The writer clearly reveals personal feelings and opinions about the topic discussed. (See **Objective**.)

Syllogism   An argument which takes two premises and joins them to produce a logical conclusion. See **deductive reasoning**.

Symbol   A person, place, or thing that exists in itself but which also stands for something else, something abstract or intangible (e.g., a flag, a tangible piece of cloth, may symbolize a nation or a political movement; an object such as a cross or a menorah may symbolize a particular religion).

Thesis or thesis statement   That part of the essay which states most clearly the writer's position or attitude. It is what the writer has to say — the chief idea or proposition advanced — about the subject. In brief essays the thesis is usually, though not always, expressed in a single sentence, and placed in the opening paragraph or paragraphs.

Tone   A writer's attitude toward the subject. A writer's involvement with the subject and attitude towards the audience determines tone. In speech, a speaker's attitude may be conveyed through tone of voice; in writing, tone is expressed chiefly through style, especially diction and sentence structure. The tone may be **objective**, appealing chiefly to the reader's intellect; or it may be **subjective**, appealing chiefly to the reader's emotions. Tone has many shades (cool, amused, mocking, cynical, bitter, joyful).

Topic sentence   The sentence in the paragraph that carries the main idea. While the thesis statement directs the development of an essay, the topic sentence directs the development of a paragraph.

Transition   The linking of parts of an essay. Depending upon the length of the essay, the transition may be a word, phrase, sentence or paragraph (e.g., "consequently," "another factor to consider," "And this brings us to our fourth and final point: the blackberries"). Transitions contribute to the smooth flow of ideas within a paragraph and between paragraphs. (See also **coherence**.)

Understatement   A form of irony which creates its effect by deliberately representing something as much less than it is in fact. In general, the speaker's emotional response is less than the response normally expected as, for example, when a speaker describes a movie star thought to be outstandingly beautiful or handsome as "not bad looking."

Unity   Oneness, the relevance of all the materials contained in an essay to its thesis or central idea. Within the paragraph, unity is achieved when all the materials relate to the topic sentence of the paragraph. (See also **coherence**.)

Index of Authors and Titles

Abuses of Advertising, The 17
ADDISON, Joseph 309
Aggressive Egg, The 641
ALLEN, Woody 3
Allowing the Mind to Wander 568
AMIS, Martin 109
ANDERSEN, Kurt 117
ANDERSON-DARGATZ, Gail 245
Another Accolade for Charter Arms
     Corp. 328
Are Feminists Alienating Women from
     the Sciences? 492
Art of Moving Pictures, The 123
ATWOOD, Margaret 314
BACON, Sir Francis 37, 250
BAKER, Russell 7
BARRECA, Regina 445
Bella Coola 401
BETTELHEIM, Bruno 123
BIBBY, Geoffrey 619
Bird and the Machine, The 199
BISSOONDATH, Neil 529
Black Like Me 559
Blown Away 109
Body in the Bog, The 619
BRODY, Hugh 253
BRONOWSKI, Jacob 631
CARSON, Rachel 191
Case Against Advertising, The 11
CASTILLO, Edward D. 131
Cathedral Square, The 666
Child's Play 4? 384
Civil Disobedience 348
CREAN, Susan 543
Dances With Wolves: Review 131
Dangerous Determination 464
DE QUINCEY, Thomas 40
De Mortuis 280
Death of a Pig 228
Discus Thrower, The 675
DOBBS, Kildare 554
DRYDEN, Ken 371
EISELEY, Loren 199
Errington, B.C. 245

FARR, Moira 464
Feeding, Feasts and Females 515
FLANNER, Janet 474
FORSTER, E.M. 379
FRANCIS, Daniel 266
FRASER, Fil 559
FREEDMAN, David H. 641
FRYE, Northrop 47
Game, The 371
GIANGRANDE, Carole 568
GOULD, Stephen Jay 650
HALDANE, J.B.S. 657
Hearing, A 253
HIGHSMITH, Patricia 384
HIMMELFARB, Gertrude 147
Historian's Opportunity, The 72
HOBAN, Russell 392
HOGGART, Richard 11
How Many Feminists Does It Take to
     Change a Light Bulb? 445
How Should One Read a Book? 95
Humanities and Science 686
I Am Canadian 529
IGLAUER, Edith 401
In the Canon, For All the Wrong
     Reasons 587
Influences 87
INGRAM, Jay 666
Is That All There Is? Tribal
     Literature 572
JOHNSON, Samuel 17
JOHNSTON, Basil H. 572
KAEL, Pauline 153
KEESHIG-TOBIAS, Lenore 583
KENNEDY, X.J. 156
KOERTGE, Noretta 492
LAURENCE, Margaret 58
LEACOCK, Stephen 209
Literature of Knowledge and the
     Literature of Power, The 40
Little Red Riding Hood Revisited 7
Loose Canons 179
LURIE, Alison 482
MacLENNAN, Hugh 411

Marilyn Monroe: The Woman Who Died Too Soon 498
Matata 554
Modest Proposal, A 338
MORRIS, Jan 418
Motive for Metaphor, The 47
MOWAT, Farley 215
Murder Among the Lovebirds 474
My Wood 379
NATOLI, Joseph 162
Nature of the North, The 215
Neo-Luddite Reflects on the Internet, A 147
New Age Daydreams [Dances With Wolves] 153
Nostalgia 286
Obligation to Endure, The 191
Of Marriage and Single Life 250
Of Studies 37
On Party-lying 309
Origin of Alien Species, The 117
ORWELL, George 21, 319
Pain of Animals, The 680
PLUMB, J.H. 280
Politics and the English Language 21
Posture Maketh the Man 650
Re-hanging the National Wallpaper: The Group of Seven and the Public Mind 266
Real Responsibilities of the Scientist, The 631
RICHLER, Mordecai 65
River Pilot Looks at the Mississippi, A 224
Roughing it in the Bush (My Plans for Moose-Hunting in the Canadian Wilderness) 209
ROYKO, Mike 328
RYBCZYNSKI, Witold 286
SALUTIN, Rick 179
SELZER, Richard 675
Shadow of Captain Bligh, The 411
Shooting an Elephant 319
SILLITOE, Alan 332
Slang Origins 3

Some Enemies of Science 657
Specifications for a Hero 430
Sport and Nationalism 332
St John's 418
STEGNER, Wallace 430
STEINEM, Gloria 498
Stop Stealing Native Stories 583
Storm Over the Amazon 238
SUZUKI, David 680
SWIFT, Jonathan 338
Taking the Missionary Position 543
TAN, Amy 587
TAYLOR, Helen 505
The Unforgiven: Histories and "Indians" 162
THOMAS, Lewis 686
THOREAU, Henry David 348
Thoughts on a Shirtless Cyclist, Robin Hood and One or Two Other Things 392
To Our Valued Customers 297
TREFIL, James 696
TRUDEAU, Garry 297
TUCHMAN, Barbara 72
TWAIN, Mark 224
Tyranny of the Clock, The 301
Unexpected Vistas 696
Unquiet Awakening, An 65
VANDERHAEGHE, Guy 87
VISSER, Margaret 515
WALKER, Martin 593
WELSH, Christine 603
Westward Oh! 593
Where the World Began 58
WHITE, E.B. 228
Who Killed King Kong? 156
WILSON, Edward O. 238
Women and Criticism 505
Women in the Shadows: Reclaiming a Métis Heritage 603
Women's Clothes — Towards Emancipation 482
WOODCOCK, George 301
WOOLF, Virginia 95
Writer's Responsibility, The 314

